Criminal Behavior and Social Systems

Criminal Behavior and Social Systems:

contributions of american sociology

edited by

Anthony L. Guenther
College of William and Mary

RAND McNALLY & COMPANY · Chicago

CONTRIBUTORS

RONALD L. AKERS
Department of Sociology
University of Washington

HOWARD S. BECKER
Department of Sociology
Northwestern University

BERNARD B. BERK
Research Social Scientist
Camarillo State Hospital, California

DONALD J. BLACK
Yale Law School
Yale University

DAVID J. BORDUA
Department of Sociology
University of Illinois

JAMES H. BRYAN
Department of Psychology
Northwestern University

ROBERT L. BURGESS
Department of Sociology
University of Washington

AARON V. CICOUREL
Department of Sociology
University of California, Santa Barbara

MARSHALL B. CLINARD
Department of Sociology
University of Wisconsin

DONALD R. CRESSEY
Department of Sociology
University of California, Santa Barbara

NORMAN K. DENZIN
Department of Sociology
University of California, Berkeley

EMILE DURKHEIM
Late of the University of Paris

PHILLIP H. ENNIS
Department of Sociology
Wesleyan University

KAI T. ERIKSON
Department of Sociology
Yale University

ROSE GIALLOMBARDO
National Opinion Research Center
University of Chicago

DANIEL GLASER
Department of Sociology
University of Southern California

FRANK E. HARTUNG
Department of Sociology
Wayne State University

JOHN I. KITSUSE
Department of Sociology
Northwestern University

EDWIN M. LEMERT
Department of Sociology
University of California, Davis

JENNIE McINTYRE
Department of Sociology
University of Maryland

v

SHELDON L. MESSINGER
Center for the Study of Law and Society
University of California, Berkeley

DONALD J. NEWMAN
School of Criminal Justice
State University of New York
   at Albany

SONYA ORLEANS
Old Westbury, New York

RICHARD QUINNEY
Department of Sociology
New York University

ALBERT J. REISS, JR.
Department of Sociology
University of Michigan

LEONARD SAVITZ
Department of Sociology
Temple University

EDWIN M. SCHUR
Department of Sociology
Tufts University

RICHARD D. SCHWARTZ
Department of Sociology
Northwestern University

THORSTEN SELLIN
Center for Studies in Criminology and
   Criminal Law
University of Pennsylvania

PHILIP SELZNICK
Center for the Study of Law and Society
University of California, Berkeley

JEROME H. SKOLNICK
Department of Sociology
University of California, San Diego

HARVEY A. SMITH
Department of Mathematics
Oakland University

ARTHUR L. STINCHCOMBE
Department of Sociology
University of California, Berkeley

EDWIN H. SUTHERLAND
Late of Indiana University

GRESHAM M. SYKES
College of Law
University of Denver

MARVIN E. WOLFGANG
Department of Sociology
University of Pennsylvania

Recently a colleague in history remarked with unconcealed envy that the reason sociology courses enroll to capacity, sociologists are recruited in a seller's market, and our research receives generous support is that we are so frightfully *relevant*. He was referring, of course, to the involvement of sociologists in understanding dramatic changes in the social order and interpersonal relations, as concentrated in studies of role conflict and its resolution, sources of political ideology, the priority of values in determining organizational structure, and the effects of restricted opportunity in the black community.

By extension, it is apparent that no greater support, emotional or financial, has been generated for a field than that concerned with lawlessness and the reaction to illegal behavior. Whether measured by congressional activity or opinion polls concentrating upon alleged "problems" of American society, criminology as a field of research, analysis, and recommendation is in an era of vitality and challenge. For this reason the present volume has been assembled; its constituent papers sample, I believe, the most comprehensive and authoritative knowledge about adult criminality. Moreover, the papers are sophisticated, in the sense that they muster competing bodies of evidence as well as alternative theories on a given topic. As George Homans and Thomas Kuhn have independently observed about the sequential development of scientific enterprise, sociologists have traditionally employed *discovery* as the criterion by which we are to be judged as scientists, but now we must construct propositions to *explain* or *predict* behavioral occurrences. The shift taking place in contemporary sociology is reflected, I hope, in the selections comprising this book.

It is appropriate to comment upon the rationale for choosing these papers from among the many fine ones available. First, those included represent major theoretical, methodological, and substantive contributions to criminology as it flourishes in this country. Second, I have sought a balance between the more orthodox interests of criminologists, exemplifed by studies of criminal statistics, the theory of differential association, and correctional systems, and the more recently developing areas such as patterns of law enforcement, victim survey research, and the sociology of law. Many of the papers are reprinted from journals not immediately accessible to the student, a few are out of print, and the one on criminological theory and victim survey research (by Daniel Glaser) is published here for the first time. In the majority of cases the complete article or chapter is reprinted, and original footnotes are reproduced for their value to the advanced reader.

An introduction to the particular subject matter prefaces each section of the book. In abbreviated fashion—for extended treatment is the province of a textbook—I raise the salient issues pertaining to each subject, point out areas of controversy, and then array a selected bibliography for use by the student who requires more detailed reading. Bibliographical references in each case identify either historically significant or highly contemporary publications, and are categorized in terms of major theoretical or empirical polemics.

Purists may be skeptical about the reference to American sociology in the subtitle of this volume, when in fact the contributors include a non-American and several nonsociologists. Their papers, however, illustrate American criminology as a school of thought or mode of analysis, in contrast with European criminology, whose assumptions, methods of research, and units of enumeration are clearly different.

The production of this volume was materially enhanced by Michael Kitzmiller, of Rand McNally, who was largely responsible for my undertaking the project, and Mrs. Gretchen English, of the College of William and Mary, who competently prepared typewritten parts of the manuscript and arranged the proliferous correspondence with authors and publishers, while somehow attending to the secretarial needs of thirteen sociologists. Finally, it is with pleasure that I record my continued indebtedness to Richard D. Schwartz, of Northwestern University, who reviewed my prospectus for the book and critically read the introductory statement for each section.

Anthony L. Guenther

September 1969
United States Penitentiary
Atlanta, Georgia

CONTENTS

Crime in Historical
and Theoretical Sociology

Behavior regarded as criminal has been a fascination to social scientists since the first observations on human affairs. But the challenge of explaining *why* illegal acts are committed, *who* commits them, and *what reactions* follow their occurrence requires more than simple observation, for evidence of law violations must be dispassionately gathered on a systematic basis and in terms of an organizing framework. The issues involved in securing data on crime will be discussed elsewhere; here, it will be informative to review the criteria for constructing explanatory models as they have developed in historical criminology.

Explanatory models, or theories of criminal behavior, are projected against the same criteria of adequacy as in any scientific enterprise. The fact that criminal acts are abrasive to the expectations of most people in the society does not mean that a radically "different" model is needed; their occurrence can be explained in terms of the same rational, calculated decision-making required for voting behavior, occupational choice, or mate selection. There was a period in the history of sociology when substantial numbers of scholars felt that the tool bag of sociological concepts and theorems useful for explaining "ordinary" social behavior was inadequate or inappropriate for the interpretation of criminal and other "deviant" behavior. At present, however, the state of sociological theory does not reflect differentiation along these lines.

After a sociologist observes patterned regularities in the phenomenon he is to explain, he must (a) postulate a relationship between the occurrence—e.g., theft by embezzlement—and antecedent conditions, (b) show that there is a causal link between the event and its antecedents, and (c) account for most, better still all, of the occurrence in terms of this link by rendering competing links and explanations implausible.

Thus one speaks of models, frameworks, or theories in connection with the study of crime because the major challenge is, and always has been, the *explanation* of lawless behavior. In addition, theory must explain the failure of crime to occur, e.g., under conditions of financial or emotional deprivation, because it will eventually be called upon to suggest preventive or eradicatory policies.

Criminological theory has developed along several lines, but it is possible to discern three analytically separable areas. On the one hand numerous investigators have inquired into the *formation of laws*, beginning with Max Weber and Emile Durkheim. These scholars, two of the most prominent figures in the development of sociology, wrote extensively about the evolution of legal regulation, and the necessity for norms prohibiting behavior that would threaten societal integrity.[1] Durkheim was the first of several authorities to point out that crimes are distinguished from other forms of deviance by their illegal character, yet not all patterns of disapproved conduct generate legal proscriptions. The question then becomes one of identifying prerequisites for the evolution of law. Since this form of social control is enacted by political authority, the relevant sociological issues are twofold: (a) what definitional processes take place so that conduct is perceived as dangerous or potentially dangerous to the community, and (b) how is community opinion about behavior deserving moral condemnation collectively translated into legal regulation?

The second major theme, *law violation* or the etiology of crime, is that body of knowledge most frequently assigned by the public to criminology. In the early days of crime study, there was suspicion that many (some said most) persons who committed breaches of the law were ignorant of the fact that such acts were prohibited, or that such persons were possessed of "overwhelming urges" and "unnatural passions." It was popular to do research on institutionalized populations such as felons or the "criminally insane," since they were *ipso facto* lawbreakers.

The degree to which biological, physiological, and constitutional explana-

---

[1] See respectively Max Rheinstein, ed., *Max Weber on Law in Economy and Society*, trans. Edward Shils and Max Rheinstein (Cambridge: Harvard University Press, 1954), chap. 5; and Emile Durkheim, *The Division of Labor in Society*, trans. George Simpson (Glencoe, Ill.: Free Press, 1933), bk. 1, chap. 5.

tions of criminality were inadequate is apparent from the reception given to sociocultural explanations. Two general models of criminal motivation seemed to prevail. The first suggested that offenders commit acts that are consistent with ambient subcultural standards, but deviant from the viewpoint of the larger society. The second, more complicated explanation depicted an actor weighing the probabilities of detection, apprehension, and adjudication against potential gain. In total rejection of biological determinism, this stance assumes rationality, selection among alternatives, and willingness to undertake risk.

The second of these models indicates that much early work was more psychological than sociological, concentrating upon how and why particular kinds of people engage in criminal acts. The sociological question, as Cohen has said, would be: "What is it about the structure of social systems that determines the kinds of criminal acts that occur in these systems and the way in which such acts are distributed within the systems?"[2]

Theoretical statements in explanation of crime are among the most urgent needs of present-day sociology. In addition, the two or three enduring over the last thirty years or so require verification and/or modification. One theory, the product of Edwin H. Sutherland, is extensively treated in Part Four (Differential Association and Crime: Theory and Research) of this book. Another, called anomie theory, originated with Durkheim in a discussion of the consequences of increased population size and density. One "abnormal form" of society, Durkheim held, was characterized by a decline in social integration, lessened commitment to the group, magnification of differences among segments of society, and heightened normlessness. He referred to this condition of the social system as anomie.

It was many years later that Robert K. Merton formulated an anomie theory of deviant behavior which pointed out the strain generated when persons are encouraged to structure their aspirations around a set of cultural goals (monetary wealth or occupational success, for example), yet are denied access to the legitimate, institutionalized means or avenues for goal achievement. This disjuncture between aspirations and opportunities may be resolved in several ways: physical or psychological withdrawal, scaling down ambitions so that they are compatible with the means at hand, or selecting an illicit (deviant) means for goal achievement.

This theory has been criticized, restated, applied, and adapted to other purposes more than any other in the sociology of deviant behavior. It is a rare attempt to account for the enactment of roles motivated to criminal behavior, with the contingency, as Cloward has pointed out, that *opportunities* for engaging in criminal acts are differentially distributed in the social order, just

---

[2] Albert K. Cohen, "The Study of Social Disorganization and Deviant Behavior," in *Sociology Today: Problems and Prospects,* ed. Robert K. Merton, Leonard Broom, and Leonard S. Cottrell, Jr. (New York: Basic Books, 1959), p. 462.

as opportunities for achieving societal goals are unevenly distributed.[3] The importance of this supplement to anomie theory becomes apparent upon inspection of arrest statistics, because much of the involvement with stolen merchandise, narcotics, gambling, and so on reflects the opportunities available in lower class society, while embezzling, price collusion, and misappropriation of funds are offenses available to white-collar occupations.

Anomie theory, however, has not received adequate verification as a set of propositions explaining criminal behavior. Yet all indications point to continuing and lively research in this area.

The third major school of criminological thought focuses on the *reaction, public and official, to law violation*. Because "crime" is a judgment conferred upon an act by legitimate authority, a number of sociologists have raised questions about the process by which such labeling takes place, the complex relations between rule makers and rule breakers, and some consequences of being labeled deviant.

One explicit concern here has been the implementation of criminal law. When an instance of behavior is suspected to be in violation of law, the authority of a series of reactive agencies is invoked: the police, courts, and prisons. Contrasting with more traditional criminology, which was devoted to crime causation, this view advocates the study of how criminal definitions are applied by the state against its citizens.

There is, one must embarrassedly admit, no adequate history of criminology available at the present time. Thorsten Sellin's "Criminology," however, might be its outline. This account ranges across the varieties of explanation originating in this country and abroad.

Durkheim's "The Normal and the Pathological" is a classical statement arguing that crime is inherent in the nature of social organization, and that it can be functional for strengthening collective sentiments about normality.

Daniel Glaser's "Cultural Influences in Crime" is a more concentrated treatment of positions taken by American criminologists, and the controversies that arose when sociologists engaged psychologists, biologists, and psychiatrists in debate over criminal conduct.

Theoretically linked with Durkheim's writing, Kai Erikson's study "Deviance and Definition" raises some interesting points about the ways deviance may serve to reestablish the boundaries of propriety, and to encourage reaffirmation of group bonds by denoting an occasion when social norms have been violated.

The concluding selection by Leonard Savitz shows how, despite a clear specification of the ideal or necessary elements of a crime, acts that qualify for such consideration often are not processed by regulatory agencies.

---

[3] Richard A. Cloward, "Illegitimate Means, Anomie, and Deviant Behavior," *American Sociological Review*, 24 (April 1959): 164–71.

For further reading in areas suggested by this brief overview, the following are among the better sources of information:

1. *The History of Inquiry into Criminal Behavior*

Fink, Arthur E. *Causes of Crime: Biological Theories in the United States, 1800–1915* (Philadelphia: University of Pennsylvania Press, 1938).

Grupp, Stanley E., ed. *The Positive School of Criminology* (Pittsburgh: University of Pittsburgh Press, 1968).

Mannheim, Hermann. *Comparative Criminology* (Boston: Houghton Mifflin, 1965), chap. 1.

Radzinowicz, Leon. *In Search of Criminology* (London: Heinemann, 1961).

Vold, George B. *Theoretical Criminology* (New York: Oxford University Press, 1958).

2. *Some Issues Confronting Criminology: Criminal Law, Acts Defined as Crimes, and Needed Research*

Clinard, Marshall B. "Criminological Research," in *Sociology Today: Problems and Prospects*, ed. Robert K. Merton, Leonard Broom, and Leonard S. Cottrell, Jr. (New York: Basic Books, 1959), pp. 509–36.

Dreher, Robert H. "Origin, Development, and Present Status of Insanity as a Defense to Criminal Responsibility in the Common Law," *Journal of the History of the Behavioral Sciences* 3 (January 1967): 47–57.

Gibbs, Jack P. "The Sociology of Law and Normative Phenomena," *American Sociological Review* 31 (June 1966): 315–25.

Goldstein, Abraham S. *The Insanity Defense* (New Haven: Yale University Press, 1967).

Schwartz, Richard D., and Miller, James C. "Legal Evolution and Societal Complexity," *American Journal of Sociology* 70 (September 1964): 159–69.

Tappan, Paul W. "Who Is the Criminal?," *American Sociological Review* 12 (February 1947): 96–102.

3. *Anomie Theory: Early Formulation, Refinement, Application, and Relation to Other Modes of Explanation*

Cloward, Richard A. "Illegitimate Means, Anomie, and Deviant Behavior," *American Sociological Review* 24 (April 1959): 164–76.

Cohen, Albert K. "The Sociology of the Deviant Act: Anomie Theory and Beyond," *American Sociological Review* 30 (February 1965): 5–14.

Dubin, Robert. "Deviant Behavior and Social Structure: Continuities in Social Theory," *American Sociological Review* 24 (April 1959): 147–64.

Lindesmith, Alfred R., and Gagnon, John. "Anomie and Drug Addiction," in *Anomie and Deviant Behavior*, ed. Marshall B. Clinard (New York: Free Press, Macmillan, 1964), pp. 158–88.

Merton, Robert K. "Social Structure and Anomie," *American Sociological Review* 3 (October 1938): 672–82.

Perrucci, Robert. *Heroes and Hopelessness in a Total Institution: Anomie Theory Applied to a Collective Disturbance* (Lafayette, Ind.: Herman C. Krannert Graduate School of Industrial Administration, Purdue University, November 1966).

Powell, Elwin H. "Crime as a Function of Anomie," *Journal of Criminal Law, Criminology, and Police Science* 57 (June 1966): 161–71.

Turk, Austin T. "Conflict and Criminality," *American Sociological Review* 31 (June 1966): 338–52.

4. *The Societal Reaction to Deviance: Statements by Proponents and Opponents*

Becker, Howard S. *Outsiders: Studies in the Sociology of Deviance* (New York: Free Press, Macmillan, 1963).

Garfinkel, Harold. "Conditions of Successful Degradation Ceremonies," *American Journal of Sociology* 61 (March 1956): 420–24.

Gibbs, Jack P. "Conceptions of Deviant Behavior: The Old and the New," *Pacific Sociological Review* 9 (Spring 1966): 9–14.

Goffman, Erving. *Stigma: Notes on the Management of Spoiled Identity* (Englewood Cliffs, N.J.: Prentice-Hall, 1963).

Gouldner, Alvin W. "The Sociologist as Partisan: Sociology and the Welfare State," *The American Sociologist* 3 (May 1968): 103–16.

Lemert, Edwin M. *Social Pathology* (New York: McGraw-Hill, 1951), chaps. 1–4.

Schur, Edwin M. *Crimes Without Victims: Deviant Behavior and Public Policy* (Englewood Cliffs, N.J.: Prentice-Hall, 1965).

1. CRIMINOLOGY

Thorsten Sellin

It is proper to use the term *criminology* to designate either (*a*) a body of scientific knowledge about crime, including its causes and prevention, the handling of offenders, and the pursuit of such knowledge regardless of where it stems from; or (*b*) a didactic discipline, which assembles, analyzes, and integrates the findings of criminological research in all scientific disciplines and indicates the best way in which they can be applied in practice to secure socially desirable ends.

Since Raffaele Garofalo (1885) invented the term, no agreement has been reached on the definition of criminology. Traditionally, it has concerned itself with the study of violations of the criminal law and of those who commit them, but opinions vary on the nature and scope of such study. Some hold that it should concentrate on the scientific investigation of the causes of crime and form a subclass of a more general catch-all discipline called "criminal science." Criminal science would be composed of many specialized branches of study, some concerned with etiology—criminology, further subdivided into biological, psychological, and sociological criminology—

Reprinted with permission of the author and the publisher from the *International Encyclopedia of the Social Sciences,* ed. David L. Sills, vol. 3, pp. 505–10. Copyright © 1968 by Crowell Collier and Macmillan, Inc.

and others with police science, substantive and procedural legal problems, and penology. By contrast, there are those who would regard all these branches as parts of criminology, a view reflected in American textbooks in particular, which consequently employ the term merely as a pedagogical device. This custom is opposed by those who see in criminology an empirical and naturalistic science, but even this more restrictive view raises problems. This is because the scientific study of offenses, offenders, and the whole complex of penal and law-enforcing institutions is carried on by researchers in a variety of scientific fields, each having its own theories, hypotheses, and techniques of investigation, which are often poorly understood, misunderstood, or rejected by researchers in other fields—either in principle or because of faulty interdisciplinary communication arising from increasing specialization in research activity. One cannot, therefore, speak of a science of criminology in the narrow sense of a discipline that possesses universally accepted theoretical concepts.

THE SEARCH FOR CAUSES

It is in the search for an understanding of why people commit crime that most research has occurred. The history of such inquiries can be said to have begun with the nineteenth century, which witnessed the development of the psychological and social sciences. Previously, indeed going back to antiquity, the problem of criminal conduct occupied the minds of natural philosophers and protoscientists, and various theories were advanced to explain it. Observers of the social scene also speculated on the causes of criminality long before sophisticated inquirers with more adequate sources of data began their studies. Generally speaking, one might say that the search for the causes of crime has been made either by those who believe that criminal conduct can be explained chiefly by the biological or mental characteristics of offenders, or by those who believe that environmental conditions and circumstances are the chief operative factors. We shall call the former the individualists and the latter the environmentalists.

The Individualists

Attempts to interpret the significance of relationships between body and mind led in ancient times to the development of *physiognomics*. This method of character diagnosis survived well into the Middle Ages, and one of its practitioners, Giambattista della Porta (1536–1615), may have been the first criminologist. He is said to have made anthropometric measurements on criminals in order to establish a typology. These medieval studies are not unlike some that appeared in the last century, and della Porta's drawings comparing human and animal faces have found counterparts in relatively recent studies by responsible scientists working with different underlying hypotheses. However, physiognomics soon fell into disrepute and remained so until Lombroso revived it in a new connection.

A different approach to the explanation of crime was that of Franz Joseph Gall (1758–1828), the greatest brain anatomist of his age, who was influenced by the faculty psychology of the time. His study of the brain and the nervous system caused him to propound a theory of the localization of brain functions, each operating through an organ in a cluster of other organs distributed over the outer layer of the brain. Criminal conduct then occurred if an overdeveloped organ of combativeness or acquisitiveness, for instance, was too stimulated. In vogue for a few decades, Gall's theory was abandoned, but it called attention to the necessity of studying the offender in order to understand his conduct. Following Gall's lead, Lauvergne (1841) studied prisoners at Toulon and described a criminal type that Lombroso later was to call a criminal by nature.

Psychiatrists were also interested in the etiology of crime. Benjamin Rush (1786), a Philadelphia physician, published an essay on the influence of physical causes on the moral faculties, in which he described persons who, although in other respects normal, became criminals because their moral faculty was impaired, a disease he called anomia. This theory, later elaborated by Philippe Pinel and Jean E. D. Esquirol, given the name "moral insanity" by James C. Prichard, and strongly defended by Prosper Despine and Henry Maudsley, took on a new lease of life in the late 1930s when the notion of the constitutional psychopathic inferior aroused a discussion that seems likely to continue.

The political revolutions of the eighteenth century may have proclaimed the equality of man, but scientists of the period were fully aware of the great variations within the human species. The prevalence of physical and mental defects, ill health, poverty, and criminality gave rise to B. A. Morel's theory of "degeneration" (1857), which held that all these phenomena were the results of a progressive pathological process in which heredity played an important role. This process led to the formation of a variety of human types, which he described in a monograph (Morel 1864) that contained many of the ideas later adopted by the Lombrosians. He also suggested the need for a science of "morbid anthropology." Dugdale's study of the Jukes (1877) shows some affinity with Morel's ideas.

In 1876 a work with the title *L'uomo deliquente* ("The Criminal Man"), by Cesare Lombroso (1835–1909), introduced a new variant among individualistic theories—the most important one, judging from its ultimate influence rather than its intrinsic value. On the basis of clinical and anatomical studies of criminals, Lombroso was convinced that the criminal was a throwback (atavism), a person who has the body and mind of our primitive ancestors, a kind of vestigial survivor from a day when mankind stood on a lower rung of the ladder of evolution, who, acting in a way natural to such a person, breaks the laws of modern society. The theory is a perfect example of the confluence of many contemporary sources of ideas. Jacob Moleschott and Friedrich K. C. L. Büchner supplied the materialistic doctrine, Charles Darwin the framework, Ernst H. Haeckel's biogenetic principle of recapitulation the mechanism that, interfered with, would account for the atavism (Mendel's discovery was still unknown), psychiatrists the concepts of moral insanity and degeneration, Paul Broca the techniques and instruments of anthropometry, the psychophysicists the methods of psychometrics, and Joseph A. de Gobineau the documentary data on the customs of primitive man.

Lombroso's theory aroused both support and opposition among researchers, not to mention the clergy or the laity represented by the legal profession. The first serious attempt to test it was done by C. B. Goring (1913), who found no support for it, and the last by E. A. Hooton, who failed to substantiate the claims he made for it. It no longer survives anywhere in its original formulation, but the orientation it represents, namely the stress on the importance of biological factors, still dominates criminological thought in Italy, the Iberian peninsula, and the Latin American countries.

A parallel avenue has been followed by the constitutionalists, seeking a correlation between somatic body types and criminality. The rediscovery of Mendel's hypothesis and the development of new psychometric devices such as intelligence tests led to numerous researches on the relationship of hereditary or psychological factors in delinquency, best demonstrated in studies of identical twins. It is within this context that we should appraise the psychoanalytic theories advanced in explanation of crime. Biological theories also fall under this head; indeed, it looks as if ancient beliefs in the role of body fluids in shaping temperaments have reappeared in a new guise in physiological studies of endocrine influences on behavior. As each new hypothesis of biological or psychological nature has appeared, or new diagnostic devices have been found (the electroencephalograph or projective psychological tests, for instance), attempts have been made to determine their usefulness in research explaining criminal conduct.

The Environmentalists

The earliest environmentalists were probably the astrologers, who believed that traits ascribed to planets were mysteriously transmitted to humans, and that persons born when certain planets were in ascendancy or conjunction were doomed to crime. In later ages, such primitive conceptions were replaced by beliefs in the effect of climate on behavior (cf. Montesquieu), systematized less than a century ago by Enrico Ferri (1881a) in his discussion of telluric factors in the etiology of crime. Today, observed seasonal changes in criminality are recognized but explained in social terms. Indeed, the contributions of the environmentalists to an understanding of criminality have been predominantly sociological. Their ideas, at first based on commonplace experience and observation, have undergone many different, if not always basic, changes, because of improved sources of data, greater methodological sophistication, and the stimulus of scientific developments of the behavioral sciences in general.

It is said that Galen, noting the malpractice of Roman physicians, claimed that their conduct was made possible only by the anonymity of city life. Had they lived in small towns, where everybody would have known them, they could not have persisted in their conduct. The effect of poverty on crime was seen by Sir John Fortescue in the fifteenth century, and described by Sir Thomas More and Juan Luis Vives in the sixteenth century. The economic and social consequences of the Black Death and the endemic wars of the following three centuries created a criminal class, the existence of which was attributed to social causes. Eighteenth-century writers like Bernard Mandeville, Henry Fielding, and Patrick Colquhoun cited police corruption, the moral contagion of prisons, poor law enforcement, gambling, the saloon, illiteracy and ignorance, etc. as responsible for criminality. Both Fielding and Colquhoun gave graphic descriptions of organized crime, as did Avé-Lallemant in Germany half a century later.

It is during the last three quarters of the nineteenth century that we discern in the social sciences a development paralleling that already described in our discussion of the individualists. In 1825 France set up the first system of judicial criminal statistics. It was to be imitated by most other European countries. These annual series of data inspired the first important statistical studies by Charles J. M. Lucas (1827) on the relation of education to crime, by Adolphe Quetelet in 1831 on the relation of age to criminality, and by André M. Guerry (1833) on economic conditions, education, sex, etc. as related to crime. To facilitate the understanding of their tables, they presented maps of France showing the distribution of some of the phenomena they investigated, a technique much employed by contemporary and later authors and revived in the present century by American social ecologists.

The socioeconomic consequences of the industrial revolution were seen as criminogenic by numerous authors, especially those influenced by the economic theories of Karl Marx. Indeed, two of them, Napoleone Colajanni (1889) and Enrico Ferri (1881b), produced the first treatises on criminal sociology. Ferri's work became particularly influential. His effort to reconcile the divergent views of the social scientists and the criminal anthropologists led to a multiple-factor approach to the study of causation, which took account of anthropological, telluric, and social factors. His earliest studies (Ferri 1881a) were statistical analyses of criminality in France since 1825.

Two French sociologists were to have considerable influence on criminological thought—Gabriel Tarde (1843–1904) and Emile Durkheim (1858–

1917). Both presented sociological theories of criminality worthy of comparison with the biological theories of men like Morel and Lombroso, and the dates of their formulation are evidence of the comparatively later maturation of sociological thought. Tarde (1890) held that as a special activity criminality was explained by the laws of imitation. The criminal represented a social class. Forms of crime originated in the upper classes and spread downward by imitation; thus an individual might be born vicious, but societal influences make him a criminal. Durkheim's best contribution was his theory of anomie, a condition that he held to be created by social evolution, as it transforms homogeneous societies into heterogeneous ones by the increasing division of labor, and by the rise of more and more social groups with divergent norms that may be in conflict with legal norms. Both of these authors, and especially Durkheim, have influenced the thinking of American criminologists.

CRIMINOLOGY IN MODERN TIMES

In this brief review, scores of names of scholars and scientists who have engaged in criminological research and who have assisted in enriching it have necessarily been omitted. And it will be noticed that, with one exception, Benjamin Rush, only Europeans have been mentioned. This is because in the United States, until the present century, studies of criminality or criminals only imitated work done abroad. The poverty of criminal statistics, which is still a problem, made the kind of social investigations done in Europe impossible. Psychologists and psychiatrists faced no such problem; the publication of Healy's *The Individual Delinquent* (1915) marked the beginning of a new era for their studies. Sociologists had to find different approaches. Before World War I, no leading American sociologist, except perhaps Charles H. Cooley, Franklin H. Giddings, or E. A. Ross, showed any theoretical interest in criminology. Courses in criminology were offered in many American colleges and universities by 1905, but they were largely concerned with social reform. Only in the last forty years has a scientific orientation grown up in American sociological research on crime, as in other sociological areas of inquiry. Such research has tended to focus on the causation of crime. Psychiatric research in criminology, clinically oriented, has also increasingly come to recognize the significance of social and cultural influences on criminal conduct.

Whereas in the United States criminological research has been done mostly by sociologists, elsewhere clinical criminology, practiced mainly by psychiatrists, dominated research until World War II. In most countries of basically Latin culture, this is still the case. Since then, however, sociological research has been gaining in importance in many countries and has reversed the psychiatric dominance, especially in northern Europe. This process has been largely due to the phenomena of postwar criminality and delinquency and to the growing familiarity with the products of American empirical criminological research, which before World War II seemed to be almost unknown outside the United States.

Sociologists have also become interested in the study of correctional institutions seen as social systems; significant research in that connection has been conducted in the United States, England, and Norway. The effectiveness of various forms of correctional treatment is being studied in many countries. Such research may be expected to have an influence on legislation on crimes, their sanctions, and correctional administration. Attempts are also being made in some countries to develop prognostic instruments useful in spotting future delinquents among young children, in the selecttion of offenders for placement on probation or parole, and in the assignment of prisoners to different types of treatment programs. In this connection, the central diagnostic clinics established by many state or national correctional departments, of which California, France, and Italy offer good examples, have aided in bringing about closer cooperation among staff representatives of the various disciplines concerned with criminal conduct.

Concurrent with the growth of scientific research activity and with the proliferation, especially in the United States, of state or local programs and agencies for the prevention of crime and delinquency and for the treatment of offenders has been the increase in the demand for criminologically trained research and treatment personnel. Pedagogical institutes of criminology, aiming to broaden the knowledge of the judiciary and of correctional administrators or candidates for such civil service offices, have existed for more than half a century at law schools in many foreign countries. Institutes combining staff research and teaching have appeared more recently. The most active are those at Cambridge, England, and Vaucresson, France. In the United States, a few universities offer programs of graduate study leading to advanced degrees related to criminology. Such courses are, with rare exceptions, designed to train teachers of criminology or correctional administrators rather than researchers; the same holds true for the offerings of the institute recently established in Japan by the United Nations.

BIBLIOGRAPHY

No adequate history of criminology exists, and the textbooks give scanty information. A broader view may be gained from Niceforo 1941; Kan 1903; Bonger 1905; Bernaldo de Quirós 1898; Antonini 1900; Montes 1911; Fink 1938; Vold 1958; Mannheim 1960. *The discussion of the scope and nature of criminology continues unabated, as witnessed by such works as* Bianchi 1956; Pelaez 1960. *Two national dictionaries of criminology are worthy of note:* Elster and Lingemann, Handwörterbuch der Kriminologie 1933–1936; *and the* Dizionario di criminologia 1943. *Good bibliographical tools are now available; especially useful are the* International Review of Criminal Policy; International Bibliography on Crime and Delinquency; Annales internationales de criminologie; Excerpta criminologica;

Current Projects in the Prevention, Control, and Treatment of Crime and Delinquency. *Textbooks are numerous. Among the many current American ones, all written by sociologists, the best known is* Sutherland and Cressey 1924. *Of foreign texts, among the leading titles are* Agge 1955; Greeff 1946; Hurwitz 1947; Bemmelen 1942; Pinatel 1963. *Many criminological journals are being published; among them, in the United States, are the* Journal of Criminal Law, Criminology, and Police Science; Archives of Criminal Psychodynamics; Journal of Research in Crime and Delinquency.

In England, the leading publication is the British Journal of Criminology. *In Germany, the* Archiv für Kriminologie *and the* Monatsschrift für Kriminologie und Strafrechtsreform *are both well-established journals, as are the Belgian* Revue de droit pénal et de criminologie, *the Dutch* Nederlands tijdschrift voor criminologie, *and the Swiss* Revue internationale de criminologie et de police technique. *France and Italy, both of which have long traditions of criminological research, produce, respectively, the* Revue de science criminelle et de droit pénal comparé *and the* Quaderni di criminologia clinica. *More extensive listings of journals will be found in* International Society of Criminology 1961. *The teaching of criminology in different countries, including the United States, is described in* International Society of Criminology 1957. *Also worth reading in this connection is* Radzinowicz 1961. *National societies for the study and promotion of scientific criminology exist in many countries. International exchange between criminologists has been organized since the late nineteenth century; no fewer than seven international congresses of "criminal anthropology" were held between 1885 and 1911. The International Society of Criminology, organized in 1937, has held such congresses in 1938, 1950, 1955, 1960, and 1965.*

AGGE, IVAR, et al., 1955. *Kriminologi.* Stockholm: Wahlström & Widstrand.

Annales internationales de criminologie. Published by the Société Internationale de Criminologie. From 1951 to 1961 it was called the *Bulletin* (of the International Society of Criminology).

ANTONINI, GIUSEPPE, 1900. *I precursori di C. Lombroso.* Turin: Bocca.

Archiv für Kriminologie: Unter Besonder Berücksichtigung der naturwissenschaftlichen Kriminalistik. Published since 1898.

Archives of Criminal Psychodynamics. Published since 1955.

BEMMELEN, JACOB M. VAN, 1958 (1942). *Criminologie: Leerbock der misdaadkunde,* 4th ed. Zwolle (Netherlands): Tjeenk Willink.

BERNALDO DE QUIRÓS, CONSTANCIO, 1911 (1898). *Modern Theories of Criminality.* Boston: Little, Brown. First published as *Las neuvas teorías de la criminalidad.*

BIANCHI, HERMANUS, 1956. *Position and Subject-Matter of Criminology: Inquiry Concerning Theoretical Criminology.* Amsterdam: North-Holland Publishing.

BONGER, WILLIAM A., 1916 (1905). *Criminality and Economic Conditions.* Boston: Little, Brown. First published as *Criminalité et conditions économiques.*

BRANHAM, VERNON C., and KUTASH, SAMUEL B., eds., 1949. *Encyclopedia of Criminology.* New York: Philosophical Library.

British Journal of Criminology. Published since 1960 by the Institute for the Study and Treatment of Delinquency. From 1950 to 1960 published as *British Journal of Delinquency.*

COLAJANNI, NAPOLEONE, 1889. *La sociologia criminale,* 2 vols. Catania (Italy): Tropea.

Current Projects in the Prevention, Control, and Treatment of Crime and Delinquency. Published from 1962 to 1964 by the National Council on Crime and Delinquency. Now published by the National Clearing House for Mental Health Information, U.S. Department of Health, Education, and Welfare, Public Health Service.

Dizionario di criminologia, 2 vols., ed. E. Florian, A. Niceforo, and N. Pende, 1943. Milan: Vallardi.

DUGDALE, RICHARD L., 1910 (1877). *The Jukes: A Study in Crime, Pauperism, Disease, and Heredity,* 4th ed. New York: Putnam.

ELSTER, ALEXANDER, and LINGEMANN, HEINRICH, eds., 1933–1936. *Handwörterbuch der Kriminologie und der anderen strafrechtlichen Hilfswissenschaften . . .* Berlin: de Gruyter.

Excerpta criminologica. A journal of abstracts, published since 1961 by the Excerpta Criminologica Foundation, Amsterdam.

FERRI, ENRICO, 1881a. *Studi sulla criminalità in Francia dal 1826 al 1878.* Rome: Botta.

FERRI, ENRICO, 1917 (1881b). *Criminal Sociology.* Boston: Little, Brown. First published as *I nuovi orizzonti del diritto e della procedura penale.* Title later changed to *Sociologia criminale.*

FINK, ARTHUR E., 1938. *The Causes of Crime: Biological Theories in the United States, 1800–1915.* Philadelphia: University of Pennsylvania Press. A paperback edition was published in 1962 by Barnes & Noble.

GAROFALO, RAFFAELE, 1914 (1885). *Criminology.* Boston: Little, Brown. First published in Italian.

GORING, CHARLES B., 1913. *The English Convict: A Statistical Study.* London: H.M. Stationery Office.

GREEFF, ÉTIENNE DE, 1947 (1946). *Introduction à la criminologie,* 2d ed. Brussels: Vandenplas.

GUERRY, ANDRÉ M., 1833. *Essai sur la statistique morale de la France.* Paris: Crochard.

HEALY, WILLIAM, 1915. *The Individual Delinquent: A Text-book of Diagnosis and Prognosis for All Concerned in Understanding Offenders.* Boston: Little, Brown.

HURWITZ, STEPHAN, 1952 (1947). *Criminology.* London: Allen & Unwin. First published in Danish.

International Bibliography on Crime and Delinquency. Published since 1963, first by the National Research and Information Center on Crime and Delinquency, National Council on Crime and Delinquency, now by the National Clearing House for Mental Health Information, U.S. Department of Health, Education, and Welfare, Public Health Service.

International Review of Criminal Policy. Published since 1952 by the United Nations, Department of Social Affairs. Contains an extensive international bibliography of criminology.

INTERNATIONAL SOCIETY OF CRIMINOLOGY, 1957. *The University Teaching of Social Sciences: Criminology.* Paris: UNESCO.

INTERNATIONAL SOCIETY OF CRIMINOLOGY, 1961. *Selected Documentation on Criminology.* Social Science Clearing House, Reports and Papers in the Social Sciences, no. 14. Paris: UNESCO. A selective bibliography for each of 25 countries.

Journal of Criminal Law, Criminology, and Police Science. Published since 1910 under various titles.

Journal of Research in Crime and Delinquency. Published since 1964 by the National Council on Crime and Delinquency and the Center for Youth and Community Studies, Howard University.

KAN, JOSEPH VAN, 1903. *Les causes économiques de la criminalité: Étude historique et critique d'étiologie criminelle.* Paris: Storck.

KINBERG, OLOF, 1935. *Basic Problems of Criminology.* Copenhagen: Levin & Munksgaard. A French revision was published in 1960 as *Les problèmes fondamentaux de la criminologie.*

LAUVERGNE, HUBERT, 1841. *Les forçats considérés sous le rapport physiologique, moral, et intellectuel.* Paris: Baillière.

LUCAS, CHARLES J. M., 1827. *Du système pénal et du système répressif en général, de la peine de mort en particulier.* Paris: Béchet.

MANNHEIM, HERMANN, ed., 1960 (1954–1960). *Pioneers in Criminology.* London: Stevens. A collection of biographies that first appeared separately in the *Journal of Criminal Law, Criminology, and Police Science.*

MANNHEIM, HERMANN, 1965. *Comparative Criminology: A Text Book,* 2 vols. London: Routledge.

MIDDENDORFF, WOLF, 1959. *Soziologie des Verbrechens.* Düsseldorf: Diederich.

Monatsschrift für Kriminologie und Strafrechtsreform. Published since 1904 under various titles.

MONTES, JERÓNIMO, 1911. *Precursores de la ciencia penal en España: Estudios sobre el delincuente y las causas y remedios del delito.* Madrid: Suárez.

MOREL, BENEDICT A., 1857. *Traité des dégénérescences physiques, intellectuelles, et morales de l'espèce humaine et des causes qui produisent ces variétés maladives.* Paris: Baillière.

MOREL, BENEDICT A., 1864. *De la formation du type dans les variétés dégénérées: Ou, nouveaux éléments d'anthropologie morbide pour faire suite à la théorie des dégénérescences dans l'espèce humaine.* Paris: Baillière.

Nederlands tijdschrift voor criminologie. Published since 1959.

NICEFORO, ALFREDO, 1949 (1941). *Criminologia,* vol. 1: *Vecchie e nuove dottrine.* Milan: Bocca.

PELAEZ, MICHELANGELO, 1960. *Introduzione allo studio della criminologia.* Milan: Giuffré.

PINATEL, JEAN, 1963. *Criminologie,* vol. 3 in Pierre Bouzat and Jean Pinatel, *Traité de droit pénal et de criminologie.* Paris: Dalloz.

Quaderni di criminologia clinica. Published since 1959.

RADZINOWICZ, LEON, 1962 (1961). *In Search of Criminology.* Cambridge: Harvard University Press.

Revue de droit pénal et de criminologie. Published since 1907.

Revue de science criminelle et de droit pénal comparé. Published since 1936 by the Centre Français de Droit Comparé, Université de Paris, Institut de Criminologie.

Revue internationale de criminologie et de police technique. Published since 1947.

RUSH, BENJAMIN, 1839 (1786). *Inquiry into the Influence of Physical Causes upon the Moral Faculty.* Philadelphia: Cist. Speech delivered before the American Philosophical Society, February 27, 1786. First published as *An Oration . . . Containing an Enquiry into the Influence of Physical Causes upon the Moral Faculty.*

SELLIN, THORSTEN, and SAVITZ, LEONARD, 1963 (1935). "A Bibliographical Manual for the Student of Criminology," 3d ed., rev. *International Bibliography on Crime and Delinquency* 1, no. 3.

SUTHERLAND, EDWIN H., and CRESSEY, DONALD R., 1960 (1924). *Principles of Criminology,* 6th ed. New York: Lippincott. First published as a textbook under the title of *Criminology,* with E. H. Sutherland as sole author.

TARDE, GABRIEL, 1912 (1890). *Penal Philosophy.* Boston: Little, Brown. First published as *La philosophie pénale.*

TULLIO, BENIGNO DI, 1945. *Trattato di antropologia criminale.* Rome: Criminalia.

VOLD, GEORGE B., 1958. *Theoretical Criminology.* New York: Oxford University Press.

2. THE NORMAL AND THE PATHOLOGICAL

Emile Durkheim

If there is any fact whose pathological character appears incontestable, that fact is crime. All criminologists are agreed on this point. Although they explain this pathology differently, they are unanimous in recognizing it. But let us see if this problem does not demand a more extended consideration.

We shall apply the foregoing rules. Crime is present not only in the majority of societies of one particular species but in all societies of all types. There is no society that is not confronted with the problem of criminality. Its form changes; the acts thus characterized are not the same everywhere; but everywhere and always, there have been men who have behaved in such a way as to draw upon themselves penal repression. If, in proportion as societies pass from the lower to the higher types, the rate of criminality, i.e., the relation between the yearly number of crimes and the population, tended to decline, it might be believed that crime, while still normal, is tending to lose this character of normality. But we have no reason to believe that such a regression is substantiated. Many facts would seem rather

Reprinted with permission of The Macmillan Company from *The Rules of Sociological Method* by Emile Durkheim, trans. Sarah A. Solovay and John H. Mueller, ed. George E. G. Catlin (New York: Free Press, Macmillan, 1950), pp. 65–75. Copyright © 1938 by George E. G. Catlin, renewed 1966 by Sarah A. Solovay, John H. Mueller, and George E. G. Catlin. Footnotes have been renumbered.

to indicate a movement in the opposite direction. From the beginning of the [nineteenth] century, statistics enable us to follow the course of criminality. It has everywhere increased. In France the increase is nearly 300 percent. There is, then, no phenomenon that presents more indisputably all the symptoms of normality, since it appears closely connected with the conditions of all collective life. To make of crime a form of social morbidity would be to admit that morbidity is not something accidental, but, on the contrary, that in certain cases it grows out of the fundamental constitution of the living organism; it would result in wiping out all distinction between the physiological and the pathological. No doubt it is possible that crime itself will have abnormal forms, as, for example, when its rate is unusually high. This excess is, indeed, undoubtedly morbid in nature. What is normal, simply, is the existence of criminality, provided it attains and does not exceed, for each social type, a certain level, which it is perhaps not impossible to fix in conformity with the preceding rules.[1]

Here we are, then, in the presence of a conclusion in appearance quite paradoxical. Let us make no mistake. To classify crime among the phenomena of normal sociology is not to say merely that it is an inevitable, although regrettable, phenomenon, due to the incorrigible wickedness of men; it is to affirm that it is a factor in public health, an integral part of all healthy societies. This result is, at first glance, surprising enough to have puzzled even ourselves for a long time. Once this first surprise has been overcome, however, it is not difficult to find reasons explaining this normality and at the same time confirming it.

In the first place crime is normal because a society exempt from it is utterly impossible. Crime, we have shown elsewhere, consists of an act that offends certain very strong collective sentiments. In a society in which criminal acts are no longer committed, the sentiments they offend would have to be found without exception in all individual consciousnesses, and they must be found to exist with the same degree as sentiments contrary to them. Assuming that this condition could actually be realized, crime would not thereby disappear; it would only change its form, for the very cause which would thus dry up the courses of criminality would immediately open up new ones.

Indeed, for the collective sentiments which are protected by the penal law of a people at a specified moment of its history to take possession of the public conscience or for them to acquire a stronger hold where they have an insufficient grip, they must acquire an intensity greater than that which they had hitherto had. The community as a whole must experience them

---

[1] From the fact that crime is a phenomenon of normal sociology, it does not follow that the criminal is an individual normally constituted from the biological and psychological points of view. The two questions are independent of each other. This independence will be better understood when we have shown, later on, the difference between psychological and sociological facts.

more vividly, for it can acquire from no other source the greater force necessary to control these individuals who formerly were the most refractory. For murders to disappear, the horror of bloodshed must become greater in those social strata from which murderers are recruited; but first it must become greater throughout the entire society. Moreover, the very absence of crime would directly contribute to produce this horror; because any sentiment seems much more respectable when it is always and uniformly respected.

One easily overlooks the consideration that these strong states of the common consciousness cannot be thus reinforced without reinforcing at the same time the more feeble states, whose violation previously gave birth to mere infraction of convention—since the weaker ones are only the prolongation, the attenuated form, of the stronger. Thus robbery and simple bad taste injure the same single altruistic sentiment, the respect for that which is another's. However, this same sentiment is less grievously offended by bad taste than by robbery; and since, in addition, the average consciousness has not sufficient intensity to react keenly to the bad taste, it is treated with greater tolerance. That is why the person guilty of bad taste is merely blamed, whereas the thief is punished. But if this sentiment grows stronger, to the point of silencing in all consciousnesses the inclination which disposes men to steal, he will become more sensitive to the offenses which, until then, touched him but lightly. He will react against them, then, with more energy; they will be the object of greater opprobrium, which will transform certain of them from the simple moral faults that they were and give them the quality of crimes. For example, improper contracts, or contracts improperly executed, which only incur public blame or civil damages, will become offenses in law.

Imagine a society of saints, a perfect cloister of exemplary individuals. Crimes, properly so called, will there be unknown; but faults which appear venial to the layman will create there the same scandal that the ordinary offense does in ordinary consciousnesses. If, then, this society has the power to judge and punish, it will define these acts as criminal and will treat them as such. For the same reason, the perfect and upright man judges his smallest failings with a severity that the majority reserve for acts more truly in the nature of an offense. Formerly, acts of violence against persons were more frequent than they are today, because respect for individual dignity was less strong. As this has increased, these crimes have become more rare; and also, many acts violating this sentiment have been introduced into the penal law which were not included there in primitive times.[2]

In order to exhaust all the hypotheses logically possible, it will perhaps be asked why this unanimity does not extend to all collective sentiments without exception. Why should not even the most feeble sentiment gather

---

[2] Calumny, insults, slander, fraud, etc.

enough energy to prevent all dissent? The moral consciousness of the society would be present in its entirety in all individuals, with a vitality sufficient to prevent all acts offending it—the purely conventional faults as well as the crimes. But a uniformity so universal and absolute is utterly impossible; for the immediate physical milieu in which each one of us is placed, the hereditary antecedents, and the social influences vary from one individual to the next, and consequently diversify consciousnesses. It is impossible for all to be alike, if only because each one has his own organism and that these organisms occupy different areas in space. That is why, even among the lower peoples, where individual originality is very little developed, it nevertheless does exist.

Thus, since there cannot be a society in which the individuals do not differ more or less from the collective type, it is also inevitable that, among these divergencies, there are some with a criminal character. What confers this character upon them is not the intrinsic quality of a given act but that definition which the collective conscience lends them. If the collective conscience is stronger, if it has enough authority practically to suppress these divergences, it will also be more sensitive, more exacting; and, reacting against the slightest deviations with the energy it otherwise displays only against more considerable infractions, it will attribute to them the same gravity as formerly to crimes. In other words, it will designate them as criminal.

Crime is, then, necessary; it is bound up with the fundamental conditions of all social life, and by that very fact it is useful, because these conditions of which it is a part are themselves indispensable to the normal evolution of morality and law.

Indeed, it is no longer possible today to dispute the fact that law and morality vary from one social type to the next, nor that they change within the same type if the conditions of life are modified. But, in order that these transformations may be possible, the collective sentiments at the basis of morality must not be hostile to change, and consequently must have but moderate energy. If they were too strong, they would no longer be plastic. Every pattern is an obstacle to new patterns, to the extent that the first pattern is inflexible. The better a structure is articulated, the more it offers a healthy resistance to all modification; and this is equally true of functional, as of anatomical, organization. If there were no crimes, this condition could not have been fulfilled; for such a hypothesis presupposes that collective sentiments have arrived at a degree of intensity unexampled in history. Nothing is good indefinitely and to an unlimited extent. The authority which the moral conscience enjoys must not be excessive; otherwise no one would dare criticize it, and it would too easily congeal into an immutable form. To make progress, individual originality must be able to express itself. In order that the originality of the idealist whose dreams transcend his century may find expression, it is necessary that the originality of the criminal, who is below the level of his time, shall also be possible. One does not occur without the other.

Nor is this all. Aside from this indirect utility, it happens that crime itself plays a useful role in this evolution. Crime implies not only that the way remains open to necessary changes but that in certain cases it directly prepares these changes. Where crime exists, collective sentiments are sufficiently flexible to take on a new form, and crime sometimes helps to determine the form they will take. How many times, indeed, it is only an anticipation of future morality—a step toward what will be! According to Athenian law, Socrates was a criminal, and his condemnation was no more than just. However, his crime, namely, the independence of his thought, rendered a service not only to humanity but to his country. It served to prepare a new morality and faith which the Athenians needed, since the traditions by which they had lived until then were no longer in harmony with the current conditions of life. Nor is the case of Socrates unique; it is reproduced periodically in history. It would never have been possible to establish the freedom of thought we now enjoy if the regulations prohibiting it had not been violated before being solemnly abrogated. At that time, however, the violation was a crime, since it was an offense against sentiments still very keen in the average conscience. And yet this crime was useful as a prelude to reforms which daily became more necessary. Liberal philosophy had as its precursors the heretics of all kinds who were justly punished by secular authorities during the entire course of the Middle Ages and until the eve of modern times.

From this point of view the fundamental facts of criminality present themselves to us in an entirely new light. Contrary to current ideas, the criminal no longer seems a totally unsociable being, a sort of parasitic element, a strange and unassimilable body, introduced into the midst of society.[3] On the contrary, he plays a definite role in social life. Crime, for its part, must no longer be conceived as an evil that cannot be too much suppressed. There is no occasion for self-congratulation when the crime rate drops noticeably below the average level, for we may be certain that this apparent progress is associated with some social disorder. Thus, the number of assault cases never falls so low as in times of want.[4] With the drop in the crime rate, and as a reaction to it, comes a revision, or the need of a revi-

---

[3] We have ourselves committed the error of speaking thus of the criminal, because of a failure to apply our rule (*Division du travail social*, pp. 395–96).

[4] Although crime is a fact of normal sociology, it does not follow that we must not abhor it. Pain itself has nothing desirable about it; the individual dislikes it as society does crime, and yet it is a function of normal physiology. Not only is it necessarily derived from the very constitution of every living organism, but it plays a useful role in life, for which reason it cannot be replaced. It would, then, be a singular distortion of our thought to present it as an apology for crime. We would not even think of protesting against such an interpretation, did we not know to what strange accusations and misunderstandings one exposes oneself when one undertakes to study moral facts objectively and to speak of them in a different language from that of the layman.

sion, in the theory of punishment. If, indeed, crime is a disease, its punishment is its remedy and cannot be otherwise conceived; thus, all the discussions it arouses bear on the point of determining what the punishment must be in order to fulfill this role of remedy. If crime is not pathological at all, the object of punishment cannot be to cure it, and its true function must be sought elsewhere.

It is far from the truth, then, that the rules previously stated have no other justification than to satisfy an urge for logical formalism of little practical value, since, on the contrary, according as they are or are not applied, the most essential facts are entirely changed in character. If the foregoing example is particularly convincing—and this was our hope in dwelling upon it—there are likewise many others which might have been cited with equal profit. There is no society where the rule does not exist that the punishment must be proportional to the offense; yet, for the Italian school, this principle is but an invention of jurists, without adequate basis.[5]

For these criminologists the entire penal system, as it has functioned until the present day among all known peoples, is a phenomenon contrary to nature. We have already seen that, for M. Garofalo, the criminality peculiar to lower societies is not at all natural. For socialists it is the capitalist system, in spite of its wide diffusion, which constitutes a deviation from the normal state, produced, as it was, by violence and fraud. Spencer, on the contrary, maintains that our administrative centralization and the extension of governmental powers are the radical vices of our societies, although both proceed most regularly and generally as we advance in history. We do not believe that scholars have ever systematically endeavored to distinguish the normal or abnormal character of social phenomena from their degree of generality. It is always with a great array of dialectics that these questions are partly resolved.

Once we have eliminated this criterion, however, we are not only exposed to confusion and partial errors, such as those just pointed out, but science is rendered all but impossible. Its immediate object is the study of the normal type. If, however, the most widely diffused facts can be pathological, it is possible that the normal types never existed in actuality; and if that is the case, why study the facts? Such study can only confirm our prejudices and fix us in our errors. If punishment and the responsibility for crime are only the products of ignorance and barbarism, why strive to know them in order to derive the normal forms from them? By such arguments the mind is diverted from a reality in which we have lost interest, and falls back on itself in order to seek within itself the materials necessary to reconstruct its world. In order that sociology may treat facts as things, the sociologist must feel the necessity of studying them exclusively.

The principal object of all sciences of life, whether individual or social,

---

[5] See Garofalo, *Criminologie*, p. 299.

is to define and explain the normal state and to distinguish it from its opposite. If, however, normality is not given in the things themselves—if it is, on the contrary, a character we may or may not impute to them—this solid footing is lost. The mind is then complacent in the face of a reality which has little to teach it; it is no longer restrained by the matter which it is analyzing, since it is the mind, in some manner or other, that determines the matter.

The various principles we have established up to the present are, then, closely interconnected. In order that sociology may be a true science of things, the generality of phenomena must be taken as the criterion of their normality.

Our method has, moreover, the advantage of regulating action at the same time as thought. If the social values are not subjects of observation but can and must be determined by a sort of mental calculus, no limit, so to speak, can be set for the free inventions of the imagination in search of the best. For how may we assign to perfection a limit? It escapes all limitation, by definition. The goal of humanity recedes into infinity, discouraging some by its very remoteness and arousing others who, in order to draw a little nearer to it, quicken the pace and plunge into revolutions. This practical dilemma may be escaped if the desirable is defined in the same way as is health and normality and if health is something that is defined as inherent in things. For then the object of our efforts is both given and defined at the same time. It is no longer a matter of pursuing desperately an objective that retreats as one advances, but of working with steady perseverance to maintain the normal state, of re-establishing it if it is threatened, and of rediscovering its conditions if they have changed. The duty of the statesman is no longer to push society toward an ideal that seems attractive to him, but his role is that of the physician: he prevents the outbreak of illnesses by good hygiene, and he seeks to cure them when they have appeared.[6]

---

[6] From the theory developed in this chapter, the conclusion has at times been reached that, according to us, the increase of criminality in the course of the nineteenth century was a normal phenomenon. Nothing is farther from our thought. Several facts indicated by us apropos of suicide (see *Suicide*, pp. 420 ff.) tend, on the contrary, to make us believe that this development is in general morbid. Nevertheless, it might happen that a certain increase of certain forms of criminality would be normal, for each state of civilization has its own criminality. But on this, one can only formulate hypotheses.

3. CULTURAL INFLUENCES IN CRIME

Daniel Glaser

The approach to crime which is distinctly sociological assumes that the criminal acquires his interest, ability, and means of self-justification in crime through his relationship to others. This conception contrasts sharply with those psychoanalytic and biological approaches which conceive of crime as the expression of innate impulses which the criminal has not learned to control.[1] It will be noted, however, that in recent years the sociological conception has been largely accepted by many persons identified with disciplines other than sociology.

THE EARLY CULTURAL EMPHASIS

The early divergence of sociological and psychological approaches to crime probably stems in part from the fact that criminals and delinquents were

Reprinted with permission of the author and the publisher from a symposium, "Crime and Correction," appearing in *Law and Contemporary Problems*, 23, no. 4 (Autumn 1958): 683–87, published by the Duke University School of Law, Durham, N.C. Copyright © 1958 by Duke University. Original title: "The Sociological Approach to Crime and Correction."

[1] Cf. August Aichhorn, *Wayward Youth*, 4 (1935); Michaels, "Delinquency and Control," *American Journal of Orthopsychiatry*, 24 (1954): 258.

referred as separate individuals to psychiatrists and psychologists, from whom diagnoses and prognoses were requested. Also, these specialists were likely to receive a disproportionate number of offenders who exhibited emotional instability or other psychological defect. In contrast, sociologists first studied crime as a statistical phenomenon, comparing the total arrest or conviction rates of different countries, cities, neighborhoods, occupations, races, social classes, and other collective units. The sociologist's problem was to explain the differences which he found in such group rates. The cases brought to his attention consisted of all persons who had official crime or delinquency records.

To the sociologist, all intergroup differences in behavior patterns were understandable only if seen as consequences of the cultures in which individuals are reared. A culture, however, was seen as understandable only in terms of its history, which antedates any single individual. To oversimplify slightly, one might say that the sociologist explained the prevalence of criminal behavior in one group and noncriminal behavior in another in the same way in which he would explain the fact that people reared in Paris talk French and people reared in Omaha talk English.

Space does not permit detailed review of nineteenth- and early twentieth-century European writings which foreshadowed this culture determinism approach. It may suffice to point out that some writings of this period which were called "sociology," like those of the Italian journalist Enrico Ferri, were not very sociological. On the other hand, the works of the French psychologist and magistrate Gabriel Tarde contained much which closely resembled the criminological writings of American sociologists forty years later.

The cultural emphasis achieved its major influence in the second quarter of the twentieth century. Its leading protagonist was the late Clifford R. Shaw, whose constant collaborator was Henry D. McKay. Their contributions were a series of statistical studies and case histories of delinquency in Chicago.[2] Among their principal findings, which have stood the test of time fairly well, were: (1) delinquency is concentrated in deteriorated slums located in those portions of a city which once were residential, but are changing to commercial and industrial districts; (2) these areas always have the highest delinquency rates, even after their population changes almost completely in national descent or race; (3) organized vice, political corruption, and most other social problems are concentrated in these areas, and case study analysis indicates that this is because social control breaks down there owing to the low social status of the residents, their newness to the urban scene, and the unattractiveness of the area for new residential investment

---

[2] Clifford R. Shaw and Henry D. McKay, *Delinquency Areas* (1929); *The Jackroller* (1930); *Natural History of a Delinquent Career* (1931); *Social Factors in Juvenile Delinquency*, published as vol. 2 of U.S. National Commission on Law Observance and Enforcement, *Report on the Causes of Crime* (1931); *Brothers in Crime* (1938).

and development; (4) as residents of these areas move elsewhere in the city, the delinquency rates of their children decrease; (5) delinquents from the high-delinquency areas have higher recidivism rates than other delinquents; (6) delinquency is usually group behavior from the outset and becomes group behavior to a greater extent as youth become more advanced in delinquency (they found that only 11.8 percent of delinquents known to the juvenile court and only 6.9 percent of all juvenile stealing cases were cases of lone delinquency); and (7) gangs are traditional in the streets of the high-delinquency areas, and youth are enculturated into delinquency in the normal course of growing up in these areas.

Shaw's approach to the study of delinquency was extended through similar research by others. Notable was F. M. Thrasher's investigation of 1,313 boys' gangs in Chicago, in which he traced the manner in which spontaneous children's play groups in the slums become transformed into unified criminal gangs through exciting disapproval and, therefore, becoming collectively involved in conflict with other gangs, police, and other adults.[3] It was shown that in the slum, the gang successfully competes with legitimate agencies to meet fundamental needs of youth for recognition, excitement, affection, and loyalty. Also, services of the gang to politicians, dealers in stolen goods, and organized vice and crime syndicates were shown to cause these agencies to reciprocate by helping the gang in resisting its enemies and by providing career opportunities for its leaders. While Chicago was the center for the Shaw-McKay-Thrasher type of research, it also was carried on in at least twenty other cities, with largely similar findings.[4]

This picture of the slum youth learning crime, as children in other cultural communities learn good manners and legitimate ambitions through enculturation, also was extended to explain the behavior of adult professional criminals. The late Edwin H. Sutherland, dean of American criminologists, annotated and published in 1937 a professional thief's account of his profession.[5] It showed how members of this profession gradually acquire a complex of highly specialized techniques, including skill in planning offenses, verbal abilities for dealing with victims and with the law, knowledge of how to dispose of stolen goods, and, if detected, the ability to "fix" a case by dealings with the police, court officials, and victims. Such knowledge is acquired only through association and cooperation with thieves, much of the former occurring in jails and prisons. As the thief becomes sophisti-

---

[3] F. M. Thrasher, *The Gang*, 2d ed. (1936).

[4] Cf. Clifford R. Shaw and Henry D. McKay, *Juvenile Delinquency and Urban Areas* (1942). A notable, but little publicized, outgrowth of this research is the shift in delinquency prevention from child-guidance clinics and settlement houses to "corner workers," "detached social group workers," slum resident committees, and "reaching out" (or "aggressive") social work. The latter locate and work with delinquents and gangs, even in the face of resistance initially, rather than waiting for them to seek counsel or aid. This approach was pioneered and still is being led, in many respects, by Shaw's Chicago Area Projects.

[5] Edwin H. Sutherland, *The Professional Thief* (1937).

cated in these professional techniques, he acquires an honorific status and looks down on more amateur offenders. Like a member of any other profession, he shares the *esprit de corps* of the profession and incorporates into his own thinking his profession's consensus of values. He thus lives in a somewhat distinct cultural world, insulated from opposing values in the larger societies.

One final work might be mentioned, a highly influential criminology textbook, *Crime and the Community*, which was written by a Columbia University professor of Latin American history, Frank Tannenbaum, assisted by Magistrate Morris Ploscowe, John Dewey, and others, including inmates of New York state prisons.[6] The literary skills of these authors enabled them to describe this process of enculturation in a much more vivid style than that usually found in sociologists' writings. The introduction to criminal careers was ascribed to "the dramatization of evil" in the arrest, jailing, and trial experience of the first offender. The procedures involved here were described as tagging the individual as a criminal, emotionally rejecting him from respectable society, and making the company of other delinquents or criminals the sole place where he can find acceptance, solace, encouragement, and even prestige. Subsequent experience is described as habituation to crime as a way of life; it becomes normal activity for the criminal and has a variety of supporting influences. Further experience with law-enforcement agencies is portrayed as a "hardening process," the ultimate result of which is the "warrior psychosis" of the professional criminal. The latter is seen as motivated by fear and by a philosophy which sees all life as a racket and which thereby justifies any means to the end of self-preservation.

THE GREAT DEBATES

The almost exclusive reliance of sociologists on enculturation as an explanation for delinquency and crime during the second quarter of this century involved them in frequently bitter debates with psychologists, psychiatrists, and biologists, as well as with legal and theological writers.

Sutherland's *Principles of Criminology*, which first appeared in 1924 and which, in its successive editions, has been by far the most successful text in criminology, from the outset criticized "psychopathy" as an etiological concept. Sutherland pointed out that some psychiatrists diagnosed almost all criminals as psychopaths, making the two terms virtually synonymous, while others used it for only a small percentage of criminals. In any case, Sutherland contended, psychopathy was too vague a concept for useful diagnosis, and if it were used as synonymous with certain patterns of crim-

---

[6] Frank Tannenbaum, *Crime and the Community* (1938).

inality, it still left these patterns to be explained. His implication was that these patterns of criminality, like others, were mainly "the result of social interactions," an interpretation consistent with much current psychiatric theory, but in contradiction to the constitutional explanation of psychopathy then implicit or explicit in most uses of this term.

Sociologists also attacked other psychological explanations for criminality, particularly low intelligence and personality. This offensive reached a high point in 1950, when two of Sutherland's students, Karl F. Schuessler and Donald R. Cressey, reviewed 113 attempts to differentiate criminals from noncriminals by means of personality tests.[7] They found that only 42 percent of these efforts yielded significant differentiations between average scores, but the deviation from the average among both the criminals and the noncriminals created so much overlap as to make none of these tests adequate for diagnosis or prediction of criminality. Furthermore, differences in education and social class between the criminal and the control groups tested, as well as the effects of imprisonment on the criminals studied (who usually were prison inmates), might account for most of the differences found in their test responses.

During this period, the enculturation explanation for crime also led many sociologists to ally themselves with psychiatrists in war against classical legalists and fundamentalist religious leaders on the free-will-versus-determinism issue. To this writer, this conflict seems to be a "phony war" in which the combatants disagree not in their conception of human behavior so much as in their taste regarding usage of the words "free will" and "determinism." In their polemical zeal, however, each side misrepresents both its own and its opponents' conceptions (a common feature of arguments). The determinists, contrary to implications conveyed in the debate, recognize that humans experience awareness of alternative possible courses of behavior and make deliberate choices between those alternatives which they perceive. And the free-will exponents, in spite of assertion in argument, recognize that the course of a human's behavior is a function of the perceptions which he has had—which is why they are so concerned that children receive "correct" teaching and preaching.

The determinist position results from the metaphysical view of the world as "interconnected," which underlies any scientific explanation for events. The free-will position grows out of different metaphysical foundations, stressing the autonomy rather than the connectedness of certain components of the universe—a stress necessary for ethical or theological evaluation of behavior. Increasingly, however, the use of different frames of reference for different types of problems is accepted in science and philosophy. The free-will-versus-determinism debate seems likely to lose its intensity

---

[7] Schuessler and Cressey, "Personality Characteristics of Criminals," *American Journal of Sociology*, 55 (1950): 476.

from this increasing awareness of the influence of conceptual frameworks on thought, from declining interest in metaphysical issues, and from the growing interests of sociologists, psychologists, and psychiatrists in voluntaristic rather than reflexive conceptions of human behavior.

The "great debates" between sociology and psychology have lost some of their former fervor. The disputes ultimately led to concessions on both sides, or more accurately, to reformulations on both sides. Sociologists succeeded impressively well in discrediting monopolistic claims of other disciplines to a single simple explanation for crime. They have, however, been less successful in formulating a single general explanation for crime on which they could agree.

4. DEVIANCE AND DEFINITION

Kai T. Erikson

It is common practice in sociology to picture deviant behavior as an alien element in society. Deviance is considered a vagrant form of human activity which has somehow broken away from the more orderly currents of social life and needs to be controlled. And since it is generally understood that this sort of aberration could only occur if something were wrong within the organization of society itself, deviant behavior is described almost as if it were leakage from machinery in poor condition: it is an incidental result of disorder and anomie, a symptom of internal breakdown.

The purpose of the following remarks will be to review this conventional outlook and to argue that it provides too narrow a framework for many kinds of sociological research. Deviation, we will suggest, recalling Durkheim's classic statement on the subject, can often be understood as a normal product of stable institutions, an important resource which is guarded and preserved by forces found in all human organizations.[1]

Reprinted with permission of the author and The Macmillan Company from *The Other Side: Perspectives on Deviance* (pp. 9–21), ed. Howard S. Becker. Copyright © 1964 by The Free Press of Glencoe, a division of The Macmillan Company. Original title: "Notes on the Sociology of Deviance." This is a slightly revised version of a paper that appeared in *Social Problems*, 9 (1962): 307–14.
[1] Emile Durkheim, *The Rules of Sociological Method*, trans. S. A. Solovay and J. H. Mueller (New York: Free Press, Macmillan, 1958).

I

According to current theory, deviant behavior is most likely to occur when the sanctions governing conduct in any given social setting seem to be contradictory[2]—as would be the case, for example, if the work rules posted by a company required one course of action from its employees and the longer-range policies of the company required quite another. Any situation marked by this kind of ambiguity, of course, can pose a serious dilemma for the individual: if he is careful to observe one set of demands imposed upon him, he runs the immediate risk of violating some other, and thus may find himself caught in a deviant stance no matter how earnestly he tries to avoid it. In this limited sense, deviance can be viewed as a "normal" social response to "abnormal" social circumstances, and we are therefore invited to assume that every act of deviation results from some imbalance within the social order—a condition of strain, anomie, or alienation.

This approach to the study of deviant behavior has generated a good deal of useful research, but it has at least one serious drawback for investigators who share an interest in what is known as "social problems." The "anomie" theory (if we may use that convenient label for a moment) is designed to account for all behavior which varies in some technical way from the norms of the community, whether or not that behavior is considered a problem by anyone else. For example, the bank teller who becomes a slave to routine and the armed bandit who relieves him of the day's receipts both register as deviants according to the logic of this scheme, since each is deviating in his own way from the ideal standards of the culture. Yet the most important difference between these men is one that the "anomie" theory cannot easily take into account: the bank teller, no matter how desperate his private needs, does not ordinarily create any concern in the rest of the community, while the bandit triggers the whole machinery of social control into vigorous action. In short, the "anomie" theory may help us appreciate the various ways in which people respond to conditions of strain, but it does not help us differentiate between those people who infringe the letter of the norm without attracting any notice and those who excite so much alarm that they earn a deviant reputation in society and are committed to special institutions like prisons and hospitals.

II

From a sociological standpoint, deviance can be defined as conduct which is generally thought to require the attention of social control agencies—that

---

[2] The best known statements of this general position, of course, are by Robert K. Merton and Talcott Parsons: Merton, *Social Theory and Social Structure*, rev. ed. (New York: Free Press, Macmillan, 1957); and Parsons, *The Social System* (New York: Free Press, Macmillan, 1951).

is, conduct about which "something should be done." Deviance is not a property *inherent in* certain forms of behavior; it is a property *conferred upon* these forms by the audiences which directly or indirectly witness them. The critical variable in the study of deviance, then, is the social audience rather than the individual actor, since it is the audience which eventually determines whether or not any episode of behavior or any class of episodes is labeled deviant.

This definition may seem a little indirect, but it has the advantage of bringing a neglected sociological issue into proper focus. When a community acts to control the behavior of one of its members, it is engaged in a very intricate process of selection. After all, even the worst miscreant in society conforms most of the time, if only in the sense that he uses the correct spoon at mealtime, takes good care of his mother, or in a thousand other ways respects the ordinary conventions of his group; and if the community elects to bring sanctions against him for the occasions when he does misbehave, it is responding to a few deviant details set within a vast array of entirely acceptable conduct. Thus it happens that a moment of deviation may become the measure of a person's position in society. He may be jailed or hospitalized, certified as a full-time deviant, despite the fact that only a fraction of his behavior was in any way unusual or dangerous. The community has taken note of a few scattered particles of behavior and has decided that they reflect what kind of person he "really" is.

The screening device which sifts these telling details out of the person's over-all performance, then, is a very important instrument of social control. We know very little about the properties of this screen, but we do know that it takes many factors into account which are not directly related to the deviant act itself: it is sensitive to the suspect's social class, his past record as an offender, the amount of remorse he manages to convey, and many similar concerns which take hold in the shifting moods of the community. This may not be so obvious when the screen is dealing with extreme forms of deviance like serious crimes, but in the day-by-day filtering processes which take place throughout the community this feature is easily observable. Some men who drink too much are called alcoholics and others are not, some men who act oddly are committed to hospitals and others are not, some men who have no visible means of support are hauled into court and others are not—and the difference between those who earn a deviant label and those who go their own way in peace depends almost entirely on the way in which the community sifts out and codes the many details of behavior to which it is witness. In this respect, the community screen may be a more relevant subject for sociological research than the actual behavior which is filtered through it.

Once the problem is phrased in this way we can ask: How does a community decide what forms of conduct should be singled out for this kind of attention? The conventional answer to this question, of course, is that society sets up the machinery of control in order to protect itself against the "harmful" effects of deviation, in much the same way that an organism mobilizes its resources to combat an invasion of germs. Yet this simple view of the matter has not always proven to be a very productive one. In the first place, as Durkheim and Mead pointed out some years ago, it is by no means clear that all acts considered deviant in a culture are in fact (or even in principle) harmful to group life.[3] In the second place, it is gradually becoming more evident to sociologists engaged in this area of research that deviant behavior can play an important part in keeping the social order intact.

This raises a number of interesting questions for sociology.

III

In recent years, sociological theory has become more and more concerned with the concept "social system"—an organization of society's component parts into a form which sustains internal equilibrium, resists change, and is boundary-maintaining. In its most abstract form, the "system" concept describes a highly complex network of relations, but the scheme is generally used by sociologists to draw attention to those forces in the social order which promote a high level of uniformity among human actors and a high degree of symmetry within human institutions. The main organizational drift of a system, then, is seen as centripetal: it acts to draw the behavior of actors toward those centers in social space where the core values of the group are figuratively located, bringing them within range of basic norms. Any conduct which is neither attracted toward this nerve center by the rewards of conformity nor compelled toward it by other social pressures is considered "out of control," which is to say deviant.

This basic model has provided the theme for most contemporary thinking about deviation, and as a result little attention has been given to the notion that systems operate to maintain boundaries. To say that a system maintains boundaries is to say that it controls the fluctuation of its constituent parts so that the whole retains a defined range of activity, a unique pattern of constancy and stability, within the larger environment.[4] Because the range of human behavior is potentially so wide, social groups maintain boundaries in the sense that they try to limit the flow of behavior within their domain so that it circulates within a defined cultural territory. Boundaries, then, are an important point of reference for persons participating in any system. A people may define its boundaries by referring to a

[3] Emile Durkheim, *The Division of Labor in Society*, trans. George Simpson (New York: Free Press, Macmillan, 1952); and George Herbert Mead, "The Psychology of Punitive Justice," *American Journal of Sociology*, 23 (1918): 577–602.

[4] Cf. Talcott Parsons, *The Social System*.

geographical location, a set of honored traditions, a particular religious or political viewpoint, an occupational specialty, a common language, or just some local way of doing things; but in any case, members of the group have some idea about the contours of the niche they occupy in social space. They know where the group begins and ends as a special entity; they know what kinds of experience "belong" within these precincts and what kinds do not.

For all its apparent abstractness, a social system is organized around the movements of persons joined together in regular social relations. The only material found in a system for marking boundaries, then, is the behavior of its participants; and the kinds of behavior which best perform this function are often deviant, since they represent the most extreme variety of conduct to be found within the experience of the group. In this sense, transactions taking place between deviant persons on the one side and agencies of control on the other are boundary-maintaining mechanisms. They mark the outside limits of the area within which the norm has jurisdiction, and in this way assert how much diversity and variability can be contained within the system before it begins to lose its distinct structure, its cultural integrity.

A social norm is rarely expressed as a firm rule or official code. It is an abstract synthesis of the many separate times a community has stated its sentiments on a given kind of issue. Thus the norm has a history much like that of an article of common law: it is an accumulation of decisions made by the community over a period of time which gradually gathers enough moral eminence to serve as a precedent for future decisions. And like an article of common law, the norm retains its validity only if it is regularly used as a basis for judgment. Each time the group censures some act of deviation, then, it sharpens the authority of the violated norm and declares again where the boundaries of the group are located.

It is important to notice that these transactions between deviant persons and agents of control have always attracted a good deal of attention in this and other cultures. In our own past, both the trial and punishment of deviant offenders took place in the public market and gave the crowd a chance to participate in a direct, active way. Today we no longer parade deviants in the town square or expose them to the carnival atmosphere of Tyburn, but it is interesting to note that the "reform" which brought about this change in penal policy coincided almost precisely with the development of newspapers as media of public information. Perhaps this is no more than an accident of history, but it is nevertheless true that newspapers (and now radio and television) offer their readers the same kind of entertainment once supplied by public hangings or the use of stocks and pillories. An enormous amount of modern "news" is devoted to reports about deviant behavior and its punishment: indeed the largest circulation newspaper in the United States prints very little else. Yet how do we explain what makes these items "newsworthy" or why they command the great attention they do? Perhaps they satisfy a number of psychological perversities among the mass audience, as commentators sometimes point out, but at the same time they constitute our main source of information about the normative contours of society. In a figurative sense, at least, morality and immorality meet at the public scaffold, and it is during this meeting that the community declares where the line between them should be drawn.

People who gather together into communities need to be able to describe and anticipate those areas of experience which lie outside the immediate compass of the group—the unseen dangers which in any culture and in any age seem to threaten its security. Traditional folklore depicting demons, devils, witches, and evil spirits may be one way to give form to these otherwise formless dangers, but the visible deviant is another kind of reminder. As a trespasser against the group norms, he represents those forces which lie outside the group's boundaries: he informs us, as it were, what evil looks like, what shapes the devil can assume. And in doing so, he shows us the difference between the inside of the group and the outside. It may well be that without this ongoing drama at the outer edges of group space, the community would have no inner sense of identity and cohesion, no sense of the contrasts which set it off as a special place in the larger world.

Thus deviance cannot be dismissed simply as behavior which *disrupts* stability in society, but may itself be, in controlled quantities, an important condition for *preserving* stability.

IV

This raises a delicate theoretical issue. If we grant that deviant forms of behavior are often beneficial to society in general, can we then assume that societies are organized in such a way as to promote this resource? Can we assume, in other words, that forces operate within the social order to recruit deviant actors and commit them to deviant forms of activity? Sociology has not yet developed a conceptual language in which this sort of question can be discussed with any ease, but one observation can be made which gives the question an interesting perspective—namely, that deviant activities often seem to derive support from the very agencies designed to suppress them. Indeed, the institutions devised by society for discouraging deviant behavior are often so poorly equipped for that task that we might well ask why this is considered their "real" function at all.

It is by now a thoroughly familiar argument that many of the institutions built to inhibit deviation actually operate in such a way as to perpetuate it. For one thing, prisons, hospitals, and similar agencies of control provide aid and shelter to large numbers of deviant persons, sometimes enhancing their survival chances in the world as a whole. But beyond this, such institutions gather marginal people into tightly segregated groups, give them an opportunity to teach one another the skills and attitudes of a deviant career, and often provoke them into employing these skills by reinforcing their sense of alienation from the rest of society.[5] It should be pointed out, furthermore, that this process is found not only in the institutions which actually confine the deviant, but throughout the general community as well.

The community's decision to bring deviant sanctions against an individual is not a simple act of censure. It is a sharp rite of transition, at once moving him out of his normal position in society and transferring him into a distinct deviant role.[6] The ceremonies which accomplish this change of status ordinarily have three related phases. They provide a formal *confrontation* between the deviant suspect and representatives of his community (as in the criminal trial or psychiatric case conference); they announce some *judgment* about the nature of his deviancy (a verdict or diagnosis, for example); and they perform an act of social *placement*, assigning him to a special role (like that of prisoner or patient) which redefines his position in society. These ceremonies tend to be events of wide public interest and usually take place in a dramatic, ritualized setting.[7] Perhaps the most obvious example of a commitment ceremony is the criminal trial, with its elaborate formality and ritual pageantry, but more modest equivalents can be found everywhere that procedures are set up to judge whether someone is deviant or not.

Now an important feature of these ceremonies in our own culture is that they are almost irreversible. Most provisional roles conferred by society— like those of the student or conscripted soldier, for example—include some kind of terminal ceremony to mark the individual's movement back out of the role once its temporary advantages have been exhausted. But the roles allotted to the deviant seldom make allowance for this type of passage. He is ushered into the deviant position by a decisive and often dramatic ceremony, yet is retired from it with hardly a word of public notice. As a result, the deviant often returns home with no proper license to resume a normal life in the community. Nothing has happened to cancel out the stigmas imposed upon him by earlier commitment ceremonies; from a formal point of view, the original verdict or diagnosis is still in effect. It should not be surprising, then, that the members of the community seem reluctant to accept the returning deviant on an entirely equal footing. In a very real sense, they do not know who he is.

A circularity is thus set into motion which has all the earmarks of a "self-

---

[5] For a good description of this process in the modern prison, see Gresham Sykes, *The Society of Captives* (Princeton: Princeton University Press, 1958). For views of two different types of mental hospital settings, see Erving Goffman, "The Characteristics of Total Institutions," *Symposium on Preventive and Social Psychiatry* (Washington, D.C.: Walter Reed Army Institute of Research, 1957); and Kai T. Erikson, "Patient Role and Social Uncertainty: A Dilemma of the Mentally Ill," *Psychiatry*, 20 (1957): 263–74.

[6] Parsons, in *The Social System*, has provided the classical description of how this role transfer works in the case of medical patients.

[7] Cf. Harold Garfinkel, "Successful Degradation Ceremonies," *American Journal of Sociology*, 61 (1956): 420–24.

fulfilling prophesy," to use Merton's fine phrase. On the one hand, it seems obvious that the community's reluctance to accept the deviant back helps reduce whatever chance he might otherwise have for a successful readjust-ment. Yet on the other hand, everyday experience seems to show that this reluctance is entirely reasonable, for it is a well-known and highly publi-cized fact that large numbers of ex-convicts return to criminal activity and that many discharged mental patients suffer later breakdowns. The com-mon assumption that deviants are not often cured or reformed, then, may be based on a faulty premise, but this assumption is stated so frequently and with such conviction that it often creates the facts which later "prove" it to be correct. If the returning deviant has to face the community's appre-hensions often enough, it is understandable that he too may begin to won-der whether he has graduated from the deviant role—and respond to the uncertainty by resuming deviant activity. In some respects, this may be the only way for the individual and his community to agree as to what kind of person he really is, for it often happens that the community is only able to perceive his "true colors" when he lapses momentarily into some form of deviant performance.

Moreover, this prophesy is found in the official policies of even the most advanced agencies of control. Police departments could not operate with any real effectiveness if they did not regard ex-convicts as an almost perma-nent population of offenders, a pool from which to draw suspects; and psy-chiatric hospitals could not do a responsible job in the community if they were not alert to the fact that ex-patients are highly susceptible to relapse. Thus the prophesy gains currency at many levels within the social order, not only in the poorly informed opinions of the community at large, but in the best informed theories of most control agencies as well.

In one form or another, this problem has been known in Western culture for many hundreds of years, and the single fact that this is so becomes a highly significant one for sociology. If the culture has supported a steady flow of deviant behavior throughout long periods of historical evolution, then the rules which apply to any form of functionalist thinking would suggest that strong forces must be at work to keep this flow intact—and this because it contributes in some important way to the survival of the system as a whole. This may not be reason enough to assert that deviant behavior is "functional," in any of the many senses of that term, but it should make us wary of the assumption that human communities are organized in such a way as to prevent deviance from occurring.[8]

This in turn might suggest that our present models of society, with their emphasis on the harmony and equilibrium of social life, do a one-sided job

---

[8] Albert K. Cohen, for example, speaking for sociologists in general, seems to take the question for granted: "It would seem that the control of deviant behavior is, by defini-tion, a culture goal" ("The Study of Social Disorganization and Deviant Behavior," in *Sociology Today*, ed. Robert K. Merton *et al.* [New York: Basic Books, 1959]), p. 465.

of representing the situation. Perhaps two different and often competing currents are found in any well-functioning system: those forces which promote a high over-all degree of conformity among its members, and those forces which encourage some degree of diversity so that actors can be deployed throughout social space to patrol the system's boundaries. These different gravitational pulls in the social system set up a constant tension of opposites, outlining the area within which human life, with all its contradiction and variety, takes place. Perhaps this is what Aldous Huxley had in mind when he wrote:

> Now tidiness is undeniably good—but a good of which it is easily possible to have too much and at too high a price. . . . The good life can only be lived in a society in which tidiness is preached and practised, but not too fanatically, and where efficiency is always haloed, as it were, by a tolerated margin of mess.[9]

V

These brief remarks are no more than a prelude to further thinking and research, and in the remaining paragraphs we will try to indicate some of the directions this line of reasoning might take.

In the first place, this paper has indirectly addressed itself to one of the oldest problems in sociology. It is all very well for an investigator to conclude that something called a "system" has certain "requirements" in respect to its participants, but the major problem for research is to ask how these needs are imposed upon the people who eventually satisfy them. Ordinarily, the fact that deviant behavior is not evenly distributed throughout the social structure is explained by declaring that something called "anomie" or "disorganization" prevails at certain sensitive points. Deviance leaks out through defects in the social structure; it occurs when the system *fails* to impose its needs on human actors. But if we consider the possibility that even the best organized collectivity needs to produce occasional episodes of deviation for the sake of its own stability, we are engaged in quite another order of inquiry. Perhaps the coherence of some social groupings is maintained only when a few juvenile offenders are enlisted to balance the conformity of an adult majority; perhaps communities can retain a sense of their own territorial identity only if they keep up an ongoing dialogue with deviants who mark and publicize the outer limits of group space; perhaps some families can remain intact only if one of its members becomes a visible deviant to serve as a focus for the rest.[10] If these supposi-

---

[9] Aldous Huxley, *Prisons: The 'Carceri' Etchings by G. B. Piranesi* (London: Trianon Press, 1949).

[10] Cf. Robert A. Dentler and Kai T. Erikson, "The Functions of Deviance in Groups," *Social Problems*, 7 (1959): 98–107.

tions prove useful, we should try to learn how a social system appoints certain of its members to deviant roles and how it encourages them to spend a period of service testing the group's boundaries. This is not to suggest that a system necessarily creates the crises which impel people into deviant activity but that it deploys these resources in a patterned, organized way.

In the second place, it is evident that cultures vary in the way they regulate deviant traffic moving back and forth from their outer boundaries. We might begin with the observation, for example, that many features of the traffic pattern in our own culture seem to have a marked Puritan cast: a defined portion of the population, largely drawn from young adult groups and from the lower economic classes, is stabilized in deviant roles and often expected to remain there indefinitely. The logic which prevails in many of our formal agencies of control and in the public attitudes which sustain them sometimes seems to echo earlier Puritan theories about predestination, reprobation, and the nature of sin. Be this as it may, different traffic patterns are found in other parts of the world which offer an interesting contrast. There are societies in which deviance is considered a natural mode of behavior for the young, a pursuit which they are expected to abandon once they move through defined ceremonies into adulthood. There are societies which give license to large groups of people to engage in deviant behavior during certain seasons or on certain days of the year. And there are societies which form special groups whose stated business is to act in ways contrary to the normal expectations of the culture. Each of these patterns regulates deviant traffic differently, yet each of them provides some institutional means for a person to give up a deviant career without any kind of permanent stigma. In either of these cases, the person's momentary commitment to deviant styles of behavior is easily reversed—when the group promotes him to manhood, declares a period of festival to be over, or permits him to give up the insignia which marked his membership in a band of "contraries." Perhaps the most interesting problem here from the point of view of pure research is to see whether these various patterns are functionally equivalent in any meaningful way. Perhaps the most interesting problem for those of us who lean over into the applied areas of the field, however, is to ask whether we have anything to learn from those cultures which permit re-entry into normal social life for persons who have spent a period of time in the deviant ranks and no longer have any special need to remain there.

5. CRIME AND THE CRIMINAL

Leonard Savitz

A collectivity of people known as a society typically operates within a particular ideal code of normative behavior called culture. A member of a society is invariably granted enormous latitude as to the actions in which he may permissibly engage. Beyond this range of "free" action, however, other behavior is proscribed; if this behavior is detected and brought to public attention, it might result in the imposition of social sanctions, the certainty, nature, and seriousness of which will depend upon the nature of the harm. For violations of minor social rules, moderate punishments are incurred; the violator of somewhat more important societal values or mores, perhaps because his deviant behavior might be injurious to others, is likely to be more seriously penalized. Still more serious are forms of behavior considered so reprehensible and threatening that members of the community are explicitly and formally prohibited from engaging in them. In civilized societies, such prohibitions usually take the form of criminal codes. Under these conditions, the prohibited action (the crime) is described in detail and the punishment made explicit, and various personnel become occupationally involved within an institution of law enforcement and are

From *Dilemmas in Criminology* (pp. 9–15), by Leonard Savitz. Copyright © 1967 by McGraw-Hill, Inc. Used by permission of McGraw-Hill Book Company and the author.

assigned the tasks of detecting, apprehending, convicting, and punishing the culpable offender. The blameworthy perpetrator of a crime, once his guilt has been established within the current system of criminal procedure, is defined as a criminal and made to suffer some established form of punishment.

Within each of the several legal jurisdictions in the United States, the appropriate legislative body determines what acts will be classified as crimes and what punishments they will incur. It also constructs and, on occasion, alters the procedure whereby a person suspected of committing a crime may formally be found guilty and considered a criminal.

It would be illuminating to discover why legislators in one jurisdiction prohibit as criminal some specific behavior, while another, equally august legislative body concludes that the identical act is not very reprehensible and does not define it as a crime. Admittedly there is universal agreement that murder, rape, robbery, burglary, and some other serious actions are "wrong in themselves" (*mala in se*) and are therefore crimes; but certain acts, such as fornication (voluntary sexual intercourse between two unmarried adults), are misdemeanors in some jurisdictions, while other jurisdictions—although perhaps judging them unattractive behavior—still do not legally prohibit them. Why this nonuniformity exists and what factors (rational and irrational) operate in the legislative decision-making processes still remain something of a mystery.

CRIME

Generally, it has been held that a crime is any act or omission prohibited by law and punishable by the state in judicial proceedings.[1] More specifically, in Anglo-Saxon law, there are five *necessary* theoretical elements in a crime:

1. *The act must involve a conscious, voluntary, external harm.* Nevertheless, the omission or neglect of legal duties will still meet this criterion. Additionally, simply conspiring to commit a crime and soliciting someone to engage in a crime are themselves misdemeanors under the common law.

2. *The act must have been legally prohibited at the time it was committed.* In effect this means that if some heartless legislature decided today to make kissing a misdemeanor, kisses committed before the passage of this law could not be made criminal offenses and would not be punishable under the law. The United States Constitution forbids the federal, state, and local governments from passing any such ex post facto laws (art. 1, sec. 9, par. 3, and sec. 10, par. 1).

3. *The perpetrator must have had criminal intent* (mens rea) *when he*

---

[1] William L. Clark and William L. Marshall, *A Treatise on the Law of Crimes,* 5th ed. (Chicago: Callaghan & Co., 1952), pp. 1–16.

engaged in the crime. If the criminal act was "willful, wanton, or done with malice," the law assumes that criminal intent was present. It must be kept in mind that if *mens rea* was lacking, the actor *cannot* be found to be a criminal; it might even be argued that in this circumstance the act itself was not a crime. The assumption of *mens rea* is sometimes difficult for someone other than a legal philosopher to comprehend. "Statutory" rape, for example, is carnal knowledge of a girl under a specific age who has given her verbal consent. Because she is under the specified age, the law says she cannot legally grant permission. The courts are not concerned with the girl's own state of mind because, in a classic legal phrase, "the law resists for her." There are cases on record in which a man, aware that rape of any type is an exceedingly serious offense, has made careful and sincere efforts to ascertain that a girl is of the age of consent, but finds later that she is really under this age. Until 1964, under these conditions a man would probably have been convicted of the crime of rape, despite his efforts to avoid committing the crime, *mens rea* being considered present because of the willful wantonness of his action.

Mens rea is also assumed in the case of "felony murder." In most states, if *anyone* is killed during the commission or attempted commission of a felony (with the sole exception of a co-felon killed by the victim or by a third party), the felon may be found guilty not only of the particular felony he was engaged in, but probably also of first-degree murder. This is so even if he had no weapon on his person, had no plans to kill anyone, or indeed was in no position to kill anyone if he had wanted to. For instance, an unarmed felon may have been committing a burglary inside a house when a police officer attempting to arrest his partner outside the house accidentally killed another policeman or some innocent third party. Under these conditions the burglar would almost certainly be guilty of first-degree murder. The law assumes, perhaps, that the offender in such cases has engaged in actions of so dangerous a nature that he should consider that someone may well die as a consequence: he therefore is culpable (blameworthy) for any death that results.[2]

Conversely, there are several conditions under which the law assumes that criminal intent does not and cannot occur. If the actor is below the age of culpability (under the common law this was seven years, but some statutory enactments have raised the age to ten years or more), if he is judged to be insane, if he was coerced into committing the act, or if the act is provably accidental, *mens rea* is deemed to be lacking; the actor is not a criminal, then, and the acts themselves are probably not crimes.

---

[2] From a rather considerable literature on this curious and most interesting phenomenon some of the most important items are: Herbert Wechsler and Jerome Michael, "A Rationale of the Law of Homicide," *Columbia Law Review* (May and December 1937): 701–61, 1261–1325; Roy Moreland, *The Law of Homicide* (Indianapolis: Bobbs-Merrill, 1952), chap. 6, pp. 42–54; Norval Morris, "The Felon's Responsibility for the Lethal Acts of Others," *University of Pennsylvania Law Review* (November 1956): 50–81.

4. *There must be a causal relationship between the voluntary miscon-duct and the legally forbidden result.* Only rarely does this requirement pose any problem. Suppose that John deliberately aims his gun and shoots Mary in the shoulder. There is certainly a direct causal relationship be-tween John's firing his pistol and the crimes of aggravated assault, assault with a deadly weapon, assault with intent to kill, and perhaps attempted murder. But suppose that the wound, although not very serious, requires some treatment, and that Mary dies during surgery to remove the bullet. The question now arises whether John has added felonious homicide to the other crimes with which he is charged. Was there a causal relationship be-tween his inflicting a flesh wound and the death of his victim?

5. *There must be some legally prescribed punishment for anyone con-victed of the crime.* These punishments can range enormously, from sus-pended sentences and fines to life imprisonment and the death penalty.

The proscribed actions that are considered crimes obviously vary not only from one jurisdiction to another but also from one time period to another. In Biblical times, for example, the Mosaic code regarded the following as capital crimes: violating the Sabbath, cursing one's parents, eating leavened bread during Passover, and oppressing the widowed and fatherless. To call these acts crimes may now seem completely absurd; yet over 2,000 years later, in colonial America, a Quaker found living in the Massachusetts Bay Colony and persons caught trading with Indians in the Virginia colony were executed as capital offenders.

There are some persistently intriguing questions which may be raised re-garding what might be thought of as the metaphysic of a crime. If a crim-inal act is committed but never comes to the attention of any public au-thority, has a crime been committed? If neither "victim" nor "offender" is aware of the fact that a criminal act has taken place, has a crime been committed? There are no "answers" to these problems. If one holds that by definition a crime implies an act which must come to the notice of public authorities, then a crime has not taken place unless this condition is met. Beyond this it must be asked, Do all crimes of necessity and by definition have culpable perpetrators who in time will be convicted of these acts and called criminals?

CRIMINAL

To this last question the answer is clearly "no." Of all crimes which become known to the police, *most* do not result in any arrest; and a very small per-centage of all crimes known to the police finally result in a formal convic-tion in a court of law. Moreover, to call someone a criminal merely because he is accused of having engaged in a crime, or because he has been arrested or held for grand jury or even placed on trial, is, in itself, to engage in criminal behavior (slander or libel) if the man so described is not convicted.

Crime is prohibited, punishable *behavior;* the criminal is the judicially proven, culpable *perpetrator* of the crime. Countries with an Anglo-Saxon legal heritage developed a rather precise set of conditions governing what evidence is admissible in determining the guilt or innocence of an accused person. By and large, the rules seem reasonable. At an earlier time in English history, very different techniques were used to prove whether the accused was a punishable offender. The so-called ordeals were, in effect, legal trials and tests of truth. The ordeals included the hot iron (carrying a red-hot bar or wearing a pair of red-hot metal gloves), boiling water (dipping one's hand into a pot of scalding water), and fire (walking on a burning pyre). If in any of these ordeals the suspect developed blisters on his hands or feet this was tantamount to a finding of guilt and he was instantly punished. We would assume that a near-miracle would be necessary for anyone not to be found guilty. However, in the cold-water ordeal (in this ordeal the accused, bound hand and foot, was lowered into a pond; if he sank to the bottom, he was considered innocent), the basic laws of nature operated in favor of the defendant.[3] Our less barbarous contemporary rules of evidence have exactly the same function as the ordeal: proving guilt or innocence. In American jurisprudence, for minor (nonindictable) offenses the determination of guilt is made by a magistrate or justice of the peace, whereas for more serious (indictable) crimes the judge or jury in a court of record makes this decision.

It has been reiterated that if a defendant is not convicted, or the conviction is not upheld by appellate courts, he is not a criminal. Are there instances when an acknowledged perpetrator of a crime is not a criminal? Certainly this might be the case under a variety of conditions. Suppose a man comes home unexpectedly and finds that he is a cuckold; in a rage at catching his indiscreet wife and her lover *flagrante delicto,* he shoots and kills the lover. At his trial he freely confesses the homicide; but the all-male jury, sympathetic to his situation and unconsciously falling back on the specious "unwritten law" allowing a wronged husband to avenge himself on the lover, acquits him. Never having been convicted, he is therefore not a criminal; but, by their verdict, did the jury not also imply that the killing itself was not a felony? Let us look at another case. A six-year-old child, brooding over the humiliations he imagines his parents have inflicted upon him, takes revenge by killing one or both of them. He is below the age of culpability and therefore is not legally responsible for his actions. Does this mean the killing itself was not criminal? Finally, one might cite the tragic case of Howard Unruh, who, some years ago in Camden, New Jersey, shot to death no fewer than thirteen neighbors and bystanders. He would seem

---

[3] John H. Wigmore, *A Kaleidoscope of Justice* (Washington, D.C.: Washington Law Book Co., 1941).

to have engaged in multiple felonious homicide; but he was declared insane and unable to stand trial. While he was, and remains to this day, institutionalized as a man who is extraordinarily dangerous and violent, he is still technically not a criminal. What is intriguing about the above examples is not that the actors are for one reason or another not criminals, but on some metaphysical plane it may be argued that, because they are not or could not be convicted, their actions—while examples of reprehensible and extremely dangerous deviant behavior—are not crimes.

It is disconcerting to note that often, even in serious research projects, the terms *crime* and *criminal* are used with considerable lack of precision. It seems to be often assumed that anyone who is arrested is necessarily a criminal. As these are basic concepts upon which the field of criminology is based, such casual indifference is somewhat difficult to understand.

Some Issues in Measurement I:
Criminal Statistics

"In view of the difficulties and inaccuracies in criminal statistics, little dependence can be placed upon them for scientific purposes."[1] Appearing in the first American criminology textbook, this observation has until very recently been an accurate commentary upon the state of criminal statistics. Despite marked advances in scope, quality, and availability, data on crime are increasingly required to reflect true *incidence* and social *distribution* of criminal acts, and to be collected in terms of underlying criminological *theory*. The latter point, that criminologists are reliant upon data gathered by public functionaries for purposes only tangential to research, has been a particularly limiting factor in the reliance that can be placed upon official statistics.

Not surprisingly, alternative means for gauging crime have developed over the years. There are at least five levels from which estimates of crime incidence may be derived, each having its distinctive limitations. First, it would be theoretically possible to survey the entire population, thereby avoiding the usual questions raised about sampling bias and "selective participation" in a study. Assuming an investigator could demonstrate that survey responses from a total population had acceptable validity, the venture would still be

---

[1] Edwin H. Sutherland, *Criminology* (Philadelphia: Lippincott, 1924).

unattractive, because the methodological impediments to and ethical issues in asking community members about their "criminal" activities would be at variance with the scientific model of research. Second, the unit of analysis might be the victims of crimes, recognizing that particular types of offenses are likely to be underreported. Recent studies suggest that this is true for crimes against property (e.g., loss covered by insurance provisions) as well as crimes against persons (e.g., rape, deception, fraud). A third level, one that has been widely exploited in this country, calls for the use of data secured and recorded by police authority. It is probably testimony to the pervasive employment of these data that more criticism and recommendation have been directed at this level than at any other, and that it has undergone the most change. Fourth, courts of law develop records in which data on the charge, plaintiff, defendant, court proceedings, and disposition must be entered. A final resource is the correctional system, where data are compiled to facilitate decisions concerning the custody and treatment of inmates. Local institutions usually perform a case analysis for each inmate, derived from inquiries sent to outside organizations, investigative agencies, and points of prior incarceration. In view of the known and highly selective character of penal establishments, comparing an institutionalized population with aggregate data on any of the other four levels would be hazardous.

While these five may appear to offer the criminologist some latitude in data collection, it should be pointed out that as one passes from the first level to the last, there is considerable selectivity of cases—most notably in terms of socioeconomic status, knowledge about and access to legal assistance, previous involvement with law-enforcement authorities, and type of offense. In the event that one decides to use official statistics, some appear to be better suited for crime-index construction than others. As Stanton Wheeler has pointed out: "A chief procedural rule is that the further removed from the actual crime incident, the less reliable the statistics. Thus indices based upon police data are better than those based on court actions because the latter include the additional biases involved in the selection of cases for court action."[2] It follows, then, that prison populations exhibit features that are improbably representative of "crime" as distributed in previous stages.

Some of the problems encountered by criminologists in having to rely upon official data sources are addressed by Cressey in "Measuring Crime Rates." He also considers evidence of "dark figure" criminality, or the commission of law-violating acts that go undiscovered by enforcement authorities.

Marvin Wolfgang's "Limitations in the Use of Official Statistics" is selected from his extensive appraisal of Uniform Crime Reports, unquestionably the most widely used source of criminal statistics. Among other things, Wolfgang

---

[2] Stanton Wheeler, "Delinquency and Crime," in Social Problems, ed. Howard S. Becker (New York: Wiley, 1966), p. 208.

reviews the development of this compilation, published by the Federal Bureau of Investigation, and discusses a variety of difficulties in the interpretation of crime data.

The papers by Donald J. Newman ("Criminal Statistics and Accommodations in Justice Administration") and by John I. Kitsuse and Aaron V. Cicourel ("Alternative Uses of Official Statistics") argue that the criminal justice system be studied in terms of its administrative routine. That is, rather than debate the adequacy of crime typology or the selectivity in a conviction process, it is fruitful to examine the actual operation of administrative legal systems that apprehend, accuse, adjudicate, and dispose of alleged offenders. As David Sudnow put it in his study of the public defender's office: "By sociologically regarding, rather than criticizing, rates of statistics and the categories employed to assemble them, one learns . . . about the 'rate producing agencies,' and the assembling process."[3] While Newman addresses himself to statistical bias introduced in court records through the use of adjudicative "accommodations," Kitsuse and Cicourel focus upon the relationship between rates of deviant behavior and the nature of decision-making rendered by control agencies.

The literature on criminal statistics is voluminous, ranging from philosophical conceptions of "crime" to refined treatments of estimated error in official records. Selected publications that illustrate major themes in this area at the present time are listed below.

1. *The Distribution of Crime in American Society*

Cressey, Donald R. "Crime," in *Contemporary Social Problems*, 2nd ed., ed. Robert K. Merton and Robert A. Nisbet (New York: Harcourt, Brace & World, 1966), pp. 136–92.

Federal Bureau of Investigation, United States Department of Justice, *Uniform Crime Reports for the United States, 1967* (Washington, D.C.: U.S. Government Printing Office, 1968).

The President's Commission on Law Enforcement and Administration of Justice, *Task Force Report: Crime and Its Impact—An Assessment* (Washington, D.C.: U.S. Government Printing Office, 1967).

Quinney, Richard. "Structural Characteristics, Population Areas, and Crime Rates in the United States," *Journal of Criminal Law, Criminology, and Police Science* 57 (March 1966): 45–52.

Wilkins, Leslie T. "Crime: Offense Patterns," in *International Encyclopedia of the Social Sciences*, ed. David L. Sills (New York: Free Press, Macmillan, 1968), vol. 3, pp. 476–83.

2. *Issues in the Employment of Criminal Statistics*

Conrad, John P. "The Unfinished Business of Criminal Statistics," in *Crime and Culture: Essays in Honor of Thorsten Sellin*, ed. Marvin E. Wolfgang (New York: Wiley, 1968), pp. 157–67.

---

[3] David Sudnow, "Normal Crimes: Sociological Features of the Penal Code in a Public Defender Office," *Social Problems,* 12 (Winter 1965): 255.

Mannheim, Hermann. "The Place of Statistics in Criminological Research I" and "The Place of Statistics in Criminological Research II: Research Statistics," *Comparative Criminology* (Boston: Houghton Mifflin, 1965), chaps. 5, 6.

Mode, Elmer B. "Probability and Criminalistics," *Journal of the American Statistical Association* 303 (September 1963): 628–40.

Pittman, David J., and Handy, William F. "Uniform Crime Reporting: Suggested Improvements," *Sociology and Social Research* 46 (January 1962): 135–43.

Sellin, Thorsten, and Wolfgang, Marvin E. *The Measurement of Delinquency* (New York: Wiley, 1964), chaps. 2–4.

Wilkins, Leslie. "New Thinking in Criminal Statistics," *Journal of Criminal Law, Criminology, and Police Science* 56 (September 1965): 277–84.

3. New Directions in the Study of Crime Occurrence

Biderman, Albert D., and Reiss, Albert J., Jr. "On Exploring the Dark Figure of Crime," *Annals of the American Academy of Political and Social Science* 374 (November 1967): 1–15.

Reiss, Albert J., Jr. "Assessing the Current Crime Wave," a paper prepared for the Conference on Crime in Urban Society, Temple University, Philadelphia, March 31, 1969.

Sudnow, David. "Normal Crimes: Sociological Features of the Penal Code in a Public Defender Office," *Social Problems* 12 (Winter 1965): 255–76.

6. MEASURING CRIME RATES

Donald R. Cressey

Numerous criminologists and correctional workers have reported their belief that the statistics on crime and criminals are among the most unsatisfactory of all social statistics. Six principal criticisms of the general statistics on crime have been made.[1] First, statistical data on the true crime rate cannot be compiled, for the simple reason that it is impossible to determine the amount of crime in any given locality at any particular time. Many crimes are not discovered. Others are discovered but not reported. Still others are reported but not recorded in any official way, so they do not appear in sets of crime statistics. Consequently, any record of crimes is at best an "index" of the total number of crimes committed.

Second, such "indexes" do not maintain a constant ratio with the true crime rate, whatever it may be. In crime statistics the variations in any set of figures cannot be considered a real index; the "index" items cannot be a sample of the whole because the whole cannot be specified.

From "Crime" by Donald R. Cressey, in *Contemporary Social Problems,* 2nd ed. (1966), ed. Robert K. Merton and Robert A. Nisbet, pp. 141–45. Reprinted by permission of the author and Harcourt, Brace & World, Inc. Footnotes have been renumbered.
[1] Donald R. Cressey, "The State of Criminal Statistics," *National Probation and Parole Association Journal,* 3 (July 1957): 230–41.

Third, variation in the conditions affecting published records of crime makes it foolhardy to compare crime rates in different jurisdictions, and it is hazardous even to compare the rates of the same jurisdiction (such as a city, county, state, or nation) in two different years.

Fourth, crime statistics are compiled primarily for administrative purposes, and for that reason they cannot be relied upon in scientific research. A scholar who develops a theory that accounts for variations in crime rates, whatever they may be, does so at great risk, for the extent of statistical error in any observed variation is unknown.

Fifth, statistics on the variations in the recorded rates for some crimes, such as white-collar crimes, are not routinely compiled. Many crimes committed by persons of upper socioeconomic status in the course of their business are handled by quasi-judicial bodies, such as the Federal Trade Commission, in order to avoid stigmatizing businessmen as criminals, in much the way that children's cases are heard in juvenile courts rather than the criminal courts used for adults, for the same reason.

Sixth, the statistics on juvenile delinquency are subject to all of these criticisms and, in addition, are inadequate because in America delinquency is not precisely defined.

"Crimes known to the police" is the set of statistics most generally accepted as the most adequate set of crime figures available. Each year the Federal Bureau of Investigation publishes a summary statement of the serious crimes known to the police departments that report to it. Table 1 summarizes these data for 1960–1966 and 1967. However, as indicated in the

TABLE 1

ESTIMATED NUMBER OF MAJOR CRIMES, AND CRIME RATES IN THE UNITED STATES, 1960–1966 AND 1967

Offense	Estimated Number of Offenses			Crimes per 100,000 Inhabitants	
	1960–1966 Average	1967	% Change	1967 Rate	% Change over 7-Year Average
Murder	9,230	12,100	+31	6.1	+25
Forcible rape	19,655	27,100	+38	13.7	+32
Robbery	123,602	202,050	+63	102.1	+56
Aggravated assault	183,428	253,300	+38	128.0	+32
Burglary	1,103,028	1,605,700	+46	811.5	+39
Larceny, $50 and over	667,886	1,047,100	+57	529.2	+50
Auto theft	421,128	654,900	+56	331.0	+49
TOTAL	2,527,957	3,802,250	+50	1,921.7	+44

SOURCE: Federal Bureau of Investigation, *Uniform Crime Reports for the United States, 1967* (Washington, D.C.: U.S. Government Printing Office, 1968), p. 61.

first three points above, this set of statistics is affected by conditions which cannot readily be taken into account in statistical reporting, conditions such as police practices, politics, laws, and public opinion. Consequently, even "crimes known to the police" may be an inadequate index of true rates. Yet the decision to use this rate is probably the best way out of a bad situation, for, as Sellin, the nation's foremost expert on crime statistics, has repeatedly pointed out, "The value of criminal statistics as a basis for measurement in geographic areas decreases as the procedure takes us farther away from the offense itself."[2] Thus, crimes known to the police probably constitute a better index of the true crime rate than the arrest rate; the arrest rate, in turn, is probably more efficient than the conviction rate; and the conviction rate probably is more effective than the imprisonment rate. The "funneling effect" of law-enforcement procedures is shown in Figure I.

Two important studies have shown that a large number of crimes are "hidden," in the sense that they do not appear in any set of crime statistics. In the first study, 1,020 men and 678 women were asked to check off which of some 49 listed offenses they had ever committed.[3] An effort was made to distribute the questionnaire to a balanced religious and racial cross section of the population, but systematic sampling procedures were not used. Most of the respondents were New Yorkers, and the group of subjects contained an excess of persons from upper socioeconomic levels. Ninety-one percent of the respondents admitted that they had committed at least one offense, excluding juvenile delinquencies, for which they could have been jailed or imprisoned. Men committed an average of eighteen offenses, and women had an average of eleven. Twenty-six percent of the men said they had committed automobile theft, 17 percent that they had committed burglary, 13 percent grand larceny, and 11 percent robbery. Among the women, 8 percent admitted at least one automobile theft, 11 percent a burglary, 11 percent a grand larceny, and 1 percent a robbery. Sixty-four percent of the men and 27 percent of the women said they had committed at least one felony, a class of serious offenses usually punishable by at least one year in the state prison.

In the second study, "white-collar crimes" were investigated.[4] These are crimes committed by persons of respectability and high social status in the course of their occupations. It was found that prosecution for this kind of crime often can be avoided because of the political or financial importance of the individuals involved, because of the difficulty of securing evidence, or because of the apparent triviality of the crimes. Also, the actions are punishable under criminal laws, but their perpetrators are often tried in

[2] Thorsten Sellin, "The Significance of Records of Crime," *Law Quarterly Review,* 67 (October 1951): 496–504.

[3] J. S. Wallerstein and C. J. Wyle, "Our Law-abiding Lawbreakers," *Probation,* 25 (March–April 1947): 107–12.

[4] Edwin H. Sutherland, *White-Collar Crime* (New York: Dryden, 1949).

FIGURE 1

Procedure in Felony Cases

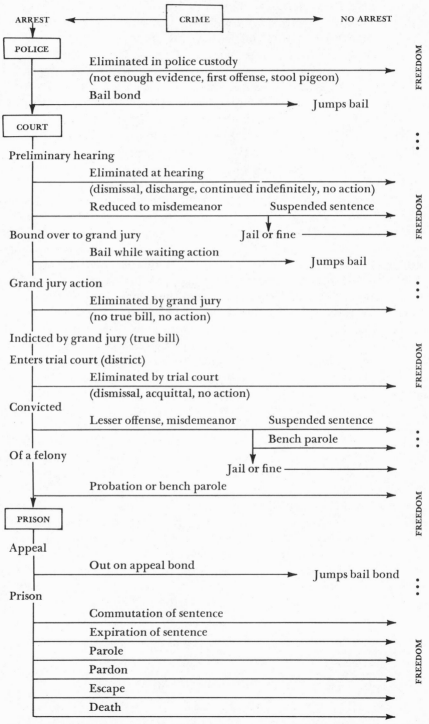

the hearings of administrative commissions and in the civil courts, rather than being subjected to the regular criminal court procedures. In a comment on the frequency of such crimes—in the form of misrepresentation of financial statements, bribery, embezzlement, tax fraud, misrepresentation in advertising, etc.—Sutherland said:

> The manufacturers of practically every class of articles used by human beings have been involved in legal difficulties . . . with more or less frequency during the last thirty years, including the manufacturers of the surgical instruments with which an infant may be assisted into the world, the bottle and nipple from which he may secure his food, the milk in his bottle, the blanket in which he is wrapped, the flag which his father displays in celebration of the event, and so on throughout life until he is finally laid away in a casket which was manufactured and sold under conditions which violated the law.[5]

More specifically, Sutherland's study of the white-collar crimes of the seventy largest mining, manufacturing, and mercantile corporations in the United States indicated that in a period of forty years every corporation had violated at least one of the laws outlawing restraint of trade, misrepresentation in advertising, infringement of patents, trademarks, and copyrights, violations of wartime regulations, and some miscellaneous activities. The corporations had a total of 307 adverse decisions on charges of restraint of trade, 222 adverse decisions on charges of infringements, 158 adverse decisions under the National Labor Relations Law, 97 adverse decisions under the laws regulating advertising, and 196 adverse decisions on charges of violating other laws. Generally, the official records indicated that the corporations violated the laws regulating trade with great frequency, but that such crimes do not appear in the official sets of statistics used as "indexes" of the true crime rate in the United States.

---

[5] Edwin H. Sutherland, "Crime and Business," *Annals of the American Academy of Political and Social Science*, 217 (September 1941): 111–18.

7. LIMITATIONS IN THE USE OF OFFICIAL STATISTICS

Marvin E. Wolfgang

A BRIEF DESCRIPTION OF THE UNIFORM CRIME REPORTS

A Committee on Uniform Crime Records was appointed at a convention of the International Association of Chiefs of Police (IACP) in 1927. In 1929, after extensive study of crime reporting, statutory designations, and police recording of various offenses throughout the country, the Committee[1] published an elaborate guide entitled *Uniform Crime Reporting: A Complete Manual for Police*. The manual attempted to establish standard categories of offenses for reporting purposes. In that same year the Committee instituted a system of uniform crime reporting on an experimental basis. The following year, the Federal Bureau of Investigation took over the system and incorporated the IACP's offense categories in its first bulletin of *Uni-*

Reprinted by permission of the author and the publisher from *University of Pennsylvania Law Review*, 111 (April 1963): 708–13 and 725–36. Original title: "Uniform Crime Reports: A Critical Appraisal." Tables and some footnotes have been renumbered.

[1] This committee was chaired by Bruce Smith, prominent police consultant and staff member of the Institute of Public Administration of New York City, and Lent D. Upson, of the Detroit Bureau of Governmental Research.

form Crime Reports.[2] The *Uniform Crime Reports (UCR)* were published
monthly, then quarterly, until 1941. Between 1942 and 1957 they were published semi-annually, and since 1958 have been published annually with a
brief, three-page quarterly preliminary report "issued for current information purposes." These reports regularly record, among other things, the
volume of crimes known to the police, offenses cleared by arrest, persons
held for prosecution, and persons released or found guilty of offenses.

The IACP Committee on Uniform Crime Records established a crime
classification based on legal categories of offenses. The original survey of
the Committee clearly showed the wide range of variation in statutory definitions of crime in the states. Therefore, offenses such as robbery, burglary,
and larceny were broadly defined so that crimes committed under each of
the varying statutes could, for statistical purposes, be embraced by the uniform classification system. Crimes were divided into two categories. The
first, originally known as Part I, included criminal homicide, rape, robbery,
aggravated assault, burglary, larceny, and automobile theft. All other
crimes were subsumed in Part II, which came to include twenty subcate-
gories, ranging from minor assaults to parking violations. Only Part I
offenses were recorded under the term "crimes known to the police"; Part II
offenses were reported according to the number of "persons charged" by
the police. Part I offenses were traditionally referred to as the "major" or
"more serious" offenses. These were assumed most likely to be reported to
the police in some consistent fashion and to maintain, more than the other
offenses, a constant ratio to the total number of committed offenses, most of
which do not come to the attention of the police. The Part I offenses came
to be used as a crime index, much like a price or cost-of-living index. The
wisdom of using police statistics for such a purpose has best been expressed
in modern times by Thorsten Sellin, who suggested that "the value of criminal statistics as a basis for the measurement of criminality in geographic
areas decreases as the procedure takes us farther away from the offense
itself."[3]

---

[2] For some early descriptive discussions, see Robinson, "History of Criminal Statistics
(1908–1933)," *Journal of Criminal Law and Criminology,* 24 (1933): 125; Warner, "Crimes
Known to the Police—An Index of Crime?," *Harvard Law Review,* 45 (1931): 307.
For a criticism of police statistics, see *Importance of Criminal Statistics* (Proceedings of
the Attorney General's Conference on Crime, Washington, D.C., 1934); Milspaugh, *Crime
Control by the National Government* (1937), pp. 235–74; Federal Bureau of Investigation,
U.S. Department of Justice, *Ten Years of Uniform Crime Reporting, 1930–1939* (1939);
Beattie, "The Sources of Criminal Statistics," *Annals of the American Academy of Politi-
cal and Social Science,* 19 (1941): 217. For some more recent comments, see Beattie, "Prob-
lems of Criminal Statistics in the United States," *Journal of Criminal Law, Criminology,
and Police Science,* 46 (1955): 178; Cressey, "The State of Criminal Statistics," *National
Probation and Parole Assn. Journal,* 3 (1957): 230; Pittman and Handy, "Uniform Crime
Reporting: Needed Improvements," paper presented at annual meeting of Society for the
Study of Social Problems, St. Louis, Mo., August 28–29, 1961.
[3] Sellin, "The Significance of Records of Crime," *Law Quarterly Review,* 67 (1951): 489
(italics in original removed); see *Research Memorandum on Crime in the Depression,*
Social Science Research Council bulletin no. 27 (1937); Sellin, "The Basis of a Crime
Index," *Journal of Criminal Law and Criminology,* 22 (1931): 335.

All of the arguments concerning the establishment of a crime index cannot be reviewed here, although some of the major problems involved in a statistical analysis of index offenses will be considered in a later section. The use of the term "crime index" in the *UCR* did not appear until 1958, although Part I offenses were traditionally used in that sense. The initial rationale for using these seven offenses as an index appeared in the original work of the Committee on Uniform Crime Records, and is still currently offered:

> The total number of criminal acts that occur is unknown, but those that are reported to the police provide the first means of a count. Not all crimes come readily to the attention of the police; not all crimes are of sufficient importance to be significant in an index and not all important crimes occur with enough regularity to be meaningful in an index. With these considerations in mind, the above crimes were selected as a group to furnish an abbreviated and convenient measure of the crime problem.[4]

The offenses listed in Part II are, therefore, those which are assumed less likely to become known to the police—because of victims' unwillingness to report them, variations in police activity, and other similar factors.

Maintenance of this system of uniform crime reporting was assigned to the FBI on September 1, 1930, by Act of Congress,[5] and has been the responsibility of that bureau ever since. In fact, the FBI has expanded the system to include data relevant to law-enforcement agencies, such as the number of police personnel and the efficiency of police activity. The FBI has no authority to compel the transmission to it of crime data from cities and separate states; instead, police agencies throughout the country are asked to cooperate by submitting their reports to the central clearinghouse in Washington. The number of cooperating police agencies has increased regularly through the years, from 400 in 1930 to 7,800 law-enforcement agencies in 1961, representing 96 percent of the total United States population. The offenses reported are violations of the criminal law of the separate states; no violations of federal law per se are tabulated or included in the *UCR*.[6] Since 1958, when important revisions were made in the presentation of data, crimes have been reported by geographical areas, following as closely as is practical definitions used by the Bureaus of the Budget and the Census. Standard metropolitan statistical areas (SMSA)—generally made up of an entire county or counties having certain metropolitan characteristics and at least one core city of 50,000 or more inhabitants—have the largest absolute population and coverage as reported in the last *UCR*

---

[4] Federal Bureau of Investigation, U.S. Department of Justice, *Uniform Crime Reports for the United States* (Washington, D.C.: U.S. Government Printing Office, 1961), p. 32 (hereafter cited as *UCR*).

[5] 45 Stat. 554 (1930), 5 U.S.C. § 340 (1958).

[6] However, the standard metropolitan statistical area containing Washington, D.C., and parts of Maryland and Virginia is now included.

(1961). The SMSA's represented 117,152,600 people, with 98.3 percent of these areas actually reporting to the FBI. "Other cities" are urban places outside the standard metropolitan statistical areas, most of which are incorporated communities of 2,500 or more inhabitants. In the last *UCR*, "other cities" contained a population of 24,185,300, with 90.7 percent of these areas actually reporting to Washington. Finally, "rural areas," which are made up of the unincorporated portions of counties outside of urban places and standard metropolitan statistical areas, had a population of 41,615,100, with 82.5 percent actually reporting. Sheriffs, county police, and many state police report crimes committed within the limits of a county but outside of cities, while the police departments within urban places report crimes committed within the city limits.

The problems of attaining uniform reporting by the 7,800 agencies which prepare crime reports on a voluntary basis are obvious. But in the past thirty-two years an elaborate machinery has been constructed to ensure increasing uniformity. A special *Uniform Crime Reporting Handbook*, instructing law-enforcement agencies how to fill out monthly forms, is provided by the FBI to all police agencies cooperating in the program. In addition, "it is standard operating procedure [for the FBI] to examine each incoming report not only for arithmetical accuracy but also, and possibly of even more importance, for reasonableness as a possible indication of errors."[7] Recognizing, however, that the variability, completeness, and correctness of the data it publishes may be subject to inaccuracies, the FBI annually prints a caveat:

> It is clear, of course, that regardless of the extent of the statistical verification processes used by the FBI, the accuracy of the data assembled under this program depends upon the degree of sincere effort exerted

---

[7] *UCR*, 1961, p. 26. "Necessary arithmetical adjustments or unusual variations are brought to the attention of the submitting agency by correspondence. During 1961, letters were addressed to contributors primarily as a result of verification and evaluation processes. Correspondence with contributors is the principal tool for supervision of quality. Not only are the individual reports studied, but also periodic trends for individual reporting units are run, as are crime rates in descending order for all units grouped for general comparability to assist in detecting variations and fluctuations possibly due to some reason other than chance. For the most part, the problem is one of keeping contributors informed of the type of information necessary to the success of this program. . . . During the calendar year 1961 there were almost 5,000 personal contacts with contributors by Special Agent personnel of the FBI" (*ibid.*, p. 27).

However, as Ronald Beattie has pointed out: "In criminal statistics gathered from many sources, it is rather obvious that despite uniform schedules and definitions, the responsibility for careful and accurate reporting of the original data rests with the reporting agencies. The greater the number of reporting agencies, the greater will be the variation in the interpretation, reliability, and consistency of reports submitted, and the greater will be the difficulty of supervising or editing these reports. The fact that 'Uniform Crime Reports' data are received from several thousand independent agencies in . . . different criminal jurisdictions, each varying from the other in definitions of crime, in organization of law-enforcement operations, and in methods of maintaining basic records, raises a real question as to how homogeneous and accurate the facts collected and published in this series may be" ("Problems of Criminal Statistics," pp. 178, 183).

by each contributor to meet the necessary standards of reporting, and, for this reason, the FBI is not in a position to vouch for the validity of the reports received.[8]

All law-enforcement agencies in the United States receive from the FBI a series of blanks, requesting information for the *UCR*. From completed forms returned by cooperating agencies, the Bureau tabulates crime rates and trends for presentation in the current quarterly preliminary reports and in the annual *UCR*. The kinds of data requested may be found in the *Uniform Crime Reporting Handbook*. For index crimes—formerly Part I offenses—the FBI requests the number of offenses reported to the police, the number of complaints that were found to be false, the number of actual or founded offenses, and the number of offenses cleared by arrest. "Cleared by arrest" means that one or more suspects have been taken into custody by the police and made available for prosecution. Only the number of founded offenses and the number of offenses cleared by arrest are reported in the *UCR*. The index crimes are the ones most completely tabulated by rates according to population groups: for instance, the age, sex, and race of persons charged; monthly variations; the type and value of property stolen and recovered; murder victims according to weapons used; and murder victims by age, sex, and race. The rural-urban distribution of index crimes is determined from the police department's location. For crimes other than those that appear in the index, the cooperating agencies report on the number of persons charged (held for prosecution) but not the number known to the police, as occurs with index crime.[9]

The most fundamental and recent changes in the *Uniform Crime Reports* occurred after the recommendations of a Consultant Committee on Uniform Crime Reporting. This committee was appointed in 1957 under the auspices of the FBI and the IACP to carry out a detailed and independent analysis of the uniform crime reporting system and to make concrete recommendations for its alteration.[10] The committee's report was published in 1958 as a special issue of the *UCR*. Twenty-two recommendations were made, all of which have been accepted as ultimate goals by the FBI

---

[8] *UCR*, 1961, pp. 27–28.

[9] Not all of the data requested from law-enforcement agencies are printed in the *UCR*. Statistics not reported include automobiles recovered by the number stolen locally and recovered locally, the number stolen locally and recovered in other jurisdictions, and the total stolen locally; aggravated assault by type of weapon–sharp object, blunt object, gun, personal weapon, explosive, and other; auto theft by joyriding and others; murder and nonnegligent manslaughter by distinction between willful killing without process of law and the justifiable killing of a felon by police and private citizens. See Pittman and Handy, *supra* note 2.

[10] The Consultant Committee was composed of Peter P. Lejins, chairman of the committee and professor of sociology at the University of Maryland; Charleton Chute, Institute of Public Administration, New York; and Stanley R. Schrotel, chief of police of Cincinnati, Ohio. Impetus for the establishment of this committee came from reaction to critical remarks about United States criminal statistics made by Thorsten Sellin in an interview which appeared in Wallace, "Crime in the U.S.," *Life*, September 9, 1957, pp. 47, 49–70.

and the IACP. However, only a few of the recommendations have thus far been carried out. The most important of these dealt with changes in statistical presentation and analysis, and with revisions in the classification of what has become known as the crime index. These alterations will be discussed in more detail below.

* * *

STATISTICAL DEFICIENCIES

A. Use of the Decennial Census

Adoption by the FBI in 1958 of a statistical recommendation from the Con-. sultant Committee eliminated one of the most glaring and consistently misleading errors of the *Reports*. Anyone not familiar with this problem could easily be misled by reading or using the crime rates for most of the years prior to 1958. Although demographers and criminologists will always be strongly in favor of criminal statistics presented in a way that expresses the incidence of crime in terms of the population capable of committing these acts, inappropriate use of such a basis vitiates the value of rates. Crude rates of crime are computed by dividing the number of crimes recorded as having been committed during a given time period by the total population during the same time period and multiplying that figure by a constant, usually 100,000. Crime rates in the *UCR* for most of the years of publication were computed only on the basis of the decennial census population, which meant that computed rates in areas in which there were tremendous population shifts were at variance with the real rates during the years immediately preceding a new census. As Daniel Bell graphically states the problem:

> One startling fact is that every ten years the number of crimes in the United States "automatically" drops—that is to say, each year, for ten years, the number of crimes mounts sharply, but in the tenth year it drops. This is not due to sunspots or some other cyclical theory, but to a single statistical pitfall. . . . The FBI rates relate crime per 100,000 population, but there is no population-accounting for intercensus years, so that the rates not only reflect the lower population base of ten years before but, more importantly, do not take into account the enormous internal migrations.[11]

California provides the best example of this phenomenon. There was a startling drop in the published crime rates for that state from 1949 to 1951. Rates for some of the Part I offenses for each of these two years were given

---

[11] Bell, *The End of Ideology* (1960), p. 139. See also Tappan, *Crime, Justice, and Correction* (1960), p. 38; Elliott, *Crime in Modern Society* (1952), p. 60.

as shown in Table 1.[12] The rate changes obviously reflected the change in computation from a 1940 census base to the 1950 base. During that decade the California population increased approximately 50 percent, or by three million inhabitants, but the 1949 numerator was still being attributed to the 1940 denominator. The three Pacific coast states increased their population about 40 percent between 1940 and 1950, yet, in effect, the number of 1949 crimes was being charged to only 60 percent of that year's population. The obvious result was an overstated rate of criminality. On the other hand, criminality in states which decreased in population was understated. This latter condition, however, was probably never so serious as the rate errors published for the Pacific states.

TABLE 1

CALIFORNIA CRIME RATES—1949, 1951

Offense	1949 Rates[a] (Based on 1940 Census)	1951 Rates[b] (Based on 1950 Census)
Criminal Homicide (a) Murder & nonnegligent manslaughter	4.97	3.5
Robbery	136.1	85.6
Aggravated assault	95.4	57.1
Burglary	756.8	523.5
Larceny	2,141.6	1,669.4
Auto theft	323.3	272.4

[a] *UCR*, 1949, p. 94.
[b] *UCR*, 1951, p. 87.

Beginning in 1953, the annual *UCR* gave passing attention to the increase in population, but there was no improvement in reporting until the Consultant Committee recommended that "in view of the differential population growth in various communities, the decennial census figures should not be used for the computation of crime rates beyond the year to which they pertain. Instead, the available annual estimates by the Bureau of the Census should be used."[13]

B. Percent Changes in the Total Volume of Index Offenses

Despite the fact that rates based on annual population estimates have appeared since 1958, another kind of statistical misrepresentation persists. Percent changes in the total volume of index offenses from one year to the

---

[12] Rape and nonnegligent manslaughter were excluded not by the author but in the original tables of the *UCR* from which these rates are taken.
[13] *UCR, Special Issue,* 1958, p. 33.

next are reported by single years or occasionally over longer time spans. Unwary readers receive a false image of the changes that are taking place in the amount of crime relative to population changes. The percent of change of the instant year over the preceding year is now given both according to population-based rates and according to the absolute number of offenses. Although this dual presentation is somewhat of an improvement, the rate changes are treated subordinately in all reports, especially in the introductory section that summarizes the data in the tricky alliteration of "crime capsule," "crime clock," "crime calender," and "crime count." This section is the one most used by newspapers, local police, and civic groups interested in crime. It is here, as well as in the current quarterly reports, that the percent change by total volume or absolute numbers, irrespective of the population base, continues to be given a prominent position and description. Trend analyses, bar charts, and pie charts are used to show how much crime has changed—usually increased—during the past year or past decade. Almost invariably these graphic presentations of criminal statistics are misleading.

It is never easy, and sometimes impossible, to find in a *UCR* issue the population base, the specific cities used, or similar items for discussion of "urban crime trends" when one wishes to make the same kind of computations that the *UCR* may make. To check on the FBI's arithmetic or to perform certain kinds of statistical analyses not found in the *UCR* is often extremely difficult or even out of the question because there may be confusion about what raw data were used or where they may be found, if at all. It is especially hard to make comparisons over time.

With these problems in mind, let us briefly examine one set of *UCR* figures to illustrate the invalidity of the traditional *UCR* method of expressing percent changes in crime. In the 1956 *Report*, the percent changes in "urban crime trends" are plotted on a chart for the period 1940 to 1956 with the 1937–39 average as the base line. Reference is made to a table[14] showing these "trends" from 1937 to 1956 for 353 cities with over 25,000 inhabitants, or a total population in 1940 of 36,408,430 and in 1950 of 42,719,693. Only a brief two-sentence reference is made to the importance of population increase.[15] The charts and many tables throughout the *Report* fail to show crime rates even for the two census years, but instead continue to express changes in each and for all the seven "serious" crimes by the absolute number of offenses. The message which the *Report* most obviously wishes to broadcast is that crime has greatly increased.

Table 2 clearly shows how incorrect this image actually is. The absolute volume change, which is the traditional *UCR* method of statistical presentation, shows that in 1950 there was 11.3 percent more crime than in 1940.

[14] *UCR*, 1956, Table 27, p. 81.
[15] *Ibid.*, p. 80.

TABLE 2

COMPARISON OF PERCENT CHANGE OF CRIMES ACCORDING TO TOTAL VOLUME AND CRIME RATES, 1940 AND 1950, FOR 353 CITIES

Part I Offenses	(A) Number of Crimes[a]		(B) Crime Rate per 100,000[b]		(C) Traditional UCR Expression of % Change of 1950 over 1940[c]	(D) % of Crime Rate Change of 1950 over 1940[d]	(E) Absolute % Difference of Col. C Minus Col. D	(F) Direction of UCR % Change
	1940	1950	1940	1950				
Murder and nonnegligent manslaughter	2,208	2,370	6.1	5.5	+ 7.3	− 9.8	17.1	Incorrect
Negligent manslaughter	1,469	1,544	4.0	3.6	+ 5.1	−10.0	15.1	Incorrect
Rape	3,207	4,994	8.8	11.6	+55.7	+32.0	23.7	Correct
Robbery	25,269	25,909	69.3	57.9	+ 2.5	−16.4	18.9	Incorrect
Aggravated assault	20,312	32,350	55.7	75.7	+59.3	+35.9	23.4	Correct
Burglary	146,361	170,708	401.1	399.6	+10.4	− 3.7	14.1	Incorrect
Larceny	391,812	425,325	1073.8	995.6	+ 8.5	− 7.3	15.8	Incorrect
Auto theft	71,350	73,521	195.5	172.1	+ 3.0	−12.0	15.0	Incorrect
TOTAL	661,988	736,721	1814.0	1724.0	+11.3	− 5.0	16.3	Incorrect

[a] Crude data are from *UCR*, 1956, pp. 80–81. The 1940 population for the 353 cities was 36,488,430; the 1950 population was 42,719,693. These are "offenses known to the police."

[b] Offenses divided by population multiplied by 100,000.

[c] The difference between the number of offenses in 1950 and 1940, divided by the number of offenses in 1940.

[d] The difference between the rate in 1950 and 1940 divided by the rate in 1940.

The range of increases was from 2.5 percent for robbery to 59.3 percent for aggravated assault. For each of the "major" offenses the change was a percentage increase. Yet, when the same data are expressed in relation to the population, the rates for each of these offenses and for all of them combined are significantly different. They then range from a decrease of 16.4 percent for robbery to an increase of 36 percent for aggravated assault. Altogether, they show a 5 percent decrease in the rate for 1950 (1,724 per 100,000) compared to 1940 (1,814 per 100,000). Only rape and aggravated assault increased, while all of the other offenses decreased.

Under the traditional *UCR* method of reporting changes, unless there is an absolute numerical reduction in all the offenses or any one in particular, there can be no percentage decrease, no matter how much the population increases. Although, as has been indicated, more accurate rates have appeared since 1958, the traditional method still receives the most graphic attention and prominent position. In the present quarterly reports, only this latter method of showing increases is used; no rates appear. Thus, my criticisms of the 1956 *Report* are still appropriate. It should also be pointed out that in the 1960 *UCR* we are told that "from 1950 to 1960, crime increased 84 percent."[16] There is no indication that this figure refers to absolute numbers, and is therefore doubly misleading. Based on rates adjusted for 1950 to include only the crimes used in the index for 1960, the increase was actually around 22 percent. Moreover, murder and nonnegligent manslaughter did not change, aggravated assault and robbery dropped slightly, and forcible rape increased slightly. The 22 percent increase was almost entirely in property offenses.

There is nothing new or esoteric about expressing changes of any phenomenon by rates per population unit. Many refinements can be made in these rates to improve their specificity, but they remain as the only appropriate and meaningful way to indicate the basic facts about changes in criminal offenses over space and time. Further and more sophisticated statistical techniques can, of course, be employed to analyze these data in terms of significant variations and correlations. But in reporting rudimentary criminal statistics, the simple rates per population unit are both sufficient and necessary. To continue publishing the traditional *UCR* expression of percent changes in volume of crime from one year or decade to another is to perpetuate almost meaningless measures. These percent changes would be useful only if the population capable of contributing to the phenomenon were perfectly stable. Such percent changes can only serve to alarm the public by creating an image of increasing crime that is either fictional or exaggerated. Local police departments are, of course, interested in knowing about volume increases in crime in their communities, for the number of police officers needed bears some relation to the volume of work.

---

[16] *UCR*, 1960, p. 12.

But the *UCR* are also designed for use by agencies and social scientists throughout the country. The primary concern of all is whether crime is in fact increasing, decreasing, or remaining stable. Unless population is static, only a population-based rate of crime can validly provide the kind of information desired.

C. The Crime Clock

The same remarks apply to the "crime clock," another device used by the FBI in the *UCR* to indicate the volume of crime. We are regularly informed that a certain number of serious crimes occurs each minute in the United States. For example, in 1961, four serious crimes occurred each minute, one murder every hour, one forcible rape every thirty-three minutes, one robbery every six minutes, one aggravated assault every four minutes, one burglary every thirty-seven seconds, one serious larceny ($50 and over) every minute, and one auto theft every one and one-half minutes.[17] If the purpose of this "crime clock" is to frighten consumers of the *UCR*, the statements probably succeed, for they are reproduced in scores of newspapers and read by millions, including congressmen, state legislators, and city councilmen who appropriate funds for police budgets. But some other document should be used for this purpose, not a responsible publication that disseminates official statistics for use by social scientists and other analysts in scholarly research. Once again, the objections are obvious. Even if the proportion of crimes to the population remained stable, the "crime clock" would move more rapidly if the population is increasing. Contrariwise, if the population were decreasing and the volume of crime remained the same, the crime rate would increase but the "crime clock" would show no change.

D. Changes in Police Performance

Another grossly misrepresented figure is that which purports to show changes in police performance by means of crimes cleared by arrest. Figure 1, reproduced from the 1960 *UCR* (page 14), is a good example. The crude data necessary for computing the presented figures did not accompany the chart, nor were they located in the text. The title of the chart is a misnomer and the impression it gives is false. Almost any reader would at first believe that police efficiency has greatly improved between 1950 and 1960 because "crimes cleared by arrest are up 71 percent over 1950." Actually, on a comparable basis, the proportion of offenses cleared by arrest based on all offenses known declined between 1950 and 1960. We are told that the number of index offenses in 1960 was 1,861,261,[18] and that this *number* was 84

---

[17] *UCR*, 1961, p. 5.
[18] *UCR*, 1960, p. 2.

percent higher than in 1950,[19] which means that there were approximately 1,011,570 offenses in 1950. There is no specific place in the 1960 *UCR* which gives the exact number of offenses cleared by arrest; only the percent of each index offense cleared is given.[20] But by multiplying this percent by the

FIGURE 1

POLICE ACTIVITY AND PERFORMANCE,
1960 OVER 1950

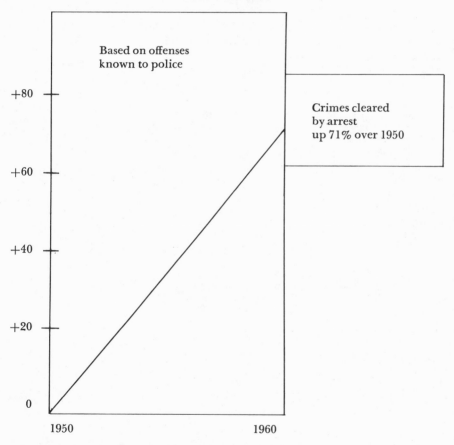

Based on offenses
known to police

Crimes cleared
by arrest
up 71% over 1950

+80

+60

+40

+20

0

1950   1960

number of offenses known, it is possible to derive the number of offenses cleared by arrest, keeping in mind that rounding may produce some variation from the true number. When this is done, the number cleared in 1960 is 572,963. Now, the 1960 *UCR* also claims that the number of offenses

[19] *Ibid.*, p. 12.
[20] *Ibid.*, p. 13.

cleared by arrest was up 71 percent in 1960 over 1950;[21] therefore, the 1950 number was about 335,066. But the clearance *rate* in 1950—offenses cleared divided by offenses known—was 33.1 percent, and in 1960 was 30.8 percent. Relatively, this means approximately a 7 percent decline $\left(\dfrac{31.1}{30.8}\right)$.[22] Therefore, if this clearance by arrest rate is to be used as an indication of police efficiency—which is sometimes a doubtful practice—their efficiency de-

FIGURE 2

PERCENT CHANGE IN THE RATE OF OFFENSES CLEARED BY ARREST, 1960 COMPARED TO 1950

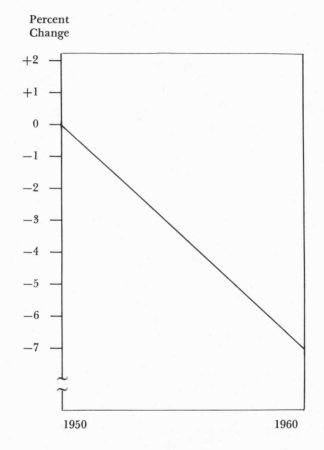

---

[21] *Ibid.*, p. 12.
[22] This could also be expressed as follows: Offenses cleared by arrest $= a$ in 1950 and c in 1960; index offenses known to the police $= b$ in 1950 and d in 1960. If $c = 1.71a$ and $d = 1.84b$, then $\dfrac{c}{d} = \dfrac{1.71a}{1.84b} = .93\dfrac{a}{b}$, which is equal to $\dfrac{30.8}{33.1}$ and means that there is a 7 percent decrease in clearance by arrest rate.

creased in 1960 as compared to 1950. Figure 2 presents this change in a manner similar to that used in the *UCR*.

Actually only two single years, a decade apart, were involved. A bar chart would therefore be more appropriate, but I am following the *UCR* pattern of illustration, which indeed makes the difference between the years appear much greater than is really the case. The rate difference is only 2.3 and might well be due to errors in the samples or in reporting variables. But even when this small difference is expressed as a percent of the 1950 clearance rate, the figure becomes — 7 percent.

E. Capacity to Commit Crime

When rates are presented in the *UCR*, they are computed per 100,000 population. This crude rate is based on an unstated assumption that all humans are equally capable of committing crimes. As Sellin has suggested, this assumption is erroneous, for criminal conduct is not evenly distributed over all segments of the population. By definition, criminal conduct generally cannot occur among children under seven years of age, and is rare among children up to at least twelve years. It predominantly appears in males between twelve and fifty years of age. The custom in some foreign countries of computing rates on the basis of the population of "punishable age" or "capable of committing a crime" represents a slight improvement. What are actually needed, but have never appeared in the *UCR*, are refined rates calculated on a population standardized for age and sex, and perhaps for other factors, depending on the availability of accurate and properly subclassified statistics of the population concerned.[23] Pittman and Handy have also suggested that

> it would be advantageous to construct age-specific, sex-specific, race-specific, and economic-status-specific rates for all crime and for particular types of crimes. This is essential since the demographic characteristics of cities, states, and regions vary considerably in the United States. Furthermore, crime rates should be constructed on standardized populations to allow for variations in state and regional population pyramids. . . .[24]

F. The Interrelationship of UCR Statistics

I have previously noted statistical deficiencies of the *UCR* classification system, especially due to the method used by police departments in reporting and scoring offenses by that system. Attributing the same "weight" of seriousness (namely, a unit of one) to each index offense also has inherent weaknesses. Equally disturbing is the fact that different levels of criminal

---

[23] Adapted from Sellin and Wolfgang, *The Measurement of Delinquency* (1964).
[24] Pittman and Handy, *supra* note 2, p. 12.

statistics are presented in the *UCR* in a fashion which does not permit analysis of their relationships. "Offenses known to the police," "offenses cleared by arrest," "persons charged," and "persons found guilty" are recorded, but it is impossible for an analyst to move directly from one statistic to another while retaining a base of offenses known. The *UCR* cannot tell us, for example, what proportion of offenses known to the police can result in the conviction of one or more perpetrators.

By referring to Table 3, which does not appear in exactly this form in the *UCR*—there is little real statistical analysis made in these *Reports*—we can note that there are significant differences between the distribution of offenses known to the police, offenses cleared by arrest, and persons charged relative to offenses known. In the *UCR*, tables cause confusion because changes in the use of population units and number of cities or agencies reporting occur from one table to another. Some of the tables showing offense distributions are based on estimates, while others are based on actual offenses known or offenders arrested. I have manipulated some of the data provided in order to maintain a consistent base for computation. The following differentials are important to the present discussion:

1. Offenses against the person (I) constitute a small proportion (8 percent, Column B) of all "major" offenses known to the police, but make up a significantly large proportion (21 percent, Column E) of offenses cleared by arrest.

2. On the other hand, offenses against property (II) constitute a large proportion (92 percent, Column B) of all "major" offenses known to the police, but make up a significantly smaller proportion (79 percent, Column E) of offenses cleared by arrest.

3. Measuring crime and types of offenses from acts committed by persons taken into custody, charged, and made available for prosecution by the police further widens the differential distribution of Type I and Type II offenses. Instead of constituting 8 percent among all offenses known, Type I offenses make up 23 percent when the universe is that of persons charged by the police (Column H). Instead of constituting 92 percent among all offenses known, Type II offenses make up 77 percent when the universe is that of persons charged (Column H).

4. This occurs because the probability of being arrested for an offense against the person (73 percent, Column C) is significantly higher than the probability of being arrested for an offense against property (27 percent, Column C).

5. This in turn results in a significantly greater ratio of persons charged by the police for offenses against the person, relative to the number of such offenses known (66 per 100, Column F), than is the ratio of persons charged for offenses against property, relative to the number of such offenses known (20 percent).

Because the *UCR* do not permit analysis to move readily from offense to

TABLE 3

INDEX CRIMES USED BY *UCR* ACCORDING TO OFFENSES KNOWN, OFFENSES CLEARED BY ARREST, AND PERSONS CHARGED—1960

	(A) Number of Offenses Known to the Police[a]	(B) Percent Distribution of Offenses Known to the Police	(C) Percent Cleared by Arrest[b]	(D) Number Cleared by Arrest[c]	(E) Percent Distribution of Offenses Cleared by Arrest	(F) Number of Persons Charged per 100 Known Offenses[d]	(G) Number of Persons Charged by Police[e]	(H) Percent Distribution of Persons Charged by Police
Type I. Offenses Against the Person								
Murder and nonnegligent manslaughter	9,140	0.49	92.3	8,436	1.47	96.8	8,848	2.01
Aggravated assault	130,230	7.00	75.8	98,714	17.23	63.3	82,436	18.80
Forcible rape	15,560	0.84	72.5	11,281	1.97	74.2	11,546	2.63
Total Type I	154,930	8.33	72.5	118,431	20.67	66.37	102,830	23.44
Type II. Offenses Against Property								
Robbery	88,970	4.78	38.5	34,254	5.98	42.8	38,079	8.69
Burglary	821,000	44.11	29.5	242,225	42.28	19.3	158,472	36.14
Auto theft	321,400	17.27	25.7	82,600	14.42	21.4	68,779	15.70
Larceny	474,900	25.51	20.1	95,455	16.65	14.8	70,285	16.03
Total Type II	1,706,370	91.67	26.6	454,534	79.33	19.67	335,615	76.56
Total	1,861,300	100.00	30.8	572,965	100.00	23.56	438,445	100.00

a Estimated number. (*UCR*, 1960, p. 2.)

b Based upon actual clearances from 2,351 cities; total population of 84,428,926. (*UCR*, 1960, p. 85.)

c Computed by applying actual clearance rates as indicated in note b to the estimated number of offenses known to the police as indicated in note a.

d Based on same unit as note b. (*UCR*, 1960, p. 85.) For example, the mean number of persons charged per 100 known offenses against the person is 66.37.

e Computed by multiplying Columns F and A.

offenders, caution must be used in interpretation. As is well known, an offense may be "cleared" by the arrest of one or of twenty persons, so long as at least one person is "made available for prosecution." On the other hand, twenty offenses may be cleared by the arrest of one person. At no time during the more than thirty years of publishing the *UCR* have these types of data been clearly defined and refined. Consequently, it never is possible for the analyst to move directly from "offenses known" or "offenses cleared by arrest" to "persons charged" by type of offense. The use of "number of persons charged per 100 known offenses" is of no help because we still know nothing about the number of offenders in each offense. For example, we are told that of each 100 murders and nonnegligent manslaughters known to the police, 96.8 persons were charged. A single case of twelve boys slaying one victim would clearly and seriously distort the meaning of this ratio.

G. Measurement of Standard Error

Finally, the number of agencies and the population units represented in the *UCR* have progressively increased. With a larger sample, the amount of variance in any computation of a standard error presumably has become smaller. The efforts of the FBI to improve the reliability of reporting, combined with the increased sample size, should have produced greater confidence in the estimates. But in none of the *Reports* is there any reference to this factor other than a caveat that the total population of the United States is not included and that the FBI cannot vouch for the accuracy of statistics from all police departments. Some of the percent changes by type of offense and for the crime index, reported yearly or over longer periods of time, would either be eliminated or otherwise statistically affected by analytical application of measures of standard error.

H. Summary

The foregoing are statistical deficiencies that a rather brief and cursory review can outline. A more complete examination might add abundant illustrations and, perhaps, other types of limitations. I have not personally compared the *UCR* with reports of other countries, but it is the kinds of deficiencies mentioned here which led Sellin to remark that "the U.S. . . . has the worst criminal statistics of any major country in the Western world."[25] The comment was made before the 1958 revisions, but there have not been sufficient improvements in the *UCR* to label it inappropriate at the present time.

---

[25] *Life*, September 9, 1957, p. 49.

8. CRIMINAL STATISTICS AND ACCOMMODATIONS IN JUSTICE ADMINISTRATION

Donald J. Newman

CRITICISMS OF CRIMINAL STATISTICS

Probably no aspect of criminology is easier to criticize and consequently has received more criticism than statistical descriptions of the crime problem. With minor exceptions statistics about crime and criminals are taken from some point in the administration of justice system, either from crime reports made to the police, arrest tabulations, or numbers of persons charged, convicted, or sentenced. Statistics taken from some point in this "conviction process" become "data" (statistics about crimes not solved or criminals uncaught are usually "estimates") and from them numerous conclusions are drawn about the nature of crime and of criminals. Both the actual value of such data and an understanding of the typical conclusions drawn from such statistics depend upon an accurate assessment of the basis of this labeling process and its operational characteristics.

Reprinted by permission of the author and the publisher from *Sociology and Social Research*, 46 (January 1962): 144–55. Original title: "The Effects of Accommodations in Justice Administration on Criminal Statistics."

This paper is based upon data gathered as a part of the American Bar Foundation's study "The Administration of Criminal Justice in the United States," with which the author has been associated.

While the critics of even the most carefully gathered crime data can base their arguments on irregularities in and discrepancies between multijurisdictional reporting systems or with some accuracy on the biased focus of such data on conventional offenses, one recurring criticism, of particular significance here, is based upon the assumption that the true universe of conventional criminal activity is much broader than crime statistics indicate. The criticism envisages the "true" crime parameter to include all statutorily proscribed conduct, whether proceeded against by enforcing agencies or not, and leads to an evaluation of these agencies as inefficient, or worse, for not enforcing legislation more effectively. This attack is based upon a conception of how criminal justice *should* work and not upon an understanding of how it does work. It illustrates the long recognized discrepancy between "law in the books" and "law in action."

THE OPERATIONAL ANALYSIS OF CRIMINAL JUSTICE ADMINISTRATION

No attempt will be made here to review the work of those who advocate better and uniform crime reporting, nor will particular emphasis be paid to documentation of spectacular breakdowns in law enforcement by corruption, bribery, and the like, as was the fashion in earlier crime surveys. Concern instead will be with analysis of the criminal justice system both in popular conception and in actual operation as the basis for crime statistics and with the meaning of data gathered from this system. Two major approaches will be taken: (1) a brief operational conception of the justice system will be presented and (2) an analysis made of accommodations at the adjudication stage. The purposes of this presentation are first of all to criticize the critics of crime data by presenting an operational image of criminal justice which challenges both the conception and premises upon which typical criticisms and evaluations are based and, secondly, to give warning about the use of conviction records as indices of the extent of crime or of types of criminals.

THE "FULL ENFORCEMENT" CONCEPTION OF CRIMINAL JUSTICE

Probably the most common image of the criminal justice process approximates what Arnold has called the "Ideal of Law Enforcement," which "repudiates the idea of compromise as immoral" and commands the state to "enforce the Law" uniformly, automatically.[1] This image relates both to

---

[1] Thurman W. Arnold, *The Symbols of Government* (New Haven: Yale University Press, 1935), p. 162.

the definition of criminal conduct and to the ways of proceeding against it. In this conception crime is defined by the words of the statutes with little allowance for administrative interpretation and none for discretion. The *nullem crimen* principle sets not only the outer limits of criminal conduct but the minimum limits as well. Not only do statutes define crime but in turn they become mandates for enforcing agencies. It becomes the duty of police, prosecutors, and courts first to search out all proscribed conduct and to invoke the process fully against those who engage in such conduct. Admitting gross inefficiencies—i.e., the police cannot possibly detect all crimes, if for no other reason because of limited resources—the assumption remains that once invoked, the conviction process runs or should run its course on the basis of legally relevant evidence, culminating in the adversary technique of trial to convict the guilty and free those against whom there is insufficient evidence. The process is complex only as law is complex but the administration is routine and mandatory with little room for discretion and none for compromise.

How widely such an image is held is debatable, yet both common criticisms of the system and the typical use to which data gathered from it are put treat it as so. The allegation of "real" crime outside administrative concern and the use of labels from the system to define the extent of "known" crime rely equally on the assumptions that crime is determined by statute, not practices, and that labels assigned convicted defendants are the statutory equivalents of their actual conduct. So to treat the administrative process is to oversimplify it, and to draw conclusions from data from the system without awareness of its operational complexity is to do it and statistics a disservice.

The administration of criminal justice is an involved and complicated process of decisions and discretionary choices of persons who administer it. Like all systems where men must decide the fate of other men, it must necessarily accommodate itself to fit rules to cases, to determine its own goals, to maintain its equilibrium, and to effectively and uniformly perform its functions. It is by no means automatic, nor does it, in theory or in practice, fit the full enforcement, maximum implementation, trial-by-combat image discussed above. At least three distinctions from this image must be made to define the basis of the justice system and its operational character as well.

The Determination of Criminal Conduct

While legislatures have the formal duty of defining criminal conduct, the list of penal statutes does not necessarily set a minimum mandate for administering agencies. Statutes define the outer limits of criminal conduct beyond which the police, courts, or other agencies cannot go, but it does *not* necessarily follow that all statutes must be fully enforced up to these limits. Statutes may be enacted as expressions of desirable morality but with no intention of full and relentless enforcement (adultery), or may be retained due to legislative oversight or consciously as strengthening the "arsenal" of prosecutors but without an expectation of general enforcement (blue laws), or be vague and not clearly limited either inadvertently, deliberately, or as a necessary limitation of all attempts to write generalizable word formulas (gambling).[2] Furthermore, the lag between the volume of criminal statutes and the resources and budget allowed to enforce them is usually such that enforcement agencies must make allocation decisions regarding which laws are to receive primary enforcement attention. The question of mandate, then, is itself a complex one, and the definition of criminal conduct more realistically one of practice within the outer limits fixed by legislation than mere reliance on the words of statutes themselves.

Discretion Within the System

The administrative process does not turn solely upon the basis of admissible evidence. There are points in the process where discretion is formally allowed and where decisions to invoke or not invoke may hinge upon bases other than evidential. The prosecutor, for example, has wide discretionary powers in deciding when and what to charge or even whether to charge at all despite sufficient evidence. Not all persons validly arrested must be charged; the prosecutor has the power *nolle prosequi*, which may be based upon extraevidential criteria.[3] In addition to the prosecutor's discretion, formally recognized discretionary powers are conferred upon the judge in sentencing and upon postconviction authorities. This discretion is not limited to legally relevant evidence but may be used to consider many cultural and psychological variables as distinguishing criteria. At least at the points of charging, sentence, and corrections, then, the system makes discretionary allowances. There are some checks, formal and otherwise, on the exercise of this discretion, but their analysis is beyond the scope of this paper. Nevertheless, here is discretion recognized and expected which, among other things, makes allegations of "disparity" in charging or sentencing less clearly a criticism of the system than if the "full enforcement ideal" were really the case.

In addition to points of recognized discretion, it is clear that discretion must be assumed at points where it is not formally permitted. The police, for example, cannot physically enforce all laws equally even if they should wish to do so.[4] And in the task of fitting laws to persons, courts must choose

---

[2] For an excellent analysis of ambiguity and the problem of defining criminal conduct, see Frank J. Remington and Victor G. Rosenblum, "The Criminal Law and the Legislative Process," *Law Forum* (1960), p. 481.

[3] Newman Baker and Earl De Long, "The Prosecuting Attorney and His Office," *Journal of Criminal Law, Criminology, and Police Science*, 25 (1935): 695.

[4] Joseph Goldstein, "Police Discretion Not to Invoke the Criminal Process: Low-Visibility Decisions in the Administration of Justice," *Yale Law Journal*, 69 (1960): 543.

among consequences of labels and sentences if they wish to individualize justice. Discretion, then, whether granted or assumed, is a part of the system[5] and forms the basis of the accommodations discussed below.

The Guilty Plea

The conviction process relies primarily on the guilty plea, not on the trial. Adversary it may be, but adversary in pleadings, not in combat. While there are fluctuations between jurisdictions, somewhere between 80 and 90 percent of all persons charged plead guilty.[6] The trial, and particularly the jury trial, is comparatively rare, considering the arrest and charging base. Not only does the guilty plea predominate adjudication but the entire conviction system operates upon an expectation of a continually high proportion of such pleas. The rather unrealistic cry is often heard that if all arrested in a single day exercised their prerogative to plead not guilty, the system would be swamped for months, or years, to come. It is, of course, highly unlikely that all cohort defendants anywhere will plead not guilty. Yet the system is so finely balanced in some congested urban court systems that even a small increment in not-guilty pleas would seriously strain trial resources.

The guilty plea has obvious advantages for the system; it not only clears the dockets and frees the prosecutor from trial efforts but at small cost assures conviction of the guilty, thus protecting the community (after all, even the best prepared trial may result in acquittal of guilty and dangerous persons), and has the further psychological advantage of recording confessions of guilt. A system built around the guilty plea presents quite a different administrative structure than one based upon trial.

ACCOMMODATIONS IN THE CONVICTION PROCESS

The term "accommodations" will be used here to refer to decisions, for the most part routine and systematic, to proceed to less than full implementation of the conviction process in spite of sufficient legal evidence to do so. The effects of such accommodations are either (a) noninvocation against persons clearly guilty of criminal conduct or (b) less than full implementation warranted by the criminal conduct of defendants and the evidence against them. Both of these affect any statistics derived from the system,

---

[5] See Charles Breitel, "Controls in Criminal Law Enforcement," *University of Chicago Law Review*, 27 (1960): 427.

[6] See American Law Institute, *A Study of the Business of the Federal Courts* (Washington, D.C., 1934); Institute of Judicial Administration, *Law-Enforcement Statistics Study* (New Jersey, 1955); and Mark S. Boerner, "Administrative Justice" (unpublished, 1959).

the first by excluding from tabulation those known to be guilty but never-theless not processed and the second by affixing criminal labels and sen-tences inconsistent with and less serious than the actual criminal conduct could warrant.

Accommodations occur at each of the major stages of the administrative process, investigation of crimes, arrest, charging, adjudication, sentencing, and postsentencing treatment. Limited space prohibits thorough analysis of each; instead one stage, adjudication, will be used in illustration. Ad-judication is, in many ways, a particularly crucial point at which to dem-onstrate such accommodations for two reasons: (a) conviction is the formal labeling stage and the crime for which defendant is convicted fixes the outer limits of his sentence and (b) adjudication is, in theory, a nondiscre-tionary phase of the process. While prosecutors have discretion in charging and the judge in sentencing, theoretically the only basis of acquittal or conviction is evidence sufficiency. Acquittal of guilty defendants is within the *power* of the judge and cannot be attacked but is not recognized as a *discretionary* choice.[7] Conviction without sufficient evidence is of course not allowable, although the guilty plea presents particular problems here in that the evidence is not ordinarily fully presented so that the judge can accurately weigh it, but the matter of selecting the crime on which to con-vict defendant and the relationship of this selection to his actual conduct is another matter. Evidently a defendant can be convicted of a less serious crime than the one of which he actually is guilty.[8]

Accommodations at adjudication fall into two major categories: (a) ac-quittal of guilty defendants in spite of evidence sufficient to convict them and (b) charge reduction in exchange for a plea of guilty. While both have some characteristics in common, they are sufficiently distinct to be viewed separately. A major difference is that the acquittal accommodation is a de-cision not to convict at all and thereby to release defendant from official control while the reduction decision retains control but modifies the label and consequent sentence.

Acquittal of Guilty Defendants

It could be argued that determination of guilt is never certain until trial has been had and that judicial acquittal of the "guilty'" is not really an accommodation at all but a finding based upon insufficient evidence to con-vict. While this might be the case if inability to convict is held to be the same as "innocent," in most routine dismissals of this nature the evidence is clearly sufficient to convict and there is little doubt, certainly no reason-able doubt, that defendant engaged in the conduct forming the basis of the arrest and charge.

---

[7] *State* v. *Evjue,* 254 Wis. 581, 37 N.W. 2d 50 (1949).
[8] See *Shelton* v. *U.S.,* 234 F (2d) 132 (1956), 242 F (2d) 101 (1957), 246 F (2d) 571 (1957), and 356 U.S. 26 (1958).

The acquittal of the guilty decision can be dichotomized as to general purposes of the judge who acquits as: (1) interpretation and review of, and possibly attempt to control, earlier investigation, arrest, and charging decisions, and (2) an attempt to individualize justice. The first category can be further refined to include (a) acquittal as a reflection of the judge's belief that the conduct is not really criminal in that it either does not fall within the legislative proscription or is not included within legislative intent as to how the law is to be interpreted or enforced, and (b) acquittal as a protest against methods used by the police in investigation or arrest. In the American Bar Foundation study judges were observed to acquit in petty gambling and adult consensual sexual-relation cases on the general grounds that the law was not intended to cover such instances. And acting in review of prior procedures, acquittal was used when police methods were felt to be unfair, although this unfairness was technically short of entrapment, illegal search, or unnecessary force. In Detroit, for example, one judge routinely acquitted both prostitutes and homosexuals when in his opinion the vice squad had "enticed" them into the criminal conduct. In addition acquittal was sometimes used as a reward for informants.

In attempting to individualize justice, judges used acquittal under the following circumstances: (a) when postconviction resources were felt to be inadequate to deal effectively with the conduct involved, particularly when alternatives short of conviction (restitution, consent to private psychiatric treatment) were available. (b) Acquittal because of the excessive cost of conviction to the defendant and the low risk of his reviolation. This occurred particularly where defendants were young, had no previous record, and/or were otherwise "respectable" persons, and the judge felt that the prior processes of arrest and charging were enough to "teach them a lesson," but that a conviction record would work some hardship beyond the formal sentence, such as loss of employment or inability to enter the armed services. (c) Acquittal because of mitigating circumstances in the case. This occurred most frequently where victim or complainant had contributed to the criminal conduct, as in assault charges growing out of barroom fights, larceny by prostitutes from their clients, and the like. (d) Acquittal in a variety of situations or unusual circumstances ranging from the low intelligence or emotional instability of certain defendants to the judicial belief that such conduct as contained in the charge is really "normal" behavior within certain racial or class subcultures.

In general, summary acquittal of the guilty did not account for a high proportion of the cases charged (although it was used in all courts studied) because cases reaching the adjudication level had already passed through police and prosecutor screens with the bulk of the decisions not to invoke the process made here. In this sense, acquittal by the court can be viewed as a review of prosecutor and police discretion, and it is likely that the values expressed here, short of personal antagonism, are rather quickly translated into police and prosecutor practices.

Charge Reduction for Reasons Other Than Sufficiency of Evidence

Whereas acquittal is outright forgiveness on the part of the court and where it is relatively infrequent because of prior screening, charge reduction is compromise, bargaining with the guilty, and a very common, almost routine practice in those jurisdictions where it is necessary to avoid mandatory sentencing provisions.

Charge reduction is a major part of a broader "negotiated plea" process,[9] and as such it affects defendants in two ways: (1) by reducing the criminal record, the "label" which attaches upon conviction, to one less than defendant's actual conduct would objectively warrant, and (2) by achieving the ordinarily less severe sentencing consequences of conviction on a lesser charge. For the most part these are related, but a case can be made that criminal records may occasionally have independent significance from sentencing provisions. Where the reduction is from felony to misdemeanor, for example, the defendant may not only markedly reduce the possible sentence but in the process avoid both the stigma and consequences of felony conviction. In other cases, however, where a felony is reduced to a lesser felony, for example, the labeling advantage is minimal, particularly where postconviction authorities, aware of bargaining, tend to treat the defendant as if he had been convicted of the original charge. The effect of discrepancies between conduct and official label on the statistical use of conviction records to generalize about conduct distribution is, however, devastating.

It is clear that the primary purpose of most charge reductions is to avoid the sentencing consequences of conviction on high charges, and it necessarily follows that charge reductions most commonly occur in those cases where there are legislative controls on judicial sentencing discretion.[10] This is most clearly illustrated where statutes fix both the minimum and maximum sentences in a given offense. In Michigan, for example, sale of narcotics carries a mandatory minimum sentence of twenty years' imprisonment, the maximum being life, without the possibility of probation. The difficulty presented by this to prosecutors and judges is that it removes the possibility of distinguishing cases once the charge has been brought and conviction recorded. Both the youthful first offender whose criminal conduct consists of selling a single marijuana cigarette to a buddy and the chronic, professional pusher face twenty years' minimum incarceration if convicted of sale. Consequently the practice is to reduce the charge in the first instance, the case of the young defendant, convicting "on the nose"

---

[9] Donald J. Newman, "Pleading Guilty for Considerations: A Study of Bargain Justice," *Journal of Criminal Law, Criminology, and Police Science,* 46 (1956): 780.

[10] Lloyd Ohlin and Frank J. Remington, "Sentencing Structure: Its Effect on the Administration of Justice," *Law and Contemporary Problems,* 23 (1958): 495.

only where there is judicial and prosecutor desire to incapacitate the organized criminal. However rationalized, whether as interpretation of the way the legislature intended the law to be used or merely as perception of differences in circumstances and defendants not accounted for in statute, charge reduction here is an attempt at equity in consequences where such equity is denied by statutory limitations or sentencing discretion.

The reduction of charges at or just prior to the adjudication stage serves certain specific purposes that would not be possible if all such discretion were left to the police at arrest or the prosecutor in bringing the original charge. In the first place, charge reduction is based upon a prior decision to convict defendant rather than to acquit him. Noninvocation of the process may be easily accomplished by the police failing to arrest or the *nolle prosequi* powers of the prosecutor, so that acquittal decisions are commonly made here. Once the decision is to convict, however, the process must be started, arrest made, and charge brought. Here various purposes of bargaining intertwine. Equity, the individualization of justice, is only a part of the motivation for the negotiated plea. As a matter of fact, charges are routinely reduced, and while the balancing of consequences between defendants may be expressed by court or prosecutor, a primary purpose of reduction is to induce defendants to plead guilty. Since every accused defendant has a right to trial, there must be a differential advantage given to that high proportion who waive this right. Where there are mandatory sentencing structures, the best inducement of guilty pleas is charge reduction to modify statutory sentencing requirements. Furthermore, in view of the categorization in some jurisdictions of certain offenses as nonprobationable, and at the same time in view of crowded prisons, charge reduction acts to lessen strains on postconviction resources as well as on the court. Thus while equity in consequences may be achieved by reducing charges in one case and not another, or by reducing further in one case, the practice has become so routine and systematic that individual differences are only occasionally offered in rationalization, with the primary benefits of this procedure relating to the system itself and not to the individual defendant.

Charge reducton at the adjudication level also means that the court has a more active role in the expression of the values involved. The judge can either initiate or directly condone bargaining, can take it into account in his sentencing decision, and in general can directly implement whatever policies or desires he has about certain types of offenders or certain laws. If bargaining were solely the province of other agencies, its visibility would be reduced and the directness of judicial check on this process lost. Since bargaining in great part is concerned with the manipulation of sentencing alternatives, negotiations at the adjudication level act to contain the sentencing decision within the province of the court.

Because any crime can be downgraded, and examples of reductions of virtually all types of felonies and misdemeanors were noted, the range of downgrading (i.e., how far the original offense is reduced) is of particular interest and the question of limits, if any, on manipulation of the original charge of particular significance. Reductions generally can be classified as either (1) reductions to lesser included offenses or (2) reductions to "illogical" lesser offenses. Some reductions bring substantial sentencing benefits, reducing the maximum punishment as much as tenfold, and of course reduction from felonies to misdemeanors reduce both sentence and record. The only limitation on the range of reductions appeared to be an inarticulated but common practice of reduction to a count which bears some categoric similarity to the original charge. Homicides, for example, involved reduction from murder to manslaughter or negligent homicide or assault or attempt, but grossly conduct-inconsistent offenses such as larceny or possession of narcotics were never arbitrarily added in place of murder unless these offenses were part of the actual conduct involved in the major crime. The "illogical" lesser offense, then, was never categorically different from the original charge; it was "illogical" ("inconsistent" would be a more accurate term) only in the sense that the added offense contained some element of proof not required in the original charge or omitted evidence of some element necessary to the major charge and was therefore somewhat inconsistent with the fact situation.

While the general overriding consideration in charge reduction is the maintenance of a steady flow of guilty pleas, specific attempts to individualize justice may underlie the reduction decision in about the same fashion as motives for acquittal of the guilty. Thus judges may concur with the prosecutor's move for reductions because (1) the conduct does not warrant the conviction record or the mandatory sentence of the greater charge, (2) the effects of conviction on the lesser count are equal to or better than conviction on the higher charge, (3) the lesser charge is more suitable because the defendant, although guilty of the greater charge, deserves a break because he is young, respectable, or otherwise deserving, (4) the lesser charge is justified by circumstances in the case which mitigate higher liability, (5) the lesser charge permits probation and thereby allows restitution or enables defendant to support his family, and (6) the lesser charge is a suitable reward for informants or states' witnesses.

Charge reduction is common, almost routine. About the same types of bargains are offered to all who wish to avail themselves of them; there was no evidence of arbitrary use nor discriminatory denial of negotiation. All in postconviction authority are aware of this process, so that a member of the Michigan Parole Board could comment: "This one is from Wayne County and it says robbery unarmed. Let's see what kind of a gun he used." Another parole official remarked: "It's almost impossible to tell what a man actually did by the formal charge under which he was sentenced." Unfortunately, the fact of charge reduction does not usually appear in judicial statistics.

CONCLUSION: THE EFFECT OF ACCOMMODATIONS ON CRIMINAL STATISTICS

The effects of the two accommodations, acquittal and reduction, on statistics gathered from the conviction process are apparent. The acquittal decision effectively removes some guilty from tabulation at conviction and sentencing stages. These are not undetected or unknown criminals, but those whose conduct and identity have been discovered but who are nevertheless released. The reduction process, on the other hand, retains control but modifies the label and the sentence of the persons convicted. To conclude that a particular criminal is a certain behavioral type from his conviction record is obviously a dubious technique. To generalize about the crime problem of a given community by the types of convictions recorded there is likewise of little value. To assume that only good-risk, minor offenders are placed on probation, as their records might indicate, is a disillusionment of many new probation officers unaware of the extent and range of bargaining. Legislators who fix severe punishments to certain crimes, such as sale of narcotics, may conclude that this punishment is effective when conviction rates decline, failing of course to take into account the accommodations available within the system to avoid legislative mandate. In short, statistics taken from the surface of the system are more likely to be inaccurate than reliable indicators of the distribution of criminal conduct involved. Failing to recognize criminal procedures as a complex pattern of decision-making, of discretionary choices of administrators, and paying little attention to the flexibility of the system in accommodating laws to cases, are errors in any conclusions based upon conviction records or for that matter tabulations taken from any point in the conviction process. A careful analysis of how the system operates, how it records its business, is a prerequisite for the use of data gathered from it.

Furthermore, to criticize statistics taken from the system because they do not include all "real" crimes or to allege inefficiency or corruption because some persons are released from the process and others are not labeled as severely as their conduct could warrant is to attribute to the system characteristics it does not have, nor necessarily should have. The "law" is no more clearly statute than practice and the desirable consequences of procedures no more clearly accurate labeling than equitable balancing of record and punishment among differing cases and defendants. A slot-machine model of administration is neither as realistic nor any more just than a system devoted to speedy disposition of cases with ample attention to due process and civil rights but with discretion to accommodate cases to law and law to persons.

9. ALTERNATIVE USES
OF OFFICIAL STATISTICS

John I. Kitsuse and Aaron V. Cicourel

Current theoretical and research formulations in the sociology of deviance are cast within the general framework of social and cultural differentiation, deviance, and social control. In contrast to the earlier moralistic conceptions of the "pathologies," the focus of description and analysis has shifted from the vagaries of morbid behavior to the patterning effects of the social-cultural environment on forms of deviant conduct. These forms of deviation are conceived as social products of the organization of groups, social structures, and institutions.

Three major lines of inquiry have developed within this general framework. One development has been the problem of explaining the rates of various forms of deviation among various segments of the population. The research devoted to this problem has produced a large body of literature in which individual, group, and areal (e.g., census tracts, regions, states, etc.) characteristics are correlated with rates of deviation. Durkheim's pioneer study of suicide is a classic example of this sociological interest. Mer-

Reprinted by permission of the authors and the Society for the Study of Social Problems from *Social Problems,* 11, no. 2 (Fall 1963): 131–39. Original title: "A Note on the Uses of Official Statistics." Footnotes have been renumbered.

The authors wish to acknowledge the support of the Youth Development Program of the Ford Foundation in facilitating the preparation of this paper.

ton's more general theory of social structure and anomie[1] may be cited as the most widely circulated statement of this problem.

The second line of investigation has been directed to the question of how individuals come to engage in various types of deviant behavior. From the theoretical standpoint, this question has been posed by the fact that although an aggregate of individuals may be exposed to the "same" sociogenic factors associated with deviant behavior, some individuals become deviant while others do not. Research into this problem has led some sociologists into the field of actuarial statistics and others to social and depth psychology to investigate differences in individual "adaptation" to the social-cultural environment. The search for the etiology of deviant behavior in individual differences has reintroduced the notion of "pathology," in the garb of "emotionally disturbed," "psychopathic personality," "weak ego structure," and other psychological concepts, which has created a hiatus between sociological and social-psychological approaches. Sutherland's differential association theory[2] represents a counterformulation which attempts to account for the etiology of deviant behavior within the general framework of "normal" learning processes.

A third line of inquiry has been concerned with the developmental processes of "behavior systems." Theory and research on this aspect of deviant behavior focuses on the relation between the social differentiation of the deviant, the organization of deviant activity, and the individual's conception of himself as deviant. Studies of the professional thief, convicts, prostitutes, alcoholics, hoboes, drug addicts, carnival men, and others describe and analyze the deviant subculture and its patterning effects on the interaction between deviant and others. The work of Lemert[3] presents a systematic theoretical and empirical integration of this interest in the sociology of deviance.

Although the three lines of investigation share a common interest in the organizational "sources" of deviant behavior, a theoretical integration between them has not been achieved. This is particularly apparent in the theoretical and methodological difficulties posed by the problem of relating the rates of deviant behavior to the distribution of "sociogenic" factors within the social structure. These difficulties may be stated in the form of two questions: (1) How is "deviant behavior" to be defined sociologically, and (2) what are the relevant rates of deviant behavior which constitute the "facts to be explained"? We shall propose that these difficulties arise as a consequence of the failure to distinguish between the social conduct which

---

[1] Robert K. Merton, *Social Theory and Social Structure,* rev. ed. (Glencoe, Ill.: Free Press, 1957), chap. 4.

[2] Edwin H. Sutherland and Donald R. Cressey, *Principles of Criminology,* 5th ed. (New York: Macmillan, 1956), chap. 4.

[3] Edwin M. Lemert, *Social Pathology* (New York: McGraw-Hill, 1951), esp. chaps. 1–4. See also Sutherland and Cressey, *op. cit.,* chaps. 12–13.

produces a *unit* of behavior (the behavior-producing processes) and organizational activity which produces a unit in the rate of *deviant* behavior (the rate-producing processes.)[4] The failure to make this distinction has led sociologists to direct their theoretical and empirical investigations to the behavior-producing processes on the implicit assumption that the rates of deviant behavior may be explained by them. We shall discuss some of the consequences of this distinction for theory and research in the sociology of deviance by examining the problems of the "appropriateness" and "reliability" of official statistics.[5]

I

The following statement by Merton is a pertinent and instructive point of departure for a discussion of the question raised above:

> Our primary aim is to discover how some *social structures exert a definite pressure upon certain persons in the society to engage in nonconforming rather than conforming conduct.* If we can locate groups peculiarly subject to such pressures, we would expect to find fairly high rates of deviant behavior in those groups, not because the human beings comprising them are compounded of distinctive biological tendencies but because they are responding normally to the social situation in which they find themselves. Our perspective is sociological. We look at variations in the *rates* of deviant behavior, not at its incidence.[6]

The central hypothesis that Merton derives from his theory is that "aberrant behavior may be regarded as a symptom of dissociation between culturally prescribed aspirations and socially structured avenues for realizing these aspirations."[7] The test of this general hypothesis, he suggests, would be to compare the variations in the rates of aberrant behavior among populations occupying different positions within the social structure. The question arises: What are the units of behavior which are to be tabulated to compile these rates of aberrant behavior?

Merton answers this question by discussing the kinds of rates which are

---

[4] The conception of the "rate-producing" processes as socially organized activities is taken from work by Harold Garfinkel, and is primarily an application of what he has termed the "praxeological rule." See Harold Garfinkel, "Some Sociological Concepts and Methods for Psychiatrists," *Psychiatric Research Reports*, 6 (October 1956): 181–95; Harold Garfinkel and Harry Brickman, "A Study of the Composition of the Clinic Patient Population of the Outpatient Department of the U.C.L.A. Neuropsychiatric Institute," unpublished manuscript.

[5] For a discussion of these problems, see Sophia M. Robison, *Can Delinquency Be Measured?* (New York: Columbia University Press, 1936). See also Sutherland and Cressey, *op. cit.*, chap. 2.

[6] Merton, *op. cit.*, p. 147. Merton's comments on the theory of social structure and anomie may be found in chap. 5 of that volume, and in "Social Conformity, Deviation, and Opportunity Structures: A Comment on the Contributions of Dubin and Cloward," *American Sociological Review*, 24 (April 1959): 177–89. See also his remarks in *New Perspectives for Research on Juvenile Delinquency*, ed. H. Witmer and R. Kotinsky (Washington, D.C.: U.S. Government Printing Office, 1956).

[7] *Social Theory and Social Structure*, p. 134.

"inappropriate," but he is less explicit about what may be considered "appropriate" data for sociological research. Discussing the relevance of his theory for research on juvenile delinquency, Merton presents two arguments against the use of "official" rates of deviant behavior. He asks:

> To what extent and for which purposes is it feasible to make use of existing data in the study of deviant behavior? By existing data I mean the data which the machinery of society makes available—census data, delinquency rates as recorded in official or unofficial sources, data on the income distribution of an area, on the state of housing in an area, and the like. . . .
>
> There is little in the history of how statistical series on the incidence of juvenile delinquency came to be collected that shows them to be the result of efforts to identify either the sources or the contexts of juvenile delinquency. These are social bookkeeping data. And it would be a happy coincidence if some of them turned out to be in a form relevant for research.
>
> From the sociological standpoint, "juvenile delinquency" and what it encompasses is a form of deviant behavior for which the epidemiological data, as it were, may not be at hand. You may have to go out and collect your own appropriately organized data rather than to take those which are ready-made by governmental agencies.[8]

Our interpretation of this statement is that for the purposes of sociological research, official statistics may use categories which are unsuitable for the classification of deviant behavior. At best such statistics classify the "same" form of deviant behavior in different categories and "different" forms in the same categories. Thus, the "sources or the contexts" of the behavior are obscured.

Merton also argues against the use of official statistics on quite different grounds. He states that such data are "unreliable" because "successive layers of error intervene between the actual event and the recorded event, between the actual rates of deviant behavior and the records of deviant behavior."[9] In this statement, the argument is that the statistics are unreliable because some individuals who manifest deviant behavior are apprehended, classified, and duly recorded while others are not. It is assumed that if the acts of all such individuals were called to the attention of the official agencies they would be defined as deviant and so classified and recorded. In referring to the "unreliability" of the statistics in this sense, however, Merton appears to suspend his "sociologically relevant" definition of deviant behavior and implicitly invokes the definitions applied by the agencies which have compiled the statistics. That is, the "unreliability" is viewed as a technical and organizational problem, not a matter of differences concerning the definition of deviant behavior.

Thus, Merton argues against the use of official statistics on two separate grounds. On the one hand, official statistics are not appropriately organized

---

[8] *New Perspectives for Research on Juvenile Delinquency*, p. 32.
[9] *Ibid.*, p. 31.

for sociological research because they are not collected by the application of a "sociologically relevant" definition of deviant behavior. On the other hand, he implies that official statistics *could* be used if "successive layers of error" did not make them "unreliable." But if the statistics are inappropriate for sociological research on the first ground, would they not be inappropriate regardless of their "unreliability"?

It is evident, however, that "inappropriate" or not, sociologists, including Merton himself,[10] do make use of the official statistics after a few conventional words of caution concerning the "unreliability" of such statistics. The "social bookkeeping data" are, after all, considered to bear some, if unknown, relation to the "actual" rates of deviant behavior that interest sociologists. But granted that there are practical reasons for the use of official statistics, are there any theoretical grounds which justify their use, or is this large body of data useless for research in the sociology of deviance? This question directs us to examine more closely the theoretical and methodological bases of the two arguments against their use.

II

The objection to the official statistics because they are "inappropriate" is, as indicated above, on definitional grounds. The argument is that insofar as the definitions of deviant behavior incorporated in the official statistics are not "sociologically relevant," such statistics are *in principle* "inappropriate" for sociological research. What then is a sociologically relevant definition of deviant behavior and what are to be considered "appropriately organized data" for sociological research?[11]

We suggest that the question of the theoretical significance of the official

---

10 For example, "Crude (and not necessarily reliable) crime statistics suggest . . ." etc. (*Social Theory and Social Structure*, p. 147). In a more extensive comment on the limitations imposed on research by the use of official statistics, Merton states: "Its decisive limitation derives from a circumstance which regularly confronts sociologists seeking to devise measures of theoretical concepts by drawing upon an array of social data which *happen* to be recorded in the statistical series established by agencies of the society—namely, the circumstance that these data of social bookkeeping which happen to be on hand are not necessarily the data which best measure the concept. . . . Pragmatic considerations of this sort are of course no suitable alternative to theoretically derived indicators of the concept" (p. 165).

11 Merton proposes to define deviant behavior in terms of the "acceptance" or "rejection" of cultural goals and/or institutionalized means. Interpreting the two terms literally, a given form of behavior (adaptation) is to be considered deviant if it is oriented by some cultural goals (to be specified by the sociologists) and/or the institutionalized means (also to be specified) which govern conduct with respect to those goals. By this definition, appropriately organized data would require that behaviors be classified in the typology of "modes of individual adaptation." But what are the operational criteria by which "acceptance" or "rejection" of cultural goals and institutionalized means are to be inferred from observed behavior? How, for example, is the sociologist to distinguish between behavior which indicates "conformity" from "overconformity" (which presumably would be classified as "ritualism"), or "retreatism" from "innovation"? Unless a set of rules for the classification of behavior as deviant can be derived from the theory, rates of deviant behavior cannot be constructed to test its validity.

statistics can be rephrased by shifting the focus of investigation from the processes by which *certain forms of behavior* are socially and culturally generated to the processes by which *rates of deviant behavior* are produced. Merton states that his primary aim is to explain the former processes, and he proposes to look at variations in the rates of deviant behavior as indices of the processes. Implicit in this proposal is the assumption that an explanation of the behavior-producing processes is also an explanation of the rate-producing processes. This assumption leads Merton to consider the correspondence between the forms of behavior which his theory is designed to explain and their distribution in the social structure as reflected in some set of statistics, including those commonly used official statistics "which are ready-made by governmental agencies."

Let us propose, however, the following: Our primary aim is to explain the *rates of deviant behavior*. So stated, the question which orients the investigation is not how individuals are motivated to engage in behavior defined by the sociologists as "deviant." Rather, the definition and content of deviant behavior are viewed as problematic, and the focus of inquiry shifts from the forms of behavior (modes of individual adaptation in Merton's terminology) to the "societal reactions" which define various forms of behavior as deviant.[12] In contrast to Merton's formulation, which focuses on forms of behavior as dependent variables (with structural pressures conceived to be the independent variables), we propose here to view the rates of deviant behavior as dependent variables. Thus, the explanation of rates of deviant behavior would be concerned specifically with the processes of rate construction.

The problem of the definition of "deviant behavior" is directly related to the shift in focus proposed here. The theoretical conception which guides us is that the *rates of deviant behavior* are produced by *the actions taken by persons in the social system* which define, classify, and record certain behaviors as deviant.[13] If a given form of behavior is not interpreted as deviant by such persons it would not appear as a unit in whatever set of rates we may attempt to explain (e.g., the statistics of local social welfare agencies, "crimes known to the police," *Uniform Crime Reports*, court records, etc.). The persons who define and activate the rate-producing processes may range from the neighborhood "busybody" to officials of law-enforcement agencies.[14] From this point of view, *deviant behavior* is behavior which is organizationally defined, processed, and treated as "strange," "ab-

---

[12] For a discussion of the concept of "societal reaction" see Lemert, *op cit.*, chap. 4.

[13] For a preliminary research application of this formulation, see John I. Kitsuse, "Societal Reaction to Deviant Behavior: Problems of Theory and Method," *Social Problems*, 9 (Winter 1962): 247–56.

[14] We recognize, of course, that many individuals may be labeled "strange," "crooks," "crazy," etc., and ostracized by members of a community, yet be unknown to the police or any other official agency. Insofar as such individuals are labeled and treated as deviants, they constitute a population which must be explained in any theory of deviance. In this paper, however, we are primarily concerned with the theoretical relevance of official statistics for the study of deviance.

normal," "theft," "delinquent," etc., by the personnel in the social system which has produced the rate. By these definitions, a sociological theory of deviance would focus on three interrelated problems of explanation: (1) how different forms of behavior come to be defined as deviant by various groups or organizations in the society, (2) how individuals manifesting such behaviors are organizationally processed to produce rates of deviant behavior among various segments of the population, and (3) how acts which are officially or unofficially defined as deviant are generated by such conditions as family organization, role inconsistencies, or situational "pressures."

What are the consequences of these definitions for the question regarding the relevance of official statistics for sociological research? First, the focus on the processes by which rates are produced allows us to consider any set of statistics, "official" as well as "unofficial," to be relevant. The question of whether or not the statistics are "appropriately organized" is not one which is determined by reference to the correspondence between the sociologist's definition of deviant behavior and the organizational criteria used to compile the statistics. Rather the categories which organize a given set of statistics are taken as given—the "cultural definitions," to use Merton's term, of deviant behavior are *par excellence* the relevant definitions for research. The specification of the definitions explicitly or implicitly stated in the statistical categories is viewed as an empirical problem. Thus, the question to be asked is not about the "appropriateness" of the statistics, but about the definitions incorporated in the categories applied by the personnel of the rate-producing social system to identify, classify, and record behavior as deviant.

Second, a unit in a given rate of deviant behavior is not defined in terms of a given form of behavior or a "syndrome" of behavior. The behaviors which result in the classification of individuals in a given deviant category are *not necessarily* similar, i.e., the "objective" manifestation of the "same" forms of behavior may result in the classification of some individuals as deviant but not others. For example, with reference to the rates of delinquency reported by the police department, we would ask: What are the criteria that the police personnel use to identify and process a youth as "incorrigible," "sex offender," "vandal," etc.? The criteria of such categories are vague enough to include a wide range of behaviors which in turn may be produced by various "sources and contexts" within the social structure.[15]

Third, the definition of deviant behavior as behavior which is organizationally processed as deviant provides a different perspective on the prob-

---

[15] In any empirical investigation of such criteria, it is necessary to distinguish between the formal (official) interpretive rules (as defined by a manual of procedures, constitution, and the like) which are to be employed by the personnel of the organization in question, and the unofficial rules used by the personnel in their deviant-processing activities, e.g., differential treatment on the basis of social class, race, ethnicity, or varying conceptions of "deviant" behavior.

lem of the "unreliability" of the official statistics. Insofar as we are primarily concerned with explaining rates rather than the forms of deviant behavior, such statistics may be accepted as a record of the number of those who have been differentiated as variously deviant at different levels of social control and treatment. The "successive layers of error" which may result from the failure of control agencies to record all instances of certain forms of behavior, or from the exclusion of cases from one set of statistics that are included in another, do not render such statistics "unreliable," unless they are assigned self-evident status. By the definition of deviance proposed here, such cases are not among those processed as deviant by the organizations which have produced the statistics and thus are not officially deviant. To reject these statistics as "unreliable" because they fail to record the "actual" rate of deviant behavior assumes that certain behavior is always deviant independent of social actions which define it as deviant.

Fourth, the conception of rates of deviant behavior as the product of the socially organized activities of social structures provides a method of specifying the "relevant structure" to be investigated. The rates are constructed from the statistics compiled by specifiable organizations, and those rates must be explained in terms of the deviant-processing activities of those organizations. Thus, rates can be viewed as indices of organizational processes rather than as indices of the incidence of certain forms of behavior. For example, variations in the rates of deviant behavior among a given group (e.g., Negroes) as reflected in the statistics of different organizations may be a product of the differing definitions of deviant behavior used by those organizations, differences in the processing of deviant behavior, differences in the ideological, political, and other organizational conditions which affect the rate-making processes.

III

We wish now to discuss briefly some recent work[16] concerning adult and juvenile criminal acts which lends support to the thesis presented above. Let us assume that an ideal system of law-enforcement would lead to the apprehension of all persons who have committed criminal acts as defined by the statutes, and adjudicated in the manner prescribed by those statutes. In the ideal case, there would be little room for administrative interpretation and discretion. The adjudication process would proceed on the basis of evidence deemed legally admissible and the use of the adversary system to convict those who are guilty and exonerate those against whom there is

---

[16] The material in this section is taken from an unpublished paper by Cicourel entitled "Social Class, Family Structure, and the Administration of Juvenile Justice," and is based on a study of the social organization of juvenile justice in two southern California communities with populations of approximately 100,000 each.

insufficient evidence.[17] Criminologists have long recognized that the practiced and enforced system of criminal law, at all levels of the process, does not fulfill this ideal conception of criminal justice strictly governed by the definitions and prescriptions of statutes. Therefore, criminal statistics clearly cannot be assumed to reflect a system of criminal justice functioning as ideally conceived, and "labels assigned convicted defendants" are not to be viewed as "the statutory equivalents of their actual conduct."[18]

What such statistics do reflect, however, are the specifically organizational contingencies which condition the application of specific statutes to actual conduct through the interpretations, decisions, and actions of law-enforcement personnel. The decisions and discretionary actions of persons who administer criminal justice have been documented by the American Bar Foundation study cited above. That study and other research[19] indicates the following:

1. There is considerable ambiguity in defining the nature of criminal conduct within the limits defined by the statutes. Categories of criminal conduct are the product of actual practices within these limits, and the decisions which must be made to provide the basis for choosing the laws which will receive the greatest attention.

2. The discretion allowed within the administration of criminal justice means that admissible evidence may give way to the prosecutor's power to determine whether or not to proceed, even in cases where there is adequate evidence to prosecute. The judge, as well as the police or the victim, also has discretion (e.g., sentencing), and some discretion is also extended to correctional institutions.

3. Most persons charged with criminal conduct plead guilty (from 80 to 90 percent, according to the references cited by Newman) and jury trials are rare. Thus, the adversary aspect of the law is not always practiced because many of the lower income offenders cannot afford lawyers and often distrust public defenders. Criminal justice depends upon a large number of guilty pleas. Many of these cases would be acquitted if there were more trials.

4. Statistics are affected by such "accommodations in the conviction process." Some offenders are excluded because they are not processed even though known to be guilty (e.g., drug addicts, prostitutes, and gamblers are often hired by the police or coerced by them to help apprehend other offenders), and the practice of relabeling offenses and reducing sentences because of insufficient evidence, "deals," and tricks (e.g., telling the defendant

---

[17] See Donald J. Newman, "The Effects of Accommodations in Justice Administration on Criminal Statistics," *Sociology and Social Research*, 46 (January 1962): 144–55 [and pp. 77–87 of this volume]; American Bar Foundation, "Administration of Criminal Justice," unpublished (1955).
[18] Newman, "The Effects of Accommodations . . . ," pp. 145–46.
[19] See *ibid.*, pp. 146–51, and the references cited.

or his lawyer that because the offender "seems like a decent person" the charge will be reduced from a felony to a misdemeanor, when in fact the prosecution finds there is insufficient evidence for either charge). These accommodations may occur at the time of arrest, or during prior or subsequent investigation of crimes, filing of complaints, adjudication, sentencing and postsentencing relations with authorities, and so on.

The significance of the American Bar Foundation study goes beyond the documentation of the usual complaints about inadequate recording, inflated recording, and the like. More importantly, it underlines the way criminal statistics fail to reflect the decisions made and discretion used by law-enforcement personnel and administrators, and the general accommodations that can and do occur. An offender's record, then, may never reflect the ambiguous decisions, administrative discretions, or accommodations of law-enforcement personnel; a statistical account may thus seriously distort an offender's past activities.

The administration of justice vis-à-vis juveniles is even more discretionary than for adults, owing to the philosophy of the juvenile court law. The juvenile offender is not officially viewed as a criminal, but rather as an adolescent who is "misdirected," "disturbed," from a "poor environment," and the like. The legal concept of an adversary system is notably absent. The philosophy, however, is differentially interpreted, with police more likely to view juveniles as adult criminals, while probation officers and some judges view the offender within the intended meaning of the law. The early work of Paul Tappan on juvenile court practices[20] shows how a juvenile court judge, on the counsel of a social worker or other "treatment-oriented" personnel, may dispose of a case in a manner which negates all previous characterizations of the offender by police, probation officer, school officials, and the like. The report of the more recent California Special Study Commission on Juvenile Justice[21] implies vaguely and in some passages flatly states that many variations of organizational procedures and interpretations by personnel differentially influence the administration of juvenile justice in California. The use of existing stereotypes and imputations of social characteristics to juvenile defendants by law-enforcement personnel routinely introduce nonlegal criteria and actions into the organizational procedures of the legal process and significantly influence the realization of judicial objectives.[22]

---

[20] *Juvenile Delinquency* (New York: McGraw-Hill, 1949).

[21] *Report of the Governor's Special Study Commission on Juvenile Justice*, pts. I and II (Sacramento: California State Printing Office, 1960).

[22] To illustrate how organizational procedures and imputations can affect official statistics, we refer to a preliminary finding by Cicourel (cited in footnote 16) which shows that one of two communities studied (Community A) has both a slightly larger population and a higher adult crime rate. Yet this community had (as of November 1962) 3,200 current cases of juveniles suspected or confirmed to be offenders. Community B, on the other hand, had approximately 8,000 current suspected or confirmed juvenile cases. Community A has two juvenile officers on its staff, while Community B has five juvenile officers.

We wish to state explicitly that the interpretation of official statistics proposed here *does not* imply that the forms of behavior which the sociologist might define and categorize as deviant (e.g., Merton's modes of adaptation) have no factual basis or theoretical importance. Nor do we wish to imply that the question of how behaviors so defined are produced by the social structure is not a sociologically relevant question. The implication of our interpretation is rather that *with respect to the problem of rates of deviant behavior* the theoretical question is: What forms of behavior are organizationally defined as deviant, and how are they classified, recorded, and treated by persons in the society?

In our discussion, we have taken the view that official statistics, reflecting as they do the variety of organizational contingencies in the process by which deviants are differentiated from nondeviants, are sociologically relevant data. An individual who is processed as "convicted," for example, is sociologically differentiable from one who is "known to the police" as criminal—the former may legally be incarcerated, incapacitated, and socially ostracized, while the latter remains "free." The fact that both may have "objectively" committed the same crime is of theoretical and empirical significance, but it does not alter the sociological difference between them. The *pattern* of such "errors" is among the facts that a sociological theory of deviance must explain, for they are indications of the organizationally defined processes by which individuals are differentiated as deviant.

Indeed, in modern societies where bureaucratically organized agencies are increasingly invested with social control functions, the activities of such agencies are centrally important "sources and contexts" which generate as well as maintain definitions of deviance and produce populations of deviants. Thus, rates of deviance constructed by the use of statistics routinely issued by these agencies are social facts *par excellence*. A further implication of this view is that if the sociologist is interested in how forms of *deviant* behavior are produced by social structures, the forms that must be explained are those which not only are defined as deviant by members of such structures but those which also activate the unofficial and/or "official" processes of social control. By directing attention to such processes, the behavior-producing and rate-producing processes may be investigated and compared within a single framework.

Some Issues in Measurement II:
Techniques and Ethics

Perhaps the most enduring sources of information on crime during the 1920s and 1930s originated through a program of studies at the University of Chicago. It was during these years that Robert Park, Ernest Burgess, and Roderick McKenzie undertook to discover the nature and distribution of "problem" behavior in metropolitan centers, using Chicago as a "natural laboratory." Park and Burgess (the latter published his "concentric zone" model of urban structure and change in 1925) made seminal contributions to ecological theory, as it was called, and their students over the years wrote research papers on a variety of behaviors considered detrimental to the welfare of society. Many of these were expanded into monographs reporting upon suicide, taxi-dance halls, prostitution, divorce, and mental disorder.

Advocates of human ecology sought to document the distribution of behaviors and life styles in social space, i.e., to account for the concentration of specific social classes or racial and ethnic minorities in certain areas of the city, and to understand the redistribution of these aggregates as the metropolis underwent economic, political, or technological change. Ecological analysis, then, was a comprehensive technique inspired by colloquial expressions of the urban mosaic: certain neighborhoods were "on the other side of the tracks," others comprised the "tenderloin" district, and every city

101

had an identifiable "black belt," "Chinatown," "skid row," and "bohemian" ("beat" in the 1950s, or "hippie" in the 1960s) district.

The Burgess model distinguished a "zone in transition" contiguous to the central business district, and ensuing research activity portrayed it as inhabited by a disproportionately male, elderly, alcoholic, unemployed, impoverished, alienated, and infirm population. By implication, many inhabitants of this zone were criminally disposed, for police surveillance was not rigorous, and the quality of interpersonal relations was predatory. Scholarly interest in this zone and its transient population was invested in the study of its major social institutions: cubicle hotels, cheap taverns, barber colleges, pawnshops, spot-labor markets, and the inevitable Salvation Army Lighthouse.

A major deficiency of ecological theorists was their failure to relate findings based upon Chicago research to data on other cities. Had they attempted this, the stability and generalizability of an ecological model might have been enhanced.

An alternative means of data-gathering consisted of the case study. Sociologists referred to this as the "life history" or "own story" technique, and one of the earliest examples of its use was by W. I. Thomas in a study of girls who turned to delinquency, prostitution, or some other social impropriety as a reaction to their inability or unwillingness to adopt the normative regulations of the general society.[1] Two other well-known works in this same tradition, but devoted to single cases, were Clifford Shaw's account of the early career of a delinquent in Chicago[2] and Sutherland's study of a career in professional theft.[3]

Among the greatest advantages of case studies were (a) their vivid portrayal of the sociocultural situation to which deviants were responsive and (b) the *subjective* evaluations deviants made of their past experiences, including rationalization and selective interpretation of occurrences during their careers. But the limitations of such studies are not unimportant, and center primarily upon the extent to which single cases constitute verification of causal links between sociocultural circumstances and ensuing behavior. Case studies, then, failed to occasion the discovery of so-called negative cases, or those that invalidated the basic hypothesis under test.

While there was probably a time in the history of sociological research when deviant, or negative, cases were embarrassing, Florian Znaniecki specifically proposed their use to reformulate erroneous or incomplete hypotheses.[4] By making statements of relationships between variables more inclusive of deviant cases, he argued, one could best generate universal predictions. In practice this called for constructing hypotheses in advance of field opera-

[1] W. I. Thomas, *The Unadjusted Girl: With Cases and Standpoint for Behavior Analysis* (Boston: Little, Brown, 1923).

[2] Clifford Shaw, *The Jack-Roller: A Delinquent Boy's Own Story* (Chicago: University of Chicago Press, 1930).

[3] Edwin H. Sutherland, *The Professional Thief* (Chicago: University of Chicago Press, 1937; Phoenix ed., 1956).

[4] Florian Znaniecki, *The Method of Sociology* (New York: Farrar & Rinehart, 1934).

tions, subjecting them to the data obtained, and marking for special study those cases that didn't fit the original hypothesis. Negative cases, then, suggested how modification of the hypothesis should be made in order to "explain" cases that falsified the earlier model.

The appearance of two empirical studies using Znaniecki's "analytic induction" technique helped to sustain interest in it for a time: Alfred R. Lindesmith's theory that opiate addiction depends upon learning that withdrawal symptoms can be alleviated by continued use of opiates,[5] and Cressey's interpretation of why persons come to violate positions of financial trust through embezzling.[6] Both studies systematically used negative cases to modify hypotheses predicting addiction and embezzling, respectively. Over the years the method of analytic induction has been subjected to heated debate, and while it is clear that many of the criticisms levied apply equally well to other methodologies, there is not much enthusiasm for this technique at present.

More recently, and largely in response to the indeterminate nature of official crime statistics, a new method for estimating true incidence has appeared. Its predecessors were "saturation surveys" done in Illinois, Oregon, Missouri, and elsewhere which attempted to enumerate crime incidence not revealed in official reports. Under stimulus of the President's Commission on Law Enforcement and Administration of Justice, a study design was undertaken to discover crimes not known to official sources by cross-sectional survey of persons victimized in recent offenses. In addition to concentrating upon *victims* as the unit of analysis, this method secured landmark data on public attitudes and behavior toward the crime problem and law enforcement.

There are at least two justifications invoked by criminologists who advocate a science of "victimology." First, it is important to redirect attention to the victim of a crime because evidence suggests that certain social and psychological characteristics predispose one to victimization. That is, persons are differentially vulnerable to criminal acts by virtue of their own negligent or even provocative behavior. The question is not whether citizens contribute to their own potential for victimization, but which features—be they attributes of personality or properties of the social order—are most likely to be associated with high victimization rates. Second, victimologists would argue that disproportionate concern has been shown for protecting the rights of suspects confronting the law, while the inconvenience, property loss, compromise of physical or mental health, and even loss of life suffered by an offended party have been neglected.

While the data obtained through victim surveys provide interesting comparisons with other estimates of true crime occurrence, there are known and important constraints upon their interpretation. Most significant among these is the conscious attempt made by respondents to minimize their complicity

[5] Alfred R. Lindesmith, *Opiate Addiction* (Bloomington, Ind.: Principia Press, 1947).
[6] Donald R. Cressey, *Other People's Money* (New York: Free Press, Macmillan, 1953).

in "sensitive" crimes: rape, gambling, narcotics, and liquor law violations. Less seriously, victims may tend to exaggerate the extent of harm perpetrated against them (particularly in insured matters), or understand the law so poorly that what they perceive to be an illegal act is not so defined by statute. It is to be expected that these limitations will be overcome as research methodology in this area becomes increasingly sophisticated.

Sociologists, since the first observations of social systems, have disagreed about ethical considerations in the role of scientific observer. There have always been differing emphases placed upon the use of methodologies that are susceptible to "reactive" bias, i.e., the distortion resulting from a respondent's knowing he is under study. So compelling is the evidence that respondents may adjust their answers to questionnaire or interview items, or modify their behavior in observational settings, that two compensatory techniques have been suggested. On the one hand, it may be possible to restructure or modify the observer's true identity so that it becomes congruent with the setting he expects to study. This tack is apparent from numerous studies in which researchers covertly participated in a role, gathering observations without the knowledge of their associates. Many of the most perceptive and revealing studies, ranging across the taxi-cab driver, professional boxer, psychiatric patient, marine radioman, Air Force enlisted man, turberculosis patient, and Alcoholics Anonymous recruit, have been products of this method. On the other hand, one can search for "nonreactive" data, i.e., those that are unresponsive to the intrusion of an observer. Among the most promising sources are archives (official and unofficial records), because they tell us not only about the substance and distribution of observations, but about the record-keeping activities of archivists themselves. We can learn a great deal from inert data sources about the processes of record-keeping as an attribute of social organization.

Disagreement about concealing one's role as observer originates in the ethical responsibilities research personnel have to their colleagues, the citizenry at large, and their study population. To be weighed against these is the probability of contaminating the research scene and its yield by revealing one's presence and intent as observer.

One of the most promising of new research methods, finally, is the application of mathematical techniques to criminological problems. Although these may take many forms, it appears that advances in operations research, such as simulation and decision theory, are most suggestive. For example, routine police activities could be subjected to a cost v. effectiveness analysis, by simulating increased manpower and redeployment of personnel in relation to changes in crimes cleared by arrest. Further, decisions about parole in correctional settings could be made by calculating probabilities for parole success associated with type of crime, institutional adjustment, strength of community ties, and extent of previous criminality, or any combination of these.

The selection by Marvin E. Wolfgang and Harvey A. Smith, "Mathematical Methods in Criminology," is part of their more extensive appeal that mathematical methods be used to improve the efficiency of crime control and treatment.

Phillip H. Ennis' "Estimates of Crime from Victim Survey Research" is a report of the criminal victimization study that he directed under sponsorship of the President's Commission on Law Enforcement and Administration of Justice. He reports the discrepancy between victim-survey crime rates and those figures obtained from official compilations, some reasons why citizens all too infrequently mobilize the police when they have been victimized, and public attitudes toward police effectiveness and honesty.

Aside from the practical issues raised by victim surveys, a number of theoretical benefits are discussed in the selection by Daniel Glaser. He argues that victim research can promote greater clarity in the concept of crime, provide a basis for measuring police effectiveness, test theory of correlates of crime such as geographical region, and offer an explanation of some police and judicial activities.

The selection by Kai T. Erikson, "Social Settings and Covert Social Participation," takes the position that misrepresenting oneself to gain access to settings otherwise unavailable incurs the risk of being unethical and unscientific. Norman K. Denzin's response debates several points related to the charges made by Erikson and proposes that many of the most significant findings of sociological research required covert observation. Finally, a rebuttal by Erikson reveals the polarized nature of this issue.

Selected references associated with methodological approaches to crime research appear below:

1. *Ecological Theory and Metropolitan Problems: Some Early Studies and Their Evaluation*

Anderson, Nels. *The Hobo* (Chicago: University of Chicago Press, 1923).

Cavan, Ruth Shonle. *Suicide* (Chicago: University of Chicago Press, 1928).

Cressey, Paul G. *The Taxi-Dance Hall* (Chicago: University of Chicago Press, 1932).

Faris, Robert E. L. *Chicago Sociology, 1920–1932* (San Francisco: Chandler, 1967), chap. 5, "Urban Behavior Research."

Madge, John. *The Origins of Scientific Sociology* (New York: Free Press, Macmillan, 1962), chap. 4, "The Chicago School Around 1930."

Reckless, Walter C. *Vice in Chicago* (Chicago: University of Chicago Press, 1933).

Schmid, Calvin F. "Urban Crime Areas: Part I," *American Sociological Review* 25 (August 1960): 527–42.

_____. "Urban Crime Areas: Part II," *American Sociological Review* 25 (October 1960): 655–78.

2. *Analytic Induction: Theory, Research, and Criticism*

Cressey, Donald R. "The Criminal Violation of Financial Trust," *American Sociological Review* 15 (December 1950): 738–43 [reproduced in Part 5 of this volume].

_____. *Other People's Money* (Glencoe, Ill.: Free Press, 1953).

Lindesmith, Alfred R. *Addiction and Opiates* (Chicago: Aldine, 1968).

Robinson, W. S. "The Logical Structure of Analytic Induction," *American Sociological Review* 16 (December 1951): 812–18.

Turner, Ralph H. "The Quest for Universals in Sociological Research," *American Sociological Review* 18 (December 1953): 604–11.

Znaniecki, Florian. *The Method of Sociology* (New York: Farrar & Rinehart, 1934).

3. *Prospects and Limitations of Victim Survey Research*

Biderman, Albert D. "Surveys of Population Samples for Estimating Crime Incidence," *Annals of the American Academy of Political and Social Science* 374 (November 1967): 16–33.

_____ and Reiss, Albert J., Jr. "On Exploring the 'Dark Figure' of Crime," *Annals of the American Academy of Political and Social Science* 374 (November 1967): 1–15.

Ennis, Phillip H. *Criminal Victimization in the U.S.: A Report on a National Survey*, Field Surveys 2, President's Commission on Law Enforcement and Administration of Justice (Washington, D.C.: U.S. Government Printing Office, 1967).

Hentig, Hans von. *The Criminal and His Victim* (New Haven: Yale University Press, 1948).

Mendelsohn, B. "The Origin of the Doctrine of Victimology," *Excerpta Criminologica* 3 (May–June 1963).

Schafer, Stephen. *The Victim and His Criminal* (New York: Random House, 1968), chap. 2, "Criminal-Victim Relationship as a Crime Factor."

4. *Debate Centering upon Concealed Observation and Its Alternative*

Mills, Theodore M. "The Observer, the Experimenter, and the Group," *Social Problems* 14 (Spring 1967): 373–81.

Polsky, Ned. "Research Method, Morality, and Criminology," *Hustlers, Beats and Others* (Chicago: Aldine, 1967), pp. 117–49.

Rainwater, Lee, and Pittman, David J. "Ethical Problems in Studying a Politically Sensitive and Deviant Community," *Social Problems* 14 (Spring 1967): 357–66.

Seeley, John R. "The Making and Taking of Problems: Toward an Ethical Stance," *Social Problems* 14 (Spring 1967): 382–89.

Webb, Eugene J.; Campbell, Donald T.; Schwartz, Richard D.; and Sechrest, Lee. *Unobtrusive Measures: Nonreactive Research in the Social Sciences* (Chicago: Rand McNally, 1966).

Yablonsky, Lewis. "Experiences with the Criminal Community," in *Applied Sociology*, ed. Alvin W. Gouldner and S. M. Miller (New York: Free Press, Macmillan, 1965), pp. 55–73.

_____ . "On Crime, Violence, LSD, and Legal Immunity for Social Scientists" (letters), *American Sociologist* 3 (May 1968): 148.

5. *Mathematical Methods in Criminological Research*

Martindale, Don. "Limits to the Uses of Mathematics in the Study of Sociology," in *Mathematics and the Social Sciences*, ed. James C. Charlesworth (Philadelphia: American Academy of Political and Social Science, June 1963), pp. 95–121. [This entire issue of the *Annals* examines the role of mathematics in the study of economics, political science, and sociology.]

Roy, Robert H. "An Outline for Research in Penology," *Operations Research* 12 (January–February 1964): 1–15.

Wolfgang, Marvin E., and Ferracuti, Franco. *The Subculture of Violence: Towards an Integrated Theory in Criminology* (London: Tavistock, 1967), pp. 292–94.

10. MATHEMATICAL METHODS IN CRIMINOLOGY

Marvin E. Wolfgang and Harvey A. Smith

INTRODUCTION

In this paper we do not attempt to survey current work in the mathematical approach to social problems or to examine the results of new criminological research. Our purpose is to suggest new directions for research and to indicate the possible utility of moving in these directions. We shall also try to point out some unresolved questions in criminology which impede the solution of certain practical problems.

We consider problems arising in the choice between alternatives and in the allocation of limited resources in the most efficient and effective manner. The types of such problems for which solutions may be found are governed by the state of knowledge and by the techniques available for utilizing this knowledge. During the past quarter century there has been a rapid development of mathematical and quasi-mathematical techniques for attacking such problems arising in business and military organizations. These techniques have become known collectively as operations research

Reprinted by permission of the authors and the United Nations Educational, Scientific, and Cultural Organization from *International Social Science Journal*, 18, no. 2 (1966): 200–202, 211–23. Footnotes have been consecutively numbered.

or operations analysis. They have been applied successfully to a wide variety of problems, including the choice between available weapons[1] for armies, the scheduling of production in factories,[2] the utilization of advertising by department stores,[3] the allocation of effort by small loan companies to collect overdue accounts,[4] and the handling of traffic in underwater tunnels.[5] We believe that the methods of operations research can be applied to the activities of the various organizations which deal with crime. Although we address our concern to methods of improving the efficiency of crime control activity, it should not be overlooked that a study of optimizing the activities of a criminal organization or of an individual criminal might also prove profitable from a scientific standpoint.

When the methods of operations research are applied to an activity, the mathematical techniques intrinsic to such research point to the need for specific quantitative information about that activity.[6] Optimizing an activity in some respect requires having a clear quantitative description of the relative desirability of various results of the activity. Once such a criterion of success has been chosen, one must determine quantitative measures of the effectiveness of various alternatives that influence the desirability of the result.

Recently the authors have been associated with an attempt to construct a quantitative measure of the relative undesirability of criminal activity. This measure seems suitable as a criterion for many purposes, but for some it would need to be supplemented. The problem of measuring the effectiveness of various alternatives necessarily cannot precede that of choosing a criterion of desirability. However, in some instances previous investigations provide data from which measures of effectiveness can be determined once the criterion is chosen. We are concerned here with the instances where existing knowledge is inadequate or is inappropriately formulated. We hope to interest criminologists in investigating further some of the mathematical techniques discussed below. We advance the point of view that the attempt to analyze practical problems mathematically provides a rich source of appropriately posed questions and that it can

---

[1] Martin L. Leibowitz and Gerald J. Lieberman, "Optimal Composition and Deployment of a Heterogeneous Local Air-Defense System," *Operations Research*, 8, no. 3: 324–37.

[2] George T. Bishop, "On a Problem of Production Scheduling," *Operations Research*, 5, no. 1: 97–103.

[3] Lawrence Friedman, "Game-Theory Models in the Allocation of Advertising Expenditures," *Operations Research*, 6, no. 5: 699–709.

[4] Morton Mitchener and Raymond P. Peterson, "An Operations Research Study of the Collection of Defaulted Loans," *Operations Research*, 5, no. 4: 522–45.

[5] Harold Greenberg and Arthur Daou, "The Control of Traffic Flow to Increase the Flow," *Operations Research*, 8, no. 4: 524–32.

[6] For discussion of broader problems of applying mathematics to social science problems, see James C. Charlesworth, ed., *Mathematics and the Social Sciences* (Philadelphia: American Academy of Political and Social Science, June 1963). Also, Fred Massarik and Philburn Ratoosh, eds., *Mathematical Explorations in Behavioral Science* (Homewood, Ill.: Richard D. Irwin, 1965); Hayward R. Alker, Jr., *Mathematics and Politics* (New York: Macmillan, 1965).

frequently provide a critique by means of which inappropriate questions can be detected.

Obviously we cannot here deal comprehensively with the applications of operations research to all problems of crime control. We shall try to give the basic ideas of some important techniques of operations research, mention some possible applications, and point out some new knowledge needed to make these applications.

Because operations research is usually practiced by interdisciplinary teams applying their knowledge and ability to the solution of special problems, the techniques applied cannot be easily delimited. Certain mathematical tools, however, have repeatedly proved useful and are widely associated with operations research. These techniques include mathematical modeling, mathematical programming, the theory of games and decisions, Markov process theory, queueing theory, combinatorics, simulation, and gaming.

* * *

THE FUNCTION AND SETTING FOR
DESIGNING MODELS IN CRIMINOLOGY

For purposes of discussion, we divide the aspects of criminal activity "chronologically" into causality, detection and apprehension, sentencing, treatment, release, and recidivism. We intend, in this section, to discuss briefly some problems in each category that seem to offer hope of substantial practical or theoretical results from the application of operations research techniques. The few mathematical models included in this section are presented not only as illustrations, but as serious efforts to operationalize specific problem areas.

The first question which must be faced in any optimization study is that of ends. What is to be optimized? What values are to prevail? What constitutes improvement? The second question is that of means. What are the operating constraints? What aspects of the situation can be changed to accomplish improvements? What are the limitations on the changes which can be introduced?

In order to study the question of ends it is necessary to find some quantitative measure of the undesirability of various criminal activities. R. H. Roy[7] has proposed an "expected total cost" model for crime, including the costs to the victim (material loss, physical and psychological trauma, etc.), the costs to the state (police efforts, court procedure, incarceration, and rehabilitation), and the costs to the criminal and his family. The objective,

---

[7] Robert H. Roy, "An Outline for Research in Penology," *Operations Research*, 12 (January–February 1964): 1–15.

in his view, is to minimize this "expected total cost." Roy's model has many advantageous features, the greatest of which seems to be the fact that the proposed measure of undesirability is expressed in monetary units. This feature facilitates evaluation of the part of the cost of different policies borne by public agencies, for frequently these costs either are available or can be readily estimated. As Roy points out, however, there are serious difficulties in attempting to assess the costs borne by the victim, the criminal, and their respective families in monetary units. Here value judgments predominate, and in using this model the principle of equal application of justice (which one might expect to be an operating constraint) might be sacrificed.

An approach to the problem of quantifying subjective response of the general populace to aggregated criminal activities has been made recently by Sellin and Wolfgang.[8] That study does not attempt to translate the resulting quantities into monetary units, however, so it cannot be integrated directly into Roy's formulation to provide a single monetary measure of expected total cost. Aside from convenience and utility, no justification or rationale for making a conversion to monetary units has been advanced by Roy.[9]

Despite the lack of a practical unified monetary formula of the type suggested by Roy, his suggestions and the results of Sellin and Wolfgang can be effective tools for optimization using a cost-effectiveness technique. The effectiveness of crime-control activities can be measured in terms of the subjective public reaction to the resulting crime situation on the Sellin-Wolfgang scale. The cost associated with these activities could be the readily available publicly borne portion of Roy's total cost, including any public payments to the victims and in the form of victim compensation—to the families of victims and offenders, in the form of relief funds, or to the offenders in the form of institutional costs.

The procedure used in making a cost-effectiveness analysis would be to fix a level of effectiveness (e.g., a crime rate as measured on the Sellin-Wolfgang scale) and then to find policies which minimize the cost. As the level of effectiveness is varied, the policies which give minimum cost will vary. This procedure allows the researcher to avoid the extremely difficult problem of balancing monetary costs against subjective values. The responsible decision-maker who will eventually allocate the funds is presented with the costs associated with attaining various levels of effectiveness and

---

[8] Thorsten Sellin and Marvin E. Wolfgang, *Measurement of Delinquency* (New York: Wiley, 1964).

[9] However, there can be good reasons for converting to monetary units. For another reference to this notion, see Leslie Wilkins, "New Thinking in Criminal Statistics," *Journal of Criminal Law, Criminology, and Police Science*, no. 56 (September 1965): 277–84.

For an emphasis on victim statistics or "consumer" data instead of on offenders, see Stanton Wheeler, "Criminal Statistics: A Reformulation of the Problem," paper presented at the Social Statistics Section, American Statistical Association, September 8, 1965, Philadelphia, Pa.

uses his own subjective judgment to balance cost against effectiveness and determine the amount to be spent.

It is of scientific interest, of course, to collect statistics on the decisions which are actually made and to consider their implications in terms of co-efficients relating subjective and monetary values, but this does not *a priori* become a vital part of the researcher's job without which progress is impossible. The objective of operations research studies of crime-control activities, therefore, can be taken as realizing the greatest effectiveness in reducing crime as measured on some appropriate scale for various fixed levels of monetary costs to the state. Equivalently, the objective could be formulated as minimizing the cost of attaining various fixed levels of crime.

The operating constraints on acceptable procedures in crime-control activity are clearly established in some cases by legal norms and constitutional guarantees. In other cases, the constraints are flexible. It may be appropriate for researchers to formulate the optimization problem with and without a particular operating constraint and submit both alternatives to the decision-maker, who must balance the subjective cost of loosening a constraint against the advantage of greater effectiveness or lower cost. For example, the use of state-operated lotteries to provide competition for the gambling activities of organized crime syndicates might be an acceptable policy even in some parts of the United States. Covert operations in which the resources of the state were used to place bets designed eventually to ruin the criminal syndicate gamblers might be an acceptable alternative or supplement to legalized gambling as a means of driving organized gambling from a community. Operation of state-supported prostitution, covert asssassination, and similar techniques which might prove quite effective would be unacceptable to decision-makers in most countries, except under most unusual circumstances. It is essential that the researcher be prepared to test the boundaries and the rigidity of the operating constraints in an imaginative manner, but it is even more imperative that he develop a realistic sense of the constraints and their elastic limits. Traditionally, overt police operations must be legal or only violate laws in minimal ways. Covert operations are allowed somewhat greater latitude; a covert agent may generally engage in minor technical offenses consistent with his assumed character while engaged in investigation of major crimes. For instance, an agent buying narcotics to obtain evidence is technically engaged in trafficking and possession. This wider latitude of covert operation should be recognized, explored, and utilized in operations research models. Whatever the permissible parameters may be, some of the secrecy problems which attach to military and commercial operations research would also be encountered in various aspects of operations research for police forces.

Operations research is traditionally carried on by small project-oriented interdisciplinary teams. They generally include both physical and social scientists in order to provide a wide range of viewpoints and techniques.

When possible, it is advantageous to include in the team high-ranking and flexible-minded members of the organization being researched. These will supply an intimate knowledge of the organization and ready access to essential contacts and information within the organization. The interdisciplinary nature of the team is of utmost importance. A team completely composed of novices in a field, while not desirable, would be preferable to a team composed of experts in the field and members of the researched organization. The latter are overwhelmingly inclined to think in traditional terms about the nature of the problem and its possible solutions. A team of novices takes longer to acquire an adequate level of knowledge about the organization, but would be more likely to see the problems in fresh terms and to propose new solutions. A judicious mixture of outside methodological and inside organizational experts will generally achieve efficient and appropriately related results more quickly while retaining the advantages of a fresh outlook.

AREAS FOR APPLICATION IN CRIMINOLOGY

Causality

When criminologists refer to causality in crime, they generally invoke the notion of remote rather than immediate causality. Although there is a cutoff point in an otherwise infinite regression causality model, most studies in causation or etiology go beyond the proximate level of police operations. For instance, the effect of poverty, the social milieu, or parental discipline rather than the absence of a policeman or the availability of a weapon is included in most criminological studies. Immediate or proximate causality will be discussed later as an aspect of police work.

From the viewpoint of social psychology, criminal acts may be divided into normal and abnormal behavior. The extreme position that all crime is normal or that all crime is abnormal could perhaps be defended, but our approach defines a dichotomy requiring research. By normal we do not mean rational or free of neurotic aggression. A criminal act involves some risk of detection and punishment; it may also involve some reward. It may well be that the expected risk involved in any criminal behavior exceeds the expected reward, so that any criminal behavior is irrational. It is also possible that because of their contracultural character, criminal acts are intrinsically manifestations of neurotic hostilities and aggressions. It must, however, be acknowledged that people are generally not rational in their decisions involving objective risk and reward. A person may willingly trade certainty of gaining or retaining a small amount for a small probability of gaining a large amount, even when the expectation (the product of the probability and the amount) is smaller. The success of gambling enterprises and lotteries is dependent precisely on this "irrational behavior." There is considerable evidence that such irrationality is also characteristic of ordinary legitimate business decisions. It can scarcely be characterized as abnormal. Moreover, some legitimate businesses are at best of questionable social utility and are such that success in them is heavily dependent on antisocial hostilities and aggressions. We shall not therefore categorize hostile and aggressive criminal behavior as abnormal when it is connected with the attainment of a goal.

It seems that a reasonable criterion of normality might be to consider the expected risks involved in an activity and the expected benefits to be derived and to ask whether the trade would normally be an appealing one, apart from questions of legitimacy, to the persons involved. Thus, shoplifting might prove to be a normal crime among the very poor, in the sense that it presents a subjectively perceived risk-reward structure normally acceptable in legitimate enterprises for these people, but might prove to be abnormal for the relatively wealthy, in the sense that a comparable risk in legitimate enterprise would be rejected.[10] It may be that the relative appeal of a high-risk–high-reward venture is a function of socioeconomic class. Also, the subjective magnitude of a reward may be strongly dependent on this factor. It is widely believed, for instance, that gambling for relatively small sums at unfavorable odds is more common among the poor. Let us suppose that the risk-reward structure of some criminal activities is such as to make them normally attractive to individuals from some segments of society, in the sense that a legitimate activity presenting an equivalent risk-reward structure would be attractive. For such crimes, increasing the probability or the severity of punishment should act as a deterrent. For crimes which have a risk-reward structure which would normally make them unattractive to all segments of society, such an approach would probably have little effect. Criminal homicide, for instance, usually has high risk and small reward, so its risk-reward structure is normally not attractive. Moreover, the volatile, visceral character of this offense is such that there are fewer cognitive variables operating than in most, and certainly in acquisitive, crimes. It might therefore be expected that increasing the risk by an increase in severity or probability of punishment would have little effect as a deterrent to homicide. Let us refer to crimes with risk-reward structures ordinarily unattractive to an individual as abnormal crimes.

Because a given crime may be classified normal or abnormal depending on the particular criminal, the model suggests that a change in the rate of normal crimes can be induced either (a) by changing the risk-reward structure or (b) by manipulating the social structure in order to change the number of people to whom the risk-reward structure will normally be

---

[10] The reader may note certain similarities to the legitimate and illegitimate opportunity structures, and the means-end schema, presented by Richard Cloward and Lloyd Ohlin in *Delinquency and Opportunity* (Glencoe, Ill.: Free Press, 1960).

appealing. The model suggests no *a priori* method for changing the rate of abnormal crimes. But in addition to being useful in examining and affecting change in rates of normal crime, the classification of crimes as normal and abnormal might be helpful in choosing methods for treatment of apprehended criminals.

Although a presumption of the model is that the rate of commission of abnormal crimes will not be affected by further increasing the probability or severity of punishment, this rate may be affected by changes in other sociological variables. A difference in economic class or education of parents, for instance, may change the statistical rate of occurrence of home environment conditions correlated with delinquent behavior of the children. Social welfare policies, therefore, could eventually have an effect on both normal and abnormal crime rates.

Of all questions raised by the model, the most fundamental is, of course, that of its validity. Does it furnish a sufficiently useful way of classifying crimes? Are perhaps all crimes abnormal from our viewpoint? Or is the actual behavior so complicated as to defy statistical classification in such a relatively simplistic manner?

The model also suggests the following questions, some of which are of interest independent of the model's validity: What are the subjective risks and rewards of various criminal activities? Can they be measured in a meaningful way? How do they vary with other sociological observables? How are subjective risks and rewards related to objective ones? What is an attractive risk-reward structure? On what sociological variables does the attractiveness or unattractiveness of a given structure depend? What portions of a given crime are normal or abnormal? What is the actual effect of varying severity and probability of punishment on the rate of commission of various crimes and on the statistical parameters of the population of criminals committing them? Finally, are social welfare programs a cost-effective means of reducing crime rates as compared with other alternatives?

Police Operations

Because a police force is a paramilitary organization, some of the same techniques employed in military operations research may be applicable to police operations. Police and military forces differ in two important respects, however. The equipment used by the police has not undergone the intensive and rapid development which has characterized military equipment in the recent past, and most police work is a continuing rather than an occasional and sporadic process. Those differences mean that the analyst will not so frequently encounter the difficulties of analyzing the use of new or relatively untried equipment and the lack of adequate information which present major difficulties in the study of military operations.

In the absence of war, it is extremely difficult to obtain adequate information on the effectiveness of alterations in military operations. Because of its continuing character, police work has the advantage of having various strategies that are subject to evaluation. Statistical information is theoretically available, albeit not systematically collected for evaluative purposes. Police operations are also more subject to experimentation without catastrophic consequences than are military operations. For these reasons, analysis of police operations should be relatively easier than that of military operations. Police work frequently includes the performance of routine services not connected with crime control, such as traffic control. While the performance of these services and the suitability of having them and crime-control operations performed by the same organization are topics for investigation, we limit ourselves to the crime-control aspects of police work.

A major question in considering crime-control operations is that of allocating resources. How much investigative effort should be allotted to which crimes? The professed ideal seems to be to work until every crime is solved. In practice, the effort allocated is a function of administrative decisions. It is quite possible that an analysis would yield a rule for assigning investigative effort to particular crimes. A similar situation has been studied successfully in small loan companies.[11] In that case, the problem was one of allocating effort to the collection of overdue accounts. By analysis of the expected results of various allocations it was possible to devise an optimal policy. Adherence to this policy was shown to be capable of producing results superior to those normally arrived at by leaving the matter to the judgment of office administrators.

While formulation of a model can best be made after thorough study of the operation, we shall sketch here a possible model for the assignment of investigative effort. We assume some measure of the relative desirability of solving each type of crime to be given, and statistics on the success in solving crimes by the application of investigative effort to be known.

To avoid analytic complications we assume that the assignment of effort is reviewed periodically rather than continuously. Presumably, the probability of success in solving a particular crime in the next time interval will depend on the effort applied to it during that interval and on the history of efforts made in previous intervals. Denote by E_0^k the current effort and by E_i^k the effort applied to crime k during the ith previous interval. The probability of obtaining a solution during the current interval will be

$$P_{j(k)}\,(E_0^k, E_i^k, \ldots, E_N^k),$$

where j denotes the type of crime and $N + 1$ is the maximum number of

[11] Mitchener and Peterson, *op. cit.*

intervals for which crimes are investigated. If we are interested only in the current interval we must maximize

$$\Sigma_k W_{j(k)} \, P_{j(k)} \, (E_0^k, E_i^k, \ldots, E_n^k)$$

by varying E_0^k subject to

$$0 < \mathrm{E}_0^k$$

and

$$\Sigma_{k=1}^K E_0^k < F$$

where K is the number of currently unsolved crimes, F is the total effort available for assignment, and W_j is the relative desirability of solving a crime of type j. While this programming problem is not linear, the behavior of the probability P can be expected to be such that the maximum can readily be computed. Such an assignment may fail to be optimum for two reasons. First, we are interested in eventual solution of the crime rather than in its immediate solution, and second, new crimes may arise during the intervals between reassignments. Theoretically, the second objection could be dealt with in the model by making the time interval being considered extremely short, but this might not be a practical solution. To deal with the first matter, let us assume that we wish to solve any crime before $N + 1$ intervals have elapsed. If N intervals have already elapsed since the initiation of the investigation, then the contribution to the sum to be maximized is, as before,

$$W_{j(k)} \, P_{j(k)} \, (E_0^k, E_i^k, \ldots, E_N^k).$$

If only $N - 1$ intervals have elapsed, however, we must take into account not only the current assigned effort but also the assigned effort during the next interval. This cannot be computed precisely because of the possible entry of new crimes into the system and the solution of old crimes during the current interval. We do, presumably, know the rate of occurrence of crimes of each type and hence the probabilities of various numbers of these crimes occurring in the current interval. Further, the probabilities of solutions of crimes during the current interval are determined by the application of effort and can thus be computed. Setting up these conditions formally, step by step working backwards, leads to complicated recursion formulas much like those discussed previously in connection with dynamic programming. Basically, the technique for developing the theory is to work backward from interval to interval and then to let the size of the interval become small. The ultimate objective of analysis would be to develop a simple algorithm for computing an optimal assignment in terms of the current inventory of unsolved crimes and their investigative histories. Hopefully, quite crude and simple rules could be devised which would give near optimum performance and be easy to implement, but this cannot be guaranteed until the analysis is made and the nature of the solution probability function P is explored. A simple rule might, for instance, take the form: A crime of j should be investigated for at most a length of time T_j, with an investigatory force $E_j(F,K)$. Analysis of the effect of applying various simple types of rules for assignment of effort is, of course, much easier than attempting to find the general optimum assignment. It is quite possible that the best approach to the practical problem would be to devise simple rules based on knowledge of the nature of the functions P and to analyze the effects of varying the parameters involved, such as T_j (the time of pursuit) in the previous example.

A problem in which an operations research approach could very likely be useful is that of patrolling. A basic question which must be asked is to what extent the functions of the patrol is inhibitive and to what extent it is detective. A patrol which never encounters a crime may simply be acting as a very effective inhibiting agent. Questions of assignment of patrol force to various areas would need study, as would questions of strategy. It seems likely that regular, and hence easily predictable, patrols would be inferior to randomized patrols in inhibiting or detecting premeditated crimes. The actual mechanics of patrol operations in terms of the modes of transportation, communication, facilities, and armament of patrollers should prove to be fruitful areas for analysis. The entire problem is analogous to the problem of anti-submarine patrol which has been studied extensively.[12] The slow-moving foot patrolman covers a region more thoroughly and is more likely to discover a crime in progress when he is nearby. Because of his slow speed, however, he is far from most of the area patrolled most of the time. Moreover, foot patrolmen are inefficient for pursuit, and their forces cannot readily be combined to deal with an emergency. Judging by similar military situations, the optimal patrol system might consist of small groups of lightly armed foot patrolmen. The function of the foot patrolman would be to act as a highly sensitive detector. Each group of foot patrolmen would be attached to a patrol car, which would serve as a pursuit vehicle, communications center and means of transportation. The foot patrolmen would be in immediate contact with their car by means of very low-powered radio transceivers. The car would rendezvous with the patrolmen and transport them to new locations according to a randomized schedule. The particular paths to be followed by the foot patrolmen and the cars between rendezvous would also be randomized. The schedule, of course, would need to be loose enough so that the patrolman is still able to serve as a good detector. A too stringent schedule might force the patrolmen to concentrate completely on being at the right place at the right time for the next rendezvous and so lower their efficiency. Even this effect is analogous to what happens to a submarine patrolling to de-

---

[12] B. O. Koopman, "Target Detection, Part II," *Operations Research*, 4, no. 5: 503–31, and "Target Detection, Part III," *Operations Research*, 5, no. 5: 613–26. Also, P. M. Morse and G. E. Kimball, *Methods of Operations Research* (Cambridge: MIT Press, 1951).

tect enemy submarines. As the patrolling submarine moves more quickly, trying to cover more territory in a fixed time, it generates more noise, masking the sounds of the enemy submarine it is trying to detect. The theory of patrol operations, most frequently with special applications to search for submarines, was one of the original topics studied by analysts during the Second World War, and a very extensive literature and body of special techniques exist on this topic. A very general exposition of the general theory of search, applicable to a wide variety of search problems, has been given by Koopman.[13]

In detective, or investigative, work the subject of correlations between events in a criminal's career might well benefit from more sophisticated analysis and interpretation than are currently used. One question which can be raised is that of the desirability of collecting and utilizing police information about the community at large and not merely about those who have previously been arrested. What factors ought to be included? Should information about the entire populace be collected, or only those satisfying certain statistical criteria? What criteria? Would collection and utilization of such data be effective in relation to their cost? Could data collection be done on an acceptable basis with respect to privacy rights? Information developed by studying correlations in criminal careers should be useful in allocating effort to the solution of crimes as well as aiding in the apprehension of particular criminals. Such information might also provide means for applying preventive measures to specific individuals rather than to whole classes.

Particular investigative activities, such as the use of informers, might be aided by analysis, and the whole topic of countering organized crime offers a challenge to the ingenuity of the research investigator. For the most part, however, as one gets more involved with the details of particular operations, the questions which arise become less sociological and tend to become questions of psychiatry, of experimental psychology, or of human engineering. An aspect of attempting to introduce new modes of organization and operation in a police department which raises questions of primarily sociological interest is the problem of command and control, i.e., the problem of organizing the command hierarchy and motivating the members so as to further the ends of the department as a whole. Like so many operations research problems, this is not capable of a direct mathematical attack, but mathematical techniques can be useful in an auxiliary manner. For instance, objective indices of performance can be created for departments or for individuals and thereby measure the degree of conformation of their performance with the overall purposes of the system. The errors which must be avoided in creating and using such indices are naïveté and credulity. A naïve index, for instance, might be the number of arrests made by

---

[13] B. O. Koopman, "The Theory of Search, Part I, Kinematic Bases," *Operations Research*, 4, no. 3: 324–46.

an individual. Application of a system of punishments or rewards based on this naïve index would probably merely result in a large volume of low-quality arrests, with each individual trying to "make his quota." Credulous use of indices, with rewards and punishments based on the use of small samples of little or no statistical significance, can lead to demoralization (because rewards and punishments may be awarded on the basis of capricious statistical fluctuations) and to ineffectiveness. To guard against such perils both sociological insight and mathematical technique are necessary.

The problem of aligning the police-force motivation with the overall crime-control system is a command and control problem on a broader scale. Solving such problems frequently involves devising means for shifting the balance of power between interest blocks and transferring control of an organization from one group to another. The use of mathematical models for such purposes is at least a possibility, and mathematical techniques may help discriminate the true state of affairs from that which may be preconceived or theoretically conjectured.

The Courts

We shall not attempt to deal with legal questions or with the alternatives of courtroom strategy which prosecutor or defense counsel could employ, although analysis would be useful. One matter which seems accessible to straightforward analysis is the effectiveness of the district attorney's office in deciding whether to pursue a case or to drop it. The questions involved here would be quite similar to those involved in the allocation of investigative efforts, and it should be possible to devise a mode providing a rule for deciding when the cost of pursuing a case is justified.

A second matter which seems clearly to be a suitable subject for analysis is that of bail policy. The decision to hold a prisoner or to grant him bail or release on recognizance should be analyzed in terms of cost to the taxpayers, the risk of imprisonment of the innocent, and the legal requirements for "reasonable" bail.

Consideration of these examples reveals that there are questions of sociological, in contrast to purely technical, interest to be investigated in connection with the operation of the legal system during the period between arrest and conviction. Again, extremely complex command and control problems are involved in dealing with political institutions such as magistrates' courts and district attorneys' offices. The present devices for aligning the interest of officeholders with the overall system objectives seem inadequate in some respects, and a study of means for their enforcement or improvement should be undertaken.[14]

---

[14] Attention should be drawn here to the commendable efforts to provide a measurement of the severity of sentencing in the administrative office of the United States courts. See James A. McCafferty, "Statistical Measurements Used by the Administrative Office of the United States Courts," paper presented at the Social Statistics Section, American Statistical Association, September 8, 1965, Philadelphia, Pa.

Treatment and Recidivism

The major problems to be dealt with in the areas of treatment and recidivism are in many ways less clear-cut than those involved in police operations. In police operations we confront a functioning organization and ask how to make its operation more efficient. The goals of police organizations are at least roughly defined and we only encounter the task of improving the definition. It seems evident that this is not the case for treatment. The first need would seem to be a definition of the aims of treatment and an evaluation of the means currently proposed for achieving them. Let us proceed by examining a possible model.

We suppose that the purpose of the crime-control system is to delay crimes (prevention being regarded as an infinite delay). To evaluate the system, therefore, it is necessary to know not only the relative weight to attribute to various crimes, but also the worth of delaying a particular crime by a given amount of time. One might hypothesize a discount rate, p, and take the current weight of a crime occurring T years in the future as p^T times the weight for an equivalent current crime. We presume that the effect of treatment is twofold. It can act on the person being treated and, by example, on the general community. We shall call the effect on the community the deterrent effect and that on the criminal the rehabilitative effect.

Omitting other relevant factors, the most effective treatment could be immediate and indiscriminate execution of all convicted criminals, for this presumably would present the strongest deterrent effect and simultaneously insure against future crimes by the criminal at relatively small cost to the state. The difficulties with this solution are that it obviously is counter to the dominant social value system, it would subject too large a universe of the population to becoming "victims" of "justice" as well as to crime, and in sum would be as socially dysfunctional as crime itself. An attempt to optimize treatment of criminals must necessarily take account of the social perception of the upper limits of severity of sanction. It is at the upper, or maximum, limit that the public begins to empathize with the convicted offender and implicitly think of themselves as conceivably subject to the penalties. Operations research need not question the public's concern with lower limits, for the issues of deterrence and of effectiveness of treatment in general are those which require research. It would be possible to devise a method of measuring the adverse impact on the general populace of inflicting various "punishments" (with given probabilities of their being "unjustly" inflicted) in much the same manner as the Sellin-Wolfgang index measures this aspect of crime. Efforts would then be made to optimize treatment with respect to both weighted future crime and weighted punishment.

This process suggests two measurements: (a) the relative weight to be attributed to various punishments; and (b) the relative weight of a punishment and a crime. The desirability of the first of these measurements has in part already been suggested by S. S. Stevens[15] in a review of the work of Sellin and Wolfgang. These questions must eventually be faced even if we accept the legally prescribed penalties as definitive because of the flexibility generally allowed by the system.

In addition to these measurements, it is desirable to know the efficacy of various treatment strategies with respect to both their deterrent effect and their rehabilitative effect. It has often been hypothesized that different treatment strategies would have different effects on different types of offenders.[16] This assumption leads to the question of whether it is possible to make a usable classification of prisoners according to the rehabilitative effects to be expected from using various treatment strategies with them. Answers to these questions would be of use in optimizing sentencing, the choice of institutional and treatment alternatives, and release policy.

The problems of institutional management also merit study, although, as we noted in discussing police operations, the problems likely to arise in such relatively specialized studies are more technical and of less broad societal interest and control. The problems of motivating institutional management might be somewhat less difficult to solve than the "command and control" problems mentioned previously, but it is still necessary to undertake their study in detail. Ex-prisoner welfare and parole activities are essentially merely alternative treatment strategies and should be studied as such.

For the optimization of treatment, it does not seem enough to use crude indicators such as the recidivism rate. We should ask, rather, how long commission of crime was delayed and how much its severity was mitigated by the treatment.[17]

CONCLUSION

We have tried to suggest the possibility of utilizing an interdisciplinary team of operations analysts, frequently working with mathematical techniques, to improve the operations of various crime-control activities. We have outlined some of the mathematical techniques appropriate to such

---

[15] S. S. Stevens, "Psychophysics of Crime and Delinquency," *Contemporary Psychology*, 10, no. 8 (1965): 356–58. This is an essay-review of Sellin and Wolfgang, *The Measurement of Delinquency*.

[16] As one type of recent research on this topic, see Robert F. Beverly, *The BGOS: An Attempt at the Objective Measurement of Levels of Interpersonal Maturity*, Research Report no. 48 (Sacramento: California Department of Youth Authority, Division of Research, October 1965).

[17] See, for example, references to these problems in Daniel Glaser, *The Effectiveness of a Prison and Parole System* (Indianapolis: Bobbs-Merrill, 1964). Current research on a halfway house, the Robert Bruce House in Newark, N.J., is making an effort to include these items in measuring effectiveness.

work and have suggested specific illustrative areas for study. It has been pointed out that frequently the questions which would be raised in the course of such study would be of broad sociological interest. The approach to these problems which is suggested has often been successful in improving military and industrial operations. Such study of crime-control activities would undoubtedly yield improvement in some areas, while it would have the possibility of making extensive advances in all phases of these activities.

11. ESTIMATES OF CRIME FROM VICTIM SURVEY RESEARCH

Phillip H. Ennis

"A skid row drunk lying in a gutter is crime. So is the killing of an unfaith-ful wife. A Cosa Nostra conspiracy to bribe public officials is crime. So is a strong-arm robbery. . . ." So states the report of the President's Commission on Law Enforcement and Administration of Justice, commonly known as the Crime Commission report, in pointing out the diversity of crime. Our recent investigation at Chicago's National Opinion Research Center re-veals that Americans are also frequent prey to incidents which may not fall firmly within the jurisdiction of criminal law, but which still leave the ordinary citizen with a strong sense of victimization—consumer frauds, landlord-tenant violations, and injury or property damage due to some-one else's negligent driving.

With the aid of a new research method for estimating national crime rates (see Appendix) the Crime Commission study has now confirmed what many have claimed all along—that the rates for a wide range of per-sonal crimes and property offenses are considerably higher than previous figures would indicate. Traditional studies have relied on the police blotter

Reprinted by permission of the author and the publisher from *Trans-action*, 4 (June 1967): 36–44. Original title: "Crime, Victims, and the Police." Copyright © 1967 by *Trans-action* magazine, St. Louis, Mo.

for information. The present research, devised and carried out by the National Opinion Research Center (NORC), tried a survey approach instead. Taking a random sample of 10,000 households during the summer of 1965, we asked people what crimes had been committed against them during the preceding year. The results—roughly 2,100 verified incidents— indicated that as many as half of the people interviewed were victims of offenses which they did not report to the police.

This finding raised several questions. How much did this very high incidence of unreported offenses alter the picture presented by the standard measures, notably the FBI's *Uniform Crime Reports (UCR)* index, based only on reported incidents? What was the situation with minor offenses, those not considered in the *UCR* index? What sorts of crimes tended to go unreported? And why did so many victims fail to contact the authorities? These were some of the issues we attempted to probe.

THE UNKNOWN VICTIMS

More than 20 percent of the households surveyed were criminally victimized during the preceding year. This figure includes about *twice as much* major crime as reported by the *UCR* index. The incidence of minor crimes —simple assaults, petty larcenies, malicious mischiefs, frauds, and so on— is even greater. According to our research, these are at least twice as frequent as major crimes. The *UCR* index includes seven major crimes, so the proliferation of petty offenses not taken into account by the index makes the discrepancy between that index and the real crime picture even greater than a consideration of major offenses alone would indicate.

Table 1 compares our figures with the *UCR* rates for the seven major crimes upon which the index is based—homicide, forcible rape, robbery, aggravated assault, burglary, larceny (over $50), and auto theft. The homicide rate projected by the survey is very close to the *UCR* rate—not surprising since murder is the crime most likely to be discovered and reported.

The survey estimate of the car theft rate is puzzlingly low. This could be because people report their cars "stolen" to the police and then find that they themselves have "misplaced" the car or that someone else merely 'borrowed" it. They may either forget the incident when interviewed or be too embarrassed to mention it. The relatively high rate of auto thefts reported to the police confirms other studies which show people are more likely to notify the police in this case than they are if they are victims of most other crimes. It may also indicate that people think the police can or will do more about a car theft than about many other offenses.

The startling frequency of reported forcible rape, four times that of the *UCR* index, underscores the peculiar nature of this crime. It occurs very often among people who know each other—at the extreme, estranged husband and wife—and there appears to be some stigma attached to the victim. Yet among the cases discovered in the survey, too few to be statistically reliable, most were reported to the police. Do the police tend to downgrade the offense into an assault or a minor sex case or put it into some miscellaneous category? This is a well-known practice for certain other kinds of crime.

TABLE 1

ESTIMATED RATES OF MAJOR CRIMES, 1965–1966

Crime	NORC Sample: Estimated Rate per 100,000	Uniform Crime Reports, 1965: Individual or Residential Rates per 100,000
Homicide	3.0	5.1
Forcible rape	42.5	11.6
Robbery	94.0	61.4[a]
Aggravated assault	218.3	106.6
Burglary	949.1	296.6[a]
Larceny ($50+)	606.5	267.4[a]
Car theft	206.2	226.0[b]
TOTAL	2,119.6	974.7

[a] The 1965 Uniform Crime Reports show for burglary and larcenies the number of residential and individual crimes. The overall rate per 100,000 population is therefore reduced by the proportion of these crimes that occurred to individuals. Since all robberies of individuals were included in the NORC sample, regardless of whether the victim was acting as an individual or as part of an organization, the total UCR figure was used for comparison.

[b] The reduction of the UCR auto theft rate by 10 percent is based on the figures of the Automobile Manufacturers Association, showing that 10 percent of all cars are owned by leasing-rental agencies and private and governmental fleets. The Chicago Police Department's auto theft personnel confirmed that about 7–10 percent of stolen cars recovered were from fleet, rental, and other nonindividually owned sources .

To what extent is crime concentrated in the urban environment? To what extent are there regional differences in crime rates? And to what extent are the poor, and especially Negroes, more or less likely to be victims of crime? Behind these questions lie alternative remedial measures, measures which range from city planning and antipoverty programs to the training and organization of police departments and the allocation of their resources throughout the nation.

THE WILD, WILD WEST

The NORC findings presented in the chart above give an overview of the crime rates for central cities in metropolitan areas, for their suburban environs, and for nonmetropolitan areas in the four main regions of the country. Figure 1 shows the crime rate (per 100,000 population) for serious crimes against the person (homicide, rape, robbery, and aggravated assault) and serious crimes against property (burglary, larceny over $50, and vehicle theft).

FIGURE 1

REGIONAL CRIMES BY TYPE OF COMMUNITY

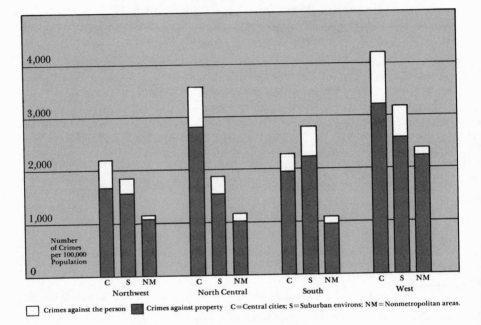

The myth of the wild West is borne out by our figures. Its present crime rate, for both property and personal crimes, is higher than that of any other region of the country. The West has almost twice the rates of the Northeast for all three types of communities. The South, in contrast, does not appear to have the high rate of violent crime that is sometimes alleged.

As one moves from the central city to the suburbs and out into the smaller towns and rural areas, the crime rates decline, but much more drastically for crimes against the person than for property crimes. The metropolitan center has a violent crime rate about *five times* as high as the smaller city and rural areas, but a property crime rate only *twice* as high.

Evidently the city is a more dangerous place than the suburbs or a small town. Yet these figures require some qualification: About 40 percent of the aggravated assaults and rapes (constituting most of the serious crimes against the person) take place *within* the victim's home; and about

ESTIMATES OF CRIME FROM VICTIM SURVEY RESEARCH

45 percent of all the serious crimes against the person are committed by someone familiar to the victim. Random "crime in the streets" by strangers is clearly *not* the main picture that emerges from these figures, even in the urban setting.

Who are the victims? Among lower income groups (under $6,000 per year) Negroes are almost twice as likely as whites to be victims of serious crimes of violence but only very slightly more likely to be victims of property crimes. Our figures show that, per 100,000 population, an estimated 748 low-income Negroes per year will be victims of criminal violence and 1,927 victims of property offenses, whereas the numbers for whites in the same income bracket are 402 and 1,829. The situation is exactly reversed for upper income groups. The wealthier Negro is not much more likely than the white to be a victim of a violent crime, but he is considerably more likely to have property stolen. His chances of losing property are 3,024 in 100,000 whereas the figure is only 1,765 for whites in the same income bracket. Burglary is the most common property crime against more affluent Negroes. The implication is that ghetto neighborhoods in which poor and richer Negroes live side by side make the latter more vulnerable to property losses than are higher income whites, who can live in more economically homogeneous areas.

Despite the fact, then, that per capita offense rates are generally acknowledged to be higher among Negroes than among whites, the incidence of whites being victimized by Negroes—an image frequently conjured up by the specter of "crime in the streets"—is relatively infrequent. Negroes tend instead to commit offenses against members of their own race. The same is true of whites. Further, to the extent that crime is interracial at all, Negroes are more likely to be victims of white offenders than vice versa. Our figures show that only 12 percent of the offenses against whites in our sample were committed by nonwhites, whereas 19 percent of the nonwhite victims reported that the persons who committed offenses against them were white.

WHO CALLS THE POLICE?

What happens when a person is victimized? How often are law-enforcement and judicial authorities involved? What changes occur in the victim's attitude and behavior as a result of the incident?

If the "right thing" to do is to call the police when you have been a victim of a crime, and there is considerable pressure to do just that, why is it that half the victimizations were not reported to the police?

The more serious the crime, the more likely it is to be reported: 65 percent of the aggravated assaults in our sample were reported to the police, but only 46 percent of the simple assaults; 60 percent of the grand larcenies, but only 37 percent of the petty larcenies. Insurance recovery also appears to play a role in the very high rate of reported auto thefts (89 percent) and reported victimizations that are the result of automobile negligence (71 percent). Victims of offenses at the border of the criminal law apparently do not think the police should be involved. Only 10 percent of the consumer fraud victims called the police, whereas 26 percent of the ordinary fraud victims (mainly those of bad checks) did so.

Those victims who said they did not notify the police were asked why. Their reasons fell into four fairly distinct categories. The first was the belief that the incident was not a police matter. These victims (34 percent) did not want the offender to be harmed by the police or thought that the incident was a private, not a criminal, affair. Two percent of the non-reporting victims feared reprisal, either physically from the offender's friends or economically from cancellation of or increases in rates of insurance. Nine percent did not want to take the time or trouble to get involved with the police, did not know whether they should call the police, or were too confused to do so. Finally, a substantial 55 percent of the nonreporting victims failed to notify the authorities because of their attitudes toward police effectiveness. These people believed the police could not do anything about the incident, would not catch the offenders, or would not want to be bothered.

The distribution of these four types of reasons for failure to notify police varies by type of crime and by the social characteristics of the victim, but two points are clear. First, there is strong resistance to invoking the law-enforcement process even in matters that are clearly criminal. Second, there is considerable skepticism as to the effectiveness of police action.

THE ATTRITION OF JUSTICE

A clue to this skepticism lies in the events which follow a call to the police. All the victims who reported an offense were asked how the police reacted and how far the case proceeded up the judicial ladder—arrest, trial, sentencing, and so forth. We have simplified the process into six stages:

1. Given a "real" victimization, the police were or were not notified.

2. Once notified, the police either came to the scene of the victimization (or in some other way acknowledged the event) or failed to do so.

3. Once they arrived, the police did or did not regard the incident as a crime.

4. Regarding the matter as a crime, the police did or did not make an arrest.

5. Once an arrest was made, there was or was not a trial (including plea of guilty).

6. The outcome of the trial was to free the suspect (or punish him "too

leniently") or to find him guilty and give him the "proper" punishment.

Figure 2 shows the tremendous attrition as the cases proceed from the bottom of the "iceberg," the initial victimization, to the top, the trial and sentencing. Failure of the police to heed a call and their rejection of the incident as a crime account for a large proportion of this attrition. Also noteworthy are the low arrest and trial rates. Once the offender is brought to trial, however, the outcome appears more balanced. About half the offenders were treated too leniently in the victim's view, but the other half were convicted and given "proper" punishment.

FIGURE 2

ATTRITION IN THE LEGAL PROCESS

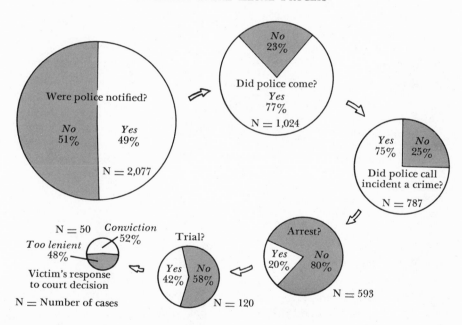

SATISFACTION AND REVENGE

How do the victims feel about this truncated legal process? Do they feel that the situation is their own fault and accept it, or are they dissatisfied with the relatively frequent failure of the police to apprehend the offender? When the victims were asked their feelings about the outcome of the incident, only 18 percent said they were very satisfied; another 19 percent were somewhat satisfied; 24 percent were somewhat dissatisfied; and 35 percent were very dissatisfied (4 percent gave no answer).

The level of satisfaction was closely related to how far the case went judicially. (See Table 2.) People who did not call the police at all were the most dissatisfied. If they called and the police did not come, about the same percentage were very dissatisfied; but peculiarly, there were more who reported that they were satisfied. An arrest lowered the dissatisfaction level, but the dramatic differences appeared when the offender was brought to trial. If he was acquitted or given too lenient a penalty (in the victim's view), dissatisfaction ran high; if he was convicted and given the "proper" penalty, the victim was generally quite pleased. This suggests that the ordinary citizen's sense of justice includes a vengeful element—a desire for punishment over and above monetary compensation for loss. Advocates of rehabilitation rather than retribution for criminals might well take such public sentiments into account.

TABLE 2
DEGREE OF SATISFACTION WITH OUTCOME OF OFFENSE

Disposition of Case	Very Satisfied	Somewhat Satisfied	Somewhat Dissatisfied	Very Dissatisfied
No notification of police	13%	18%	28%	41%
Police did not respond to notification	22	22	18	38
Police did not consider incident a crime	24	26	24	26
Crime, but no arrest	20	23	27	30
Arrest, but no trial	33	21	22	24
Acquittal or too lenient penalty	17	13	26	44
Conviction and "proper" penalty	60	16	12	12

Quite independent of the judicial outcome of the case is its impact on the daily life and feelings of the victim and his family. Slightly more than 40 percent of the victims reported increased suspicion and distrustfulness along with intensified personal and household security measures. It appears that it is the unpredictability of the event and the sense of invasion by strangers rather than the seriousness of the crime that engenders this mistrust. With these strong feelings and the frequent lack of knowledge about the identity of the offender, victimization may well exacerbate existing prejudice against the groups typically blamed for social disorder and crime.

POLICE POPULARITY POLL

How does the public feel about the police? The survey asked all the crime victims and a comparably large sample of nonvictims a series of questions probing their attitudes on how well the local police do their job, how respectful they are toward the citizenry, and how honest they are. Items concerning the limits of police authority and exploring the functions of the police were also included.

Several conclusions emerged. Upper income groups are consistently more favorable in their evaluation of the police and are more in favor of augmenting their power than those with lower incomes. Negroes at all income levels show strong negative attitudes toward the police. (See Tables 3 and 4.)

Table 3 shows rather clearly that Negroes, regardless of income, estimate police effectiveness lower than whites do, with Negro women being even more critical than Negro men of the job the police are doing. Furthermore, Negroes show a smaller shift in attitude with increasing income than do whites, who are more favorable in their opinion of police effectiveness as their income rises.

TABLE 3

Positive Opinions on Local Police Effectiveness
(Percentage who think police do an excellent
or good job in enforcing the law)

Sex	White		Nonwhite	
	Less than $6,000	$6,000 or More	Less than $6,000	$6,000 or More
Male	67%	72%	54%	56%
Female	66	74	39	43

Table 4 shows that Negroes are also sharply more critical than whites are of police honesty. Here there are no income differences in attitude among white males. Women at higher income levels, both white and Negro, appear to be relatively less suspicious of police honesty. It is difficult to say how much these attitude differences are attributable to actual experience with police corruption and how much they express degrees of general hostility to the police. In either case the results indicate a more negative attitude toward the police among Negroes than among whites.

The next question probed a more personal attitude toward the police—their respectfulness toward "people like yourself." Almost 14 percent of the Negroes answered that it was "not so good." Less than 3 percent of the whites choose this response. This represents a much more critical attitude by Negroes than by whites, with hardly any differences by sex or income. There is some tendency, however, for very low-income people of both races and sexes to feel that the police are not sufficiently respectful to them.

One further conclusion is more tentative. It appears that there is no *one* underlying attitude toward the police. The police have many and sometimes only slightly related jobs to do in society. For example, they have a role both in suppressing organized gambling and in maintaining civil order. Most people (73 percent) feel the police should stop gambling even though it brings a good deal of money into the community. A significant minority (21 percent) feel the police should act only on complaints, and only 2 percent said the police should not interfere with gambling at all. With respect to police control of demonstrations for civil and political rights, on the other hand, a slight majority (54 percent) say police should

TABLE 4

OPINIONS ON THE HONESTY OF NEIGHBORHOOD POLICE

| | Males | | | |
| | White | | Nonwhite | |
Police are ...	Less than $6,000	$6,000 or More	Less than $6,000	$6,000 or More
Almost all honest	65%	67%	33%	33%
Most honest, few corrupt	24	26	47	41
Almost all corrupt	3	1	9	19
Don't know	8	6	11	7
	Females			
	White		Nonwhite	
Police are ...	Less than $6,000	$6,000 or More	Less than $6,000	$6,000 or More
Almost all honest	57%	65%	24%	35%
Most honest, few corrupt	27	29	54	49
Almost all corrupt	2	0	10	4
Don't know	14	6	12	12

not interfere if the protests are peaceful; 40 percent say police should stop all demonstrations; and 3 percent feel demonstrations should be allowed under any and all circumstances. Negroes are much more permissive about demonstrations than whites, and somewhat more permissive about gambling. Among lower income Negroes there is a significant relation between permissiveness on gambling and a strong prodemonstration attitude. But whites show no such consistent attitudes on the two issues. They tend to favor police intervention in gambling but not in rights demonstrations.

A more dramatic example of discontinuities in attitudes toward police has to do with limitations on their power. A national cross-section of citizens was asked:

> Recently some cities have added civilian review boards to their police departments. Some people say such boards offer the public needed protection against the police, and others say these boards are unnecessary

and would interfere with good police work and morale. In general, would you be in favor of civilian review boards or opposed to them?

In favor	45%
Opposed	35
Don't know	20

Do you favor giving the police more power to question people, do you think they have enough power already, or would you like to see some of their power to question people curtailed?

Police should have more power	52%
Have enough power already	43
Should curtail power	5

The police sometimes have a hard time deciding if there is enough evidence to arrest a suspect. In general, do you think it is better for them to risk arresting an innocent person rather than letting the criminal get away, or is it better for them to be really sure they are getting the right person before they make an arrest?

Risk arresting innocent	42%
Be really sure	58

The Supreme Court has recently ruled that in criminal cases the police may not question a suspect without his lawyer being present, unless the suspect agrees to be questioned without a lawyer. Are you in favor of this Supreme Court decision or opposed to it?

In favor	65%
Opposed	35

The significance of these results is their lack of consensus. On none of the questions is there overwhelming agreement or disagreement. Opinions are split almost in half, with the exception that hardly anyone is in favor of curtailing present police powers. The advocates of extending police authority in questioning suspects are almost balanced by those who think the police have enough power to do their job. Further, there is lack of internal agreement on the specific facets of the question. Being in favor of a civilian review board does not necessarily make a person support the Supreme Court decision on interrogation of suspects. Nor does a preference for having the police risk arresting the innocent rather than letting a criminal go free strongly predict being in favor of granting more power to the police in questioning people.

It is not clear why attitudes toward the police are so scattered. Perhaps police power is too new an issue on the national scene to have its components hammered into a clear and cohesive whole. Local variations in police practices may also blur the situation. It appears we are only at the beginning of a long process of relocating the police in the political spectrum.

As the federal presence in local law enforcement enlarges, both the shape of crime and the nature of law enforcement itself will change. Accurate crime statistics will be essential ·in monitoring these changes and in evaluating the worth of new programs designed to protect the public from the growing threat of invasion and victimization by criminal acts.

APPENDIX

FINDING THE VICTIMS

The study reported here is one of the major research efforts to have provided hard figures for the President's Crime Commission report. Its survey approach originated from well-known difficulties with police statistics. Those difficulties included the lack of comparability of criminal statistics in different cities; the fact that "crime waves" could be made to appear and disappear with changes in the system of reporting; the failure to include some kinds of criminal activities in statistical reports or to differentially report certain types of crimes; and, perhaps most important, the impossibility of estimating how much crime was not being reported to the police.

The excellent work of the FBI's *Uniform Crime Reports*, upon which the *UCR* index of major crime is based, repaired only some of these difficulties because these reports still drew on local police records. Was there another way to measure crime that did not rely on the police? Could a survey method do the job? These were the questions that D. Gale Johnson, dean of the social sciences at the University of Chicago, asked Peter H. Rossi, director of the National Opinion Research Center (NORC), in 1962.

The inquiry was of more than academic interest, for Chicago's crime statistics had just been jogged upward by the new police superintendent, Orlando Wilson, pointing out in dramatic fashion all the difficulties just outlined. In Chicago, as well as nationally, important policy questions—what resources had to be given to the police and how they were to be allocated—depended upon accurate social bookkeeping on the amount and distribution of crime.

After considerable experimentation NORC concluded that a survey of individual *victims* of crime could feasibly supply national estimates. Moreover, such estimates were now imperative. The crime problem was becoming more serious daily, and the President's commission had already begun its investigation.

The study's focus on individual victims meant that some crimes could not be measured. People were simply not going to report their participation in illegal activities such as violation of gambling, game, or liquor laws, abortion, or the use of narcotics. Crimes against corporations or other large institutions were also excluded.

Crimes of violence and property crimes against the individual were the main targets. Defining such crimes turned out to be a problem. For example, many people said they had been "robbed" (personally held up) when in fact they had been "burglarized" (had had property stolen from their homes, cars, etc.). Was a fist fight in the schoolyard really an assault? Was being given a bad check by a friend a fraud, a basis for a civil law suit, or just a private matter? Was the man's coat really taken, or did he leave it in the bar? A "stolen" pocketbook may simply have been lost, and a "consumer fraud" have been no more than sharp dealing.

A variety of tactics were used to identify and reduce these potential errors. First, interviewers were instructed to allow the respondents plenty of time to recollect about each type of crime. Then, when an incident was recalled, the special questionnaire form probed intensively into the matter—what had happened, when and where, whether there were witnesses, whether the police were called, the extent of injuries, loss, and damage, and the direct and indirect costs. Was there an arrest, a trial? If not, what was the outcome?

The 3,400 "crimes" reported in the interviews were then reviewed by two different staff members, evaluating each case independently. To check this evaluation procedure, a team of lawyers from the American Bar Foundation and two detectives from the Chicago police department were asked to make independent evaluations of NORC's interviews. The results were most encouraging, with substantial agreement in between 75 and 80 percent of the cases.

The evaluation outcome reduced the initial 3,400 reported victimizations to about 2,100. These 2,100 offenses—ranging all the way from murder to victimizing incidents typically treated as private matters—were felt to realistically represent the experience of the American people with crime.

12. VICTIM SURVEY RESEARCH: THEORETICAL IMPLICATIONS

Daniel Glaser

Traditionally the volume of crime in any area is measured by tabulating the crimes reported to or by its police departments. Victim survey research, by asking a representative sample of the population whether they have suffered from any of various types of crime in a recent period, provides a new type of evidence on the volume of crime. This creates new ways of testing hypotheses deduced from prior criminological theory. However, it may be even more important as a basis for theory and research on agencies for social control. Let us consider first the comparisons and contrasts such surveys can promote in the concepts by which we classify crime.

CLASSIFICATION OF CRIMES BY CONCEPTION OF THE VICTIM

Assuming we define "victim" as the person or organization injured by a crime, victim survey research immediately forces us to differentiate acts designated by law as "crime" according to how definitely their victims can

Prepared especially for this volume. Based upon an invited paper presented at the annual meeting of the American Sociological Association, San Francisco, 1967.

136

be specified. On the one hand, there are those acts in which there is clearly a deliberately injured individual or corporate victim: the persons or organizations whose money or other property a criminal takes or damages, or whom the criminal consciously seeks to injure. We may call offenses with such intended victims "predatory crimes." They include theft, burglary, forgery, fraud, assault, rape, and murder, as legally defined. In comparison with other types of offenses, there is relatively little difficulty in identifying the victims in these acts, either by studying persons named as victims in police and court records (as von Hentig, Wolfgang, Schafer, and others in the new specialty of "victimology" have done), or by discovering victims through asking samples of the general population if specific offenses have been committed against them (as is done in victim survey research). Sometimes research is hampered because the victim is not immediately or ever aware that he has been deliberately injured, as in much shoplifting and fraud, but we have relatively little conceptual difficulty in defining the victim whenever we know of the occurrence of such crimes.

Crimes that are not clearly predatory form a scale with respect to the problem of defining a victim. Perhaps closest to predatory offenses are "public disorder crimes," where there is generally someone who complains because he is an unwilling audience to the disorder, or the police act as sole complainants. These offenses include such misdemeanors as public drunkenness, excessive noisemaking, and indecent exposure. Here there is usually no allegation of intent to injure a victim, and often no clear injury. Although they are the most frequent basis for arrest in the United States, they generally are not considered a serious social problem because the damage done any victim usually is considered negligible in comparison with the damage from predatory crimes.

A second marginal category consists of "negligence crimes," where no intent to injure is alleged, although they create either injured victims or an increase in the probability of unintentional victimization, as in reckless driving, speeding, and some other acts which are illegal on grounds that they endanger the public. These crimes, especially those involving autos, are a serious social problem, for the injuries to persons and property are several times as great as those clearly ascribed to predatory crimes. However, conceptually they are a relatively distinct category because of the presumption of no intent to victimize.

Further from predatory offenses, in terms of the clear existence of a victim, is any crime in which, instead of someone taking another's possessions or intentionally injuring him, the person whom the law defines as criminal is selling a commodity or a service to a willing purchaser. These "service crimes" include such things as sale of moonshine liquor or narcotics and sale of illegal services, such as prostitution and gambling. In these criminal transactions, as in legitimate economic exchanges, all participants usually gain satisfaction and do not consider themselves victims: the purchaser gets what he wishes to buy, at a price he is willing to pay, and the seller receives the payment which he requests. Insofar as being a customer of such services is also a crime, we have what might be called "consumption crimes," the extreme opposite of predatory crimes in our scale of victimization.

Thus, the first valuable contribution we can gain for criminological theory from victim research is more lucidity for the murky concept of crime. Victim research, of necessity, narrows our focus to predatory offenses. Criminologists still concern themselves with public disorder, negligence, and service or consumption crimes, and even in international and historical comparative research with "treason" and "illegal status" offenses. However, each of these has functional implications in understanding a society, and poses problems for social control different from those of predatory crimes. Each of these other types of crime also has less universality, as types of individual behavior punishable by the state, than predatory crime. At any rate, victim research forces us to observe and to think about predatory crimes separately from other types of crime.

EPIDEMIOLOGICAL RESEARCH:
THE INTERACTION OF METHODOLOGY AND THEORY

Cressey has suggested that criminological theory has two distinct problems: to account for the development of individual cases of crime, and to account for the epidemiology of crime, particularly the trend, the density, and the geographic and demographic distribution of various types of crime.[1] Let us consider first the most publicized finding of the first national victim survey research project, the one conducted by the National Opinion Research Center (henceforth called NORC) in 1965 for the President's Commission on Law Enforcement and the Administration of Justice.[2] I refer to the finding that over twice as much major crime was reported by victims as had been reported to the police and tabulated in the *Uniform Crime Reports*. This will be the first of several illustrations of the difficulty of separating theoretical implications of survey research from the methodological implications with which they interact.

Data on the frequency of crime, or on any other phenomenon, are significant for theory only if they can be correlated with something else. However, even viewing the NORC total alone, without correlating it with anything,

---

[1] Donald R. Cressey, "Epidemiology and Individual Conduct: A Case from Criminology," *Pacific Sociological Review*, 3, no. 2 (Fall 1960): 47–58.
[2] Phillip H. Ennis, "Crimes, Victims, and the Police," *Trans-action*, 4, no. 7 (June 1967): 36–44; Phillip H. Ennis, *Criminal Victimization in the U.S.: A Report on a National Survey*, Field Surveys II of the President's Commission on Law Enforcement and Administration of Justice (Washington, D.C.: U.S. Government Printing Office, 1967).

we find that, like much previous research in criminology, it is significant for the doubts it casts on many prevailing beliefs. For example, the FBI's *Uniform Crime Reports* for 1967 indicates that major crimes have increased 71 percent in the past seven years. This poses tremendous theoretical problems, for there has not been nearly a 71 percent increase in these seven years in anything generally designated as a cause of crime, such as urbanization, lack of opportunity, cultural deprivation, social isolation, family disorganization, the proportion of the population that is youthful, or the proportion that is youthful and has these various other problems. However, the NORC evidence is that less than 45 percent of major crime was covered in the 1965 *Uniform Crime Reports'* findings of very large percent increases in crime each year during the 1960's.

A 71 percent increase in the completeness of crime reporting by police forces to the FBI between 1960 and 1967 would create a 71 percent increase in the *Uniform Crime Reports'* total, even if the actual crime rate stayed constant. The NORC survey concluded that FBI data on major crimes in 1965 were 45 percent complete. Let us assume that for 1967 they were 50 percent complete. If they were only 29.2 percent complete in 1960, the increase to 50 percent complete in 1967 would be a 71 percent increase. That the current FBI coverage may represent an appreciable increase in completeness from preceding years is suggested by the success of many organizations, notably the FBI, in promoting growth in the size and training of police forces. There has also been a modernization of police data collection and tabulation systems. Metropolitan and state police forces have been a major market for the hardware and software of computers and systems engineers, the "new Utopians" of the 1960's. These trends probably have promoted increased completeness in police crime recording. They are the only explanations for such phenomena as the 202 percent increase in the Kansas City crime rate from 1959 to 1961, the 95 percent increase in the Buffalo crime rate from 1961 to 1963, and the 72 percent increase in the Chicago crime rate from 1959 to 1960.[3] Regularly repeated victim survey research should indicate how much fluctuation occurs in the actual crime rate, independently of changes in the adequacy of police data collection. Therefore, such surveys would indicate how much of the increase in official crime rates is due merely to increases in completeness of coverage.

It follows that, in the interest of both theory and practice on social control, victim survey research should not be viewed as a replacement for police reports on the volume of crime, but as a continually necessary supplement to police figures. If both police and victim survey crime rates are tabulated, information on the difference between these rates may be just

---

[3] President's Commission on Law Enforcement and Administration of Justice, *The Challenge of Crime in a Free Society* (Washington, D.C.: U.S. Government Printing Office, 1967), p. 25.

as valuable as either rate alone. For maximum scientific and practical utility, victim surveys should be repeated regularly by a permanent national staff, in a standardized manner, and the FBI's current *Uniform Crime Reports* should also be continued. Repeated victim survey research would not only reveal more accurately than the police figures the trend of predatory crime rates in this country, but in conjunction with tabulations like those now made by the FBI it would also show the proportion of the total volume of crime which comes to the attention of law-enforcement agencies. Variations in the discrepancy between victim survey and police tabulations could be a major guide for the comparative study of police systems with a view to identifying factors related to differences in their effectiveness.

In addition to providing a standard for the assessment of police effectiveness, victim survey data may be useful for testing theory on the ecological correlates of crime. However, any criminological theory based on correlates of the less complete crime-rate data of the *Uniform Crime Reports* could still be relatively sound if the discrepancy between these rates and victim survey rates were distributed in the same manner as the actual rates. The value of a correlation coefficient, after all, is unchanged when all values of one variable have a constant added, or have a constant multiplier. However, if the underreporting error of police data varies markedly with theoretically important correlates of crime, then revelation of this error should stimulate revision of criminological theory. Therefore, in appraising theoretical implications of victim research, we are bound to consider also the methodological question of the scope and correlates of error in both victim survey and police-reported crime rates.

A striking feature of the NORC victim survey data is that the discrepancy between their figures and the police-reported figures published in the *Uniform Crime Reports* varies markedly according to type of offense. The victim-reported burglary is over three times as frequent as police-reported burglary, victim-reported rates for grand larceny and for aggravated assault are over twice as high as police-reported rates, and victim-reported rates of robbery are about 50 percent above police-reported rates. On the other hand, victim-reported car theft is only four-fifths of police-reported rates, and victim survey rates for homicide are only three-fifths of official rates.

Let us consider the probable validity of the NORC figures by offense. It is a built-in consequence of the household sampling procedure alone that the burglary, larceny, and robbery figures of the NORC victim survey, although much more frequent than police data, still underrepresent crimes of this type, by omitting many crimes against corporations. With respect to larceny, Cameron found that stores report only a small fraction of the shoplifters whom they apprehend, and it is probable that they never are aware of most of the shoplifting and pilfering that is conducted in their premises.[4] The University of Michigan survey for the President's Commission more rigorously confirmed this.[5] In reporting the Bureau of Social Science Research survey for the President's Commission, Biderman has analyzed a variety of evidence of error in victim research; they were predominantly errors of underreporting property offenses.[6]

Automobile theft, unlike other property offenses, is reported not as frequently by the NORC survey as by police reports, although this discrepancy is small enough to be a function of sampling error, as is suggested by the fact that its direction varies by region. The high value of autos, the pressure to report car theft because of registration and insurance, and the high police recovery rate for stolen autos apparently make police-reported auto-theft rates sufficiently complete that victim survey research will not yield appreciably more accurate data on this offense. However, burglary and larceny other than auto theft are two-thirds of major offenses according to the FBI and three-fourths of major offenses according to the NORC survey. Actual rates of these offenses, including offenses against corporations and undetected shoplifting and pilfering, apparently exceed police-reported rates to an even greater extent than the NORC data suggest.

For crimes against persons, the relative discrepancy between victim survey and official crime rates by type of crime is a more complex function of reporting variables. For example, the NORC figures indicate about one rape per 1,250 females per year, while the FBI figures indicate about one per 4,300 females. Yet confidential interviews by sociologists Kirkpatrick and Kanin with 291 coeds at a midwest university indicated that about one in 15 suffered "aggressively forceful attempts at sex intercourse in the course of which menacing threats of coercive infliction of physical pain were employed."[7] This implies rape or attempted rape, yet none of these episodes had been reported to authorities. Since rape is an offense of which the victim is usually ashamed, the proportion which would be reported by the victims to survey interviewers probably is less than the proportion reported to university health-service specialists in an office interview under conditions more conducive to frank revelation of sex experiences.

This university research suggests that underreporting of rape—certainly

---

[4] Mary Owen Cameron, *The Booster and the Snitch* (New York: Free Press, Macmillan, 1964), chap. 1.

[5] Albert J. Reiss, Jr., and associates, *Studies in Crime and Law Enforcement in Major Metropolitan Areas*, vols. 1 and 2, Field Surveys III of the President's Commission on Law Enforcement and Administration of Justice (Washington, D.C.: U.S. Government Printing Office, 1967). This is hereafter referred to as the University of Michigan survey, as it was administered by the Survey Research Center and other units of the University of Michigan.

[6] Albert D. Biderman and associates, *Report of a Pilot Study in the District of Columbia on Victimization and Attitudes Toward Law Enforcement*, Field Survey I of the President's Commission on Law Enforcement and the Administration of Justice (Washington, D.C.: U.S. Government Printing Office, 1967).

[7] C. Kirkpatrick and E. Kanin, "Male Sex Aggression on a University Campus," *American Sociological Review*, 22 (1957): 52–58.

of rape attempts—remains extensive in both police and NORC statistics. Yet of the rape incidents reported to NORC, three-fourths were said by the respondents to have been reported to the police. Since police-reported rape rates were only a fourth of the NORC rates, the three-fourths-reporting claims of NORC respondents suggest that even that fraction of rape reported to the police is underreported by them, perhaps reflecting definitional problems with this offense. Indeed, while improved knowledge of sexual offense rates will depend upon victim survey research, optimum field methods probably would resemble those of the Kinsey Foundation more closely than those of NORC. It is noteworthy that the Bureau of Social Science Research survey in Washington, D.C., used different questions and received more reporting of sex offenses than the NORC national survey. In summary, probably all available statistics on sex-offense rates are too questionable to warrant efforts at epidemiological generalization. It is quite possible that any correlates of sex-offense rates are as much a function of interviewing personnel and procedures as they are of the actual occurrence of these offenses.

Only one homicide was reported in the NORC survey, perhaps because an inquiry as to whether there were any murders in the household in the past year is not the best way to measure the frequency of this offense. The certificates on cause of death prepared by physicians, and tabulated in U.S. Public Health Service *Vital Statistics* reports, probably yield more accurate data on homicide than are likely to be gathered by either victim survey or police reports.

The borderline between simple and aggravated assaults and the borderline between simple assaults and altercations not considered crime are both vague. Accordingly, it is quite probable that variations in the customarily tolerated vigor of expressing interpersonal opposition may greatly affect variations in the reporting of assaults both to the police and to victim surveyors. In "polite society" a shove or a slap may be conceived as assault, while in high-violence groups only an intensive effort to beat up or to wound would be either reported to the police or recalled in a household survey. However, this type of error was apparently reduced considerably in the NORC survey by the survey staff's independent classification of all reported assaults as simple or aggravated. Thus differential reporting on assaults by socioeconomic class (of either victim or assaulter) and classification of the assault by the survey staff probably explain why middle-class assault rates obtained by NORC were higher on simple assault and lower on aggravated assault than lower-class rates. The major advantage of the victim survey in assault tabulation is revealed by the fact that in a third of the aggravated-assault cases and over half the simple assaults the victims did not report their assaults to the police, most often on the grounds that they considered it a private matter. Indeed, probably many intrahousehold assaults are also not reported to survey interviewers. However, we can assume that, despite lingering omissions and definitional problems, victim survey research probably provides much more complete and accurate statistics on the frequency and distribution of assault than are available from police reports.

The first section of this paper suggested that victim survey research is clearly applicable only to predatory offenses. This section concluded that such research would not improve our knowledge on rates of homicide, rape, or auto theft. These comprise approximately one-fourth of all major predatory crimes according to the FBI, but scarcely more than one-tenth according to the NORC survey. For the remaining majority of predatory offenses, the NORC survey indicates new geographic correlates.

The South has long had this country's highest murder rates, and FBI data indicated that it also had the highest assault rates. The NORC victim survey, however, finds assault rates in the South less than half those of the West, only about three-fourths those of the north-central states, and only a few percent higher than rates for the northeastern states. The West, which always had the highest rates for most crimes according to the FBI, retains this distinction in the NORC survey. For the largest category of offenses, burglary and larceny, the relative ranks of the South and North-east decrease somewhat and that of the North-central states increases, in NORC figures.

Since we have assumed that the NORC rates are more valid than police rates with respect to assault, we are confronted with the fact that NORC data reverse the conclusion previously supported by both homicide and assault rates, that a subculture of violence distinguishes the South. The NORC data, however, are further broken down by type of community. These indicate that the regional difference in assault rates is concentrated in the central cities of metropolitan areas. In all regions except the South, central cities have the highest assault rates. For central cities, western rates are over three times southern rates, north-central rates are almost twice those of the South, and even northeastern rates are higher than southern rates. Since southern cities are, on the whole, less segregated than those else-where, one could hypothesize that *violence varies directly with the segregation of recent migrants from high-violence areas,* or *with the size of the ghettoes into which they are segregated.* It should be noted that the South still has the highest homicide rates; what seems to be differently distributed than we assumed heretofore is the frequency of nonlethal violence.

THE NEW VICTIMOLOGY

Our discussion thus far has dealt with victim survey information on crime rates. These differ not in kind, but in being more complete and therefore presumably more accurate than crime rates collected by the police. Victim survey research, of course, by covering crimes more completely, also enhances the completeness of statistics on attributes of victims, but data on victims also are available from police and court records, and led to the growing field of "victimology."[8] In general, the NORC data confirm leading conclusions on victims developed previously from police data, such as the predominance of Negro victims among crimes by Negroes, and the predominance of white victims among crimes by whites. Omission of corporation victims in the NORC data possibly leads to their underreporting the extent of interracial confrontation in crime, since we may assume that there is a predominance of whites among the white-collar employees representing corporation victims of both Negro and white crimes. There is also little not previously indicated by police figures in the survey data on the ecology of risk, such as their finding that middle- and upper-class persons, of either race, are victimized most if they live near the slums. However, much more important is the distinctly new kind of victimology data which survey research adds to the police-record information. These new data are concerned with victim attitudes.

The hardest data on attitudes toward the police yielded by victim surveys are not the verbal opinions they compile regarding the police, but the reports they collect on whether or not crime victims notify the police. These reports on actions express the attitudes of the respondents better than their evaluative words. For property crimes, at least, the hypothesis which survey data seem to support is simply: *The proportion of total crimes that are reported by victims to the police varies directly with the proportion of reported crimes on which the police act effectively*. Vicious circles obviously can develop here: the less successfully police cope with crimes reported to them, the smaller will be the proportion that is reported to them, and hence the less successfully they can cope with them. Beneficent circles, however, can also occur: the more successfully the police cope with crime, the larger the proportion of offenses of which they will be told. This may be one reason why improved police work leads to higher police-reported crime statistics: more crime is reported to good police forces, in addition to better records being kept by them. Regularly collected victim survey crime rates could break this particular circle of higher apparent crime rates with improved policing, due to lower discrepancy between police-reported rates and actual rates.

Attitudes toward the police reported by victims in evaluative language

---

[8] For systematic reviews of this literature, see Albert Morris, "What About the Victims of Crime?," *Correctional Research*, United Prison Assn. of Massachusetts bulletin no. 16 (November 1966); Stephen Schafer, *The Victim and His Criminal: A Study in Functional Responsibility* (New York: Random House, 1968); President's Commission on Law Enforcement and the Administration of Justice, "Victimology," *Technical Papers* (Washington, D.C.: U.S. Government Printing Office, 1967); Ezzat Abdel Fattah, "Quelques problèmes posés à la justice pénale par la victimologie," *Annales Internationales de Criminologie*, 5, no. 2 (1966): 335–361.

reflect primarily the intervening variable in reporting offenses or not reporting them, which is perceived probability of police effectiveness. The most frequent reason given for not reporting property crimes to the police is simply doubt that the police will do anything about them. With crimes against persons the intervening variables are more complex: the most frequent reasons given for not reporting assault and rape to the police were belief that these offenses were personal matters, not of police concern; doubts of police effectiveness were only the second most frequent reason for not reporting these offenses.

In addition to probing reasons for nonuse of the police by crime victims, the survey technique permits inquiry on the satisfaction obtained by those who call the police. The NORC findings suggest that retribution by punishment of the offender remains the ultimate objective of those who have suffered from a crime, despite predominant growth in public support for nonpunitive approaches to changing offenders. However, these data also show that punishment does not really get to be an issue in almost nine-tenths of the cases. This is because, according to the victims, the police did not even come when called in a quarter of the cases; in a quarter of those in which they did come, they did not treat the offense as a crime; and they made an arrest in only a fifth of the cases which they did define as crimes. Obviously, data on the variation of these percentages by police system, by offense, by attributes of the victim, and by neighborhood will be a tremendous asset for identifying the differential effectiveness of various police forces, and for guiding theory and research to account for such variations.

Survey research was used as a means of determining the general public's knowledge and attitudes with respect to various components of law enforcement and administration of justice, even before such surveys included inquiries on victimization.[9] However, the tremendous potential utility of public knowledge and opinion surveying has hardly begun to be realized by law-enforcement agencies, despite the fact that police and court effectiveness depends so much on community support.

The NORC survey confirmed prior impressions that a less favorable attitude toward the police prevails among nonwhites than among whites. It was surprising only in finding relatively little relationship of these orientations to income within racial groups, but distinctly more negative orientations toward the police in nonwhite women than in nonwhite men. There is no breakdown by age. The University of Michigan survey was highly detailed and specific in its probes on types of illegal action that the respondents actually saw police commit or believed they committed. There

---

[9] Royal Commission on the Police, *The Relations Between the Police and the Public*, Appendix IV to the Minutes of Evidence (London: H.M. Stationery Office, 1962); John P. Clark, "Isolation of the Police: A Comparison of the British and American Situations," *Journal of Criminal Law, Criminology, and Police Science*, 56, no. 3 (September 1965): 307–19.

would certainly be merit in analysis of these attitudes by integration indices for communities and for police forces, and by many other attributes of communities and of police policy and procedure.

VICTIM SURVEYS AND
JUDICIAL POLICY

If victim surveys had been administered routinely for some years, we might not now be in such a poor position to assess the unintended consequences of Supreme Court decisions designed to regulate the police. There were indications in the analyses of American Bar Foundation surveys, by Herman Goldstein and by Wayne La Fave,[10] that police choice of procedures, whether legal or illegal, tends to be a function of what they perceive as most efficiently reducing what we might call the "net heat" they encounter. If police receive complaints about gambling, prostitution, or pocket-picking, for example, these complaints are often reduced with a much smaller investment of police manhours by harassment of gamblers, prostitutes, or suspected pickpockets in those neighborhoods where their visibility generates complaints than by seeking convictions against them. Accordingly, police commonly deal with these offenders by picking up suspects without formally booking, or they book and lock up without expecting to seek or to achieve convictions. Achieving convictions is conceived as requiring a much greater effort for a given amount of reduction in the total demands for action confronted by the police.

Similarly, if police encounter pressure to reduce burglary, theft, and strong-arm robbery in commercial, amusement, or middle-class residential areas, they are especially prone to stop any persons who look suspicious to them in these areas. Their "probable cause" as ground for arrest is often not that which traditionally stands up in court, but instead a combination of considerations such as the hour of the day and the general appearance and conduct of the suspects, which indicate to the police a high probability that they are dealing with thieves, burglars, or strong-armers. Furthermore, when the response of those stopped suggests to the police an even higher probability that they have stopped criminally oriented persons, there is an increase in their incentives to interrupt the activities of these suspects by any action for which police can expect not to receive complaints.

The sequence described above is especially evident in the action of

---

[10] Herman Goldstein, "Police Discretion: The Ideal vs. the Real," *Public Administration Review*, 23, no. 3 (September 1963): 140–48; Wayne R. La Fave, "The Police and Nonenforcement of the Law," *Wisconsin Law Review*, 1962), no. 1 (January 1962): 104–37, and no. 2 (March 1962): 179–239; Wayne R. La Fave, *Arrest: The Decision to Take a Suspect into Custody* (Boston: Little, Brown, 1965).

police who have reason to believe that those whom they stop under suspicious circumstances are drug addicts. This is because addiction, in our society, is highly correlated with professional burglary and theft. The police judgment, essentially, is that their action most effective in reducing complaints is to pick up the most suspicious persons they stop. Then, of course, they look for further evidence; they will frisk those stopped, both for police protection from possible concealed weapons and for the drugs or ostensibly stolen goods that frisking may yield. But if the police perception of their probable success in gaining a conviction is low, and if, in their judgment, the probability is high that the persons stopped are causes of police problems, the police will be inclined to use against these persons any devices other than convictions that are available to them. Thus, police perception that gaining a conviction has become much more difficult, whether this perception is accurate or not, may well increase their inclination to use alternatives to obtaining a conviction in their efforts to reduce the "heat" they encounter from crime rates.

What I am hypothesizing in the foregoing—stimulated by a limited amount of police and court observation—is that judicial effort to make the police more lawful frequently has the unintended consequence, at least temporarily, of making the police more lawless. The police perception that it will be harder to cope with their problems by lawful means, even if it is an inaccurate perception, may become a self-fulfilling prophecy if it leads to less police effort at employing lawful procedures. When such a development increases police inclination to harass persons whom they suspect cause their problems, rather than to initiate prosecution against them (or if they initiate prosecution as part of the harassment, with little expectation of obtaining a conviction), then police grounds for stopping and frisking can be expected increasingly to reflect their personal prejudices and their beliefs in the effectiveness of violence.

One can reasonably hypothesize that an increase in police expression of their personal prejudices and more ready use of violence may occur simply because of a drop in police interest in obtaining a conviction. This could decrease the role of the courts as a partial check on police expression of prejudice and on the use of unlawful violence. It may well be that the development of such a shift in police behavior has occurred in recent years, simultaneously with the growth of militant movements for increased power among minority groups and others toward whom some police may be prejudiced. This would make inevitable a progressive escalation of conflict between such police and these persons. Had we already had more frequent public opinion surveys, more sharply focused in sampling and in question construction to pinpoint the locations and the dimensions of public hostility to law enforcement (and confidential surveys of police attitudes), we might have had a major resource for understanding and correcting some causes of large-scale law-enforcement breakdowns.

CONCLUSION

I have tried to show that victim survey research, like much other research on social problems, has implications that are both theoretical and practical. It is noteworthy that this type of research burgeoned primarily because the President's Commission prodded sociologists to a greater concern with explaining scientifically and recommending practical remedies for the contrast between the actual and the ideal in crime control. This differs greatly from the traditional preoccupations of commissions and of many criminologists, who have been more concerned with denouncing and accusing than with theoretical analysis and scientific research. Finally, I hope I have demonstrated that theorizing is continually necessary if we are to increase the value of victim survey research for both theory and practice.

13. SOCIAL SETTINGS AND COVERT PARTICIPANT OBSERVATION

Kai T. Erikson

At the beginning of their excellent paper on the subject, Howard S. Becker and Blanche Geer define participant observation as "that method in which the observer participates in the daily life of the people under study, either openly in the role of researcher or covertly in some disguised role. . . ."[1]

The purpose of this paper is to argue that the research strategy mentioned in the last few words of that description represents a significant ethical problem in the field of sociology. In point of sheer volume, of course, the problem is relatively small, for disguised participant observation is probably one of the rarest research techniques in use among sociologists. But in point of general importance, the problem is far more serious—partly because the use of disguises seems to attract a disproportionate amount of interest both inside and outside the field, and partly because it

Reprinted by permission of the author and the Society for the Study of Social Problems from *Social Problems*, 14, no. 4 (Spring 1967): 366–73. Original title: "A Comment on Disguised Observations in Sociology."

This paper was read at the annual meeting of the Society for the Study of Social Problems, Chicago, 1965.

[1] Howard S. Becker and Blanche Geer, "Participant Observation and Interviewing: A Comparison," *Human Organization*, 16 (1957): 28–32.

offers a natural starting point for dealing with other ethical issues in the profession.

In recent years, a handful of studies have been reported in the literature based on the work of observers who deliberately misrepresented their identity in order to enter an otherwise inaccessible social situation. Some of these studies have already provoked a good deal of comment—among them, for instance, the cases of the anthropologist who posed as a mental patient by complaining of symptoms he did not feel,[2] the sociologists who joined a gathering of religious mystics by professing convictions they did not share,[3] the Air Force officer who borrowed a new name, a new birth date, a new personal history, a new set of mannerisms, and even a new physical appearance in order to impersonate an enlisted man,[4] and the group of graduate students who ventured into a meeting of Alcoholics Anonymous wearing the clothes of men from other social classes than their own and the facial expressions of men suffering from an unfortunate disability.[5]

In taking the position that this kind of masquerading is unethical, I am naturally going to say many things that are only matters of personal opinion; and thus the following remarks are apt to have a more editorial flavor than is usual for papers read at professional meetings. But a good deal more is at stake here than the sensitivities of any particular person, and my excuse for dealing with an issue that seems to have so many subjective overtones is that the use of disguise in social research affects the professional climate in which all of us work and raises a number of methodological questions that should be discussed more widely.

I am assuming here that "personal morality" and "professional ethics" are not the same thing. Personal morality has something to do with the way an individual conducts himself across the range of his human contacts; it is not local to a particular set of occupational interests. Professional ethics, on the other hand, refer to the way a group of associates define their special responsibility to one another and to the rest of the social order in which they work. In this sense, professional ethics often deal with issues that are practical in their application and limited in their scope: they are the terms of a covenant among people gathered together into a given occupational group. For instance, it may or may not be ethical for an espionage agent or a journalist to represent himself as someone he is not in the course of gathering information, but it certainly does not follow that the conduct of

---

[2] William C. Caudill *et al.*, "Social Structure and Interaction Processes on a Psychiatric Ward," *American Journal of Orthopsychiatry*, 22 (1952): 314–34.

[3] Leon Festinger, Henry W. Riecken, and Stanley Schacter, *When Prophecy Fails* (Minneapolis: University of Minnesota Press, 1956).

[4] Mortimer A. Sullivan, Stuart A. Queen, and Ralph C. Patrick, Jr., "Participant Observation as Employed in the Study of a Military Training Program," *American Sociological Review*, 23 (1958): 660–67.

[5] John F. Lofland and Robert A. Lejeune, "Initial Interaction of Newcomers in Alcoholics Anonymous: A Field Experiment in Class Symbols and Socialization," *Social Problems*, 8 (1960): 102–11.

a sociologist should be judged in the same terms; for the sociologist has a different relationship to the rest of the community, operates under a different warrant, and has a different set of professional and scientific interests to protect. In this sense, the ethics governing a particular discipline are in many ways local to the transactions that discipline has with the larger world.

The argument to be presented here, then, is that the practice of using masks in social research compromises both the people who wear them and the people for whom they are worn, and in doing so, violates the terms of a contract which the sociologist should be ready to honor in his dealings with others. There are many respects in which this is true, but I will be dealing here in particular with the relationship between the sociologist and (a) the subjects of his research, (b) the colleagues with whom he works (c) the students he agrees to teach, and (d) the data he takes as his subject matter.

The first of these points has to do with the responsibilities a sociologist should accept toward other institutions and other people in the social order. It may seem a little cranky to insist that disguised observation constitutes an ugly invasion of privacy and is, on that ground alone, objectionable. But it is a matter of cold calculation to point out that this particular research strategy can injure people in ways we can neither anticipate in advance nor compensate for afterward. For one thing, the sheer act of entering a human transaction on the basis of deliberate fraud may be painful to the people who are thereby misled; and even if that were not the case, there are countless ways in which a stranger who pretends to be something else can disturb others by failing to understand the conditions of intimacy that prevail in the group he has tried to invade. Nor does it matter very much how sympathetic the observer is toward the persons whose lives he is studying: the fact of the matter is that he does not *know* which of his actions are apt to hurt other people, and it is highly presumptuous of him to act as if he does—particularly when, as is ordinarily the case, he has elected to wear a disguise exactly because he is entering a social sphere so far from his own experience.

So the sheer act of wearing disguises in someone else's world may cause discomfort, no matter what we later write in our reports; and this possibility raises two questions. The first, of course, is whether we have the right to inflict pain at all when we are aware of these risks and the subjects of the study are not. The second, however, is perhaps more important from the narrow point of view of the profession itself: so long as we suspect that a method we use has at least *some* potential for harming others, we are in the extremely awkward position of having to weigh the scientific and social benefits of that procedure against its possible cost in human discomfort, and this is a difficult business under the best of circumstances. If we happen to harm people who have agreed to act as subjects, we can at least argue that they knew something of the risks involved and were willing to contribute to that vague program called the "advance of knowledge." But when we do so with people who have expressed no readiness to participate in our researches (indeed, people who would presumably have refused if asked directly), we are in very much the same ethical position as a physician who carries out medical experiments on human subjects without their consent. The only conceivable argument in favor of such experimentation is that the knowledge derived from it is worth the discomfort it may cause. And the difficulties here are that we do not know how to measure the value of the work we do or the methods we employ in this way, and, moreover, that we might be doing an extraordinary disservice to the idea of detached scholarship if we tried. Sociologists cannot protect their freedom of inquiry if they owe the rest of the community (not to mention themselves) an accounting for the distress they may have inadvertently imposed on people who have not volunteered to take that risk.

The second problem with disguised observation to be considered here has to do with the sociologist's responsibilities to his colleagues. It probably goes without saying that research of this sort is liable to damage the reputation of sociology in the larger society and close off promising areas of research for future investigators. This is true in the limited sense that a particular agency—say, for example, Alcoholics Anonymous—may decide that its integrity and perhaps even its effectiveness were violated by the appearance of sociologists pretending to be someone else and deny access to other students who propose to use an altogether different approach. And it is also true in the wider sense that any research tactic which attracts unfavorable notice may help diminish the general climate of trust toward sociology in the community as a whole. So long as this remains a serious possibility, the practice of disguised observation becomes a problem for everyone in the profession; and to this extent, it is wholly within the bounds of etiquette for one sociologist to challenge the work of another on this score.

This objection has been raised several times before, and the answer most often given to it is that the people who are studied in this fashion—alcoholics or spiritualists or mental patients, for example—are not likely to read what we say about them anyway. Now this argument has the advantage of being correct a good deal of the time, but this fact does not prevent it from being altogether irrelevant. To begin with, the experience of the past few years should surely have informed us that the press is more than ready to translate our technical reports into news copy, and this means that we can no longer provide shelter for other people behind the walls of our own anonymity. But even if that were not the case, it is a little absurd for us to claim that we derive some measure of protection from the narrowness of our audience when we devote so much time trying to broaden it. The fact is that we are increasingly reaching audiences whose confidence we cannot afford to jeopardize, and we have every right to be afraid that such people may close their doors to sociological research if they learn to become too suspicious of our methods and intentions.

The third objection to be raised here, if only as a note in passing, concerns the responsibilities the profession should accept toward its students. The division of labor in contemporary sociology is such that a considerable proportion of the data we use in our work is gathered by graduate students or other apprentices, and this proportion is even higher for research procedures that require the amount of energy and time necessary for participant observation. Of the dozen or more observers who took part in the studies I have cited, for example, all but one were graduate students. Now a number of sociologists who have engaged in disguised observation have reported that it is apt to pose serious moral problems and a good deal of personal discomfort, and I think one might well argue that this is a heavy burden to place on any person who is, by our own explicit standards, not yet ready for professional life. I am not suggesting here that students are too immature to make a seasoned choice in the matter. I am suggesting that they should not be asked to make what one defender of the method has called "real and excruciating moral decisions" while they are still students and presumably protected from the various dilemmas and contentions which occupy us in meetings like this—particularly since they are so likely to be academically, economically, and even psychologically dependent upon those elders who ask them to choose.[6]

The fourth objection I would like to raise here about the use of undercover observation is probably the most important—and yet the most remote from what is usually meant by the term "ethics." It seems to me that any attempt to use masquerades in social research betrays an extraordinary disrespect for the complexities of human interaction, and for this reason can only lead to bad science. Perhaps the most important responsibility of any sociologist is to appreciate how little he really knows about his intricate and elusive subject matter. We have at best a poor understanding of the human mind, of the communication signals that link one mind to another, or the social structures that emerge from those linkages—and it is the most arrant kind of oversimplification for us to think that we can assess the effect which a clever costume or a few studied gestures have on the social setting. The pose might "work" in the sense that the observer is admitted into the situation; but once this passage has been accomplished, how is he to judge his own influence on the lives of the people he is studying? This is a serious problem in every department of science, of course, and a good deal of time has been devoted to its solution. But the only way to cope with the problem in even a preliminary way is to have as clear a picture as possible of the social properties that the observer is introducing into the situation, and this

---

[6] To keep the record straight, I might add that I first became interested in these matters when I was a graduate student and applied for one of the observer posts mentioned here.

is altogether impossible if we ourselves are not sure who he is. We can *impersonate* other modes of behavior with varying degrees of insight and skill, but we cannot *reproduce* them; and since this is the case, it seems a little irresponsible for a sociologist to assume that he can enter social life in any masquerade that suits his purpose without seriously disrupting the scene he hopes to study.

When people interact, they relate to one another at many different levels at once, and only a fraction of the messages communicated during that interchange are registered in the conscious mind of the participant. It may be possible for someone to mimic the conventional gestures of fear, but it is impossible for him to reproduce the small postural and chemical changes which go with it. It may be possible for a middle-class speaker to imitate the broader accents of lower-class speech, but his vocal equipment is simply not conditioned to do so without arousing at least a subliminal suspicion. It may be possible for a trained person to rearrange the slant of his body and reset his facial muscles to approximate the bearing of someone else, but his performance will never be anything more than a rough imposture. Now we know that these various physiological, linguistic, and kinetic cues play an important part in the context of human interaction, but we have no idea how to simulate them—and what is probably more to the point, we never will. For one thing, we cannot expect to learn in a matter of hours what others have been practicing throughout a lifetime. For another, to imitate always means to parody, to caricature, to exaggerate certain details of behavior at the expense of others, and to that extent any person who selects a disguise will naturally emphasize those details which *he* assumes are most important to the character he is portraying. In doing so, of course, he is really only portraying a piece of himself. It is interesting to speculate, for example, why the Air Force lieutenant mentioned earlier thought he needed to present himself as a near-delinquent youth with a visible layer of personal problems in order to pose as an enlisted man. Whatever the reasoning behind this particular charade, it would certainly be reasonable for someone to suspect that it tells us more about the investigators' impression of enlisted men than it does about the men themselves—and since we have no way of learning whether this is true or not, we have lost rather than gained an edge of control over the situation we are hoping to understand. What the investigators had introduced into the situation was a creature of their own invention, and it would be hardly surprising if the results of their inquiry corresponded to some image they had in advance of the enlisted man's condition. (It is perhaps worth noting here that impersonation always seems easier for people looking down rather than up the status ladder. We find it reasonable to assume that officers "know how" to portray enlisted men or that sociologists have the technical capacity to pose as drunks or religious mystics, but it is not at all clear that the reverse would be equally true.)

This, then, is the problem. If we provide observers with special masks and coach them in the "ways" of the private world they are hoping to enter, how can we learn what is happening to the people who meet them in this disguise? What information is registered in the unconscious minds of the other people who live in that world? How does the social structure accommodate to this peculiar invasion?

It is clear, I think, that something happens—something over which we have no control. Let me relate two incidents drawn from the studies mentioned earlier. The first has to do with the Air Force officer who posed as an enlisted man. In their report of the study, the investigators used several pages of a short paper to describe the elaborate masquerade they had fashioned for the observer and the coaching he had received in the ways of the adolescent subculture. "So successful was the tutoring," reads the brief report, "that when the time for 'enlistment' arrived, the recruiting sergeant . . . suggested that the observer not be accepted by the Air Force because by all appearances he was a juvenile delinquent."[7] And later, during an interview with a service psychologist, the observer was recommended for reclassification on the grounds that he appeared quite anxious over the death of his father. Now these events may indeed suggest that the pose was successful, for the observer *was* trying to look somewhat delinquent and *did* have a story memorized about the death of his father in an auto accident. But who would care to argue that the diagnosis of the sergeant and the psychologist were inaccurate? Surely something was wrong, and if they perceived an edge of uneasiness which reminded them of anxiety or detected a note of furtiveness which looked to them like delinquency, they may only have been responding to the presence of a real conflict between the observer and his mask. We may leave it to the psychoanalysts to ask whether vague anxieties about "killing" one's father are an unlikely impression for someone to leave behind when he is parading around with a new name, a new background, a new history, and, of course, a new set of parents. The authors of the article tell us that the observer "did have something of a problem to transform himself from a 27-year-old, college trained commissioned officer into a 19-year-old, near-delinquent high school graduate," and this is certainly easy to believe.[8] What is more difficult to believe is that such a transformation is possible at all—and if it is not, we can have very little confidence in the information gathered by the observer. Since we do not know to what kind of creature the enlisted men were responding, we do not know what sense to make of what they said and did.

The second example comes from the study of the apocalyptic religious group. At one point in the study, two observers arrived at one of the group's

---

[7] Sullivan, Queen, and Patrick, *op. cit.*, p. 663.
[8] Stuart A. Queen, "Comment," *American Sociological Review*, 24 (1959): 399–400.

meeting places under instructions to tell quite ordinary stories about their experience in spiritualism in order to create as little commotion as possible. A few days afterwards, however, the leader of the group was overheard explaining that the two observers had appeared upset, excited, confused, and unsure of their errand at the time of their original visit, all of which helped confirm her suspicion that they had somehow been "sent" from another planet. In one sense, of course, this incident offered the observers an intriguing view of the belief structure of the cult, but in another sense, the leader's assessment of the situation was very shrewd: after all, the observers *had* been sent from another world, if not another planet, and she may have been quite right to sense that they were a bit confused and unsure of their errand during their early moments in the new job. "In both cases," the report informs us, the visits of the observers "were given as illustrations that 'strange things are happening.' "[9] Indeed, strange things *were* happening; yet we have no idea how strange they really were. It is almost impossible to evaluate the reaction of the group to the appearance of the pair of observers because we do not know whether they were seen as ordinary converts or as extraordinary beings. And it makes a difference, for in the first instance the investigators would be observing a response which fell within the normal range of the group's experience, while in the second instance they would be observing a response which would never have taken place had the life of the group been allowed to run its own course.

My point in raising these two examples, it should be clear, is not to insist on the accuracy of these or any other interpretations, but to point out that a wide variety of such interpretations is possible so long as one has no control over the effects introduced by the observer. A company of recruits with a disguised officer in its midst is simply a different kind of organization than one without the same ingredient; a group of spiritualists which numbers as many as eight observers among its twenty or so members has a wholly different character than one which does not—and so long as we remain unable to account for such differences, we cannot know the meaning of the information we collect.

In one of the most sensible pieces written on the subject, Julius Roth has reminded us that all social research is disguised in one respect or another and that the range of ethical questions which bear on the issue must be visualized as falling on a continuum.[10] Thus, it is all very well for someone to argue that deliberate disguises are improper for sociologists, but it is quite another matter for him to specify what varieties of research activity fall within the range of that principle. Every ethical statement seems to lose its crisp authority the moment it is carried over into marginal

---

[9] Festinger, Riecken, and Schacter, *op. cit.*, pp. 241–42.
[10] Julius A. Roth, "Comments on 'Secret Observation,' " *Social Problems*, 9 (1962): 283–84.

situations where the conditions governing research are not so clearly stipulated. For instance, some of the richest material in the social sciences has
been gathered by sociologists who were true participants in the group
under study but who did not announce to other members that they were
employing this opportunity to collect research data. Sociologists live careers
in which they occasionally become patients, occasionally take jobs as steel
workers or taxi drivers, and frequently find themselves in social settings
where their trained eye begins to look for data even though their presence
in the situation was not engineered for that purpose. It would be absurd,
then, to insist as a point of ethics that sociologists should always introduce
themselves as investigators everywhere they go and should inform every
person who figures in their thinking exactly what their research is all about.

But I do think we can find a place to begin. If disguised observation sits
somewhere on a continuum and is not easily defined, this only suggests that
we will have to seek further for a relevant ethic and recognize that any line
we draw on that continuum will be a little artificial. What I propose, then,
at least as a beginning, is the following: first, that it is unethical for a
sociologist to *deliberately misrepresent* his identity for the purpose of
entering a private domain *to which he is not otherwise elegible;* and second, that it is unethical for a sociologist to *deliberately misrepresent* the
character of the research in which he is engaged. Now these negative sanctions leave us a good deal of leeway—more, perhaps, than we will eventually want. But they have the effect of establishing a stable point of
reference in an otherwise hazy territory, and from such an anchored position as this we can move out into more important questions about invasion of privacy as an ethical issue.

In the meantime, the time has probably come for us to assume a general
posture on the question of disguised participant observation even if we are
not yet ready to state a specific ethic, and a logical first step in this direction
would be to assess how most members of the profession feel about the
matter. I am not suggesting that we poll one another on the merits of
adopting a formal code, but that we take some kind of unofficial reading
to learn what we can about the prevailing climate of opinion in the field.
If we discover that a substantial number of sociologists are uncomfortable
about the practice, then those who continue to employ it will at least know
where they stand in respect to the "collective conscience" of their discipline. And if we discover that only a scattering of sociologists are concerned about the matter, we will at least have the satisfaction of knowing
that the profession—as a profession—has accepted the responsibility of
knowing its own mind.

14. ON THE ETHICS OF
DISGUISED OBSERVATION

Norman K. Denzin
and a reply by Kai T. Erikson

Four papers recently published in this journal on the ethics of social research point to an important and as yet unresolved aspect of the sociologist's work.[1] In brief the questions are: "To whom is the sociologist responsible when he makes his observations?" "Does he have the right to observe persons who are unaware of his presence?" And, "What are the ethical consequences of those disguised observations that may disturb, alter, or cause discomfort to those observed?" Ten years ago Shils argued that sociologists have no right to make observations on persons who have not consented to be observed.[2] In several senses the papers to which I make reference follow Shils' dictum; however, it is the paper by Erikson on the ethical consequences of disguised observations that most directly adheres

Reprinted by permission of the authors and the Society for the Study of Social Problems from *Social Problems*, 15, no. 4 (Spring 1968): 502–506.

[1] *Social Problems*, 14 (Spring 1967). See the papers by Rainwater and Pittman, Erikson, Mills, and Seeley.

[2] Edward A. Shils, "Social Inquiry and the Autonomy of the Individual," in Daniel Lerner, ed., *The Human Meaning of the Social Sciences* (Cleveland: Meridian, 1959), pp. 114–57.

to Shils' position, and it is to this paper that I direct my comments.[3]

Erikson states that observations by the sociologist that either covertly or in some way deliberately disguise the role or intent of the investigator pose significant ethical problems for the sociologist in his relationship to his subjects, his colleagues, his students, and his data. I turn to each of Erikson's arguments and present the counterposition which he submits is either unethical or ethically ambiguous.

First, a comment on my position.[4] I disagree with those who suggest the sociologist has no right to observe those who have not given their consent. I suggest the sociologist has the right to make observations on anyone in any setting to the extent that he does so with scientific intents and purposes in mind. The goal of any science is not willful harm to subjects, but the advancement of knowledge and explanation. Any method that moves us toward that goal, without unnecessary harm to subjects, is justifiable. The only qualification is that the method employed not in any deliberate fashion damage the credibility or reputation of the subject. The sociologist must take pains to maintain the integrity and anonymity of those studied —unless directed otherwise. This may require the deliberate withholding of certain findings from publication entirely, or until those observed have moved into positions where they could be done no harm.[5] My position holds that no areas of observation are in an *a priori* fashion closed to the sociologist, nor are any research methods in an *a priori* fashion defined as unethical. This position is clearly at odds with that of Shils and Erikson.

Erikson's first argument against disguised observation is that it represents an invasion of privacy of those studied. Such an interpretation, of course, assumes the sociologist can define beforehand what is a private and what is a public behavior setting. Cavan's recent findings suggest that any given behavior setting may, depending on the time of day and categories of participants present, be defined as either public or private in nature.[6] The implication is that the "privateness" of a behavior setting becomes an empirical question. To categorically define settings as public or private potentially ignores the perspective of those studied and supplants the sociologist's definitions for those studied. Erikson continues his argument by suggesting that when sociologists gain entry into private settings via disguised roles they potentially cause discomfort to those observed. Because

---

[3] Kai T. Erikson, "A Comment on Disguised Observation in Sociology," *Social Problems*, 14, no. 4 (Spring 1967): 366–73.

[4] See my *The Substance of Sociological Theory and Method: An Interactionist Interpretation* (Chicago: Aldine, tentative title, in process), chap. 14, "The Ethics of Social Research," where this is more fully elaborated.

[5] This draws from Howard S. Becker, "Problems in the Publication of Field Studies," in Arthur J. Vidich, Joseph Bensman, and Maurice R. Stein, eds., *Reflections on Community Studies* (New York: Wiley, 1964), pp. 267–84.

[6] Sheri Cavan, *Liquor License: An Ethnography of Bar Behavior* (Chicago: Aldine, 1966).

the sociologist lacks the means to assess this induced discomfort, he has no right to disguise his intent or role in the research process.

If the research of Goffman is taken seriously, the statement that wearing masks, or disguising one's intents, raises ethical questions and causes discomfort during the research process may be challenged, for the proper question becomes not whether wearing a mask is unethical (since no mask is any more real than any other), but, rather, "Which mask should be worn?"[7] There is no straightforward answer; for we, as sociologists, assume a variety of masks or selves depending on where we find ourselves (e.g., the classroom, the office, the field, etc.). Who is to say which of these are disguised and which are real? My position is that any mask not deliberately donned to injure the subject is acceptable. To assert that an assumed role during the research process is necessarily unethical and harmful is meaningless in this context.

Second, Erikson argues that the sociologist who assumes a disguised role jeopardizes the broader professional community because in the event of exposure he could simultaneously close doors to future research, while tainting the image of his profession. My position is that any research method poses potential threats to fellow colleagues.[8] The community surveyed twice annually for the past ten years can just as easily develop an unfavorable image of sociology and refuse to be studied as can a local Alcoholics Anonymous club studied by a disguised sociologist. Every time the sociologist ventures into the outside world for purposes of research he places the reputation of the profession on the line, and to argue that disguised observations threaten that reputation more than the survey or the experiment ignores the potential impact these methods can and often do have.

Third, Erikson argues that we, as sociologists, owe it to our students not to place them in situations where they might have to assume a disguised research role. The assumption of such roles, Erikson suggests, places moral and ethical problems on the investigator and students should not have this burden placed on them. My position, based on my own and the experiences related by other colleagues, is that this feeling of uncertainty and ethical ambiguity can just as easily arise from the circumstances surrounding the first interview with an irate housewife in a social survey. Certain persons feel more comfortable in the role of disguised observer than in the roles of survey interviewer, known participant observer, or laboratory

---

[7] Erving Goffman, *The Presentation of Self in Everyday Life* (New York: Doubleday, 1959).

[8] Quite obviously, discovery in the disguised role, or the publication of findings from a study in which the research role was not clearly established, can have damaging effects, as the "Springdale" incident indicated. See Arthur J. Vidich and Joseph Bensman, "The Springdale Case: Academic Bureaucrats and Sensitive Townspeople," in Vidich, Bensman, and Stein, *op. cit.*, pp. 313–49, for a review of the circumstances surrounding this incident. This is not the point at issue, however.

observer, for example. Therefore the belief that encounters with subjects when in the role of disguised observer cause more investigator discomfort may be questioned. I suggest there is nothing inherent in the role that produces ethical or personal problems for the investigator. Instead, it is hypothesized that this represents definitions brought into the role and not definitions inherent in the role itself.

Erikson's fourth argument is that data gathered via the disguised method are faulty because an observer lacks the means to assess his disruptive effects on the setting and those observed. I propose that sociologists sensitive to this problem of disruption employ the method of post-observational inquiry, recently adopted by psychologists, during which the investigator asks the subject what he thought the experiment entailed.[9] After completing observations in the disguised role our presence could be made public and those observed could then be questioned concerning our effect on them. Such a procedure would (1) provide empirical data on our perceived disruptive effect, thereby allowing an assessment of this effect, and (2) allow us to measure empirically the amount of discomfort or harm our disguised presence created. Further, the investigator might make greater use of his day-to-day field notes to measure his own perceived impact.[10] Every time the sociologist asks a question of a subject, he potentially alters behavior and jeopardizes the quality of subsequent data. It seems unreasonable to assume that public research methods (e.g., surveys) do not also disrupt the stream of events under analysis. To argue that disguised roles cause more disruption seems ill-founded and, at the very least, is an empirical question.

Erikson concludes by noting that sociologists never reveal everything when they enter the field. I suggest we not only never reveal everything, but frequently this is not possible because we ourselves are not fully aware of our actual intentions and purposes (e.g., long-term field studies).

Summarizing his position, Erikson offers two ethical dictates: (1) it is unethical to deliberately misrepresent our identity to gain entry into private domains otherwise denied us; and (2) it is unethical to misrepresent the character of our research deliberately.

My reactions are perhaps in the minority among contemporary sociologists, but they indicate what I feel is a necessary uneasiness concerning the argument that sociologists are unethical when they investigate under disguise or without permission. To accept this position has the potential of making sociology a profession that studies only volunteer subjects. I suggest

---

[9] See Martin T. Orne, "On The Social Psychology of the Psychological Experiment: With Particular Reference to Demand Characteristics and Their Implications," in Carl W. Backman and Paul F. Secord, eds., *Problems in Social Psychology* (New York: McGraw-Hill, 1966), pp. 14–21.

[10] Benjamin D. Paul, "Interview Techniques and Field Relationships," in A. L. Kroeber, ed., *Anthropology Today* (Chicago: University of Chicago Press, 1953), pp. 430–541, presents strategies for this use of field notes.

that such an argument misrepresents the very nature of the research process because sociologists have seldom stood above subjects and decided whom they had the right to study and whom they were obligated not to study. Instead, we have always established our domain during the process of research, largely on the basis of our own personal, moral, and ethical standards. In retrospect this can be seen to be so given the fact that such categories of persons as housewives, homosexuals, mental patients, prostitutes, and so on are now viewed as acceptable and legitimate persons for observation.

To conclude, I suggest that, in addition to these ethical questions, sociologists might also concern themselves with the fact that at this point in their scientific career they lack the automatic moral-legal license and mandate to gain entry into any research setting; nor do they have the power to withhold information from civil-legal authorities after their data have been obtained.[11] As Project Camelot recently demonstrated, sociology (as a profession and science) has little power in the eyes of the public and broader civil-legal order. To cast ourselves in a position which sanctions research only on what persons give us permission to study continues and makes more manifest an uncomfortable public status. Certainly this need not be the case, as the current examples of psychiatry, medicine, the clergy, and the law indicate.

That my position involves ethical issues of the highest order cannot be denied, for I have placed the burden of ethical decision on the personal-scientific conscience of the individual investigator.[12] My value position should be clear, for I feel sociologists who have assumed those research roles and strategies Erikson calls unethical have contributed more substantive knowledge to such areas as small-group research than have those who have assumed more open roles. But again this is a matter of individual, as well as collective, scientific conscience and standards. The entry into any scientific enterprise potentially threatens someone's values —be it other sociologists or members of some society. We must always ask ourselves, "Whose side are we on?"[13] Unfortunately, I feel Erikson's position removes from the hands of the sociologist the right to make this decision. But perhaps, rather than engaging in polemics and debate, we might as a profession open these matters up to public discussion and empirical inquiry.[14]

NORMAN K. DENZIN

---

[11] Ned Polsky also points to this issue in his *Hustlers, Beats, and Others* (Chicago: Aldine, 1967), pp. 117–49.

[12] This is also Becker's conclusion. See Becker, *op. cit.*

[13] Howard S. Becker, "Whose Side Are We On?," *Social Problems*, 14 (Winter 1967): 239–48.

[14] I am currently engaged in a series of studies with Rita James Simon at the University of Illinois which will provide empirical data for a number of issues that to this point can only be taken at face value, or be resolved by personal choice.

An issue not treated in this note is the efficacy and ethicality of unobtrusive measures of observation in sociology. My position would sanction their use but, as I interpret

A REPLY TO DENZIN

I have been asked to make my remarks as brief as possible in the interests of preserving space, so I will respond to what I regard the more important of Professor Denzin's arguments in essentially the order that he presented them. Professor Denzin is certainly correct that his position is radically at odds with my own. He contends that any research method is justified so long as it is designed to advance scientific knowledge and does not willfully harm human subjects. This principle, I take it, would admit to the roster of legitimate research techniques not only such practices as disguised observation, but the use of wiretapping and eavesdropping devices of one sort or another, and all the rest of the contrivances that come from the new technology of espionage. I suspect that most sociologists—perhaps even Professor Denzin—would prefer to draw a line somewhere short of this. If so, the main point at issue here is not whether sociologists should respect some limits in their search for data, but whether the deliberate use of masks falls inside or outside that line.

My objections to disguised observation are based on a broader set of considerations than are mentioned in Denzin's review. I feel that sociologists should not invade the privacy of other persons, no matter how genial their intentions or how impressive their scientific credentials, because the practice is damaging both to the climate of a free society and to the integrity of the profession that permits it. Now this is largely a personal reflection and I cannot see much point in arguing about it. But even if I agreed with Denzin that the case should rest with the subjects themselves, I would still have serious reservations about disguised observation. This is because I do not think that Denzin or I or anyone else really *knows* when we are harming other people; and, so long as this continues to be the case, it seems to me that we have no right to let others take the risks for projects that happen to mean something to us without first obtaining their informed consent. I am not at all sure that I know what "informed consent" is, but it is evident that disguised observation does not fit under the heading.

I made four general points in my original article and Professor Denzin has discussed them in order. Regarding the first, I agree that it is sometimes difficult to distinguish between "private" and "public" settings in any objective fashion, but I propose the following rule of thumb: Whenever an investigator goes to all the trouble of disguising his own identity and introducing himself as someone he knows he is not in order to enter a social sphere to which he is not otherwise eligible, then it is fair to infer (a) that *he,* at least, defines that sphere as private, and (b) that he expects others in that situation to define it similarly. Moreover, I think it is simply not true that "no mask is any more real than any other," and in this asser-

---

Erikson, he would not. See Eugene J. Webb *et al., Unobtrusive Measures: Nonreactive Research in the Social Sciences* (Chicago: Rand McNally, 1966), where a catalogue of these measures is presented.

tion I would claim to be a student of Goffman's too. Every man plays many parts, to be sure; but every sane and moral man knows that certain roles in the repertory of his culture are proper for him to play while others are not, and it seems to me that we are completely forgetting what we know about the nature of human personality and the development of social selves if we view the matter as flatly as Denzin suggests. It is one thing for him and me to shift social gears as we move in a reasonably defined orbit from the office to the classroom and out into the field, but it is quite another thing for us to emulate those of our colleagues who join a group of alcoholics dressed in clothes picked out of a garbage can or who impersonate enlisted men while receiving the pay and privileges of officers. The elaborate disguises that most employers of the method have devised in order to "pose" (their word) as someone they are not should be testimony enough to the fact that they are aware of the difference; and, if this is not persuasive, we need only consider what would happen if an unlicensed stranger were to appear in a professional gathering and present himself as an instructor of sociology. We might denounce it as a fraud, diagnose it as a delusion, or pass it off as a prank, but few of us would experience any difficulty determining whether the mask was real or not.

As for the second point, Professor Denzin offers a compelling argument and I will yield. It is of course true that other forms of sociological research have a potential for closing doors to future investigation. I happen to feel that the risks here are considerably greater, but Denzin is correct to suppose that this estimate is based as much on conviction as it is on information.

As for the third point, it may be that Denzin has me there, too. I have no particularly good reasons to insist that students are more compromised while engaged in undercover observation than they are, say, when confronting irate housewives during a door-to-door survey. Granting this, I am left the choice either of arguing that students should be protected from this latter practice as well, or of withdrawing as gracefully as possible. I think a strong case might be made for the first of these options, but instead I will retreat to the second—noting only that my original intention was to point out the incongruities one sees in the arguments of sociologists who discuss the moral ambiguities of disguised observation and then send students out to do the work.

The fourth point is in many ways the critical one, and here I suspect that Professor Denzin has confused the kind of undercover work I was discussing in my paper with other forms of small-group research. He contends that we could measure the effect that disguised observation has on subjects by following up the attempt with such methods as post-observational inquiry and the like. Now I think it is reasonable to assume that researchers wear masks primarily when they cannot show their faces, and I cannot imagine why people who will not respond to a more open kind of investigation in the first instance should submit to a few cheerful rounds of interviewing in the second. People who have seen their trust violated, their privacy invaded, their personal worlds exposed, are not likely to be the most cooperative or reliable informants—unless, of course, Denzin is proposing that a second wave of observers should dress in costumes and follow the first, in which case all the objections I raised earlier are simply doubled. I agree that some empirical evidence would be valuable here: my problem is that no one to date has come up with any and I doubt very much that anyone ever will. The conditions that prompt investigators to wear disguises are almost always conditions that discourage any reasonable hope of measuring the disruptive influence of the observer.

The fact that the position I recommend limits our field of observation to volunteers is, I agree, something of an inconvenience; but any ethical stance is a limitation on one's freedom of movement and I cannot see that this is a reasonable objection. From a purely scientific point of view, after all, it is also an inconvenience that physicians cannot experiment on the persons of patients. The presumption in our society has always been that some things are more important than the needs of researchers.

In this connection, Denzin is concerned that sociologists do not enjoy the license to "gain entry into any research setting" and proposes that this privilege be extended to us. What he fails to appreciate is that none of the professions he lists enjoy this license *when they are engaged in research,* but only when they are serving the interests of clients. If we were to find ourselves dealing only with volunteers, we would certainly be limiting our terrain; but we would then be in exactly the same position as those physicians and lawyers whose status Professor Denzin is so anxious for us to share. The only investigators I can think of who enjoy privileges when engaged in the business of gathering information for their own professional purposes are policemen and espionage agents, and I doubt very much that any of us would like to operate with the general level of trust and respect that they command.

In short, my main disagreement with Professor Denzin is his assumption —stated implicitly, at least—that what is good for sociology is inherently ethical. His "value position," as he informs us near the end of his remarks, is that researchers "who have assumed those research roles and strategies . . . have contributed more substantive knowledge . . . than have those who assumed more open roles." I do not think that this is true by any means, but, even if it were, it would not strike me as the firmest moral ground on which to build a professional ethic. Surely the case should be decided on other merits.

I do not know whether Denzin is in the minority or not, as he seems to feel; but he has stated his case with refreshing candor and I admire his willingness to join the discussion in so straightforward a fashion.

Kai T. Erikson

Differential Association and Crime: Theory and Research

Primarily in response to the contention that criminal behavior was biologically or psychologically determined, Edwin H. Sutherland formulated a theory of criminality that since has attained major stature among American sociologists. First published in 1939, the theory continues to generate frequent and vigorous debate, and has stimulated more empirical research in criminology than any competing theory. The magnitude of its impact, moreover, is signified by the variety of ways it has been used to explain noncriminal social behavior.

Three decades of test, modification, and assessment, however, have failed to produce a conclusive verification of Sutherland's theory. Of the many reasons for this, the most serious appears to be the difficulty experienced in operationalizing—making testable—the propositions comprising the theory. Some problems arise because Sutherland's writings are inexplicit; others originate when an attempt is made to explain variations in the criminality of individuals, as contrasted with explaining aggregate data on crime.

Sutherland began his theory by building upon the accepted proposition that behavior, including some that qualifies as criminal, is learned through interpersonal relations. While criminologists during the early decades of the twentieth century may have concentrated excessively upon socially "disorganized" areas of the city, or upon one's abnormal, pathological associates, suspicion arose in many quarters that criminality is somehow related to the *quality* of interpersonal patterns. Thus, it was not the culturally disorganized urban area as such that generated crime, or the undesirable companions, but the *symbolic* influence these had upon the careers of persons involved. According to this view, development of criminal behavior is normatively prescribed by a subculture whose ideological content is preponderantly unfavorable to law compliance. Put differently, a disposition to criminality is furnished through interpersonal communication with persons whose normative standards are in opposition to those of the general community.

The most striking feature is the extent to which Sutherland's theory departed from traditional explanations of crime based upon emotional disorder, psychopathology, or some inherent physiological characteristic of the offender. By emphasizing crime as *learned* behavior, he was able to call attention to such parameters as the sources of learned content, the relative effectiveness of various learning mechanisms, and the ideological transformations necessary to sustain a criminal identity. Learning of criminal conduct, then, involves such symbolic content of interpersonal communications as values, rationalizations, norms, and attitudes.

Some investigators, however, have pointed out that deviants need not learn an entirely different subcultural content. Alternatively, they may feel committed to a dominant, perhaps middle-class normative system, yet manage to justify their departure from these behavioral expectations by a process of rationalization.[1] In the case of delinquency, specific techniques are developed which effectively neutralize normative violation. Thus the delinquent remains committed to norms of the larger society, but *qualifies* them so that deviation is acceptable. Among the more frequent opted mechanisms is denial that a harm has been done (for example, automobile theft is defined as "borrowing" a car) and denial of the victim (because homosexuals are "fags" and shopkeepers are "crooked," injury to them is viewed as rightful punishment). The essential point here is that these techniques involve rationalizations important for justifying and supporting definitions unfavorable to law compliance. The conflicts that techniques of neutralization generate are cogently pointed out by Sykes and Matza: *"Delinquency is based upon what is essentially an unrecognized extension of defenses to crime, in the form of justifications for delinquency that are seen as valid by the delinquent, but not by the legal system, or society at large."*[2]

A major reinterpretation of Sutherland's theory of differential association was suggested by Glaser under the rubric "differential identification." Sutherland had stated that criminal behavior is learned through interaction and participation in groups composed of significant role models. Glaser took ex-

---

[1] Gresham M. Sykes and David Matza, "Techniques of Neutralization: A Theory of Delinquency," *American Sociological Review*, 22 (December 1957): 664–70.

[2] *Ibid.*, p. 666 (emphasis in the original).

ception to the necessity for participation, arguing that one's criminality is a voluntaristic process in which past identifications as well as present circumstances determine selection of persons with whom one will identify, and from whose perspective criminal behavior seems acceptable. Although many of the same problems in testing differential association are duplicated here, some preliminary evidence supports the notion that learning of criminal patterns requires identification and role-playing with criminalistic models.

Most prominent theories of criminal behavior regularly attract proponents and empirical testers, as well as some who would oppose the theory on logical grounds, or question its explanatory power. By any measure, differential association has commanded an impressive amount of thinking and investigation. The cumulative effects of research stimulated by the differential association model during the last decade offer serious challenge to George Vold's deprecating remarks: "The differential association theory has provided an exciting episode in criminological thinking. Through a fortunate combination of words and illustrations in its first formulation, it seemed to offer much more than it has been able to deliver."[3]

The first selection in this section, Glaser's "Differential Association: Retrospect and Prospect," is a succinct statement of Sutherland's theory, covers many of the most frequent criticisms and shortcomings, and indicates what is needed to test its explanatory power.

Frank E. Hartung's paper extends the differential-association principle by showing how the white-collar thief (embezzler) develops and uses a vocabulary of motives in much the same way that delinquents employ techniques of neutralization.

In an examination of behavior to which the label "crime" is applied, but which apparently is not learned in the manner predicted by the differential-association theory, Cressey's selection focuses upon the degree to which compulsive crimes are exceptions to the theory.

Finally, in answer to critics (Weinberg, Caldwell, and Cressey, among others) who felt that psychological processes were given short shrift in the differential-association theory, Robert L. Burgess and Ronald L. Akers propose a modification incorporating the learning-theory principles of operant and respondent conditioning. By making this theoretical revision, they specify more precisely how individuals become deviant, and what sustains both deviant behavior and the pattern of reinforcement.

Further reading in differential-association theory and research is provided in the following sources:

1. *The Origin and Development of Differential-Association Theory*
Cressey, Donald R. "An Introduction to the Theory of Differential Association," *De-*

---

[3] George Vold, *Theoretical Criminology* (New York: Oxford University Press, 1958), p. 198.

linquency, Crime, and Differential Association (The Hague: Martinus Nijhoff, 1964), chaps. 1–4, pp. 3–78.

Sutherland, Edwin H. "Development of the Theory," in *The Sutherland Papers*, ed. Albert K. Cohen, Alfred R. Lindesmith, and Karl F. Schuessler (Bloomington: Indiana University Press, 1956), pp. 13–29.

Vold, George. "Crime as Normal Learned Behavior," *Theoretical Criminology* (New York: Oxford University Press, 1958), pp. 183–202.

2. *Suggested Modifications of the Differential-Association Model*

Cloward, Richard A., and Ohlin, Lloyd E. *Delinquency and Opportunity: A Theory of Delinquent Gangs* (New York: Free Press, Macmillan, 1960), chap. 6, "Illegitimate Means and Delinquent Subcultures."

De Fleur, Melvin L., and Quinney, Richard. "A Reformulation of Sutherland's Differential Association Theory and a Strategy for Empirical Verification," *Journal of Research in Crime and Delinquency* 3 (January 1966): 1–22.

Glaser, Daniel. "Criminological Theories and Behavioral Images," *American Journal of Sociology* 61 (March 1956): 433–44.

Glueck, Sheldon. "Theory and Fact in Criminology," *British Journal of Delinquency* 7 (October 1956): 92–109.

Jeffery, C. R. "Criminal Behavior and Learning Theory," *Journal of Criminal Law, Criminology, and Police Science* 56 (September 1965): 294–300.

Liska, Allen E. "Interpreting the Causal Structure of Differential Association Theory," *Social Problems* 16 (Spring 1969): 485–92.

3. *Differential Association: Its Empirical Test and Application*

Akers, Ronald L.; Burgess, Robert L.; and Johnson, Weldon T. "Opiate Use, Addiction, and Relapse," *Social Problems* 15 (Spring 1968): 459–69.

Cressey, Donald R. "Changing Criminals: The Application of the Theory of Differential Association," *American Journal of Sociology* 61 (September 1955): 116–20.

Glaser, Barney G. " 'Differential Association' and the Institutional Motivation of Scientists," *Administrative Science Quarterly* 10 (June 1965): 82–97.

Matthews, Victor. "Differential Identification: An Empirical Note," *Social Problems* 15 (Winter 1968): 376–83.

Reiss, Albert J., Jr., and Rhodes, Lewis. "An Empirical Test of Differential Association Theory," *Journal of Research in Crime and Delinquency* 1 (January 1964): 5–18.

Short, James F., Jr. "Differential Association as a Hypothesis: Problems of Empirical Testing," *Social Problems* 8 (Summer 1960): 14–25. [This issue is devoted largely to a consideration of differential association theory and research.]

Stratton, John R. "Differential Identification and Attitudes Toward the Law," *Social Forces* 46 (December 1967): 256–62.

Volkman, Rita, and Cressey, Donald R. "Differential Association and the Rehabilitation of Drug Addicts," *American Journal of Sociology* 69 (September 1963): 129–42.

15. DIFFERENTIAL ASSOCIATION: RETROSPECT AND PROSPECT

Daniel Glaser

EVOLUTION OF THE THEORY

The term "criminology" is reported to have been coined by the popular press in the late nineteenth century as an abbreviation for "criminal anthropology" (9). Its use in much of Europe still connotes primarily the physical anthropological study of criminals. A latent function of academic sociology in America appears to have been to serve as a repository for left-over areas of societal or cultural study not clearly claimed by social science departments established before sociology. Accordingly, criminology, along with demography and the study of inventions, acquired an academic resting place in sociology which is rather unique to the United States. In Europe, criminology still is most commonly a specialty of law or medicine faculties; in the United States it has turned up in departments other than sociology at only a few institutions.

With the proliferation and expansion of sociology departments in American universities in the early twentieth century, and with the public in-

Reprinted by permission of the author and the publisher from Daniel Glaser, "The Differential-Association Theory of Crime," in *Human Behavior and Social Processes*, ed. Arnold M. Rose (Boston: Houghton Mifflin, 1962), pp. 425–42.

creasingly demanding attention to "the crime problem" after World War I, the 1920's and 1930's saw a rapid increase in the number of American sociologists who became specialists in criminology. Their problem was to "explain" crime, and in this connection, they first had to cope with the older European literature in criminology, of strong biological orientation, which was extensively republished in the United States during the second decade of the twentieth century. Criminology textbooks and courses by American sociologists during the period between the two world wars, and some even today, devote more time to summarizing and attacking the nonsociological literature on crime than to presenting substantive sociological propositions.

During the early twentieth century, many nonsociologists modified earlier biological explanations of crime. In Italy, Marxist influence led Ferri and others to try to blend economic and biological explanations (7). In France, drawing from experience as a magistrate and from his postulated "laws of imitation," Gabriel Tarde interpreted crime as a product of human association, reaching conclusions strikingly similar to much sociological writing several decades later (25). The psychiatrist Healy in the United States (15) and the psychologist Burt (1) in Britain each examined hundreds of delinquents, listing as "causes of delinquency" any presumed deviation from normalcy which they encountered, including deviations in health, intelligence, family conditions, education, and numerous other variables.

The first major contribution by American sociologists to empirical knowledge on crime was made at the University of Chicago by a series of studies providing systematic evidence that young criminals are highly associated with each other. Thrasher reported the actual or alleged names and locations of 1,313 gangs among juvenile delinquents in Chicago, and showed the functions these gangs served in delinquency (26). Shaw and McKay presented statistics, maps, and case studies which showed, among other things, that delinquency was concentrated in a limited portion of the city, that about 90 percent of delinquents committed their offenses in company with other delinquents, and that their ties with other offenders and other sources of social support for criminal attitudes became more extensive the more they participated in crime (21).

In the first textbooks on criminology written by sociologists, which appeared in the 1920's, and in most such works still today, the basic formulation of theory is essentially the same as that of most nonsociologist writers, including early writers like Ferri, Healy, and Burt, whom we have cited. This is the so-called "multicausal" or "multiple factor" theory of crime. Its essence is that crime is a consequence of many causes, of which the most often cited include mental deficiency, economic distress, broken homes, association with criminals, and personality defects. The principal polemics of these theorists are against anyone who, they charge, overemphasizes a single factor.

Differences between sociologists and other multiple-factor theorists have not been great with respect to the variety of causes recognized. Rather, differences have arisen from the relatively high weight which sociologists give to association with criminals and enculturation in criminal sub-cultures, and their lesser emphasis on alternative "causes." However, most presumed correlates of crime cited by others are included in the socio-logical multi-factor catalogues.

In this setting, when as a young sociologist at the University of Illinois Edwin H. Sutherland was asked to teach criminology and to prepare a text in that field, he readily assimilated multi-causal theory. As he put it: "I took pride in my broadmindedness in including all kinds of factors and in not being an extremist like the geographic determinists, the economic determinists, the biological determinists, or the mental-tester determinists" (2, p. 14). This was apparent in 1924 when his *Criminology* appeared. Fifteen years later, however, after a series of intellectual stimulations at the University of Minnesota (1926–1929), the University of Chicago (1930–1935), and Indiana University thereafter, he says:

> It was my conception that a general theory should take account of all the factual information regarding crime causation. It does this either by organizing the multiple factors in relation to each other or by abstract-ing from them certain common elements [2, p. 18].

He also felt association alone to be inadequate as an explanation for crime since:

> . . . some people who reside in delinquency areas commit crimes, some do not. Any concrete condition is sometimes associated with criminal behavior and sometimes not. Perhaps there is nothing that is so fre-quently associated with criminal behavior as being a male. But it is obvious that maleness does not explain criminal behavior. I reached the general conclusion that a concrete condition cannot be a cause of crime, and that the only way to get a causal explanation of criminal behavior is by abstracting from the varying concrete conditions things which are universally associated with crime [2, p. 19].

The third edition of Sutherland's text, isued in 1939 as *Principles of Criminology*, contained the first publication of his "differential associa-tion" theory. In essence, it asserts: (*a*) the techniques and the "specific direction of motives, drives, rationalizations and attitudes" of criminal behavior are learned in interaction with other persons within intimate personal groups; (*b*) almost always in American society a person encoun-ters a mixture of behavior which defines the legal codes as rules to be observed and behavior favorable to violation of the legal codes, and hence he experiences "culture conflict in relation to the legal codes"; (*c*) the principle of differential association "refers to both criminal and anti-criminal associations and has to do with counteracting forces" affecting one's definition of appropriate behavior; the principle is that "a person becomes delinquent because of an excess of definitions favorable to viola-tion of law over definitions unfavorable to violation of law"; (*d*) the learn-ing of criminal and anti-criminal behavior "involves all of the mechanisms that are involved in any other learning," is an expression "of the same needs and values," and is a function of the "frequency, duration, priority, and intensity" of differential associations with criminal and with anti-criminal behavior (2, pp. 8–10; 24, pp. 77–79).

As Sutherland interpreted his theory, all of the conditions predom-inantly—yet incompletely—correlated with crime, such as poverty, pa-rental neglect, or personal traits, "have a causal relation to criminal be-havior only as they affect the person's associations" (2, p. 25). Strongly influenced by Lindesmith at Indiana to strive to employ Znaniecki's "ana-lytic induction" method of theory formation, Sutherland endeavored to phrase and to rephrase his theory so that it would account for the genesis of every case of crime which he encountered (2, pp. 17–18; 28). He par-ticularly urged sociological study of those offenses commonly interpreted as having a genesis not readily accounted for by differential association, such as kleptomania, pyromania, incest, embezzlement, white-collar crimes, and offenses allegedly committed under the influence of alcohol by persons who do not commit crimes when not under alcohol. If his theory would not account for these offenses, then his method would oblige him to revise his theory, or to divide crimes into categories each of which has a distinct genesis, then limit his theory to the class of crimes the genesis of which it explained. His posthumous papers suggest that he expected the theory to be revised from such research, but that he had not yet encountered what he considered to be adequate evidence for its systematic revision or de-limitation.

THE THEORY'S STRUGGLE FOR EXISTENCE

Sutherland's theory was presented in nine propositions on two pages of his text. Illustration, elaboration, and interpretation of these nine proposi-tions were not systematic in the rest of that volume. In the two-page formu-lation, the nine propositions and the commentary which is provided for each are rather dissimilar in scope. Indeed, it is not clear whether "differ-ential-association theory" refers only to the sixth proposition, on "excess of definitions favorable to criminal behavior" (which he identifies as the "principle" of differential association), to all nine propositions taken col-lectively, or to the entire chapter in which they appear. His students and followers, notably Cressey, refer to the two-page, nine-proposition formula-tion as the theory, and we have taken this view (but have attempted a tighter integration of the theory, mostly in Sutherland's own words, in the four-segment synopsis presented in the preceding section).

Given this deficiency of formulation, and the polemical orientation especially characteristic of the literature of would-be sciences such as criminology, it is understandable that Sutherland's theory came under attack.

Cressey lists several errors of those critics who, he says, "do not always understand what Sutherland was talking about." Most serious, perhaps, is the error of assuming that the theory is concerned only with criminal behavior patterns, neglecting Sutherland's simultaneous reference to *anti-criminal* patterns at almost every point of his theory. This error is understandable, however, since Sutherland applies his theory almost entirely to data on criminals, rather than to data on anti-criminals, ex-criminals, or other noncriminals. Secondly, Sutherland referred to association with patterns of *behavior,* but many of his supporters (including this writer) and most of his opponents frequently express his theory in terms of association with *types of persons,* criminal or anti-criminal. As Cressey points out: "One can learn criminal behavior patterns from persons who are not criminals, and one can learn anti-criminal behavior patterns from . . . professional crooks . . . and gangsters." Another type of error cited by Cressey is the practice of treating differential association as referring only to the learning of techniques for crime, rather than acquiring motivations and rationalizations. Still another type of misrepresentation sets forth the theory as concerned only with the "raw ratio of associations"—their frequency alone—neglecting Sutherland's stress on priority, intensity, and duration of differential association (6).

It was primarily in order to achieve more effective communication of what I conceived as Sutherland's theory that I proposed some years ago a reformulation of the theory as "differential identification," with the basic principle: "A person pursues criminal behavior to the extent that he identifies himself with real or imaginary persons from whose perspective his criminal behavior seems acceptable" (10). Later, it was also suggested that "differential reference" or even "differential learning" might be more adequate than "differential association" to convey in modern social-psychological language Sutherland's ascription of crime to the net effect of social learning, including socially derived motivation (11). Korn and McCorkle seem to be reformulating Sutherland's theory as differential "commitment" to various groups, adding an interesting and testable principle of "intensiveness" and "extensiveness" of commitments, but not basically altering Sutherland's image of the social genesis of crime (16, chap. 14).

A second group of criticisms of Sutherland's theory can be distinguished as those which expect the theory to apply to the explanation of phenomena other than criminal behavior. For example, some writers seem to want the theory to account for the origin of criminal and anti-criminal association. While this is an area of inquiry to which one might reasonably progress in the course of applying differential-association theory, it clearly takes one to types of theory designed for other purposes, such as accounting for concentration of certain conditions in the slums, or for aspects of social stratification. A somewhat different form of unreasonable expectation by critics of differential association is the claim that the theory does not account for personality conditions associated with crime. This is unreasonable in that they have not demonstrated that any specific personality attributes other than criminal orientations and rationalizations, which are accounted for by differential-association theory, are regular antecedents of crime. Thus far investigations have shown that persons involved in crime are quite diverse with respect to noncriminal attributes of personality commonly investigated by personality tests.

A third variety of criticism of Sutherland's theory consists of claims that the theory does not fit certain categories of crime. Some of these claims pose issues as to whether the behavior considered can properly be called "crime," such as "unpremeditated" or "adventitious" offenses, and some juvenile delinquency (like delinquent but noncriminal disobedience to parents). Most other such claims involve unusual offenses, like pyromania, and have never been tested by research. Only two of these claims which the writer has thus far encountered seem to come from extensive research which clearly indicates that differential-association theory does not account for the genesis of the offense. These involve the crimes of trust violation and simple check forgery (4, 17).

A fourth major type of criticism of differential association is the observation that criminal behavior obviously occurs in part as a function of differential opportunities to commit criminal or noncriminal acts as alternative means to a given end. While there are arguments for and against the proposition that over any appreciable period of time almost everyone has opportunities to commit crime, it certainly is not true that everyone always has access to noncriminal means to attain his ends. There is increasing evidence that large segments of the population shift to economically oriented crime primarily when opportunities for legitimate employment diminish (13). Sutherland observed that differential association accounts for differences in recourse to crime in a given state of economic distress, but it might be usefully complemented by a theory taking into account the inverse relationship between some crime and opportunities for noncriminal achievement of the goals of crime.

TESTABILITY

The final type of criticism to be considered is that which contends that differential-association theory cannot be tested. This charge, if valid, would render the theory unacceptable, since it is a canon of science that any theory must be capable of being subjected to empirical tests which conceivably could prove it false (20). In this connection, Glueck inquires: "Has anybody actually counted the number of definitions favorable to violation of law and definitions unfavorable to violation of law, and demonstrated that in the pre-delinquency experience of the vast majority of delinquents and criminals, the former exceeds the latter?" (14). While the answer to this would at first appear to be negative, it should be noted that an abstract theory is not tested directly by empirical observation; it is validated or invalidated by tests of operational hypotheses deduced from the abstract theory. Our problem is to consider whether differential-association theory generates testable hypotheses.

Glueck's reference to definitions favorable or unfavorable to violation of law comes from Sutherland's sixth proposition, called by Sutherland "the principle of differential association." However, seen as a whole, the nine propositions of his theory specify that several aspects of orientation to criminal and anti-criminal behavior (technique, rationalizations, etc.) are learned as a function of several aspects of association (priority, intensity, intimacy, etc.), and only in this context does the "principle of differential association" become meaningful. In this context the "definitions" phraseology seems to be a means of making a summary reference to the net effect of social learning processes, that is, all that is learned which is relevant to one's consideration of violation or nonviolation of the legal codes.

It follows from the foregoing interpretation that one way to test Sutherland's theory without actually counting what Glueck calls the "number" of definitions would be to measure indices of the aspects of association specified in the theory, and to measure their correlation with observable criminal behavior, assuming the definitions to be an intervening variable. Sutherland's "definitions" term seems to come from W. I. Thomas' "definition of the situation," and in today's behavioral science idiom he might have used the term "orientations." At any rate, in the light of the foregoing analysis, the theory may be considered testable if operational indices of association and of criminal behavior can be deduced. The "definitions" concept then becomes an intervening variable, conceptualized but not directly indicated, in this respect resembling the concept "genes" in genetic theory and the concept "atom" in chemical theory, despite the vast differences between these theories.

The phrase "epistemic correlation" has been employed to designate the extent to which a particular type of observation is indicative of an abstractly conceived condition (19, chap. 7). Since Sutherland asserts that most people, at least in America, experience both criminal and anti-criminal associations, and several aspects of each are relevant (priority, intensity, etc.), many indices of association are available. Indeed, indices of opposite types of association may be observed in any subject. It would follow that there will be only an imperfect epistemic correlation between any single type of relevant observation and the net association of subjects with criminal and anti-criminal behavior.

Some tests of differential association are diagrammed in Table 1. These happen to be tests in which the hypotheses were validated. However, three major sources of limitation in testability, rather than invalidity of differential-association theory, could account for findings of no significant correlation between the observations (set in roman type) connected by arrows:

TABLE 1

FOUR EMPIRICAL TESTS OF DIFFERENTIAL ASSOCIATION THEORY

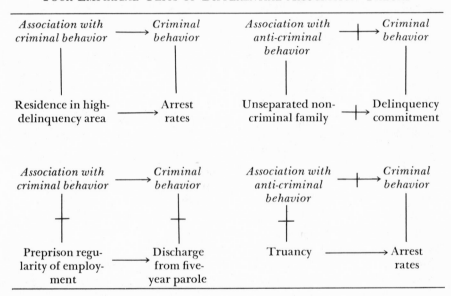

Key:
    Concepts: italicized phrases
    Observations (operationally defined indices): roman phrases
    Positive epistemic correlations: plain vertical lines
    Negative epistemic correlations: vertical lines with short cross-line
    Positive theoretical relationships: plain arrows connecting concepts
    Negative theoretical relationships: cross-lined arrows connecting concepts
    Hypothesis of positive correlation: plain arrows connecting observations
    Hypothesis of negative correlation: cross-lined arrows connecting observations
Note that there must be an even number of negative correlations or negative theoretical relationships. (This system of diagramming was learned by the author at the American Sociological Society meetings in Detroit in 1956 from Professor Robert Hamblin, now of Washington University in St. Louis.)

1. Epistemic correlations between the total associations with which differential-association theory is concerned and any available index of these associations necessarily are limited because each index reflects only a segment of an individual's total associations (school, family, neighborhood, and so on).

2. Each index for those segments can be assumed to signify only the

relative extent of criminal or anti-criminal association there; residence in high-delinquency areas, for example, can be assumed to signify more exposure to pro-criminal behavior than residence in low-delinquency areas in most cases, but not necessarily a predominant influence of criminal over anti-criminal influences.

3. Since known criminal behavior is relatively infrequent in the general population, its relationship to antecedents is not likely to be manifested with statistical significance unless samples are extremely large, or are especially selected so that the group in which criminal behavior is manifest approaches 50 percent of the sample. The lower the epistemic correlation, the more this sampling requirement of high "antecedent probability" of the criterion event (criminal behavior) becomes necessary for evidence of any relationship (18). That is why criminological causation research is most fruitful in analysis of recidivism for known delinquent or criminal populations (where it occurs in about half of the cases), or in comparison of a matched delinquent or criminal group with a nondelinquent or noncriminal control group.

Sutherland's theory deals with the net influence of criminal and anti-criminal association, while the tests illustrated in Table 1 involve only one of these types of association. However, there is much evidence that many indices of association with criminal behavior are highly correlated with one another (criminal records, truancy, residence in high-delinquency area, and the like), that many indices of association with anti-criminal behavior are also highly intercorrelated (regularity of work record, cohesiveness of family, and so on), and that there is an inverse relationship between these two groups of indices. That is why, in Table 1, the same indices can be designated as having a positive epistemic correlation with association with criminal behavior or a negative correlation with association with anti-criminal behavior.

A numerical score which might be assumed to be correlated with the net ratio of definitions favorable and unfavorable to crime acquired through association conceivably could be procured by multiple-correlation analysis. This is the method employed in criminological prediction research, using more or less sophisticated systems of deriving weights. (The discriminant-function method, of course, involves a much more rational analysis than the so-called Burgess or Glueck weighting systems.)

Unfortunately, integrated tests are not available in criminological prediction literature because studies thus far have always mixed predictors which can be deduced to be indices of association with criminal or anti-criminal behavior and predictors which cannot readily be deduced as such indices. In a recent survey of this literature, however, I have shown that the group of predictors having the highest association with an index of criminal behavior (parole violation or delinquency) in each study includes a markedly higher proportion of predictors deducible from differential-association theory than the group of predictors having the lowest association with the index of criminal behavior (12). The most effective predictors deducible from the theory and positively related to later violation or delinquency are indices of the extent of prior criminal record, truancy, and alienation from parents; those with highest negative relationships are regularity of prior work record, age at first arrest, and age at first leaving home. Among the poorest predictors have been measures of physical strength, number of siblings, dominant parent, and psychological test scores.

Two major exceptions to support of differential-association theory in criminological prediction research are that the most effective predictors also include type of prior offense and immediate job expectation. At least one of the types of prior offense highly associated with recidivism, forgery, cannot reasonably be inferred to be more of an index of prior association with criminal behavior than the less recidivistic type of offense (17). Job expectation may be an index of prior regularity of work record, but insofar as it is a function of involuntary unemployment due to fluctuations in the business cycle, it also reflects differential opportunity somewhat independent of prior associations.

Much more direct indices of differential association have been employed by Short, who procured from delinquents and nondelinquents responses to a series of questions on the delinquency of their first friends, most often seen friends, longest known friends, and best friends. These were presumed indicative, respectively, of priority, frequency, duration, and intensity of delinquent association. The results generally supported Sutherland's theory, particularly for boys rather than girls, for older rather than younger boys, for institutionalized rather than noninstitutionalized delinquents, and especially with respect to the most intense—"best friend"—associations (22). Later, Short asked delinquents and nondelinquents questions on both the delinquency and the anti-criminality of their best friends. This yielded even more marked and consistent support for differential-association theory (23).

Wheeler has validated differential-association theory with a rather unique index of what might be called definitions favorable to conformity to conventional moral codes. He procured reformatory staff and inmate opinions on the most proper conduct of several alternatives in a series of hypothetical prison situations in which an actor was faced with a complex moral choice. Inmates most deviant from staff in their choices were judged lowest in conformity. These were the inmates with earliest and most frequent arrests, which was taken as an index of priority and frequency of contact with criminal patterns. An unanticipated finding was a low negative relationship between number of correctional institution commitments (taken as an index of intensity of contact with criminal patterns) and conformity to staff moral norms. Wheeler interprets this as due to the high number of alcoholic forgers in his sample who were both highly conforming in moral choices and frequently committed to institutions (27).

A misperception of the function of theory may develop if we accept without qualification Short's conclusion that operationalization of Sutherland's variables, at which Short has brilliantly led the way, enhances knowledge if it leads to "transformation of the theory by specification" (23). As Philipp Frank points out with repeated illustrations from the history of science, a major function of abstract theory is to serve as a code for summarizing myriad detailed observations; these are the observations which validate operational hypotheses deduced from the theory. The generalizations of theory which are validated become accepted as the principles of a science. These principles lose their utility for the analysis of new types of data if they lose their generality.

The foregoing does not mean that theory should not be revised to fit unanticipated findings, but the canon of parsimony in science creates pressure for drastic reconceptualization wherever a theory must become too highly qualified and cumbersome in order to account for observations. As Frank says: "Every acceptance of a debatable theory is due to a compromise between . . . agreement with facts and efficiency as a code" (8, p. 341). A theory is most useful if a diversity of useful hypotheses can readily be deduced from it (that is, if it can be operationalized in many ways for analysis of many problem situations). A theory's validity is never known conclusively or finally, although increased confidence may be inspired if there is a diversity as well as a high volume of validating test results.

SURVIVAL OF THE FITTEST THEORY

Commenting on the utility of the phlogiston theory of oxidation for 150 years after evidence contradicting it was known, but before the significance of oxygen was recognized, James B. Conant writes:

> Does it argue for the stupidity of the experimental philosophers of that day? Not at all; it merely demonstrates that in complex affairs of science one is concerned with trying to account for a variety of facts and with welding them into a conceptual scheme; one fact is by itself not sufficient to wreck the scheme. A conceptual scheme is never discarded because of a few stubborn facts with which it cannot be reconciled; a conceptual scheme is either modified or replaced by a better one, never abandoned with nothing left to take its place [3, p. 173].

In the light of the criticisms discussed in the preceding section, let us consider whether differential-association theory should be replaced by an alternative theory already available, or whether a modification of differential-association theory can be suggested to make it more adequately meet the effective criticisms which it has encountered.

The most prevalent theory in American criminology textbooks is multiple causation, which asserts that crime is a function of numerous variables, but does not indicate their interrelationship. Unless a testable proposition is set forth to rank, weight, or otherwise interrelate multiple variables, the proposition that crime is a function of many variables does not provide a basis for deducing hypotheses which observation could prove false. One can always subdivide or find a correlate of any variable which might be proposed as a basis for an alternative theory. This makes multicausal theory untestable, and for this reason, it cannot be considered a scientific conclusion.

The other leading competitor of differential-association theory in criminological literature is the psychoanalytic view of crime as a breakdown of controls over innate impulses, or other breakdown or absence-of-control theories analogous to the psychoanalytic model. While this may be useful for encompassing certain behavior called "delinquency" in some literature, such as temper tantrums, it fails to account for the social sources of learning in what the courts more commonly call delinquency and crime (see 12 for fuller discussion).

By comparison with its principal competitors, then, differential association stands fairly secure.

Earlier, this paper indicated some deficiencies of Sutherland's formulation in communicating what his supporters have interpreted as his meaning. Several modes of reformulating Sutherland's theory were noted. It also was reported that two types of criticism of differential-association theory have been supported by research. The first is that the theory does not account for most cases of at least two types of offense, trust violation and forgery. The second is that the theory does not take adequately into account the extent to which the genesis of crime is a function of fluctuations in opportunity for noncriminal achievement of the goals of crime.

The peculiar association between much persistent lone forgery and chronic alcoholism makes more adequate theory for that type of forgery highly dependent on development of a more satisfactory theory of the etiology of chronic alcoholism. While there may be other felonies in addition to forgery and trust violation which are peculiarly independent of a social learning process, Cressey has pointed out the questionable basis for assuming this independence in most so-called compulsive crimes (5). Our analysis leaves the conclusion that differential association still is the most satisfactory theory for interpreting the great bulk of major crimes, particularly larceny, burglary, and robbery, which comprise 90 percent of felonies tabulated in the FBI's *Uniform Crime Reports*.

For guidance in predicting the criminality of the majority of currently convicted offenders, who show appreciable evidence of both criminal and anti-criminal orientations, I have suggested that a "differential anticipation" theory of criminality might be developed to conceptualize simultaneously both the principles of differential-association theory and the influence of fluctuations in noncriminal opportunities (12). Since this type of prediction problem continually confronts judicial and correctional officials, such a frame of reference may be eminently practical. It is hoped that the elaboration and testing of such a formulation can be achieved in the currently burgeoning research in federal, state, and local judicial and correctional systems. Every theory such as differential association, which evolved from efforts to encompass conceptually an accumulation of empirical data, risks being but a step in the further evolution of theory, as long as procurement of new data continues.

REFERENCES

1. BURT, CYRIL. *The Young Delinquent* (London: University of London, 1925).
2. COHEN, ALBERT; LINDESMITH, ALFRED; and SCHUESSLER, KARL, eds. *The Sutherland Papers* (Bloomington: Indiana University Press, 1956).
3. CONANT, JAMES B. *Science and Common Sense* (New Haven: Yale University Press, 1951).
4. CRESSEY, DONALD R. "Application and Verification of the Differential Association Theory," *Journal of Criminal Law and Criminology* 43 (May–June 1952): 43–52.
5. ———. "Differential Association and Compulsive Crimes," *Journal of Criminal Law, Criminology, and Police Science* 45 (May–June 1954): 29–40.
6. ———. "Epidemiology and Individual Conduct: A Case from Criminology," *Pacific Sociological Review* 3 (Fall 1960): 47–58.
7. FERRI, ENRICO. *Criminal Sociology* (Boston: Little, Brown, 1917).
8. FRANK, PHILIPP. *Philosophy of Science* (Englewood Cliffs, N.J.: Prentice-Hall, 1957).
9. GEIS, GILBERT. "Sociology, Criminology, and Criminal Law," *Social Problems* 7 (Summer 1959): 40–47.
10. GLASER, DANIEL. "Criminality Theories and Behavioral Images," *American Journal of Sociology* 61 (March 1956): 433–44.
11. ———. "The Sociological Approach to Crime and Correction," *Law and Contemporary Problems* 23 (Autumn 1958): 683–702.
12. ———. "Differential Association and Criminological Prediction," *Social Problems* 7 (Summer 1960): 2–6.
13. ———, and RICE, KENT. "Crime, Age, and Employment," *American Sociological Review* 24 (October 1959): 679–86.
14. GLUECK, SHELDON. "Theory and Fact in Criminology," *British Journal of Delinquency* 7 (October 1956): 92–109.
15. HEALY, WILLIAM. *The Individual Delinquent* (Boston: Little, Brown, 1924).
16. KORN, RICHARD R., and McCORKLE, LLOYD W. *Criminology and Penology* (New York: Holt-Dryden, 1959).
17. LEMERT, EDWIN M. "The Behavior of the Systematic Check Forger," *Social Problems* 6 (Fall 1958): 141–49.
18. MEEHL, PAUL E., and ROSEN, ALBERT. "Antecedent Probability and the Efficiency of Psychometric Signs, Patterns, or Cutting Scores," *Psychological Bulletin* 52 (May 1955): 194–216.
19. NORTHROP, F. S. C. *Logic of the Sciences and the Humanities.* (New York: Macmillan, 1947).
20. POPPER, KARL. *The Logic of Scientific Discovery* (New York: Basic Books, Inc., 1959).

21. SHAW, CLIFFORD R., and McKAY, HENRY D. *Delinquency Areas.* (Chicago: University of Chicago Press, 1929).
22. SHORT, JAMES F., JR. "Differential Association with Delinquent Friends and Delinquent Behavior," *Pacific Sociological Review* 1 (Spring 1958): 20–25.
23. ————. "Differential Association as a Hypothesis: Problems of Empirical Testing," *Social Problems* 7 (Summer 1960): 14–25.
24. SUTHERLAND, EDWIN H., and CRESSEY, DONALD R. *Principles of Criminology,* 5th ed. (Philadelphia: Lippincott, 1955).
25. TARDE, GABRIEL. *Penal Philosophy* (Boston: Little, Brown, 1912).
26. THRASHER, FREDERICK M. *The Gang* (Chicago: University of Chicago Press, 1927).
27. WHEELER, STANTON H. "Social Organization in a Correctional Community." Unpublished Ph.D. dissertation, University of Washington, Seattle, 1958.
28. ZNANIECKI, FLORIAN. *The Method of Sociology* (New York: Farrar & Rinehart, 1934).

16. DIFFERENTIAL ASSOCIATION AND THE ATYPICAL OFFENDER

Frank E. Hartung

The development and the use of vocabularies of motives are by no means confined to some juveniles learning to be delinquent and some others learning to be lawful. The same process characterizes both the criminal and the lawful adult, and may be observed with particular clarity in the adult offender commonly known as the "embezzler." Before analyzing the sociological research dealing with this type of offender, we shall find it useful, by way of comparison, to see him through the perspective of a recent popular study, *The Thief in the White Collar*, by Jaspan and Black.[1] According to the claim made on the dust jacket of the book, Jaspan is one of the foremost management consultants in the United States, president of Norman Jaspan Associates, management engineers, and of its "fact-finding" division, Investigations, Inc. His firm's clients include many large and small manufacturing, service, and retail establishments; and his firm operates throughout Canada and the United States. With hardly more than one ex-

Reprinted from *Crime, Law, and Society* (pp. 125–36), by Frank E. Hartung, by permission of the author and the Wayne State University Press. Copyright © 1965 by Wayne State University Press.
[1] Norman Jaspan with Hillel Black, *The Thief in the White Collar* (Philadelphia: Lippincott, 1960).

ception the cases in the book were drawn from the files of his firm. It may be that the book was written for business firms and the potential embezzlers whom they employ. Jaspan does establish one thing beyond question, to judge from his interpretation of his firm's experience: embezzlement has become endemic in American business. White-collar employees, both rank-and-file and supervisory and executive, steal about four million dollars from their employers every working day. More than one billion dollars was stolen in 1960. The United States Department of Justice's *Uniform Crime Reports* shows that in 1960 American police departments reported that burglars, pickpockets, robbers, and automobile thieves stole only 570 million dollars' worth. Jaspan estimated that as of today employees of banks have embezzled between ten million to twenty-five million dollars still to be discovered. Such estimates are statistically worthless because they cannot be checked.

When I first began to read *The Thief in the White Collar*, I decided merely to sample it here and there, because it seemed, at first glance, to be only another hastily—which is to say, badly—written book. I had not read very far in it, however, before it became fascinating. As a result of his company's experience in finding that such things as embezzlement, the theft of goods, kickbacks, and cheating on expense accounts are so common as to have become an integral part of the culture of business, Jaspan has a message for employers. Even though never explicitly stated, it is perhaps the more forcefully communicated for being implicit. The message is: Pay your employees adequately or your niggardliness will cause them to embezzle; treat them decently and ascertain their personal problems or your indifference and ignorance may cause them to embezzle; always distrust both them and the security personnel whom you hire to check on them; conduct your own personal and unannounced checks on your security personnel. Mr. Jaspan never asks or considers the question, Who will check on the honesty of the employers?

This book may serve an end never intended by its authors. By their sympathetic interpretation of the embezzler they may help to perpetuate the vocabulary of motives employed by such people since time out of mind. Their conception of *cause* constitutes, in my judgment, a vocabulary of motives for the committing of embezzlement! It seems to me, for example, that in the first pages of the book Jaspan provides a white-collar formulation of two often-repeated motives used by delinquents, and also by adults who commit serious crimes. He asserts not only that "everyone has larceny in his heart," or that "everyone has his own racket," but also (p. 12) that "most people will try to cheat on their income tax if they think they can get away with it." He presents no supporting evidence. Perhaps he had his own clients in mind. We read (p. 101) that a Mrs. Burton was possessed by an "irrational hunger" for "conspicuous consumption," the "same senseless desire that we all have."

In addition to learning that crooks and honest people all have the same senseless desires and motives, the man or woman contemplating embezzlement may take heart when reading of "the fact" that "chance and luck are responsible for the detection of most white collar thieves."[2] An interesting project would be a comparative study of vocabularies of motives according to social class and education. It will be recalled that delinquents make use of *irresponsibility* and *a higher loyalty*. They present themselves as being subjects moved around by agencies beyond their control, such as the slum, a broken home, a drunken mother, or a worthless father; or they might claim, "I did it for a friend." Jaspan presents these two motives to the embezzler in a more elegant and esthetic form. "The Honest Crooks" of his fifth chapter "have in common the fact that circumstances over which they had no control forced them to commit their dishonest acts." We should understand the "forces that drive" the white-collar thief.[3] Continuing the discussion with reference to the white-collar accomplice in crime, who also is an "honest crook," Jaspan notes that "there is often a mitigating circumstance, for the individual he is protecting usually is a close relative, friend or loved one."

The creation of a role that the potential embezzler can enact frees him of responsibility, supplying further motivation for his offense. In this instance the role is that of a sick person and—as everyone knows—the sick person is not responsible for his sickness. Thus we are informed that a thief by the name of Jean "couldn't help herself. She was a kleptomaniac."[4] If Jaspan were familiar with the psychiatric literature he would know that the diagnosis of kleptomania depends at least as much on what goes on in the head of the psychiatrist as on what goes into the pocket of the thief. White-collar crime, we are told, is a disease; perhaps "it may be possible to detect the first symptoms of the disease, and perhaps, in many instances, even prevent the original infection."[5] The medical metaphor is misleading, even if it does help a man to talk himself into being a thief. Jaspan seems to take it literally. We are informed (p. 154) that "horses, cards and dice have become the largest single causative factor in white collar crime." On the next page we find that "gambling is a disease, the causes of this bacillus are numerous. . . . The bacillus of this disease, of course, feasts on a ready supply of cash." Jaspan even quotes from a bank teller in grammar typical of a third-grade street-corner boy, "It got like a disease." That quotation, of course, presents the embezzling bank teller as the passive subject of an active agent that he could not control. Six pages later gambling has grown so large that "it is a national disease." "The Insecure Executive" (the title of Chapter 7) will be interested in the motivation supplied to John Russell

---

[2] *Ibid.*, p. 37.
[3] *Ibid.*, pp. 92 and 26.
[4] *Ibid.*, p. 93.
[5] *Ibid.*, p. 26.

Cooney: "The cause of his thefts was the promise of a salary raise that was fulfilled too late."

It seems to me that Jaspan and Black understand neither Sutherland's conception of white-collar crime nor Cressey's analysis of the violation of financial trust. Sutherland studied white-collar crime as perpetrated by businessmen in the conduct of their *business* and not of their *personal* affairs. Jaspan makes no reference to this conception and type of white-collar crime. Perhaps the reason is that the United States Department of Justice may investigate Jaspan's employers (that is, his firm's clients), whereas Jaspan investigates their employees.[6]

Cressey's book, *Other People's Money*, is a study in the criminal violation of financial trust. Where Cressey's book is scientific and analytical, Jaspan and Black's is sympathetic and moralistic, and may contribute to the criminal's vocabulary of motives. (The comments on Jaspan's book are concerned with the validity of its analysis. While they indicate that the book may provide motivation to potential embezzlers, that is not relevant to its evaluation. The logico-empirical validity of a theory, and the actual or potential uses made of that theory, are two quite different things. The scientific evaluation of a theory can, as a matter of course, be concerned only with validity, and not with possible misuse.)

Cressey's research on the criminal violation of financial trust is of great significance both for a general theory of criminality and for a general theory of human, or sociocultural, behavior. The theory of differential association has been attacked on several grounds. One of the criticisms is that some types of criminals are exceptions to it. Two of the supposed exceptions are (1) persons such as embezzlers, with no previous criminal record and no known past or present criminal friends, and (2) murderers, nonprofessional shoplifters, and persons who commit crimes of passion under emotional stress.[7] These two classes do not, in my opinion, constitute exceptions to the social-psychological and sociological analysis of human conduct. One great merit of that analysis is that it makes possible the bringing within the purview of a single theory the widest range of sociocultural behavior. It renders unnecessary the postulation or invention of pathologies in order to explain morally disapproved behavior. It cannot, however, account for cases of strict liability and negligence, which, Jerome Hall has suggested, should be excluded from the rules of criminal law.

The legal category "embezzlement" does not, Cressey found, refer to a homogeneous class of criminal behavior, because of variations in the definitions of legal terms from one state to another. He developed the concept

---

[6] See Frank E. Hartung, "A Vocabulary of Motives for Embezzlers," *Federal Probation*, 25 (December 1961): 68–69.

[7] For an enumeration of supposed exceptions to the theory of differential association, and a bibliography of the criticisms, see the article by Donald R. Cressey, "Epidemiology and Individual Conduct: A Case from Criminology," *Pacific Sociological Review*, 3 (Fall 1960): 47–58, esp. nn. 37–49.

"criminal violation of financial trust" to refer to a homogeneous class. Two criteria must be met in order for a given case to be included. First, a person must have accepted a position of financial trust in good faith. This criterion is practically identical with the legal definition that the "felonious intent" in embezzlement must be formulated *after* taking the position. Second, the person must have violated that trust by committing a crime.[8] The central problem of Cressey's research was to ascertain whether a definite sequence or concurrence of events is always present when the criminal violation of trust occurs and never present when the violation is absent, and the correlated problem, to explain genetically the presence or absence of those events. Cressey formulated the following hypothesis, which he subsequently tested and confirmed:

> Trusted persons become trust violators when they conceive of themselves as having a financial problem which is nonshareable, are aware that this problem can be secretly resolved by violation of the position of financial trust, and are able to apply to their own conduct in that situation verbalizations which enable them to adjust their conceptions of themselves as trusted persons with their conception of themselves as users of the entrusted funds or property.[9]

The nonshareable financial problem was so defined by the violator. Another person might not have defined it thus. *A*, for example, could lose a considerable amount of money at the race track daily; but the loss, even if it constituted a personal problem for him, would not be defined by him as being a nonshareable problem. For *B*, however, the financial problem created by his loss would be defined as nonshareable. He would thus find it impossible to discuss the problem with his wife, best friend, or employer. People may have nonshareable problems of a nonfinancial character, for example, whether or not to obtain a divorce. Such nonfinancial, nonshareable problems are usually not solvable by obtaining more money either legitimately or through the violation of financial trust. Thus not all trusted persons who have nonshareable problems become trust violators; but according to the present research and theory, all criminal violators of financial trust have what *they* define as nonshareable financial problems. All of the situations involved in producing nonshareable financial problems were concerned with either status-seeking or status-maintaining activities. Since, however, status seeking or maintaining seems to be universal, engaging in these activities does not differentiate the trust violators from nonviolators.[10]

In addition to defining a financial problem as nonshareable, the violator

---

[8] Donald R. Cressey, *Other People's Money: A Study in the Social Psychology of Embezzlement* (Glencoe, Ill.: Free Press, 1953), p. 20.

[9] *Ibid.*, p. 30.

[10] "Status-seeking, status-gaining, status-maintaining, irrespective of the unit, time and place, is universal insofar as human relationships are concerned" (Samuel Haig Jameson, "Principles of Human Interaction," *American Sociological Review*, 10 [February 1945]: 6–7).

of trust must identify his position and knowledge *to himself* as providing the means of solving it. He must also apply certain motives to his own conduct that will allow him to use this means. The identification of the opportunity for trust violation and the development of motivation occur together.[11] The realization by the violator that he can solve his problem criminally is indicated by his use of such phrases as "it occurred to me," or "it dawned on me," that the entrusted funds or property could be used personally. Trusted persons know that positions of trust can be criminally violated, even when they have no nonshareable financial problem, and so do most other adults. I have already referred to a small part of the literature dealing with fraud and embezzlement in particular and white-collar crime in general.[12] In many cases of trust violation, the people trained to discharge the routine duties of a position have at the same time been trained in the skills necessary for the violation of trust. The technical skill necessary to the violation is the same technical skill necessary to hold the position in the first place. When violators perpetrate their criminal violations, they do not depart from ordinary occupational routines in which they are skilled. Thus, "Accountants use checks which they have been entrusted to dispose of, sales clerks withhold receipts, bankers manipulate seldom-used accounts or withhold deposits, real estate men use deposits entrusted to them, and so on." As an example Cressey quotes from an accountant who "never even thought of stealing" the money that passed across his desk outside of normal routine. "It was a matter of routine with me; I simply followed out the routine I had every day."[13]

If a person in a position of financial trust defines his financial problem as being nonshareable, realizes that he can solve it illegally, and at the same time applies to his own conduct verbalizations enabling him to adjust his conception of himself as a trusted person with his conception of himself as a user of the entrusted funds, he will violate that trust. When these three components are in conjunction, the criminal violation of trust will occur; when any one of them is absent there will be no such violation.

This hypothesis makes use of the social-psychological theory of motivation mentioned briefly in the discussion of the development of a vocabulary of motives by delinquent boys and boys who are becoming delinquent. The process through which the criminal violator of financial trust develops and uses motives is basically the same process through which the boys proceed. The adult violator uses a language enabling him to conceive of the violation of trust as being essentially noncriminal and also as either justified or as irresponsible behavior over which he can exert no control. Cressey uses the term "rationalization" to refer to this use of language by the violator. As we indicated previously, this use of the term emphasizes that the be-

---

[11] The following paragraphs are a brief summary of the complex third and fourth chapters in Cressey, *op. cit.*

[12] Cressey cites other references (*ibid.*, pp. 79, 173–74).

[13] *Ibid.*, p. 84.

havior in question is deliberate and purposive and in part results from the way in which the actor conceives of himself in relation to others. The rationalization is the actor's motivation, as we said before, and this applies to the criminal violator. His motive is a linguistic construct organizing his behavior in a particular situation. The use of the motive makes his behavior intelligible to himself. Its use may or may not make his behavior understandable to others, depending on whether they accept or reject his vocabulary of motives. If they accept his rationalization they will define his behavior as "understandable," even if they disapprove of or condemn it, and even if they may think him "stupid," or "not very smart." If others reject the criminal violator's rationalization, they will define his behavior as "unintelligible," or "senseless," or "impulsive," or "unmotivated."

Significant rationalizations were always present *before* the criminal violation of financial trust in all the cases in the study now being discussed. It was often found that the rationalization was abandoned after the violation was discovered. The trusted person can violate his trusted position because he is able to rationalize. The use of these rationalizations in trust violation is not separable from their sources. Just as the delinquent boys were able to draw upon the cultural store of motives, the trust violators "discovered" or "rediscovered" the cultural store of motivations sanctioning trust violation and applied them to their own conduct. The trust violators thus came into effective contact with cultural patterns of thought and action. Association with other criminals was unnecessary, and, as Cressey has said, could not be demonstrated. He has suggested the following definitions of situations calling for the violation of financial trust, and thus amounting to justifications for the crime: "Some of our most respectable citizens got their start in life by using other people's money temporarily." He quotes from Alexander Dumas's *The Money Question:* "What is business? That's easy. It's other people's money, of course." "In the real estate business there is nothing wrong about using deposits before the deal is closed." "All people steal when they are in a difficult position."

The trust violator gives a personal touch to the above rationalizations: "My intent is only to use this money temporarily, so I am 'borrowing,' not 'stealing' "; "My immediate use of real estate deposits is 'ordinary business' "; "I have been trying to live an honest life but I have had nothing but troubles so to hell with it."[14] In applying motives such as these to his behavior, the violator of financial trust may have some comfort in the knowledge that reactions by others to "borrowing" in order to solve a nonshareable problem are very different from their reactions to "stealing." Thus, like the delinquent drawing upon the rationalizations of his peers and the larger community . . . the trust violator can observe himself as being "all right" because the rationalizations upon which he has drawn sanction and support him in his actions.

---

[14] *Ibid.*, p. 96.

The criminal violator of financial trust is a man who almost by definition has had no criminal record, no known criminal friends and associates, and who for a greater or lesser number of years has been well established as a respectable member of his community. And still he becomes a criminal. As I have tried to indicate above, this does not constitute an exception to the theory of differential association. The violator of trust is involved in the sociocultural process from the beginning to the end of his crime. Starting with his having learned his occupation socioculturally, he has encountered a financial problem. By linguistic means—a conversation confined wholly to himself—he has defined his problem as being nonshareable. He cannot even discuss it with his wife! The definition of his problem is based upon his system of values, and upon his conception of himself in relation to others who are significant to him—"What *will* they think of me?"—and his values and self-conception are purely sociocultural.

Through the continued private use of language he informs himself that he knows how to solve his problem. By the same means he draws upon cultural resources in the form of motives applicable in his situation, finds a vocabulary of adjustment, and criminally violates his position of financial trust. Through his private conversation he has "conned" or talked or verbally manipulated himself into a situation in which he can perpetrate his crime.

Physical contact with others already criminal is therefore not always necessary to the development of criminality in a given individual. It seems, however, that effective contact with appropriate sociocultural sources and processes, in the form of patterns of thought and action, is always necessary. This type of offender's criminality is learned socioculturally, in the process of symbolic communication, including his self-conversations.

It will have been noticed that the criminal violator of financial trust and the career delinquent have one thing in common: Their criminality is learned in the process of symbolic communication, dependent upon cultural sources for patterns of thought and action, and for systems of values and vocabularies of motives. The criminality and the life history of the two types of offenders is, however, quite different. The delinquent who engages in delinquency as a financial means is most likely to be a more completely developed criminal than the trust violator. A boy who is reared in an area with a high rate of delinquency might have a well-developed pattern of criminality, Sutherland and Cressey say, "by age twelve or fourteen." Some might object that twelve years is a bit too young, and it could be that one should set the years at twelve to sixteen, or fourteen to sixteen. But whatever the range of years, the significant fact is that by about twelve to about sixteen years such a boy is criminally developed in the sense that criminal conceptions of law, person, and property have been accepted by him as values upon which to act.

Such a boy is deliberate in committing his crimes: he plans how to perpetrate them, plots possible escape routes, and soon learns to consider securing immunity if caught. If his precautions are inadequate—as they often are—his apprehension and subsequent possible detention and commitment to a juvenile correctional institution do not constitute crises for him. He does not like detection or detention but he can accept them as part of his life, an occupational hazard, so to speak, "just as a newsboy who has made what provision he could against the rain takes the rain as a part of his life." He may, and in fact often does, gain in prestige among his peers if he is committed to a correctional institution. In addition, the career delinquent of sixteen years of age is likely to have had about five to six years, and it seems in many cases as much as about eight years, of active and intensive experience with other delinquents. If the boy is on the way to becoming an adult burglar or robber, there is considerable evidence to show that his delinquency has had a typical development: from trivial to serious offenses, from a game to a livelihood, and from membership in a loosely organized boy's gang to a rather tightly organized gang of adolescents.[15] In those years he will have engaged in a wide range of offenses. Usually they begin with petty pilfering and truancy, and proceed to such offenses as shoplifting, purse-snatching, strong-arming, and burglary.

The career of the trust violator is quite different. First, as we said before, he is most likely not to have had a previous record, even though typically he is middle-aged when detected. Second, his education, occupation, residence, friends, and leisure-time activities usually set him in a social class higher than that of the delinquent. Third, even though his crime is deliberate and he attempts to avoid detection, he fails to plan for the securing

---

[15] See a short bibliography for this in Sutherland and Cressey, *Principles of Criminology*, 6th ed., pp. 219–20. The two brief quotations in this and the previous paragraph are from the same source. Their chap. 12, "Processes in Criminal Behavior," presents a more detailed comparison of the life histories of the career delinquent and the trust violator.

McCleery has presented a vivid description of a different although related result of the continued private use of language that supports the present analysis of the vocabulary of motives. The thief in the white collar talks himself into a criminal violation of his position of financial trust. The isolated inmate in the incorrigible unit of a maximum-security prison—which is physically separate from the other units—may talk himself into a mental hospital. The days and months during which his illusions are developed are seldom interrupted by contact with reality or by challenging skepticism. The isolate has no one but himself to convince that he is blameless and the victim of a complex plot. McCleery says that:

> A fairly common product of this condition is a note written to the Warden [which] with minor variations, will express the idea that the inmate has complete power over the prison system. It will assert that unless the Warden stops "them" from trying to poison or hurt him, the inmate and God will destroy the system. If these notes find their way through official channels, the inmate may be transferred to a mental hospital where his condition is diagnosed apart from the situation that produced it. Prison inmates, however, recognize it as an extreme form of a common affliction they call "stir crazy." In its extreme form it manifests itself in the individual's not wanting to be released from prison, or from the incorrigible unit, or from his isolation cell. More rational inmates fear and resist going "stir crazy," but they do not resent it in others. They recognize it as a way of adjusting to confinement and distinguish it from the "cracking up" which comes with [the] inability to take punishment [Richard H. McCleery, "Authoritarianism and the Belief System of Incorrigibles," in *The Prison*, ed. Donald R. Cressey (New York: Holt, Rinehart & Winston, 1961), p. 289].

of immunity if caught. Fourth, even though he may be three or four times as old as the career delinquent, his arrest constitutes a serious crisis for him that he cannot take in his stride. His arrest and conviction, and the attendant publicity, are a disgrace to him. He loses status even though some segment of the community may sympathize with him without condoning what he did. The trust violator is therefore typically not as fully developed a criminal as a sixteen-year-old delinquent is likely to be.

The career delinquent and the criminal violator of financial trust are like and unlike each other in ways significant to our further discussion. They are similar in that both are dependent upon and make use of culturally supplied vocabularies of motives. They are different in that the delinquent makes use of a more systematized and widely held vocabulary of motives openly and explicitly discussed and accepted by his peers. At least one important motive—the denial of responsibility—is also widely accepted by persons in positions of legal authority who use that motive to explain the delinquency of the boy. Furthermore, the conception of cause and effect that marks mechanistic theories imparts to this motive the respectability and persuasive power of science. The delinquent has a relative psychical advantage in that his motivation is constantly validated by other significant people. Knowledge that he is conforming to acceptable motives helps him to justify his delinquency to himself. Policemen, reporters, parents, and newspapers confirm the delinquent's motive when, in a case involving adolescent offenders from the middle class and upper class, a parent says, "I don't understand why he stole; my boy had everything he needed."[16] Those boys have no motive that is acceptable to respectable society; hence, their delinquency is described as "having no cause," or as "senseless," or as "unmotivated."

Because the delinquent is conforming to an acceptable and independently validated motive, he does not have to contend with his conscience very much. This state of affairs is one reason why he is sometimes described as "displaying no remorse." Another and perhaps major reason is that "displaying no remorse" is an interpretation made by an examiner. The criminal violator of financial trust, in contrast, does not find such a constant validation in his personal experience. He has only himself and the impersonal cultural source of his motivation. The sanction for his behavior is not systematized and not as widely accepted as the delinquent's. The trust violator is therefore not as emancipated from his conscience. When apprehended he may experience great shame and guilt through rejecting his previous criminal rationalization, and agreeing with respectable society that what he did was criminal.

---

[16] For an example, see the *New York Times*, June 25, 1961, and the photograph accompanying the story, "14 Who Had No Cause for Crime in Court for 'Trial of Plenty.'"

17. DIFFERENTIAL ASSOCIATION AND COMPULSIVE CRIMES

Donald R. Cressey

The differential association theory, which is considered by most sociologists as the best formulation to date of a general theory of criminality, holds, in essence, that criminality is learned in interaction with others in a process of communication. Specifically, the hypothesis is that criminality is learned from observations of definitions favorable to law violation, the learning including both the techniques of committing crime and the "specific direction of motives, drives, rationalizations and attitudes." The ratio between such definitions and others unfavorable to law violation determines whether or not a person becomes criminal.[1]

This generalization is stated in universal form, presumably as a description of the etiology of all criminal behavior. Hence, the discovery of cases of criminal behavior whose genesis and development have not followed such a process would call for either a modification of the generalization or a redefinition of the concept "crime."[2] The important point in the

Reprinted by permission of the author and the publisher from the *Journal of Criminal Law, Criminology, and Police Science* (Northwestern University School of Law), copyright © 1954, vol. 45, no. 1 (May–June 1954): 29–40. Original title: "The Differential Association Theory and Compulsive Crimes."

[1] E. H. Sutherland, *Principles of Criminology* (New York: Lippincott, 1947), pp. 6–9.
[2] Many criminologists now argue that crime is not a homogeneous phenomenon and

theory is that all criminal behavior is learned in a process of social interaction, and to prove or disprove the theory we must carefully examine behavior to which the label "crime" is applied but which does not appear to have been learned in such interaction.[3]

For example, crimes which in the criminal law are based upon strict liability rather than on proof of intent almost immediately appear as possible exceptions. Careful examination of the characteristics of such offenses might logically call for a redefinition of the concept "crime," rather than a revision of the generalization, although either procedure would be scientifically permissible.[4] As another example, "situational crimes" or "crimes of passion," such as an assault or murder perpetrated after a period of antagonistic or irritating behavior on the part of the victim, present an apparent exception to the generalization and should be examined carefully for the purpose of determining whether they are real exceptions.

Also apparently exceptional to the theory are the so-called "compulsive crimes," such as kleptomania and pyromania. It is the objective of this paper to reexamine the "compulsive crime" concept with an aim to determining in a preliminary way whether such behavior must remain as exceptional.

THE LEGAL-PSYCHIATRIC CONTROVERSY

Before such reexamination can be made, however, it is necessary to review briefly the three fundamental points in the legal-psychiatric controversy about whether behavior said to be "compulsive" also is "crime." The issues are fairly clear. First, in the criminal law, under the M'Naghten rules, the stigma "insanity," not "crime," is applied to legally harmful behavior perpetrated under circumstances such that the defendant was unable to distinguish between right and wrong. This is to say, in more general terms, that he was unable to contemplate the normative consequences of his acts. If it is observed that a so-called "compulsive criminal" *did* contemplate the

---

that it is therefore unwise to attempt universal scientific generalizations about it. While there is merit in this argument, it is not pertinent to the present discussion. See Donald R. Cressey, "Criminological Research and the Definition of Crimes," *American Journal of Sociology*, 56 (May 1951): 546–51.

[3] Some apparent exceptions to the theory were pointed out by Sutherland himself. See his "The Relation Between Personal Traits and Associational Patterns," in Walter C. Reckless, *The Etiology of Delinquent and Criminal Behavior*, Social Science Research Council bulletin no. 50 (New York, 1943), pp. 131–37.

[4] One argument for the first course of action already has been made. Hall holds that strict liability offenses have so little in common with other crimes that they should not be included in the ambit of the criminal law. Jerome Hall, *Principles of Criminal Law* (Indianapolis: Bobbs-Merrill, 1947), pp. 280, 296. Such a redefinition of the crime concept, incidentally, would have serious effects upon current generalizations about "white-collar crimes," many of which are of a strict liability type.

normative consequences of his behavior, the behavior is classed as crime, rather than as insanity.

Second, psychiatrists insist that some of the behavior which results in legal harm ("compulsive crime") has essentially the same characteristics as does compulsive behavior generally. As a general category of neuroses ("psychasthenia," "anankastic reactions," etc.), compulsive acts are described as irresistible behavior which the person in question often recognizes as irrational but is subjectively compelled to carry out.[5] Such acts are considered as irrational because they are thought to be prompted by a subjective morbid impulsion which the person's "will" or "judgment" or "ego" cannot control.[6] In other words, behavior described as compulsive is thought to be completely determined by the inner impulse or compulsion, and while the genesis of the compulsion might lie in a social context, once it has been formed it apparently operates as an entity, agent, or element in itself. Thus, the overt act is considered as prompted entirely "from within," and present contact with values concerning morality, decency, or correctness of the overt behavior in no way affects the actor, in the last analysis, either in deterring him from acting or in encouraging him to act.[7]

It is argued by psychiatrists, then, that in cases of "compulsive crime" the actor *does* know right from wrong and does contemplate the normative consequences of his acts (i.e., he recognizes the behavior as irrational, foolish, wrong, illegal, etc.), but *nevertheless* exhibits the behavior because it is prompted from within by a force which he is powerless to resist.[8] If the legal harm resulting from such behavior actually is crime, then it obviously is exceptional to the differential association theory. The "criminality" in "compulsive crime" would depend not upon former contacts with differential values concerning law-abidingness, but upon a nonsocial agent or process.

---

[5] Cf. Roy M. Dorcus and G. Wilson Shaffer, *Textbook of Abnormal Psychology* (Baltimore: Williams & Wilkins, 1941), p. 364.

[6] Malamud, for example, indicates that psychasthenias or anankastic reactions "have in common the fact that the patients feel themselves compelled by some inner force and against their own will or reason to think, act or feel in an abnormal manner," and that compulsive acts are "forms of behavior which the person carries out consciously without knowing the reason for such activity or for reasons which he knows have no logical foundation" (William Malamud, "The Psychoneuroses," in *Personality and the Behavior Disorders*, ed. J. McV. Hunt [New York: Ronald Press, 1944], pp. 851–52). Cf. Franz Alexander and Hugo Staub, *The Criminal, the Judge, and the Public* (New York: Macmillan, 1931), pp. 149–50.

[7] Cf. Gregory Zilboorg, "Misconceptions of Legal Insanity," *American Journal of Orthopsychiatry*, 9 (July 1939): 540–53.

[8] Lorand, for example, cites three case histories as evidence that "compulsive stealing" is a subconscious act of aggression against the parents or parent surrogates. He points out that there were faults in the critical appreciation of the factors of reality, and that "all showed an overwhelmingly strong instinctual drive which clouded the function of critical faculty. They were unable, consciously, to resist, and they could not prevent the breaking through of strong drives from within which lead to stealing" (Sandor Lorand, "Compulsive Stealing," *Journal of Criminal Psychopathy*, 1 [January 1940]: 247–53). Cf. Malamud, *op. cit.*

Third, some jurists have adopted a position similar to that of the psychiatrists. This is apparent from the fact that the courts of about fourteen states hold that the consequences to the actor of the perpetration of a legal harm can be avoided by showing that while the defendant knew right from wrong, his behavior was prompted by an "irresistible impulse."[9] While there is disagreement among psychiatrists, it appears that most of them agree with the legal theory of those jurisdictions allowing the irresistible-impulse defense, and many of them contend that those judges not allowing it are backward, ignorant, or stubborn.[10]

MENTALISTIC ASSUMPTIONS OF LAW AND PSYCHIATRY

This divergence in opinion and viewpoint is enhanced by the fact that an assumption of "mind" is implicit in the psychological orientations of both psychiatry and criminal law, so that each discipline has a "mentalistic" approach to human behavior. In criminal law, the "right and wrong test" assumes the existence of a mind which, when normal and mature, operates in such a way that the human has conscious freedom to choose rationally whether or not a crime shall be committed. The mind impels the person only in the direction he wishes to be impelled. But a mind which is immature or "diseased" cannot make intelligent choices, and a defendant possessing such a mind is considered incapable of entertaining crim-

---

[9] E. R. Keedy, "Irresistible Impulse as a Defense in Criminal Law," *University of Pennsylvania Law Review*, 100 (May 1952): 956–93. The "irresistible impulse" and "compulsive crime" concepts seem to have at their base the same assumptions inherent in the old faculty psychology concepts "moral perversion," "moral imbecility," "inhibitory insanity," "affective mania," "monomania," etc., each of which implied a psychological disorder which has no connection with the "intellect" or "knowing" or "reasoning" faculties. See Lawson G. Lowrey, "Delinquent and Criminal Personalities," in *Personality and the Behavior Disorders*, ed. J. McV. Hunt (New York: Ronald Press, 1944), pp. 799–801. Most modern psychiatrists claim that theirs is not a faculty psychology since what was formerly considered as emotional and intellectual faculties is now considered as one— the total personality. But while this "integration" theory is affirmed by psychiatrists as they oppose the M'Naghten rules, it is denied when they support notions of "compulsive crime" or "irresistible impulse." See the discussion by Jerome Hall, *op. cit.*, pp. 523–24.

[10] Wertham is a noteworthy exception. This psychiatrist writes that "the criminal law which makes use of the conception of irresistible impulse is not an advance belonging to the present 'scientific social' era. It is a throwback to, or rather a survival of, the previous 'philosophical psychological' era. The concept of irresistible impulse derives from a philosophical, speculative, synthetic psychology. It forms no part of and finds no support in the modern dynamic psychoanalytic study of mental process" (New York University School of Law, *Social Meaning of Legal Concepts—Criminal Guilt* [New York: New York University Press, 1950], p. 164). Elsewhere the same author has stated that there is nothing in the whole field of psychopathology which corresponds to the irresistible impulse, and that compulsions play no role in criminal acts (Frederic Wertham, *The Show of Violence* [New York: Doubleday, 1949], pp. 13–14). Bromberg and Cleckley recently stated a similar position: "The concept of sudden 'irresistible impulse' in an otherwise perfectly normal organism is unsupported by modern psychiatric knowledge" (Walter Bromberg and Hervey M. Cleckley, "The Medico-Legal Dilemma—A Suggested Solution," *Journal of Criminal Law, Criminology, and Police Science*, 42 [March–April 1952]: 729–45).

inal intent. Such an assumption tends to equate rationality and sanity, and it is necessary to fixing "responsibility" for acts.[11] Although psychiatrists often denounce this jurisprudential assumption on the ground that it ignores the facts of science,[12] their denunciation is possible only because of emphasis on a different mentalistic construct. In writing of "compulsive crime," at least, most psychiatrists assume a mind with only one significant difference from the one assumed by most jurists. Here, the mind is said to be subject to casual emotional experiences, especially early sexual experiences, which give it characteristics such that at the present moment of action it completely determines the person's choice—and, consequently, his overt behavior—in a manner which usually is completely unconscious and unknowable without the help of a psychiatrist. The deeply hidden emotional forces of the mind are thought to compel the actor even if he knows the action is illegal, and he has no choice in whether the action shall be undertaken. The chief difference between such psychological forces or "mainsprings of action" and instinctive "mainsprings of action" is that the former are "unconscious."[13]

Mentalistic assumptions of both kinds must be clarified and supplemented in order to determine whether "compulsive criminality" is exceptional to the differential association theory. As long as criminality is said to have its etiology in a rather mysterious "mind," "soul," "will," or "unconscious," there will be no possible way for generalizations about criminality to be subjected to empirical tests or observations which would settle the issue. Also, so long as "compulsiveness," as traditionally described, must be determined by specialists rather than judges or juries, jurists will resist discussion of it in their courts and the legal-psychiatric controversy will continue.

A SOCIOLOGICAL THEORY OF MOTIVATION

Behavior traditionally considered as "compulsive crime" can be handled and clarified without the assumption of "mind" or a basic biological or

---

[11] For discussion of the differences between "responsibility," "causation," and "accountability," see Arnold W. Green, "The Concept of Responsibility," *Journal of Criminal Law and Criminology*, 33 (January–February 1943): 392–94; and Bromberg and Cleckley, *op. cit.*

[12] See, *e.g.*, Edward Glover, "The Diagnosis and Treatment of Delinquency," in *Mental Abnormality and Crime*, ed. L. Radzinowicz and J. W. C. Turner, vol. 2 of *English Studies in Criminal Science* (London: Macmillan, 1949), pp. 279–80.

[13] See Benjamin Karpman, "An Attempt at a Re-evaluation of Some Concepts of Law and Psychiatry," *Journal of Criminal Law and Criminology*, 38 (September–October 1947): 206–17. Foote has pointed out that in spite of the seductive appeal which is exerted by the hope of reducing human behavior to some simple and permanent order through finding certain "basic" imperatives underlying it, criticism has negated every specific naming of the "mainsprings of action" (Nelson N. Foote, "Identification as the Basis for a Theory of Motivation," *American Sociological Review*, 16 (February 1951): 14–22.

psychic imperative by application of the sociological hypothesis that there are differences in the degree to which acts are controlled by the linguistic constructs (words or combinations of words) which the actor has learned from his social groups. Since the use of linguistic constructs depends upon contacts with social groups, this amounts to differences in the degree to which the actor participates in group experiences. In sociological "role theory," differences of this kind are considered differences in the motivation of the actor, although this concept is used in a sense quite different from the use in psychiatry. Motivation here refers to the process by which a person, as a participant in a group, symbolically (by means of language) defines a problematic situation as calling for the performance of a particular act, with symbolically anticipated consummation and consequences.[14] Motives are not inner, biological mainsprings of action but linguistic constructs which organize acts in particular situations,[15] the use of which can be examined empirically. The key linguistic constructs which a person applies to his own conduct in a certain set of circumstances are motives; the complete process by which such verbalizations are used is motivation.

The great difference between this conception of motivation and the notion that motives are biological or are deeply hidden in the "unconscious" may be observed in the use of the concept "rationalization" in the two systems. In psychiatry it usually is said that one "merely rationalizes" (*ex post facto* justification) behavior which "has really been prompted by deeply hidden motives and unconscious tendencies."[16] In the other system, which uses a nonmentalistic conception of motivation, it is held that one does not necessarily "merely rationalize" behavior already enacted but acts because he has rationalized. The rationalization is his motive. When such rationalizations or verbalizations are extensively developed and systematized, the person using them has a sense of conforming because they give him a sense of support and sanction.[17] An individual in our society, for example, may feel fairly comfortable when he commits an illegal act in connection with his business, for, after all, "business is business." But not all verbalizations are equally developed or systematized, and in some instances the use of the verbalizations does not, therefore, receive such extensive support and sanction. The individual in these instances does not have a comfortable sense of conforming. The person in the above example probably would not feel as comfortable if his illegal act were perpetrated

---

[14] *Ibid.*

[15] Cf. C. Wright Mills, "Situated Actions and Vocabularies of Motive," *American Sociological Review*, 5 (December 1940): 904–13.

[16] Arthur P. Noyes, *Textbook of Modern Psychiatry* (Philadelphia: Saunders, 1940), p. 49. See also, for example, William A. White, *Insanity and the Criminal Law* (New York: Macmillan, 1923), p. 9; and Benjamin Karpman, *op. cit.*

[17] For an excellent discussion of this point, see A. R. Lindesmith and A. S. Strauss, *Social Psychology* (New York: Dryden Press, 1949), pp. 307–10.

according to the verbalization "all businessmen are dishonest." As conceptualized in sociology, then, motives are treated as "typical vocabularies (linguistic constructs) having ascertainable functions in delimited societal situations"[18] and, as such, they may be examined empirically.

Using this conception of motivation, it is immediately apparent that not all behavior is equally motivated; there are differences in the degree to which behavior is linguistically controlled. Certainly some behavior is performed with almost no social referent, i.e., with the use of no shared verbalization. For instance, behavior which is physiologically autonomous is clearly nonmotivated, since the release of energy appropriate to performing the behavior does not depend upon the application of a linguistic construct. Similarly, if one's behavior has been so conditioned by his past experiences that he behaves automatically, in the way that Pavlov's dogs behaved automatically at the sound of the bell, he is not motivated.[19] However, it is equally certain that other behavior cannot be enacted unless the actor has had rather elaborate and intimate contact with linguistic constructs, which are, by definition, group products. Such behavior is motivated, and it may be distinguished from automatic behavior by the fact that it has reference to means and ends. If a person defines a situation as one in which there are alternatives, if there is evidence of planning, evidence of delaying small immediate gains for larger future gains, or evidence of anticipation of social consequences of acts, he is motivated.

APPLICATION OF THE MOTIVATION THEORY TO "COMPULSIVE CRIME"

When this theory of motivation is applied to the problem at hand, it may be seen that if behavior traditionally considered as "compulsive crime" were clearly nonmotivated or autonomous, then the legal-psychiatric controversy would have been resolved long ago, since, if such were the case, the behavior easily could be subsumed under the legal concept "insanity." If "compulsions" "in" a person "came out" in the same way that his whiskers "come out," then even in the most "anti-psychiatric" court there would be no question of his legal responsibility, and his behavior would not, in fact, be designated as crime. In this case, there would be no problem about whether the behavior were an exception to the differential association theory, for the behavior would lie outside the definition of the phenomenon (crime) with which the differential association theory is concerned. Nonmotivated behavior of this kind which resulted in legal harm

---

[18] C. Wright Mills, *op. cit.*
[19] Genuinely fetishistic behavior probably is of this kind.

would not be unlike the behavior of a sleeping or drugged person whose hand was guided by another to the trigger of a gun aimed at a victim's head. Such behavior is not planned by the actor, and precautions against detection are not taken because the ability to use the language symbols normally pertinent to the situation is absent or deficient.[20] If behavior is nonmotivated, the actor cannot possibly entertain ."criminal intent."

In most cases now labeled "kleptomania," "pyromania," etc., however, the actors appear to be motivated in the same way that other criminals are motivated. Consequently they are, in the terminology of the criminal law, "responsible." They select secluded places in which to perpetrate their acts, plan their activities in advance, realize that they will be arrested if detected, and do many other things indicative that there is a conscious normative referent in their behavior. Certainly most acts traditionally described as "compulsive crime" are clearly quite different from autonomous behavior having no normative components,[21] in spite of the fact that the two are usually assumed to be identical or at least very similar. While it is not easy to classify precisely certain acts as motivated or nonmotivated, since men do not always explicitly articulate motives,[22] the sociological framework at least affords an opportunity to classify correctly the great proportion of the acts ordinarily labeled "compulsive crime." In that framework, illegal conduct which is motivated would be classed as "crime" and illegal acts which were nonmotivated would be classed as "compulsion" and would fall within the legal category "insanity."

----

[20] Although it is not recommended, because it probably would lead to even more confusion than now exists, the criminal law theory which exempts some persons from liability because they lack "responsibility" might easily be restated in these terms. Those persons—generally psychotics and very young children—who are now excused on the ground that they cannot distinguish between right and wrong either have not acquired or have lost the ability to control language symbols. In fact, on a level which now seems very unsophisticated, this principle was recognized in the criminal law as early as the thirteenth century when Bracton formulated what erroneously has been called the "wild beast test."

[21] Possibly it was the observation of this same difference which led Alexander and Staub to argue that while the impulse in kleptomania, pyromania, and compulsive lying is an unconscious one, an impulse foreign to the ego, yet the act is not completely unconscious, as is the case, they hold, in compulsive neuroses generally (*op. cit.,* pp. 95–97). See also Robert H. Gault, *Criminology* (New York: Heath, 1932), pp. 163–66, where kleptomania and pyromania are used as illustrations of the psychopathic personality. That is, they are considered as "a form of outlet for a nature that is unbalanced by reason of the dominance of the egocentric disposition. . . . They take what does not belong to them not so much as a result of blind impulsion; not *quite* 'blind impulsion' because the kleptomaniac is at pains to conceal not only his act but the products of his stealing. . . . We are forced to conclude that in the general run of instances of this nature we are dealing with unreasoned impulsion to get goods to amplify one's store, to gratify one's desire for possession and therefore magnify one's self. In other words, here is the egocentric disposition. This language suggests a purposive character of the behavior—and it is so that it results in obtaining goods." However, Lichtenstein, Stekel, and many others claim that the evidence of deliberation and intent in the acts of pyromaniacs and kleptomaniacs does not in and of itself signify sanity (Perry M. Lichtenstein, *A Doctor Studies Crime* [New York: Van Nostrand, 1934], p. 182; Wilhelm Stekel, *Peculiarities of Behavior* [New York: Liveright, 1924], vol. 1, p. 258).

[22] C. Wright Mills, *op. cit.*

NONSCIENTIFIC CRITERIA OF COMPULSIVE CRIMINALS

Accurate classification of this kind would be valuable, since in the current system it appears that compulsive crime concepts are no less "wastebasket categories" than is the "psychopathic personality" concept. Casual observation indicates, at least, that the application of the "compulsive crime" label often accompanies the inability of either the subject or the examiner to account for the behavior in question *in terms of motives which are current, popular, and sanctioned in a particular culture or among the members of a particular group within a culture.* For example, one criterion, usually overlooked, for designating behavior "kleptomania" rather than "theft" is apparent lack of economic need for the item on the part of the person exhibiting the behavior. This may be observed in at least two different ways. First, the probability that the term "kleptomania" will be applied to a destitute shoplifter is much lower than the probability that it will be applied to a wealthy person performing the same kind of acts. "Kleptomania," then, often is simply a shorthand way of saying, as the layman does,. "That woman is rich and can buy almost anything she desires. She has no need (economic) to steal. She must be crazy."[23] An interesting but erroneous assumption in such logic is that the behavior of normal persons committing property crimes is explainable in terms of economic need.[24] This assumption, coupled with the empirical observation that wealthy persons sometimes do commit major property crimes, led to the erroneous conclusion by two sociologists that such crimes must be prompted by "greed" rather than "need."[25] Among psychiatrists, contradiction of the same assumption, through observation of the fact that wealthy persons do sometimes commit minor property crimes, results in the notion that larcenous behavior of wealthy persons must be "compulsive." The economic status of the observer probably is of great importance in determining whether he thinks a person is not in economic need and is

---

[23] Compare: "In kleptomaniacs we have individuals who steal, but their stealing has a number of important differences from ordinary theft. For one thing, the purely predatory element present in common theft is lacking here. The subject steals not because of the value and the money he gets from the stolen articles—that is, not for their mercenary value—but entirely for what they mean to him emotionally and symbolically. One often observes this in rich women who have no need for the article they steal and, in point of actual fact, dispose of the article almost immediately after it has been stolen. While the symbolic nature of such stealing is often evident on the surface, we not infrequently come across cases of stealing the nature of which is not so obvious, so that one is puzzled to figure out whether we are dealing with kleptomania or ordinary theft. Many such case are found in our prisons" (Benjamin Karpman, "Criminality, Insanity, and the Law," *Journal of Criminal Law and Criminology,* 39 (January–February 1949): 584, 605.

[24] For evidence to the contrary, see E. H. Sutherland, *White Collar Crime* (New York: Dryden Press, 1949).

[25] Harry Elmer Barnes and Negley K. Teeters, *New Horizons in Criminology* (New York: Prentice-Hall, 1945), p. 43. The conclusion does not appear in the second edition (1951) of this book.

consequently compulsive. Whether or not the misconduct is considered "disproportionate to any discernible end in view"[26] conceivably will depend a great deal upon the attitudes of the examiner rather than upon those of the offender. That is, a poor person might consider that a middle-class person had no need to steal and that his stealing must be the result of "greed" or a "compulsion," while a middle-class person probably will entertain this notion only as it refers to upper-class persons whose incomes far exceed his. If all psychiatrists were poverty-stricken, the proportion of shoplifters called "kleptomaniacs" probably would be much higher than it is. And if it is assumed that the larcenous behavior of wealthy persons is, because they are wealthy, "compulsive," then there is little opportunity for determination of possible contacts with behavior patterns conducive to crime.

Second, the absence, from the observer's standpoint, of economic need is used as a criterion for designating persons as "kleptomaniacs" in cases in which the particular articles taken appear to be of no immediate use to the subject. For example, Alexander and Staub do not consider as kleptomanic the behavior of a physician (a "neurotic criminal") who had been taking medical books and supplies, but his "theft of porcelain figures which were new and actually of no value is more in the nature of a kleptomanic act," and Wallerstein has stated that a case "was hardly kleptomania in the usual sense because the articles were pawned or sold for money."[27] Although they have not been explored in this connection, Veblen's arguments about the great desirability in our culture of acquiring money merely as a means of accumulating economically "useless" goods might have a bearing here.[28] If his thesis were followed it would seem, at least, that there is little logical justification for designating as "criminal" the behavior of one who stole money with which to buy "useless" goods while at the same time designating as "compulsive" the stealing of the goods themselves.

This criterion also is used for designating even poor persons as "kleptomaniacs" in instances of repetitive taking of what appear to be economically useless goods. However, the fact that mere repetitive taking need not indicate a compulsion may be illustrated by the case of a gang of boys who went from store to store in a large city stealing caps. They would enter a store and each boy would steal a cap, leaving his own on the counter. The group would then move to another store where the stolen caps would be left on the counter, and new ones would be stolen. This practice would continue until the gang members became bored with the game. It is not difficult to distinguish such behavior from what is called kleptomania because

---

[26] William Healy, *The Individual Delinquent* (Boston: Little, Brown, 1918), p. 771.

[27] Alexander and Staub, *op. cit.*, p. 168; James S. Wallerstein, "Roots of Delinquency," *Nervous Child,* 6 (October 1947): 399–412 .

[28] See Thorstein Veblen, *The Theory of the Leisure Class* (New York: Vanguard Press, 1938); and Louis Schneider, *The Freudian Psychology and Veblen's Social Theory* (New York: King's Crown Press, 1948).

it was perpetrated by a number of boys acting together, because it appears to have been done as play,[29] and, most important, because it was perpetrated by boys closely approaching the cultural stereotype of the delinquent or criminal. Even a psychoanalyst probably would not assume that the caps were sex symbols or fetishes, although it is not inconceivable that he would do so.[30] However, if one of the boys at a later date repeated alone the same kind of thefts, the probability that he would be labeled a kleptomaniac would be high. And if the boy were a member of a wealthy family, the probability of his being labeled a kleptomaniac would be even higher.

In fire-setting cases the absence of obvious economic need also is used, in the traditional system of thought, as a criterion for applying the term "pyromania," but here the absence of other popular motives is used as well. If it can be determined easily that one burned property in order to collect insurance, in order to get revenge, or in an attempt to conceal a criminal act, or if there is ground for believing that he had some other conventional motive, then the probability that he will be designated a "pyromaniac" is low. However, if none of these is immediately apparent,[31] and especially in instances where the thing burned has no great economic value, the probability that the term will be applied is much higher. Traditionally, pyromania has been, then, like kleptomania, a residual category.[32]

In contrast to what appears to be current practice, when sociological theory of motivation is used the apparent inability of a person to explain

---

[29] In discussing legal problems of kleptomania, Hall says, "But mere repetition tends to prove habit, not abnormality" (*op. cit.*, p. 517). See also H. M. Tiebout and M. E. Kirkpatrick, "Psychiatric Factors in Stealing," *American Journal of Orthopsychiatry*, 2 (April 1932): 114–23 .

[30] Karpman reports the case of a man who burglarized women's apartments, taking both money and female intimate garments. By using this case as an illustration of "fetishistic kleptomania" he puts great emphasis upon the taking of the garments and almost ignores the taking of money ("Criminality, Insanity, and the Law"). Gault has made the following significant statement about such practices: "*The attempt that some have made to lay the foundation for cases of this nature in repressed sex motives and to interpret the objects stolen as so many symbols that they have in relation to the sex aspect of experience is a very unconvincing procedure. . . .* The case is doubtless not so simple. The sex urge is only one of the many that actuate the human organism. For instance, let us assume that a clothespin or a rubber hose found among the stolen goods of a kleptomaniac is a symbol. Symbol of what? The answer, according to the present writer's opinion, is that *its symbolic character depends upon what the investigator is interested in finding*" (*op. cit.*, pp. 163–66; italics not in the original).

[31] One investigator states that of all the varieties of incendiarists, the pyromaniac is most difficult to detect "because of the lack of motive" (Camille F. Hoyek, "Criminal Incendiarism," *Journal of Criminal Law and Criminology*, 41 (March–April 1951): 836–45.

[32] Psychoanalysts make much of the assumed sexual symbolism in cases of noneconomically motivated incendiarism. Thus, in one case of repeated burning of grass on vacant lots it was asserted that the lots symbolized the subject's father, that by driving onto the lot with his father's automobile the subject identified himself with his father and his sex organ and performed the act of incest on his mother, that the subject's efforts to help in extinguishing the fires was symbolic of an unconscious wish to atone for his sin, and that the splashing of water on the fire was a symbolic repetition of a regression to the urethral phase of his libidinal development, in which phase the subject was said to have had erections which were relieved by urinating. Ernest Simmel, "Incendiarism," in *Searchlights on Delinquency*, ed. K. R. Eissler (New York: International Universities Press, 1941), pp. 90–101.

his actions to the police, to a psychiatrist, or even to himself, is not considered sufficient for classifying those actions "compulsive." Using that theory, it may be observed that most criminals, in fact, when asked to explain their acts either recite the popular motives involved or respond that they do not know. For example, one might say, as did a criminal who had stolen a whole truckload of groceries, "I didn't want to take them but I had to because I was hungry." This response may be compared with that of a person arrested for taking small objects from a store: "I didn't want to take them but I just had to take them," and with that of a person who had burned an automobile, "I just wanted to stir up some excitement." As indicated above, such rationalizations are not necessarily *ex post facto* justifications for acts—and if they are not, then there is no logical justification for classifying one person as a "thief" and the others as "compulsive." Motives are circumscribed by the actor's learned vocabulary.

SOCIOLOGICAL ROLE THEORY APPLIED TO "COMPULSIVE CRIME"

But sociological theory can do more than correctly classify the large proportion of defendants said to be compulsive. The literature on role theory provides a framework not only for understanding the behavior of such defendants, but for understanding their inability to account for their behavior as well. Closely related to the theory of motivation which has been outlined is that aspect of role theory which deals with the relationship between the person's identification of himself as a "social object" and his subsequent behavior.[33] In order to play a social role one must anticipate the reactions of others by taking the role implicitly before it is taken overtly. He must look at himself from another's point of view. By hypothesizing the reactions of others the person looks upon himself as an object and, consequently, identifies himself as a particular kind of object. He then performs the role which is appropriate to the kind of social object with which he has identified. The vocabulary of motives employed in the performance of the role also is a corollary of this self-identification. But at various times and in different situations the person may identify himself differently, so that he is able to play many, often even conflicting, social roles. Again, his identification of who he is and what he is determines the roles he plays.[34]

For example, one might in the course of a day identify himself as a father in one situation, as a husband in another situation, and as a property owner in another situation. The motives employed in the performance

---

[33] For a general discussion of this subject, see George H. Mead, *Mind, Self, and Society* (Chicago: University of Chicago Press, 1934).
[34] See the discussion by Nelson Foote, *op. cit.*

of each role will reflect his particular identification. A similar phenomenon may exist in respect to so-called "compulsive crime." For example, a person might in some situations identify himself as a kleptomaniac, since that construct is now popular in our culture, and a full commitment to such an identification includes the use of motives which, in turn, release the energy to perform a so-called compulsive act. The more positive the conviction that one is a kleptomaniac, the more automatic his behavior will appear. The subject's behavior in particular situations, then, is organized by his identification of himself according to the linguistic construct "kleptomania" or its equivalent. In the framework of role theory, it is this kind of organization which makes the behavior recognizably recurrent in the life history of the person. The fact that the acts are recurrent does not mean that they are prompted from within, but only that certain linguistic symbols have become usual for the person in question.

If this theory were applied, we would not expect apprehended shoplifters, some of whom conceive of themselves as kleptomaniacs, to provide a logically consistent or even "correct" explanation for their behavior. For example, one who has behaved according to a set of linguistic constructs acceptable to himself in one role (kleptomaniac) might later discover that both the behavior and the constructs are unacceptable to himself in another role he is playing or desires to play (father, property owner). In that case there will be a high probability of denial to himself in the second role that "he" behaved at all. His conception of himself from one point of view results in denial of the action: "I wasn't myself when (or if) I did that," "I wasn't feeling well that day," "I couldn't be the criminal you seek—I couldn't do a thing like that," etc. On the other hand, his continued conception of himself according to the symbolic constructs which were used in behaving in the first place probably will result in open confession that "he" behaved: "Stop me before I do it again," "I have no control of myself," "That which is 'in' me comes out in situations like that." "I did it and I'm glad," etc.

In interviewing persons who, according to role theory, have identified with "compulsive criminals" of some sort, we should not expect them to realize that "who they are" depends upon language symbols and hence upon arbitrary ascriptions by others. One who identifies himself as a "kleptomaniac," for example, will be prone to accept such a conception of himself as ultimate reality. Even those observers or examiners who use the traditional notion that compulsive behavior is an expression of an "inner spring of action" have considered the subject's conception of himself as absolute rather than as a group product. As one sociologist has pointed out, "Because our learning has more often than not been perfected to the point where cognitive judgments in standardized situations are made instantaneously, and the energy for performing the appropriate behavior is released immediately, it has been an easy mistake for many observers to suppose that the organic correlates came first and even account for the definition of the situation, rather than the reverse."[35]

In our present state of knowledge we cannot be entirely sure how one gets committed to particular identities and motives in the first place, but, as indicated, the process certainly is one of social learning. The differential association theory is a theory of social learning specifically applied to criminal behavior, and it contends that, in the terminology used above, the identifications and motives of criminals are acquired through direct personal contacts with persons sharing those identifications and motives. This theory may have many defects, in that it does not precisely or adequately describe or integrate all the aspects of the processes by which criminality is learned, but it describes the processes by which one becomes a "compulsive" criminal as well as it describes the processes by which one becomes a "noncompulsive" criminal. "Compulsive criminality," as traditionally described, is not of such a nature that it is necessarily an exception to the differential association theory.

SUMMARY AND CONCLUSIONS

1. The assertion that "the latent forces of such phenomena as compulsive stealing and fire-setting are understood"[36] is not warranted.

2. If the traditional assumption that all "compulsive crime" is motivated entirely "from within" is correct, then the use of the words "compulsive" and "crime" together is erroneous. If the behavior actually were prompted "from within," it would be subsumed under the legal concept "insanity," not "crime."

3. Reexamination of "compulsive crime" concepts in the framework of sociological theories of motivation, identification, and role-playing indicates that most of the legally harmful behavior traditionally labeled "compulsive" actually is "motivated" and has a developmental history which is very similar to that of other "motivated" behavior. That legally harmful behavior which is automatic ("nonmotivated") cannot be considered as crime.

4. Since the developmental processes in so-called "compulsive criminality" are the same as the processes in other criminality, "compulsive crimes" are not, because of something in their nature, exceptional to the differential association theory. Upon closer empirical examination it probably will be demonstrated that criminality which traditionally has been assumed to be "personal" is actually a group product, and this criminality will become of more concern to the sociologist than has been the case in the past.

---

[35] *Ibid.*
[36] Robert M. Lindner, *Stone Walls and Men* (New York: Odyssey Press, 1946), p. 323.

18. DIFFERENTIAL ASSOCIATION AND MODERN BEHAVIOR THEORY

Robert L. Burgess and Ronald L. Akers

INTRODUCTION

In spite of the body of literature that has accumulated around the differential association theory of criminal behavior,[1] it has yet to receive crucial

Reprinted by permission of the authors and the Society for the Study of Social Problems from *Social Problems*, 14, no. 2 (Fall 1966): 128–47. Original title: "A Differential Association–Reinforcement Theory of Criminal Behavior."

[1] By 1960, Cressey had collected a 70-item bibliography on the theory; see Edwin H. Sutherland and Donald R. Cressey, *Principles of Criminology*, 6th ed. (Philadelphia: Lippincott, 1960), p. vi. He has presented an exhaustive review of the mistaken notions, criticisms, attempted reformulations, and empirical tests of the theory contained in a sizable body of literature (Donald R. Cressey, "Epidemiology and Individual Conduct: A Case from Criminology," *Pacific Sociological Review*, 3 [Fall 1960]: 47–58). For more recent literature, see Donald R. Cressey, "The Theory of Differential Association: An Introduction," *Social Problems*, 8 (Summer 1960): 2–5; James F. Short, Jr., "Differential Association as a Hypothesis: Problems of Empirical Testing," *Social Problems*, 8 (Summer 1960): 14–25; Henry D. McKay, "Differential Association and Crime Prevention: Problems of Utilization," *Social Problems*, 8 (Summer 1960): 25–37; Albert J. Reiss, Jr., and A. Lewis Rhodes, "An Empirical Test of Differential Association Theory," *Journal of Research in Crime and Delinquency*, 1 (January 1964): 5–18; Harwin L. Voss, "Differential Association and Reported Delinquent Behavior: A Replication," *Social Problems*, 12 (Summer 1964): 78–85; Siri Naess, "Comparing Theories of Criminogenesis," *Journal of Research in Crime and Delinquency*, 1 (July 1964): 171–80; C. R. Jeffery, "Criminal Behavior and Learning Theory," *Journal of Criminal Law, Criminology, and Police Science*, 56 (September 1965): 294–300.

empirical test or thorough restatement beyond Sutherland's own revision in 1947. Recognizing that the theory is essentially a learning theory, Sutherland rephrased it to state explicitly that criminal behavior is learned as any behavior is learned. In Cressey's two revisions of the textbook, the theory has been deliberately left unchanged from Sutherland's revision. Thus, the theory as it stands now is postulated upon the knowledge of the learning process extant twenty to twenty-five years ago.[2]

Sutherland himself never was able to test directly or find specific empirical support for his theory, but he was convinced that the two-edged theory —(1) genetic differential association and (2) structural differential social organization—accounted for the known data on the full range of crimes, including conventional violations and white-collar crimes.[3] The theory has received some other empirical support,[4] but negative cases have also been found.[5] The attempts to subject the theory to empirical test are marked by inconsistent findings both within the same study and between studies, as well as by highly circumscribed and qualified findings and conclusions. Whether the particular researcher concludes that his findings do or do not seem to support the theory, nearly all have indicated difficulty in operationalizing the concepts and recommend that the theory be modified in such a way that it becomes more amenable to empirical testing.

Suggested theoretical modifications have not been lacking, but the difficulty with these restatements is that they are no more readily operationalized than Sutherland's.[6] One recent paper, however, by De Fleur and

---

[2] The original formal statement appeared in Edwin H. Sutherland, *Principles of Criminology*, 3rd ed. (Philadelphia: Lippincott, 1939), pp. 4–8. The terms "systematic" and "consistency," along with some statements referring to social disorganization and culture conflict, were deleted in the revised theory. Two sentences stating that criminal behavior is learned were added, and the terms "learned" and "learning" were included in other sentences. The modalities of duration, priority, and intensity were added. The revised theory is in Sutherland and Cressey, *op. cit.*, pp. 77–79. For Cressey's discussion of why he left the theory in its 1947 form, see *ibid.*, p. vi.

[3] *Ibid.*, pp. 77–80; Edwin H. Sutherland, *White Collar Crime* (New York: Holt, Rinehart & Winston, 1961), pp. 234–56 (originally published 1949). See also Cressey's "Foreword," p. x.

[4] John C. Ball, "Delinquent and Non-Delinquent Attitudes Toward the Prevalence of Stealing," *Journal of Criminal Law, Criminology, and Police Science*, 48 (September–October 1957): 259–74; James F. Short, "Differential Association and Delinquency," *Social Problems*, 4 (January 1957): 233–39; Short, "Differential Association with Delinquent Friends and Delinquent Behavior," *Pacific Sociological Review*, 1 (Spring 1958): 20–25; Short, "Differential Association as a Hypothesis"; Voss, *op. cit.*; Donald R. Cressey, "Application and Verification of the Differential Association Theory," *Journal of Criminal Law, Criminology, and Police Science*, 43 (May–June 1952): 47–50; Cressey, *Other People's Money* (Glencoe, Ill.: Free Press, 1953), pp. 147–49; Daniel Glaser, "Differential Association and Criminological Prediction," *Social Problems*, 7 (Summer 1960): 7–10.

[5] Marshall Clinard, *The Black Market* (New York: Rinehart, 1952), pp. 285–329; Clinard, "Rural Criminal Offenders," *American Journal of Sociology*, 50 (July 1944): 38–45; Edwin M. Lemert, "An Isolation and Closure Theory of Naive Check Forgery," *Journal of Criminal Law, Criminology, and Police Science*, 44 (September–October 1953): 293–307; Reiss and Rhodes, *op. cit.*; Cressey, "Application and Verification of the Differential Association Theory," pp. 51–52; Cressey, *Other People's Money*, pp. 149–51; Glaser, *op. cit.*, pp. 12–13.

[6] See Daniel Glaser, "Criminality Theories and Behavioral Images," *American Journal of Sociology*, 61 (March 1956): 433–44; Glaser, "Differential Association and Criminological Prediction," pp. 10–13; Naess, *op. cit.*, pp. 174–79.

Quinney,[7] offers new promise that the theory can be adequately operationalized. They have presented a detailed strategy for making specific deductions for empirical testing. But while they have clarified the problems in the derivation and generation of testable hypotheses from differential association, they still see its empirical validation as a very difficult, though not impossible, task.

Regardless of the particular criticisms, the exceptions taken, and the difficulties involved in testing and reformulating the theory that have been offered, few take exception to the central learning assumptions in differential association. If we accept the basic assumption that criminal behavior is learned by the same processes and involves the same mechanisms as conforming behavior, then we need to recognize and make use of the current knowledge about these processes and mechanisms. Neither the extant statement of the theory nor the reformulations of it make explicit the nature of the underlying learning process involved in differential association. In short, no major revisions have been made utilizing established learning principles.

That this type of revision of the theory is needed has been recognized and some criticism of differential association has revolved around the fact that it does not adequately portray the process by which criminal behavior is learned. But as Cressey explains: "It is one thing to criticize the theory for failure to specify the learning process accurately and another to specify which aspects of the learning process should be included and in what way."[8]

Sutherland, of course, was as interested in explaining the "epidemiology" of crime as in explaining how the individual comes to engage in behavior in violation of the law, and insisted that the two explanations must be consistent.[9] Differential social organization (normative conflict) has been successful in "making sense" of variations in crime rates. But differential association has been less sucessful in explicating the process by which this differential organization produces individual criminality. This seems to be due not to the lack of importance of associations for criminal behavior but "rather to the fact that the theory outran the capacity of either psychology or social psychology to give adequate, scientific answers to the question of why there are such qualitative (selective) differences in human association."[10]

It now appears, however, that there is a body of verified theory which is

---

[7] Melvin De Fleur and Richard Quinney, "A Reformulation of Sutherland's Differential Association Theory and a Strategy for Empirical Verification," *Journal of Research in Crime and Delinquency*, 3 (January 1966): 13.

[8] Cressey, "Epidemiology and Individual Conduct," p. 54.

[9] Sutherland and Cressey, *op. cit.*, p. 80; Albert K. Cohen, Alfred R. Lindesmith, and Karl F. Schuessler, eds., *The Sutherland Papers*, Social Science series no. 15 (Bloomington: Indiana University Press, 1956), pp. 5–42. That Sutherland intended an explanation of the twofold problem of rates of crime and individual criminal behavior is, of course, the basic point of Cressey's paper "Epidemiology and Individual Conduct."

[10] George B. Vold, *Theoretical Criminology* (New York: Oxford University Press, 1958), p. 198.

adequate to the task of accurately specifying this process. Modern learning theory seems capable of providing insights into the problem of uniting structural and genetic formulations. While sociologists know a great deal about the structure of the environment from which deviants come, we know very little about the determining variables operating within this environment. The burden of criminological theory today is to combine knowledge of structural pressures with explanations of "why only *some* of the persons on whom this pressure is exerted become non-conformists."[11]

It is for this reason that the recent effort by C. R. Jeffery to reexamine differential association in light of modern learning theory marks a new departure in the abundance of thinking and writing that has characterized the intellectual history of this theory.[12] In spite of their intricate axiomatization of the theory, De Fleur and Quinney, for example, recognize that even they have left the learning process in differential association unspecified. But, they note, "modern reinforcement learning theory would handle this problem. . . ."[13] This is precisely what Jeffery proposed to do, and to the extent that this objective is served by discussing learning theory and criminal behavior together, he is at least partially successful. However, Jeffery does not in fact make it clear just how Sutherland's differential association theory may be revised. His explanation incorporates differential reinforcement: "[A] criminal act occurs in an environment in which in the past the actor has been reinforced for behaving in this manner, and the aversive consequences attached to the behavior have been of such a nature that they do not control or prevent the response."[14] This statement, as it stands, bears no obvious or direct relation to Sutherland's differential association, and nowhere else does Jeffery make it clear how differential reinforcement is a reformulation of differential association. Jeffery does discuss modern learning principles, but he does not show how these principles may be incorporated within the framework of Sutherland's theory, nor how these principles may lead to explanations of past empirical findings.

Jeffery's theory and his discussion of criminal behavior and learning theory remain not so much incorrect as unconvincing. His presentation of learning principles is supported wholly by reference to experiments with lower organisms and his extension to criminal behavior is mainly through anecdotal and illustrative material. The potential value and impact of Jeffery's article is diminished by not calling attention to the already large and growing body of literature in experimental behavioral science, especially evidence using human subjects, that has direct implications for dif-

---

[11] Cressey, "Theory of Differential Association," p. 5.
[12] Jeffery, *op. cit.*
[13] De Fleur and Quinney, *op. cit.*, p. 3.
[14] *Ibid.*, p. 295.

ferential association theory. We are basically in agreement with Jeffery that learning theory has progressed to the point where it seems likely that differential association can be restated in a more sophisticated and testable form in the language of modern learning theory. But that restatement must be attempted in a thorough fashion before we can expect others to accept it. Jeffery begins to do this and his thoughts are significant, but they do not take into account the theory as a whole.

The amount of empirical research in the social psychology of learning clearly has shown that the concepts in learning theory are susceptible to operationalization. Therefore, applying an integrated set of learning principles to differential association theory should adequately provide the revision needed for empirical testing. These learning principles are based on literally thousands of experimental hours covering a wide range of the phylogenetic scale and more nearly constitute empirically derived *laws* of behavior than any other set of principles. They enable the handling of a great variety of observational as well as experimental evidence about human behavior.

It is the purpose of this paper to take the first step in the direction to which Jeffery points. A restatement of the theory, not an alternative theory, will be presented, although, of necessity, certain ideas not intrinsic to differential association will have to be introduced and additions will be made to the original propositions. It should be pointed out that De Fleur and Quinney have been able to demonstrate that Sutherland's propositions, when stated in the form of set theory, appear to be internally consistent. By arranging the propositions in axiomatic form, stating them in logical rather than verbal symbols, they have brought the theoretical grammar up to date.[15] Such is not our intention in this paper at all. We recognize and appreciate the importance of stating the propositions in a formal, deductive fashion. We do feel, however, that this task is, at the present time, subsidiary to the more urgent task of: (1) making explicit the learning process, as it is now understood by modern behavioral science, from which the propositions of differential association can be derived; (2) fully reformulating the theory, statement by statement, in light of the current knowledge of this learning process; and (3) helping criminologists become aware of the advances in learning theory and research that are directly relevant to an explanation of criminal behavior.[16] No claim is made that this constitutes a final statement. If it has any seminal value at all, that is, if it provokes a serious new look at the theory and encourages further effort in this direction, our objective will have been served.

---

[15] De Fleur and Quinney, *op. cit.*

[16] Our main concern here, of course, is with the nine statements of the theory as a genetic explanation of the process by which the individual comes to engage in illegal behavior. We do not lose sight of the fact, however, that this must be integrated with explanations of the variation and location of crime.

DIFFERENTIAL ASSOCIATION AND
MODERN BEHAVIOR THEORY

In this section the nine formal propositions in which Sutherland expressed his theory will be analyzed in terms of behavior theory and research and will be reformulated as seven new propositions. (See Table 1, page 232.)

1. "Criminal behavior is learned"; 8. "The process of learning criminal behavior by association with criminal and anti-criminal patterns involves all of the mechanisms that are involved in any other learning."

Since both the first and eighth sentences in the theory obviously form a unitary idea, it seems best to state them together. Sutherland was aware that these statements did not sufficiently describe the learning process,[17] but these two items leave no doubt that differential association theory was meant to fit into a general explanation of human behavior, and as such is unambiguously stated in the prefatory remarks of the theory: an "explanation of criminal behavior should be a specific part of a general theory of behavior."[18] Modern behavior theory as a general theory provides us with a good idea of what the mechanisms are that are involved in the process of acquiring behavior.[19]

According to this theory, there are two major categories of behavior. On the one hand, there is reflexive or *respondent* behavior, which is behavior that is governed by the stimuli that elicit it. Such behaviors are largely associated with the autonomic system. The work of Pavlov is of special significance here. On the other hand, there is *operant* behavior: behavior which involves the central nervous system. Examples of operant behavior include verbal behavior, playing ball, driving a car, and buying a new suit. It has been found that this class of behavior is a function of its past and present environmental consequences. Thus, when a particular operant is followed by certain kinds of stimuli, that behavior's frequency of occurrence will increase in the future. These stimuli are called reinforcing stimuli or reinforcers[20] and include food, money, clothes, objects of various

---

[17] Sutherland and Cressey, *op. cit.*, p. 54.

[18] *Ibid.*, p. 75.

[19] It should be mentioned at the outset that there is more than one learning theory. The one we will employ is called behavior theory. More specifically, it is that variety of behavior theory largely associated with the name of B. F. Skinner (*Science and Human Behavior* [New York: Macmillan, 1953]). It differs from other learning theories in that it restricts itself to the relations between observable, measurable behavior and observable, measurable conditions. There is nothing in this theory that denies the existence, or importance, or even the inherent interest of the nervous system or brain. However, most behavioral scientists in this area are extremely careful in hypothesizing intervening variables or constructs, whether they are egos, personalities, response sets, or some sort of internal computers. Generally they adopt the position that the only real value of a construct is its ability to improve one's predictions. If it does not, then it must be excluded in accordance with the rule of parsimony.

[20] It has been said by some that a tautology is involved here. But there is nothing tautological about classifying events in terms of their effects. As Skinner, *op. cit.*, pp. 72–73, has noted, this criterion is both empirical and objective. There is only one sure way of telling whether or not a given stimulus event is reinforcing to a given individual under

sorts, social attention, approval, affection, and social status. This entire process is called positive reinforcement. One distinguishing characteristic of operant behavior as opposed to respondent behavior, then, is that the latter is a function of its antecedent stimuli, whereas the former is a function of its antecedent environmental consequences.

Typically, operant and respondent behaviors occur together in an individual's everyday behavior, and they interact in extremely intricate ways. Consequently, to understand fully any set of patterned responses, the investigator should observe the effects of the operants on the respondents as well as the effects of the respondents on the operants. The connections between operant and respondent behaviors are especially crucial to an analysis of attitudes, emotional and conflict behaviors.

In everyday life, different consequences are usually contingent upon different classes of behavior. This relationship between behavior and its consequences functions to alter the rate and form of behavior as well as its relationship to many features of the environment. The process of operant reinforcement is the most important process by which behavior is generated and maintained. There are, in fact, six possible environmental consequences relative to the law of operant behavior. (1) A behavior may produce certain stimulus events and thereby increase in frequency. As we have indicated above, such stimuli are called positive reinforcers and the process is called positive reinforcement. (2) A behavior may remove, avoid, or terminate certain stimulus events and thereby increase in frequency. Such stimuli are termed negative reinforcers and the process negative reinforcement. (3) A behavior may produce certain stimulus events and thereby decrease in frequency. Such stimuli are called aversive stimuli or, more recently, punishers.[21] The entire behavioral process is called positive punishment. (4) A behavior may remove or terminate certain stimulus events and thereby decrease in frequency. Such stimuli are positive reinforcers and the process is termed negative punishment. (5) A behavior may produce or remove certain stimulus events which do not change the behavior's frequency at all. Such stimuli are called neutral stimuli. (6) A behavior may no longer produce customary stimulus events and thereby decrease in frequency. The stimuli which are produced are neutral stimuli, and the process extinction. When a reinforcing stimulus no longer functions to increase the future

given conditions, and that is to make a direct test: observe the frequency of a selected behavior, then make a stimulus event contingent upon it and observe any change in frequency. If there is a change in frequency, then we may classify the stimulus as reinforcing to the individual under the stated conditions. Our reasoning would become circular, however, if we went on to assert that a given stimulus strengthens the behavior *because* it is reinforcing. Furthermore, not all stimuli, when presented, will increase the frequency of the behavior which *produced* them. Some stimuli will increase the frequency of the behavior which *removes* them, still others will neither strengthen nor weaken the behavior which produced them. See Robert L. Burgess and Ronald L. Akers, "Are Operant Principles Tautological?," *Psychological Record*, 16 (July 1966): 305–12.

[21] N. H. Azrin and D. F. Hake, "Conditioned Punishment," *Journal of the Experimental Analysis of Behavior*, 8 (September 1965): 279–93.

probability of the behavior which produced it, we say the individual is satiated. To restore the reinforcing property of the stimulus we need only deprive the individual of it for a time.[22]

The increase in the frequency of occurrence of a behavior that is reinforced is the very property of reinforcement that permits the fascinating variety and subtlety that occur in operant as opposed to respondent behavior. Another process producing the variety we see in behavior is that of *conditioning*. When a primary or unconditioned reinforcing stimulus such as food is repeatedly paired with a neutral stimulus, the latter will eventually function as a reinforcing stimulus as well. An illustration of this would be as follows. The milk a mother feeds to her infant is an unconditioned reinforcer. If the food is repeatedly paired with social attention, affection, and approval, these latter will eventually become reinforcing, as will the mother herself as a stimulus object. Later these *conditioned reinforcers* can be used to strengthen other behaviors by making these reinforcers contingent upon those new behaviors.

Differential reinforcement may also alter the form of a response. This process is called *shaping* or *response differentiation*. It can be exemplified by a child learning to speak. At first, the parent will reinforce any vocalization, but as time wears on, and as the child grows older, the parent will differentially reinforce only those responses which successfully approximate certain criteria. The child will be seen to proceed from mere grunts to "baby talk" to articulate speech.[23]

Of course, organisms, whether pigeons, monkeys, or people, do not usually go around behaving in all possible ways at all possible times. In short, behavior does not occur in a vacuum; a given behavior is appropriate to a given situation. By appropriate we mean that reinforcement has been forthcoming only under certain conditions, and it is under these conditions that the behavior will occur. In other words, differential reinforcement not only increases the probability of a response, it also makes that response more probable upon the recurrence of conditions the same as or similar to those that were present during previous reinforcements. Such a process is called *stimulus control* or *stimulus discrimination*. For example, a child when he is first taught to say "daddy" may repeat it when any male is present, or even, in the very beginning, when any adult is present. But through differential reinforcement, the child will eventually speak the word "daddy" only when his father is present or in other "appropriate" conditions. We may say that the father, as a stimulus object, functions as a discriminative stimulus (S^D) setting the occasion for the operant verbal re-

---

[22] See Jacob L. Gewirtz and Donald M. Baer, "Deprivation and Satiation of Social Reinforcers as Drive Conditions," *Journal of Abnormal and Social Psychology*, 57 (1958): 165–72.

[23] This seems to be the process involved in learning to become a marijuana user. By successive approximations, the user learns (from others) to close on the appropriate techniques and effects of using marijuana. See Howard S. Becker, *Outsiders* (New York: Free Press, Macmillan, 1963), pp. 41–58.

sponse "daddy" because in the past such behavior has been reinforced under such conditions.

It has also been discovered that the pattern or schedule of reinforcement is as important as the amount of reinforcement. For example, a *fixed-interval* schedule of reinforcement, where a response is reinforced only after a certain amount of time has passed, produces a lower rate of response than that obtained with reinforcement based on a *fixed-ratio* schedule, where a response is reinforced only after a certain number of responses have already been emitted. Similarly a response rate obtained with a fixed-ratio schedule is lower than that obtained with a *variable-ratio* schedule, where reinforcement occurs for a certain proportion of responses randomly varied about some central value. A schedule of reinforcement, then, refers to the response *contingencies* upon which reinforcement depends. All of the various schedules of reinforcement, besides producing lawful response characteristics, produce lawful extinction rates, once reinforcement is discontinued. Briefly, behavior reinforced on an intermittent schedule takes longer to extinguish than behavior reinforced on a continuous schedule.

This concept, schedules of reinforcement, is one the implications of which are little understood by many behavioral scientists, so a few additional words are in order. First of all, social reinforcements are for the most part intermittent. One obvious result of this fact is the resistance to extinction and satiation of much social behavior, desirable as well as undesirable. This is not peculiar to human social behavior, for even lower organisms seldom are faced with a continuous-reinforcement schedule. Nevertheless, reinforcements mediated by another organism are probably much less reliable than those produced by the physical environment. This is the case because social reinforcement depends upon behavioral processes in the reinforcer which are not under good control by the reinforcee. A more subtle, though essentially methodological, implication of this is that because most social behaviors are maintained by complex intermittent schedules which have been shaped over a long period of time, a social observer newly entering a situation may have extreme difficulty in immediately determining exactly what is maintaining a particular behavior or set of behaviors. Nor can the individual himself be expected to be able to identify his own contingencies of reinforcement.[24]

An important aspect of this theory is the presentation of the general ways that stimuli and responses can be formed into complex constellations of stimulus-response events. Although the basic principles are simple and must be separated to be distinguished and studied, in actual life the principles function in concert, and consist of complex arrays and constellations.[25] Such complexity can be seen in the fact that single S-R events may be com-

---

[24] Crossey encountered this problem in trying to get trust violators to reconstruct past associations (*Other People's Money*, p. 149).

[25] Arthur Staats, "An Integrated-Functional Learning Approach to Complex Human Behavior," Technical Report no. 28 (Tempe: Arizona State University, 1965).

bined into sequences on the basis of conditioning principles. That is, responses can be thought to have stimulus properties. In addition, more than one response may come under the control of a particular stimulus. Thus, when the stimulus occurs, it will tend to set the occasion for the various responses that have been conditioned to it. These responses may be competitive, that is, only one or the other can occur. When this is so, the particular response which does occur may also depend upon other discriminative stimuli present in the situation that control only one or the other response. Finally, while some of the stimuli to which an individual responds emanate from the external environment, social and otherwise, some come from his own behavior. An individual is, then, not only a source of responses, he is also a source of some stimuli—stimuli that can affect his own behavior.

The most general behavioral principle is the law of operant behavior, which says that behavior is a function of its past and current environmental consequences. There have been numerous studies with children[26] as well as adults[27] which indicate that individual behavior conforms to this law. Of much more interest to sociologists is an experiment designed by Azrin and Lindsley in 1956[28] to investigate cooperative social behavior. Their study demonstrated that cooperative behavior could be developed, maintained, eliminated, and reinstated solely through the manipulation of the contingency between reinforcing stimuli and the cooperative response. This basic finding has received much subsequent support. It has also been demonstrated that not only cooperative behavior, but also competitive behavior and leading and following behavior are functions of their past and present consequences.

Another of the behavioral principles we mentioned was that of stimulus discrimination. A discriminative stimulus is a stimulus in the presence of which a particular operant response is reinforced. Much of our behavior has come under the control of certain environmental, including social, stimuli because in the past it has been reinforced in the presence of those stimuli. In an experiment by Donald Cohen,[29] a normal thirteen-year-old boy named Justin, when placed under identical experimental conditions, emitted different behavior depending upon whether his partner was his mother, brother, sister, friend, or a stranger. The results of this investigation demonstrated that Justin's social behavior was differentially controlled by reinforcement; but it also demonstrated that his behavior was

---

26 See, for example, S. W. Bijou and P. T. Sturges, "Positive Reinforcers for Experimental Studies with Children—Consumables and Manipulatables," *Child Development*, 30 (1959): 151–70.

27 J. G. Holland, "Human Vigilance," *Science*, 128 (1959): 61–67; Harold Weiner, "Conditioning History and Human Fixed-Interval Performance," *Journal of the Experimental Analysis of Behavior*, 7 (September 1964): 383–85.

28 N. H. Azrin and O. R. Lindsley, "The Reinforcement of Cooperation Between Children," *Journal of Abnormal and Social Psychology*, 52 (January 1956).

29 Donald J. Cohen, "Justin and His Peers: An Experimental Analysis of a Child's Social World," *Child Development*, 33 (1962).

different depending upon the social stimuli present, thus reaffirming the principle of stimulus discrimination. In other words, the dynamic properties of his social behavior, whether cooperative, competitive, leading, or following, were controlled by his previous extra-experimental history with his teammates, although the experimenter could change those behaviors by experimentally altering the contingencies of reinforcement. It is, of course, almost a truism to say that an individual behaves differently in the presence of different people. The significance of this experiment, however, is that the investigator was able to isolate the determining variables and the principles by which they operated to produce this common phenomenon.

While this is by no means a complete survey of the relevant experimental tests of the behavioral principles outlined above, it may serve to point out that many forms of "normal" social behavior function according to the law of operant behavior. But what about "deviant" behavior? Can we be sure these same principles are operating here? Unfortunately there have been no studies which attempt to test directly the relevance of these behavioral principles to criminal behavior. But there have been several experimental investigations of deviant behaviors emitted by mental patients. For example, in a study by Ayllon and Michael,[30] it was shown that the bizarre behaviors of psychotics functioned according to these learning principles. In this particular study various behavioral problems of psychotic patients were "cured" through the manipulation of reinforcement contingencies. Such principles as extinction, negative and positive reinforcement, and satiation were effectively utilized to eliminate the unwanted behaviors.[31] This study was one of the first experimental tests of the contention that not only conforming but also many unusual, inappropriate, or undesirable behaviors are shaped and maintained through social reinforcement. In another experiment Isaacs, Thomas, and Goldiamond[32] demonstrated that complex adjustive behaviors can be operantly conditioned in long-term psychotics by manipulating available reinforcers.

In yet another investigation,[33] the personnel of a mental hospital ward for schizophrenics recorded the behavior of the patients and provided consequences to it according to certain preestablished procedures. Without going into the many important details of this long investigation, we may note that in each of the six experiments that were carried out, the results demon-

---

[30] T. Ayllon and J. Michael, "The Psychiatric Nurse as a Behavioral Engineer," *Journal of the Experimental Analysis of Behavior*, 2 (1959): 323–34.

[31] There is, of course, no intention on our part to equate "mental" illness or similarly severe behavior problems with criminal behavior. The only connection that we are making is that both may be seen to function according to the same basic behavioral principles and both may be in opposition to established norms.

[32] W. Isaacs, J. Thomas, and I. Goldiamond, "Application of Operant Conditioning to Reinstate Verbal Behavior in Psychotics," *Journal of Speech and Hearing Disorders*, 25 (1960): 8–12.

[33] T. Ayllon and N. Azrin, "The Measurement and Reinforcement of Behavior of Psychotics," *Journal of the Experimental Analysis of Behavior*, 8 (November 1965): 357–83.

strate that reinforcement was effective in maintaining desired performances, even though these were "back-ward" psychotics who had resisted all
previous therapy, including psychoanalysis, electroshock therapy, lobot-
omies, and so forth.

> In each experiment, the performance fell to a near zero level when
> the established response-reinforcement relation was discontinued. . . .
> The standard procedure for reinforcement had been to provide tokens
> . . . [exchanged] for a variety of reinforcers. Performance decreased
> when this response-reinforcement relation was disrupted (1) by deliver-
> ing tokens independently of the response while still allowing exchange
> of tokens for the reinforcers (Exp II and III), (2) by discontinuing the
> token system entirely but providing continuing access to the reinforcers
> (Exp IV), or (3) by discontinuing the delivery of tokens for a previously
> reinforced response while simultaneously providing tokens for a differ-
> ent, alternative response (Exp I and VI). Further, the effectiveness of
> the reinforcement procedure did not appear to be limited to an all-or-
> none basis. Patients selected and performed the assignment that pro-
> vided the larger number of tokens when reinforcement was available
> for more than one assignment (Exp V).[34]

Again, we cannot review all of the relevant literature, yet perhaps the
three investigations cited will serve to emphasize that many forms of deviant behavior are shaped and maintained by various contingencies of reinforcement.[35] Given this experimental evidence, we would amend Sutherland's first and eighth propositions to read: 1. *Criminal behavior is learned
according to the principles of operant conditioning.*

2. "Criminal behavior is learned in interaction with other persons in
the process of communication."

As De Fleur and Quinney have noted, the major implication of this
proposition is that symbolic interaction is a necessary condition for the
learning of criminal behavior.[36] Of direct relevance to this is an experiment
designed to test the relative significance of verbal instructions and reinforcement contingencies in generating and maintaining a certain class of
behaviors.[37] In brief, the results indicated that behavior could not be maintained solely through verbal instructions. However, it was also discovered
that it was an extremely arduous task to shape a set of complex behaviors
without using verbal instructions as discriminative stimuli. Behavior was
quickly and effectively developed and maintained by a combination of

---

[34] *Ibid.*, p. 381.
[35] See also J. J. Eysenck, ed., *Experiments in Behaviour Therapy* (New York: Pergamon
Press, Macmillan, 1964); L. Krasner and L. Ullman, *Research in Behavior Modification*
(New York: Holt, Rinehart & Winston, 1965); L. Ullman and L. Krasner, *Case Studies in
Behavior Modification* (New York: Holt, Rinehart & Winston, 1964).
[36] De Fleur and Quinney, *op. cit.*, p. 3.
[37] T. Ayllon and N. Azrin, "Reinforcement and Instructions with Mental Patients,"
Journal of the Experimental Analysis of Behavior, 7 (1964): 327–31.

verbal instructions *and* reinforcement consequences. Symbolic interaction is, then, not enough; contingencies of reinforcement must also be present.

From the perspective of modern behavior theory, two aspects of socialization are usually considered to distinguish it from other processes of behavioral change: (1) Only those behavioral changes occurring through learning are considered relevant; (2) only the changes in behavior having their origins in interaction with other persons are considered products of socialization.[38] Sutherland's theory may, then, be seen to be a theory of differential socialization, since he, too, restricted himself to learning having its origin in interaction with other persons. While social learning is, indeed, important and even predominant, it certainly does not exhaust the learning process. In short, we may learn (and, thus, our behavior would be modified) without any direct contact with another person. As such Sutherland's theory may be seen to suffer from a significant lacuna in that it neglected the possibility of deviant behavior being learned in nonsocial situations. Consequently, to be an adequate theory of deviant behavior, the theory must be amended further to include those forms of deviant behavior that are learned in the absence of social reinforcement. Other people are not the only source of reinforcement, although they are the most important. As Jeffery[39] has aptly noted, stealing is reinforcing in and by itself, whether other people know about it and reinforce it socially or not. The same may be said to apply to many forms of aggressive behaviors.[40]

There are many studies which are relevant to social interaction and socialization on the one hand, and Sutherland's second proposition on the other. For example, in a study by Lott and Lott[41] it was found that when child A was reinforced in the presence of child B, child A would later select child B as a companion. The behavior of selecting child B was not the behavior that was reinforced. The experimental conditions simply paired child B with positive reinforcement. In accordance with the principle of conditioning, child B had become a conditioned positive reinforcer. As such any behavior which produced the presence of child B would be strengthened, such behaviors, for example, as verbal responses requesting child B's company. Thus as Staats[42] has noted, the results of this study indicate that the concepts of reinforcing stimuli and group cohesion are related when analyzed in terms of an integrated set of learning principles.

---

[38] Paul F. Secord and Carl W. Backman, *Social Psychology* (New York: McGraw-Hill, 1964).

[39] Jeffery, *op. cit.*

[40] For some evidence that aggressive behavior may be of a respondent as well as an operant nature, see N. Azrin, R. Hutchinson, and R. McLaughlin, "The Opportunity for Aggression as an Operant Reinforcer During Aversive Stimulation," *Journal of the Experimental Analysis of Behavior,* 8 (May 1965): 171–80.

[41] B. E. Lott and A. J. Lott, "The Formation of Positive Attitudes Toward Group Members," *Journal of Abnormal and Social Psychology,* 61 (1960): 297–300.

[42] Arthur Staats, *Human Learning* (New York: Holt, Rinehart & Winston, 1964), p. 333.

Glaser[43] has attempted to reformulate Sutherland's differential association theory in terms of social identification. It should be recognized, however, that identification as well as modeling and imitative behavior (which are usually associated with identification) comprise just one feature of the socialization process. Furthermore, such behavior may be analyzed quite parsimoniously with the principles of modern behavior theory. For example, in a study by Bandura and Ross,[44] a child experienced the pairing of one adult with positive reinforcers. Presumably this adult would become a conditioned reinforcer. And indeed, later it was found that the child imitated this adult more than it did an adult who was not paired with positive reinforcers. That is, the one adult, as he became a stronger reinforcer, had also become a stronger S^D for imitating or following behavior. Thus, Bandura's and Ross's results demonstrate that imitating or following behavior is at least in part a function of the reinforcing value of people as social stimuli.

> On the basis of these results it is suggested that a change in the reinforcing value of an individual will change his power as a stimulus controlling other people's behavior in various ways. An increase in the reinforcing value of an individual will increase verbal and motor approach, or companionable responses, respectful responses, affectionate behavior, following behavior, smiling, pleasant conversation, sympathetic responses and the like.[45]

The relevance of these studies is that they have isolated some of the determining variables whereby the behavior of one person is influenced or changed by the behavior of another as well as the principles by which these variables operate. We have, of course, only scratched the surface. Many other variables are involved. For instance, not all people are equally effective in controlling or influencing the behavior of others. The person who can mediate the most reinforcers will exercise the most power. Thus, the parent, who controls more of his child's reinforcers, will exercise more power than an older sibling or the temporary "baby sitter." As the child becomes older and less dependent upon the parent for many of his reinforcers, other individuals or groups such as his peers may exercise more power. Carrying the analysis one step further, the person who has access to a large range of aversive stimuli will exert more power than one who has not. Thus a peer group may come to exercise more power over a child's behavior than the parent even though the parent may still control a large share of the child's positive reinforcers.

In addition to the reinforcing function of an individual or group, there

---

43 Glaser, "Criminality Theories and Behavioral Images."
44 A. Bandura, D. Ross, and S. Ross, "A Comparative Test of the Status Envy, Social Power and the Secondary Reinforcement Theories of Identification Learning," *Journal of Abnormal and Social Psychology*, 67 (1963): 527–34.
45 Staats, *Human Learning*, p. 333.

is, as seen in the Cohen and the Bandura and Ross studies, the discriminative stimulus function of a group. For example, specific individuals as physical stimuli may acquire discriminative control over an individual's behavior. The child in our example above is reinforced for certain kinds of behaviors in the presence of his parent, thus the parent's presence may come to control this type of behavior. He is reinforced for different behaviors in the presence of his peers, who then come to set the occasion for this type of behavior. Consequently this proposition must be amended to read: 2. *Criminal behavior is learned both in nonsocial situations that are reinforcing or discriminative and through that social interaction in which the behavior of other persons is reinforcing or discriminative for criminal behavior.*

3. "The principal part of the learning of criminal behavior occurs within intimate personal groups."

In terms of our analysis, the primary group would be seen to be the major source of an individual's social reinforcements. The bulk of behavioral training which the child receives occurs at a time when the trainers, usually the parents, possess a very powerful system of reinforcers. In fact, we might characterize a primary group as a generalized reinforcer (one associated with many reinforcers, conditioned as well as unconditioned). And, as we suggested above, as the child grows older, groups other than the family may come to control a majority of an individual's reinforcers, e.g., the adolescent peer group.

To say that the primary group is the principal molder of an individual's behavioral repertoire is not to ignore social learning which may occur in other contexts. As we noted above, learning from social models can be adequately explained in terms of these behavioral principles. The analysis we employed there can also be extended to learning from the mass media and from "reference" groups. In any case, we may alter this proposition to read: 3. *The principal part of the learning of criminal behavior occurs in those groups which comprise the individual's major source of reinforcements.*

4. "When criminal behavior is learned, the learning includes (*a*) techniques of committing the crime, which are sometimes very complicated, sometimes very simple; (*b*) the specific direction of motives, drives, rationalizations, and attitudes."

A study by Klaus and Glaser,[46] as well as many other studies,[47] indicates that reinforcement contingencies are of prime importance in learning various behavioral techniques. And, of course, many techniques, both simple

---

[46] D. J. Klaus and R. Glaser, "Increasing Team Proficiency Through Training" (Pittsburgh: American Institute of Research, 1960).

[47] See Robert L. Burgess, "Communication Networks and Behavioral Consequences," forthcoming.

and complicated, are specific to a particular deviant act, such as jimmying, picking locks of buildings and cars, picking pockets, short- and big-con techniques, counterfeiting and safecracking. Other techniques in criminal behavior may be learned in conforming or neutral contexts, e.g., driving a car, signing checks, shooting a gun, etc. In any event, we need not alter the first part of this proposition.

The second part of this proposition does, however, deserve some additional comments. Sutherland's major focus here seems to be motivation. Much of what we have already discussed in this paper often goes under the general heading of motivation. The topic of motivation is as important as it is complex. This complexity is related to the fact that the same stimulus may have two functions: it may be both a reinforcing stimulus and a discriminative stimulus controlling the behavior which is followed by reinforcement.[48] Thus, motivation may be seen to be a function of the processes by which stimuli acquire conditioned reinforcing value and become discriminative stimuli. Reinforcers and discriminative stimuli here would become the dependent variables; the independent variables would be the conditioning procedures previously mentioned and the level of deprivation. For example, when a prisoner is deprived of contact with members of the opposite sex, such sex reinforcers will become much more powerful. Thus, those sexual reinforcers that are available, such as homosexual contact, would come to exert a great deal of influence and would shape behaviors that would be unlikely to occur without such deprivation. And, without going any further into this topic, some stimuli may be more reinforcing, under similar conditions of deprivation, for certain individuals or groups than for others. Furthermore, the satiation of one or more of these reinforcers would allow for an increase in the relative strength of others.

Much, therefore, can be learned about the distinctive characteristics of a group by knowing what the available and effective reinforcers are and the behaviors upon which they are contingent. Basically, we are contending that the nature of the reinforcer system and the reinforcement contingencies are crucial determinants of individual and group behavior. Consequently, a description of an individual's or group's reinforcers, and an understanding of the principles by which reinforcers affect behavior, would

---

[48] A central principle underlying this analysis is that reinforcing stimuli, both positive and negative, elicit certain respondents. Unconditioned reinforcers elicit these responses without training, conditioned reinforcers elicit such responses through respondent conditioning. Staats and Staats (*Complex Human Behavior* [New York: Holt, Rinehart & Winston, 1964]) have characterized such respondents as "attitude" responses. Thus, a positive reinforcer elicits a positive attitude. Furthermore, these respondents have stimulus characteristics which may become discriminative stimuli setting the occasion for a certain class of operants called "striving" responses for positive reinforcers and escape and/or avoidance behaviors for negative reinforcers. These respondents and their attendant stimuli may be generalized to other reinforcing stimuli. Thus, striving responses can be seen to generalize to new positive reinforcers since these also will elicit the respondent responses and their characteristic stimuli which have become S^D's for such behavior.

be expected to yield a great deal of knowledge about individual and group deviant behavior.

Finally, the rationalizations which Cressey identifies with regard to trust violators and the peculiar extensions of "defenses to crimes" or "techniques of neutralization" by which deviant behavior is justified, as identified by Sykes and Matza,[49] may be analyzed as operant behaviors of the escape or avoidance type which are maintained because they have the effect of avoiding or reducing the punishment that comes from social disapproval by oneself as well as by others. We may, therefore, rewrite this proposition to read: 4. *The learning of criminal behavior, including specific techniques, attitudes, and avoidance procedures, is a function of the effective and available reinforcers, and the existing reinforcement contingencies.*

5. "The specific direction of motives and drives is learned from definitions of the legal codes as favorable or unfavorable."

In this proposition, Sutherland appears to be referring, at least in part, to the concept "norm," which may be defined as a statement made by a number of the members of a group, not necessarily all of them, prescribing or proscribing certain behaviors at certain times.[50] We often infer what the norms of a group are by observing reaction to behavior, i.e., the sanctions applied to, or reinforcement and punishment consequences of, such behavior. We may also learn what a group's norms are through verbal or written statements. The individual group member also learns what is and is not acceptable behavior on the basis of verbal statements made by others, as well as through the sanctions (i.e., the reinforcing or aversive stimuli) applied to his behavior (and other norm violators) by others.

Behavior theory specifies the place of normative statements and sanctions in the dynamics of acquiring "conforming" or "normative" behavior. Just as the behavior and even the physical characteristics of the individual may serve discriminative functions, verbal behavior, and this includes normative statements, can be analyzed as S^D's. A normative statement can be analyzed as an S^D indicating that the members of a group ought to behave in a certain way in certain circumstances. Such "normative" behavior would be developed and maintained by social reinforcement. As we observed in the Ayllon-Azrin study[51] of instructions and reinforcement contingencies, such verbal behavior would not maintain any particular class of behaviors if it were not at least occasionally backed by reinforcement consequences. Extending their analysis, an individual would not "conform" to a norm if he did not have a past history of reinforcement for such con-

---

[49] Cressey, *Other People's Money*, pp. 93–138; G. M. Sykes and David Matza, "Techniques of Neutralization: A Theory of Delinquency," *American Sociological Review*, 22 (December 1957): 664–70.

[50] George C. Homans, *Social Behavior: Its Elementary Forms* (New York: Harcourt, Brace & World, 1961).

[51] Ayllon and Azrin, "Reinforcement and Instructions with Mental Patients."

forming behavior. This is important, for earlier we stated that we can learn a great deal about a group by knowing what the effective reinforcers are and the behaviors upon which they are contingent. We may now say that we can learn a great deal about an individual's or a group's behavior when we are able to specify, not only what the effective reinforcers are, but also what the rules or norms are by which these reinforcers are applied.[52] For these two types of knowledge will tell us much about the types of behavior that the individual will develop or the types of behaviors that are dominant in a group.

For example, it has often been noted that most official criminal acts are committed by members of minority groups who live in slums. One distinguishing characteristic of a slum is the high level of deprivation of many important social reinforcers. Exacerbating this situation is the fact that these people, in contrast to other groups, lack the behavioral repertoires necessary to produce reinforcement in the prescribed ways. They have not been and are not now adequately reinforced for lawful or normative behavior. And as we know from the law of operant reinforcement, a reinforcer will increase the rate of occurrence of any operant which produces it. Furthermore, we would predict that given a large number of individuals under similar conditions, they are likely to behave in similar ways. Within such groups, many forms of social reinforcement may become contingent upon classes of behaviors which are outside the larger society's normative requirements. Norms and legal codes, as discriminative stimuli, will only control the behavior of those who have experienced the appropriate learning history. If an individual has been, and is, reinforced for such "normative" behavior, that behavior will be maintained in strength. If he has not been and is not now reinforced for such behaviors, they would be weak, if they existed in his repertoire at all. And, importantly, the reinforcement system may shape and maintain another class of behaviors which do result in reinforcement, and such behaviors may be considered deviant or criminal by other members of the group. Thus we may formulate this proposition to read: 5. *The specific class of behaviors which are learned and their frequency of occurrence are a function of the reinforcers which are effective and available, and the rules or norms by which these reinforcers are applied.*

6. "A person becomes delinquent because of an excess of definitions favorable to violation of law over definitions unfavorable to violation of law."

This proposition is generally considered the heart of Sutherland's theory; it is the principle of differential association. It follows directly from proposition 5, and we must now refer back to that proposition. In proposition 5,

---

[52] Staats and Staats, *op. cit.*

the use of the preposition "from" in the phrase "learned from definitions of the legal codes as favorable or unfavorable" is somewhat misleading. The meaning here is not so much that learning results *from* these definitions as it is that they form part of the *content* of one's learning, determining which direction one's behavior will go in relation to the law, i.e., law-abiding or lawbreaking.

These definitions of the law make lawbreaking seem either appropriate or inappropriate. Those definitions which place lawbreaking in a favorable light in a sense can be seen as essentially norms of evasion and/or norms directly conflicting with conventional norms. They are, as Sykes and Matza and Cressey note, "techniques of neutralization," "rationalizations," or "verbalizations" which make criminal behavior seem "all right" or justified, or which provide defenses against self-reproach and disapproval from others.[53] The principle of negative reinforcement would be of major significance in the acquisition and maintenance of such behaviors.

This analysis suggests that it may not be an "excess" of one kind of definition over another in the sense of a cumulative ratio, but rather in the sense of the relative amount of discriminative stimulus value of one set of verbalizations or normative statements over another. As we suggested in the last section, normative statements are, themselves, behaviors that are a function of reinforcement consequences. They, in turn, may serve as discriminative stimuli for other operant behaviors (verbal and nonverbal). But recall that reinforcement must be forthcoming, at least occasionally, before a verbal statement can continue as a discriminative stimulus. Bear in mind, also, that behavior may produce reinforcing consequences even in the absence of any accompanying verbal statements.

In other terms, a person will become delinquent if the official norms or laws do not perform a discriminative function and thereby control "normative" or conforming behavior. We know from the law of differential reinforcement that that operant which produces the most reinforcement will become dominant if it results in reinforcement. Thus, if lawful behavior did not result in reinforcement, the strength of the behavior would be weakened, and a state of deprivation would result, which would, in turn, increase the probability that other behaviors would be emitted which are reinforced, and such behaviors would be strengthened. And, of course, these behaviors, though common to one or more groups, may be labeled deviant by the larger society. And such behavior patterns themselves may acquire conditioned reinforcing value and subsequently be enforced by the mem-

---

[53] Sykes and Matza, *op. cit.;* Cressey, *Other People's Money,* pp. 93–138; Cressey, "The Differential Association Theory and Compulsive Crimes," *Journal of Criminal Law, Criminology, and Police Science,* 45 (May–June 1954): 29–40; Cressey, "Social Psychological Foundations for Using Criminals in the Rehabilitation of Criminals," *Journal of Research in Crime and Delinquency,* 2 (July 1965): 45–59. See revised proposition 4.

bers of a group by making various forms of social reinforcement, such as social approval, esteem, and status, contingent upon that behavior.

The concept "excess" in the statement "excess of definitions favorable to violation of law" has been particularly resistant to operationalization. A translation of this concept in terms of modern behavior theory would involve the "balance" of reinforcement consequences, positive and negative. The law of differential reinforcement is crucial here. That is, a person would engage in those behaviors for which he had been reinforced most highly in the past. (The reader may recall that in the Ayllon-Azrin study with schizophrenics, it was found that the patients selected and performed those behaviors which provided the most reinforcers when reinforcement was available for more than one response.) Criminal behavior would, then, occur under those conditions where an individual has been most highly reinforced for such behavior, and the aversive consequences contingent upon the behavior have been of such a nature that they do not perform a "punishment function."[54] This leads us to a discussion of proposition 7. But first let us reformulate the sixth proposition to read: 6. *Criminal behavior is a function of norms which are discriminative for criminal behavior, the learning of which takes place when such behavior is more highly reinforced than noncriminal behavior.*

7. "Differential associations may vary in frequency, duration, priority, and intensity."

In terms of our analysis, the concepts frequency, duration, and priority are straightforward enough. The concept *intensity* could be operationalized to designate the number of the individual's positive and negative reinforcers that another individual or group controls, as well as the reinforcement value of that individual or group. As previously suggested, the group which can mediate the most positive reinforcers and which has the most reinforcement value, as well as access to a larger range of aversive stimuli, will exert the most control over an individual's behavior.

There is good reason to suspect, however, that Sutherland was not so much referring to differential associations with other persons as differential associations with criminal *patterns*. If this supposition is correct, then this proposition can be clarified by relating it to differential contingencies of reinforcement rather than differential social associations. From this perspective, the experimental evidence with regard to the various schedules

---

[54] This, then, is essentially differential reinforcement as Jeffery presents it. We have attempted to show how this is congruent with differential association. Further, while Jeffery ignores the key concepts of "definitions" and "excess," we have incorporated them into the reformulation. These definitions, viewed as verbalizations, become discriminative stimuli; and "excess" operates to produce criminal behavior in two related ways: (1) verbalizations conducive to law violation have greater discriminative stimulus value than other verbalizations, and (2) criminal behavior has been more highly reinforced and has produced fewer aversive outcomes than has law-abiding behavior in the conditioning history of the individual.

of reinforcement is of major importance. There are three aspects of the schedules of reinforcement which are of particular importance here: (1) the *amount* of reinforcement: the greater the amount of reinforcement, the higher the response rate: (2) the *frequency* of reinforcement, which refers to the number of reinforcements per given time period: the shorter the time period between reinforcements, the higher the response rate; and (3) the *probability* of reinforcement, which is the reciprocal of responses per reinforcement: the lower the ratio of responses per reinforcement, the higher the rate of response.[55]

Priority, frequency, duration, and intensity of association with criminal persons and groups are important to the extent that they insure that deviant behavior will receive greater amounts of reinforcement at more frequent intervals or with a higher probability than conforming behavior. But the frequency, probability, and amount of reinforcement are the crucial elements. This means that it is the coming under the control of contingencies of reinforcement that selectively produces the criminal definitions and behavior. Consequently, let us rewrite this proposition to read:
7. *The strength of criminal behavior is a direct function of the amount, frequency, and probability of its reinforcement.*

9. "While criminal behavior is an expression of general needs and values, it is not explained by those general needs and values since noncriminal behavior is an expression of the same needs and values."

In this proposition, Sutherland may have been reacting, at least in part, to the controversy regarding the concept "need." This controversy is now essentially resolved. For we have finally come to the realization that "needs" are unobservable, hypothetical, fictional inner-causal agents which were usually invented on the spot to provide spurious explanations of some observable behavior. Furthermore, they were inferred from precisely the same behavior they were supposed to explain.

While we can ignore the reference to needs, we must discuss values. Values may be seen as reinforcers which have salience for a number of the members of a group or society. We agree with Sutherland to the extent that he means that the nature of these general reinforcers do not necessarily determine which behavior they will strengthen. Money, or something else of general value in society, will reinforce any behavior that produces it. This reinforcement may depend upon noncriminal behavior, but it also may become contingent upon a set of behaviors that are labeled as criminal. Thus, if Sutherland can be interpreted as meaning that criminal and noncriminal behavior cannot be maintained by the same set of reinforcers, we

---

[55] R. T. Kelleher and L. R. Gollub, "A Review of Positive Conditioned Reinforcement," *Journal of the Experimental Analysis of Behavior*, October 1962, pp. 543–97. Because the emission of a fixed ratio or variable ratio of responses requires a period of time, the rate of responding will indirectly determine the frequency of reinforcement.

TABLE 1

A DIFFERENTIAL ASSOCIATION–REINFORCEMENT
THEORY OF CRIMINAL BEHAVIOR

Sutherland's Statements	Reformulated Statements
1. "Criminal behavior is learned."	1. Criminal behavior is learned according to the principles of operant conditioning.
8. "The process of learning criminal behavior by association with criminal and anti-criminal patterns involves all of the mechanisms that are involved in any other learning."	
2. "Criminal behavior is learned in interaction with other persons in a process of communication."	2. Criminal behavior is learned both in nonsocial situations that are reinforcing or discriminative and through that social interaction in which the behavior of other persons is reinforcing or discriminative for criminal behavior.
3. "The principal part of the learning of criminal behavior occurs within intimate personal groups."	3. The principal part of the learning of criminal behavior occurs in those groups which comprise the individual's major source of reinforcements.
4. "When criminal behavior is learned, the learning includes (a) techniques of committing the crime, which are sometimes very complicated, sometimes very simple; (b) the specific direction of motives, drives, rationalizations, and attitudes."	4. The learning of criminal behavior, including specific techniques, attitudes, and avoidance procedures, is a function of the effective and available reinforcers, and the existing reinforcement contingencies.
5. "The specific direction of motives and drives is learned from definitions of the legal codes as favorable or unfavorable."	5. The specific class of behaviors which are learned and their frequency of occurrence are a function of the reinforcers which are effective and available, and the rules or norms by which these reinforcers are applied.
6. "A person becomes delinquent because of an excess of definitions favorable to violation of law over definitions unfavorable to violation of law."	6. Criminal behavior is a function of norms which are discriminative for criminal behavior, the learning of which takes place when such behavior is more highly reinforced than noncriminal behavior.
7. "Differential associations may vary in frequency, duration, priority, and intensity."	7. The strength of criminal behavior is a direct function of the amount, frequency, and probability of its reinforcement.
9. "While criminal behavior is an expression of general needs and values, it is not explained by those general needs and values since noncriminal behavior is an expression of the same needs and values."	9. (Omit from theory.)

must disagree. However, it may be that there are certain reinforcing consequences which only criminal behavior will produce, for the behavior finally shaped will depend upon the reinforcer that is effective for the individual. Nevertheless, it is the reinforcement, not the specific nature of the reinforcer, which explains the rate and form of behavior. But since this issue revolves around contingencies of reinforcement which are handled elsewhere, we will eliminate this last proposition.

CONCLUDING REMARKS

The purpose of this paper has been the application of the principles of modern behavior theory to Sutherland's differential association theory. While Sutherland's theory has had an enduring effect upon the thinking of students of criminal behavior, it has, till now, undergone no major theoretical revision, despite the fact that there has been a steady and cumulative growth in the experimental findings of the processes of learning.

There are three aspects of deviant behavior which we have attempted to deal with simultaneously, but which should be separated. First, how does an individual *become* delinquent, or how does he learn delinquent behavior? Second, what *sustains* this delinquent behavior? We have attempted to describe the ways in which the principle of modern behavior theory are relevant to the development and maintenance of criminal behavior. In the process, we have seen that the principle of differential reinforcement is of crucial importance. But we must also attend to a third question, namely, what sustains the pattern or *contingency* of reinforcement? We only have hinted at some of the possibly important variables. We have mentioned briefly, for example, structural factors such as the level of deprivation of a particular group with regard to important social reinforcers, and the lack of effective reinforcement of "lawful" behavior[56] and the concomitant failure to develop the appropriate behavioral repertoires to produce reinforcement legally.[57] We have also suggested that those behaviors which do result in reinforcement may themselves gain reinforcement value and be enforced by the members of the group through the manipulation of various forms of social reinforcement, such as social approval and status, contingent upon such behaviors.[58] In short, new norms may develop and these may be termed delinquent by the larger society.

[56] Robert K. Merton, *Social Theory and Social Structure* (Glencoe, Ill.: Free Press, 1956), pp. 161–95. For a more complete discussion of social structure in terms relevant to this paper, see Robert L. Burgess and Don Bushell, Jr., *Behavioral Sociology*, Parts IV and V, forthcoming.

[57] *Ibid.*, and Richard A. Cloward, "Illegitimate Means, Anomie, and Deviant Behavior," *American Sociological Review*, 24 (April 1959): 164–77.

[58] Albert K. Cohen, *Delinquent Boys: The Culture of the Gang* (Glencoe, Ill.: Free Press, 1955).

There are many other topics that are of direct relevance to the problem of deviant behavior which we have not been able to discuss given the requirements of space. For instance, no mention has been made of some outstanding research in the area of punishment. This topic is, of course, of prime importance in the area of crime prevention. To illustrate some of this research and its relevance, it has been found experimentally that the amount of behavior suppression produced by response-contingent aversive stimuli is a direct function of the intensity of the aversive stimulus, but that a mild aversive stimulus may produce a dramatic behavior-suppression if it is paired with reinforcement for an alternative and incompatible behavior. Furthermore, it has been discovered that if an aversive stimulus is repeatedly paired with positive reinforcement, and reinforcement is not available otherwise, the aversive stimulus may become a discriminative stimulus (S^D) for reinforcement and, consequently, not decrease the behavior's frequency of occurrence.

There are, in conclusion, numerous criteria that have been used to evaluate theories. One such set is as follows:

1. The amount of empirical support for the theory's basic propositions.
2. The "power" of the theory, i.e., the amount of data that can be derived from the theory's higher-order propositions.
3. The controlling possibilities of the theory, including (a) whether the theory's propositions are, in fact, *causal* principles, and (b) whether the theory's propositions are stated in such a way that they suggest possible *practical* applications.

What dissatisfaction there has been with differential association can be attributed to its scoring low on these criteria, especially 1 and 3. We submit that the reformulated theory presented here answers some of these problems and better meets each of these criteria. It is our contention, moreover, that the reformulated theory not only specifies the conditions under which criminal behavior is learned, but also some of the conditions under which deviant behavior in general is acquired. Finally, while we have not stated our propositions in strictly axiomatic form, a close examination will reveal that each of the later propositions follow from, modify, or clarify earlier propositions.

Criminal Careers and
Behavior Systems

The early stages of a science are frequently devoted to constructing a typology of the variable or variables under investigation. If it is of any scientific value, the typology must meet a number of requirements, including a precise statement of its intent, an explicit set of defining characteristics on the basis of which classification may be undertaken, and logical reason to believe the differentiated types form a single typology.

The fact that everyday activities require frequent, and often strategic, use of taxonomies is so obvious that we tend to overlook the job confronting any scientist who imposes order upon his data. Nowhere has the task been more arduous than in criminology, and probably no field of inquiry has a more extensive graveyard of discarded taxonomies.

Typologies have been essential to the work of criminologists since the original need to identify types of criminals. While distinguishing varieties of criminals did not originate with Cesare Lombroso, his work at the turn of the century is well known to criminological historians. Eclectic, subjective, and with an obvious biological model in mind, Lombroso extensively analyzed "criminaloid," "political," "born," "insane," and "habitual" offenders. Similarly, his colleague Enrico Ferri proposed a typology composed of "born," "insane," "passional," "occasional," and "habitual" offenders. While these early criminologists may have differed in the extent to which they emphasized biological determinants of crime, or the proportion of criminals belonging to each category, their central deficiency was to concentrate upon sources of criminal motivation as the sole criterion for classification.

More recently, sociologists have pointed out that two conceptual dimensions other than personal motivation to crime deserve consideration: the act itself, whether legally or ethically defined, and the victim. Newly developing interest in victimology research [see Part Three of this book] underscores the victim's role in being exploited; for example, the social situations in which he routinely operates, the persons with whom he associates, and his styles of interaction with both familiar and unfamiliar persons.

A criminal typology, no matter how "exhaustive" of its subject matter, is inherently limited in its ability to capture the dynamic, patterned features of much criminal behavior. For this reason, investigators began some years ago to develop the concept of behavior systems, which directed attention to behavioral aspects of crimes and offenders. The distinguishing properties of a criminal behavior system, according to one authority, include

> the social roles the offender plays, the degree of his identification with crime, his conception of himself as a criminal, his patterns of association with others who are criminals or noncriminals, his continuation and progression in crime, the way in which he commits offenses, the relation of his behavior to his personality traits, and the degree to which criminal behavior has become part of his total life organization.[1]

Some of the most enthralling work being done by research criminologists concentrates upon the system attributes of "naïve" check forgery, embezzling, sex offenses, prostitution, homicide, chronic drunkenness, confidence swindling, pool hustling, and organized, syndicated crime.

In short, behavior systems analysis has become an attractive orientation because it emulates three themes fundamental to the sociological perspective: (a) it is not just a category of acts and offenders, but includes any traditions, rules of conduct (perhaps professional norms), and symbols of solidarity; (b) behavior is not unique to any individual, but is common to most or all —reflecting the central sociological features of patterning and repetition; and (c) since collective participation in the behavior system is characteristic, the most salient feature is the feeling of *identification* among participants.[2]

An additional attraction of the behavior-systems approach is its emphasis upon the *career* features of some offenders. By and large, the preponderance

---

[1] Marshall B. Clinard, "Criminological Research," in *Sociology Today: Problems and Prospects,* ed. Robert K. Merton, Leonard Broom, and Leonard S. Cottrell, Jr. (New York: Basic Books, 1959), p. 522.

[2] Edwin H. Sutherland and Donald R. Cressey, *Principles of Criminology,* 7th ed. (Philadelphia: Lippincott, 1966), p. 289.

of crime is committed by persons who are not acting out of idiosyncratic and spontaneous motives, but who have "programmed" lawlessness into their daily routine.

The concept of career has enjoyed use in many contexts, e.g., in reference to developmental organizations such as educational systems and work establishments. It is also appropriate for understanding a sequence of stages in behavioral deviance, and the list of reported criminal careers—jackrolling, professional theft, and economically motivated homosexuality, to name just a few—is extensive. Not surprisingly, sociologists have learned that a common set of elements appears to be involved in both criminalistic and non-criminalistic careers: recruitment, training, identification, and retention. Since a great deal is known about these elements as they operate in the case of dentists, assembly-line operatives, psychiatric aides, and taxi-cab drivers, the convergence of information on criminal careers with data on those who pursue "normal" activities holds a great deal of promise.

After reviewing some past work in criminal typology, Marshall B. Clinard and Richard Quinney generate a behavior-systems model comprising eight types of criminality. These are systematically employed in their *Criminal Behavior Systems*, from which the first selection in this section is taken.

Howard S. Becker's paper "Deviant Careers" portrays a sequential paradigm of career transformation, drawing upon a range of deviance from homosexuality to marijuana use. Of particular interest is his contention that reactions of others to the deviant are important determinants of his progression through the sequence.

The career of a deviant may involve transforming his personal ideology in the direction of increased distance between his values and those of the general community, or increased commitment to a deviant role. Edwin M. Lemert's paper "Primary and Secondary Deviation" describes the effects of continued deviance upon role behavior and self-conception.

"The Professionalization of Theft" is taken from Sutherland's classic account of an accomplished pickpocket, *The Professional Thief*. Although the materials are essentially from a single case, it is clear that professional theft presumes knowledge of the mores, skills, and verbalizations exclusive to and shared by followers of that career.

One of the few studies of criminality employing the analytic induction model, Cressey's paper on trust violators reveals the perspective taken by persons committing acts of embezzlement. They must begin by reasoning that they have a financial problem that cannot be alleviated through legitimate means, nor can they share the problem with anyone else. Next, they must possess the requisite skills for violation, and have access to a position of trust. Finally, they "adjust" their misuse of entrusted funds by conceiving the act as a "temporary loan."

The final paper in this section, James H. Bryan's "Apprenticeships in Prostitution," emphasizes not the personality structure of participants, but rather their recruitment and initial training period. Data support the view that early call-girl socialization is essential to the establishment of an adequate clientele, avoidance of trouble, and the maintenance of a favorable self-conception.

Selections from the enormous literature on behavior systems and deviant careers are provided below for the interested reader.

1. *Typologies in Criminology: History and Analysis*

Clinard, Marshall B., and Quinney, Richard. *Criminal Behavior Systems* (New York: Holt, Rinehart & Winston, 1967).

Driver, Edwin D. "A Critique of Typologies in Criminology," *Sociological Quarterly* 9 (Summer 1968): 356–73.

Gibbons, Don C. *Changing the Lawbreaker* (Englewood Cliffs, N.J.: Prentice-Hall, 1965), chap. 2, "Causal Analysis and Offender Typologies," and chap. 3, "Two Candidate Typologies."

Gibbs, Jack P. "Needed: Analytical Typologies in Criminology," *Southwestern Social Science Quarterly* 40 (March 1960): 321–29.

Glaser, Daniel. "National Goals and Indicators for the Reduction of Crime and Delinquency," *Annals of the American Academy of Political and Social Science* 371 (May 1967): 104–26.

McKinney, John C. *Constructive Typology and Social Theory* (New York: Appleton-Century-Crofts, 1966).

Roebuck, Julian B. "Approaches to Criminal Typology," *Criminal Typology* (Springfield, Ill.: Charles C. Thomas, 1967), pp. 3–30.

2. *Diverse Research in Criminal Behavior Systems*

Bell, Daniel. "Crime as an American Way of Life," *The End of Ideology* (New York: Free Press, Macmillan, 1960), pp. 115–36.

Camp, George M. *Nothing to Lose: A Study of Bank Robbery in America.* Unpublished Ph.D. dissertation, Yale University, 1967.

Clinard, Marshall B. *The Black Market: A Study of White Collar Crime* (New York: Rinehart, 1952).

Cressey, Donald R. *Other People's Money* (Glencoe, Ill.: Free Press, 1953).

————. *Theft of the Nation: The Structure and Operations of Organized Crime in America* (New York: Harper & Row, 1969).

Geis, Gilbert, ed. *White-Collar Criminal: The Offender in Business and the Professions* (New York: Atherton Press, 1968).

Lemert, Edwin M. "The Behavior of the Systematic Check Forger," *Social Problems* 6 (Fall 1958): 141–49.

Polsky, Ned. "The Hustler," *Hustlers, Beats, and Others* (Chicago: Aldine, 1967), pp. 41–116.

Roebuck, Julian. "The Negro Numbers Man as a Criminal Type: The Construction and Application of a Typology," *Journal of Criminal Law, Criminology, and Police Science* 54 (March 1963): 48–60.

Sutherland, Edwin H. *White Collar Crime* (New York: Holt, Rinehart & Winston, 1949).

Wolfgang, Marvin E. *Patterns in Criminal Homicide* (Philadelphia: University of Pennsylvania Press, 1958).

3. *Behavior Patterns, Deviant Careers, and Criminality*

Baum, Martha, and Wheeler, Stanton. "Becoming an Inmate," in *Controlling Delinquents,* ed. Stanton Wheeler (New York: Wiley, 1968), pp. 153–85.

Becker, Howard S. *Outsiders: Studies in the Sociology of Deviance* (New York: Free Press, Macmillan, 1963), chap. 3, "Becoming a Marijuana User."

—— and Strauss, Anselm L. "Careers, Personality, and Adult Socialization," *American Journal of Sociology* 62 (November 1956): 253–63.

Gibbons, Don C. *Society, Crime, and Criminal Careers* (Englewood Cliffs, N.J.: Prentice-Hall, 1968), chap. 10, "Causal Analysis: The Study of Role-Careers."

Goffman, Erving. "The Moral Career of the Mental Patient," *Asylums: Essays on the Social Situation of Mental Patients and Other Inmates* (Chicago: Aldine, 1962), pp. 125–69.

Matza, David. *Delinquency and Drift* (New York: Wiley, 1964), chap. 6, "Drifting into Delinquency."

Roth, Julius A. *Timetables: Structuring the Passage of Time in Hospital Treatment and Other Careers* (Indianapolis: Bobbs-Merrill, 1963).

19. THE BEHAVIOR SYSTEMS APPROACH TO CRIMINAL TYPOLOGY

Marshall B. Clinard and Richard Quinney

TYPOLOGIES BASED ON SOCIAL BEHAVIOR SYSTEMS

The division of criminal behavior into social behavior typologies consists of more than merely dividing the phenomena of crime into "classes." The construction of types consists of the formation of a *configuration or pattern of variables linked in specified ways*. Classifications of crime are typologies when they are composed of constructed types rather than classes of phenomena.

If crime is to be studied as a social phenomenon, it is necessary to delineate types of criminal behavior according to the social context of the criminal offender and the criminal act. A number of such types have been developed. Two European criminologists of the last century, Mayhew and Moreau, proposed criminal types based on the way in which crime is related to the various *activities* of the criminal. Mayhew distinguished between professional criminals, who earn their living through criminal

Reprinted by permission of the authors and the publisher from Marshall B. Clinard and Richard Quinney, *Criminal Behavior Systems* (New York: Holt, Rinehart & Winston, 1967), pp. 7–18. Footnotes have been renumbered.

activity, and accidental offenders, who commit criminal acts as a result of unanticipated circumstances. Moreau added one other type of criminal to Mayhew's types. Recognizing that many of the criminals who commit crimes against the person cannot be included in either of Mayhew's types, Moreau designated the "habitual criminal" as one who continues to commit criminal acts for such diverse reasons as a deficiency in intelligence and lack of self-control.

Lindesmith and Dunham, with an awareness of the Mayhew-Moreau criminal types, devised a continuum of criminal behavior ranging from the *individualized criminal* to the *social criminal*.[1] The criminal acts of the individualized criminal are committed for diverse and personal reasons, with the behavior finding little cultural support. The criminal behaviors of the social criminal, on the other hand, are supported and prescribed by group norms. The social criminal through his criminal behavior achieves status and recognition within a group. In addition, while the social criminal uses means which are illegitimate, the goals he seeks, such as economic gain and security, are valued by the broader culture. The types of criminals found between the extremes share in varying degrees the characteristics of one or the other polar types. In the individualized category is the situational or accidental criminal, for example, a murderer who prior to the crime was a law-abiding person. In the social category is the professional criminal, such as the racketeer or the confidence man. Lindesmith and Dunham also employ a third type, *habitual-situational*. This type is utilized to classify all those criminals who actually are not professional, but are more than situational or accidental offenders. This type of criminal is described as the offender who, while not a professional, is constantly in trouble with the legal authorities, committing in a somewhat fortuitous and free-wheeling manner such crimes as robbery and larceny, intermixed with legitimate economic activities. A slum juvenile delinquent might be described as *habitual-situational*. This trichotomy, while consisting of rather broad categories, does not, however, appear to be exhaustive. For instance, as Lindesmith and Dunham themselves suggest, white-collar crime committed by persons in the upper socioeconomic groups does not seem to fit in any one of the three categories. It is not a situational or accidental crime, since in many cases the individual criminal may have committed the crime continuously over a lifetime. It is not a professional crime, for in many cases (such as embezzlement) the offender may be a situational criminal. Also, it is not a habitual-situational crime, for Lindesmith and Dunham definitely describe this type as being overt in nature, and white-collar crime is characterized by anything but overtness. More important, research subsequent to the development of this typology has indicated con-

---

[1] Alfred R. Lindesmith and H. Warren Dunham, "Some Principles of Criminal Typology," *Social Forces,* 19 (March 1941): 307–14.

siderable group and social factors in such offenses as murder, aggravated assault, and forcible rape, which they had tended to regard as of the individual type.

Another scheme with a somewhat different inflection has been developed by Gibbons and Garrity.[2] They suggest that a significant difference among criminals is the chronological age at which the offender is defined by society as a criminal. They express this difference as a dichotomy: (1) that group of offenders defined as criminals from the time of their first criminal act, and (2) that group of offenders not defined as criminal until late in life, though committing criminal acts early in life. Gibbons and Garrity understand this dichotomous scheme to differentiate respectively between the criminal whose total life orientation is guided by criminal groups and the criminal whose life orientation is largely guided and reinforced by non-criminal groups.

While it may be true that the chronological age at which the offender is labeled a criminal is an excellent predictor of the criminal patterns of the offender, in terms of constructing a typology this information is of little value, since it is simpler to use the actual behavior patterns, which are accessible, to type the offenders, rather than causal indicators of these patterns. For a typology is not a predictive device; rather it is a device employed to order and describe parsimoniously data from which potential predictive statements are generated.

A number of criminologists have stressed the vocational aspects of certain forms of crime. They have seen that some crimes are committed by persons who pursue criminal behavior as a career. Reckless has suggested three criminal careers: ordinary, organized, and professional.[3] As career crimes, these three types of crime are similar in that they usually involve property offenses for the purpose of gain; the criminals tend to specialize in particular violations; the commission of the offenses requires various degrees of skill and experience; crime is pursued as a way of life; and career criminals continue in crime for a long period of time, possibly for a lifetime. In terms of differences among the career types, ordinary criminals represent the lowest rank of career crime. They engage in conventional crimes, such as robbery, larceny, and burglary, which require limited skill. Ordinary criminals lack the organization to avoid arrest and conviction. Organized criminals, on the other hand, through a high degree of organization are able, without being detected or convicted, to specialize in activity which can be operated as a large-scale business. Force, violence, intimidation, and bribery are used to gain and maintain control over

---

[2] Don C. Gibbons and Donald L. Garrity, "Some Suggestions for the Development of Etiological and Treatment Theory in Criminology," *Social Forces*, 38 (October 1963): 51–58.

[3] Walter C. Reckless, *The Crime Problem*, 3d ed. (New York: Appleton-Century-Crofts, 1961), chaps. 9 and 10.

economic activity. Special types of organized crime include various forms of racketeering, control of gambling and prostitution, and the distribution of narcotics. Professional criminals, as the third type of career criminals, are highly skilled and are thus able to obtain considerable amounts of money without being detected. Because of organization and contact with other professional criminals, these offenders are able to escape conviction. Professional criminals specialize in offenses which require skill rather than violence, such as confidence games, pickpocketing, shoplifting, sneak thievery, and counterfeiting. While this distinction is important and largely valid insofar as it goes, it is limited to those who make an occupation or career out of crime. Many persons who commit illegal acts are not career criminals.

Using a more comprehensive typology by emphasizing the career patterning of offenders, Clinard has developed a classification based on a continuum of criminal behavior systems.[4] At one extreme is the noncareer offender and at the other the career offender. The criminal types constructed in the typology vary according to such characteristics as the social roles of the offender, the degree of identification with crime, conception of the self, pattern of association with others, progression in crime, and the degree to which criminal behavior has become part of the life organization of the person. On the basis of these criteria, he has ranged criminal behavior along a continuum with subtypes under each, of the criminally insane, extreme sex deviate, occasional offender, prostitute and homosexual, habitual petty offender, white-collar criminal, ordinary career criminal, organized criminal, and professional criminal.

A significant typology of criminal offenders has been constructed by Gibbons in terms of offense patterns, self-image, normative orientation, and other social psychological characteristics.[5] Types, to Gibbons, are primarily role-careers in which identifiable changes occur in different offender types.

> There are some criminal patterns in which role-performance is begun and terminated in a single illegal act, and there are others in which involvement in the deviant role continues over several decades or more, as in the instance of professional criminals. Some delinquent roles lead to adult criminality, whereas other delinquent roles are terminal ones, for they do not normally precede or lead to involvement in adult deviation. In turn, some criminal roles have their genesis in juvenile delinquent behavior, whereas other forms of adult criminality develop in adulthood and are not presaged by delinquent careers. Then, too, some role-careers involve more changes

[4] Marshall B. Clinard, *Sociology of Deviant Behavior,* rev. ed. (New York: Holt, Rinehart & Winston, 1963), chap. 8.

[5] Don C. Gibbons, *Changing the Lawbreaker: The Treatment of Delinquents and Criminals* (Englewood Cliffs, N.J.: Prentice-Hall, 1965). He also sets up a program of treatment for each type.

in the component episodes of the pattern than do others. Semiprofessional property offenders are one illustration. This pattern begins at the onset of minor delinquent acts in early adolescence. Such a career line frequently leads to more serious forms of delinquency with advancing age: repeated police contacts, commitment to juvenile institutions, "graduation" into adult forms of illegal activity, and more contacts with law enforcement and correctional agencies. Over this lengthy developmental sequence, the social-psychological characteristics of offenders also change. For example, the degree of hostility toward policemen and correctional agents exhibited by the adult semiprofessional criminal is likely to be considerably greater than the antagonism demonstrated by the same person at an early age. The same comment could be made regarding changes in self-image, attitudes, and other matters.[6]

A uniform frame of reference employing the criteria of "definitional dimensions" and "background dimensions" is used by Gibbons. The definitional dimensions consist of: (1) the nature of the offense behavior, (2) the interactional setting with others in which the offense takes place, (3) the self-concept of the offender, (4) attitudes toward society and agencies of social control such as the police, and (5) the steps in the role career of the offender. There are four aspects of the "background dimensions" of each type: (1) social class, (2) family background, (3) peer-group associations, and (4) contact with defining agencies such as the police, courts, and prisons.

On this basis Gibbons sets up fifteen adult types and nine juvenile types:

Adult Types	*Juvenile Types*
Professional thief	Predatory gang delinquent
Professional "heavy" criminal	Conflict gang delinquent
Semiprofessional property criminal	Casual gang delinquent
Property offender—"one-time loser"	Casual delinquent, nongang member
Automobile thief—"joyrider"	Automobile thief— "joyrider"
Naïve check forger	Drug user—heroin
White-collar criminal	Overly aggressive delinquent
Professional "fringe" violator	Female delinquent
Embezzler	"Behavior problem" delinquent[7]
Personal offender—"one-time loser"	
"Psychopathic" assaultist	
Violent sex offender	
Nonviolent sex offender— nonviolent "rapo"	
Nonviolent sex offender— statutory rape	
Narcotic addict—heroin	

Gibbons provides a description of each type. Unfortunately, some of his types are not sharply delineated and tend to overlap or be unclear as to

---

[6] *Ibid.*, pp. 51–52.
[7] *Ibid.*, chap. 3.

their specific characteristics. Other types depart from an essentially general group and cultural frame of reference and present a largely individualistic psychological orientation which is somewhat contradictory to the overall frame of reference.

A somewhat different typology has been developed by Cavan, which gives principal consideration to the public reaction to crime and the criminal's reaction to the public.[8] In an analysis of the interaction between the public and the criminal, seven types of criminal behavior are constructed: (1) criminal contraculture (professional crime, robbery, burglary), (2) extreme underconformity (for example, embezzlement), (3) minor underconformity (for example, occasional drunkenness), (4) "average" conformity (minor pilfering), (5) minor overconformity (exactness in obeying laws and moral codes), (6) extreme overconformity (attempts to reform society by persuasion and legal means), and (7) ideological contraculture (strenuous efforts to remodel society, possibly through the use of illegal means). Because societal reaction is crucial to the criminal's self-concept and subsequent behavior, it is an important variable to be included in a typology of crime.

An indication of the importance of the typological approach in modern criminology can be seen in the attention devoted to the subject in some recent criminology textbooks. Bloch and Geis, for example, give considerable attention to types of criminal behavior systems and to the social and cultural structure in which criminal behavior systems arise.[9] Their types of criminal behavior systems include professional criminals, organized crime, homicides and assaults, sexual offenders, property offenders, white-collar offenders, juvenile delinquents, and petty and miscellaneous offenders.

PRINCIPLES OF CRIMINAL TYPOLOGY

Ideally, a typology of crime should be constructed on the basis of a general, underlying theory of crime. No matter how implicit, some assumptions are always present concerning the nature and etiology of crime. In addition, the particular selection of characteristics and variables which ultimately determine the types in the system is guided by the interests of the criminologist. In other words, the purpose at hand determines how the typology is to be constructed. For example, if the purpose of the typology is to view crime in terms of public reaction, then one set of characteristics will be used. Likewise, another purpose will require a different typology. Also, the level of explanation desired by the criminologist will play a part in the particular selection of characteristics in the typology.

---

[8] Ruth Shonle Cavan, *Criminology*, 3d ed. (New York: Crowell, 1962), chap. 3.
[9] Herbert A. Bloch and Gilbert Geis, *Man, Crime, and Society* (New York: Random House, 1962).

General characteristics for the construction of typologies can be developed in the course of criminological research. With the use of such a technique as factor analysis, for example, common characteristics of offenders can be found.[10] These dimensions in turn can be used in the construction of a typological system. Typologies can also be constructed through the use of findings from other research studies of various kinds of crime and delinquency.[11] Once such typologies are constructed, and with the addition of terms, concepts, and postulates, typologies can serve as axiomatic theories whereby further statements regarding types of crime can be deduced.[12]

Related to the selection of characteristics underlying typologies is the problem of the phenomena to be included in the typology. There has been the tendency in criminology, especially in the development of typologies, to avoid distinguishing between the subclasses of phenomena included in the study of crime. The phenomena associated with crime include *criminal behavior, the criminal,* and *criminality.* These phenomena represent the areas of study in criminology.[13] Criminal behavior refers to the behavioral aspects of the violation of the law and the criminal refers to the person who violates the law. Criminality refers to the official status conferred upon behavior and persons by authorities within a political unit. There is thus the possibility of constructing separate typologies of criminal behavior, criminals, and criminality.

The distinction between criminal behavior, the criminal, and criminality is crucial in the attempt to construct types in criminology. Typologies will differ markedly from one another according to the particular phenomena upon which they are based. For example, if a typology is based on criminals, the emphasis will be on such matters as life histories of offenders, self-conceptions, attitudes, and social background factors. On the other hand, if the objective is a typology of criminal behavior, attention will be focused on such matters as the mode of operation, the overt criminal act, the situation in which the offense occurs, opportunities to commit crime, subcultural norms, relationships between offenders, and structural aspects of the larger society. A typology based on criminality would consist

---

[10] Employed on the ecological level in Calvin F. Schmid, "Urban Crime Areas: Part I," *American Sociological Review,* 25 (August 1960): 527–42.

[11] Don C. Gibbons and Donald L. Garrity, "Definition and Analysis of Certain Criminal Types," *Journal of Criminal Law, Criminology, and Police Science,* 53 (March 1962): 27–35; and John W. Kinch, "Continuities in the Study of Delinquent Types," *Journal of Criminal Law, Criminology, and Police Science,* 53 (September 1962): 323–28.

[12] Clarence Schrag, "A Preliminary Criminal Typology," *Pacific Sociological Review,* 4 (Spring 1961): 16.

[13] Various views on this subject are presented in Austin T. Turk, "Prospects for Theories of Criminal Behavior," *Journal of Criminal Law, Criminology, and Police Science,* 55 (December 1964): 454–61; Clarence R. Jeffery, "The Structure of American Criminological Thinking," *Journal of Criminal Law, Criminology, and Police Science,* 46 (January–February 1956): 658–72; Marvin E. Wolfgang, "Criminology and Criminologists," *Journal of Criminal Law, Criminology, and Police Science,* 54 (June 1963): 155–62.

of characteristics that relate to the conditions and processes by which persons and behaviors become defined as criminal. In addition, a typology might be constructed which would combine the three classes of phenomena associated with crime. Such a typology would consider the fact that persons and behaviors with certain characteristics are more likely to be defined as criminal than are persons and behaviors with other characteristics.

Other problems connected with underlying principles in the construction of criminal typologies can be described briefly as follows: (1) Multidimensional typologies: It is conceivable that any number of characteristics could be used in the construction of a criminal typology. In the construction of any typology, decisions must be made regarding the number of characteristics to be included and the kind of measurement to be used. (2) Exhaustiveness: There is the question of whether or not a typology should include the entire universe of crime or should be limited in scope. (3) Homogeneity of types: An objective of a typology may be the division of crime into types such that the types are homogeneous, that is, so that the behaviors within a given type are subject to a single explanation. This objective is related to the level of abstraction of both the types and the theories to explain the types. (4) Types and behavior systems: Types of crime do not necessarily represent behavior systems. Since some types of crime may not be systematic in that they do not consist of, among other things, social relationships and cultural norms, not all types can be studied as behavior systems. (5) Juvenile delinquency: While minors and adults are handled differently before the law, many of the offenses of juveniles are behaviorally the same as those of adults. Therefore, in constructing types, there may be little reason to create separate types for minors and adults. It may be more realistic and theoretically sound to integrate various forms of juvenile delinquency into typologies of crime.

Whatever the basis of typological construction, the trend in criminology is clearly toward further study of types of crime. In the development of typologies we cannot, however, expect to achieve a typological system which can be agreed upon by all criminologists as being the most desirable. To be certain, there will be classifications which will at various times be more popular than others. But there are a number of reasons why we cannot look forward to a single typology in criminology.

First, as already mentioned, typologies differ according to the purposes which they are to serve. Since there will continue to be a multitude of purposes, including levels of analysis and degrees of generality, there will be a number of typologies. Second, there is the fact that crime is relative. That is, the definitions of crime change from time to time and from place to place. Therefore, the behaviors and persons to be included in a typology will vary according to time and place. It may be that future typologies will be developed which will include the crimes of other historical periods.

Third, theory within criminology will continue to develop. As this happens, typologies will be altered. Finally, theories, theoretical frameworks, and the related typologies will change as the orientations of criminologists change. Inevitably, as with all intellectual trends, the interests of criminologists will be attuned to the developments in the larger society.

A TYPOLOGY OF CRIME

In the approach to typological construction used in this book, types of crime are constructed according to *systems* of criminal behavior. As heuristic devices, types are necessarily constructed as "systems." McKinney has noted, "The constructed type is a special kind of concept in that it consists of a set of characteristics wherein the relations between the characteristics are held constant for the purposes at hand. Hence, the type is a pragmatically constructed 'system.' "[14] Criminal behavior systems are constructed types that serve as a means by which concrete occurrences can be compared and understood within a system of characteristics that underlie the types.

Accordingly, eight types of criminal behavior are constructed:

1. Violent personal crime
2. Occasional property crime
3. Occupational crime
4. Political crime
5. Public-order crime
6. Conventional crime
7. Organized crime
8. Professional crime

The typological construction is based upon four characteristics: (1) the criminal career of the offender, (2) the extent to which the behavior has group support, (3) correspondence between criminal behavior and legitimate behavior patterns, and (4) societal reaction.

1. *Criminal career of the offender:* the extent to which criminal behavior is a part of the offender's career. Includes conception of self, identification with crime, progression in crime, and the degree to which criminal behavior has become a part of the life organization of the offender.
2. *Group support of criminal behavior:* the extent to which the offender's criminal behavior is supported by the norms of the group or groups

---

[14] John C. McKinney, *Constructive Typology and Social Theory* (New York: Appleton-Century-Crofts, 1966), p. 7.

to which he belongs. Includes the differential association of the offender with criminal and noncriminal norms, the social roles of the offender, and the integration of the offender into social groups.

3. *Correspondence between criminal behavior and legitimate behavior patterns:* the extent to which the type of criminal behavior is consistent with legitimate patterns of behavior in the society. Includes the degree to which the criminal behavior corresponds to the valued goals and means that are regarded as legitimate by the dominant power segments of society. Includes the extent of conflict between value systems.

4. *Societal reaction:* The extent to which society reacts to the criminal behavior. Includes the various forms of informal reaction, such as disapproval and censure, and the forms of official reaction, such as enforcement of law, prosecution, convictions, and sentencing.

The types of criminal behavior systems in the typology are shown in Table 1. Eight distinct patterns of crime are delineated in relation to the four characteristics. The career continuum is used to order the criminal behavior systems. The ranking of the criminal behavior systems on each continuum is based on available research evidence.

There are undoubtedly other ways of dividing crime into types along the career continuum in reference to group support of criminal behavior, correspondence between criminal behavior and legitimate behavior patterns, and societal reaction. The behaviors and associated phenomena that run along the continua have been, for our purposes, abstracted and segmented into eight distinct types. The typology serves the purpose of allowing us to present existing research on various forms of crime.

The eight types of criminal behavior systems which we have constructed may be summarized as follows:

1. *Violent Personal Crime.* Includes such forms of criminal activity as murder, assault, and forcible rape. The offenders do not conceive of themselves as criminals. They are often persons without previous records, but because of certain circumstances commit a personal offense. The offenses are not directly supported by any group, though there may be subcultural definitions which are favorable to the general use of violence. The behaviors are in sharp contrast to the middle-class values of the society. There is a strong reaction to the offenses.

2. *Occasional Property Crime.* Includes some auto theft, shoplifting, check forgery, and vandalism. The offenders do not usually conceive of themselves as criminals and are able to rationalize their criminal behavior. They are usually committed to the general goals of society and find little support for their behavior in group norms. The offenses are in violation of the

TABLE 1
TYPOLOGY OF CRIMINAL BEHAVIOR SYSTEMS

Classification Characteristics	1 Violent Personal Crime	2 Occasional Property Crime	3 Occupational Crime	4 Political Crime
Criminal career of the offender	*Low* Crime not part of offender's career; usually does not conceive of self as criminal	*Low* Little or no criminal self-concept; does not identify with crime	*Low* No criminal self-concept; occasionally violates the law; part of one's legitimate work; accepts conventional values of society	*Low* Usually no criminal self-concept; violates the law out of conscience; attempts to change society or correct perceived injustices; desire for a better society
Group support of criminal behavior	*Low* Little or no group support, offenses committed for personal reasons; some support in subcultural norms	*Low* Little group support; individual offenses	*Medium* Some groups may tolerate offenses; offender integrated in groups	*High* Group support; association with persons of same values; behavior reinforced by group
Correspondence between criminal behavior and legitimate behavior patterns	*Low* Violation of values on life and personal safety	*Low* Violation of value on private property	*High* Behavior corresponds to pursual of business activity; "sharp" practices respected; "buyer beware" philosophy; hands-off policy	*Medium* Some toleration of protest and dissent, short of revolution; dissent periodically regarded as a threat (in times of national unrest)
Societal reaction	*High* Capital punishment; long imprisonment	*Medium* Arrest; jail; short imprisonment, probation	*Low* Indifference; monetary penalties, revocation of license to practice, seizure of product, or injunction	*High* Strong disapproval; regarded as threat to society; prison
Legal categories of crime	Murder, assault, forcible rape, child molesting	Some auto theft, shoplifting, check forgery, vandalism	Embezzlement, fraudulent sales, false advertising, fee splitting, violation of labor-practice laws, antitrust violations, black-market activity, prescription violation	Treason, sedition, espionage, sabotage, radicalism, military draft violations, war collaboration, various protests defined as criminal

TABLE 1 *(Continued)*

5	6	7	8
Public-order Crime	*Conventional Crime*	*Organized Crime*	*Professional Crime*
Medium	*Medium*	*High*	*High*
Confused self-concept; vacillation in identification with crime	Income supplemented through crimes of gain; often a youthful activity; vacillation in self-concept; partial commitment to a criminal subculture	Crime pursued as a livelihood; criminal self-concept; progression in crime; isolation from larger society	Crime pursued as a livelihood; criminal self-concept; status in the world of crime; commitment to world of professional criminals
Medium	*High*	*High*	*High*
Partial support for behavior from some groups; considerable association with other offenders	Behavior supported by group norms; status achieved in groups; principal association with other offenders	Business associations in crime; behavior prescribed by the groups; integration of the person into the group	Associations primarily with other offenders; status gained in criminal offenses; behavior prescribed by group norms
Medium	*Medium*	*Medium*	*Medium*
Some forms required by legitimate society; some are economic activities	Consistent with goals of economic success; inconsistent with sanctity of private property; behavior not consistent with expectations of adolescence and young adulthood	Illegal services received by legitimate society; economic risk values; large-scale control also employed in legitimate society	Engaged in an occupation; skill respected; survival because of cooperation from legitimate society; law-abiding persons often accomplices
Medium	*High*	*Medium*	*Medium*
Arrest; jail; prison; probation	Arrest; jail; probation; institutionalization; parole; rehabilitation	Considerable public toleration; arrest and sentence when detected; often not visible to society; immunity through politicians and law officers	Rarely strong societal reaction, most cases "fixed"
Drunkenness, vagrancy, disorderly conduct, prostitution, homosexuality, gambling, traffic violation, drug addiction	Robbery, larceny, burglary, gang theft	Racketeering, organized prostitution and commercialized vice, control of drug traffic, organized gambling	Confidence games, shoplifting, pickpocketing, forgery, counterfeiting

values of private property. Societal reaction often involves arrest, especially for the offender who already has a criminal record.

3. *Occupational Crime.* Includes embezzlement, fraudulent sales, false advertising, price fixing, fee splitting, black-market activity, prescription violation, and antitrust violation. Violators do not conceive of themselves as criminals and rationalize their behavior as being merely a part of their daily work. Their behavior may be tolerated by their peers. They accept conventional values and attempt to seek a greater share of the rewards in the conventional world. The illegal behavior corresponds to the social and economic philosophy of the achievement of ends in the society. Because such crime is committed by persons in high-status positions and the violation of law is often complex and not highly visible, there is little reaction from the public when these violations occur.

4. *Political Crime.* Includes treason, sedition, espionage, sabotage, military draft violations, war collaboration, radicalism, and the various other forms of protest which may be defined as criminal. The offenders occasionally violate the law when they feel that illegal activity is essential in achieving necessary changes in society. The offenders are committed to the larger society or to an order which they are trying to bring about. Their behavior is prescribed and supported by their own groups. Democratic societies are based on the right to petition, yet societal reaction is strong when such behavior is regarded as a threat to the society.

5. *Public-Order Crime.* Includes drunkenness, vagrancy, disorderly conduct, prostitution, homosexuality, traffic violation, and drug addiction. The violators may conceive of themselves as criminals when they are repeatedly defined as criminals by others. They may vacillate between criminal values and the values of a larger social order. They may associate with other offenders. There is some correspondence between the illegal behavior of public-order offenders and legitimate patterns. Some of the forms of public-order crime (for example, prostitution) are desired by parts of the legitimate society. Other forms (for example, drunkenness and vagrancy) are regarded as merely representative of "failure" in the existing economic system. There may be informal punitive reaction as well as arrest and limited incarceration.

6. *Conventional Crime.* Includes robbery, larceny, burglary, and gang theft. The offenders pursue crime as a part-time career, usually supplementing a legitimate income through crimes of gain. Many juvenile gang members may be beginning a career in illegal activity. While there may be some identification with the larger society, there is likely to be greater commitment to a criminal subculture. There is usually association with other

offenders. The behavior corresponds to the goals of economic success; but there is public reaction to the behavior because the value on the sanctity of private property is violated.

7. *Organized Crime.* Includes racketeering, organized prostitution, organized gambling, and control of narcotics. The offenders pursue crime as a livelihood. In the lower echelons they conceive of themselves as criminals, associate primarily with other criminals, and are isolated from a larger social order. In the top levels the individuals associate as well with persons of legitimate society and often reside in the better residential areas. There is considerable correspondence between the illegal activities of organized crime and legitimate society. The principles of large-scale enterprise are shared by legitimate society. Illegal services desired by legitimate society are provided by organized crime. The public tolerates organized crime, partly because of the desired services it provides and partly because of the difficulty in dealing with its operation.

8. *Professional Crime.* Includes confidence games, shoplifting, pickpocketing, forgery, and counterfeiting. Professional criminals pursue crime as a livelihood and as a way of life. They conceive of themselves as criminals, associate with other criminals, and have high status in the world of crime. They are usually isolated from the larger society and are committed to a career of crime. There is some correspondence between professional crime and dominant behavior patterns in that professional criminals are, after all, engaged in full-time employment. Also, law-abiding persons are sometimes involved as accomplices in an attempt to obtain money in a quick and easy manner. Societal reaction is not usually strong. Many cases of professional crime are "fixed" in the course of legal processing.

20. DEVIANT CAREERS

Howard S. Becker

A useful conception in developing sequential models of various kinds of deviant behavior is that of *career*.[1] Originally developed in studies of occupations, the concept refers to the sequence of movements from one position to another in an occupational system made by any individual who works in that system. Furthermore, it includes the notion of "career contingency," those factors on which mobility from one position to another depends. Career contingencies include both objective facts of social structure and changes in the perspectives, motivations, and desires of the individual. Ordinarily, in the study of occupations, we use the concept to distinguish between those who have a "successful" career (in whatever terms success is defined within the occupation) and those who do not. It can

Reprinted with permission of the author and The Macmillan Company from *Outsiders: Studies in the Sociology of Deviance* (pp. 24–39), by Howard S. Becker. Copyright © 1963 by The Free Press of Glencoe, a division of The Macmillan Company. Footnotes have been renumbered.

[1] See Everett C. Hughes, *Men and Their Work* (New York: Free Press, Macmillan, 1958), pp. 56–67, 102–15, and 157–68; Oswald Hall, "The Stages of the Medical Career," *American Journal of Sociology*, 53 (March 1948): 243–53; and Howard S. Becker and Anslem L. Strauss, "Careers, Personality, and Adult Socialization," *American Journal of Sociology*, 62 (November 1956): 253–63.

also be used to distinguish several varieties of career outcomes, ignoring the question of "success."

The model can easily be transformed for use in the study of deviant careers. In so transforming it, we should not confine our interest to those who follow a career that leads them into ever increasing deviance, to those who ultimately take on an extremely deviant identity and way of life. We should also consider those who have a more fleeting contact with deviance, whose careers lead them away from it into conventional ways of life. Thus, for example, studies of delinquents who fail to become adult criminals might teach us even more than studies of delinquents who progress in crime.

*   *   *

The first step in most deviant careers is the commission of a nonconforming act, an act that breaks some particular set of rules. How are we to account for the first step?

People usually think of deviant acts as motivated. They believe that the person who commits a deviant act, even for the first time (and perhaps especially for the first time), does so purposely. His purpose may or may not be entirely conscious, but there is a motive force behind it. We shall turn to the consideration of cases of intentional nonconformity in a moment, but first I must point out that many nonconforming acts are committed by people who have no intention of doing so; these clearly require a different explanation.

Unintended acts of deviance can probably be accounted for relatively simply. They imply an ignorance of the existence of the rule, or of the fact that it was applicable in this case, or to this particular person. But it is necessary to account for the lack of awareness. How does it happen that the person does not know his act is improper? Persons deeply involved in a particular subculture (such as a religious or ethnic subculture) may simply be unaware that everyone does not act "that way" and thereby commit an impropriety. There may, in fact, be structured areas of ignorance of particular rules. Mary Haas has pointed out the interesting case of interlingual word taboos.[2] Words which are perfectly proper in one language have a "dirty" meaning in another. So the person, innocently using a word common in his own language, finds that he has shocked and horrified his listeners who come from a different culture.

In analyzing cases of intended nonconformity, people usually ask about motivation: Why does the person want to do the deviant thing he does? The question assumes that the basic difference between deviants and those who conform lies in the character of their motivation. Many theories have

---

[2] Mary R. Haas, "Interlingual Word Taboos," *American Anthropologist*, 53 (July–September 1951): 338–44.

been propounded to explain why some people have deviant motivations and others do not. Psychological theories find the cause of deviant motivations and acts in the individual's early experiences, which produce unconscious needs that must be satisfied if the individual is to maintain his equilibrium. Sociological theories look for socially structured sources of "strain" in the society, social positions which have conflicting demands placed upon them such that the individual seeks an illegitimate way of solving the problems his position presents him with. (Merton's famous theory of anomie fits into this category.)[3]

But the assumption on which these approaches are based may be entirely false. There is no reason to assume that only those who finally commit a deviant act actually have the impulse to do so. It is much more likely that most people experience deviant impulses frequently. At least in fantasy, people are much more deviant than they appear. Instead of asking why deviants want to do things that are disapproved of, we might better ask why conventional people do not follow through on the deviant impulses they have.

Something of an answer to this question may be found in the process of commitment through which the "normal" person becomes progressively involved in conventional institutions and behavior. In speaking of commitment,[4] I refer to the process through which several kinds of interests become bound up with carrying out certain lines of behavior to which they seem formally extraneous. What happens is that the individual, as a consequence of actions he has taken in the past or the operation of various institutional routines, finds he must adhere to certain lines of behavior, because many other activities than the one he is immediately engaged in will be adversely affected if he does not. The middle-class youth must not quit school, because his occupational future depends on receiving a certain amount of schooling. The conventional person must not indulge his interest in narcotics, for example, because much more than the pursuit of immediate pleasure is involved; his job, his family, and his reputation in his neighborhood may seem to him to depend on his continuing to avoid temptation.

In fact, the normal development of people in our society (and probably in any society) can be seen as a series of progressively increasing commitments to conventional norms and institutions. The "normal" person, when he discovers a deviant impulse in himself, is able to check that impulse by thinking of the manifold consequences acting on it would produce for

---

[3] Robert K. Merton, *Social Theory and Social Structure* (New York: Free Press, Macmillan, 1957), pp. 131–94.

[4] I have dealt with this concept at greater length in "Notes on the Concept of Commitment," *American Journal of Sociology*, 66 (July 1960): 32–40. See also Erving Goffman, *Encounters: Two Studies in the Sociology of Interaction* (Indianapolis: Bobbs-Merrill, 1961), pp. 88–110; and Gregory P. Stone, "Clothing and Social Relations: A Study of Appearance in the Context of Community Life" (unpublished Ph.D. dissertation, Department of Sociology, University of Chicago, 1959).

him. He has staked too much on continuing to be normal to allow himself to be swayed by unconventional impulses.

This suggests that in looking at cases of intended nonconformity we must ask how the person manages to avoid the impact of conventional commitments. He may do so in one of two ways. First of all, in the course of growing up the person may somehow have avoided entangling alliances with conventional society. He may, thus, be free to follow his impulses. The person who does not have a reputation to maintain or a conventional job he must keep may follow his impulses. He has nothing staked on continuing to appear conventional.

However, most people remain sensitive to conventional codes of conduct and must deal with their sensitivities in order to engage in a deviant act for the first time. Sykes and Matza have suggested that delinquents actually feel strong impulses to be law-abiding, and deal with them by techniques of neutralization: "justifications for deviance that are seen as valid by the delinquent but not by the legal system or society at large." They distinguish a number of techniques for neutralizing the force of law-abiding values.

> In so far as the delinquent can define himself as lacking responsibility for his deviant actions, the disapproval of self or others is sharply reduced in effectiveness as a restraining influence. . . . The delinquent approaches a "billiard ball" conception of himself in which he sees himself as helplessly propelled into new situations. . . . By learning to view himself as more acted upon than acting, the delinquent prepares the way for deviance from the dominant normative system without the necessity of a frontal assault on the norms themselves. . . .
>
> A second major technique of neutralization centers on the injury or harm involved in the delinquent act. . . . For the delinquent . . . wrongfulness may turn on the question of whether or not anyone has clearly been hurt by his deviance, and this matter is open to a variety of interpretations. . . . Auto theft may be viewed as "borrowing," and gang fighting may be seen as a private quarrel, an agreed upon duel between two willing parties, and thus of no concern to the community at large. . . .
>
> The moral indignation of self and others may be neutralized by an insistence that the injury is not wrong in light of the circumstances. The injury, it may be claimed, is not really an injury; rather, it is a form of rightful retaliation or punishment. . . . Assaults on homosexuals or suspected homosexuals, attacks on members of minority groups who are said to have gotten "out of place," vandalism as revenge on an unfair teacher or school official, thefts from a "crooked" store owner—all may be hurts inflicted on a transgressor, in the eyes of the delinquent. . . .
>
> A fourth technique of neutralization would appear to involve a condemnation of the condemners. . . . His condemners, he may claim, are hypocrites, deviants in disguise, or impelled by personal spite. . . . By attacking others, the wrongfulness of his own behavior is more easily repressed or lost to view. . . .
>
> Internal and external social controls may be neutralized by sacrific-

ing the demands of the larger society for the demands of the smaller
social groups to which the delinquent belongs such as the sibling
pair, the gang, or the friendship clique. . . . The most important point
is that deviation from certain norms may occur not because the norms
are rejected but because other norms, held to be more pressing or
involving a higher loyalty, are accorded precedence.[5]

In some cases a nonconforming act may appear necessary or expedient to
a person otherwise law-abiding. Undertaken in pursuit of legitimate interests, the deviant act becomes, if not quite proper, at least not quite improper. In a novel dealing with a young Italian-American doctor we find a
good example.[6] The young man, just out of medical school, would like to
have a practice that is not built on the fact of his being Italian. But, being Italian, he finds it difficult to gain acceptance from the Yankee practitioners of his community. One day he is suddenly asked by one of the
biggest surgeons to handle a case for him and thinks that he is finally being admitted to the referral system of the better doctors in town. But when
the patient arrives at his office, he finds the case is an illegal abortion. Mis-
takenly seeing the referral as the first step in a regular relationship with the
surgeon, he performs the operation. This act, although improper, is thought
necessary to building his career.

But we are not so much interested in the person who commits a deviant
act once as in the person who sustains a pattern of deviance over a long
period of time, who makes of deviance a way of life, who organizes his
identity around a pattern of deviant behavior. It is not the casual experi-
menters with homosexuality (who turned up in such surprisingly large
numbers in the Kinsey Report) that we want to find out about, but the
man who follows a pattern of homosexual activity throughout his adult
life.

One of the mechanisms that lead from casual experimentation to a more
sustained pattern of deviant activity is the development of deviant motives
and interests. . . . Here it is sufficient to say that many kinds of deviant activity spring from motives which are socially learned. Before engaging in
the activity on a more or less regular basis, the person has no notion of the
pleasures to be derived from it; he learns these in the course of interaction
with more experienced deviants. He learns to be aware of new kinds of
experiences and to think of them as pleasurable. What may well have been
a random impulse to try something new becomes a settled taste for something already known and experienced. The vocabularies in which deviant
motivations are phrased reveal that their users acquire them in interaction
with other deviants. The individual *learns*, in short, to participate in a
subculture organized around the particular deviant activity.

---

[5] Gresham M. Sykes and David Matza, "Techniques of Neutralization: A Theory of
Delinquency," *American Sociological Review*, 22 (December 1957): 667–69.
[6] Guido D'Agostino, *Olives on the Apple Tree* (New York: Doubleday, Doran, 1940).
I am grateful to Everett C. Hughes for calling this novel to my attention.

Deviant motivations have a social character even when most of the activity is carried on in a private, secret, and solitary fashion. In such cases, various media of communication may take the place of face-to-face interaction in inducting the individual into the culture. . . . Pornographic pictures . . . [are] described to prospective buyers in a stylized language. Ordinary words [are] used in a technical shorthand designed to whet specific tastes. The word "bondage," for instance, [is] used repeatedly to refer to pictures of women restrained in handcuffs or straightjackets. One does not acquire a taste for "bondage photos" without having learned what they are and how they may be enjoyed.

One of the most crucial steps in the process of building a stable pattern of deviant behavior is likely to be the experience of being caught and publicly labeled as a deviant. Whether a person takes this step or not depends not so much on what he does as on what other people do, on whether or not they enforce the rule he has violated. Although I will consider the circumstances under which enforcement takes place in some detail later, two notes are in order here. First of all, even though no one else discovers the nonconformity or enforces the rules against it, the individual who has committed the impropriety may himself act as enforcer. He may brand himself as deviant because of what he has done and punish himself in one way or another for his behavior. This is not always or necessarily the case, but may occur. Second, there may be cases like those described by psychoanalysts in which the individual really wants to get caught and perpetrates his deviant act in such a way that it is almost sure he will be.

In any case, being caught and branded as deviant have important consequences for one's further social participation and self-image. The most important consequence is a drastic change in the individual's public identity. Committing the improper act and being publicly caught at it place him in a new status. He has been revealed as a different kind of person from the kind he was supposed to be. He is labeled a "fairy," "dope fiend," "nut," or "lunatic," and treated accordingly.

In analyzing the consequences of assuming a deviant identity let us make use of Hughes' distinction between master and auxiliary status traits.[7] Hughes notes that most statuses have one key trait which serves to distinguish those who belong from those who do not. Thus the doctor, whatever else he may be, is a person who has a certificate stating that he has fulfilled certain requirements and is licensed to practice medicine; this is the master trait. As Hughes points out, in our society a doctor is also informally expected to have a number of auxiliary traits: most people expect him to be upper-middle-class, white, male, and Protestant. When he is not there is a sense that he has in some way failed to fill the bill. Similarly, though skin color is the master status trait determining who is Negro and who is white,

---

[7] Everett C. Hughes, "Dilemmas and Contradictions of Status," *American Journal of Sociology*, 50 (March 1945): 353–59.

Negroes are informally expected to have certain status traits and not to have others; people are surprised and find it anomalous if a Negro turns out to be a doctor or a college professor. People often have the master status trait but lack some of the auxiliary, informally expected characteristics; for example, one may be a doctor but be female or Negro.

Hughes deals with this phenomenon in regard to statuses that are well thought of, desired, and desirable (noting that one may have the formal qualifications for entry into a status but be denied full entry because of lack of the proper auxiliary traits), but the same process occurs in the case of deviant statuses. Possession of one deviant trait may have a generalized symbolic value, so that people automatically assume that its bearer possesses other undesirable traits allegedly associated with it.

To be labeled a criminal one need only commit a single criminal offense, and this is all the term formally refers to. Yet the word carries a number of connotations specifying auxiliary traits characteristic of anyone bearing the label. A man who has been convicted of housebreaking and thereby labeled criminal is presumed to be a person likely to break into other houses; the police, in rounding up known offenders for investigation after a crime has been committed, operate on this premise. Further, he is considered likely to commit other kinds of crimes as well, because he has shown himself to be a person without "respect for the law." Thus, apprehension for one deviant act exposes a person to the likelihood that he will be regarded as deviant or undesirable in other respects.

There is one other element in Hughes' analysis we can borrow with profit: the distinction between master and subordinate statuses.[8] Some statuses, in our society as in others, override all other statuses and have a certain priority. Race is one of these. Membership in the Negro race, as socially defined, will override most other status considerations in most other situations; the fact that one is a physician or middle-class or female will not protect one from being treated as a Negro first and any of these other things second. The status of deviant (depending on the kind of deviance) is this kind of master status. One receives the status as a result of breaking a rule, and the identification proves to be more important than most others. One will be identified as a deviant first, before other identifications are made. The question is raised: "What kind of person would break such an important rule?" And the answer is given: "One who is different from the rest of us, who cannot or will not act as a moral human being and therefore might break other important rules." The deviant identification becomes the controlling one.

Treating a person as though he were generally rather than specifically deviant produces a self-fulfilling prophecy. It sets in motion several mechanisms which conspire to shape the person in the image people have of

---

[8] *Ibid.*

him.[9] In the first place, one tends to be cut off, after being identified as deviant, from participation in more conventional groups, even though the specific consequences of the particular deviant activity might never of themselves have caused the isolation had there not also been the public knowledge and reaction to it. For example, being a homosexual may not affect one's ability to do office work, but to be known as a homosexual in an office may make it impossible to continue working there. Similarly, though the effects of opiate drugs may not impair one's working ability, to be known as an addict will probably lead to losing one's job. In such cases, the individual finds it difficult to conform to other rules which he had no intention or desire to break, and perforce finds himself deviant in these areas as well. The homosexual who is deprived of a "respectable" job by the discovery of his deviance may drift into unconventional, marginal occupations where it does not make so much difference. The drug addict finds himself forced into other illegitimate kinds of activity, such as robbery and theft, by the refusal of respectable employers to have him around.

When the deviant is caught, he is treated in accordance with the popular diagnosis of why he is that way, and the treatment itself may likewise produce increasing deviance. The drug addict, popularly considered to be a weak-willed individual who cannot forgo the indecent pleasures afforded him by opiates, is treated repressively. He is forbidden to use drugs. Since he cannot get drugs legally, he must get them illegally. This forces the market underground and pushes the price of drugs up far beyond the current legitimate market price into a bracket that few can afford on an ordinary salary. Hence the treatment of the addict's deviance places him in a position where it will probably be necessary to resort to deceit and crime in order to support his habit.[10] The behavior is a consequence of the public reaction to the deviance rather than a consequence of the inherent qualities of the deviant act.

Put more generally, the point is that the treatment of deviants denies them the ordinary means of carrying on the routines of everyday life open to most people. Because of this denial, the deviant must of necessity develop illegitimate routines. The influence of public reaction may be direct, as in the instances considered above, or indirect, a consequence of the integrated character of the society in which the deviant lives.

Societies are integrated in the sense that social arrangements in one sphere of activity mesh with other activities in other spheres in particular ways and depend on the existence of these other arrangements. Certain kinds of work lives presuppose a certain kind of family life . . .

---

[9] See Marsh Ray, "The Cycle of Abstinence and Relapse Among Heroin Addicts," *Social Problems*, 9 (Fall 1961): 132–40.

[10] See *Drug Addiction: Crime or Disease?*, Interim and Final Reports of the Joint Committee of the American Bar Association and the American Medical Association on Narcotic Drugs (Bloomington: Indiana University Press, 1961).

Many varieties of deviance create difficulties by failing to mesh with expectations in other areas of life. Homosexuality is a case in point. Homosexuals have difficulty in any area of social activity in which the assumption of normal sexual interests and propensities for marriage is made without question. In stable work organizations such as large business or industrial organizations there are often points at which the man who would be successful should marry; not to do so will make it difficult for him to do the things that are necessary for success in the organization and will thus thwart his ambitions. The necessity of marrying often creates difficult enough problems for the normal male, and places the homosexual in an almost impossible position. Similarly, in some male work groups where heterosexual prowess is required to retain esteem in the group, the homosexual has obvious difficulties. Failure to meet the expectations of others may force the individual to attempt deviant ways of achieving results automatic for the normal person.

Obviously, everyone caught in one deviant act and labeled a deviant does not move inevitably toward greater deviance in the way the preceding remarks might suggest. The prophecies do not always confirm themselves, the mechanisms do not always work. What factors tend to slow down or halt the movement toward increasing deviance? Under what circumstances do they come into play?

One suggestion as to how the person may be immunized against increasing deviance is found in a recent study of juvenile delinquents who "hustle" homosexuals.[11] These boys act as homosexual prostitutes to confirmed adult homosexuals. Yet they do not themselves become homosexual. Several things account for their failure to continue this kind of sexual deviancy. First, they are protected from police action by the fact that they are minors. If they are apprehended in a homosexual act, they will be treated as exploited children, although in fact they are the exploiters; the law makes the adult guilty. Second, they look on the homosexual acts they engage in simply as a means of making money that is safer and quicker than robbery or similar activities. Third, the standards of their peer group, while permitting homosexual prostitution, allow only one kind of activity, and forbid them to get any special pleasure out of it or to permit any expressions of endearment from the adult with whom they have relations. Infractions of these rules, or other deviations from normal heterosexual activity, are severely punished by the boy's fellows.

Apprehension may not lead to increasing deviance if the situation in which the individual is apprehended for the first time occurs at a point where he can still choose between alternate lines of action. Faced, for the first time, with the possible ultimate and drastic consequences of what he

---

[11] Albert J. Reiss, Jr., "The Social Integration of Queers and Peers," *Social Problems*, 9 (Fall 1961): 102–20.

is doing, he may decide that he does not want to take the deviant road, and turn back. If he makes the right choice, he will be welcomed back into the conventional community; but if he makes the wrong move, he will be rejected and start a cycle of increasing deviance.

Ray has shown, in the case of drug addicts, how difficult it can be to reverse a deviant cycle.[12] He points out that drug addicts frequently attempt to cure themselves and that the motivation underlying their attempts is an effort to show nonaddicts whose opinions they respect that they are really not as bad as they are thought to be. On breaking their habit successfully, they find, to their dismay, that people still treat them as though they were addicts (on the premise, apparently, of "once a junkie, always a junkie").

A final step in the career of a deviant is movement into an organized deviant group. When a person makes a definite move into an organized group—or when he realizes and accepts the fact that he has already done so—it has a powerful impact on his conception of himself. A drug addict once told me that the moment she felt she was really "hooked" was when she realized she no longer had any friends who were not drug addicts.

Members of organized deviant groups of course have one thing in common: their deviance. It gives them a sense of common fate, of being in the same boat. From a sense of common fate, from having to face the same problems, grows a deviant subculture: a set of perspectives and understandings about what the world is like and how to deal with it, and a set of routine activities based on those perspectives. Membership in such a group solidifies a deviant identity.

Moving into an organized deviant group has several consequences for the career of the deviant. First of all, deviant groups tend, more than deviant individuals, to be pushed into rationalizing their position. At an extreme, they develop a very complicated historical, legal, and psychological justification for their deviant activity. The homosexual community is a good case. Magazines and books by homosexuals and for homosexuals include historical articles about famous homosexuals in history. They contain articles on the biology and physiology of sex, designed to show that homosexuality is a "normal" sexual response. They contain legal articles, pleading for civil liberties for homosexuals.[13] Taken together, this material provides a working philosophy for the active homosexual, explaining to him why he is the way he is, that other people have also been that way, and why it is all right for him to be that way.

Most deviant groups have a self-justifying rationale (or "ideology"), although seldom is it as well worked out as that of the homosexual. While such rationales do operate, as pointed out earlier, to neutralize the con-

---

[12] Ray, *op. cit.*

[13] *One* and *The Mattachine Review* are magazines of this type that I have seen.

ventional attitudes that deviants may still find in themselves toward their own behavior, they also perform another function. They furnish the individual with reasons that appear sound for continuing the line of activity he has begun. A person who quiets his own doubts by adopting the rationale moves into a more principled and consistent kind of deviance than was possible for him before adopting it.

The second thing that happens when one moves into a deviant group is that he learns how to carry on his deviant activity with a minimum of trouble. All the problems he faces in evading enforcement of the rule he is breaking have been faced before by others. Solutions have been worked out. Thus, the young thief meets older thieves who, more experienced than he is, explain to him how to get rid of stolen merchandise without running the risk of being caught. Every deviant group has a great stock of lore on such subjects and the new recruit learns it quickly.

Thus, the deviant who enters an organized and institutionalized deviant group is more likely than ever before to continue in his ways. He has learned, on the one hand, how to avoid trouble and, on the other hand, a rationale for continuing.

One further fact deserves mention. The rationales of deviant groups tend to contain a general repudiation of conventional moral rules, conventional institutions, and the entire conventional world.

21. PRIMARY AND SECONDARY DEVIATION

Edwin M. Lemert

In an earlier book[1] I proposed the concept of secondary deviation to call attention to the importance of the societal reaction in the etiology of deviance, the forms it takes, and its stabilization in deviant social roles or behavior systems. Sympathetic reception of the idea by a number of reputable sociologists and by unheralded teachers in the field has encouraged me to undertake further clarification of the concept and to articulate it with some of the newer ideas which have come out of sociological studies of deviance.

The notion of secondary deviation was devised to distinguish between *original* and *effective* causes of deviant attributes and actions which are associated with physical defects and incapacity, crime, prostitution, alcoholism, drug addiction, and mental disorders. Primary deviation, as contrasted with secondary, is polygenetic, arising out of a variety of social, cultural, psychological, and physiological factors, in either adventitious or recurring combinations. While it may be socially recognized and even de-

From Edwin M. Lemert, *Human Deviance, Social Problems, and Social Control*, pp. 40–41, 50–51, 53–55, copyright © 1967. Reprinted by permission of Prentice-Hall, Inc., Englewood Cliffs, N.J. Footnotes have been renumbered.
[1] Edwin M. Lemert, *Social Pathology* (New York: McGraw-Hill, 1951), pp. 75f.

fined as undesirable, primary deviation has only marginal implications for the status and psychic structure of the person concerned. Resultant problems are dealt with reciprocally in the context of established status relationships. This is done either through *normalization,* in which the deviance is perceived as normal variation—a problem of everyday life— or through management and nominal controls which do not seriously impede basic accommodations people make to get along with each other.

Secondary deviation refers to a special class of socially defined responses which people make to problems created by the societal reaction to their deviance. These problems are essentially moral problems which revolve around stigmatization, punishments, segregation, and social control. Their general effect is to differentiate the symbolic and interactional environment to which the person responds, so that early or adult socialization is categorically affected. They become central facts of existence for those experiencing them, altering psychic structure, producing specialized organization of social roles and self-regarding attitudes. Actions which have these roles and self-attitudes as their referents make up secondary deviance. The secondary deviant, as opposed to his actions, is a person whose life and identity are organized around the facts of deviance.

Parenthetically it needs comment that all or most persons have physical attributes or histories of past moral transgressions, even crimes, about which they are sufficiently self-conscious to have developed techniques for accepting and transforming or psychologically nullifying degrading or punitive societal reactions. Recognition of this compromised state of mankind led Goffman in his sensitive analysis of stigma to hold that secondary deviation is simply the extreme of a graded series of moral adaptations, found among "normal" persons as well as those with socially obtrusive stigma.[2] I believe, however, that this overlooks the fact that stigma involves categorical societal definitions which depict polarized moral opposites, and also that self-definitions or identities are integral in the sense that individuals respond to themselves as moral types.

Moreover, whereas Goffman addresses himself to the question of how persons manage stigma and mitigate its consequences, secondary deviation concerns processes which create, maintain, or intensify stigma; it presumes that stigma may be unsuccessfully contained and lead to repetition of deviance similar or related to that which originally initiated stigmatization. Also, it does not exclude the possibility that stigmatized deviance may be strategic, willful, or readily accepted as a solution to problems of the person standing in a stigmatized position.

The way in which a person presents himself in public encounters, particularly in an attenuated, pluralistic society, does much to direct the

---

[2] Erving Goffman, *Stigma* (Englewood Cliffs, N.J.: Prentice-Hall, 1962), p. 127.

kinds of reactions others make to him and by such means he protects cherished aspects of his identity. However, to dwell upon the cognitive, dramatic details of face-to-face interaction is to grapple with only part of the thorny question of secondary deviance. Over and beyond these are macrocosmic, organizational forces of social control through which public and private agencies actively define and classify people, impose punishments, restrict or open access to rewards and satisfactions, set limits to social interaction, and induct deviants into special, segregated environments.[3]

Although the ideas of personal adaptation and maladaptation rest uneasily in a kind of sociological limbo, the conception of primary and secondary deviance inclines thought in their direction, or at least toward some comparable terms. Their consideration makes it clear that awareness of unenviable features of the self is a complex rather than a simple reciprocal of societal insults to identity, and, further, that adaptations can turn into maladaptations on the person's own terms.[4] This comes to light where efforts at validating the self are complicated by distinct feelings of hopelessness, entrapment, or loss of control over actions presumed to be volitional. These can be observed in certain forms of deviance best described as self-defeating; their peculiar, illogical manifestations speak of underlying difficulty or dilapidation in the communication process by which self and other are constituted.

*   *   *

PROCESS AND SECONDARY DEVIANCE

The most general process by which status and role transitions take place is socialization. As it has been applied to the study of deviants, the concept has been further circumscribed to designate such processes as criminalization, prisonization, "sophistication," "hardening," pauperization, addiction, conversion, radicalization, professionalization, and "mortification of self." All of these speak in varying degrees of a personal progression or differentiation in which the individual acquires: (1) morally inferior status; (2) special knowledge and skills; (3) an integral attitude or "world view"; and (4) a distinctive self-image based upon but not necessarily coterminous with his image reflected in interaction with others.

The earliest descriptions of deviant socialization current in sociology came from Shaw's documents on delinquent careers. These were likened to

---

[3] John Kitsuse and Aaron Cicourel, "A Note on the Uses of Official Statistics," *Social Problems*, 11 (1963): 131–39.

[4] On this point see Messinger's criticism of Goffman. Sheldon Messinger, "Life as a Theatre," *Sociometry*, 25 (1962): 98–109.

natural histories and so titled, but their descriptive content was derived from the delinquent's "own story," as related to an interviewer.[5] From a present-day perspective these studies appear to have been colored by Shaw's unconcealed interest in reform and the probable interest of the respondent in supporting Shaw's views. Valuable as the stories were and still are for certain purposes, they carried unavoidable overtones of nineteenth-century entrepreneurial ideology in reverse, resembling "sad tales," or reminiscent of Hogarth's *Rake's Progress,* or early moral propaganda tracts which portray prostitution as the "road to ruin."

The deviant-career concept also has been linked with or partly derived from an occupational model, examples of which are found in the descriptions of criminal behavior systems, such as thieving, and the marginal deviance of dance musicians.[6] The occupational parallel, of course, can be demonstrated in the professionalization of some types of thieves, prostitutes, political radicals, vagrants, bohemians (beatniks), beggars, and to some extent the physically handicapped. In contrast to these, however, there is little indication of an occupational orientation among alcoholics, mentally disordered persons, stutterers, homosexuals, and systematic check forgers.

Closer examination of the career concept suggests that its application to deviance should be guarded. I doubt, for example, that the notion of "recruitment" of persons to most kinds of deviance can be any more than a broad analogy. While learning specialized knowledge from other deviants is a condition of some deviance, it is not so for all, and the notion that deviants serve an "apprenticeship" may be more figurative than literal where it is applicable. A career denotes a course to be run, but the delineation of fixed sequences or stages through which persons move from less to more serious deviance is difficult or impossible to reconcile with an interactional theory. Furthermore, no incontrovertible evidence has yet been marshaled to justify the belief that prodromal signs of deviance exist— either in behaviors or in personality syndromes such as "predelinquent," "prepsychotic," or "addiction-prone." The flux and pluralism of modern society make concepts of drift, contingency, and risk far more meaningful in deviance than inevitability or linear progress.

A more defensible conception of deviant career is that of recurrent or typical contingencies and problems awaiting someone who continues in a

---

[5] Clifford Shaw, *The Jack-Roller* (Chicago: University of Chicago Press, 1930). Goffman uses the concept "moral career" as a broad orientation to changes over time basic and common to persons in a social category. He regards it as a two-sided perspective which shifts back and forth between the self and its significant society. Erving Goffman, "The Moral Career of the Mental Patient," *Psychiatry,* 22 (1959): 123–42.

[6] E. H. Sutherland, *The Professional Thief* (Chicago: University of Chicago Press, 1937); Howard Becker, *Outsiders* (New York: Free Press, Macmillan, 1963), chaps. 5, 6; C. Cambor, Gerald Lesowitz, and Miles Miller, "Creative Jazz Musicians: a Clinical Study," *Psychiatry,* 25 (1960): 1–15; Raymond Mack, "The Jazz Community," *Social Forces,* 38 (1960): 211–22.

course of action, with the added notion that there may be theoretically "best" choices set into a situation by prevailing technology and social structure. There is some predictive value of a limited or residual nature in concepts like "turning points" or "points of no return," which have been brought into the sociological analysis of careers. These allow it to be said that persons having undergone certain changes will not or cannot retrace their steps; deviant actions act as social foreclosures which qualitatively change meanings and shift the scope of alternatives within which new choices can be made.[7] Even here a caveat is necessary, for alcoholics, drug addicts, criminals, and other deviants do sometimes make comebacks in the face of stigma, and an early history of deviance may in some instances lead to success in the conventional world.

* * *

THE SECONDARY DEVIANT

Devaluation of the self on society's terms ordinarily has a sequel of internal or psychic struggle, greatest where the sense of continuity of the self is massively threatened. Some persons never move beyond this state, overtly striving to conform at times, at others entangling themselves with deviance. Terms like "unorganized" or "transitional" deviance may be apt descriptions of their actions for certain purposes. Assuming that the person moves further toward deviance, the abatement of his conflicts usually follows discovery that his status as deviant, although degraded, is by no means as abysmal as represented in moral ideologies. The blinded war veteran learns that blindness is not a stark tragedy but more like a "damned nuisance," and that life is possible, particularly if a lot of "charitable" people would leave him alone. The prostitute soon realizes that her new life is sometimes rough and unpredictable, and that arrest is a hazard, but it is not a life of shame. Having discovered the prosaic nature of much of his life under a new status, the deviant, like other people, usually tries to make out as best he can.[8] What happens will be conditioned by several factors:[9] (1) the clarity with which a role or roles can be defined; (2) the possession

---

[7] See Lemert, *Social Pathology*, chap. 4; also Becker, *Outsiders*, chap. 2; for a careful evaluation and critique of attempts to predict delinquency, see Jackson Toby, "An Evaluation of Early Identification and Intensive Treatment Programs for Predelinquents," *Social Problems*, 13 (1965): 161–75.

[8] This may be likened to playing a game with new and not very favorable rules. Tannenbaum described it in connection with the professional criminal: "After a while he accepts it [the game] as a matter of course. He bargains upon the amount of freedom he may have, hopes for escape, for total freedom from arrest, but bargains with fate and gives hostages to freedom, calculates his chances and accepts the inevitable with stoicism" (Frank Tannenbaum, "The Professional Criminal," *Century Magazine,* 110 (1925): 584).

[9] I am indebted for these ideas to William Robinson, who some years ago in a seminar at UCLA suggested them as a parsimonious summary of Leonard Cottrell's article "The Adjustment of the Individual to His Age and Sex Roles," *American Sociological Review*, 7 (1942): 617–20.

or acquisition of attributes, knowledge, and skills to enact, improvise, and invent roles; and (3) the motivation to play his role or roles.

A great deal can be said, mostly illustrative, about the first two items. Confidence men, for example, have clearly defined occupational roles in a criminal world, but not many persons are recruited to the roles because they lack the requisite skills and knowledge for this exacting form of thievery. In decided contrast, there are few or no specialized roles available to stutterers, save perhaps that of a clown or an entertainer. Fashioning their own roles is difficult because effective speech is a requirement for most social roles. Consequently they are reduced to filling conventional occupational roles usually below their educational or skills level, becoming, in a figurative sense, ridiculous or strangely silent hewers of wood and haulers of water. Somewhere between the two extremes of confidence man and stutterer is the drug addict, most of whom in our society are excluded from conventional occupations and tend to be excluded from professional or organized criminal pursuits. However, they may elect to be petty thieves, burglars, prostitutes, hustlers, stool pigeons, or choose to peddle drugs to other addicts.

While the social roles available to deviants vary in number, kind, and degree of stigmatization, there is always some basis for adaptation or a modus vivendi open to the deviant. Moreover, attributes can be faked or concealed and some measure of skills and knowledge learned, whether they be means of filling the leftover, low-status roles of conventional society or those more explicitly defined as immoral or criminal. Such conclusions furnish the more pertinent one that secondary deviance to a large extent becomes a phenomenon of motivation.

MOTIVATION AND LEARNING

If motivation to exploit the possibilities of degraded status and to play a deviant role are critical aspects of transition to secondary deviance, then analysis is pushed toward some form of learning theory, preferably one which accounts for the variable social meanings of satisfactions, rewards, and punishments. This enters an area little trod by sociologists and to some extent looked upon as an alien if not sterile preoccupation of psychologists. Yet notwithstanding the criticism that the laws of learning have been largely formal and devoid of content, the outlook is less bleak than sometimes pictured—particularly where efforts have been made to bring together dynamic personality theory and ego psychology with newer formulations of the learning process.

If nothing else, common sense dictates that some variant of the law of effect be made part of the explanation of secondary deviance. This is true even in the face of the formidable task of specifying what is rewarding or punishing to human beings, whose actions in contrast to those of the rest of the animal world are complicated by symbolic learning and delayed gratification. Restated and applied to deviance, the law of effect is a simple idea that people beset with problems posed for them by society will choose lines of action they expect to be satisfactory solutions to the problems. If the consequences are those expected, the likelihood that the action or generically similar action will be repeated is increased. If the consequences are unsatisfactory, unpleasant, or make more problems than they solve, then the pattern of action will be avoided.[10] The fact that anticipation of satisfactions or expectation of punishments is a cognitive process based upon symbolic learning as well as experience does not vitiate the principle of effect; it only reasserts the long-standing need to show how individuals evaluate their own responses in a world where the accommodations of others become means to ends. The absence of any well-worked-out theory for doing this leaves the field open to several propositions which may be suitable for further study of the process of evaluation connected with secondary deviance:

1. Defining one's self as deviant is instrumental in seeking out means of satisfaction and mitigating stigmatization. The redefinition of self leads to reinterpretation of past experiences, which in turn reduces inner tensions and conflict. Ends and means are more easily sorted out, and personal accommodations established necessary to utilize available alternatives.

2. The value hierarchy of the degraded individual changes, in the process of which ends become means and means become ends. Conventional punishments lose their efficacy with loss of status. Experiences at one time evaluated as degrading may shift full arc to become rewarding. The alcoholic is an example; deeply ashamed by his first stay in jail, he may as years go by come to look upon arrest as a means of getting food, shelter, and a chance to sober up.

3. Persons who renounce higher status are less affected by the promise of remote satisfactions and more by those within their immediate ken. This is related to the degree of degradation, and also to incarceration or hospital sojourns which determine the point in personal life cycles at which evaluations are made. Deprivation and long experience with highly specific systems of sanctions within control institutions reinforce a world view of the attainable over the achievable.

4. Once deviance becomes a way of life the personal issue often becomes the costs of making a change rather than the higher status to be gained through rehabilitation or reform. Such costs are calculated in terms of the time, energy, and distress seen necessary to change.

---

[10] The law of effect was originally stated by the psychologist E. L. Thorndike. For a discussion of his principle and learning theory in general, see O. Hobart Mowrer, *Learning Theory and Behavior* (New York: Wiley, 1960), chap. 1.

22. THE PROFESSIONALIZATION OF THEFT

Edwin H. Sutherland

The essential characteristics of the profession of theft, as described by the professional thief in the preceding section of this book, are technical skill, status, consensus, differential association, and organization. Two significant conclusions may be derived from analysis of these characteristics. The first is that the characteristics of the profession of theft are similar to the characteristics of any other permanent group. The second is that certain elements run through these characteristics which differentiate the professional thieves sharply from other groups. The similarities and differences will be indicated in the following elaboration of these characteristics and of the implications which may be derived from them.

I. THE PROFESSION OF THEFT AS A COMPLEX OF TECHNIQUES

The professional thief has a complex of abilities and skills, just as do physicians, lawyers, or bricklayers. The abilities and skills of the professional thief are directed to the planning and execution of crimes, the disposal of stolen goods, the fixing of cases in which arrests occur, and the control of other situations which may arise in the course of the occupation. Manual dexterity and physical force are a minor element in these techniques. The principal elements in these techniques are wits, "front," and talking ability. The thieves who lack these general abilities or the specific skills which are based on the general abilities are regarded as amateurs, even though they may steal habitually.[1] Also, burglars, robbers, kidnapers, and others who engage in the "heavy rackets" are generally not regarded as professional thieves, for they depend primarily on manual dexterity or force. A few criminals in the "heavy rackets" use their wits, "front," and talking ability, and these are regarded by the professional thieves as belonging to the profession.

The division between professional and nonprofessional thieves in regard to this complex of techniques is relatively sharp. This is because these techniques are developed to a high point only by education, and the education can be secured only in association with professional thieves; thieves do not have formal educational institutions for the training of recruits.[2] Also, these techniques generally call for cooperation which can be secured only in association with professional thieves. Finally, this complex of techniques represents a unified preparation for all professional problems in the life of the thief. Certain individuals, as lone wolves, develop to a high point the technique of executing a specific act of theft—e.g., forgery —but are quite unprepared in plans, resources, and connections to deal with emergencies such as arrest.

Because some of the techniques are specific, professional thieves tend to specialize on a relatively small number of rackets that are related to one another. On the other hand, because of the contacts in the underworld with criminals of all kinds and because of the generality of some of the techniques of crime, professional thieves frequently transfer for longer or shorter periods from their specialty to some other racket. In some cases they like the new racket better than the old and remain in the new field. In many cases they dislike the new racket. Hapgood's thief was primarily a pickpocket; he participated occasionally in burglaries but never liked burglary and remained at heart a pickpocket; he wrote regarding burglary:

---

[1] Several statistical studies of habitual thieves, defined in terms of repeated arrests, have been published. Some of these are excellent from the point of view of the problems with which they deal, but they throw little light on professional thieves because they do not differentiate professional thieves from other habitual thieves. See Roland Grassberger, *Gewerbs- und Berufsverbrechertum in den Vereinigten Staaten von Amerika* (Vienna, 1933); Fritz Beger, *Die rückfälligen Betrüger* (Leipzig, 1929); Alfred John, *Die Rückfallsdiebe* (Leipzig, 1929).

[2] Stories circulate at intervals regarding schools for pickpockets, confidence men, and other professional thieves. If formal schools of this nature have ever existed, they have probably been ephemeral.

"It is too dangerous, the come-back is too sure, you have to depend too much on the nerve of your pals, the 'bits' [prison sentences] are too long, and it is very difficult to 'square' it."[3]

The evidence is not adequate to determine whether specialization has increased or decreased. Cooper asserts that it has decreased and explains the decrease as due to the war, prohibition, and the depression. He asserts specifically that confidence men, who a generation ago would have been ashamed to engage in any theft outside of their own specialty, are now engaging in banditry, kidnaping, and other crimes, and he gives a detailed description of a conference of confidence men held in Chicago in which they attempted to formulate a code which would prohibit their colleagues from excursions outside their own field.[4] Byrnes showed in 1886 in his history of professional criminals in America that many thieves participated for longer or shorter times in crimes outside their own special field.[5]

II. THE PROFESSION OF THEFT AS STATUS

The professional thief, like any other professional man, has status. The status is based upon his technical skill, financial standing, connections, power, dress, manners, and wide knowledge acquired in his migratory life. His status is seen in the attitudes of other criminals, the police, the court officials, newspapers, and others. The term "thief" is regarded as honorific and is used regularly without qualifying adjectives to refer to the professional thief. It is so defined in a recent dictionary of criminal slang: "Thief, n. A member of the underworld who steals often and successfully. This term is applied with reserve and only to habitual criminals. It is considered a high compliment."[6]

Professional thieves are contemptuous of amateur thieves and have many epithets which they apply to the amateurs. These epithets include "snatch-and-grab thief," "boot-and-shoe thief," and "best-hold cannon." Professional thieves may use "raw-jaw" methods when operating under excellent protection, but they are ashamed of these methods and console themselves with the knowledge that they could do their work in more artistic manner

---

[3] Hutchins Hapgood, *Autobiography of a Thief* (New York, 1903), p. 107.

[4] Courtney R. Cooper, *Ten Thousand Public Enemies* (Boston, 1935), pp. 271–72; "Criminal America," *Saturday Evening Post*, 207 (April 27, 1935): 6. A confidence man, when asked regarding this conference of confidence men in Chicago, said that Cooper's writings regarding it should have been entitled "Mythologies of 1935."

[5] Thomas Byrnes, *Professional Criminals of America* (New York, 1886). Grassberger (*op. cit.*) has several ingenious methods of measuring the extent of specialization, but the conclusions apply to habitual criminals in general rather than to professional thieves, and the habitual criminals in general probably have less tendency to specialize than do the professional thieves.

[6] Noel Ersine, *Underworld and Prison Slang* (Upland, Indiana, 1935).

if necessary. They will have no dealings with thieves who are unable to use the correct methods of stealing.

Professional thieves disagree as to the extent of gradations within the profession. Some thieves divide the profession into "big-time" and "small-time" thieves on the basis of the size of the stakes for which they play, on the preparations for a particular stake, and on connections. A confidence man who regarded himself as "big-time" wrote as follows regarding a shoplifter:

> While he is undoubtedly a professional thief, I should a few years ago [before he was committed to prison] have been ashamed to be seen on the street with him. I say this not out of a spirit of snobbishness but simply because for business reasons I feel that my reputation would have suffered in the eyes of my friends to be seen in the company of a booster [shoplifter].

On the other hand, the thief who wrote this document insisted that there are no essential gradations within the profession:

> I have never considered anyone a small-time thief. If he is a thief, he is a thief—small-time, big-time, middle-time, eastern standard, or Rocky Mountain, it is all the same. Neither have I considered anyone big-time. It all depends on the spot and how it is handled. I recall a heel touch [sneak theft] at ten one morning which showed $21 and three hours later the same troupe took off one for $6,500 in the same place. Were they small-time in the morning and big-time in the afternoon? The confidence men who play against a store [using a fake gambling club or brokerage office] expect to get large amounts. But there is considerable interchange, some working for a time at short con and then at elaborate con rackets. Those who play against a store know those who engage in short con; if not, they have many mutual friends.

The difference in opinion is quite similar to the difference that would emerge if lawyers or doctors were discussing the gradations within their professions. In any case there is pride in one's own position in the group. This pride may be illustrated by the action of Roger Benton, a forger, who was given a signed blank check to fill out the amount of money he desired; Benton wrote a big "Void" across the face of the check and returned it to the grocer who gave it to him. He explains, "I suppose I had too much professional pride to use it—after all, I was a forger who took smart money from smart banks, not a thief who robbed honest grocerymen."[7]

III. THE PROFESSION OF THEFT AS CONSENSUS

The profession of theft is a complex of common and shared feelings, sentiments, and overt acts. Pickpockets have similar reactions to prospective victims and to the particular situations in which victims are found. This

---

[7] *Where Do I Go from Here?* (New York: Lee Furman, Inc., 1936), p. 62.

similarity of reactions is due to the common background of experiences and the similarity of points of attention. These reactions are like the "clinical intuitions" which different physicians form of a patient or different lawyers form of a juryman on quick inspection. Thieves can work together without serious disagreements because they have these common and similar attitudes. This consensus extends throughout the activities and lives of the thieves, culminating in similar and common reactions to the law, which is regarded as the common enemy. Out of this consensus, moreover, develop the codes, the attitudes of helpfulness, and the loyalties of the underworld.

The following explanation of the emphasis which thieves place on punctuality is an illustration of the way consensus has developed:

> It is a cardinal principle among partners in crime that appointments shall be kept promptly. When you "make a meet" you are there on the dot or you do not expect your partner to wait for you. The reason is obvious. Always in danger of arrest, the danger to one man is increased by the arrest of the other; and arrest is the only legitimate excuse for failing to keep an appointment. Thus, if the appointment is not kept on time, the other may assume arrest and his best procedure is to get away as quickly as possible and save his own skin.[8]

One of the most heinous offenses that a thief can commit against another thief is to inform, "squeal," or "squawk." This principle is generally respected even when it is occasionally violated. Professional thieves probably violate the principle less frequently than other criminals for the reason that they are more completely immune from punishment, which is the pressure that compels an offender to inform on others. Many thieves will submit to severe punishment rather than inform. Two factors enter into this behavior. One is the injury which would result to himself in the form of loss of prestige, inability to find companions among thieves in the future, and reprisals if he should inform. The other is loyalty and identification of self with other thieves. The spontaneous reactions of offenders who are in no way affected by the behavior of the squealer, as by putting him in coventry, are expressions of genuine disgust, fear, and hatred.[9] Consensus is the basis of both of these reactions, and the two together explain how the rule against informing grows out of the common experiences of the thieves.

Consensus means, also, that thieves have a system of values and an *esprit de corps* which support the individual thief in his criminal career. The distress of the solitary thief who is not a member of the underworld society of criminals is illustrated in the following statement by Roger Benton at the time when he was an habitual but not a professional forger:

---

[8] *Ibid.*, p. 269.
[9] Philip S. Van Cise, *Fighting the Underworld* (Boston, 1936), p. 321; Josiah Flynt Willard, *Tramping with Tramps* (New York, 1899), pp. 23–24, and *My Life* (New York, 1908), pp. 331–40.

I had no home, no place to which I could return for sanctuary, no friend in the world to whom I could talk freely. . . . I was a lone man, my face set away from those of my fellows. But I didn't mind—at least I didn't think I minded. [A little later he became acquainted in St. Louis with Nero's place, which was a rendezvous for theatrical people.] I liked Nero. I liked the crowd that gathered in his place and I wanted my evening entertainment there to continue. And I found that I was hungrier for human companionship than I had known. Here I found it. . . . It was a gay interlude and I enjoyed it thoroughly, and neglected my own work [forgery] while I played and enjoyed the simple, honest friendships of these children of the stage. [Still later] I could not rid myself of the crying need for the sense of security which social recognition and contact with one's fellows and their approval furnishes. I was lonely and frightened and wanted to be where there was someone who knew me as I had been before I had become a social outcast.[10]

Among the criminal tribes of India the individual was immersed almost completely in a consistent culture and felt no distress in attacking an outsider because this did not make him an enemy in any group which had significance for him. Nowhere in America, probably, is a criminal so completely immersed in a group that he does not feel his position as an enemy of the larger society. Even after Roger Benton became a member of the underworld as a professional forger, he felt lonely and ill at ease: "I was sick of the whole furtive business, of the constant need to be a fugitive among my fellows, of the impossibility of settling down and making a home for myself, and of the fear of imprisonment."[11]

The professional thief in America feels that he is a social outcast. This is especially true of the professional thieves who originated in middle-class society, as many of them did. He feels that he is a renegade when he becomes a thief. Chic Conwell states that the thief is looking for arguments to ease his conscience and that he blocks off considerations about the effects of his crimes upon the victims and about the ultimate end of his career. When he is alone in prison, he cannot refrain from thought about such things, and then he shudders at the prospect of returning to his professional activities. Once he is back in his group, he assumes the "bravado" attitudes of the other thieves, his shuddering ceases, and everything seems to be all right. Under the circumstances he cannot develop an integrated personality, but the distress is mitigated, his isolation reduced, and his professional life made possible because he has a group of his own in which he carries on a social existence as a thief, with a culture and values held in common by many thieves. In this sense, also, professional theft means consensus.[12]

---

[10] *Op. cit.*, pp. 62, 66–67, 80–81.

[11] *Ibid.*, p. 242.

[12] The document in Part I provides internal evidence of the lack of integration of the professional thief. The tone of the first chapters is significantly different from the tone of

IV. THE PROFESSION OF THEFT AS DIFFERENTIAL ASSOCIATION

Differential association is characteristic of the professional thieves, as of all other groups. The thief is a part of the underworld and in certain respects is segregated from the rest of society. His place of residence is frequently in the slums or in the "white-light" districts where commercial recreations flourish. Even when he lives in a residential hotel or in a suburban home, he must remain aloof from his neighbors more than is customary for city dwellers who need not keep their occupations secret.

The differential element in the association of thieves is primarily functional rather than geographical. Their personal association is limited by barriers which are maintained principally by the thieves themselves. These barriers are based on their community of interests, including security or safety. These barriers may easily be penetrated from within; since other groups also set up barriers in their personal association, especially against known thieves, the thieves are, in fact, kept in confinement within the barriers of their own groups to a somewhat greater extent than is true of other groups. On the other hand, these barriers can be penetrated from the outside only with great difficulty. A stranger who enters a thieves' hangout is called a "weed in the garden." When he enters, conversation either ceases completely or is diverted to innocuous topics.

Many business and professional men engage in predatory activities that are logically similar to the activities of the professional thief. But the widow-and-orphan swindler does not regard himself as a professional thief and is not so regarded by professional thieves. Each regards the other with contempt. They have no occasion to meet and would have nothing to talk about if they did meet. They are not members of the same group.

The final definition of the professional thief is found within this differential association. The group defines its own membership. A person who is received in the group and recognized as a professional thief is a professional thief. One who is not so received and recognized is not a professional thief, regardless of his methods of making a living.

Though professional thieves are defined by their differential association, they are also a part of the general social order. It would be a decided mistake to think of professional thieves as absolutely segregated from the rest

---

the last chapter. In the first chapters the thief is idealized and described in a jaunty manner; in the last chapter the thief is frustrated and regards himself as the principal "sucker." This difference in tone is not due to changes which occurred in the thief during the course of his work on the document, for the materials were not organized in their present form until he had completed his work; some portions of the last chapter were written previous to much of the first chapters. The inconsistency in tone is related to the topics under consideration. The thief assumed one tone when discussing the techniques and the internal relations of the profession and a different tone when discussing the relation of the profession to the larger society.

of society. They live in the midst of a social order to which they are intimately related and in many ways well adjusted. First, the thief must come into contact with persons in legitimate society in order to steal from them. While, as a pickpocket, he may merely make physical contact with the clothes and pocketbooks of victims, as a confidence man he must enter into intimate association with them. This intimacy is cold-blooded. The feelings are expressed as by an actor on a stage, with calculations of the results they will produce. He is like a salesman who attempts to understand a prospective customer only as a means of breaking down sales resistance and realizing his own objective of increased sales.

Second, he has some personal friends who are law-abiding in all respects. He is generally known to these friends as a thief. In his relations with these friends the reciprocity of services does not involve criminality on either side.

Third, he receives assistance from persons and agencies which are regarded as legitimate or even as the official protectors of legitimate society. In such persons and agencies he frequently finds attitudes of predatory control[13] which are similar to his own. The political machine which dominates the political life of many American cities and rural districts is generally devoted to predatory control. The professional thief and the politician, being sympathetic in this fundamental interest in predatory control, are able to cooperate to mutual advantage. This involves cooperation with the police and the courts to the extent that these agencies are under the control of the political machine or have predatory interests independent of the machine. The thief is not segregated from that portion of society but is in close and intimate communication with it not only in his occupational life but in his search for sociability as well. He finds these sympathizers in the gambling places, cabarets, and houses of prostitution, where he and they spend their leisure time.

Fourth, the professional thief has the fundamental values of the social order in the midst of which he lives. The public patterns of behavior come to his attention as frequently as to the attention of others. He reads the newspapers, listens to the radio, attends the picture shows and ball games, and sees the new styles in store windows. He is affected just as are others by the advertisements of dentifrices, cigarettes, and automobiles. His interest in money and in the things that money will buy and his efforts to secure "easy money" fit nicely into the pattern of modern life. Though he has consensus within his own profession in regard to his professional activities, he also has consensus with the larger society in regard to many of the values of the larger society.

---

[13] I am indebted for this term, "predatory control," to my colleague Dr. A. B. Hollingshead. It seems to be a proper term to apply to the salesman, described above, to the thief, to many politicians, and to others.

V. THE PROFESSION OF THEFT AS ORGANIZATION

Professional theft is organized crime. It is not organized in the journalistic sense, for no dictator or central office directs the work of the members of the profession. Rather it is organized in the sense that it is a system in which informal unity and reciprocity may be found. This is expressed in the *Report of the* [Chicago] *City Council Committee on Crime* as follows:

> While this criminal group is not by any means completely organized, it has many of the characteristics of a system. It has its own language; it has its own laws; its own history; its traditions and customs; its own methods and techniques; its highly specialized machinery for attack upon persons and particularly upon property; its own highly specialized modes of defense. These professional criminals have inter-urban, interstate and sometimes international connections.[14]

The complex of techniques, status, consensus, and differential association which have been described previously may be regarded as organization. More specifically, the organization of professional thieves consists in part of the knowledge which becomes the common property of the profession. Every thief becomes an information bureau. For instance, each professional thief is known personally to a large proportion of the other thieves, as a result of their migratory habits and common hangouts. Any thief may be appraised by those who know him, in a terse phrase, such as "He is O.K.," "He is a no-good bastard," or "Never heard of him." The residue of such appraisals is available when a troupe wishes to add a new member, or when a thief asks for assistance in escaping from jail.

Similarly, the knowledge regarding methods and situations becomes common property of the profession. "Toledo is a good town," "The lunch hour is the best time to work that spot," "Look out for the red-haired sales-lady—she is double-smart," "See Skid if you get a tumble in Chicago," "Never grift on the way out," and similar mandates and injunctions are transmitted from thief to thief until everyone in the profession knows them. The discussions in the hangouts keep this knowledge adjusted to changing situations. The activities of the professional thieves are organized in terms of this common knowledge.

Informal social services are similarly organized. Any thief will assist any other thief in a dangerous situation. He does this both by positive actions, such as warning, and by refraining from behavior that would increase the danger, such as staring at a thief who is working. Also, collections are taken in the hangouts and elsewhere to assist a thief who may be in jail or the wife of a thief who may be in prison. In these services reciprocity is assumed, but there is no insistence on immediate or specific return to the one who performs the service.

---

[14] P. 164.

The preceding description of the characteristics of the profession of theft suggests that a person can be a professional thief only if he is recognized and received as such by other professional thieves. Professional theft is a group way of life. One can get into the group and remain in it only by the consent of those previously in the group. Recognition as a professional thief by other professional thieves is the absolutely necessary, universal, and definitive characteristic of the professional thief. This recognition is a combination of two of the characteristics previously described, namely, status and differential association. A professional thief is a person who has the status of a professional thief in the differential association of professional thieves.

Selection and tutelage are the two necessary elements in the process of acquiring recognition as a professional thief. These are the universal factors in an explanation of the genesis of the professional thief. A person cannot acquire recognition as a professional thief until he has had tutelage in professional theft, and tutelage is given only to a few persons selected from the total population.

Selection and tutelage are continuous processes. The person who is not a professional thief becomes a professional thief as a result of contact with professional thieves, reciprocal confidence and appreciation, a crisis situation, and tutelage. In the course of this process a person who is not a professional thief may become first a neophyte and then a recognized professional thief. A very small percentage of those who start on this process ever reach the stage of professional theft, and the process may be interrupted at any point by action of either party.

Selection is a reciprocal process, involving action by those who are professional thieves and by those who are not professional thieves. Contact is the first requisite, and selection doubtless lies back of the contacts. They may be pimps, amateur thieves, burglars, or they may be engaged in legitimate occupations as clerks in hotels or stores. Contacts may be made in jail or in the places where professional thieves are working or are spending their leisure time. If the other person is to become a professional thief, the contact must develop into appreciation of the professional thieves. This is not difficult, for professional thieves in general are very attractive. They have had wide experience, are interesting conversationalists, know human nature, spend money lavishly, and have great power. Since some persons are not attracted even by these characteristics, there is doubtless a selective process involved in this, also.

The selective action of the professional thieves is probably more significant than the selective action of the potential thief. An inclination to steal is not a sufficient explanation of the genesis of the professional thief. Everyone has an inclination to steal and expresses this inclination with more or less frequency and with more or less finesse. The person must be appreciated by the professional thieves. He must be appraised as having an adequate equipment of wits, front, talking ability, honesty, reliability, nerve, and determination. The comparative importance of these several characteristics cannot be determined at present, but it is highly probable that no characteristic is valued more highly than honesty. It is probably regarded as more essential than mental ability. This, of course, means honesty in dealings within their own group.

An emergency or crisis is likely to be the occasion on which tutelage begins. A person may lose a job, get caught in amateur stealing, or may need additional money. If he has developed a friendly relationship with professional thieves, he may request or they may suggest that he be given a minor part in some act of theft. He would, if accepted, be given verbal instructions in regard to the theory of the racket and the specific part he is to play. In his first efforts in this minor capacity he may be assisted by the professional thieves, although such assistance would be regarded as an affront by one who was already a professional. If he performs these minor duties satisfactorily, he is promoted to more important duties. During this probationary period the neophyte is assimilating the general standards of morality, propriety, etiquette, and rights which characterize the profession, and he is acquiring "larceny sense." He is learning the general methods of disposing of stolen goods and of fixing cases. He is building up a personal acquaintance with other thieves, and with lawyers, policemen, court officials, and fixers. This more general knowledge is seldom transmitted to the neophyte as formal verbal instructions but is assimilated by him without being recognized as instruction. However, he is quite as likely to be dropped from participation in further professional activities for failure to assimilate and use this more general culture as for failure to acquire the specific details of the techniques of theft.

As a result of this tutelage during the probationary period, he acquires the techniques of theft and consensus with the thieves. He is gradually admitted into differential association with thieves and given tentative status as a professional thief. This tentative status under probation becomes fixed as a definite recognition as a professional thief. Thereby he enters into the systematic organization which constitutes professional theft.

A person who wished to become a professional thief might conceivably acquire some knowledge of the techniques and of the codes by reading the descriptions of theft in newspapers, journals, and books. Either alone or in the company of two or three others he might attempt to use these techniques and to become a self-made professional thief. Even this, of course, would be tutelage. Aside from the fact that hardly ever is the technique of a theft described in such a manner that it can be applied without personal assistance, this part of the skill of the thief is only a part of the requirements for a successful career. This person would not have that indefinite body of appreciations which is called "larceny sense," nor would he have the personal acquaintances with and confidence of fences, fixers, and policemen which are necessary for security in professional theft. He would quickly land in prison, where he would have a somewhat better opportunity to learn how to steal.

A person who is a professional thief may cease to be one. This would generally result from a violation of the codes of the profession or else from inefficiency due to age, fear, narcotic drugs, or drink. Because of either failure he would no longer be able to find companions with whom to work, would not be trusted by the fixer or by the policemen, and therefore he would not be able to secure immunity from punishment. He is no longer recognized as a professional thief, and therefore he can no longer be a professional thief. On the other hand, if he drops out of active stealing of his own volition and retains his abilities, he would continue to receive recognition as a professional thief. He would be similar to a physician who would be recognized as a physician after he ceased active practice.

23. TRUST VIOLATION AS WHITE-COLLAR OR OCCUPATIONAL CRIME

Donald R. Cressey

The notion that a scientist must seek to formulate generalizations which include all of the cases of the phenomena with which he is concerned has been brought to the attention of sociologists many times.[1] The perfect form of scientific knowledge is assumed to be universal generalizations which permit the discernment of exceptions, thus making possible the perfecting or refinement of generalizations. However, this notion, which is essentially an assumption regarding the proper design for scientific research, has been applied only rarely in criminology, and never in an attempt to formulate a sociological theory of trust violation. In fact, while the criminal violation of financial trust poses serious problems for theoretical criminology, text-

Reprinted by permission of the author and the American Sociological Association from *American Sociological Review*, 15 (December 1950): 738–43. Original title: "The Criminal Violation of Financial Trust."

[1] G. H. Mead, "Scientific Method and the Individual Thinker," in John Dewey, *Creative Intelligence* (New York: Holt, 1917); A. D. Ritchie, *Scientific Method: An Inquiry into the Character and Validity of Natural Laws* (New York: Harcourt, Brace, 1923), pp. 53–83; F. Znaniecki, "Social Research in Criminology," *Sociology and Social Research*, 12 (April 1928): 307–22; F. Znaniecki, *The Method of Sociology* (New York: Farrar & Rinehart, 1934), pp. 232–33; Kurt Lewin, *A Dynamic Theory of Personality* (New York: McGraw-Hill, 1935), pp. 18–24; A. R. Lindesmith, *Opiate Addiction* (Bloomington, Ind.: Principia, 1947), pp. 12–14; R. H. Turner, "Statistical Logic in Social Research," *Sociology and Social Research*, 32 (January–February, 1948): 697–704.

book writers and other sociologists who have offered theories of criminal causation have for the most part ignored it.[2] As a result, almost all publications on trust violation have been issued by persons or agencies primarily interested in the techniques used or in prevention of the crime, and the vast majority of the explanations given in the literature merely repeat and emphasize popular views. Few of the explanations have been convincing since little attempt at an integration with an explicit theory has been made.

On the contrary, most of the current explanations are of a multiple-factor type, usually stated in terms of the way the trust violator spends the funds which he has dishonestly obtained. Thus, "gambling," "drink," and "extravagant living" are listed as causes of embezzlement, even if behavior of this kind is not present in even a majority of the cases.[3] Such conceptions are in general more in the nature of attempts to place blame or to indicate immorality than they are explanations of the behavior. For example, if it is said that a trust violator who has been considered a "pillar of the community" and a trusted and loyal employee actually has been gambling with his own and his company's money, an indication of immorality has been revealed, but his behavior has not been explained. Equally in contrast to the assumption regarding proper scientific methodology are those conceptions which assert that trust violation is caused by an assumed hidden variable, such as "moral weakness" or "tensions,"[4] or by weakness in the systems of checks on the trusted person.[5] The latter "explanation" merely states, in a sense, that trust violation is caused by the existence of institutions whose functioning depends upon varying degrees of trust.[6]

The central problem of this study is that of providing an explanation in keeping with the assumption of proper scientific method and generalization by determining whether a definable sequence of events is always present when trust violation is present, and never present when trust violation is absent. A major related problem is that of accounting for the presence in individual cases of the events which make up the sequence which differentiates violators from nonviolators. These two problems are closely re-

---

[2] Only three sociologists have published detailed accounts of research on the subject: E. Redden, "Embezzlement: A Study of One Kind of Criminal Behavior, with Prediction Tables Based on Fidelity Insurance Records" (Ph.D. dissertation, University of Chicago, 1939); Svend Riemer, "Embezzlement: Pathological Basis," *Journal of Criminal Law and Criminology*, 32 (November–December 1941): 411–23; S. Lottier, "Tension Theory of Criminal Behavior," *American Sociological Review*, 7 (December 1942): 840–48.

[3] See, for example, United States Fidelity and Guaranty Co., *1001 Embezzlers* (Baltimore, 1937), and *1001 Embezzlers Post War* (Baltimore, 1950); J. Edgar Hoover, "National Bank Offenses," *Journal of Criminal Law and Criminology*, 24 (September–October 1933): 655–63; V. Peterson, "Why Honest People Steal," *ibid.*, 38 (July–August 1947): 94–103.

[4] Cf. H. Koppel, "Other People's Money," *Collier's*, 67 (April 16, 1921): 11–12; J. Edgar Hoover, *op. cit.*; S. Lottier, *op. cit.*

[5] Cf. George E. Bennet, *Fraud: Its Control Through Accounts* (New York: Century, 1930), p. 22; L. A. Pratt, *Bank Frauds: Their Detection and Prevention* (New York: Ronald, 1947), pp. 7–10.

[6] Hall has pointed out that the economic system in our modern society presupposes business transactions based on a considerable amount of trust (Jerome Hall, *Theft, Law, and Society* [Boston: Little, Brown, 1935]).

lated since the events in the person-situation complex at the time trust violation occurs cannot be completely separated from the prior life experiences of the trust violator. However, only the first problem, that concerned with what Lewin calls "systematic" causation, in contrast to "historical" or "genetic" causation,[7] will be discussed here.

Hypotheses in regard to the first problem, the problem of systematic causation, were formulated progressively. When an hypothesis was formulated, a search for negative cases was conducted, and when such cases were found the hypothesis was reformulated in light of them. The behavior to be explained in this manner was at first defined as embezzlement, and a legal definition of that crime was used.[8] Upon contact with cases, however, it was almost immediately discovered that the term is not used in a consistent manner in the jurisdiction where the research was conducted, and that many persons whose behavior was adequately described by the legal definition actually had been sentenced to the penitentiary on some other charge. Consequently, the legal definition was abandoned and in its place two criteria for inclusion of any particular case in the study were established: (a) The person must have accepted a position of trust in good faith. This is similar to the implication of the legal definition that the "felonious intent" in embezzlement must have been formulated *after* the time of taking possession. All legal definitions are in agreement in this respect. (b) The person must have violated the trust. These criteria permit the inclusion of almost all persons convicted for embezzlement and in addition a proportion of those convicted for larceny by bailee, forgery, and confidence game.

The main source of direct information in regard to the behavior now called "the criminal violation of financial trust" was interview material obtained in informal contacts over a period of five months with all prisoners whose behavior met the criteria and who were confined at the Illinois State Penitentiaries at Joliet.[9] In some cases we were able to write verbatim

---

[7] Kurt Lewin, "Some Social and Psychological Differences between the United States and Germany," *Character and Personality*, 4 (June 1936): 265–93. For a discussion of these two types of explanation in criminology, see E. H. Sutherland, *Principles of Criminology* (Philadelphia: Lippincott, 1947), p. 5; and J. F. Brown and D. W. Orr, "Field Theoretical Approach to Criminology," *Journal of Criminal Psychopathology*, 3 (October 1941): 236–52.

[8] "The fraudulent appropriation to his own use or benefit of property or money entrusted to him by another, on the part of a clerk, agent, trustee, public officer or other person acting in a fiduciary capacity" (*Black's Law Dictionary* [St. Paul, Minn.: West Publishing Co., 1933], p. 633). Almost all studies pertinent to the current research have been studies of embezzlement. But since this term has been used to denote the behavior of all fidelity bond defaulters, the criminal behavior of all persons employed in banks, and the behavior of swindlers as well as embezzlers, it is obvious that the factual conclusions of the studies are not immediately comparable in all respects. The varied usage of the term is due to oversight on the part of some investigators, but it is also due in part to the existence of a variety of legal definitions among the states and foreign countries.

[9] Determination of whether or not a particular prisoner's behavior met the criteria was made by examination of documents in his personal file and by preliminary or "screening" interviews. The document most heavily relied upon for this purpose was the "State's Attorney's Report" (the official statement of facts in each case), but other documents, such as

notes during the interviews without disturbing the subject, but in other cases it seemed appropriate to make only outline notes, and in some cases no notes could be taken at all. In the last two instances the content of the interview was written down in the subject's own words as soon as he left the room.

The length and frequency of interviews with individual subjects depended to a large extent upon the subject himself. Those subjects who seemed reluctant to talk were seen more frequently than those with whom a friendly and confidential relationship was established early in the process, but those who could not present the details of their cases and backgrounds, even if they so desired, were not interviewed as frequently as those who were able to do so. That is, "good" subjects were interviewed more often and more extensively than were "poor" subjects—those whose intelligence, educational background, and vocabulary restricted the communication of their experiences. Those who described their behavior fluently became crucial cases, their testimony causing the abandonment of the hypotheses which had guided the research up to the time they were encountered. The new hypotheses were then checked against the less fluent cases.

The initial hypothesis, which was abandoned almost immediately, was that positions of financial trust are violated when the incumbent has learned in connection with the business or profession in which he is employed that some forms of trust violations are merely "technical violations" and are not really "illegal" or "wrong," and, on the negative side, that they are not violated if this kind of definition of the behavior has not been learned. This hypothesis was suggested by Sutherland in his writings on white-collar crime.[10] In the interviews, however, many trust violators expressed the idea that they knew the behavior to be illegal and wrong at all times and that they merely "kidded themselves" into thinking that it was not illegal. Others reported that they knew of no one in their business or profession who was carrying on practices similar to theirs and some of them defined their offenses as theft rather than as trust violation.

In view of these negative cases, a second hypothesis, which included some of the "multiple factor" ideas of gambling and family emergencies, as well as the potential trust violators' attitudes toward them, was formulated. This hypothesis was in part derived from Riemer's statement that the "opportunities" inherent in trust positions form "temptations" if the

---

reports of the Chicago Crime Commission, letters from former employers and from friends and relatives, and the prisoner's statement upon admission to the institution also were consulted. In the screening interviews the subjects were never asked the question "Did you accept your position of trust in good faith?" but instead the interviewer waited for the subject to give the information spontaneously. Ordinarily, evidence of acceptance in good faith came out in the first interview in the form of statements such as the following: "I had no idea I was going to do this until the day it happened." Evidence of acceptance in bad faith was presented, for example, as follows: "My case isn't like embezzlement because I knew when I took their money that I was going to use it for myself." .

[10] E. H. Sutherland, *White Collar Crime* (New York: Dryden, 1949).

incumbents develop antisocial attitudes which make possible an abandonment of the folkways of business behavior.[11] The formulation was that positions of trust are violated when the incumbent structures a real or supposed need for extra funds or extended use of property as an "emergency" which cannot be met by legal means, and that if such an emergency does not take place trust violation will not occur. This hypothesis proved fruitful, but like the first one it had to be revised when persons were found who claimed that while an emergency had been present at the time they violated the trust, other, perhaps even more extreme, emergencies had been present in earlier periods when they did not violate it. Others reported that there had been no financial emergency in their cases, and a few "explained" their behavior in terms of antagonistic attitudes toward the employer or feelings of being abused, underpaid, or discriminated against in some other way.

The next revision shifted the emphasis from emergency to psychological isolation, stating that persons become trust violators when they conceive of themselves as having incurred financial obligations which are considered as not socially sanctionable and which, consequently, must be satisfied by a private or secret means. Negatively, if such nonshareable obligations are not present, trust violation will not occur. This hypothesis had the advantage of calling attention to the fact that not all emergencies, even if they are created by prior "immoral" behavior on the part of the trusted person, are important to trust violation. It had been suggested by La Piere and Farnsworth, who cite Sutherland as having shown that in cases of white-collar crime the person is frequently confronted "with the alternative of committing a crime or losing something he values above his integrity,"[12] but it was brought into the present study by a suggestion from a prisoner who stated that he believed that no embezzlement would ever occur if the trusted person always told his wife and family about his financial problems, no matter what the consequences. However, when the cases were reexamined in light of this hypothesis it was found that in a few of them there was nothing which could be considered as financial *obligation*, that is, as a debt which had been incurred in the past and for which the person at present felt responsible. Also, in some cases there had been nonsanctionable obligations at a prior time, and these obligations had not been alleviated by means of trust violation. It became increasingly apparent at this point that trust violation could not be attributed to a single event, but that its explanation could be made only in terms of a sequence of events, a process.

Again the hypothesis was reformulated, emphasizing this time not financial *obligations* which were considered as not socially sanctionable and hence as nonshareable, but nonshareable *problems* of that nature. This hypothesis also pointed up the idea that not only was a nonshareable

---

[11] Svend Riemer, *op. cit.*
[12] R. T. La Piere and P. R. Farnsworth, *Social Psychology* (New York: McGraw-Hill, 1949), p. 344.

problem necessary, but that the person had to possess (a) knowledge or awareness of the fact that the problem could to some extent be solved by means of trust violation and (b) the technical skills necessary for such violation. Negative cases appeared, however, in instances where men reported that what they considered a nonshareable problem had been present for some period of time and that they had known for some time before the violation took place that the problem could be solved by violating their position of trust by using a particular skill. Some stated that they did not violate the trust at the earlier period because the situation was not in sharp enough focus to "break down their ideas of right and wrong."

Such statements suggested the final revision, which took the following form: Trusted persons become trust violators when they conceive of themselves as having a financial problem which is nonshareable, have the knowledge or awareness that this problem can be secretly resolved by violation of the position of financial trust, and are able to apply to their own conduct in that situation verbalizations which enable them to adjust their conceptions of themselves as trusted persons with their conceptions of themselves as users of the entrusted funds or property.

This hypothesis proved to be far superior to the others, and no evidence necessitating its rejection has been found as yet. In all of the cases interviewed the sequence has been found to be present, and when cases were examined with a view to answering the question: "Why did these men not violate their trust at an earlier period?" it was seen that in earlier periods one or more of the events in the sequence had not been present. A search of cases reported in the literature also showed no negative cases, though it should be pointed out that in many of the reports crucial information which would either contradict or affirm the hyothesis is not given. A similar search of about 200 unpublished cases collected by E. H. Sutherland in the 1930's, before he had formulated the differential association theory, likewise showed no negative cases.

The events present in the process cannot be considered in great detail here. However, brief comments about the sequence are in order.

(1) Criteria of an objective nature in regard to the degree of "shareability" which specific types of problems have in our culture were not set up, but instead the subject's definition of the situation was used as a datum.[13] Consequently, a list which would exhaust all of the possible problems which could be considered as nonshareable and which might play a part in the etiology of trust violation is not conceivable. For purposes of illustration, however, we may cite one type of problem which is frequently so defined.

This type of problem is that which the trusted person considers to have

---

[13] Evidence of the presence of nonsharable problems was found in the language used by trust violators. None of them, of course, used the words "nonshareable problem," but many of them stated that they were "ashamed" to tell anyone of a certain situation or that they had "too much false pride" to get help from others.

resulted from the violation of the obligations "ascribed" to his position of trust, that is, those obligations of a nonfinancial nature which are expected of persons in consequence of their incumbency in positions of financial trust. Just as persons in trusted positions have obligations not to violate the trust by taking funds, most of them also have obligations, for example, to maintain an enviable position in the community and to refrain from certain types of gambling and from what may be loosely described as riotous living.[14] When persons incur financial responsibilities as a result of violation of these ascribed obligations they often consider that they must be kept secret, and meeting them becomes a nonshareable problem.

The concept of the nonshareable problem and consideration of the type of nonshareable problem just discussed help to make understandable the reported high incidence of "wine, women, and wagering" in the behavior of embezzlers and other trust violators, but these modes of behavior are not used as explanatory principles. In fact, it appears that the use of them as explanations of trust violation merely indicates lack of understanding of the problem.[15]

(2) A nonshareable problem becomes a stimulus to violation of a position of trust only when the position is perceived as offering a private solution to this specific problem. In addition to having a financial problem which he feels he cannot share with persons who, from a more objective point of view, could help him, the trusted person must have a certain amount of knowledge or information about trust violation in general, and he must be able to apply that general information to his own specific situation. The presence of this event is often indicated by trust violators in their use of the language "it occurred to me" or "it dawned on me" that the entrusted funds could be used for such-and-such purpose. This "dawning" or "insight" or "perception" that the nonshareable problem can and may be solved by trust violation involves both knowledge of this fact and a "rationalization" of the behavior.

(3) The verbalizations ("rationalizations") used by trust violators are reflections of contact with cultural ideologies which adjust for the person contradictory ideas in regard to criminality on the one hand and in regard to integrity, honesty, and morality on the other. Upon the appearance of a nonshareable problem the trusted person applies to his own situation a ver-

---

[14] E. C. Hughes has pointed out that in addition to the specifically determining traits, a complex of "auxiliary traits" is expected of incumbents of certain statuses ("Dilemmas and Contradictions of Status," *American Journal of Sociology*, 50 [March 1945], 353–59). In law, this type of obligation is called an "obediential obligation" since it is a consequence of a situation or a relationship, not of a contract (*Black's Law Dictionary*, p. 1274).

[15] We do not mean to imply that statistical studies of personal and social traits as selective factors in trust violation have no place. A study, for example, showing a precise relationship between the presence of certain personal and social traits and the structuring of a financial problem as nonshareable would be extremely valuable. What we wish to imply is that such studies of selective factors, even if properly carried out, do not solve the problem of etiology. Cf. A. R. Lindesmith, *op. cit.*, pp. 157–58.

balization which the groups in which he has had membership have applied to others, or which he himself has applied to the behavior of others. This is his motivation.[16] The hypothesized reactions of others to "borrowing" (criminal behavior) in order to solve a nonshareable problem, for example, are much different from the hypothesized reactions to "stealing" or "embezzling," and the trusted person behaves accordingly. It is because of an ability to hypothesize reactions which will not consistently and severely condemn his criminal behavior that the trusted person takes the role of what *we* have called the "trust violator." *He* often does not think of himself as playing that role, but instead thinks of himself as playing another role, such as that of a special kind of borrower or businessman.

The final hypothesis in its complete form made it possible to account for some of the features of trust violation and for some individual cases of that behavior which could not be accounted for by other hypotheses. However, the fact that it was revised several times probably means that future revision will be necessary if negative cases are found. The location by another investigator of persons who have violated positions of trust which were accepted in good faith, but in whose behavior the sequence was not present, will call for either a new revision of the hypothesis or a redefinition of the behavior included in the scope of the present hypothesis.

---

[16] Cf. C. Wright Mills, "Situated Actions and Vocabularies of Motive," *American Sociological Review*, 5 (December 1940): 904–13.

24. APPRENTICESHIPS IN PROSTITUTION

James H. Bryan

While theoretical conceptions of deviant behavior range from role strain
to psychoanalytic theory, orientations to the study of the prostitute have
shown considerable homogeneity. Twentieth-century theorizing concerning this occupational group has employed, almost exclusively, a Freudian
psychiatric model. The prostitute has thus been variously described as masochistic, of infantile mentality, unable to form mature interpersonal relationships, regressed, emotionally dangerous to males, and as normal as the
average women.[1] The call girl, the specific focus of this paper, has been
accused of being anxious, possessing a confused self-image, excessively dependent, demonstrating gender-role confusion, aggressive, lacking internal
controls, and masochistic.[2]

Reprinted by permission of the author and the Society for the Study of Social Problems
from *Social Problems*, 12, no. 3 (Winter 1965): 287–97.
    [1] H. Benjamin, "Prostitution Reassessed," *International Journal of Sexology*, 26 (1951):
154–60; H. Benjamin and A. Ellis, "An Objective Examination of Prostitution," *International Journal of Sexology*, 29 (1955): 100–105; E. Glover, "The Abnormality of Prostitution," in *Women*, ed. A. M. Krich (New York: Dell, 1953); M. H. Hollander, "Prostitution, the Body, and Human Relatedness," *International Journal of Psychoanalysis*, 42
(1961): 404–13; M. Karpf, "Effects of Prostitution on Marital Sex Adjustment," *International Journal of Sexology*, 29 (1953): 149–54; J. F. Oliven, *Sexual Hygiene and Pathology*
(Philadelphia: Lippincott, 1955); W. J. Robinson, *The Oldest Profession in the World*
(New York: Eugenics Publishing Co., 1929).
    [2] H. Greenwald, *The Call Girl* (New York: Ballentine, 1960).

The exclusive use of psychoanalytic models in attempting to predict behavior, and the consequent neglect of situational and cognitive processes, has been steadily lessening in the field of psychology. Their inadequacy as models for understanding deviancy has been specifically explicated by Becker, and implied by London.[3] The new look in the conceptualization and study of deviant behavior has focused on the interpersonal processes which help define the deviant role, the surroundings in which the role is learned, and limits upon the enactment of the role. As Hooker has indicated regarding the study of homosexuals, one must consider not only the personality structure of the participants, but also the structure of their community and the pathways and routes into the learning and enactment of the behavior.[4] Such "training periods" have been alluded to by Maurer in his study of the con man, and by Sutherland in his report on professional thieves. More recently, Lindesmith and Becker have conceptualized the development of drug use as a series of learning sequences necessary for the development of steady use.[5]

This paper provides some detailed, albeit preliminary, information concerning induction and training in a particular type of deviant career: prostitution, at the call-girl level. It describes the order of events, and their surrounding structure, which future call girls experience in entering their occupation.

The respondents in this study were thirty-three prostitutes, all currently or previously working in the Los Angeles area. They ranged in age from eighteen to thirty-two, most being in their mid-twenties. None of the interviewees were obtained through official law-enforcement agencies, but seven were found within the context of a neuropsychiatric hospital. The remaining respondents were gathered primarily through individual referrals from previous participants in the study. There were no obvious differences between the "psychiatric sample" and the other interviewees on the data to be reported.

All subjects in the sample were call girls. That is, they typically obtained their clients by individual referrals, primarily by telephone, and enacted the sexual contract in their own or their clients' place of residence or employment. They did not initiate contact with their customers in bars, streets, or houses of prostitution, although they might meet their customers

[3] H. S. Becker, *Outsiders: Studies in the Sociology of Deviance* (New York: Free Press, Macmillan, 1963). Also see *The Other Side*, ed. H. S. Becker (New York: Free Press, Macmillan, 1964); P. London, *The Modes and Morals of Psychotherapy* (New York: Holt, Rinehart & Winston, 1964). For recent trends in personality theory, see N. Sanford, "Personality: Its Place in Psychology," and D. R. Miller, "The Study of Social Relationships: Situation, Identity, and Social Interaction." Both papers are presented in *Psychology: A Study of a Science*, ed. S. Koch, vol. 5 (New York: McGraw-Hill, 1963).

[4] Evelyn Hooker, "The Homosexual Community," *Proceedings of the XIV International Congress of Applied Psychology* (1961), pp. 40–59. See also A. Reiss, "The Social Integration of Queers and Peers," *Social Problems*, 9 (1961): 102–20.

[5] D. W. Maurer, *The Big Con* (New York: Signet, 1940); H. S. Becker, *Outsiders;* E. H. Sutherland, *The Professional Thief* (Chicago: University of Chicago Press, 1937); A. R. Lindesmith, *Opiate Addiction* (Bloomington, Ind.: Principia, 1947).

at any number of locations by prearrangement. The minimum fee charged per sexual encounter was $20. As an adjunct to the call-girl interviews, three pimps and two "call boys" were interviewed as well.[6]

Approximately two-thirds of the sample were what are sometimes known as "outlaw broads"; that is, they were not under the supervision of a pimp when interviewed. There is evidence that the majority of pimps who were aware of the study prohibited the girls under their direction from participating in it. It should be noted that many members of the sample belonged to one or another clique; their individually expressed opinions may not be independent.

The interviews strongly suggest that there are marked idiosyncrasies from one geographical area to another in such practices as fee splitting, involvement with peripheral occupations (e.g., cabbies), and so forth. For example, there appears to be little direct involvement of peripheral occupations with call-girl activities in the Los Angeles area, while it has been estimated that up to 10 percent of the population of Las Vegas is directly involved in activities of prostitutes.[7] What may be typical for a call girl in the Los Angeles area is not necessarily typical for a girl in New York, Chicago, Las Vegas, or Miami.

Since the professional literature (e.g., Greenwald, Pomeroy) concerning this occupation and its participants is so limited in quantity, and is not concerned with training per se, the present data may have some utility for the social sciences.[8]

All but two interviews were tape-recorded. All respondents had prior knowledge that the interview would be tape-recorded. The interviewing was, for the most part, done at the girls' place of work and/or residence. Occasional interviews were conducted in the investigator's office, and one in a public park. Interviews were semistructured and employed open-ended questions. One part of the interview concerned the apprenticeship period or "turning out" process.

THE ENTRANCE

> I had been thinking about it [becoming a call girl] before a lot. . . .
> Thinking about wanting to do it, but I had no connections. Had I not
> had a connection, I probably wouldn't have started working. . . . I
> thought about starting out. . . . Once I tried it [without a contact]. . . .

---

[6] This definition departs somewhat from that offered by Clinard. He defines the call girl as one dependent upon an organization for recruiting patrons and one who typically works in lower-class hotels. The present sample is best described by Clinard's category high-class independent professional prostitute (M. B. Clinard, *Sociology of Deviant Behavior* [New York: Rinehart, 1957]).

[7] E. Reid and O. Demaris, *The Green Felt Jungle* (New York: Pocket Books, 1963).

[8] H. Greenwald, *op. cit.*; W. Pomeroy, "Some Aspects of Prostitution" (unpublished paper).

> I met this guy at a bar and I tried to make him pay me, but the thing is,
> you can't do it that way because they are romantically interested in you,
> and they don't think that it is on that kind of basis. You can't all of a
> sudden come up and want money for it, you have to be known before-
> hand. . . . I think that is what holds a lot of girls back who might work.
> I think I might have started a year sooner had I had a connection.
> You seem to make one contact or another . . . if it's another girl or a
> pimp or just someone who will set you up and get you a client. . . . You
> can't just, say, get an apartment and get a phone in and everything and
> say, "Well, I'm gonna start business," because you gotta get clients from
> somewhere. There has to be a contact.

Immediately prior to entrance into the occupation, all but one girl had
personal contact with someone professionally involved in call-girl activities (pimps or other call girls). The one exception had contact with a customer of call girls. While various occupational groups (e.g., photographers)
seem to be peripherally involved, often unwittingly, with the call girl, there
was no report of individuals involved in such occupations being contacts
for new recruits. The novice's initial contact is someone at the level at
which she will eventually enter the occupation: not a streetwalker, but a
call girl; not a pimp who manages girls out of a house of prostitution, but
a pimp who manages call girls.

Approximately half of the girls reported that their initial contact for
entrance into the profession was another "working girl." The nature of
these relationships is quite variable. In some cases, the girls have been long-
standing friends. Other initial contacts involved sexual relationships between a Lesbian and the novice. Most, however, had known each other less
than a year, and did not appear to have a very close relationship, either
in the sense of time spent together or of biographical information exchanged. The relationship may begin with the aspiring call girl soliciting
the contact. That is, if a professional is known to others as a call girl,
she will be sought out and approached by females who are strangers:[9] "I
haven't ever gone out and looked for one. All of these have fell right into
my hands. . . . They turned themselfs out. . . . They come to me for help."

Whatever their relationship, whenever the professional agrees to aid the
beginner, she also, it appears, implicitly assumes responsibility for training
her. This is evidenced by the fact that only one such female contact referred
the aspirant to another girl for any type of help. Data are not available as
to the reason for this unusual referral.

If the original contact was not another call girl but a pimp, a much
different relationship is developed and the career follows a somewhat different course. The relationship between pimp and girl is typically one of
lovers, not friends:

---

[9] A point also made in the autobiographical account of a retired call girl: Virginia
McManus, *Not for Love* (New York: Dell, 1960), p. 160.

> . . . because I love him very much. Obviously, I'm doing this mostly for him. . . . I'd do anything for him. I'm not just saying I will, I am. . . . [After discussing his affair with another woman] I just decided that I knew what he was when I decided to do this for him and I decided I had two choices—either accept it or not, and I accepted it, and I have no excuse.

Occasionally, however, a strictly business relationship will be formed:

> Right now I am buying properties, and as soon as I can afford it, I am buying stocks. . . . It is strictly a business deal. This man and I are friends, our relationship ends there. He handles all the money, he is making all the investments and I trust him. We have a legal document drawn up which states that half the investments are mine, half of them his, so I am protected.

Whether the relationship is love or business, the pimp solicits the new girl.[10] It is usually agreed that the male will have an important managerial role in the course of the girl's career, and that both will enjoy the gains from the girl's activities for an indefinite period: "Actually a pimp has to have complete control or else it's like trouble with him. Because if a pimp doesn't, if she is not madly in love with him or something in some way, a pimp won't keep a girl."

Once the girl agrees to function as a call girl, the male, like his female counterpart, undertakes the training of the girl, or refers the girl to another call girl for training. Either course seems equally probable. Referrals, when employed, are typically to friends and, in some cases, wives or ex-wives.

Although the data are limited, it appears that the pimp retains his dominance over the trainee even when the latter is being trained by a call girl. The girl trainer remains deferential to the pimp's wishes regarding the novice.

APPRENTICESHIP

Once a contact is acquired and the decision to become a call girl made, the recruit moves to the next stage in the career sequence: the apprenticeship period. The structure of the apprenticeship will be described, followed by a description of the content most frequently communicated during this period.

The apprenticeship is typically served under the direction of another call girl, but may occasionally be supervised by a pimp. Twenty-four girls

---

[10] Two of the pimps denied that this was very often so and maintained that the girls will solicit them. The degree to which they are solicited seems to depend upon the nature and extent of their reputations. It is difficult to judge the accuracy of these reports as there appears to be a strong taboo against admitting to such solicitation.

in the sample initially worked under the supervision of other girls. The classroom is, like the future place of work, an apartment. The apprentice typically serves in the trainer's apartment, either temporarily residing with the trainer or commuting there almost daily. The novice rarely serves her apprenticeship in such places as a house of prostitution, motel, or on the street. It is also infrequent that the girl is transported out of her own city to serve an apprenticeship. Although the data are not extensive, the number of girls being trained simultaneously by a particular trainer has rarely been reported to be greater than three. Girls sometimes report spending up to eight months in training, but the average stay seems to be two or three months. The trainer controls all referrals and appointments, novices seemingly not having much control over the type of sexual contact made or the circumstances surrounding the enactment of the contract.

The structure of training under the direction of a pimp seems similar, though information is more limited. The girls are trained in an apartment in the city in which they intend to work and for a short period of time. There is some evidence that the pimp and the novice often do not share the same apartment, as might the novice and the girl trainer. There appear to be two reasons for the separation of pimp and girl. First, it is not uncommonly thought that cues which suggest the presence of other men displease the girl's customers:

> Well, I would never let them know that I had a lover, which is something that you never let a john know, because this makes them very reticent to give you money, because they think you are going to go and spend it with your lover, which is what usually happens.

(Interestingly, the work of Winick suggests that such prejudices may not actually be held by many customers.)[11] Secondly, the legal repercussions are much greater, of course, for the pimp who lives with his girl than for two girls rooming together. As one pimp of nineteen years' experience puts it:

> It is because of the law. There is a law that is called the illegal cohabitation that they rarely use unless the man becomes big in stature. If he is a big man in the hustling world, the law then employs any means at their command....

Because of the convenience in separation of housing, it is quite likely that the pimp is less directly involved with the day-to-day training of the girls than the call-girl trainer.

The content of the training period seems to consist of two broad, interrelated dimensions, one philosophical, the other interpersonal. The former refers to the imparting of a value structure, the latter to "do's" and "don'ts" of relating to customers and, secondarily, to other "working girls"

---

[11] C. Winick, "Prostitutes' Clients' Perception of the Prostitute and Themselves," *International Journal of Social Psychiatry*, 8 (1961–62): 289–97.

and pimps. The latter teaching is perhaps best described by the concept of a short-range perspective. That is, most of the "do's" and "don'ts" pertain to ideas and actions that the call girl uses in problematic situations.[12] Not all girls absorb these teachings, and those who do incorporate them in varying degrees.

Insofar as a value structure is transmitted, it is that of maximizing gains while minimizing effort, even if this requires transgressions of either a legal or moral nature. Frequently, it is postulated that people, particularly men, are corrupt or easily corruptible, that all social relationships are but a reflection of a "con," and that prostitution is simply a more honest or at least no more dishonest act than the everyday behavior of "squares." Furthermore, not only are "johns" basically exploitative, but they are easily exploited; hence they are, in some respects, stupid. As explained by a pimp: "[In the hustling world] the trick or the john is known as a fool. . . . This is not the truth. . . . He [the younger pimp] would teach his woman that a trick was a fool."

Since the male is corrupt, or honest only because he lacks the opportunity to be corrupt, then it is only appropriate that he be exploited as he exploits. "Girls first start making their scores—say one guy keeps them for a while or maybe she gets, you know, three or four grand out of him, say a car or a coat. These are your scores. . . ." The general assumption that man is corrupt is empirically confirmed when the married male betrays his wife, when the moralist, secular or religious, betrays his publicly stated values, or when the "john" "stiffs" (cheats) the girl. An example of the latter is described by a girl as she reflects upon her disillusionment during her training period.

> It is pretty rough when you are starting out. You get stiffed a lot of times. . . . Oh, sure. They'll take advantage of you any time they can. And I'm a trusting soul, I really am. I'll believe anybody till they prove different. I've made a lot of mistakes that way. You get to the point, well, Christ, what the heck can I believe in people, they tell me one thing and here's what they do to me.

Values such as fairness with other working girls, or fidelity to a pimp, may occasionally be taught. To quote a pimp:

> So when you ask me if I teach a kind of basic philosophy, I would say that you could say that. Because you try to teach them in an amoral way that there is a right and wrong way as pertains to this game . . . and then you teach them that when working with other girls to try to treat the other girl fairly because a woman's worst enemy in the street [used in both a literal and figurative sense] is the other woman and only by treating the other women decently can she expect to get along. . . . Therefore the basic philosophy, I guess, would consist of a form of honesty, a form of sincerity and complete fidelity to her man [pimp].

---

[12] H. S. Becker, Blanche Geer, E. C. Hughes, and A. L. Strauss, *Boys in White* (Chicago: University of Chicago Press, 1961).

It should be noted, however, that behavior based on enlightened self-interest with concomitant exploitation is not limited to customer relationships. Interviewees frequently mentioned a pervasive feeling of distrust between trainer and trainee, and such incidents as thefts or betrayal of confidences are occasionally reported and chronically guarded against.

Even though there may be considerable pressure upon the girl to accept this value structure, many of them (perhaps the majority of the sample) reject it.

> People have told me that I wasn't turned out, but turned loose instead. . . . Someone who is turned out is turned out to believe in a certain code of behavior, and this involves having a pimp, for one thing. It also involves never experiencing anything but hatred or revulsion for "tricks," for another thing. It involves always getting the money in front [before the sexual act] and a million little things that are very strictly adhered to by those in the "in group," which I am not. . . . Never being nice or pleasant to a trick unless you are doing it for the money, getting more money. [How did you learn that?] It was explained to me over a period of about six months. I learned that you were doing it to make money for yourself so that you could have nice things and security. . . . [Who would teach you this?] [The trainer] would teach me this.[13]

It seems reasonable to assume that the value structure serves, in general, to create in-group solidarity and to alienate the girl from "square" society, and that this structure serves the political advantage of the trainer and the economic gains of the trainee more than it allays the personal anxieties of either. In fact, failure to adopt these values at the outset does not appear to be correlated with much personal distress.[14] As one girl describes her education experiences:

> Some moral code. We're taught, as a culture . . . it's there and after awhile you live, breathe, and eat it. Now, what makes you go completely against everything that's inside you, everything that you have been taught, and the whole society, to do things like this?

Good empirical evidence, however, concerning the functions and effectiveness of this value structure with regard to subjective comfort is lacking.

A series of deductions derived from the premises indicated above serve to provide, in part, the "rules" of interpersonal contact with the customer. Each customer is to be seen as a "mark," and "pitches" are to be made.

> [Did you have a standard pitch?] It's sort of amusing. I used to listen to my girl friend [trainer]. She was the greatest at this telephone type

---

[13] The statements made by prostitutes to previous investigators and mental helpers may have been parroting this particular value structure and perhaps have misled previous investigators into making the assumption that "all whores hate men." While space prohibits a complete presentation of the data, neither our questionnaire nor interview data suggest that this is a predominant attitude among call girls.

[14] There is, from the present study, little support for the hypothesis of Reckless concerning the association of experience trauma and guilt with abruptness of entry into the occupation (W. C. Reckless, *The Crime Problem* [New York: Appleton-Century-Crofts, 1950]).

> of situation. She would call up and cry and say that people had come to
> her door. . . . She'd cry and she'd complain and she'd say, "I have a bad
> check at the liquor store, and they sent the police over," and really . . .
> a girl has a story she tells the man. . . . Anything, you know, so he'll
> help her out. Either it's the rent or she needs a car, or doctor's bills, or
> any number of things.

Any unnecessary interaction with the customer is typically frowned
upon, and the trainee will receive exhortations to be quick about her business. One girl in her fourth week of work explains ("What are some of the
other 'don'ts' that you have learned about?"): "Don't take so much time. . . .
The idea is to get rid of them as quickly as possible." Other content taught
concerns specific information about specific customers.

> She would go around the bar and say, now look at that man over there,
> he's this way and that way, and this is what he would like and these are
> what his problems are. . . .
> She would teach me what the men wanted and how much to get,
> what to say when I got there . . . just a line to hand them.

Training may also include proprieties concerning consuming alcohol
and drugs, when and how to obtain the fee, how to converse with the customers, and, occasionally, physical and sexual hygiene. As a girl trainer explains:

> First of all, impress cleanliness. Because on the whole, the majority of
> girls, I would say, I don't believe there are any cleaner women walking
> the streets, because they've got to be aware of any type of body odor. . . .
> You teach them to French [fellatio] and how to talk to men.
> [Do they (pimps) teach you during the turning-out period how to
> make a telephone call?] Oh, usually, yes. They don't teach you, they
> just tell you how to do it and you do it with your good common sense,
> but if you have trouble, they tell you more about it.

Interestingly, the specific act of telephoning a client is often distressing
to the novice and is of importance in her training. Unfortunately for the
girl, it is an act she must perform with regularity, as she does considerable
soliciting.[15] One suspects that such behavior is embarrassing for her because it is an unaccustomed role for her to play—she has so recently come
from a culture where young women do *not* telephone men for dates. Inappropriate sex-role behavior seems to produce greater personal distress
than does appropriate sex-role behavior even when it is morally reprehensible. "Well, it is rather difficult to get on the telephone, when you've
never worked before, and talk to a man about a subject like that, and it is
very new to you."

What is omitted from the training should be noted as well. There seems
to be little instruction concerning sexual techniques as such, even though
the previous sexual experience of the trainee may have been quite limited.
What instruction there is typically revolves around the practice of fellatio.

---

[15] The topic of solicitation will be dealt with in a forthcoming paper.

There seems to be some encouragement not to experience sexual orgasms with the client, though this may be quite variable with the trainer. "... and sometimes, I don't know if it's a set rule or maybe it's an unspoken rule, you don't enjoy your dates." "Yes, he did [teach attitudes]. He taught me to be cold."

It should be stressed that, if the girls originally accepted such instructions and values, many of them, at least at the time of interviewing, verbalized a rejection of these values and reported behavior which departed considerably from the interpersonal rules stipulated as "correct" by their trainers. Some experience orgasms with the customer, some show considerable affect toward "johns," others remain drunk or "high" throughout the contact.[16] While there seems to be general agreement as to what the rules of interpersonal conduct are, there appears to be considerable variation in the adoption of such rules.

A variety of methods are employed to communicate the content described above. The trainer may arrange to eavesdrop on the interactions of girl and client and then discuss the interaction with her. One trainer, for example, listened through a closed door to the interaction of a new girl with a customer, then immediately after he left discussed, in a rather heated way, methods by which his exit may have been facilitated. A pimp relates:

> The best way to do this [teaching conversation] is, in the beginning, when the phone rings, for instance . . . is to listen to what she says and then check and see how big a trick he is and then correct her from there. . . .
>
> With every one of them [trainees] I would make it a point to see two guys to see how they [the girls] operate.

In one case a girl reported that her pimp left a written list of rules pertaining to relating to "johns." Direct teaching, however, seems to be uncommon. The bulk of whatever learning takes place seems to take place through observation. "It's hard to tell you, because we learn through observations." "But I watched her and listened to what her bit was on the telephone."

To summarize, the structure of the apprenticeship period seems quite standard. The novice receives her training either from a pimp or from another more experienced call girl, more often the latter. She serves her initial two to eight months of work under the trainer's supervision and often serves this period in the trainer's apartment. The trainer assumes responsibility for arranging contacts and negotiating the type and place of the sexual encounter.

The content of the training pertains both to a general philosophical stance and to some specifics (usually not sexual) of interpersonal behavior with customers and colleagues. The philosophy is one of exploiting the

---

[16] In the unpublished paper referred to above, Pomeroy has indicated that, of thirty-one call girls interviewed, only 23 percent reported never experiencing orgasms with customers.

exploiters (customers) by whatever means necessary and defining the colleagues of the call girl as being intelligent, self-interested, and, in certain important respects, basically honest individuals. The interpersonal techniques addressed during the learning period consist primarily of "pitches," telephone conversations, personal and occasionally sexual hygiene, prohibitions against alcohol and dope while with a "john," how and when to obtain the fee, and specifics concerning the sexual habits of particular customers. Specific sexual techniques are very rarely taught. The current sample included a considerable number of girls who, although capable of articulating this value structure, were not particularly inclined to adopt it.

CONTACTS AND CONTRACTS

While the imparting of ideologies and proprieties to the prospective call girl is emphasized during the apprenticeship period, it appears that the primary function of the apprenticeship, at least for the trainee, is building a clientele. Since this latter function limits the degree of occupational socialization, the process of developing the clientele and the arrangements made between trainer and trainee will be discussed.

Lists ("books") with the names and telephone numbers of customers are available for purchase from other call girls or pimps, but such books are often considered unreliable. While it is also true that an occasional pimp will refer customers to girls, this does not appear to be a frequent practice. The most frequent method of obtaining such names seems to be through contacts developed during the apprenticeship. The trainer refers customers to the apprentice and oversees the latter in terms of her responsibility and adequacy in dealing with the customer. For referring the customer, the trainer receives 40 to 50 percent of the total price agreed upon in the contract negotiated by the trainer and customer.[17] The trainer and trainees further agree, most often explicitly, on the apprentice's "right" to obtain and to use, on further occasions, information necessary for arranging another sexual contract with the "john" without the obligation of further "kickback" to the trainer. That is, if she can obtain the name and telephone number of the customer, she can negotiate another contract without fee splitting. During this period, then, the girl not only is introduced to other working colleagues (pimps and girls alike), but also develops a clientele.

---

[17] The fee-splitting arrangement is quite common at all levels of career activity. For example, cooperative activity between two girls is often required for a particular type of sexual contract. In these cases, the girl who has contracted with the customer will contact a colleague, usually a friend, and will obtain 40–50 percent of the latter's earnings. There is suggestive evidence that fee-splitting activities vary according to geographical areas and that Los Angeles is unique for both its fee-splitting patterns and the rigidity of its fee-splitting structure.

There are two obvious advantages for a call girl in assuming the trainer role. First, since there seems to be an abundant demand for new girls, and since certain service requirements demand more than one girl, even the well-established call girl chronically confronts the necessity for making referrals. It is then reasonable to assume that the extra profit derived from the fee-splitting activities, together with the added conveniences of having a girl "on call," allows the trainer to profit considerably from this arrangement. Secondly, contacts with customers are reputedly extremely difficult to maintain if services are not rendered on demand. Thus, the adoption of the trainer role enables the girl to maintain contacts with "fickle" customers under circumstances where she may wish a respite from the sexual encounter without terminating the contacts necessary for reentry into the call-girl role. It is also possible that the financial gains may conceivably be much greater for most trainers than for most call girls, but this is a moot point.

A final aspect of the apprenticeship period that should be noted is the novice's income. It is possible for the novice, under the supervision of a competent and efficient trainer, to earn a great deal of money, or at least to get a favorable glimpse of the great financial possibilities of the occupation and, in effect, be heavily rewarded for her decision to enter it. Even though the novice may be inexperienced in both the sexual and interpersonal techniques of prostitution, her novelty on the market gives her an immediate advantage over her more experienced competitors. It seems quite likely that the new girl, irrespective of her particular physical or mental qualities, has considerable drawing power because she provides new sexual experience to the customer. Early success and financial reward may well provide considerable incentive to continue in the occupation.

A final word is needed regarding the position of the pimp vis-à-vis the call girl during the apprenticeship period. While some pimps assume the responsibility for training the girl personally, as indicated above, as many send the novice to another girl. The most apparent reason for such referral is that it facilitates the development of the "book." Purposes of training appear to be secondary for two reasons: (1) The pimp often lacks direct contact with the customers, so he personally cannot aid directly in the development of the girl's clientele. (2) When the pimp withdraws his girl from the training context, it is rarely because she has obtained adequate knowledge of the profession. This is not to say that all pimps are totally unconcerned with the type of knowledge being imparted to the girl. Rather, the primary concern of the pimp is the girl's developing a clientele, not learning the techniques of sex or conversation.

The apprenticeship period usually ends abruptly, not smoothly. Its termination may be but a reflection of interpersonal difficulties between trainer and trainee, novice and pimp, or between two novices. Occasionally termination of training is brought about through the novice's discovery and subsequent theft of the trainer's "book." Quite frequently, the termination is due to the novice's developing a sufficient trade or other business opportunities. The point is, however, that no respondent has reported that the final disruption of the apprenticeship was the result of the completion of adequate training. While disruptions of this relationship may be due to personal or impersonal events, termination is not directly due to the development of sufficient skills.

DISCUSSION AND SUMMARY

On the basis of interviews with thirty-three call girls in the Los Angeles area, information was obtained about entrance into the call-girl occupation and the initial training period or apprenticeship therein.

The novice call girl is acclimated to her new job primarily by being thoroughly immersed in the call-girl subculture, where she learns the trade through imitation as much as through explicit tutoring. The outstanding concern at this stage is the development of a sizable and lucrative clientele. The specific skills and values which are acquired during this period are rather simple and quickly learned.

In spite of the girls' protests and their extensive folklore, the art of prostitution, at least at this level, seems to be technically a low-level skill. That is, it seems to be an occupation which requires little formal knowledge or practice for its successful pursuit and appears best categorized as an unskilled job. Evidence for this point comes from two separate sources. First, there seems to be little technical training during this period, and the training seems of little importance to the career progress. Length or type of training does not appear correlated with success (i.e., money earned, lack of subjective distress, minimum fee per "trick," etc.). Secondly, the termination of the apprenticeship period is often brought about for reasons unrelated to training. It seems that the need for an apprenticeship period is created more by the secrecy surrounding the rendering or the utilization of the call-girl service than by the complexity of the role. In fact, it is reasonable to assume that the complexity of the job confronting a streetwalker may be considerably greater than that confronting a call girl. The tasks of avoiding the police, sampling among strangers for potential customers, and arrangements for the completion of the sexual contract not only require different skills on the part of the streetwalker, but are performances requiring a higher degree of professional "know-how" than is generally required of the call girl.[18]

---

[18] Needless to say, however, all of the sample of call girls who were asked for status hierarchies of prostitution felt that the streetwalker had both less status and a less complex job. It *may* well be that the verbal exchange required of the call girl requires greater knowledge than that required of a streetwalker, but the nonverbal skills required of the streetwalker may be considerably greater than those of the call girl.

As a pimp who manages both call girls and "high-class" streetwalkers explains:

> The girl that goes out into the street is the sharper of the two, because she is capable of handling herself in the street, getting around the law, picking out the trick that is not absolutely psycho . . . and capable of getting along in the street. . . . The streetwalker, as you term her, is really a prima donna of the prostitutes . . . her field is unlimited, she goes to all of the top places so she meets the top people. . . .

The fact that the enactment of the call-girl role requires little training, and the introduction of the girl to clients and colleagues alike is rather rapid, gives little time or incentive for adequate occupational socialization. It is perhaps for this reason, rather than, for example, reasons related to personality factors, that occupational instability is great and cultural homogeneity small.

In closing, while it appears that there is a rather well-defined apprenticeship period in the career of the call girl, it seems that it is the secrecy rather than the complexity of the occupation which generates such a period. While there is good evidence that initial contacts, primarily with other "working girls," are necessary for entrance into this career, there seems no reason, at this point, to assume that the primary intent of the participants in training is anything but the development of an adequate clientele.

Control Systems I:
The Police and Law Enforcement

The enforcement of law by formal agencies of social control is a task relegated to so many diverse organizations that to speak of "the police" is grossly to simplify a complex network of protective services. Regulatory functions are performed by the county sheriff and his deputies, metropolitan police bureaucracies, state agencies, and a variety of federal units including the Post Office Department, Secret Service, Internal Revenue Service, immigration authorities, Bureau of Narcotics, and of course the Federal Bureau of Investigation. As an example of the responsibility assigned to a federal agency, the Post Office Department through its system of inspectors investigates cases of postal robbery, mail theft, postal burglary, embezzlement, mail fraud, and obscenity. One of the most complex features of law enforcement in the United States is the distribution of authority throughout political jurisdictions so that police control is the province of a single agency. Of course, cooperation is often found between, say, state and federal investigators, and the infrequency with which a conviction obtained in a lower court is overturned by a higher court because the case was prosecuted by an inappropriate jurisdiction signifies an efficient allocation of authority.

In this country law-enforcement authorities are assumed to have a deterrence function; that is, their major role is to prevent the occurrence of criminal acts. Paradoxically, most of their activities are devoted to (a) following up lawbreaking through detection and recording of incidents, apprehension of suspects, and gathering physical or verbal evidence for subsequent use by judicial bodies, or (b) performing services tangential to law enforcement, e.g., traffic control, or assisting indisposed or disoriented persons.

The problems confronted by police in the discharge of their duties usually originate independent of technical issues. Law-enforcement officers, with the notable exception of FBI special agents, are accorded low prestige on the supposition that they are haphazardly recruited, poorly trained, sadistic, and subject to political corruption. Yet in marked contrast to this public image, police are given wide powers of decison-making, perform an indispensable service, encounter regular and frequent danger and challenge to their authority, and must develop great skill in legal and investigative spheres. To illustrate public belief that law-enforcement authorities are inefficient or ineffective, it is necessary only to note the high frequency with which persons fail to mobilize police facilities when a crime has been perpetrated against them.

Of all the agencies charged with responsibility for crime control—police systems, the courts, and correctional institutions—law-enforcement agencies have been most neglected by criminological research. In part this came about because police systems were made inaccessible to social scientists, whose fact-finding ventures may have been potentially threatening to agencies accustomed to charges of laxity and political manipulation. It is now fashionable for criminologists to study law-enforcement establishments, and police administrators concerned with professionalizing their personnel increasingly realize the benefits of collaborative research.

The comparative novelty of metropolitanization helps to explain why police have so recently become a significant unit of social control. Large cities are so new in this country that their law-enforcement facilities have reached present proportions only in the last decade or two. Metropolitan police systems, despite an actual loss of resident population in many cities during the last several years, have continued to grow and diversify. This is due in part to the concentration of disprivileged, disenfranchised segments of the population in inner-city areas, where the problems of prevention and control have always been demanding and complex.

The same pattern appears among suburban or "urban fringe" areas, whose accelerated growth has tended to outstrip their means for regulating disorderly and lawless conduct. It is noteworthy here that field studies of community police problems done under the aegis of the Omnibus Crime Control and Safe Streets Act of 1968 show serious jurisdictional impediments to investigation and apprehension inherent in autonomous city and suburban police facilities.

The problem of coordination, however, is a political and technical challenge best addressed through the expertise of police science. There are in fact many technical limitations to police effectiveness, such as the development of communications systems, gathering of physical and other types of evidence, securing adequate laboratory facilities, proper deployment of man-power, and the cultivation of informers.

Sociologists, on the other hand, have mainly attended to three other avenues of investigation. First, they have concentrated upon occupational issues in the performance of the *police role*. Prominent among empirical projects in this vein are studies of role conflict, selective recruitment of "personality types," technical and interpersonal skills that patrolmen are expected to develop, and consequences of police specialization. Second, sociologists are engaged in the study of *police system organization*, with special consideration being given to internal differentiation, problems of supervision and discipline, attempts at professionalization, and centralization of control. Third, there have been a number of very recent studies of *police relations with the community*, beginning with police views of community expectations and community attitudes toward the policeman's role. Other important work is being done on the decision-making associated with search, investigation, arrest, detention, and confession, and how decisions are a function of the type of crime, public sentiment about the priorities of illegal acts, status of the suspect, and personal inclination of the victim.

The paper by Albert J. Reiss, Jr., and David J. Bordua, "Environment and Organization: A Perspective on the Police," examines some characteristics of communities related to the legal basis for their governance, and salient features of modern urban communities which affect the social structure of law enforcement.

Jerome H. Skolnick's selection makes three points: first, there is a basic incompatibility between a democratic ethos and restraints upon police behavior demanded by the "rule of law"; second, there are limitations in the extent to which police professionalization can take place; and third, the policeman's self-conception is a function of community expectations and an associated ideology of professionalization.

In Arthur L. Stinchcombe's contribution, the distribution of crimes, arrest and conviction rates, and police practice are shown to be clearly different for public, as opposed to private, social locations. Related to this is the allocation of subsections of police departments to cope with public- and private-section crimes.

The paper by Reiss and Donald J. Black explores the degree to which police behavior is affected by exclusionary rules such as the *Miranda* decision. Data on suspect interrogations show that since officers always have evidence for arrest apart from interrogation itself, an exclusionary rule will have little effect on the liability of suspects to criminal charges.

Reporting on an unusual study, Jennie McIntyre demonstrates that there is general belief among the public that crime is increasing, fear that lawbreaking will in all probability take the form of an attack upon the person by a stranger, and hope that changes in daily habits will optimize safety. She also shows that persons tend to recommend stern treatment of offenders in the aggregate, but are disposed to leniency and a concern for individual rights in concrete cases.

The selected bibliography that follows is intended to serve as a partial guide to the literature bearing upon the sociology of law enforcement and the police.

1. *Occupational and Other Issues in the Police Role*

Cumming, Elaine; Cumming, Ian M.; and Edell, Laura. "Policeman as Philosopher, Guide, and Friend," *Social Problems* 12 (Winter 1965): 276–86.

Esselstyn, T. C. "The Social Role of the County Sheriff," *Journal of Criminal Law, Criminology, and Police Science* 44 (July–August 1953): 177–84.

McNamara, John H. "Uncertainties in Police Work: The Relevance of Police Recruits' Backgrounds and Training," in *The Police: Six Sociological Essays*, ed. David J. Bordua (New York: Wiley, 1967), pp. 163–252.

Niederhofer, Arthur. *Behind the Shield: The Police in Urban Society* (Garden City, N.Y.: Doubleday, 1967).

Skolnick, Jerome H. *Justice Without Trial: Law Enforcement in a Democratic Society* (New York: Wiley, 1966), chap. 3, "A Sketch of the Policeman's 'Working Personality.'"

Terris, Bruce J. "The Role of the Police," *Annals of the American Academy of Political and Social Science* 374 (November 1967): 58–69.

Wilson, James Q. *Varieties of Police Behavior* (Cambridge: Harvard University Press, 1968).

2. *Police Effectiveness, Community Relations, and the Maintenance of Order*

Bordua, David J., and Reiss, Albert J., Jr., "Command, Control, and Charisma: Reflections on Police Bureaucracy," *American Journal of Sociology* 72 (July 1966): 68–76.

_____. "Law Enforcement," in *The Uses of Sociology*, ed. Paul F. Lazarsfeld, William H. Sewell, and Harold L. Wilensky (New York: Basic Books, 1967), pp. 275–303.

Gibbons, Don C. "Crime and Punishment: A Study in Social Attitudes," *Social Forces* 47 (June 1969): 391–97.

Nelson, Harold A. "The Defenders: A Case Study of an Informal Police Organization," *Social Problems* 15 (Fall 1967): 127–47.

Peterson, Virgil W. "Local and State Law Enforcement Today," *Current History* 53 (July 1967): 8–14. (This entire issue is devoted to U.S. crime and law enforcement.)

The President's Commission on Law Enforcement and Administration of Justice. *Task Force Report: The Police* (Washington, D.C.: U.S. Government Printing Office, 1967).

Skolnick, Jerome H. *Justice Without Trial: Law Enforcement in a Democratic Society* (New York: Wiley, 1966), chap. 1, "Democratic Order and the Rule of Law."

Westley, William A. "Violence and the Police," *American Journal of Sociology* 49 (July 1953): 34–41.

Wilson, James Q. "Police Morale, Reform, and Citizen Respect: The Chicago Case," in *The Police: Six Sociological Essays*, ed. David J. Bordua (New York: Wiley, 1967), pp. 137–62.

3. *Discretionary Decision-Making: The Confrontation of Police and Public*

Bittner, Egon. "Police Discretion in Emergency Apprehension of Mentally Ill Persons," *Social Problems* 14 (Winter 1967): 278–92.

_____. "The Police on Skid Row: A Study of Peace Keeping," *American Sociological Review* 32 (October 1967): 699–715.

Driver, Edwin D. "Confessions and the Social Psychology of Coercion," *Harvard Law Review* 82 (November 1968): 42–61.

La Fave, Wayne R. *Arrest: The Decision to Take a Suspect into Custody* (Boston: Little, Brown, 1965).

Piliavin, Irving, and Briar, Scott. "Police Encounters with Juveniles," *American Journal of Sociology* 70 (September 1964): 206–214.

Skolnick, Jerome H. *Justice Without Trial: Law Enforcement in a Democratic Society* (New York: Wiley, 1966), chap. 4, "Operational Environment and Police Discretion," and chap. 5, "The Confrontation of the Suspect."

Wilson, James Q. "The Police and the Delinquent in Two Cities," in *Controlling Delinquents*, ed. Stanton Wheeler (New York: Wiley, 1968), pp. 9–30.

25. ENVIRONMENT AND ORGANIZATION: A PERSPECTIVE ON THE POLICE

Albert J. Reiss, Jr., and David J. Bordua

INTRODUCTION

This chapter presents a general perspective on the metropolitan police as an object of sociological research. The chapter is neither a detailed presentation of formal research hypotheses nor a presentation of research findings. An organizational perspective on the consequences of police relations to the environing system is presented as an orienting image within which more specific theoretical and empirical work can proceed.[1] Several topics are selected to illustrate the general application of the perspective. The facts are gleaned from general observation, research under way, and the literature on the police.

POLICE AND THE ENVIRONING SYSTEM

The municipal police as an organizational system is especially adapted to

Reprinted by permission of the authors and the publisher from *The Police: Six Sociological Essays*, ed. David J. Bordua (New York: Wiley, 1967), pp. 25–48.

[1] We attempt to make explicit what is often left implicit in research programs—the generalized "image" out of which more specific work flows. See, for example, Daniel Glaser, "Criminality Theories and Behavioral Images," *American Journal of Sociology*, 61 (March 1951): 433–44.

an analysis that stresses its relations with the organized environment and its boundary transactions and moves from these to consideration of internal differentiation and problems of integration, coordination, and control. All organizations can be so studied, of course, but since Weber the broad fashion among sociologists has been to focus on the internal structure of organizations and on task differentiation as it is manifested within the organization. Unlike many organizations, however, the police have as their fundamental task the creation and maintenance of, and their participation in, external relationships. Indeed, the central meaning of police authority itself is its significance as a mechanism for "managing" relationships.

Directing traffic, investigating complaints, interrogation, arresting suspects, controlling mobs and crowds, urging prosecutors to press or drop charges, testifying in court, participating with (or battling, as the case may be) probation officers in juvenile court, presenting budget requests to the city council, pressing a case with the civil service commission, negotiating with civil rights groups, defense attorneys, reporters, irate citizens, business groups, other city services, and other police systems—even such an incomplete list indicates the probable values of a perspective that emphasizes transactions and external relationships. The list also indicates something else of considerable significance. All of these transactions can be and often are antagonistic ones. Because of the complexity of organizational relationships with the environment, apparent even from a partial listing of police activities, we have chosen to concentrate our discussion of the external environment of the police and its internal consequences by selecting a few basic environmental features. These are the nature of the legal system, the nature of violative activity, and civic accountability. They are brought to bear upon a variety of organizational transactions and internal processes, especially on problems of production, strategy and tactics, and command and control.

The basic social mechanisms available to the police all flow from their role in the legal system. Yet, the legal system broadly considered is the source of some of the most severe problems of adaptation faced by the police. Because of this dual involvement with law, much of our early discussion of external relations deals with the police and the legal system. The legal system is not a seamless web of tightly articulated rules and roles, however, but a loose-jointed system held together at many points by microsystems of antagonistic cooperation and discretionary decisions.

Modern metropolitan police exist only in view of the fact that communities are legally organized.[2] The problem of the external parameters of police operation and organization, in its broadest sense, inheres both in the nature of the urban community and in the nature of the legal system.

---

[2] Something like police can occur in societies that would ordinarily not be termed legally organized. See Richard D. Schwartz and James C. Miller, "Legal Evolution and Societal Complexity," *American Journal of Sociology*, 70 (September 1965): 159–69.

Indeed, the fundamental position of the police may be conceived as mediating between the two. On the one hand, the police are a fundamental representative of the legal system and a major source of raw material for it. On the other, the police adapt the universalistic demands of law to the structure of the locale by a wide variety of formal and informal devices.

Later we discuss several features of the modern urban community as they impinge on the social structure of law enforcement. In this section we concentrate on some key aspects of the legal system and on the implications of the fact that the governance of communities is done by legal rather than other means. The broad designation "legal system" may be broken into the "legality" component, the "legal content" component, the "legal order" component, and the "government" component.[3]

The value of these distinctions will perhaps be more apparent if we discuss first the one most familiar—the "legal content" component. By this, we mean simply the actual content of laws. The importance for our purposes is that even modern societies differ considerably in the substances of the things they make illegal, and violations under them differ considerably in their impact on police strategy and tactics. A prime example is the well-known tendency of American society to make illegal many service crimes such as gambling.

By the "government" component we mean simply that the legal system is always organized politically into larger or smaller, more or less centralized, units. Even further, powers of government may be separated or combined in various patterns. Thus in the United States the police are organized to parallel the federal structure of local, state, and national government. Although the matter of levels of government has been widely discussed as a central "problem" in police administration, we are not particularly concerned with the matter here, since our focus is on the single community rather than intergovernmental aspects of the context of police operations.[4]

The third aspect of the legal system is the "legal order" component. By this we mean the complex apparatus involved in the administration of justice, especially those aspects with which the police are likely to come into contact routinely, such as the prosecutor and the courts. Because of the unique significance of this aspect of the legal system, we will devote considerable attention to it.

---

[3] Except for the government component, the division follows closely that proposed by Roscoe Pound, who also discusses the confusions centering around the various uses of the terms "law" and "legal" (Roscoe Pound, "The Sociology of Law," in *Twentieth Century Sociology*, ed. Georges Gurwitch and Wilbert E. Moore [New York: Philosophical Library, 1945]).

[4] See the somewhat outraged treatment of Donal E. J. MacNamara, "American Police Administration at Mid-Century," *Public Administration Review*, 10 (Summer 1950): 181–89.

Finally, the "legality" component to which we now give special attention refers only to the procedural aspects of the exercise of legal power.

LEGALITY, POLICE, AND COMMUNITY

In one sense, the police provide the primeval social service—protection of life and property. Unlike some other social services, however, the existence of a public agency largely precludes the performance of the service on a private basis. The very existence of the modern police signifies that in the broadest sense the exchange of property and the infliction of injury may take place only under definite rules. Moreover, disputes arising out of property exchange or personal altercation may be resolved only within definite limits. The body of legal rules that specify the acceptable modes of procedure in the resolution of disputes may collectively be deemed the canons of *legality*. The basic elements of legality—objective definitions of right, "due process," notice, citizen compliance, and official accountability —are primarily aspects of the ways citizens are treated rather than descriptions of specific statutes or judicial rulings. In the Anglo-Saxon tradition, the courts provide the primary definitions of legality in this sense with varying admixtures of legislative action and constitutional undergirding.

A society based upon such procedural and value premises, however, presents two closely intertwined problems. We can anchor the discussion of them by defining them very generally in terms of the subsystem relations involved. The first is the citizen-to-citizen relationship.

Within very broad limits, citizens must generally avail themselves of police services rather than resort to "self-help" in dealing with problems of person or property. The existence of police symbolizes not only that the citizen will be protected from the violator but that the violator will be protected from the citizen. One way the police serve the cause of legality, therefore, is to assure by their presence and performance that a set of rules prevails which make it *unnecessary* for the citizen to be continually prepared to defend himself or his property. We may, in fact, partly define the "maintenance of law and order" as the maintenance of a set of social conditions such that over the society as a whole, the expectation of attack on person or property has a probability below the level at which the citizenry resorts to "self-help." The maintenance of these conditions is always problematic, and in some localities of American society, "law and order" is sustained only with difficulty.

Comparison of the linkage among legality, police, and community in criminal law areas with the corresponding linkage in civil law is of sociological interest. The two great divisions of the law of civil wrongs—torts and contracts—involve much the same concern with the avoidance of "self-help" as a response to injury. Indeed, the traditional distinction in jurisprudence between civil remedies and criminal sanctions, with the former accruing to the injured party and the latter to the "state," obscures similarities between the two areas.

In the area of civil wrongs, especially tort law, the law is reactive rather than proactive, i.e., the legal system does not patrol or search out wrongs and take action but rather leaves to private initiative the invocation of the legal process. Closely related to the reactive stance of civil law is a very broad presumption favoring the private ordering of conduct and even of the resolution of disputes.[5] Thus legal ethics seem clear. The lawyer may not behave like a patrolman and search out tort victims or sufferers from breach of contract to encourage civil suits. Compare this doctrine of legal restraint with the doctrine of "aggressive patrol," which figures so prominently in modern police thinking.

On close examination many of the stark differences between the organization of civil remedies and the organization of criminal sanctions become less clear-cut. They perhaps can be seen most clearly if we look from the perspective of the private arrangement system itself. The determinants of the decision to call the police, for example, to deal with a neighborhood juvenile, are presumably complex but not totally unlike the decision to sue for damages.[6] A large part of police intervention is initiated by the victim. Moreover, the police have as one of their fundamental responsibilities the determination of when a "victim's" complaint in fact warrants formal action. No crime may have been committed, or if there is one, it may be so minor that department policy dictates only cursory attention. Like the civil lawyer, the policeman also becomes sensitive to subtleties of private vengeance masquerading as public duty.

Beyond these elements of "victims" initiating police activity, police "adjudication" policy, and their upholding of "disinterested" canons of legality, the operating procedures of police bear other similarities to civil procedure. Foremost among these is the tendency of police to let stand, or even to encourage, private settlement of disputes—even where violence may be present or likely. Among the "private arrangements" that the police may protect are their own relationships with categories of violators.

This aspect of policing is discussed in more detail later on, but at this point it is appropriate to indicate that the police in a sense are a service without clients. The police serve the public as a collectivity rather than distributively.[7] Enforcement must be initiated where there is no personal

---

[5] For a jurisprudential discussion of the significance of private ordering with a sociological cast, see Henry M. Hart, Jr., and Albert M. Sacks, *The Legal Process: Basic Problems in the Making and Application of Law* (Cambridge, Mass., tentative edition, mimeo, 1958), chap. 1.

[6] Or, indeed, the decision to be sticky about formal contractual provisions in business dealings. Stewart Macaulay, "Non-contractual Relations in Business: A Preliminary Study," *American Sociological Review*, February 1963, pp. 55–69.

[7] See the discussion of commonweal organizations in Peter M. Blau and W. Richard Scott, *Formal Organizations* (San Francisco: Chandler, 1962), p. 54.

victim or/and complainant. Given the lack of guidelines either from the public as client or from a specific victim or complainant as client, the police can become in effect their own clients. We take this to be one of the fundamental features in the oft mentioned tendency of the police to develop a supermoralistic perspective and to see themselves as engaged in a "private" war on crime. Of basic significance here is that the courts and the police are in a relationship of "antagonistic cooperation" so that the legal order itself can be described only with difficulty as the "client" of the police.

Thus in many ways the respect for private ordering that is formal in civil law is informal in criminal law. Unlike the civil side, a large organized body of officials—the police—intervene between law and practice and may come to participate in such private arrangements themselves. From this perspective it is useful to see the police not as discretionless ministerial officers but as somewhat analogous to the practicing attorney, whose roles as advocate, counselor, and officer of the court are not totally dissimilar (though better legitimated) to the roles played by the policeman.[8]

Informal practice allows the police to vary their relationship to the many private dispute-settling procedures available; hence, the degree to which formal legality is extended to (or imposed upon) different groups in the population varies considerably.[9] Among the private arrangements that the police may allow to stand is the use of violence among subordinate or peripheral groups in the society. The most outstanding instance until recently has been the willingness of the American police to respect intraracial violence among Negroes, thus implicitly defining the Negro population in a sense as a group "without the law." Correlatively, the police established private arrangements with the Negro violator that included their extrajudicial use of force as a substitute for "due process." Whether such private adjudication is less predictable, less merciful, and less just seems open to dispute, but such arrangements clearly imply that a segment of the population is operationally treated as outside the pale of legality.

---

[8] There is a considerable law review literature on police discretion and what we have termed private arrangements involving the police. Most useful for the sociologist is the work of La Fave: Wayne R. La Fave, *Arrest: The Decision to Take a Suspect into Custody* (Boston: Little, Brown, 1965). Also, Wayne R. La Fave, "The Police and Nonenforcement of the Law—Part I," *Wisconsin Law Review*, 1962, no. 1 (January 1962): 104–37 and "The Police and Nonenforcement of the Law—Part II," *Wisconsin Law Review*, 1962, no. 2 (March 1962): 179–239. See also Joseph Goldstein, "Police Discretion Not to Invoke the Criminal Process: Low-Visibility Decisions in the Administration of Justice," *Yale Law Journal*, 69, no. 543 (1960): 543–94, and Edward L. Barrett, Jr., "Police Practices and the Law—From Arrest to Release or Charge," *California Law Review*, 50, no. 1 (March 1962): 11–55.

[9] Informal practice in the police area may often be highly formalized. Indeed, it may even be written down. Formal, written department policy and procedure may be considered informal with respect to the law. Operating norms at all levels in police organizations may differ from either the law or department written rules. One of the more puzzling aspects of the control of police by the courts is the fact that the courts rarely take judicial notice of written police department rules and decide cases as though the individual policeman were a free agent. See the comparison of court rulings and police manuals in Goldstein, *op. cit.*

The broader problem involved here is, of course, the central one of the conditions under which membership in the *state* supersedes membership in other collectivities as a determinant of both formal and operative rights. Historical developments for at least two centuries have tended to define state membership, that is, citizenship as prevailing over other statuses in determining individual rights. Nevertheless, here as elsewhere there have been many lags between formal declaration and informal practice.[10]

Up to this point we have tried to establish a general perspective that emphasizes the similarities between civil and criminal legal operations. The key points here are (1) that many features that are formal in the civil law are "informal" in the criminal law; (2) that the relations between private ordering and public determination are important in both areas; (3) that large areas of police operation are closer to the reactive model of civil adjudication than to the generally held proactive model of criminal process; (4) that the maintenance of legality as *between citizens* always involves some balance of police willingness either to "respect" or to override private arrangements; and (5) that the conditions under which citizens invoke the criminal process may determine the nature and boundaries of subsystem solidarity as well as of police behavior.

We purposely have emphasized the role of the police in securing as well as symbolizing legality between citizens since this is a relatively neglected aspect of the larger problem. The other face of the legality problem is that of the relations between the citizenry and the police. Since this aspect of the problem has received much more attention, we will make only a few general remarks in the discussion of police in the legal order.

THE POLICE IN THE LEGAL ORDER

Liberal democratic societies stemming from the English tradition formally organize enforcement of the law and the maintenance of order *within* the society in both the military and the police but principally in the police. The extension of the role of law in legality, due process, the exercise of discretion, and enacting justice when accusations or arrests are made is formally organized in the public prosecutor and the courts. This functional separation of powers in which ordinarily the police are expected to enforce the law and the judiciary to determine the outcome of events creates

---

[10] T. H. Marshall proposes a historical scheme from which much of the above has been drawn. He argues that the lower classes were first the recipients of civil legal status and then later of welfare or social rights as adjuncts of citizenship. In the United States, at least, one can argue that large segments of the population had access to unemployment and old-age insurance *before* developing any meaningful access to civil legality. This is true even in the formal sense for Negroes in the South, for example (T. H. Marshall, *Citizenship and Social Class* [Cambridge: Cambridge University Press, 1950]).

problems for both organizations and appears to account for some aspects of police organization and work.

Although the police are formally organized to enforce the law and maintain public order, it is apparent they are involved at the same time in enacting justice. It is important to note that all three key terms—order, legality, and justice—are ambiguous terms in any social system. But what philosophers, social scientists, and lawyers have argued over for centuries the police must do every day. The point requires little documentation. A policeman on duty, for example, when confronted with a situation of law enforcement or threat to public order must make decisions about the evidence and whether the act violates the law. Decisions to hold for investigation, to arrest or release, or to enforce order likewise require the extension of legality. His decision may, and often does, involve him at the same time in dispensing equity. Police, in short, make important decisions that affect outcome. They either do justice or limit the judicial function of courts, particularly by determining the nature of the evidence and who is to be held for adjudication.

Court decisions to dismiss charges are often viewed by the police as a rejection of their decisions. Such decisions may be particularly galling to the officer, since he regards his rules of knowing as more valid than the court's rules of evidence in making a decision. Futhermore, court decisions to dismiss offenders or to return offenders to the community often affect police work, as released offenders frequently create problems for continued law enforcement. The most obvious examples of this kind occur in police work with juveniles, vagrants, and habitual drunks. Police dissatisfaction with rehabilitation workers such as probation officers likewise stems in part from the fact that they have been unable to control disposition of the case; today's probationers are not infrequently tomorrow's work.

Police dissatisfaction with the administration of justice by the courts results in their doing justice, a tendency to settle things outside the courts to be sure that "justice is done." Nowhere is this more apparent than when police are expected to continue law enforcement involving violators that the court sends back to the community. The police then may take the law in their own hands and dispense justice, even if it means using violence. The continuing conflict between the police and the courts over admissibility of evidence, techniques of interrogation, the status of the confession, and the use of force, together with their separate definitions of justice, is likewise a consequence of the separation of powers.

Transactions among police officers, public prosecutors, and the judiciary not infrequently have the effect of subverting the goals of law enforcement, since each is in a position to sanction the other's behavior. That individual or collective sanctions do not always achieve the intended goal is clear when the effect of sanctions of one part on another is examined. A single example may serve as an illustration.

Judges often negatively sanction police officers for failing to develop cases that meet court standards. It is not uncommon for a judge to criticize publicly from the bench an officer new to the service with a terse statement that fails to explain the grounds constituting an effective case. This judicial practice leaves the young officer in a quandary that often leads him to turn to the informal police system for advice about responses to judicial practice. Not infrequently this course of action leads to poor police technique and the development of cases where there is no intention to prosecute. Such responses lead to further judicial criticism that department administrators may ultimately perceive as an unwillingness by the court to convict. At this juncture, however, police practice may have deteriorated to the point where the court could not convict, if it would. Negative sanctions by the court and prosecutors thus lead to a deterioration of police practice which subverts judicial goals.

There is no necessary reason why these systems must be related in a cumulative set of negative sanctions. Police, prosecutors, and jurists sometimes take steps to cope with predicaments caused by negative sanctions, evolving practices that moderate these effects. They provide, for example, for prosecutors to advise officers prior to their appearance in court, though, to be sure, prosecutors may use officers for their own intended sanctions of judicial behavior. The conflict between police practice and legality stems in part, however, from the fact that American courts traditionally resist giving advisory opinions and from the fact that jurists and prosecutors, as lawyers, do not perceive that they have an educational obligation toward the officers or their clients in the situation.

The legally defined end of a police department is to enforce the law. The measure of success of a police department is presumably some measure of the degree to which it has in fact enforced the law. There are two major ways that success gets defined for departments. The first kind is a measure of aggregate success, whether of a crime rate, arrests, crimes cleared by arrest, convictions, or value of stolen property recovered. The second is the success it has in meeting public demands to solve a particular crime problem, as, for example, when a crime outrages the public conscience.

Police are relatively free to define their own criteria of success in crimes known to them, arrests made, and crimes cleared through arrest, despite national attempts to standardize the criteria. They can determine a successful arrest per se and satisfy themselves when a case has been cleared by arrest. They can recover stolen property incident to arrest and clearance, or independent of it, as is often the case for stolen autos. Their productivity record in these areas, however, can be compared with that of other cities through the uniform crime reporting system organized through the FBI. The media of communication hold the local police system accountable for its record in this system.

So far as the public is concerned, police departments generally have a low success rate in the proportion of crimes cleared through arrest. Only about one in four offenses known to the police is generally cleared by arrest.[11] Clearance through arrest is greater for crimes against persons than crimes against property and for misdemeanors such as vagrancy, drunkenness, and disorderly conduct, though the latter bring few credits in the public ledger. The low success rate in crimes cleared by arrest creates a dilemma for the police administrators in their efforts to maintain a public image of themselves as productive in a market-oriented society. It is neither sufficient nor publicly acceptable for American police to justify themselves by their roles as simple representatives of moral or legal order.[12] They are under considerable pressure from local organizations such as the newspapers and crime commissions and from the FBI, who interpret the statistics in relation to their own goals, goals that not infrequently conflict with those of the police department.

The dilemma created by the necessity to maintain a public image of success in the face of aggregative measures of lack of success can readily lead to the manipulation of the statistics to create a favorable public image. Police departments, in fact, build up their *volume* of production largely out of misdemeanors rather than felonies, out of crimes against property rather than against persons, and in these days from juveniles and traffic. Tradition-oriented departments often artificially inflate their success rate by getting arrested persons to "cop out" to additional offenses or by charging offenses to an arrested person on the basis of a *modus operandi*.

The separation of enforcement from outcome creates additional dilemmas for the department in defining its success rate. Assuming legal police conduct, it is through convictions only that the penal sanctions presumed efficacious in reducing crimes can be forthcoming. And it is also through conviction only that the police's sense of justice can be vindicated. The conviction rate, however, is subject to police control only within narrow limits. Both prosecutors and courts intervene. The courts do so with the avowed purpose of scrutinizing police conduct, especially when legality as well as violation of the law is defined as an issue. While department arrest figures may define the policeman's success, acquittals in court may define his failures.

These dilemmas in defining success are partially resolved by the development of a complex bargaining process between police and prosecutors, the shifting of departmental resources in directions of maximum payoff

---

[11] Federal Bureau of Investigation, U.S. Department of Justice, *Crime in the United States: Uniform Crime Reports—1965* (Washington, D.C.: U.S. Government Printing Office, 1966), Table 8, pp. 97ff. A total clearance rate of 26.3 percent is reported for seven major crimes. Clearance rates varied from 90.5 percent for murder to 19.6 percent for larceny (*ibid.*, p. 97).

[12] Compare Banton's analysis of the degree to which the police in Scotland justify themselves by simply existing as symbols of order: Michael Banton, *The Policeman in the Community* (New York: Basic Books, 1965).

from a conviction point of view, the development of a set of attitudes that define the police as alone in the "war on crime," and the elaboration of success measures that do not require validation by the courts.

All major metropolitan departments elaborate measures of success that they can manipulate independent of the prosecutor and the courts. Investigations of organized crime are publicized, though there is relatively little success in conviction in relation to the effort expended. Arrests under public pressure of well-known gangsters or crackdowns on prostitution, gambling, or narcotics peddling have their symbolic public relations value even if it is difficult to secure convictions, and they make undue claim on limited resources. Successful prosecution of the most serious or violent crimes against persons, such as homicide, forcible rape, and aggravated assault, likewise are used for their symbolic value, though they account for only a small volume of all crimes known to the police.[13]

Police concern for clearance of crimes through arrest is not infrequently a response to immediate public pressures that they maintain a safe community as well as to the more general and continuing one that they are an effective and efficient department. The police, for example, may come under fire when a neighborhood is plagued by a series of assaults or strong-arm robberies or when the "public" is offended by any specific crime. Police concern then shifts to clearing up these particular crimes so that they may reduce public pressure by an announcement that the perpetrators have been brought into custody.

Police administrators are confronted with a dilemma in their effort to manipulate the image of crime in the community. To justify increases in manpower and budget before municipal agencies, they are compelled to emphasize the high volume of crime in the community and the difficulties they face in meeting it with the resources available to them. At the same time, this emphasis can easily be interpreted as failure.

The individual policeman likewise is production oriented; his successes are arrests and acquittals are his failures. The successful policeman quickly learns what the police system defines as successes. These become his arrests. When he is not supported by the judicial system for what he regards as right action, he tends to take the law into his own hands, often by making a decision not to arrest or by making an arrest where there is no intention to prosecute.[14] In this way the police officer sanctions the judicial system for what he defines as its failure to make him a success.

Separation of enforcement from outcome also has an effect on police attitudes. The refusal of the courts to convict or of prosecutors to prosecute

---

[13] Federal Bureau of Investigation, *op. cit.*, p. 47. These three offenses accounted for 8.1 percent of the total number of index crimes reported for 1965. The index crimes are all major crimes. The annual report of any large city department will show that these "public outcry" offenses are *quantitatively* a much smaller proportion of all crimes known to the police.

[14] See the sources cited in footnote 8, *supra*.

may rest on what seem to the police the most artificial of formalities. Police are aware as well that this lack of support attributes failure to them. Their sense of justice may be outraged. Collective subcultural modes of adjustment are a common protective response to such dilemmas and contradictions. For the police this adjustment consists in part in the development of a collective identity wherein the police are viewed as the true custodians of morality and justice. In the words of one police administrator:

> Police get conditioned to the idea that we are the only people with our finger in the criminal dike in this country. They feel that everyone else "lets him go." Police differ from the D.A. The D.A. is satisfied with the conviction, finding him guilty. But police want him punished. They become outraged when the result of their work is ignored. "What if they let him off, I get him tomorrow: those bastards kiss him on the cheek and let 'em go," is their attitude of how the D.A. and the judge handle *their* cases.

Thus the police want an outcome that signifies for them that their effort has been appreciated and that morality has been upheld. This for them is what is meant by justice being done.

Many police see two broad classes of violators—those who deserve to be punished and those who do not. For the police, justice is done by *them* when they let a man go; he does not deserve to be punished. But justice must be done by *some other means* when they arrest. This they regard as the moral obligation of the prosecutor and the courts.

Mention has been made that the separation of enforcement from outcome forces the police into a bargaining situation that includes violators, prosecutors, defense attorneys, and courts. The public prosecutor is usually the central figure in this process. Bargaining relationships of the police are undoubtedly more complexly patterned and determined than current information allows us to assess. Three important points can be made here, however. The first is that the police are hedged in by officials whose formal discretion is greater than their own. The second is that although the prosecutor and the judge are the traditional figures, the system of justice has come to include others, such as probation officers and juvenile court officials, with whom the police must also enter into a bargaining relationship. Finally, all of these bargaining relationships are ones in which the role incumbents are potentially hostile to the police. As Stinchcombe has recently noted, adjunctive officials of the courts, particularly rehabilitation or welfare officials, are hired wholly or in part as a set of official opponents of the police.[15]

The formal linkage of the police to the prosecutor's office and the court has other implications for their adaptation. Interpersonal contact between police and court personnel involve both an inequality relationship and

---

[15] Arthur L. Stinchcombe, "The Control of Citizen Resentment in Police Work" (unpublished paper).

a reversal of roles. Normally, police are in a position of authority vis-à-vis the citizen; in a substantial number of situations, they are in a superior status position as well. When they are not, police use tactics to assert authority in the situation. Furthermore, police work generally places an officer in the role of interrogator, a role requiring that little information be given to suspects. Now in contacts with the courts, role situations are reversed. Police are generally below the status of officials they deal with in the courts, particularly with men of the bar and bench, and they are interrogated. Under certain circumstances, they are subject to cross-examination. This kind of contact brings with it all the suspicion and hostility generated between status unequals where roles are reversed and authority is displaced. The ambivalence of the police toward both the administration of justice and its role incumbents is further exacerbated under these conditions. This status reversal plus the generalized lower prestige of police when taken together with the institutionalized distrust of police built into the trial process creates a situation where the police not only feel themselves balked by the courts but perhaps, even more fundamentally, feel themselves dishonored.

The involvement of police in the legal order may also be looked at from the point of view of the legal remedies available in the event of illicit police conduct. For the citizen they are largely civil remedies against the individual policeman. Usually, the citizen does not sue the police department for false arrest or battery; he sues the policeman. The officer's conduct, however, may have been well within the reasonable limits of departmental policy or regulation. The relatively unpredictable and *ex post facto* nature of judicial decision may exacerbate the problem for the policeman, even though the usually broad wording of applicable provisions of the law of arrest afford the officer much protection. This anomalous disjuncture between authority and liability is presumably one source of the oft-noticed solidarity of police systems. If effecting the department's mission lays the officer open to suit, clearly a norm of secrecy and mutual support is a highly likely result. The blue curtain descends between staff and line and the department and the outer world.

The balancing and correlative fact that police chiefs may be liable to sanctions by political and governmental officials even though immune from suit acts in much the same way. "Formal" informal mechanisms such as secret department trials, requests for resignation, and liability defense funds develop as ways of containing this dilemma.

Although the civil suit is in principle available to citizens, it is rarely used. There seem to be several reasons for this in addition to the fact that policemen are usually not able to pay large judgments. The segments of the population most likely to sue are (or were) least likely to be involved with the police. Those most involved with the police, the "depressed populations," are simultaneously unlikely to use the courts in general, because they are fearful of police reprisal and too impoverished to afford counsel.

The very structure of judicial control of the police means—as in recent U.S. Supreme Court decisions—that rulings about the illegality of police practices toward offenders must come in the form of upsetting the convictions of criminals.[16] Judicial rulings that announce new procedural limitations on the police are of necessity *ex post facto*, and therefore difficult to predict. Given this situation, it is no wonder that in the system for maintaining law and order other people have the law and police get stuck with the order.

Recent decisions of the Court also highlight basic differences between the police and the courts regarding their organizational requirements for the legality and legal content components and set the stage for organizational conflict. The police organization generally requires high specificity of the legal content component in the decision to arrest but relative ambiguity of the legality component in enforcement and processing situations. The courts, in contrast, insist upon high specificity of the legality component in their position of judicial control of the police (or the protection of citizen rights) while tolerating relative ambiguity in the statement of legal content in the interest of case law.

VIOLATIVE ACTIVITY AND ORGANIZATIONAL STRATEGY AND TACTICS

Police departments are organized primarily to carry out a reactive rather than proactive strategy. This is in sharp contrast with some intelligence systems geared to a proactive strategy. A majority of the line in any major metropolitan police system is allocated to units that react to communications that the police are wanted at some time and place. The communications center is the heart of the modern operating system. Patrol is the single largest division. Geared essentially to react, patrol belies its name. To be sure, some units, such as tactical patrol, conduct both proactive and reactive operations, and others, such as vice control, are principally proactive, but on balance patrol is organized to respond to commands that are reactions to requests originating outside the department. To understand how it happens that police departments operate primarily with a reactive strategy, we must turn to the organization of the environing system and the development of police transactions with individuals and organizations beyond its boundaries.

Before the evolution of modern police systems the citizen was paid for giving information on crimes and the whereabouts of criminals to proper

---

[16] *Mapp* v. *Ohio*, 367 U.S. 643 (1961); *Kerr* v. *California*, 374 U.S. (1963); *Escobedo* v. *Illinois*, 84 U.S. 1785 (1964).

authorities. But in Western societies there has been a gradual evolution from the citizen as paid informant and prosecutor to the citizen as a responsible complainant accompanied by a delegation of responsibility to the police for the enforcement of the law and to the prosecutor for pursuing formal charges. As a consequence of these changes the social sources of information on violations have changed. Police strategy and tactics become proactive, and special units—for example, vice and traffic control divisions—are developed to deal with violations where the individual citizen is not directly threatened and hence does not mobilize the police.[17] Information on crimes of this nature must generally originate, therefore, with police work, including the use of the undercover agent and the otherwise abandoned practice of paid informants. Correlatively, where police rely almost exclusively on the citizen complainant for origination of information on crimes against a person or his property, their strategy and tactics are generally reactive. Patrol is the initial unit assigned to respond, and the detective bureau follows.

Only in a superficial sense may police be said to solve crimes or to enforce the law. The organization of the society, the nature of violative activity, and the organization of a police department make it impossible to locate a population of subjects who have violated the law or to solve most crimes.

The social organization of behavior that violates the law and of how it is communicated to the police, when coupled with organizational problems in the allocation of limited resources to the solution of crimes, makes it impossible for the police to generate most of the inputs they process. These conditions also largely determine the internal differentiation of the police department and the strategy and tactics each unit adopts to process violations of the law. We shall turn first to examine ways in which communications about violations of the law create problems for the police in solving crimes and how the police organization adapts to these problems.

In a democratic society, the major volume of police work derives from an external source, the citizen complaint, rather than from an internal organizational source, police detection of crimes committed. The major element occasioning a complaint by an American citizen is that he sees himself as a "victim" experiencing a personal loss. Citizens are unlikely to mobilize the police or to report violations in which they are not actually victims. In all other cases, the citizen tends to define enforcement of the law as a police responsibility. This means that many violations are known to citizens but not reported to the police because they lack direct personal

---

[17] As Skolnick notes, there are those violative acts where the individual citizen is directly offended: there is a crime against him as a private individual or against his property; and there are those violative acts where the citizen is involved only in the collective sense: there is some threat to the social order as defined by the legal norms. See Jerome H. Skolnick and J. Richard Woodworth, "Police, Suspects, and Prosecutors" (paper read at the annual meetings of the American Sociological Association, Los Angeles, September 2, 1963).

involvement in the violative activity. Even when the person is a victim, he may not necessarily make his complaint known, since citizen complaint is responsive to public and police norms and expectations about communicating violations of the law.

Police definitions of the status of "victim" constitute one such set of expectations. Certain deviants—for example, homosexuals and prostitutes—do not usually report crimes against themselves, since they cannot afford to take the risk. In other cases, the citizen responds to collectively defined expectations of treatment by the police, as, for example, the Negro's response to expectations of "white man's" justice or police brutality. Indeed, much of the post-Second World War reported increase in crime in American cities may be due to the changing relationship between the Negro public and the police rather than to an actual increase in violative behavior. Negroes now seem more willing to report crimes against themselves.

There are a number of norms that govern the role of citizen as compainant. Beyond the fact that enforcement of the law is defined primarily as a police and not a citizen responsibility, there are powerful norms governing the role of informant in our society. Norms about "squealing" and "minding one's own business" control the reporting of citizen information about violations. There are also norms about "not getting involved with the law" and general citizen distrust of involvement with interrogation by lawyers or policemen.

Indeed, the integrity of private systems and relations among them may require that citizens withhold compaint. Such matters as the protection of individual integrity, family honor, or the opportunity to continue in business have priority in the American normative system over obligation to report violations or violators to the police. Finally, though we rely in our society on self-enforcement of conduct, the normative system works against reporting one's own violations. Though the police are charged with the detection of deviation, they are least likely to be sought out for confession of deviation. Deviation from the law may be acknowledged to the self, to the cleric, lawyer, friend, or therapist, but not to the police.

The nature of violative activity markedly affects the way police organization can cope with it. The popular image of how one effectively deals with crimes is through detective work. Yet, in a very important sense, police work does not rest on solving crimes through an inductive process of investigation beginning with evidence that leads ultimately to a violator. Rather, crimes are most often solved through a process of attaching persons known as violators to known violations.

Police work in response to citizen complaint usually begins and concludes solely as an intelligence operation; no arrest is made. The intelligence fed into the police system is on a crime that has been committed with, in many cases, little or no information on who may have committed it. The problem seemingly is one, then, as the public says, of solving the crime. Though a majority of crimes must remain unsolved, for reasons under discussion here, even among those solved, only a minority can be said to be cleared through the inductive work of the detective division.

A majority of the cases that are cleared by arrest may be said to solve themselves in the sense that the violator is "known" to the complainant or to the police at the time the crime initially comes to the attention of the police. Whether the prosecutor and the courts will concur is another matter, but there is little doubt that the policeman operates in such situations by having a citizen sign a complaint or by making an arrest. Evidence technicians and detectives may work on such cases, but their task is one of linking the enforcement to the prosecution and adjudication systems by providing evidence, not one of solving crimes.

Though good data are lacking on the matter, there is good reason to claim that the second largest proportion of all crimes cleared by arrest is "solved" by arresting otherwise known violators. The arrest of a person for a crime often results in solving other crimes known to the police, since a major element of police practice is to utilize the arrested person and knowledge of his current offense as a means of clearing other crimes. Such well-known police practices as interrogating the suspect to obtain confession to other crimes and presenting him for identification in a show-up are standard practices for clearing unsolved crimes, as are less well-known ones such as charging the violator with unsolved crimes or simply assigning them to him in the department's records on the basis of a *modus operandi*. It is not uncommon to find that an arrest carries with it the solution to a half-dozen other crimes, particularly for crimes of robbery and larceny.

One of the major problems for the modern metropolitan police force, as it centralizes command and control and draws its personnel away from operations that are based in local areas, is to maintain adequate intelligence on potential or known violators. There is good reason to conclude that the pattern of crimes solved by arrest changes with centralization of command and control, since it compels the department to place greater reliance on formal intelligence systems and means of crime solution.

The enforcement of the law is not simply a matter of maintaining an intelligence system on crimes and criminals and allocating organizational resources to deal with them in response to either citizen mobilization or police work. The organization of the larger society affects the organization of operating police units and their strategy and tactics in yet other ways.

Society is organized to make the detection of some violative behavior and the location of some violators more difficult than others. Consider just the matter of how a residential organization can affect the policing of the public. A public housing project with buildings twenty stories high, each containing several hundred families, poses somewhat different problems of crime detection and arrest than policing of the same area when it consisted of tenement houses.

Apart from considerations of the territorial and corporate organization of a population, the legal norms and order exercise an enormous impact on the exercise of coercive authority. A distinctive feature of modern liberal states is their use of the monopoly of violence to guarantee the boundaries of small, autonomous social systems like the private place and the citizen's right to privacy in public places. Police access to private places is guaranteed by the right of surveillance when there is reason to believe that a crime has been committed; and entry, search of the person and of places, and seizure of evidence are warranted under legally specified conditions. The right of the citizen to privacy and the right of state access to private matters forms one of the principal dialectical concerns in the organization of modern states and their police systems.

The laws defining police access to private places have consequences for the organization of staff and line units in police departments and in the strategy and tactics they adopt. Stinchcombe emphasizes that the differential distribution of crimes in public and private places, when coupled with the greater legal accessibility police have to public as over and against private places, affects both the volume of police work and structural differentiation within the department.[18] He argues that police are organized through patrol to operate in public places and therefore act much more on their own initiative in them; entry into private places is generally only on compaint or warrant.[19] It is true, of course, that police are in a better position to make an "on-view" arrest in a public rather than in a private place because of norms governing their access to private places. But it is also true that police are more likely to respond to complaints in both public and private places than they are to make an on-view arrest. This fact stems primarily from two conditions: the nature of occurrence of crime, and the allocation of limited organizational resources.

Whenever the nature of the crimes is such that the police cannot readily forecast a high probability of occurrence in a particular public or private location at a particular time, they must be organized primarily as a reactive organization. Many crimes in public as well as private places are of this form. These crimes are most likely to involve coercion in private life and disorders and nuisances in public places. Whether they are homicides, assaults, robberies, burglary, larceny, drunkenness, disorderly conduct, collective disturbances, or traffic accidents, police must in the nature of the case be organized to react to the occurrence of the crime when they are *not* present, for there is usually low predictability of occurrence of these types of crime, given the resources in manpower available.

A major problem police face in norms governing access to private places is the limitation they place on proactive strategies and tactics. Vice pro-

---

[18] Arthur L. Stinchcombe, "Institutions of Privacy in the Determination of Police Administrative Practice," *American Journal of Sociology*, 69 (September 1963): 158.

[19] *Ibid.*, p. 152.

vides an excellent example. It operates "in the open" if a police department does not adopt a proactive strategy, since citizens who participate in
such activities are unlikely to sign complaints that constitute a legal case.
When a department "puts the heat on," however, vice can retreat into
private places. This then necessitates an alteration in police tactics for
dealing with vice. Progressively, as the legally acceptable means for access
to these places become operationally difficult, the police resort to undercover roles or to use tactics designed to control public aspects of vice, for
example, harassment.

Police organization and work, moreover, are substantially affected by
the ways in which the violation is socially organized. To oversimplify, we
might say that the more organized the violative activity, the less effective
police are in dealing with the violation. Modern metropolitan police departments are perhaps least effective in dealing with organized crime. The
literature on police work and the public press emphasizes that this is
largely a consequence of the territorial limitations on operations of a
metropolitan police force. By simple deduction, it is assumed that a police
force coextensive with the organized activity would "solve" the problem
of organized crime. Stinchcombe argues that it is difficult to deal with illegitimate businesses and dangerous organizations because of the barriers
of privacy.[20]

Though there is merit in both arguments, they oversimplify the problem. While a national police force may well be more effective in coping
with organized crime, the fact of the matter is that organized crime is more
difficult to deal with precisely because it is highly organized. Similarly,
while access to private places limits police effectiveness in dealing with
organized crime even when access is gained through warrant or other
means, it generally fails because of the difficulty in attacking the higher
echelon organization. Operations in private places may be closed only to
reopen elsewhere or to take to operating in public places, since the criminal organization adapts its strategy and tactics to those of the police. For
the intelligence and operating units of the police, one has the counter-
intelligence units of organized crime.

We have noted that the more formally organized the criminal activity,
the less effective police are in dealing with it. To this we should add that
at the opposite extreme, the absence of informal organization of criminal
activity, in at least its social patterning, also contributes to the problem of
policing. The police are organized principally to respond to stimuli
generated by citizen complaint and for surveillance in public places. Furthermore, many of their standard investigative techniques—for example,
informants and *modus operandi* files—presuppose an "underworld," a
loosely organized community of persons more or less habitually involved
in committing crimes.

---

[20] *Ibid.*, p. 155.

Police administrators face a major policy question of how available resources are to be allocated to inputs into the department and their processing within the department. Mention has been made of the fact that these problems place limits on the allocation of manpower to situations where crimes may occur and dictate a primarily reactive strategy even for occurrences in public places. The technology of policing now makes possible the mobilization of men to react quickly over relatively long distances so that where possible even foot patrol gives way to mobile patrol. Some police departments organize tactical units to deal with large public assemblies as they occur at various places and times, but on the whole most public as private places do not have police on duty. Most places of business, for example, are left without police on duty, as are most public streets; rather, mobile units are assigned to territories to respond to situations requiring police as they arise in public or private places.

Similarly in the organization's processing of information on crimes, the department faces an enormous problem of allocating scarce resources. A police department must on any day turn out a volume equivalent on the average to its intake. This means that on the average it cannot afford to allocate resources to very many cases on other than a routine basis. Every department will alter assignments within a detective bureau for a particularly "big case" that public pressure presses for solution. But it cannot afford so to assign men for a long time or for many cases without leaving much other work undone.

Although this is not the place to go into the matter, quite clearly both the volume of crime known to the police and the proportion cleared by arrest constitute some function of how much resources it takes to gain knowledge of a particular crime and clear it by arrest. No department can exceed its resource capacity. Since beyond a certain point the amount of resources necessary to clear a crime exceeds the willingness of the society to allocate additional resources, it perhaps is not surprising that three out of four crimes known to the police will remain unsolved. One caveat, of course, must be entered to any such statement. There undoubtedly is, in the nature of the case, a large number of crimes that will remain unsolved regardless of the resources allocated to their solution, since the information required to solve them never can become available in the police system. No police department can know more crime than its resources make possible for it to know in that given period of time nor solve more than its resources make possible. From a social organization point of view, the crime in any social system is a function of organizational capabilities to know it.

The heavily reactive nature of police operations means not only that the client-complainant system defines the conditions under which police are called at all, but also that the private system that includes the complainant, and in many cases also the offender, dominates the social stage upon which police intervention takes place. The police must react to calls for service by going out into every conceivable kind of social situation. Unlike many modern bureaucratic professions, the police must develop techniques for structuring these social situations, situations over which they ordinarily have little control. The basic tactic for doing so is to "take charge," if only to freeze the situation before any escalation of the offense can occur or evidence of it can be altered. The basic instrument in this strategy is authority. Failing its effectiveness, the basic backstop is force.

Uncoerced responsiveness to police authority in the immediate situation, that is, respect—uncoerced in the immediate situation, at least—is the most valuable resource available to the police. Much excessive police coercion can be attributed either to the perception that respect must be reestablished in a situation where it has broken down or to building up future respect credits in populations where police expect disrespect as a routine matter.[21]

Citizen respect for police authority in this context corresponds to the patient's respect for medical competence in the doctor-patient relationship. Unlike medical practice in modern clinics and hospitals, however, many clients of the police on call are not preprocessed by the routines of admission or readmission, nor are the clients always ill in the sense that they are aware of need and dependent upon the physician. Perhaps the proclivity of the police to prefer to deal with persons who have prior arrest records arises from the fact that they are preprocessed. The use of force by the policeman in a sense is an attempt to create in his clients, usually in offenders but sometimes also in complainants, the same capacity for subservience that the physician can count on because of illness on the one hand and office or hospital routines on the other.

We can discern here one of the fundamental sources of misunderstanding between police and rehabilitation personnel in the system for administering criminal justice. The police are the preprocessing agency that not only enforces the basic transition from independence to subservience but also delivers the newly processed clients to a social setting already dominated by rehabilitation.

---

[21] William A. Westley, "Violence and the Police," *American Journal of Sociology*, 49 (August 1953): 34–41.

26. POLICE DILEMMA, PROFESSIONALIZATION, AND COMMUNITY EXPECTATIONS

Jerome H. Skolnick

The traditional concern of criminology and of writers on "social control" is the maintenance of order in society. This study suggests that such a view is limited both philosophically and sociologically. "Social control" must deal not merely with the maintenance of order, but with the quality of the order that a given system is capable of sustaining and the procedures appropriate to the achievement of such order. Thus, a given set of social and legal conditions may lead to order in a stable democracy but not in a stable totalitarianism. Meaningful sociological analysis of order cannot, therefore, be value-free, because such a posture falsely assumes the equivalence of all types of order.

This research rejects the "value-free" approach, and concentrates instead upon the social foundations of legal procedures designed to protect democratic order. In the workings of democratic society, where the highest stated commitment is to the ideal of legality, a focal point of tension exists between the substance of order and the procedures for its accomplishment. "The basic and anguishing dilemma of form and substance in law can be alleviated, but never resolved, for the structure of legal domination retains

Reprinted by permission of the author and the publisher from *Justice Without Trial* (New York: Wiley, 1966), pp. 230–45.

its distinguishing features only as long as this dilemma is perpetuated."[1] This dilemma is most clearly manifested in law-enforcement organizations, where both sets of demands make forceful normative claims upon police conduct.

In addition to this fundamental dilemma, there are further complications. Neither form nor substance, law nor order, is an entirely clear conception; and what it means for police to use law to enforce order is also somewhat problematic. The empirical portion of this study looked into the question of how the police themselves conceive the meaning of "law" and "order" to find out how these conceptions develop and are implemented in police practices. Social conditions in the varying assignments of police heightened or diminished the conflict between the obligations of maintaining order and observing the rule of law.

This chapter considers the implications of the research. First we summarize findings about these issues and suggest that the dilemma of the police in democratic society arises out of the conflict between the extent of initiative contemplated by nontotalitarian norms of work and restraints upon police demanded by the rule of law. Second, we consider the meaning of police professionalization, pointing out its limitations according to the idea of managerial efficiency. Finally, we discuss how the policeman's conception of himself as a craftsman is rooted in community expectations, and how the ideology of police professionalization is linked to these expectations. Thus, this chapter focuses upon the relation between the policeman's conception of his work and his capacity to contribute to the development of a society based upon the rule of law as its master ideal.

OCCUPATIONAL ENVIRONMENT AND THE RULE OF LAW

Five features of the policeman's occupational environment weaken the conception of the rule of law as a primary objective of police conduct. One is the social psychology of police work, that is, the relation between occupational environment, working personality, and the rule of law. Second is the policeman's stake in maintaining his position of authority, especially his interest in bolstering accepted patterns of enforcement. Third is police socialization, especially as it influences the policeman's administrative bias. A related factor is the pressure put upon individual policemen to "produce"—to be efficient rather than legal when the two norms are in conflict. Finally, there is the policeman's opportunity to behave inconsistently with the rule of law as a result of the low visibility of much of his conduct.

Although it is difficult to weigh the relative import of these factors, they

---

[1] Reinhard Bendix, *Nation-Building and Citizenship* (New York: Wiley, 1964), p. 112.

all seem analytically to be joined to the conception of policeman as *crafts-man* rather than as *legal actor*, as a skilled worker rather than as a civil servant obliged to subscribe to the rule of law. The significance of the conception of the policeman as a craftsman derives from the differences in ideology of work and authority in totalitarian and nontotalitarian societies. Reinhard Bendix has contended that the most important difference be-tween totalitarian and nontotalitarian forms of subordination is to be found in the managerial handling of problems of authority and sub-ordination.[2]

Subordinates in totalitarian society are offered little opportunity to introduce new means of achieving the goals of the organization, since subordination implies obedience rather than initiative. As Bendix says, ". . . managerial refusal to accept the tacit evasion of rules and norms or the uncontrolled exercise of judgment is related to a specific type of bu-reaucratization which constitutes the fundamental principle of totalitarian government."[3] By contrast, in nontotalitarian society, subordinates are encouraged to introduce their own strategies and ideas into the working situation. Bendix does not look upon rule violation or evasion as neces-sarily subverting the foundations of bureaucratic organization, but rather sees these innovations as "strategies of independence" by which the em-ployees "seek to modify the implementation of the rules as their personal interests and their commitment (or lack of commitment) to the goals of the organization dictate."[4] In brief, the managerial ideology of nontotali-tarian society maximizes the exercise of discretion by subordinates, while totalitarian society minimizes innovation by working officials.[5]

This dilemma of democratic theory manifests itself in every aspect of the policeman's work, as evidenced by the findings of this study. In explain-ing the development of the policeman's "working personality," the dan-gerous and authoritative elements of police work were emphasized. The combination of these elements undermines attachment to the rule of law in the context of a "constant" pressure to produce. Under such pres-sure, the variables of danger and authority tend to alienate the policeman from the general public, and at the same time to heighten his perception of symbols portending danger to him and to the community. Under the same pressure to produce, the policeman not only perceives possible crim-inality according to the symbolic status of the suspect; he also develops a stake in organized patterns of enforcement. To the extent that a suspect

---

[2] See his *Work and Authority in Industry* (New York: Harper Torchbook, 1963) and *Nation-Building and Citizenship*.

[3] *Work and Authority*, p. 446.

[4] *Ibid.*, p. 445.

[5] There is, perhaps, some ambiguity in this posing of the situation of the worker in totalitarian society. Police in a totalitarian society may have the opportunity to exercise a great deal of "initiative." See Simon Wolin and Robert M. Slusser, eds., *The Soviet Secret Police* (New York: Praeger, 1957); and Jacques Delarue, *The Gestapo*, trans. Mervyn Sevill (New York: Morrow, 1964).

is seen as interfering with such arrangements, the policeman will respond negatively to him. On the other hand, the "cooperative" suspect, that is, one who contributes to the smooth operation of the enforcement pattern, will be rewarded. Accordingly, a detailed investigation was made of exchange relations between police and informers, in part to ascertain how informers are differentially treated according to the extent to which they support enforcement patterns, and partly to analyze how the policeman creates and uses the resources given to him.

In attempting to enrich his exchange position, the policeman necessarily involves the prosecutor in supporting his enforcement needs. The prosecutor, of course, also has a stake in the policeman's work performance, since the policeman provides him with the raw materials of prosecutorial achievement. Our observations suggested, however, that although he is ultimately the policeman's spokesman, the prosecutor performs a quasi-magisterial function by conveying a conception of legality to the policeman.

Most interesting, of course, is the basis on which the prosecutor's greater attachment to legality rests. We may point here to pertinent differences between policeman and prosecutor. One, of course, has to do with socialization. The prosecutor is a product of a law school, with larger understanding and appreciation of the judiciary and its restraints, especially constitutional ones. The policeman, on the other hand, generally has less formal education, less legal training, and a sense of belonging to a different sort of organization. Such differences in background go far to explain the development of the policeman's conception of self as a craftsman, coupled with a guildlike affirmation of worker autonomy. The policeman views himself as a specialist in criminological investigation, and does not react indifferently either to having his conclusions challenged by a distant judiciary or to having "obstacles" placed in his administrative path. He therefore views the judiciary, especially the appellate courts, as saboteurs of his capacity to satisfy what he sees as the requirements of social order. Each appellate decision limiting police initiative comes to be defined as a "handcuffing" of law enforcement, and may unintentionally sever further the policeman's attachment to the rule of law as an overriding value. In addition, the policeman is offended by judicial assumptions running contrary to probabilistic fact—the notion of due process of law staunchly maintains a rebuttable presumption of innocence in the face of the policeman's everyday experience of an administrative presumption of regularity.

Although the prosecutor is legally accorded a wider area of discretion than the policeman, the setting of the policeman's role offers greater opportunity to behave inconsistently with the rule of law. Police discretion is "hidden" insofar as the policeman often makes decisions in direct interaction with the suspect. The prosecutor typically serves at most as adviser to these dealings. Whether it is a question of writing out a traffic citation, of arresting a spouse on a charge of "assault with a deadly weapon," or of apprehending an addict informer, the policeman has enormous power; he may halt the legal process right there. Such discretionary activity is difficult to observe. By contrast, prosecutorial discretion frequently takes place at a later stage in the system, after the initial charge has been made public. The public character of the charge may restrict the prosecutor's discretion in practice more than the policeman's, even though the scope of the prosecutor's discretion is far wider in theory.

Internal controls over policemen reinforce the importance of administrative and craft values over civil libertarian values. These controls are more likely to emphasize efficiency as a goal rather than legality, or, more precisely, legality as a means to the end of efficiency. Two analyses were made along these lines. One was of the clearance rate as an internal control process. Here it was suggested that the policeman operates according to his most concrete and specific understanding of the control system, and that the clearance-rate control system emphasizes measures stressing the detective's ability to "solve" crimes. It was further shown how it is possible for this control system to reverse the penalty structure associated with substantive criminal law by rewarding those evidencing a high degree of criminality. Thus, persons with greater criminal experience are frequently better "equipped" to contribute to the "solution" of crimes, thereby enhancing the policeman's appearance as a competent craftsman. The introduction of this control system into police work was analyzed to illustrate a response to the difficulties experienced by organizations that produce a fundamentally intangible service, or at least where "output" is subject to a variety of interpretations. Such an organization requires internal measures of the competence of employees, plus a set of measures (which may be the same) for assessment by outside evaluators.

The dilemma of democratic society requiring the police to maintain order and at the same time to be accountable to the rule of law is thus further complicated. Not only is the rule of law often incompatible with the maintenance of order but the principles by which police are governed by the rule of law in a democratic society may be antagonistic to the ideology of worker initiative associated with a nontotalitarian philosophy of work. In the same society, the ideal of legality rejects discretionary innovation by police, while the ideal of worker freedom and autonomy encourages such initiative. Bureaucratic rules are seen in a democracy as "enabling" regulations, while the regulations deriving from the rule of law are intended to constrain the conduct of officials.

The conflict between the democratic ideology of work and the legal philosophy of a democracy brings into focus the essential problem of the role of the police. The police are not simply "bad guys" or "good guys," authoritarians or heroes. Nor are they merely "men doing their jobs." They are legal officials whose tendencies to be arbitrary have roots in a conception of the freedom of the worker inhering in the nontotalitarian ideology of the relation between work and authority, a conception carried out in the context of police work. Seeing themselves as craftsmen, the police tend to conduct themselves according to the norms pertaining to a working bureaucracy in democratic society. Therefore, the more police tend to regard themselves as "workers" or "craftsmen," the more they demand a lack of constraint upon initiative. By contrast, *legal actors* are sympathetic toward the necessity for constraint and review.

PROFESSIONALISM AND POLICE CONDUCT

The idea of professionalism is often invoked as the solution to the conflict between the policeman's task of maintaining order and his accountability to the rule of law. The meaning of this idea, however, is by no means clear. In sociology, there have been two main traditions, one emphasizing professional ideals and values, the other stressing technical competence. In Durkheim's view, what is distinctive about the idea of "professional" groups is not merely that such groups have high status, or high skill, or a politically supported monopoly over certain kinds of work, or a distinctive structure of control over work—most important is an infusion of work and collective organization with moral values, plus the use of sanctions to insure that these moral values are upheld. Arguing against the laissez-faire doctrines of the classical economists, for example, Durkheim pleaded for the introduction of morality into economic life:

> [W]hen we wish to see the guilds reorganized on a pattern we will presently try to define, it is not simply to have new codes superimposed on those existing; it is mainly so that economic activity should be permeated by ideas and needs other than individual ideas and needs . . . with the aim that the professions should become so many moral *milieux* and that these (comprising always the various organs of industrial and commercial life) should constantly foster the morality of the professions. As to the rules, although necessary and inevitable, they are but the outward expression of these fundamental principles. It is not a matter of co-ordinating any changes outwardly and mechanically, but of bringing men's minds into mutual understanding.[6]

An alternative concept of "professionalism" is associated with a managerial view emphasizing rationality, efficiency, and universalism. This view envisages the professional as a bureaucrat, almost as a machine calculating alternative courses of action by a stated program of rules, and possessing the technical ability to carry out decisions irrespective of personal feelings. As Weber says:

---

[6] Emile Durkheim, *Professional Ethics and Civic Morals*, trans. Cornelia Brookfield (Glencoe, Ill.: Free Press, 1958), p. 29.

> Above all, bureaucratization offers the optimal possibility for the reali-
> zation of the principle of division of labor in administration accord-
> ing to purely technical considerations, allocating individual tasks to
> functionaries who are trained as specialists and who continuously add
> to their experience by constant practice. "Professional" execution in
> this case means primarily execution "without regard to person" in
> accordance with calculable rules.[7]

In the effort to introduce fairness, calculability, and impersonality into
an American administration of criminal justice that was often riddled
with corruption and political favoritism, most writers who have seriously
examined police have also tended to subscribe to reforms based upon the
managerial conception of "professional." Reviewing the works of such
police reformers as O. W. Wilson or William Parker, we find that the conception of "professional" emphasizes managerial efficiency based upon a
body of "expert" knowledge. A recently completed volume by law professor
Wayne La Fave contains a similar point of view. In his concluding chapter, La Fave advocates a conception of the police as an administrative
agency, with, presumably, the presumptions of regulation associated with
such "expertise." He writes:

> The development of police expertness should be encouraged, and its
> existence should be recognized when appropriate. . . . There is need,
> and ample precedent in other fields, for the development of methods
> of communicating the existence of police expertness to trial or appel-
> late courts which are called upon to decide arrest issues. The relation-
> ship between the court and the economic regulatory agency might
> serve as a model in the absence of a more highly developed proposal.[8]

There are, however, costs in developing a professional code based upon
the model of administrative efficiency. Such a conception of professionalism not only fails to bridge the gap between the maintenance of order and
the rule of law; in addition it comes to serve as an ideology undermining
the capacity of police to be accountable to the rule of law. The idea of
organization based on principles of administrative efficiency is often misunderstood by officials who are themselves responsible for administering
such organizations. In practice, standardized rules and procedures are frequently molded to facilitate the tasks of acting officials. The materials of
this study have clearly demonstrated that the policeman is an especially
"nonmechanical" official. As Bruce Smith says:

> The policeman's art . . . consists in applying and enforcing a multi-
> tude of laws and ordinances in such degree or proportion and in such
> manner that the greatest degree of protection will be secured. The
> degree of enforcement and the method of application will vary with

---

[7] *Max Weber on Law in Economy and Society*, ed. Max Rheinstein, trans. Max Rheinstein and Edward Shils (Cambridge: Harvard University Press, 1954), p. 350.

[8] Wayne R. La Fave, *Arrest: The Decision to Take a Suspect into Custody* (Boston:
Little, Brown, 1965), pp. 512–13.

each neighborhood and community. There are no set rules, nor even general principles, to the policy to be applied. Each policeman must, in a sense, determine the standard to be set in the area for which he is responsible. Immediate superiors may be able to impress upon him some of the lessons of experience, but for the most part such experience must be his own. . . . Thus he is a policy-forming police administrator in miniature, who operates beyond the scope of the usual devices for control. . . .[9]

Smith may be making his point too strongly. Nevertheless, as a system of organization, bureaucracy can hope to achieve efficiency only by allowing officials to initiate their own means for solving specific problems that interfere with their capacity to achieve productive results. Some of these procedures may arise out of personal feelings—for example, relations between police and traffic violators—while others may become a routine part of the organizational structure. Examination of a procedural code, for example, would disclose no reference to the systematic use of informants. Given the task of enforcing crimes without citizen complainants, however, it becomes necessary for police to develop alternative methods to those used to apprehend violators in "standard" or "victimizing" crimes. These techniques of apprehension may demand considerable organization and skill on the part of the individual official, skill not so much in a formal administrative sense as in the sense of knowledge and ability to work within the effective limits of formal organization. As described, for example, the informer system requires so much ability that an aesthetic of execution has come to be associated with its use; it has become such an intrinsic component of police work that the abilities of the "professional" detective have come to be defined in terms of capacity to utilize this system.

As a bureaucratic organization, however, the police and governmental institutions, increasingly and generally, have a distinctive relationship to the development of the rule of law. The rule of law develops in response to the innovations introduced by officials to achieve organizational goals. It is certainly true, as Bendix asserts, that "a belief in legality means first and foremost that certain formal procedures must be obeyed if the enactment or execution of a law is to be considered legal."[10] At the same time, while legality may be seen as comprising a set of unchanging ideals, it may also be seen as a working normative system which develops in response to official conduct. The structure of authoritative regulations is such that legal superiors are not part of the same organization as officials and are expected to be "insensitive" to "productive capacity" as contrasted with legality. Thus, for example, a body of case law has been emerging that attempts to define the conditions and limits of the use of informants. Legality, there-

---

[9] Bruce Smith, *Police Systems in the United States* (New York: Harper & Row, 1960), p. 19.

[10] Bendix, *op. cit.*, p. 112.

fore, develops as the other side of the coin of official innovation. As such, it is both a variable and an achievement. To the extent that police organizations operate mainly on grounds of administrative efficiency, the development of the rule of law is frustrated. Therefore, a conception of professionalism based mainly on satisfying the demands of administrative efficiency also hampers the capacity of the rule of law to develop.

The police are increasingly articulating a conception of professionalism based on a narrow view of managerial efficiency and organizational interest. A sociologist is not surprised at such a development. Under the rule of law it is not up to the agency of enforcement to generate the limitations governing its actions, and bureaucrats typically and understandably try to conceal the knowledge of their operations so that they may regulate themselves unless they are forced to make disclosures. But the police in a democracy are not merely bureaucrats. They are also, or can be conceived of as, legal officials, that is, men belonging to an institution charged with strengthening the rule of law in society. If professionalism is ever to resolve some of the strains between order and legality, it must be a professionalism based upon a deeper set of values than currently prevails in police literature and the "professional" police department studied, whose operations are ordered on this literature.

The needed philosophy of professionalism must rest on a set of values conveying the idea that the police are as much an institution dedicated to the achievement of legality in society as they are an official social organization designed to control misconduct through the invocation of punitive sanctions. The problem of police in a democratic society is not merely a matter of obtaining newer police cars and a higher order of technical equipment, or of recruiting men who have to their credit more years of education. What must occur is a significant alteration in the ideology of police, so that police "professionalization" rests on the values of a democratic legal order, rather than on technological proficiency.

No thoughtful person can believe that such a transformation is easily achieved. In an article estimating the prospects for the rule of law in the Soviet Union, Leonard Schapiro has written, "It is perhaps difficult for dictators to get accustomed to the idea that the main purpose of law is, in fact, to make their task more difficult."[11] It is also hard for police officials in a democracy to accept this idea. In the same article, Schapiro reports the case of two professors who were criticized for urging the desirability of adopting certain principles of bourgeois law and criminal procedure, arguing that observance of legal norms must prevail over expediency in government legislation and administration. They were officially criticized for incorrectly understanding "the role of legal science in the solution of the

---

[11] Leonard Schapiro, "Prospects for the Rule of Law," *Problems of Communism*, 14 (March–April 1965): 2.

practical tasks of government,"[12] a criticism not too different from the sort often leveled by "professional" police administrators in the United States against those who, for example, insist that the police must act legally for their evidence against the accused to be admitted. The argument is always essentially the same: that the efficient administration of criminal law will be hampered by the adoption of procedures designed to protect individual liberties. The police administrators on the whole are correct. They have been given wide and direct responsibility for the existence of crime in the community, and it is intrinsically difficult for them to accustom themselves to the basic idea of the rule of law: "that the main purpose of law is, in fact, to make their task more difficult."

THE COMMUNITY AND POLICE CONDUCT

If the police are ever to develop a conception of *legal* as opposed to *managerial* professionalism, they will do so only if the surrounding community demands compliance with the rule of law by rewarding police for such compliance, instead of looking to the police as an institution solely responsible for controlling criminality. In practice, however, the reverse has been true. The police function in a milieu tending to support, normatively and substantively, the idea of administrative efficiency that has become the hallmark of police professionalism. Legality, as expressed by both the criminal courts community with which the police have direct contact and the political community responsible for the working conditions and prerogatives of police, is a weak ideal. This concluding section will attempt to locate the main sources of support for the managerial concept of police professionalism.

A posthumously published article by Professor Edmond Cahn distinguishes between "the imperial or official perspective" on law and "the consumer perspective."[13] The official perspective, according to the author, is so called "because it has been largely determined by the dominant interests of rulers, governors, and other officials."[14] In contrast, the "consumer" perspective reflects the interests and opinions of those on the receiving end of law. In the "consumer" view, therefore, constraints on the decision-making powers of officials are given more importance than the requirements of the processing system and those who carry out its administration. Cahn adds, in addition, that "a free and open society calls on its official processors to perform their functions according to the perspective of consumers."[15] At

---

[12] *Ibid.*, p. 7.
[13] "Law in the Consumer Perspective," *University of Pennsylvania Law Review,* 112 (November 1963): 1–21.
[14] *Ibid.*, p. 4.
[15] *Ibid.*, p. 9.

the same time that he argues against it, however, Cahn demonstrates in his own article the empirical strength of the presumption of correctness in official conduct. So in large part do the materials in this study.

The "official perspective" is most persuasive because it operates as the "established" mode of law enforcement, in the broadest sense of that term. The administration of criminal justice has become a major industry in modern urban society. FBI data show that during 1963 there were 4,437,786 arrests reported by 3,988 police agencies covering areas totaling 127 million in population. In California alone during 1963 there were 98,535 adult felony arrests and 595,992 adult misdemeanor arrests. There were in addition 244,312 arrests of juveniles.[16] During 1962 to 1963, the District Attorney of Los Angeles County had a staff of 546 (with 180 lawyers) and a budget of just over $4,800,000.[17]

Under these circumstances of mass administration of criminal justice, presumptions necessarily run to regularity and administrative efficiency. The negation of the presumption of innocence permeates the entire system of justice without trial. All involved in the system, the defense attorneys and judges, as well as the prosecutors and policemen, operate according to a working presumption of the guilt of persons accused of crime. As accused after accused is processed through the system, participants are prone to develop a routinized callousness, akin to the absence of emotional involvement characterizing the physician's attitude toward illness and disease. That the accused is entitled to counsel is an accepted part of the system, but this guarantee implies no specific affirmation of "adversariness" in an interactional sense. Indeed, the most respected attorneys, prosecuting and defense alike, are those who can "reasonably" see eye to eye in a system where most defendants are guilty of some crime.

The overwhelming presence of the "official" system of justice without trial provides normative support for the policeman's own attachment to principles of administrative regularity in opposition to due process of law. Under such circumstances, it should not be surprising to find the policeman adopting the "official" perspective too, since his role is to make the initial decision as to whether a charge has been warranted. Having made the charge, he of all people can hardly be expected to presume the innocence of the defendant. He has, in practice, listened to the defendant's story and assured himself of the latter's culpability. In his own mind, there are numerous guilty parties whom he has not arrested because he does not feel their cases will hold up in court, even though he is personally convinced of their guilt to a moral certainty. Police may feel most strongly about the "irrationality" of due process, but in fact other role players in the system

---

[16] Edward L. Barrett, "Criminal Justice and the Problem of Mass Production," in *The Courts, the Public, and the Law Explosion*, ed. Harry W. Jones (Englewood Cliffs, N.J.: Prentice-Hall, 1965), p. 95.

[17] *Ibid.*, p. 98.

of criminal justice may also be observed to be more concerned with efficiency than legality. If the policeman is the strongest advocate of a "rational bureaucratic" system emphasizing factual over legal guilt, it may well be simply because it is the definition of his ability as a worker that is most affected by the application of the rule of law.

An "order" perspective based upon managerial efficiency also tends to be supported by the civic community. The so-called power structure of the community, for example, often stresses to the police the importance of "keeping the streets clear of crime." The La Loma County grand jury, composed of "prominent" citizens—mainly businessmen and bankers—typically expresses concern not over violations of due process of law, but over a seemingly ever-rising crime rate and the inability of police to cope with it. Similarly, the Westville *Courier,* the city's only newspaper, makes much of crime news, exaggerating criminality and deploring its existence. The police, quite sensitive to press criticism, find little support for the rule of law from that quarter. Indeed, when a newspaper runs an editorial, or a political figure emphasizes the importance of "making the streets safe for decent people," the statements are rarely qualified to warn law-enforcement officials that they should proceed according to the rule of law. On the contrary, such injunctions are typically phrased as calls for zealous law enforcement or strict law enforcement. James Q. Wilson has described this as the "problem of the crusade." As he says:

> Even if the force has but one set of consistent ends specified for it by the commissioner or superintendent, and even if adherence to those ends is enforced as far as possible, it is almost inevitable that there will come a time when the commissioner will decide that something must be done "at all costs"—that some civic goal justifies any police means. This might be the case when a commissioner is hard pressed by the newspapers to solve some particularly heinous crime (say, the rape and murder of a little girl). A "crusade" is launched. Policemen who have been trained to act in accord with one set of rules ("Use no violence." "Respect civil liberties." "Avoid becoming involved with criminal informants.") are suddenly told to act in accord with another rule—"catch the murderer"—no matter what it costs in terms of the normal rules.[18]

The emphasis on the maintenance of order is also typically expressed by the political community controlling the significant rewards for the police—money, promotions, vacations. Mayors, city councilmen, city managers draw up police budgets, hire and fire chiefs of police, and call for "shake-ups" within the department. Even the so-called liberal politician is inclined to urge police to disregard the rule of law when he perceives circumstances as exceedingly threatening. Thus, Wilson adds:

---

[18] James Q. Wilson, "The Police and Their Problems: A Theory," *Public Policy,* 12 (1963): 199.

When Fiorello La Guardia became mayor of New York City he is said to have instructed his police force to adopt a "muss 'em up" policy toward racketeers, to the considerable consternation of groups interested in protecting civil liberties. The effort to instill one set of procedural rules in the force was at cross-purposes with the effort to attain a certain substantive end.[19]

In contrast to that of political authority, the power of appellate courts over the police is limited. In practice, the greatest authority of judges is to deny the merit of the prosecution. Thus, by comparison to the direct sanctions held by political authority, the judiciary has highly restricted *power* to modify police behavior. Not only do appellate courts lack direct sanctions over the police but there are also powerful political forces that, by their open opposition to the judiciary, suggest an alternative frame of reference to the police. By this time, however, the police have themselves become so much a part of this same frame of reference that it is often difficult to determine whether it is the political figure who urges "stricter law enforcement" on the policeman or the law-enforcement spokesman who urges the press and the politician to support his demands against laws "coddling criminals," by which he typically means rulings of appellate courts upholding constitutional guarantees, usually under the Fourth, Fifth, Sixth, and Fourteenth Amendments. Whether the policeman is the "man in the middle," as Wilson portrays him, and as police prefer to present themselves, or whether police have by this time come to be the tail wagging the press and the politician, is the subject for another study. Beyond doubt, however, there are enough forces within the community, perhaps by now including the police themselves, to provide the working policeman with a normative framework praising managerial efficiency and opposing due process of law.

CONCLUSION

This chapter has indicated how the police respond to the pressures of the dilemma of having two sets of ideals thrust upon them. As workers in a democratic society, the police seek the opportunity to introduce the means necessary to carry out "production demands." The means used to achieve these ends, however, may frequently conflict with the conduct required of them as legal actors. In response to this dilemma, police "experts" have increasingly adopted a philosophy of professionalism based upon managerial efficiency, with the implied hope that advancing technology will somehow resolve their dilemma. As indicated, it has not, and by its very assumptions cannot. First of all, in those areas where violations of the rule of law occur, advanced technology often results in greater violation. Technological ad-

---

[19] *Ibid.*

vances in the form of wiretaps, polygraphs, stronger binoculars, and so forth only make the police more competent to interfere with individual liberty. Secondly, the model of efficiency based on bureaucracy simply does not work out in practice. Warren Bennis has catalogued the limitations of bureaucracy in general, and such limits are certainly applicable to large urban police forces. The following is a sample:

1. Bureaucracy does not adequately allow for personal growth and development of mature personalities.
2. It develops conformity and "group-think."
3. It does not take into account the "informal organization" and the emergent and unanticipated problems.
4. Its systems of control and authority are hopelessly outdated.
5. It has no adequate juridical process.
6. It does not possess adequate means for resolving differences and conflicts between ranks, and most particularly, between functional groups.
7. Communication and innovative ideas are thwarted or distorted due to hierarchical division.[20]

The working policeman is well aware of the limitations of "scientific" advances in police work and organization. He realizes that his work consists mostly of dealing with human beings, and that these skills are his main achievement. The strictures of the rule of law often clash with the policeman's ability to carry out this sort of work, but he is satisfied to have the argument presented in terms of technological achievement rather than human interaction, since he rightly fears that the public "will not understand" the human devices he uses, such as paying off informers, allowing "fences" to operate, and reducing charges, to achieve the enforcement ends demanded of him.

Police are generally under no illusions about the capacity of elected officials and the general public to make contradictory demands upon them. A certain amount of lip service may be paid to the need for lawful enforcement of substantive criminal law, but the police are rarely, if ever, rewarded for complying with or expanding the area of due process of law. On the contrary, they are rewarded primarily for apprehension of so-called notorious criminals, for breaking "dope rings," and the like. As a matter of fact, police are often much more sophisticated about their practices than the politicians who reward them. Police, for example, generally recognize the complexities of the meaning of such a term as "hardened criminal" and of the difficulties involved in carrying out a system of enforcement in line with the strictures of due process of law. The working detective who has used an individual as an informant for years, who has developed a relationship with the man in which each can depend on the word of the other, is not taken in by newspaper exaggerations of the man's "criminal" character.

---

[20] Warren Bennis, "Beyond Bureaucracy," *Trans-action*, 2 (July–August 1965): 32.

Finally, the dilemma can never be resolved since it contains a built-in dialectic. Appellate decisions upholding the integrity of procedural requirements may well move large segments of the community to a greater concern for the security of the substantive ends of criminal law. Especially when the police are burdened with the responsibility of enforcing unenforceable laws, thereby raising the spectre of a "crime-ridden" community,[21] decisions that specifically protect individual liberty may increase the pressure from an anxious community to soften these, and thus contain the seeds of a more "order-oriented" redefinition of procedural requirements. Over the past twenty years, courts have been increasingly indulgent of the rights of the accused. Whether this trend will continue, or whether the courts will redefine "due process of law" to offer legitimacy to what is presently considered unlawful official behavior, may well be contingent upon the disposition of the civic community.

If this analysis is correct in placing ultimate responsibility for the quality of "law and order" in American society upon the citizenry, then the prospects for the infusion of the rule of law into the police institution may be bleak indeed. As an institution dependent on rewards from the civic community, police can hardly be expected to be much better or worse than the political context in which they operate. When the political community is itself corrupt, the police will also be corrupt. If the popular notion of justice reaches no greater sophistication than that "the guilty should not go free," then the police will respond to this conception of justice. When prominent members of the community become far more aroused over an apparent rise in criminality than over the fact that Negroes are frequently subjected to unwarranted police interrogation, detention, and invasions of privacy, the police will continue to engage in such practices. Without widespread support for the rule of law, it is hardly to be expected that the courts will be able to continue advancing individual rights, or that the police will themselves develop a professional orientation as *legal* actors, rather than as efficient administrators of criminal law.

[21] Police statistics also contribute to this perception. See Gilbert Geis, "Statistics Concerning Race and Crime," *Crime and Delinquency*, April 1965, pp. 142–50.

27. POLICE PRACTICE, TYPES OF CRIMES, AND SOCIAL LOCATION

Arthur L. Stinchcombe

Legal institutions in general depend on rare events, such as arrests or civil court cases, to structure the field in which frequent events take place. This makes the operation of legal institutions very difficult to study, except when fairly comparable types of frequent events operate in strikingly different legally structured fields. The institutions of liberty generally, and of legally protected privacy in particular, have the characteristic that rare events, such as a case being thrown out of court because the law of search and seizure has been violated, structure the field in which the everyday activity of police is carried out. The many types of crimes that police deal with are very differently situated with respect to the legal institutions of privacy, as we shall try to demonstrate in the first part of this paper.

Certain statistics on the arrest and conviction rates for different types of crimes as well as pieces of common knowledge can be used to explore the different characteristics of police administrative practice in these different legally structured fields. We will then try to show that police administrative

Reprinted by permission of the author and the publisher from *American Journal of Sociology*, 69 (September 1963): 150–60. Copyright © 1963 by the University of Chicago. Original title: "Institutions of Privacy in the Determination of Police Administrative Practice."

practice with respect to different types of crime varies strikingly and systematically with the relation of the crimes to the legal institutions of privacy. This paper then tries to conduct an empirical study of that kind of "structural effect" on which the regulatory power of the law depends, namely, an effect on the behavior of many of an action by the courts that specifically applies only to the action of a few.

The order of presentation will be as follows: First I shall outline some well-known characteristics of the legal institutions by which "private places" are defined, and the effects of the growth of large cities on the social structure of "public places." Then I shall outline the relation of certain types of crime to these legal institutions and show how the location of crimes with respect to private and public places affects the organized activities of the police in handling these crimes. Since the police "organization" is made up of organized activities with respect to crime, this is really an indirect approach to studying the effect of social structure on organizational structure. To show this more clearly, in the final part of the section I shall summarize the way that the socially determined activities of police for particular types of crime are organized into police subsections with different characteristics.

LEGAL RELATIONS OF POLICE POWER TO PRIVACY

Most of our daily life is lived in a number of small, bounded social systems, such as families, schools, factories, clubs, etc., that have their own norms, goals, and facilities. The maintenance of the boundaries of these systems is necessary to their free and autonomous development. If agents of the state or strange private citizens could enter these systems arbitrarily and interfere with interaction within them, they cannot develop freely.

The central practical boundaries are such mundane things as walls, doors, window shades, and locks. But in modern society few of these are made to withstand a concerted effort by a group of men to breach them (in contrast to feudal societies, for example). Yet these fragile doors and windows effectively prevent police or private citizens from interfering with our sleep, our classrooms, our toolbenches, or our bars, at least most of the time. This is because a door is a legal entity of great importance: legitimate concerted social efforts to break down a door may take place only on legally defined occasions. These occasions are defined in the law of arrest[1] and the law of search and seizure,[2] and therefore, derivatively, in the criminal law.

---

[1] A good summary of the law of arrest is R. M. Perkins, "The Law of Arrest," *Iowa Law Review*, 25 (1940): 201–89.

[2] See E. W. Machen, Jr., *The Law of Search and Seizure* (Chapel Hill: University of North Carolina Press, 1950).

The legal defense of doors and walls and windows means that small social systems which have legal possession of a place can maintain *continuous, discretionary* control over who crosses their boundaries. And this discretion may be enforced against agents of the state unless they have legal cause to penetrate the system or are invited in. Whenever such continuous discretionary control is maintained, the law speaks of "private places." The legal existence of "private places," then, is the main source of the capacity of small social systems to maintain their boundaries and determine their own interaction without interference from the outside. The distinctive feature of a modern *liberal* state is that it uses the monopoly of violence (which all modern industrial states have) to guarantee the boundaries of small, autonomous social systems.

The central importance in our society of the private places created in this way is indicated by two facts. First, in Maryland, a state not much less free than others, a man entirely without access to private places is legally unfree:

> Every person, not insane, who wanders about in this state and lodges in market houses, market places, or in other public buildings [note that some of these "public buildings" are "private property"], or in barns, outhouses, barracks, or in the open air, without having any lawful occupation in the city, town, or country in which he may so wander, and without having any visible means of support, shall be deemed to be a tramp, and to be guilty of a misdemeanor, and shall be subject to imprisonment, at the discretion of the Court or Justice of the Peace hearing the charge, for a period of not less than thirty days nor more than one year. This section not to apply to Allegany County.[3]

That is, if a man is not a member of some organization or family or other group that has control over a "private place" (which may, of course, be "public property," as for instance a county hospital), then he has to *satisfy a policeman* that his occupation in the area is lawful, and has to make visible his means of support (except in Allegany County). Access to private places is itself sufficient evidence that a man has a legitimate relation to the social structure; without that evidence, special evidence of legitimate occupation has to be provided. "Occupation" here means any legitimate activity, not specifically a job.

The second fact indicating the importance of the legal definition of private places is that unless continuous discretionary control of access to a piece of property is maintained (creating a "private place"), police may freely enter and supervise interaction and arrest without a warrant: "An officer in uniform or in citizen's clothes may enter any public house, if open, as other people enter, for the purpose of detecting or suppressing crime, and having peaceably entered, may arrest for any offense committed

---

[3] H. E. Flack, ed., *The Annotated Code . . . of Maryland, 1951*, art. 27, sec. 666.

in his presence.[4] (Apparently a common-law rule, as cases are cited for authority rather than statutes.)

A man's affairs are never, then, legally free of police supervision except within private places. Police may not legally, of course, forbid actions in public places that are not prohibited by law. But there is a fundamental difference between conducting the affairs of a small social system in such a manner that no crimes committed shall *come to the attention* of the police, and conducting them so that a physically present policeman will approve. In the first case, the problem is to prevent complaints, perhaps by agreement; in the second, the problem is to satisfy the police, rather than other members of the system, that all is as it should be. Few of us ever see a policeman in those places where we spend most of our time; a "tramp" sees one wherever he goes, and the policeman has the discretionary power to "run him in."

DISTRIBUTION OF PRIVATE PLACES AND URBAN-RURAL POLICE PRACTICE

The concentration of the population into cities concentrates intensively used "public places" within a small geographical area, thus greatly reducing the amount of "public" area per person and making professional control of public places much more economical. At the same time the size and anonymity of the city decrease the chance of small social systems to control the behavior of their members in public. In a small village, activity in public places easily comes to the attention of the family, the priest, the employer, and the peers of the offender. Further, in larger cities there are much stronger norms about "deliberately not noticing" the behavior of other people. This means that in cities, much more behavior is inquired into *only* by the police.

That is, in cities it is economically possible to patrol public places, and at the same time it is functionally necessary. City police can therefore depend much more on their own presence and information for the detection of crime (especially certain types of crime) than can a rural police force. To a large degree (except for the patrol of main highways) rural police depend on complaints from people who are injured or know of a crime rather than on their own patrol.

Besides leading to differential structural conditions of police practice, intensively used public places pose new problems. The most important are, of course, traffic jams and accidents. But also, extensive traffic creates opportunities for the use of public places for private profit in ways that cre-

---

[4] *Instructions . . . and Digest of the Statutes, Ordinances and Decisions* (Baltimore: Baltimore Police Department, 1939), p. 13.

ate a "nuisance." Soliciting for prostitution, begging, street vending, speechmaking, all become profitable uses of public places when the traffic gets heavy enough. The control of these "nuisances" is easily done without access to private places, along with other patrol duties.

The increasing predominance of patrol of public places means that policemen act much more on their own initiative. Much or all of the evidence that justifies arrest will be collected by the policeman on the spot. The arrest often need not involve any invasion at all of private places. Consequently these arrests are much more likely than are those in rural areas to be arrests without a warrant, and therefore without prior check by the judiciary, or to be a direct summons to appear in court (as in traffic cases).

ARRESTS INVOLVING ENTRY
INTO PRIVATE PLACES

Private autonomy alone cannot guarantee liberty in the sense in which we understand it today. Feudal manors or plantations in the ante bellum South were much more autonomous and free of state interference than modern factories and business places. But this private autonomy did not create liberty in the modern sense because the police power was privately appropriated and consequently not exercised according to "due process of law." The practical implication of this is that besides *not* entering small systems *except* on legally defined occasions, *entering* them *on* those occasions is a duty of the police in liberal societies. A primary function of the criminal law is the limitation of coercion within small social systems.

But once the small systems are entered by the state, "due process of law" means mainly a set of procedures which guarantee that the autonomy of individuals and small social systems will be restored as quickly as possible if a crime has not in fact been committed. And it means that the process of investigating and legally establishing the existence of a crime shall not so far damage the individuals and small social systems that they cannot function after they have been found innocent.

Due process thus involves a grading of coercion, applied by the police, into arrest and seizure of evidence, coerced appearance in court, and coerced paying of the penalty of crime. Each of these grades of coercion changes the legal status of the presumed offender. Each of these changes of the legal condition of the presumed offender must be justified by evidence of a probability that a crime has been committed and probability that the defendant committed the crime. The probabilities increase with the increase in severity of coercion. The probability required to justify arrest (by a police officer at least) is not as high as that required to coerce an appearance in court (a "prima facie case"). To justify conviction the commission of a crime must be established "beyond reasonable doubt." We now have sufficient background to discuss the structural location of different types of crime with respect to the institutions of privacy and the effect of this structural distribution on police practice.

THE EFFECT OF THE SOCIAL LOCATION OF DIFFERENT CRIMES ON POLICE PRACTICE

It is immediately evident that different types of crime will be distributed differently with respect to the institutions of privacy. For instance, wife-beating rarely goes on in public places. Soliciting for prostitution requires some systematic contact with an anonymous public through a pimping apparatus. Except for call girls and prostitutes in well-known houses, this requires soliciting (often by the woman herself) in some public places. But prostitution takes place in private places. Burglary consists in the invasion of the private place of another, generally in secret, which results in a complaint against an unknown person. The person's identity has to be established by the police. Murder generally takes place within small social systems, behind doors. Riots take place in streets and other public places.

Of course these variations in the social location of crimes imply differences in police practice. Information relevant to each stage of the criminal process comes to the police in different ways, different degrees and kinds of coercion have to be applied for different purposes, different things have to be proved with the evidence. There are differences in the number and types of private places that have to be penetrated, and in the amount of preparation of the case previous to this penetration. The kinds of people who commit different types of crime have different stability of social ties, which makes due process work differently.[5] We may distinguish the following types of crime.

Coercion in Private Life

The application of force or other coercion in private life is either controlled and adjusted within the small social system (as when a wife puts up with a beating), or it is not. When it is not, the crimes are, generally speaking, "crimes of passion." Probably the legally defined crimes with the highest proportion originating in this way are incest and murder,[6] but

---

[5] A statistical reflection of this could be obtained by computing the proportion of appeals to higher courts of convictions for those types of crime that indicate weak connection to the social structure, such as vagrancy, and comparing this with the rate of appeals for other types of crimes with approximately the same penalties.

[6] For instance, in a study in Denmark, 57.0 percent of murder victims were relatives, 30.8 percent acquaintances (ranging from "close" to "met the day before"), and only 12.2 percent strangers (see K. Svalastoga, "Homicide and Social Contact in Denmark," *American Journal of Sociology*, 62 (1956): 37–41.

some unknown proportion of other crimes against persons (rape, aggravated assault) originate the same way.

Such crimes generally result either in complaint to the police or in such heinous crimes that access to private places is hardly a difficulty, at least for investigation. Because the people who participate in small social systems are highly visible once the system is penetrated, and because often the complainant knows perfectly well who coerced whom, arrests are fairly easy to make. Crimes against persons generally have a high proportion of "crimes known to the police" that are "cleared by arrest" (see Table 1).

TABLE 1

PROPORTION OF CRIMES KNOWN TO THE POLICE
"CLEARED BY ARREST," AND PROPORTION OF
THOSE CHARGED WHO ARE CONVICTED,
FOR VARIOUS CRIMES

Crime	Percentage Cleared by Arrest	Percentage Convicted
Crimes indicating coercion in private life:		
Murder, including nonnegligent manslaughter	92.7	59.4
Forcible rape	73.6	43.0
Aggravated assault	64.7	43.9
Crimes indicating coercion in public places:		
Robbery	42.5	64.8
Crimes indicating invasion of private places of another:		
Burglary	30.7	71.4
Larceny (over $50)	20.9	72.6
Auto theft	26.2	67.5
Crimes indicating individual public disorder:		
Vagrancy	N.a.	77.5
Disorderly conduct	N.a.	86.5
Drunkenness	N.a.	69.7

Computed from Federal Bureau of Investigation, *Uniform Crime Reports—1959* (Washington, D.C.: U.S. Government Printing Office, 1960), Tables 12 and 14.

But the same conditions that produce easy arrests create another characteristic of enforcement against these crimes, namely, that arrests quite often do not result in conviction. Legal responsibility of the assailant must be established. His intentions are not immediately obvious from the nature of the act (as they are, for example, in burglary). The kind of passionate conflicts that lead to murders rarely make the motives of the crime absolutely clear. In the highly intensive interaction between the presumed offender and the victim, the crime may have been provoked, for example, by requiring self-defense, or by consent before the presumed rape of a woman.

In addition, conviction before a jury generally requires that the defendant be judged not only legally but also morally responsible for the crime. In spite of the legal tradition, rape of a prostitute or murder of a really oppressive husband seems to be a lesser crime. Evidence of moral responsibility is much harder to produce in crimes of passion. Finally, complaint to the police is something of a betrayal of those to whom we have close personal ties. Once the complaint is made, and the immediate danger and anger past, the personal ties or embarrassment of the complainant quite often reassert themselves, and the main source of evidence refuses to testify further.

The processing of the presumed offender then typically takes the following form: the arrest may be made on a warrant after preliminary investigation, but fairly often the offender is still at the scene and is arrested without a warrant; after the arrest supporting evidence must be collected by skilled investigation, both questioning and examination of physical clues; this is generally challenged very carefully and fully in court. A fairly general administrative pattern then is for uniformed patrol police to be called first; they come and take control of the scene and of the relevant evidence, and perhaps make arrests. Then the work passes to the detective force, which tries to establish the case (and generally takes credit for the conviction or blame for the poor case).

Crimes against persons in public places tend to depart from this pattern in several respects. In the first place, the officer is much more likely to happen on the scene, so that his own information is sufficient to justify arrest. Second, the assailant is generally unknown and not intimately tied to the victim. Consequently the location of the assailant may be more of a problem. In the case of strange assailants, however, the establishment of legal and moral responsibility is easier if they are located, and there is less motivation for the complainant to drop the case. The only crime for which statistics are given that uniformly falls in this category is robbery. As expected, the proportion cleared by arrest is somewhat smaller (42.5 percent) and the proportion of charges leading to conviction considerably higher (64.8 percent). ("Robbery" refers to taking things from persons, generally strangers, by violence or threat of violence.)

Crimes against persons, then, normally take place within the boundaries of morally dense small social systems. They come to the attention of the police typically through complaint, and arrests are usually easy to make. But conviction is very problematic, and requires detailed investigation of high skill.

Illegitimate Businesses and "Dangerous" Organizations

Illegitimate businesses, such as prostitution, the illegal narcotics trade, and gambling in most of the United States, use the institutions of privacy

to cloak activities that the society chooses to suppress. "Dangerous" organizations such as revolutionary or conspiratorial political parties stand in
approximately the same relation to the institutions of privacy. These types
of crime do not have "victims" in the same sense as do theft or murder.
Instead the "victim" is an active participant in the system, either as a
customer or as a party member. Consequently complaints do not come
from within the system to the same degree that they do with crimes against
persons. On the other hand, illegitimate businesses do not generally
(directly) create disorder in public places. This means that patrol alone
does not produce evidence justifying arrest or conviction. And although
revolutionary political organizations must produce speech in public places,
the speech is generally tempered enough (or if not tempered, ineffective
enough) not to threaten the peace.

These conditions set the stage for the characteristic police practices in
this field: "undercover" work, harassment, and regulation of the (relatively
epiphenomenal) public aspects of the business. The prevalence of "undercover" work follows directly from the nature of the offense: the fact that
it does not produce complaints, and that it takes place behind the barriers
that protect privacy. Secret police activity is more prevalent in societies
where the government routinely invades and distorts the functioning of
small social systems; it is more prevalent within liberal societies when the
suppression of illegitimate business or "dangerous" organizations is demanded by law and police policy.

By harassment I mean periodic or continuous enforcement of laws not
normally enforced against the general public against people in illegitimate
businesses or "dangerous" organizations. For instance, street soliciting of
various kinds may be held to be a nuisance, but this is more likely to be
enforced against prostitutes than against the Salvation Army, and the
quality of evidence required to arrest prostitutes may be negligible.[7] Or
a license required for "street vendors" may be required of the salesman
of radical newspapers, though no other news vendors have been required
to have licenses.

Harassment is easy to carry out because the participants are quite often
infamous, without many friends who will appear in public in their defense, and personally demoralized, without a conviction of their own innocence. This is, of course, more true of people who run illegitimate businesses than of those who belong to "dangerous" organizations. The pattern of harassment produces a degree of discretionary power over illegitimate business by police. This discretion may be privately appropriated by
the officer or by a political machine and used to "tax" illegitimate business.

The third pattern of law-enforcement activity often produced by illegiti-

---

[7] For the situation in London, see Anonymous, *Women of the Streets* (London: British
Social Biology Council, Secker & Warburg, 1955), pp. 18–23.

mate business or "dangerous" organizations is tight regulation of public manifestations. In Baltimore, for example, the set of bars in which solicitation for prostitution goes on is concentrated in a relatively small area, and during the evening hours this area is very heavily patrolled. This prevents street soliciting and obnoxious forms of "barking" of the strip shows (prevalent, at least several years ago, in San Francisco), prevents the bars from serving minors, keeps bars closed after hours, and generally maintains public decorum without substantially disturbing the business. The same pattern is found in many large cities in the area set aside for "lunatic fringe" speakers. Heavy patrol helps prevent speakers' being attacked, prevents potential riots from getting very far, prevents audiences from interrupting traffic, and so forth.

The general problem presented to police by illegitimate business or "dangerous" organizations, then, is that "crimes" do not become "known to the police."[8] When they do become known, conviction is generally relatively easy for the demoralized employees of illegitimate businesses, and for "dangerous" organizations depends on the public temper and the mood of the Supreme Court. In liberal societies, activity by secret police posing as customers of illegitimate businesses or as members of "dangerous" organizations tends to be concentrated in this field. The barriers of privacy require that the police get permission to enter where the "crime" is being carried on, and they have difficulty getting that permission if they are openly policemen. Harassment and corruption are both latent consequences of the legal suppression of systems that function behind barriers of privacy.

Invasion of Private Places by Criminals

Burglary, much larceny, and trespass involve the invasion of the private place of another without permission, generally in secret. These crimes present distinctive enforcement problems because they very often result in complaint to the police, yet the secrecy of the act makes it difficult to locate offenders. Relatively few of the "crimes known to the police" are "cleared by arrest." The proportion is lower than that of crimes against persons, either in public (robbery) or in private (see Table 1 above).

Unless they are caught in the act (which is the main way complaints of trespass originate), the offenders can generally be caught only by physical evidence (e.g., possession of contraband), by informers, or by confession. Confession quite generally happens only when the offender is arrested on some other charge or illegally arrested "on suspicion," and some informing takes place under the same conditions.

---

[8] Statistics on "crimes known to the police" are not given for these offenses in the *Uniform Crime Reports*, probably for the reasons given above.

If enough evidence has been collected to connect a particular person with the crime to justify arrest, there is generally enough evidence to justify conviction. Contraband does not change its testimony out of love or pity. The act itself communicates its intention much better than does, say, the act of killing someone. The establishment of legal and moral responsibility is therefore not so difficult, and most arrests result in convictions.

These are crimes, then, where both arrest and preparation of evidence are generally the job of specialized investigative police. These police must be highly trained in scientific analysis of physical evidence, must have contacts in the underworld for information, and may find a period of questioning arrested people "under pressure" very useful. Although relatively few arrests are made, generally on the basis of carefully collected evidence and therefore on a warrant, a large share of these result in conviction. These are the crimes, and not the murders that figure so heavily in detective stories, which produce the ideal typical pattern of "detective" activity. A latent consequence of this type of crime is the "third degree."

Disorder and Nuisance in Public Places

The regulation of public places is the central responsibility of patrol police. We may distinguish three main types of public disorder: individual, collective, and structural. Perhaps the ideal type of individual disorder is "drunk and disorderly." By "collective disorder" I refer primarily to riot, parades that get out of hand, and other types of collective behavior, though in unusual circumstances private military groups may create collective disorder. By "structural disorder" I refer especially to the modern phenomenon of the traffic jam. No crowd or individual "wills" a traffic jam.

1. Individual disorder in public places consists mainly of doing things that would be entirely legitimate if done in private, such as getting too drunk to stand up, or sleeping on park benches. Other individual disorder, such as soliciting for prostitution or begging, may be illegal even if done in private, but is in fact relatively safe there.

This means first of all that there is a good deal of difference in the "commission" of these "crimes" according to the degree of access people have to private places. Homeless men are obviously more likely to commit the crime of vagrancy, which is the crime of being a homeless man. And if they get drunk, homeless men are more likely to have to sleep it off in the street. Since there is a rough correlation between social class and access to private places (particularly *enough* private places to cover most of one's social life), individual public disorder is related to social class even if the behavior of all classes is the same.

The fact that the "commission" of individual disorder is an index of the lack of connection to small social systems results in a main characteristic of these offenders, that they have not the will, the money, the friends, or the reputation to make good use of their legal right to defend themselves. For will depends on social support of intimates; money for defense often comes from the collective resources (or credit) of a small system; friends are products of intimate interaction; and reputation is generally dependent on a guaranty of good behavior by a small system. Those whose ties to small systems are weak are at a disadvantage in all these ways. Hearings before a police-court magistrate in these cases are generally purely formalities; it is assumed by all concerned, including the defendant, that the presumed offender is guilty. The only question that remains to be decided is how much *noblesse oblige* the magistrate should show. As Table 1 shows, the conviction rates for these crimes are quite high, and this is not the result of the sterling qualities of the evidence.

The information on which arrest is based is generally collected entirely by the patrolman, and he has a relatively wide degree of discretion about whether behavior constitutes "disorder." Arrests are almost entirely without a warrant. The fact that police information rather than complaint starts the proceedings means that there are no "crimes known to the police" that have not been solved. The FBI has the good sense not to try to report how many people were drunk or disorderly on the streets of the nation during the year. Investigative police are hardly ever involved.

In summary, the substitution of police for small bounded social systems in the government of the streets produces discretionary power in the hands of the police, particularly over population groups that are unlikely to defend themselves vigorously and effectively in court. The arrest is rarely justified to a judicial officer before it takes place, nor afterward except by the word of the policeman. When conviction does not follow an arrest, it is generally due to *noblesse oblige* rather than to defense by the presumed offender.

2. Collective public disturbances are quite often the immediate stimulus to the formation of quasi-military uniformed police forces. The London Metropolitan Police were partly an answer to the impending Chartist agitation; many state police forces in the United States were originally designed as a more controllable and delicately adjusted mechanism than the National Guard for dealing with industrial disturbances. Since police forces are almost always in a minority in a riot, their military organization is essential in this field.

Collective public disturbances by their nature involve questions of political legitimacy, the channels of political expression, the nature and role of the military, and other very complex topics. These are beyond the scope of this paper. Briefly, however, police are appropriate tools only for temporary control of acting crowds and are rarely competent to defeat an organized military effort by a social movement (unless they have much more military organization than American police do, as the Spanish

Guardia Civil), and rarely have much to do with the basically political process of channeling the discontent that results in riot. Their competence does extend to expressive crowds that get out of hand, but, as the reams of material on the collective disturbances surrounding the House Un-American Activities Committee hearings in San Francisco in the spring of 1960 show, the ultimate questions are not police questions.

3. Structural disorder in public places, as opposed to collective disorder, arises from the disorderly effects of individual "innocent" actions. A traffic jam or a smog problem is at most attributable to "negligence" of individuals, that is, to *their* not taking account of the structural effects of their actions. More often, the traffic jam could not have been avoided by people as individuals, even if they tried. Traffic control then consists in the regulation of otherwise innocent action that would have unfortunate consequences if not regulated.

Since the "offenses" do not offend the moral sensibilities of the population, being convicted is not much of a defamation. There are few reasons to protest innocence except to avoid the penalty, but the penalty for "minor" infractions cannot be very great. Though generally preserved in fiction, the whole adversary procedure is generally dispensed with, and all the complicated changes of status of due process are done away with. Patrolmen have factual discretionary power to levy penalties for traffic infractions. The police here play the peculiar role of administrators of the anonymous masses, rather than the role of detectors and punishers of crime.

DETERMINATION OF DIVISION OF LABOR IN POLICE PRACTICE

We may briefly group these socially determined activities into the functional divisions they normally have in police departments:

1. Traffic patrol and other patrol of structural disorder, which enforce regulations not involving moral turpitude of those who break the law. Typically due process of law is irrelevant to the processing of offenders, arrests are uncommon, and when made are made without a warrant. Enforcement does not involve the invasion of private places.

2. Street patrol (including radio cars), especially in downtown areas, to control individual offenses in public places and to be quickly available in cases of coercion within small social systems. The offenses generally involve some degree of moral disapproval, but the friendlessness and lack of resources of the defendants largely eliminates due process of law. Information is obtained primarily by the patrolman's observation, on which both arrest and conviction are based. Arrests are generally without a warrant.

3. Investigative work, generally involving complaint from a small social system, which has to be turned into acceptable evidence of crime. The

crimes may be against people within these small systems, in which case arrest is easy (often done by patrolmen) but conviction difficult. Or it may involve the invasion of private places by criminals, in which case arrest is difficult but conviction is easy. Most arrests made on warrants and with focus on due process derive from this area. But these kinds of offenses create pressures toward the "third degree," toward illegal search and seizure. It is police activity in this area that makes the police force a heroic and newsworthy enterprise, rather than merely a technical device for administering the streets of a city. And much police ideology about "hardened criminals" derives from work in this area. Many of the differences between federal police and local police, generally attributed to the federal agents' greater competence or the greater control by federal courts (e.g., the fact that federal police generally arrest on a warrant), are attributable instead to their work being almost entirely investigative.

4. Undercover work, in which fraud is used to get inside social systems otherwise protected by the institutions of privacy. Subversion and illegitimate business are the main offenses dealt with.

5. Quasi-military action, in which the problem is to apply coercion to control the public riot of some social movement. There quite often are few arrests. Perhaps most of the military trappings of police departments derive from their historical origin in the control of rioting.

CONCLUSIONS

The argument of this paper is that differences in police practice with respect to different types of crime are closely related to the social location of these types of crime vis-à-vis the institutions of privacy. We would be on more solid ground if direct classifications of crimes of one type (such as murder) were made by social location, rather than depending on the known correlation of murder with private places. Then we could determine whether murders that took place between mutually anonymous people showed a systematically different administrative pattern than murders among kin, eliminating the possibility that other features of murder explain the differences in administration noted. Or people arrested for a crime could be systematically classified by the solidity of their connection to small social structures, to see how much of the variation in the operation of due process of law in criminal matters really derives from differences in the strength of the social ties of the offender.

Second, the indexes of differences between administrative practices for different types of crime used here are extraordinarily crude. While this may convince us that there must have been a strong difference in reality to create a difference in such crude measures, and hence indicate that further research is worthwhile, many of the more interesting hypothesized relations cannot be tested by these data. For instance, the proportion of witnesses changing their testimony or refusing to testify further for different types of crime (either the crude types we have used here, or refined social-location types as suggested above) could be computed, to see whether this indeed explains any of the variation between the conviction rates of murder and burglary. Likewise, the proportion of times the compainant named a suspected offender, the length of time between complaint and arrest, the official status of the officer making an arrest, the proportions of arrests where a warrant was previously obtained, the number of entries into private places by police officers in the course of enforcement, and so on, could be precisely computed.

From knowledge of the characteristic social location of different types of crime, we can make predictions about the structural changes that are likely to take place in a subsection of a police department when a new crime is added to its responsibility. If the crime has a fundamentally different social location than the crimes that have traditionally been the responsibility of the subsection, then we would predict that new specialized roles will be developed in the subsection to deal with the new crime. On the other hand, if the new crime is fundamentally similar in social location to the crimes previously dealt with, responsibility for it will probably be added to the role obligations of old roles. For instance, if the control of the narcotics trade (an illegitimate business) is newly added to a police subsection which has previously dealt with burglary, murder, and other crimes of a different kind, we would predict that narcotics law enforcement will quite quickly become the responsibility of specially designated officers. If a newly serious narcotics problem is made the responsibility of a police subsection that already handles illegitimate businesses, such as a vice squad, we would expect much less pressure toward specialization. Any actual study would have to take account of other forces that help determine the degree of specialization, such as the size of police departments. Both the establishment of such a phenomenon and an exploration of the dynamics of role differentiation under these circumstances would increase our knowledge of the causes of the division of labor in organizations.

As for the general problem of studying the causal relations between rare events and frequent events, which is in some ways the foundation of the problem of studying authority, we have less to say. It is commonly alleged in police circles that Supreme Court cases on admissible evidence (e.g., whether evidence will be admitted that is collected in an "unreasonably long" period between arrest and appearance before a magistrate) will have a large effect on the efficiency of police practice. I am less hopeful. It seems that with our present research technology, the connection between such rare events and the frequent events on which we can collect statistics must remain a qualitative step in the research process. The definition of private and public places in the law and its application to the situations in which different types of crime are committed is an example of such a qualitative step in this paper. Presumably there is a long chain of events on a large scale, structuring rewards and constraints in police practice, and structuring criminal behavior of different types with respect to the norms established and continually enforced in a few court cases. This chain of events should, in theory, be amenable to study. But it is often a matter of historical time and of rather subtle readjustments of other rare events (such as promotions of policemen) to the new situation, so that in practice such studies are extremely difficult to carry out. It seems to me that if sociology is to enter in a systematic way into the empirical study of the sociology of law, the technique of combining qualitative judgments of which norms apply to which behavior, with statistical study of that behavior, is going to need substantial development. I hope that the strong relations among variables derived in this qualitative way, found in Table 1, help to provide motivation for more attention to this problem.

28. INTERROGATION AND THE CRIMINAL PROCESS

Albert J. Reiss, Jr., and Donald J. Black

The legal system in American society is a loosely articulated set of sub-systems. Where the criminal law is concerned, the subsystems are law enforcement, the public prosecutor, legal counsel, the judiciary, and corrections. The legitimacy and administrative responsibility for any of them may derive from different government jurisdictions, giving rise to problems of mutual cooptation and control. Nowhere within the legal system is there formal provision for organizational subordination of one subsystem to the other so that decisions in any one subsystem can be directly and effectively enforced in others by administrative or other organizational sanctions. The law itself, rather than organizational implementation, generally governs such relationships.

Though each subsystem is highly dependent upon the others and they are hierarchically organized so that the outputs of one become the inputs of another, each is more highly integrated around its focal orientation than around an orientation that is common to the legal system. This paper focuses on conflict over legitimacy of means that arises between the police in the law-enforcement system and the appellate courts in the judicial system. It examines a current controversy over the legality of means of interro-

Reprinted by permission of the authors and the publisher from *The Annals of the American Academy of Political and Social Science*, 374 (November 1967): 47–57.

gation. The conduct of interrogation by the police has received much attention since the *Escobedo* and *Miranda* decisions of the United States Supreme Court.[1]

All subsystems within the legal system may be regarded in organizational terms as primarily information- and people-processing systems. The law-enforcement system is the major originating point for both people and information about them as they are processed in the legal system. Given the loose articulation of units in the system and their divergent ends, conflict arises as to the means which each organization may use to achieve its immediate organizational ends vis-à-vis those of the legal system qua legal system.

PROCEDURAL CONFLICT IN THE LEGAL SYSTEM

Conflict between the judicial and the law-enforcement subsystems is, in a broad sense, endemic in the legal system, particularly conflict between the appellate courts and the police. The judicial system, especially its higher courts, is organized to articulate a moral order—a system of values and norms—rather than an order of behavior in public and private places. By contrast, the police are organized to articulate a behavior system—to maintain law and order. Theirs is a system of organizational control. Nowhere is this more apparent than in their processing of people and information.

Indeed, the justices of our highest courts and the police officer on patrol represent almost opposite poles in their processing of people and information. The officer in routine patrol is principally oriented toward maintenance of behavior systems and is least likely to interpret the law as he exercises discretion in making decisions. By contrast, a justice of the Supreme Court is least likely to see organizational and behavioral consequences of his decisions and most likely to interpret the law in terms of a moral order.

The police organization bears the major responsibility for implicating persons in the criminal legal system and for gathering information that the public prosecutor may effectively process in the courts. While the information for a case that may be prosecuted effectively in the courts is governed by rules of evidence and procedure, the organizational emphasis of the police is upon generating information that links a person with a criminal event or helps to maintain public order. The appellate courts, however, control the criteria for admissibility of evidence, including the legitimacy (legality) of the means for securing it. Their criteria are established by the moral system of the law rather than in terms of organizational criteria of effective enforcement of the law.

To be sure, the appellate courts are enmeshed in the balancing of inter-

---

[1] *Escobedo* v. *Illinois*, 378 U.S. 478 (1964); *Miranda* v. *Arizona*, 384 U.S. 436 (1966).

ests and in the pursuit of such abstract ends as the protection of society and the maintenance of justice. Both ends and interests, however, get defined in terms of a moral order. Where judicial interpretation is concerned, the courts may respond to behavioral and organizational changes, but within the confines of articulating a moral order that is the law. Where law enforcement is concerned, the police may respond to behavioral and organizational changes, but within the confines of organizational control of behavior.

There is an important sense in which the relevance of information to law enforcement differs from its relevance to the courts. Again, this arises from the variation in their functions within the legal system. For the police, the end of securing information is to increase their knowledge of crimes and the solution of crimes by the arrest of persons. Along with the public prosecutor, they have an investment in "making it stick," but their organizational concern is less for the legitimacy of means than for the rather immediate end of enforcing behavior standards. For the appellate courts, information is relevant to the body of the law; it is an issue of law rather than of organizational effectiveness.

Despite a spate of scientific criminology for developing laboratory evidence by police organizations and despite a spate of rules regarding such evidence, the core of information for both systems remains that secured and presented by oral statement. For the police, as for the courts, the oral interview is crucial in supplying information. Whether dignified by names such as interrogation or testimony, it is a structure of question and answer in social encounters, be it the private or public setting, the station house or courtroom, the office or chambers. Until recently, however, the procedures for eliciting such oral information, whether by the police, lawyers, or judicial officers, have received relatively little formal attention.

Admittedly, there is a considerable body of rules governing the admissibility of evidence in trial proceedings. Such rules generally relate to the conduct of matters *within* the immediate jurisdiction of the court, such as the admissibility of hearsay during the trial. Given the loose articulation of subsystems within the legal system and the absence of any formal central authority to enforce conformity across subsystems, the major means any subsystem has for controlling others in the legal system is through its own operating organization. For the police, control of other subsystems is exercised through the discretionary decision to arrest. For the courts, it is exercised through the control of the admissibility of evidence, particularly by means of the exclusionary rule. *Miranda* is a case in point.

When the court establishes criteria for admissibility, however, it does so within the context of a specific legal issue rather than in terms of a generic legal or organizational problem. Thus, *Miranda* does not come to terms with the general issue of the interview as a mode of gaining information, nor of the role of interrogation, for that matter. Rather, the decision states criteria for the admissibility of admissions or confessions, criteria that relate to the rights of persons with respect to self-incrimination.

Like the police, the behavioral scientist is oriented toward behavior in organizational systems. In designing behavioral research that has relevance to legal issues, not unlike the police he confronts problems of operationalizing legal concepts. This becomes apparent when one attempts to undertake research with respect to the legal issues relating to interrogation, particularly if one regards recent decisions as early cases in a potential series of decisions that may have relevance to information gained through questioning of suspects.

The *Miranda* v. *Arizona* decision of the United States Supreme Court makes it obligatory for police officers, *inter alia,* to apprise suspects of their constitutional rights before "in-custody interrogation" if the admission gained from the interrogation is to be admissible as evidence. It is far from clear when an "in-custody" situation legally begins, when questioning becomes interrogation, or when information becomes an admission. Furthermore, from an organizational point of view, the limiting of police practices by controlling admissibility of evidence secured through "in-custody interrogation" within an interrogation room of a station house logically opens the way to greater use of interrogation in field settings. Moreover, for the behavioral scientist, there is a general question of the kinds of information available for processing in the system apart from interrogation. Would the elimination of all questioning within in-custody situations eliminate a major source of information? These are difficult matters for operationalization if they are to have relevance to questions at issue in the legal system.

This paper reports selected findings pertaining to interrogations in encounters between police officers and suspects in patrol settings. For purposes of the field study, an interrogation was defined operationally as any questioning of a probing nature that went beyond mere identification of the person and that led to defining the person as a suspect or offender. The field patrol officer, unlike the detective or officer who interrogates in the now stereotyped setting of the interrogation room at the station, must use an interview or questioning to define the situation and the participants in it. Both the assertion of some authority and the development of facts are essential elements in such a process.[2]

Furthermore, in field patrol work, the officer usually encounters suspects in the situation where an event is presumed to have occurred and generally at a point relatively immediate to the event itself. By way of contrast, the detective usually encounters a suspect at a time and place removed from the occurrence of the event—either at the station where the suspect has been brought for questioning or in a public or private place where he

---

[2] David J. Bordua and Albert J. Reiss, Jr., "Sociology in Law Enforcement," in *Uses of Sociology,* ed. Paul F. Lazarsfeld, William Sewell, and Harold Wilensky (New York: Basic Books, 1967).

seeks information from the suspected person. Interrogation or questioning thus may play a somewhat different role for the two types of officers. Yet
in both cases, a central question is how much is gained by questioning or
admission that would aid in conviction over and above that already gained
from other sources of evidence. If there is a witness to a criminal event
prior to questioning of the arrested person by detectives at the station,
what is added through interrogation?

THE OBSERVATION STUDY

The data for this paper were gathered through direct observation by thirty-
six observers in high-crime-rate police precincts of Boston, Chicago, and
Washington, D.C., during the summer of 1966.[3] It should be emphasized
that the information pertains only to questioning of suspects by uniformed
police officers in encounters of field patrol. To the degree that *Miranda* is
strictly interpreted as applying to in-custody interrogations in a station
house, the data are not immediately relevant to the frontal issue raised in
that decision; rather, they relate more to questions concerning the extension of the *Miranda* rule to field settings.[4]

Patrolmen are the first police to enter most crime situations and hence
the first to have contact with any suspects available in the immediate setting. Typically, the police are mobilized to handle incidents in one of two
major ways. The great majority of incidents handled by patrolmen arise
subsequent to a citizen complaint by telephone followed by a "dispatch"
to the patrol car. The second major way in which the police become involved in incidents is through "on-view" work—police intervention in a
field situation that occurs at the officer's discretion rather than in response to a radioed command. The "stop-and-frisk" is an example of an
on-view incident. The two types of mobilization carry with them differential opportunities for discretionary action and differential limiting conditions on how the officer exercises his discretion.

Moreover, the way the police are mobilized to deal with incidents affects
the kind of evidence they secure, and hence the relative importance of ques-

---

[3] See Donald J. Black and Albert J. Reiss, Jr., "Patterns of Behavior in Police and Citizen Transactions," in *Studies in Crime and Law Enforcement in Major Metropolitan
Areas*, ed. Albert J. Reiss, Jr., U.S. President's Commission on Law Enforcement and Administration of Justice Field Survey III (Washington, D.C.: U.S. Government Printing
Office, 1967).

[4] *State* v. *Intogna*, 419 P. 2d 59 (Arizona, 1966). The court explained "custodial interrogation" to mean questioning when a person "has been taken into custody or otherwise
deprived of his freedom in any significant way." This definition was then applied to an
interrogation that occurred in a field setting, with the conclusion that "a defendant questioned by an officer with a drawn gun within three feet of him was deprived of his freedom in a significant way." This case was tried before *Miranda*, but the court followed the
interpretation of *Escobedo* given in *Miranda* to rule on the admissibility of the defendant's admission. *Intogna*, then, represents an early extension of *Miranda* to field settings.

tioning of suspects. The police must link evidence to crimes *and* to violators. Specifically, they must demonstrate that a criminal or other violation has occurred (evidence of a crime) and that a particular person is liable for it (evidence of guilt). Broadly speaking, there are two major kinds of evidence that can be offered in each case—oral and physical. Most oral testimony is by way of witnessing an event or acknowledging participation in it.

Evidence of guilt is differentially available depending upon the type of mobilization in field settings. In on-view encounters with suspects, the major evidence of guilt lies in the testimony of the officer as complainant and witness. Physical evidence such as a weapon in the suspect's possession, stolen property, and the like usually depends as well upon the officer's testimony that it was found in the crime setting or on the suspect. Questioning of the suspect and an admission from him may add little to what is available from the officer in on-view encounters.

Evidence of guilt in dispatched encounters of the police with suspects usually rests upon the testimony of others who are witnesses to the event. This arises from the simple fact that the officer usually arrives after the offense has occurred. Even when there is some physical evidence lending weight to the belief that a crime has occurred, the officer has to rely on testimonial evidence as to who is suspect. Without a sworn complaint in such situations, "probable cause" may not be satisfied. Questioning of suspects and admission thus may loom large as factors in whether or not an officer arrests in dispatched situations, particularly when conflicting statements are made by complainants and suspects. The role that questioning plays in police work then may depend to a great extent on how the officer enters a situation and on what kind of oral testimony is available to him.

CHARACTERISTICS OF FIELD INTERROGATIONS

Patrolmen conduct interrogations in only about one-third of their encounters with suspects. The proportion is roughly the same in dispatched situations and on-view situations. The frequency with which patrol officers interrogate is greater than that with which they conduct personal and property searches, as only one-fifth of the police-suspect transactions included a search. However, in almost one-third of the encounters where an interrogation took place, a search of person, property, or both also was conducted.

One characteristic of field interrogations distinguishing them from those conducted in an interrogation room at a police station is that, not uncommonly, more than one suspect is questioned at the same time. In over one-third of the interrogations observed, two or more persons were questioned, and in about one-fifth, three or more were questioned. That the field interrogation is so often a confrontation between group and group places it somewhat at odds with popular stereotypes of the interrogation as an encounter between one or more officers and a lone suspect. In the absence of other patrol units to lend assistance, the classic technique of separating suspects for interrogation is often unavailable to officers in a field setting. The support and surveillance given by his fellows may well mitigate some of the suspect's vulnerability in such field confrontations.

Most field interrogations—about three-fourths—took place only in a field setting, usually on the street or in a private place such as a dwelling. Nine in ten included interrogation at the field setting, some also involving questioning during transportation to the police station itself. Less than 5 percent of the suspects were interrogated only at the station.

Not only did most occur far from an interrogation room, but a substantial majority involved temporary field detention before the suspect was either formally arrested or released. About one-half of the suspects were detained for less than ten minutes and three-fourths for less than twenty minutes. Nearly all of these persons were released in the field setting. Over nine-tenths of the suspects were detained less than forty minutes; nevertheless, about 5 percent were detained an hour or more before the police made a decision to book or release.

There was a good deal of variety in the content of the questions asked. Field interrogations often have more to do with ascertaining whether or not someone *might* be criminally liable than with extracting a self-incriminating statement from a person already suspected. Mere information-gathering aimed at structuring the facts in the situation is perhaps the major concern of a patrolman entering a possible crime situation. Detectives, by contrast, ordinarily begin their investigation after the preliminary structuring of the situation by patrol officers. Consequently, about three-fourths of the interrogations had as a manifest aim something other than obtaining an oral admission of guilt from the suspect. The questions frequently concerned such matters as what specifically occurred; the discrepancies in the versions of the parties involved; whether or not, indeed, the alleged incident occurred at all; and the like. This is not to say, however, that such seemingly innocuous probes rarely elicit admissions or incriminating statements. It is during this process that suspects quite often make admissions voluntarily.

INTERROGATION OF ADULT SUSPECTS

There were 248 encounters in which an adult suspect was interrogated in a field setting by the police. The type of evidence available to the officer on guilt of the suspect is clearly a function of how the officer entered the setting. Of the 248 encounters where an adult suspect was questioned, 116 (47 percent) eventuated in an arrest; exactly one-fourth of the arrests were made in on-view settings. In 93 percent of the on-view arrests, as contrasted with 42 percent of the dispatched arrests, the officer would have been able to offer some testimony that a crime event took place in his presence or that he had both evidence and observation that the suspect was definitely linked to the crime, for example, the suspect had a stolen car in his possession. The differences are even greater considering the fact that in 66 percent of all on-view arrests, as compared with 24 percent of all dispatched arrests, the *only* evidence available was the on-view testimony of the officer that the offense occurred in his presence.

Considering the interrogation situation where the officer did not make an arrest, a similar pattern with sharper contrast prevails. For 94 percent of the on-view encounters, the only evidence available to the officer that the suspect committed the crime would have been his own testimony, while that was true for only 11 percent of all dispatched situations. Put another way, in dispatched encounters, the officer more often must rely upon evidence from others to satisfy the criteria of a legal arrest. Indeed, considering the arrests for Part I offenses, when the officer was dispatched he had to rely upon other evidence in twenty-two of twenty-nine arrests that were booked, whereas the officer witnessed the three Part I on-view offenses where there was an arrest and booking.

While officers need to rely on other evidence less often in Part II offenses that are booked, the same pattern is evident. Of forty-two dispatched Part II offenses booked, fifteen had to be made solely on other evidence, while for only one of the twenty-three on-view bookings did the officer have to rely upon other evidence.

Clearly, too, an officer is much less likely to make an on-view arrest for a felony than for a misdemeanor. But three of the thirty-two bookings for Part I offenses were on-view, whereas twenty-three of the sixty-five Part II bookings were on-views. This difference undoubtedly arises from the fact that felonies typically occur in private, as contrasted with public places; hence felonies in progress are not generally visible to the officer on patrol. The police usually are mobilized to a felony situation by a complainant. Here is a case where the law of arrest complements the empirical pattern of the organization of crime. In felony situations, the law requires only "reasonable grounds" or "probable cause" before a legal arrest is made, whereas in misdemeanor situations there generally is the "in-presence" or "warrant" requirement for an arrest to be made.

THE PRODUCTIVITY OF FIELD INTERROGATIONS

Recall that a rather broad definition of interrogation was used in the field observation study such that it was considered an interrogation when the officer was directing his questioning toward identifying elements of the crime and assurances that it constituted a bona fide arrest situation. Often he may not have been attempting to elicit a self-incriminating statement as an admission of guilt or a confession *per se*. The officer interrogated in 31 percent of the 801 nontraffic encounters with adult suspects. That interrogation was not integral to making a field arrest and booking is apparent from the fact that in 54 percent of the 198 Part I and Part II bookings of adults there was no interrogation. Correlatively, the officer interrogated in 25 percent of the 603 nontraffic encounters with adult suspects where he did not eventually book a suspect. Indeed, only 39 percent of all 248 interrogations for Part I and Part II offenses led to a booking.

On the whole, the kind of interrogation that the officer conducts in field settings is relatively unproductive of admissions. Of the 116 *arrests* (including suspects never booked) that included interrogation by officers, 91 (78 percent) did not eventuate in admission. Of the 132 encounters where persons were interrogated and not arrested, 121 (92 percent) did not involve an admission. About 86 percent of all encounters involving interrogation did not result in an admission. This is substantially below the figure reported for in-station interrogations, where about 50 percent of all interrogated suspects are reported to make an admission.[5]

Considering only Part I crimes classified as felonies, the situation is not substantially different. Among adult suspects interrogated, there were twenty-seven arrests for felonies and seventeen felonies where there was no arrest. Somewhat more than 80 percent of the encounters with felons did not result in an admission when interrogation took place. Since 78 percent of all interrogations of arrested persons did not lead to an admission, there is almost no difference in admissions among arrested persons depending upon the seriousness of the criminal charge. In encounters with nonarrested persons, however, a somewhat greater percent of encounters with nonarrested felons (15 percent) than of *all* encounters with nonarrested persons (8 percent) resulted in an admission. In any case, admission on interrogation in field settings did not make suspects substantially more liable to arrest.

The kind of interrogation conducted in field settings seems remarkably unproductive of admissions of guilt. Of all admissions in field situations, more were made voluntarily prior to questioning than were made after questioning. Among encounters with arrested persons, there were 25 admissions out of 116 interrogations; 68 percent of these were voluntary admissions before questioning, and the questioning served only to provide the officer with additional information or evidence. Among those not ar-

---

[5] A study by the Georgetown University Law Center's Institute of Criminal Law and Procedure found that of the defendants questioned by the police, 34 percent were interrogated only at the time and place of arrest, 35 percent at the police precinct, and 25 percent at both places. Of the suspects interrogated, 45 percent were reported by their attorneys to have given statements. See "Miranda Impact," Georgetown University News Service, July 9, 1967.

rested, there were only 11 admissions in 132 interrogations. Of these, 45 percent were voluntary. Assuming that *Miranda* admits of voluntary confessions under nearly all circumstances, questioning in field settings is at least modestly productive of admissions that clearly would be allowed as evidence in court.[6]

A surprising fact is that admissions after questioning are less productive of arrest than are voluntary admissions in field settings. Of the twenty-two voluntary admissions before interrogation, 77 percent eventuated in arrest; of the fourteen admissions after questioning, 57 percent resulted in arrest.

Among the fifty-eight encounters with suspected felons, six resulted in voluntary admissions and three included admissions after questioning. Five of the six, including voluntary admissions, led to an arrest, compared with one of the three admissions after questioning. Though the numbers are so small as to render the comparison of doubtful value, voluntary admission seems more linked to arrest than does admission following interrogation.

INTERROGATIONS AND EVIDENCE

It is difficult to determine how important interrogation is in producing evidence that eventuates in conviction. Given the fact that evidence is evaluated at each step of a criminal proceeding and not all of it enters the trial proceeding or judicial determination, there is no *a priori* way of assessing outcomes validly on the basis of evidence. Indeed, given the high proportion of pleas of guilt entered by the defendant, the role of evidence itself is moot in many proceedings. These and other factors make it difficult to determine how important interrogation is in a pattern of evidence.

Nonetheless, certain questions can be asked of the data that are relevant to the general problem of the role of interrogation in a pattern of evidence. One such question concerns how often an admission would be the only form of evidence available. Each interrogation involving a suspect was examined to determine what evidence was available to the patrol officer making the investigation. While detailed information was available on the kind of evidence, a simple distinction was made as to whether the evidence was available to the officer by dint of his personal observation of the alleged offense or through acquisition of physical evidence or testimony by others. In some situations, of course, both, or even all three kinds, were available to the officer.

The striking pattern is that of the fifty felonies committed by adults who

---

[6] During the observation period, the *Miranda* warning rarely was given to suspects in field settings. A citizen was apprised of at least one of the rights specified in the *Miranda* decision in 3 percent of the police encounters with suspects. In only three cases were all four rights mentioned in *Miranda* used in the warning. Even when suspects were apprised of their rights, there is no evidence that they were less likely to make admissions. See Black and Reiss, *op. cit.*, pp. 102–109.

were subsequently interrogated, there were only three instances where the officer needed to rely upon interrogation to secure evidence. None of these three cases involved an arrest, however. Further, the three interrogations where there was no evidence failed to yield admissions. All admissions therefore were made when there was other evidence or officer testimony as to occurrence of the event and the implication of the suspect. This suggests that people admit or confess when they are aware that "the evidence is against them."

In three of the thirty felonies where there was an arrest and booking, the officer's only evidence was his own observation. For six of the bookings, the offense was observed by the officer and there also was other evidence; in twenty-one bookings his case rested upon witnesses or other evidence. In those eight arrests for felonies where the suspect was released without booking, all involved reliance upon other evidence, including witnesses or complaints. Generally, these are situations in which the complainant refuses to sign a complaint that could lead to effective prosecution of the felony. *For every felony arrest, then, whether the suspect was booked or not, the officer would not have needed to interrogate to offer evidence in support of the arrest.* While it could be argued that, for the eight felony suspects released without booking, an admission could have substituted for the failure of the complainant to sign a complaint, none of these suspects made an admission to the officer.

For the twenty felony situations where no arrest was made, the officer could have relied on his own testimony in two cases and evidence from others in fifteen cases. In only three cases was he left essentially without evidence in the field setting, and in each of these the interrogation failed to yield an admission.

It should be clear, then, that in the large majority of cases where an officer interrogates in a field setting following an allegation about a felony, he does have some basis for proceeding, apart from any admission from the suspect, whether or not he actually makes an arrest.

CONCLUSION

The relative absence of formal provision for the resolution of conflict in the American legal system results in each organization's controlling others in the system through constraints on the processing of people and information as inputs to their own organization. This paper has focused on the specific case where the courts attempt to control the behavior of law-enforcement officers through the exclusionary rule, particularly as set forth in the *Miranda* decision. The data presented relate to arrest and interrogation of suspects in field patrol settings, situations to which *Miranda* potentially may be extended. Furthermore, the data from field settings are of relevance in that they relate to the question of how necessary in-custody interrogation is, given prior processing of suspects in the field patrol setting.

Unfortunately, no study has been undertaken that views suspects in process from the field setting where arrest takes place through processing in custody, public prosecution, and trial proceedings. In the absence of such general processing studies, the relevance of data on interrogations in field settings for legal issues is debatable. Nonetheless, a few observations are offered, addressed to the specific issues of whether the liability of suspects to criminal charges is substantially reduced by *Miranda* warnings and whether the rate of arrest, in turn, would be substantially affected by their introduction into field settings.

The data for this paper on interrogations of suspects in field patrol settings show that arresting officers always had evidence apart from the interrogation itself as a basis for arrest. Indeed, voluntary admissions were substantially more frequent than were admissions following interrogation. For the most part, however, interrogation was unproductive of admissions in the field setting. It would appear, then, that the introduction of *Miranda*-type warnings into field settings would have relatively little effect on the liability of suspects to criminal charges, particularly in felony cases —assuming current police behavior with respect to arrest.

Nonetheless, it is difficult to define the point at which *Miranda*-type warnings should be given in field settings. Quite clearly, the officer in field patrol must process information by questioning in field settings in order to define the situation and the roles of participants in it. At the very least, he must often use questioning to define the roles of complainant and suspected offender. Conceivably, the introduction of such warnings very early in the process of contact with citizens could affect the liability of suspects to criminal charges adversely from the perspective of the legal system.

The extension of warnings against self-incrimination to field settings is presumed to affect the rate of arrest adversely. The general profile of police work that emerges from this investigation, however, suggests that this argument is less forceful than many presume. The extent to which patrolmen exercise their discretion not to invoke the criminal process—even in felony situations—when there is adequate evidence for an arrest raises a serious question of whether this effect of the discretionary decision on liability for criminal charges is not greater than any potential effect of *Miranda* warnings.

The extent to which the police exercise discretion to arrest bears on the issue of the consequences of procedural restrictions in two ways. First, it makes clear the fact that the volume of cases which police generate as inputs for the prosecutor and the courts is far from a maximum, given contemporary police practice. Second, their practices throw into relief the degree to which the law-enforcement system deviates from a prosecution-oriented model to a community-oriented or behavioral-system-oriented model of "justice." The release of offenders at police discretion, for whatever reason, renders ineffective any control system based on limitation of their outputs as inputs, as is the case with the exclusionary rule.

A great deal of the conflict between the police and the courts over interrogation procedures may have less impact on the police system than is generally believed. Nevertheless, within the police system, its consequences may be greater for detectives than for routine patrol officers. This difference in consequences may be directly related to the greater organizational distance from criminal violators at which detectives do investigative work. In-station interrogation, unlike routine patrol interrogation, is more prosecution-oriented; hence, existing procedural restrictions on interrogation may be more consequential than would be an extension of those restrictions.

29. PUBLIC ATTITUDES TOWARD CRIME AND LAW ENFORCEMENT

Jennie McIntyre

Public concern about crime is neither new nor surprising. An interest which was once manifested in attendance at the public punishment of offenders is now expressed in reaction to the news media's reports of crime and criminals in the local community, the nation, and farther afield.[1] Especially since the growth of the mass news media, there have been, from time to time, surges of public alarm concerning current crime waves. A legal scholar who recently reviewed the literature of the last fifty years noted that in each and every decade, there were prominent articles about the need for strong measures to meet the then-current crisis in crime.[2] From time to time, there were commissions appointed or committees

Reprinted by permission of the author and the publisher from *The Annals of the American Academy of Political and Social Science*, 374 (November 1967): 34–46.

In addition to sources cited herein, the writer has drawn upon the following: unpublished consultant papers prepared by Albert D. Biderman for the National Crime Commission, a search of its archives by the Roper Public Opinion Center, and assistance of Albert H. Cantril in searching recent attitude surveys.

[1] For discussions of shifting interpretations of crime as well as the functions of public interest, see Leon Radzinowicz, *Ideology and Crime* (New York: Columbia University Press, 1966); and Kai T. Erikson, "Notes on the Sociology of Deviance," *Social Problems*, 9 (Spring 1962): 307–14.

[2] Yale Kamisar, "When the Cops Were Not 'Handcuffed,'" *New York Times Magazine*, November 7, 1965.

formed to investigate what was seen as intolerable increases in crime. It may be that there has always been a crime crisis.

Sometimes these crime waves have been synthetic, manufactured by journalists. Lincoln Steffens, for example, describes his own creation of a crime wave accomplished by giving headline treatment to the ordinary occurrences of the day.[3] The intensity of the current concern regarding crime may be due in part, not to fabrication, but rather to the excellence of news coverage.

An entire nation reads of the fearful mass killing of eight nurses in Chicago and the apparently senseless shooting of thirteen passers-by on a Texas campus by a person not known to them. The unpredictable nature of such violence becomes the more fearful and immediate as citizens across the land view the scene and hear the tales of witnesses on television news programs. The public's perception of the incidence of crime as well as the intensity of its reaction may be influenced by the fact that it receives reports of violent crime drawn from a larger pool of crime-incident reports than ever before.

Nationally oriented communications media tend to draw attention to crime as a national problem. Other conditions, too, encourage the perception of a national crime wave rather than the local phenomenon portrayed by Steffens. The crimes which draw the most attention are urban occurrences. While the primarily rural population of an earlier day could view crime as a characteristic of remote and not quite moral cities, the primarily urban population of today perceives urban crime as more directly threatening. In spite of perennial concern, there is some reason to believe that public concern about crime as a national problem is at an unprecedented level.

An understanding of the attitudes of the public regarding crime, the level of concern, the manner in which this concern affects the lives of people, the beliefs regarding the causes of crime, and the appropriate methods of coping with the problem is for some purposes of as much consequence as an understanding of the nature and extent of crime itself. For the public attitudes on these issues to some extent determine the feasibility of alternative methods of crime prevention and law enforcement. The National Crime Commission in 1966 undertook to assess these attitudes through an analysis of national public opinion polls and surveys conducted for the Commission. . . .

HEIGHTENED CONCERN ABOUT CRIME

The national public opinion polls in recent years provide some evidence of

_____

[3] Lincoln Steffens, *The Autobiography of Lincoln Steffens* (New York: Harcourt, Brace, 1931), pp. 285–91.

the heightened concern about crime.[4] Until recently, crime was given only peripheral attention by national pollsters. When completely open-ended questions were asked by a Gallup poll about the problems facing the nation, international problems invariably topped the lists; until recently, crime was not mentioned by enough persons to appear on the list of top problems. In 1966, when the National Opinion Research Center (NORC) conducted a national survey for the Crime Commission, interviewers asked citizens to pick from a list of six major domestic problems the one to which they had been paying the most attention recently.[5] Crime was the second most frequently selected from this list; only race relations was picked by more persons. (Lower-income nonwhites placed more emphasis on education than crime.)

When local community problems are considered, juvenile delinquency takes on added significance. In 1963 Gallup asked a sample of adults to select the top problem facing their community from a list of thirty-nine. Juvenile delinquency was picked by more persons than almost any other problem; only local real estate taxes were named more frequently. The third most frequently named, the need for more recreational areas, was probably related to the concern with juvenile delinquency.

Whether more concerned about adult or juvenile crime, most people think that the crime situation in their own community is getting worse, and while substantial numbers think the situation is staying about the same, hardly anyone sees improvement. A Gallup survey in April 1965 showed that this pessimistic perception of the problem prevailed among men and women, well educated and less well educated, and among all age, regional, income, and city-size groupings. When citizens in Washington, D.C., were interviewed by the Bureau of Social Science Research (BSSR) the next year, 75 percent thought that crime had been getting worse in that city during the past year; 16 percent thought it was about the same.[6]

SOURCES OF ATTITUDES

For the large majority of people, attitudes about crime and crime trends apparently are derived largely from vicarious sources. Whether we judge

---

[4] Surveys by George Gallup, Director, American Institute of Public Opinion, Princeton, New Jersey, will be referred to as Gallup polls. Those by Louis Harris, public opinion analyst, will be cited as Harris surveys.

[5] Phillip Ennis, *Criminal Victimization in the United States: A Report of a National Survey*, President's Commission on Law Enforcement and Administration of Justice Field Survey II (Washington, D.C.: U.S. Government Printing Office, 1967); hereinafter referred to as the NORC study.

[6] Albert D. Biderman, Louise A. Johnson, Jennie McIntyre, and Adrianne W. Weir, *Report on a Pilot Study in the District of Columbia on Victimization and Attitudes Toward Law Enforcement*, President's Commission on Law Enforcement and Administration of Justice Field Survey I (Washington, D.C.: U.S. Government Printing Office, 1967); hereinafter referred to as the BSSR study.

volume from crimes known to the police or from the far more generous estimates from public surveys conducted for the Crime Commission, its incidence is not so great as to make personal victimization the major determinant of people's perceptions of the crime problem. This is manifestly true of crimes of violence, which, although relatively rare, are the focus of most people's fears. The experience of being robbed or assaulted might well have a most profound effect on the attitudes and habits of a victim, but such experiences are infrequent.

Even taking into consideration the more common, less serious offenses, most people are not victimized sufficiently often for these experiences to make a major impact on their lives. Neither are those offenses which do occur sufficiently important in people's lives to be remembered vividly for any length of time. These are among the conclusions derived from the intensive methodological work undertaken by the BSSR for the Commission. . . . It was necessary to devise and refine special interviewing techniques in order to facilitate recall of incidents of victimization, particularly those that had happened more than a short time prior to the interview. When people were asked about the worst thing that had happened to them that could be called a crime, few remembered anything that had not happened recently.

The seriousness of the incidents recounted to interviewers further suggests that the experiences of victimization are not remembered for any length of time by most people. If persons being interviewed remembered all criminal victimizations, they could be expected to recount numerous trivial incidents, the minor offenses, such as vandalism and bicycle theft, which occur most frequently. Such was not the case, and the seriousness of the incidents reported to interviewers was much the same as that of those reported to police. It appears that many minor incidents are simply brushed aside and forgotten. Even the more serious offenses, such as burglary, usually involved relatively small monetary loss. Inferentially, then, most incidents of victimization do not appear to constitute very important events in a person's life experience.

If the experience of victimization is not a major event in the lives of most people, it is understandable that this experience does not determine their attitudes regarding crime. The surveys conducted for the commission found little statistical relationship between the experience of victimization and attitudes toward most aspects of the crime problem. The BSSR applied an index of exposure to crime, which included victimization of self, victimization of friends, and having personally witnessed any offense.[7] Scores on this index did not correlate with responses to a variety of questions on attitudes toward crime and toward law enforcement. Nor was

---

[7] BSSR study, p. 126.

crime exposure related to anxiety about crime. Victims were neither more nor less likely to believe that crime was increasing or to express a sense of uneasiness about their personal safety. The one exception appeared in the case of the Negro male. Negro men who have been the victims of even one criminal incident were more apprehensive about their safety.[8]

The NORC study similarly found little relationship between the experience of victimization and concern about crime.[9] Those who had been victims did worry about the possibility of burglary and robbery somewhat more frequently than did the nonvictims. The difference between men and women was greater than that between victims and nonvictims, however; so that women who had been victimized more often worried than men who had. Victims and nonvictims were equally likely to have taken strong household security measures, however: 57 percent of victims and 58 percent of nonvictims had high scores on an index of precautionary behavior which included locking doors during the daytime and keeping a watchdog or weapons for protection.

Anxiety about crime was not a simple function of living in areas where crimes are frequent occurrences. The BSSR study in Washington, D.C., found that the average level of concern with crime in a predominantly Negro precinct that had one of the highest rates of crime in the city, according to police data, was lower than it was in another Negro precinct that had a lower crime rate.[10]

Perhaps the most direct evidence that people form their attitudes about crime on the basis of something other than experience can be found in their own statements. After respondents in Washington were asked for their estimate of an increase or decrease in crime in the city, they were asked where they had obtained their information on this subject. A preponderant majority said that they got their information either from the news media or from what they heard people say.

But if the actual experience of victimization is not a major determinant of attitudes about crime, there is another sense in which vulnerability does influence fear. In the survey in Washington, D.C., the BSSR constructed an index of anxiety about crime.[11] This index reflected a general concern for personal safety as well as the belief that crime is increasing. It found that Negro women had the highest average score, followed by Negro men, white women, and white men. The greater concern of Negroes is consistent with the risks of victimization suggested by police statistics. An analysis of police records in Chicago, for example, indicates that Negroes are far more likely to be the victims of a serious offense against the person than are white

---

[8] *Ibid.*, p. 127.
[9] NORC study.
[10] BSSR study, p. 125.
[11] *Ibid.*, p. 121.

persons.[12] The greater anxiety of women than men is not consistent with what is known of the victimization risks, however, and one would have to look for alternative explanations. Anxiety scores were lower at the higher income levels for both Negroes and whites.

CRIME WORSE ELSEWHERE

If most people do not base their attitudes on personal experience, neither do they rely on their understanding of the experiences of others in their immediate environs. While most people questioned thought that the situation is terrible and getting worse all the time, they nevertheless believed that they are relatively safe near their own homes. In the NORC study for the Commission, 60 percent of those questioned compared their own neighborhood favorably to other parts of the community in which they lived, with regard to the likelihood that their home would be broken into, while only 14 percent thought that their area presented a greater hazard.[13] This is true even in areas which are considered crime-ridden by the police—areas which might terrify many suburban dwellers. In the BSSR survey in Washington precincts with average to high crime rates, only one out of five respondents thought that the chances of being beaten were greater in his neighborhood than in other parts of the city.[14] Almost half of the national sample interviewed by NORC said that there was no place in their own city (or suburb or county) where they would not feel safe. Two-thirds of the respondents said that they feel safe walking alone when it is dark if they are in their own neighborhood.[15]

CENTRAL ROLE OF FEAR FOR THE PERSON

When citizens in Washington were asked what steps they had taken to protect themselves from crime, they spontaneously spoke of avoiding danger on the streets.[16] They said that they stayed home at night or used taxis, or they avoided talking to strangers. Others spoke of measures to protect themselves and their property at home; they kept firearms or watchdogs or put stronger locks on the doors and windows. In the districts sur-

---

[12] Albert J. Reiss, Jr., "Probability of Victimization for Major Crimes Against the Person by Race and Sex Status of Victims and Offenders," in *Studies in Crime and Law Enforcement in Major Metropolitan Areas*, ed. Albert J. Reiss, Jr., President's Commission on Law Enforcement and Administration of Justice Field Survey III (Washington, D.C.: U.S. Government Printing Office, 1967); hereinafter referred to as Reiss studies.
[13] NORC study, Table 47, p. 76.
[14] BSSR study, p. 121.
[15] NORC study.
[16] BSSR study, pp. 128–30.

veyed in Boston and Chicago by the University of Michigan, five out of every eight said that they had changed their habits in one or more of these ways because of the fear of crime.[17] No one mentioned efforts to avoid loss through fraud or overly sharp loan practices or any kind of swindle. It was clear that the crimes which they feared were crimes which might endanger their personal safety, especially attack by a stranger.

The national survey by NORC suggests the same conclusion. While two-thirds of those interviewed feel safe walking in their neighborhoods, one-third do not. Over 80 percent lock their doors at night, and 25 percent lock them during the daytime when family members are at home. Twenty-eight percent said their dogs were primarily watchdogs, and 37 percent, that firearms in the home were kept at least partly for protection.[18]

Possibly indicative of the concern of the public is the reaction of citizens to a question posed in the NORC survey: "If you were walking down the street alone around here in the evening and heard footsteps coming from behind, and turned to see a stranger rapidly approaching, what would you do?" A large majority interpreted the situation as dangerous. One-fourth of the respondents said they would "do nothing, just keep right on walking," but the most frequent reply was "Run as fast as I could or call for help."[19] This fear of personal victimization is becoming more intense. In recent years, Harris surveys have found that each year 50 percent of their respondents have said that they are more worried about their personal safety on the streets than they were in the previous year.

Although many persons felt relatively safe in their own neighborhoods, they were not thereby indifferent or unconcerned about personal safety for themselves or their families. Respondents in Washington, D.C., were asked whether they had thought more about the neighborhood or the house when they had selected their current residence. The largest number said that the neighborhood was most important, and nearly as many said that neighborhood and house were of equal importance.[20] Although some respondents selected a location because of its convenience or aesthetic qualities, 56 percent had placed greatest emphasis on the safety or moral characteristics of the neighborhood. Having selected a location which, within the alternatives available, seemed safe, most felt relatively secure. Nonetheless, 24 percent of the respondents in Washington felt that there was so much trouble in the area that they would like to move. In the areas studied in Boston and Chicago, 20 percent thought that they would like to move because of crime; 30 percent wanted to move out of the higher-crime-rate district in Boston.[21]

---

[17] Reiss studies, vol. 1, sec. 2, p. 103.
[18] NORC study, Table 44, p. 74.
[19] *Ibid.*
[20] BSSR study, p. 119.
[21] Reiss studies, p. 31.

SIGNIFICANCE OF THE FEAR OF CRIME

The crimes which the public fears most, crimes of violence, are those which occur least frequently. People are much more tolerant of crimes against property. The average citizen probably suffers the greatest economic loss as a result of crimes against businesses and public institutions which pass on their losses in the form of increased prices and taxes. Nevertheless, most shoplifters are never arrested, and employees suspected of dishonesty are either warned or dismissed.[22]

Furthermore, violence and the threat of violence do not present as great a hazard as do other risks in an industrial society. The number of accidental injuries calling for medical attention or restricted activity of one day or more[23] is far greater than the 1.8 offenses per 1,000 Americans involving violence or threat of violence.[24] Inadequate medical care is another example of risk which does not provoke the same horror as violence. A recent study found the quality, numbers, and distribution of ambulances and other emergency services severely deficient, and estimated that as many as 20,000 persons die each year as a result of inadequate emergency medical care.[25]

Death or injury as a result of violence, however, has a different significance than death by accident or improper care, a significance consistent with the repugnance with which Americans view violence. Recent studies have shown that there is a widespread consensus on the relative seriousness of different types of crimes.[26] Offenses involving physical assaults against the person are the most feared, and the greatest concern is expressed about those in which a weapon is used.

The precautions which people take to protect themselves indicate that underlying the fear of crime is a profound fear of strangers. They are afraid that some unknown person will accost them on the street or break into their homes and take their property or attack them personally. Again, the fears are not consistent with the objective risks. Not only are the risks of injury by violence slight relative to the risks of injury or death from other causes, but the risk of serious attack by strangers is about half as great as it is from persons well known to the victim.[27] Injuries in the case of assault

[22] Donald J. Black and Albert J. Reiss, Jr., "Problems and Practices for Protection Against Crime Among Businesses and Organizations," in Reiss studies.

[23] National Safety Council, *Accident Facts* (Chicago: National Safety Council, 1966), p. 2.

[24] U.S. Department of Justice, Federal Bureau of Investigation, *Crime in the United States: Uniform Crime Reports* (Washington, D.C.: U.S. Government Printing Office, 1965), p. 3.

[25] Data obtained by interview from American College of Surgeons, Washington, D.C., 1966.

[26] Thorsten Sellin and Marvin E. Wolfgang, *The Measurement of Delinquency* (New York: Wiley, 1964), Table 69, p. 289.

[27] For a review of findings on the relationship between victim and offender, see President's Commission on Law Enforcement and Administration of Justice, *Task Force Report: Crime and Its Impact—An Assessment* (Washington, D.C.: U.S. Government Printing Office, 1967), pp. 14–15.

are not only more common but more serious when the victim and offender know each other well. This hazard does not even stop at the self, for suicide is twice as common as homicide.

This fear of strangers is impoverishing the lives of many Americans. People stay behind the locked doors of their homes rather than walk in the street at night. Poor people take taxis because they are afraid to walk or use public transportation. Sociable people are afraid to talk to those they do not know. Society is suffering from what the economists would label opportunity costs. When people stay home, they are not enjoying the pleasurable and cultural opportunities in their communities; they are not visiting their friends as frequently as they might. The general level of sociability is diminished. Some are restricting their earning opportunities, as when they ignore job openings in some neighborhoods. Hospital administrators in large cities report difficulty in staffing for night duty. Administrators and officials interviewed by the University of Michigan survey team report that Parent-Teacher Association meetings at night are poorly attended, that library use is decreasing and recreational facilities remain unused, because of stories of robberies and purse-snatching.[28]

As social interaction is reduced and fear of crime becomes fear of the stranger, the social order is further damaged. Not only are there fewer persons on the streets and in public places than there might be, but persons who are afraid may show a lack of concern for each other. The logical consequences of this reduced sociability, mutual fear, and distrust can be seen in the reported incidents of bystanders indifferent to cries for help.

RELIANCE ON LAW ENFORCEMENT

The surveys regarding beliefs about the causes of crime indicate a pronounced concern with the morals of the country and the moral training of the country's youth. Few persons blamed social conditions or law enforcement. When Gallup asked the causes of crime, most persons who were interviewed gave answers which could be categorized as poor parental guidance or inadequate home life and supervision of teenagers. "Breakdown of moral standards" was also frequently mentioned. Persons interviewed by Harris blamed disturbed and restless teenagers most frequently. Unemployment, racial problems, broken homes, and low moral standards were next in importance.

When Harris asked why people become criminal rather than for an explanation of the crime rate, then the emphasis on moral training became explicit. Sixty-eight percent of the persons interviewed believed that upbringing or bad environment were the main causes. Many of the other

---

[28] Stephen Cutler and Albert J. Reiss, Jr., "Crimes Against Public and Quasi-Public Organizations in Boston, Chicago, and Washington, D.C.," in Reiss studies.

causes named, such as broken homes or wrong companions, could also indicate a concern with the moral training and discipline of youth. Few persons suggested innate defects, and even fewer blamed police failure in any of these polls.

Although a majority saw crime as the consequence of a moral breakdown, most tended to believe that stricter law enforcement was the way to cope with the current crime problem. The BSSR survey in Washington, D.C., asked citizens what they thought was the most important thing that could be done to cut down crime in their city.[29] Responses were classified as to whether a repressive measure, a measure of social amelioration, or one of moral inculcation was being advocated. Sixty percent recommended repressive measures such as more police, police dogs, stiffer sentences, or "cracking down on teenagers." Forty percent believed that the solution lay in social amelioration or moral inculcation. These included such measures as more jobs, recreation and youth programs, better housing, improved police-community relations, better child-training, religious training and revival, community leadership, or simply inculcating discipline. Only 3.5 percent would rely solely on moral measures.

Another indication that many people believe repressive measures, rather than amelioration of social conditions or moral training of youth, to be the more effective means of cutting down crime lies in attitudes about court actions. The BSSR study in Washington, D.C., asked whether the sentences given by courts in that city were generally too lenient or too harsh. Most respondents, including Negroes, thought that the courts were too lenient. A Gallup survey in 1965 also found that a majority of persons interviewed believed that the courts do not deal harshly enough with criminals; only 2 percent said "too harshly."

Reliance on strict policing and law enforcement is somewhat tempered and not altogether repressive, however. When NORC asked whether the main concern of the police should be with preventing crimes or with catching criminals, over 60 percent placed the emphasis on prevention.[30] Gallup asked respondents how they would deal with a hypothetical youth caught stealing an automobile. The most frequent responses were to give him another chance, be lenient.

When the fate of an actual person is to be decided, the demand for stern treatment of the lawbreaker is further relaxed. The clearest illustration of this in studies undertaken for the Commission can be seen in the survey of employers carried out by the University of Michigan in Boston, Chicago, and Washington, D.C.[31] Only 19 percent of the employers who reported larcenies, fraud, forgery, embezzlement, or misuse of company property by employees said that they had called the police. The most frequent way

---

[29] BSSR study, p. 134.
[30] NORC study, p. 59.
[31] Black and Reiss, *op. cit.*

of handling the offenders was discharge, but in other instances a transfer or demand for restitution sufficed.

More police, more stringent policing, less leniency by the courts—this is how a substantial segment of the population would undertake to reduce crime—except when they are confronted with the necessity of deciding the fate of a particular individual. A smaller proportion of the public believed that social changes could reduce the amount of crime; only a very few suggested improving the moral fiber of the country—although a majority believed that inadequate moral training was responsible for an increase in crime.

CITIZEN RESPONSIBILITY FOR CRIME REDUCTION

Persons who believe that poor upbringing and moral training of youth are a major cause of crime might be willing to assume some responsibility for improved discipline. A Gallup survey which asked adults whether they would be willing to devote one evening a month to working with juvenile delinquents or trying to solve juvenile delinquency problems did, indeed, uncover a considerable potential responsibility. Sixty percent said that they would be willing to spend an evening each month in such activities. On the other hand, citizens in one precinct in Washington were asked whether they had ever "gotten together with other people around here, or has any group or organization you belong to met and discussed the problem of crime or taken some sort of action to combat crime?" Only 12 percent answered affirmatively. Neither did most persons believe that they could do anything about the crime in their own neighborhoods. Just over 17 percent thought that they could do anything.

When administrators and officials of public and quasi-public organizations were asked about the most effective remedies for crime, they suggested the amelioration of social conditions far more frequently than did members of the general public.[32] They also recommended improvement of the moral fiber of the population and better training of youth much more often than the general public. Perhaps because of their broader view of crime reduction, they were also able to see more ways in which they might help to reduce crime. A number thought that they might cooperate with the police in ways calculated to make law enforcement easier. A number thought that they might cooperate in neighborhood and community programs, particularly by donating money for youth and recreation groups. The greatest number of suggestions involved what might be termed an extension of the organization's services. Electric-company executives considered more and brighter street lights; park officials, more recreational

---

[32] Cutler and Reiss, *op. cit.*

activities; and school administrators, more youth programs and adult education. Others believed that they might further community goals through integration of work crews and support of community-relations programs. Although most persons have not become involved in any activity intended to prevent or reduce crime, there does exist the potential for citizen involvement when responsible persons are convinced of its value.

AMBIVALENCE TOWARD LAW ENFORCEMENT

There is a convergence of attitudes and preferences expressed by large numbers of the citizens interviewed which would tend to predispose them to a preference for strong police agencies, unhampered in their efforts to apprehend and convict criminals. A large majority believes that the crime situation is terrible and getting worse. Accounts of crime rates arouse fears of crimes of violence; the quest for safety becomes an important factor in the ordering of personal lives. Their beliefs regarding the causes of crime notwithstanding, a majority would rely on more strict law enforcement and stern treatment of offenders to lower the crime rate. Few seriously considered any personal efforts to reduce crime, even in their own neighborhoods, either by themselves or in concert with other citizens.

It is not surprising, then, to find considerable willingness to permit whatever practices the police consider important. A majority of those interviewed in Washington, D.C., 73 percent, agreed that the police ought to have leeway to act tough when they have to.[33] More than half (56 percent) agreed that there should be more use of police dogs, while fewer than one-third disagreed. Few respondents consistently endorsed either restricting or enlarging police powers, however. Many who take a permissive attitude on one issue refuse to do so on another; more than half of those who oppose the greater use of police dogs are in favor of police freedom to act tough. Neither was there a strong relationship between attitudes toward these issues and more general attitudes toward the police. Respondents were characterized as more or less favorable toward policemen, according to their responses to a six-item scale. Nearly half (47 percent) of those who did not favor police toughness or more police dogs nevertheless indicated strong respect and sympathy for policemen.

A similar ambivalence was observed in the results of the national survey conducted by NORC.[34] Forty-five percent favored civilian review boards (35 percent opposed them; 20 percent were uncertain or indifferent); 52 percent believed that the police should have more power; 42 percent, that police should risk arresting an innocent person rather than risk missing

---

[33] BSSR study, p. 146.
[34] NORC study.

a criminal; and 65 percent favored the ruling that police may not question a suspect without his lawyer being present or the suspect's consent to be questioned without counsel. Most persons were in favor of enlarging police powers on some issues and restricting it on others; only 25 percent were consistently for or against permitting greater powers to the police.

The surveys conducted for the Commission found a strong concern for the civil rights of the individual, including the person who is a suspect or offender, in spite of a wish for strict law enforcement. This is particularly apparent when the issue of rights is explicit. In the districts studied in Boston, Chicago, and Washington, D.C., citizens were asked whether they thought that "too much attention is being paid to the rights of people who get into trouble with the police."[35] In each of the three cities, fewer than half (38 percent) agreed. As was true concerning the issue of police practices, this concern for the individual was not derogatory of the police. In Washington, D.C., more than half of those who took a rights position on this question also expressed strong sympathy and respect for the police.

In addition to a tradition of concern for individual rights, a belief that the police discriminate in the way that they treat various groups may account for some of the ambivalence regarding law enforcement. In Washington, D.C., the BSSR study found that 60 percent of the Negro men, 49 percent of the Negro women, and 27 percent of the white citizens thought that Negroes get worse treatment than other people.[36] Among the comments of these respondents were that the police pick on Negroes more, that they are rude to Negroes, use brutality and physical force, or else ignore Negroes more than other people. Others expressed the belief that affluent citizens get better treatment than the poor. In Washington, D.C., half of the persons interviewed agreed that people who have money for lawyers do not have to worry about the police. In Boston and Chicago, there was a tendency for citizens in the predominantly white districts to point out rich and respectable citizens as recipients of more favorable treatment, while citizens in the predominantly nonwhite districts pointed to the less favorable treatment of Negroes by police.[37]

When another issue was posed in economic rather than racial terms, there was again a strong indication of concern with rights of the individual. Almost three-quarters of the persons questioned by the NORC study approved the Supreme Court decision that the state must provide a lawyer to suspects who want one but cannot afford to pay the lawyer's fee.[38] Not only does a strong majority approve the decision, but no income, sex, or racial group opposes it.

---

[35] BSSR study, p. 149, and Reiss studies, p. 82.
[36] BSSR study, p. 144.
[37] Reiss studies, pp. 43–47.
[38] NORC study, Table 40, p. 70.

NONREPORTING OF CRIMES TO THE POLICE

Americans who believe that crime control is strictly a matter for the police and the courts nevertheless frequently fail to take the one action that they as citizens must take if the police and courts are to intervene in any particular situation. Although the surveys undertaken for the Commission represent a more intensive effort to measure the magnitude of nonreported crime than any in the past, students of crime have long recognized the phenomenon of *le chiffre noir* and speculated on the reasons for its existence. In the current studies, persons who were interviewed were asked not only whether they had reported any given incident to the police but also their reasons for not doing so when they had not.[39] The victim's reluctance to get involved was one of the most frequently cited reasons for not calling the police. Sometimes he did not want to take the time to call the police and present evidence, often fearing that this might necessitate spending time in court and away from work.

Some who had witnessed incidents which they thought were crimes denied any responsibility in the matter. An illustration of this sentiment is a comment sometimes made to interviewers: "I am not my brother's keeper." Others said that they did not think that the victim would want the police to be notified or indicated a concern for the offender. The NORC study found that for all classes of offenses except serious crimes against the person, the police were less likely to be notified if the offender were personally known to the victim than if he were a stranger.

The fear of reprisal or other unfortunate consequences sometimes deterred victims or witnesses from notifying the police of an incident. Some feared personal harm might come from the offender or his friends; others, that they themselves would become the subjects of police inquiry or action. Other consequences which the victim might wish to avoid include cancellation of insurance or an increase in rates.

The most frequently cited reason for not calling the police was a resigned belief that any efforts would be useless. The victim simply accepted his losses as irrevocable. This was particularly true in the cases of malicious mischief and vandalism, where it often seemed that there were no clues. The damage could not be undone, nor could the police be expected to apprehend and punish the offender.

Often the victim believed that his evidence was insufficient to convince either the police or the courts that a crime had indeed been committed. This was the reason given by nearly half of the employers who said they had not reported cases of employee dishonesty to the police.[40] Given the belief in the ineffectiveness of a call to police, they preferred the more

---

[39] BSSR study, Tables 3–23 and 3–24, pp. 154–55; NORC study, Table 24, p. 44.
[40] Black and Reiss, *op. cit.*

simple and direct method of discharging or otherwise punishing the employee. (Ironically, these same employers often relied on police records for the purpose of screening prospective employees.)

It has been noted that persons interviewed during the national study were far more likely to fail to notify the police if the offender were a relative or person well known to the victim than a stranger. The employer not only knows but is in a special relationship to the employee whom he suspects of dishonesty. In a similar manner, a businessman who cashes a check for a customer has assumed some measure of responsibility for his relationship with this customer. It may be, then, that an undefined sense of responsibility for his own victimization sometimes deters the individual from calling the police. The employers and businessmen who were interviewed had refrained from calling the police more frequently in instances of employee dishonesty and bad checks than shoplifting. Lacking any special relationship with the shoplifter, the businessman could more readily report his offense.

Other persons did not notify the police because of their own uncertainty of what ought to be done. Sometimes they were not sure of what was taking place at the time, or they did not know whether it was a crime or what was the proper procedure for reporting the incident. For these persons, more knowledge of what constitutes reason for calling the police and how to do so would probably increase the rate of reporting. In those cities in which the police department is actively enlisting the aid of the public, dissemination of this information has been effective. Efforts to increase the rate of crime reporting by citizens would have to take into account also the reluctance of most to get involved, to take responsibility for reporting, and to be willing to spend time testifying.

SUMMARY AND CONCLUSIONS

Analysis of the findings of the public opinion polls and the surveys conducted for the Commission indicates a widespread concern about crime, both as a national problem and as a problem in assuring personal safety. Persons who were interviewed expressed a belief that crime is increasing. They tend to equate crime with crimes of violence and to fear most violence at the hands of strangers in unfamiliar surroundings. Crimes against the person are far less common than those against property, and an unknown person is the least likely assailant.

Because of their fear of strangers many people restrict their activities. They forgo opportunities for pleasure or cultural enrichment, and they become less sociable, more suspicious. The level of interaction and mutual trust in the society is reduced; public places may become less safe than they otherwise might be. The crime rate is blamed on a breakdown in morals, and especially on inadequate training and discipline of young people. As a threat to the moral and social order, it becomes fearful even to persons who live in relatively safe circumstances and have no personal experience with crime.

Although attributing an increase in crime to lowered moral standards, most persons would depend on the police and courts for stern treatment of offenders in order to diminish the level of crime. Not as many, but none-theless a substantial proportion, would recommend increased employment opportunities and other improved social conditions to combat crime. Along with the reliance on law-enforcement officials, there was willingness to permit the police considerable latitude in their efforts to apprehend and convict criminals. This apparent harshness toward offenders was immediately mitigated when the issue of the rights of the individual was posed. Some of this concern is related to the belief that there is discrimination against economic and racial groups. Finally, the recommendation for stern treatment of wrongdoers is further tempered when the fate of an individual offender is considered.

Control Systems II:
Establishments for Adjudicated Offenders

Whatsoever is brought upon thee, take cheerfully,
And be patient when thou art changed to a low estate,
For gold is tried in fire
And acceptable men in the furnace of adversity.

—*Wall inscription*
United States Penitentiary
Terre Haute, Indiana

A final step in the administration of justice is to decide whether, and for how long, adjudicated offenders will be incarcerated. Both the conferral of guilt and imprisonment are such vivid reminders of the imperfections of man and the social order that elaborate philosophical and technical justifications for the court decision have been put forth. Yet if there is one unambiguous conclusion about the effectiveness of correctional policy, it is that a period of social isolation and penitence will rarely modify inmates in socially approved directions.

Considering that some 1.3 million persons are sequestered in federal, state, or municipal institutions on any given day, it is not surprising that criminologists have long been interested in the structure and operation of prison systems. Important shifts, however, have taken place in the focus of prison research, as well as in the methods by which evidence is accumulated.

Perhaps most attention has been given in recent times to the organizational features that prisons share with other "people-processing" or "people-changing" establishments. People-processing organizations such as universities, which are largely developmental in function, are structurally differentiated from mental hospitals and correctional systems, which have the primary function of resocialization. At the same time, however, both types of organizations must establish standards by which personnel may be admitted, make explicit a normative order governing conduct, provide appropriate (perhaps new) social identities, and define short- and long-range goals. As Stanton Wheeler has phrased it, if institutional processes focus upon social objects such as inmates, "the primary purpose is to change the knowledge, beliefs, attitudes, or skills of those who pass through the system."[1]

Some organizations, such as the manufacturing plant, process nonsocial, and therefore nonreactive, objects. Others, directed essentially to people-changing, are distinguished by the ability of their constituents to respond in collective fashion. It was precisely the adaptation to "the pains of imprisonment" that led Gresham M. Sykes to observe:

> There are no exits for the inmate in the sense of a device or series of devices which can completely eliminate the pains of imprisonment. But if the rigors of confinement cannot be completely removed, they can at least be mitigated by the patterns of social interaction established among the inmates themselves.[2]

The development of inmate culture appears to have been one of the earliest yet most enduring fascinations of criminologists. Since inmates undergo a socialization process that Donald Clemmer termed "prisonization"—"the taking on in greater or less degree of the folkways, mores, customs, and general culture of the penitentiary"[3]—the organizational form supporting this is in many ways a microcosm of the larger society. It thus invites attention to such features of free community socialization as differentiation of roles, the evolution of identities, structural properties like the inequalities of power relationships, and distribution of prestige. Because of their "total" character, prison establishments vividly portray the consequences of human, albeit monosexual, interaction.

Finally, correctional objectives, whether formulated by political authority, the administrators of institutions, or inmate councils, have always been criti-

---

[1] Stanton Wheeler, "The Structure of Formally Organized Socialization Settings," in Orville G. Brim, Jr., and Stanton Wheeler, Socialization after Childhood (New York: Wiley, 1966), p. 57.

[2] Gresham M. Sykes, The Society of Captives (Princeton, N.J.: Princeton University Press, 1958), p. 82 (emphasis in original).

[3] Donald Clemmer, The Prison Community (New York: Rinehart, 1958, orig. pub. 1940), p. 299.

cized for their inconsistencies. It is argued that traditional goals—reformation, incapacitation, and retribution—are inherently abrasive, and that the most sensitive index of this is an enormous recidivism rate. Only recently, following the establishment of progressive innovations such as work-release programs, have systematic efforts been made to measure correctional effectiveness.

Cressey's "The Prison and Organizational Goals," taken from a lengthy paper on social-system attributes of correctional settings, emphasizes some issues in the philosophy of punishment. Included is a review of societal attitudes and reactions toward imprisoned offenders.

The selections by Sykes and Messinger and by Rose Giallombardo are analyses of inmate value systems and normative expectations as reflected in the role networks of male and female prisons, respectively. Evidence is presented to the effect that inmate roles are differentiated along lines of prestige, power, verbal and physical adroitness, and commitment to staff or inmate norms.

Bernard Berk's paper "Informal Organization and Inmate Attitudes in Three Types of Prisons" reports upon a comparative study of institutions. Differing widely with respect to their "treatment" as opposed to "custodial" orientation, the research sites are hypothesized to have contrasting inmate attitudes toward the institution, staff, and programs.

For the interested reader, selected publications on correctional system theory and research are listed below.

1. *Prison Goals and the Concept of Effectiveness*

Cressey, Donald R. "Contradictory Directives in Complex Organizations: The Case of the Prison," *Administrative Science Quarterly,* 4 (June 1959): 1–19.

Glaser, Daniel. *The Effectiveness of a Prison and Parole System* (Indianapolis: Bobbs-Merrill, 1964).

——— and Stratton, John R. "Measuring Inmate Change in Prison," in *The Prison: Studies in Institutional Organization and Change,* ed. Donald R. Cressey (New York: Holt, Rinehart & Winston, 1961), pp. 381–92.

McCleery, Richard H. "The Governmental Process and Informal Social Control," in *The Prison: Studies in Institutional Organization and Change,* ed. Donald R. Cressey (New York: Holt, Rinehart & Winston, 1961), pp. 149–88.

Ohlin, Lloyd E. "Conflicting Interests in Correctional Objectives," in Richard A. Cloward, et al., *Theoretical Studies in Social Organization of the Prison* (New York: Social Science Research Council, 1960), pp. 111–29.

Schrag, Clarence. "The Correctional System: Problems and Prospects," *Annals of the American Academy of Political and Social Science* 381 (January 1969): 11–20. (This entire issue, edited by John P. Conrad, is devoted to "The Future of Corrections.")

2. *Organizational Features of Prison Systems*

Cressey, Donald R. "Prison Organizations," in *Handbook of Organizations,* ed. James G. March (Chicago: Rand McNally, 1965), pp. 1023–70.

Street, David. "The Inmate Group in Custodial and Treatment Settings," *American Sociological Review* 30 (February 1965): 14–39.

Mayer N. Zald, "Power Balance and Staff Conflict in Correctional Institutions," *Administrative Science Quarterly* 7 (June 1962): 22–49.

3. The Process of Socialization in Correctional Establishments

Atchley, Robert C., and McCabe, M. Patrick. "Socialization in Correctional Communities: A Replication," *American Sociological Review* 33 (October 1968): 774–85.

McCorkle, Lloyd W., and Korn, Richard. "Resocialization Within Walls," *Annals of the American Academy of Political and Social Science* 293 (May 1954): 80–98.

Wheeler, Stanton. "Socialization in Correctional Institutions," in *Handbook of Socialization Theory and Research*, ed. David A. Goslin (Chicago: Rand McNally, 1969), pp. 1005–1023.

4. Inmate Modes of Adaptation and Response to Imprisonment

Clemmer, Donald. *The Prison Community* (New York: Rinehart, 1958, orig. pub. 1940), chaps. 4–8.

Garabedian, Peter G. "Social Roles and the Process of Socialization in the Prison Community," *Social Problems* 11 (Fall 1963): 139–52.

Goffman, Erving. "On the Characteristics of Total Institutions: The Inmate World," in *The Prison: Studies in Institutional Organization and Change*, ed. Donald R. Cressey (New York: Holt, Rinehart & Winston, 1961), chap. 1.

Irwin, John, and Cressey, Donald R. "Thieves, Convicts, and the Inmate Culture," in *The Other Side: Perspectives on Deviance*, ed. Howard S. Becker (New York: Free Press, Macmillan, 1964), pp. 225–45.

Seeman, Melvin. "Alienation and Social Learning in a Reformatory," *American Journal of Sociology* 69 (November 1963): 270–84.

Ward, David A., and Kassebaum, Gene G. "Homosexuality: A Mode of Adaptation in a Prison for Women," *Social Problems* 12 (Fall 1964): 159–77.

5. Role Behavior and Ideologies of Prison Staff

Giallombardo, Rose. *Society of Women: A Study of a Women's Prison* (New York: Wiley, 1966), chap. 3, "Characteristics of the Staff," and chap. 4, "Organization of the Staff and Relations with Inmates."

Goffman, Erving. "On the Characteristics of Total Institutions: Staff-Inmate Relations," in *The Prison: Studies in Institutional Organization and Change*, ed. Donald R. Cressey (New York: Holt, Rinehart & Winston, 1961), chap. 2.

Grusky, Oscar. "Role Conflict in Organization: A Study of Prison Camp Officials," *Administrative Science Quarterly* 3 (March 1959): 452–72.

Sykes, Gresham M. "The Corruption of Authority and Rehabilitation," *Social Forces* 34 (December 1956): 257–62.

———. *The Society of Captives* (Princeton, N.J.: Princeton University Press, 1958), chap. 2, "The Regime of the Custodians."

30. THE PRISON AND ORGANIZATIONAL GOALS

Donald R. Cressey

In recent years, variations in the effectiveness and efficiency of different kinds of organizations and in the conditions under which these organizations arise, persist, and change have been studied in many settings, ranging from broad administrative systems to specific governmental and military hierarchies, factories, and hospitals. Almost all such studies could have been made in prisons, which contain systems of a military type designed to keep inmates within walls, industrial systems to maintain the prison and produce goods, and professional or "service" systems to rehabilitate inmates. Moreover, the prison as a whole is a governmental organization designed to administer the activities of the persons in the various roles in these and other subsidiary systems.

Prisons, however, provide more than a convenient opportunity for verifying observations already made by students of social organizations.[1] In

Reprinted by permission of the author and the publisher from *Handbook of Organizations,* ed. James G. March (Chicago: Rand McNally, 1965), pp. 1023–30. Original title: "Prison Organizations." Footnotes have been added.

[1] The material in this and the following three paragraphs is taken from Donald R. Cressey, "Limitations on Organization of Treatment in the Modern Prison," in Richard A. Cloward *et al., Theoretical Studies in Social Organization of the Prison* (New York: Social Science Research Council, 1960), pp. 78–110.

two principal respects, prisons seem to differ significantly from factories and similar organizations. First, the administrative hierarchies of prisons are organized down to the lowest level. In factories, there are separate hierarchies of management personnel and of workers, and research has been concerned with the relations of these roles to each other and to their organizational purpose, production. The lowest-status employee in a prison, in contrast, is both a manager and a worker. He is managed in a system of regulations and controls from above, but he also manages in a presumably concordant system the inmates who are in his charge. He is a low-status worker in interaction with management, but a higher-status foreman, "officer," or treatment agent in interaction with inmates. The guard, who in traditional prisons is at the bottom of a hierarchical system which manages his job of managing men, has no counterpart in the business and industrial world. The closest analogy would be the overseer of a crew of slaves, who would be viewed as "outside" the organization designed to utilize their labor effectively. Even this analogy is fallacious except as guards may serve as foremen of inmate industrial or maintenance crews. Most guards have nothing to do but stand guard: they do not "use" inmates productively any more than they themselves are used productively by prison managers. Guards manage and are managed in organizations where management is an end, not a means.

Second, as prisons have grown in size and as concepts of good penology have changed, new services and roles have been added without regard to those already existing. This process seems different from that accompanying similar growth of other bodies, for the new roles have been organized around purposes that are little related to each other. In all prisons there is a line organization of custodial ranks, ranging from warden to guard, and salary differentials and descriptive titles indicate that a chain of command is expected within this hierarchy. However, although all employees are responsible to the warden, there is no clear expectation that the institution should consist solely of a hierarchy of custodial ranks in reference to which all positions are integrated. Systems of nonline positions, such as those of professional personnel and industrial foremen and superintendents, are essentially separate and have their own salary differentials and titles. They are part of neither the custodial chain of command nor staff organizations. Noncustodial personnel are not advisers to the custodians in the sense that the experts of various sorts who make up the staff organization of factories are advisers, providing specialized knowledge to assist the line organization with its task of production.[2] The structure of prisons provides for three principal hierarchies devoted, respectively, to keeping, using, and serving inmates, but not for the integration of their divergent purposes.

---

[2] M. Dalton, "Conflicts Between Staff and Line Managerial Officers," *American Sociological Review*, 15 (1950): 342–51.

The separate organizations concerned with keeping and with serving inmates, for example, not merely are overlapping, but have entirely different and partly contradictory purposes.

The objectives of each hierarchy require that its roles and processes of role integration take definite forms. The model of an organization for giving help and treatment to inmates is an archetypical mental hospital; for using inmates, an industrial organization such as a lumber camp, where employees both work and live together; for keeping them, a prison on the order of the early Pennsylvania institutions, where all inmates were kept in solitary confinement. Each organization includes a specific kind of relationship between employees and inmates; a specific pattern of authority, communication, and decision-making; and a specific system for distributing rewards and punishments. These features vary significantly among the different kinds of organization. . . .

Little is known about the processes of modification and accommodation taking place when the three hierarchies are expected to function as parts of an overall organization. There has been little systematic observation of the resulting consequences for each subsidiary organization. There is need for description and analysis of organizational problems stemming from administrative attempts to transform the total system into an organization consistent with only one or another of the subsidiaries. For example, some prison administrators seem committed to establishing, in the presence of treatment and productive organizations, a total system modeled on the custodial archetype.[3] Other administrators, in the presence of productive and custodial organizations, strain to establish and maintain a total system consistent with the treatment archetype. . . .

THE PRISON AND SOCIETY

The variety of occupational activities and organizational patterns characterizing modern prisons has grown out of changing conceptions, in the society as a whole, of what ought to be done to, with, and for criminals. Later sections of this chapter try to show how both conforming behavior and deviant behavior among prison staff members are related to the social pressures arising out of the organizational conditions within which the behavior takes place. It is necessary, therefore, to review briefly some of the history of prisons in order to show how these organizational conditions came into existence. It is erroneous to believe that the prison administrator

---

[3] R. L. Jenkins, "Treatment in an Institution," *American Journal of Orthopsychiatry*, 11 (1941): 85–91; Lloyd E. Ohlin, *Sociology and the Field of Corrections* (New York: Russell Sage Foundation, 1956); H. Powelson and R. Bendix, "Psychiatry in Prison," *Psychiatry*, 14 (1951): 73–86; L. N. Robinson, "Contradictory Purposes in Prisons," *Journal of Criminal Law and Criminology*, 37 (1947): 449–57.

is free to organize and develop his prison in any way he considers efficient. The activities which his staff must perform are sharply and rather specifically determined by groups outside the prison itself.

In contemporary American society, there are at least four distinguishable attitudes toward the control of crime, and each of them incorporates a program of action for correctional agencies and institutions.[4] First, there is a desire for retribution. At least since Hammurabi, it has been generally accepted that the criminal deserves to suffer simply because he is a criminal. Taking individual revenge is now usually illegal and/or immoral, but contemporary America does maintain a powerful legal organization for corporate imposition of suffering on offenders. Most of us view this system of officially punishing criminals as highly desirable. By acting collectively to take revenge on criminals, society is said to reinforce its anticriminal values. From this point of view, the future of the offender is unimportant.

Next, there is a desire that suffering be imposed on criminals as a deterrent to potential criminals. Again, the future effects of punishment on the society, not on the criminal, are viewed as the important consideration. The basic notion is that infliction of pain on offenders serves to arouse in others a fear of perpetrating the offense: swift and certain punishment of crime will arouse in noncriminals a fear of transgression. In a narrow perspective, the desire for punishment as a deterrent is based on the assumption that individuals carefully calculate the future consequences of their contemplated acts and do not commit them if they are likely to stimulate punishment. In a broader perspective, the assumption is that administration of the criminal law's penal sanctions by police, courts, and prisons, among others, has long-run effects upon public morality.[5]

Third, in contemporary America there is an obvious desire for protection against the criminal. Whether he is punished or not, the offender must be physically isolated so that the community is safe from him. The attitude here is directed neither at the criminal's fate nor at the indirect effects which punishment has on society's morality. Rather, the criminal is viewed as dangerous, like a poisonous snake or a tornado, and the conclusion is that he must be controlled.

Finally, there is in our society a desire to reduce crime rates by changing criminals. A high crime rate is the result either of a large number of people committing one crime each or of a few people committing many crimes. Hence, although punishment of the offender may deter many potential criminals, the offender himself must be reformed or rehabilitated if the crime rate is to be substantially reduced. This attitude, of course, is congruent with the notion that society must be protected from criminals; the

---

[4] Edwin H. Sutherland and Donald R. Cressey, *Principles of Criminology*, 6th ed. (Philadelphia: Lippincott, 1960), pp. 460–61.

[5] Emile Durkheim, *The Division of Labor in Society* (Glencoe, Ill.: Free Press, 1947), pp. 70–110.

desire for reformation is merely an implied variation of the proper action to be taken in order to achieve protection from criminals.

These four attitudes are not new. For about 250 years, prison administrators have been charged with implementing each of them. They continue to be charged with such implementation, and this means that prisons must somehow exact retribution, deter potential criminals, and incapacitate and reform convicted criminals. In other words, contemporary prison programs, like those of two centuries ago, are to make life unpleasant for men who have made others' lives unpleasant, to isolate criminals so they cannot commit crimes during certain periods of time, and to reduce crime rates both by deterring the general public from criminal behavior and by reforming criminals. But the conceptions of the proper *procedures* for implementing these attitudes have changed considerably, even in the twentieth century.

In early prisons, few organizational problems arose in connection with meeting these expectations. According to the dominant notions about correctional procedures at the time, each could be fulfilled by an organization designed to inflict punishments of an intensity now labeled "severe." Within the prison walls which were to protect society from dangerous criminals, a rigorous, monotonous, and unpleasant regime was to fill the social needs for retribution, deterrence, and reformation. Gradually, however, conceptions of the proper means to be used for achieving these goals have shifted. First, serious doubts arose about whether there is a social need for retribution and deterrent punishments more severe than "mere" deprivation of liberty. There has been a trend toward the notion that punishment by deprivation of liberty should be substituted for punishment by infliction of physical pain. Next, serious doubts about the necessary degree of severity of punishment and the necessary degree of control have arisen. There has been a trend toward reducing the severity of punishments. Then, more recently, serious doubts have arisen about whether reformation can be achieved by punishment of any kind, including deprivation of liberty. There has been a trend toward increasing acceptance of the notion that reformation, rehabilitation, or "correction" of criminals can be achieved only through nonpunitive treatment methods.

Psychological versus Physical Punishment

Punishment as an instrument of public justice is pain and suffering purposively inflicted on criminals by the state because of some value, such as deterrence or reformation, it is assumed to have. Significantly, the pain and suffering need not be physical: punishment can be deprivation of anything the members of the society cherish, such as money or liberty. One relevant point to note in this connection is that imprisonment as a system for dealing with criminals was hardly known until the time of the great democratic revolutions in the eighteenth century.[6] Until the last part of that century, the primary use of incarceration was for persons awaiting trial; after trial, pain was inflicted on the guilty by corporal punishment. It was no mere coincidence that imprisonment arose when it did, nor is it merely a coincidence that imprisonment has remained the dominant method of dealing with serious offenders in democratic countries. As democracy developed, so did an appreciation of liberty, and restriction of freedom by imprisonment, rather than imposition of physical pain, has come to be regarded as a proper system of punishing criminals. It was in the early democratic period that the current system of criminal laws, each law calling for a measured amount of loss of freedom and thus a measured amount of pain, was initiated.

However, substitution of this kind of suffering for more direct physical suffering has been slow and incomplete. The history of imprisonment is in part a story of the gradual but as yet unfinished modification of the principle that men are sent to prisons *for* punishment rather than *as* punishment. Invention of the notion that criminals should be punished by "mere" deprivation of their freedom, rather than by imposition of physical pain, was not readily accepted by all the groups having significant interests in prisons, and it is not widely accepted, without qualifications, even today. However, in the early days of democracy, people seemed even less sure of themselves than at present, for administrators were more often expected to inflict pain on prisoners while at the same time depriving them of their freedom. In the extreme, prisoners were required to walk treadmills, turn cranks, carry a cannonball for prescribed periods, and to perform other painful tasks. They also were conscientiously forced to live in unpleasant physical surroundings, often depending upon charity for their maintenance. Few opportunities for diversions such as participation in religious services were provided, presumably on the ground that this would mitigate the conditions of suffering which the criminal was thought both to deserve and to need. In this system, reformation was to be produced by the same physically punitive devices which fulfilled the needs for retribution and deterrent punishments.

Prisons soon abandoned harsh corporal punishments and punitive labor as a regime for supplementing the suffering which mere incarceration was expected to produce. Yet "mere incarceration" has never been consistently defined and has meant many things to many people, as has been true of the concept "liberty." In early institutions, such as the Walnut Street Jail in Philadelphia at the end of the Revolutionary War,[7] it meant mere perimeter control, with freedom to commit crime and engage in debauchery within the prison walls. Even today in some prisons perimeter control is

---

[6] Cressey, "Rehabilitation Theory and Reality, I: The Pain of Restriction," *California Youth Authority Quarterly*, 10 (1957): 6–9.

[7] R. C. Gray, *Prison Discipline in America* (London: Murray, 1848).

stressed, although inmates are not granted the degree of freedom within the walls that they had in the earlier institutions. Such things as petty rackets, stealing, the manufacture, purchase, and consumption of alcohol, homosexuality, fighting, gambling, and other unsupervised activities are not necessarily condoned in these institutions, but they are not prevented either. When these conditions become known to significant outsiders, strong pressures are placed on the administrators to "clean up" and "tighten up" their institutions, pressures which ordinarily arise from assumptions that such prisons are not sufficiently punitive, and therefore are not sufficiently reformative. Further, because the prisoners for whom only perimeter control is exercised do not themselves necessarily develop and maintain high standards of sanitation and hygiene, humanitarian as well as penological considerations enter into evaluations of such institutions as "bad." Control of actions *within* the prison, then, not mere confinement behind walls, becomes a necessary part of punitive imprisonment.

An early and extreme response to this modified interpretation of the meaning of "mere incarceration" was continuous confinement of all prisoners in isolation. "Perimeter control" was in the Pennsylvania institutions in the early nineteenth century extended to the individual inmate, who was confined to a cell. The "abuses" as well as the relatively non-punitive and nonreformative conditions of freedom within the walls were corrected by solitary confinement under conditions of physical discomfort. Such ultimate restriction of liberty was clearly within the intent of the principle that criminals were to be both punished and reformed by mere incarceration: confinement in solitary would be unpleasant and feared but, at the same time, would make prisoners penitent. This system is used for a small minority of the men in present-day prisons, but it has been abandoned as a general regime principally on the theoretical ground that it is "too restrictive" or punitive, and therefore not reformative.

Another early interpretation of the proper mode of handling men whose freedom is being restricted for punitive and reformative purposes was different from the solitary-confinement interpretation only in degree. Inmates were to be allowed some physical mobility within the walls, but every effort was made to insure that a maximum number of their actions and choices was *directed* by prison employees.

A conception of liberty which makes it possible to take this middle ground between interpretation of deprivation of liberty as only perimeter control and interpretation of it as complete individual control has remained the most popular conception today. Control of inmate actions within the prison, not mere confinement behind walls and not individual isolation, has come to be synonymous with imprisonment. Even here there are variations, however, for there is by no means complete consensus on what "individual freedom" and "liberty" mean. One conception of deprivation of liberty has it that regulation of almost all the details of the prisoner's life shall be attempted, while a different conception dictates that a much smaller degree of control shall be used. The different ideological positions involved are the same as those which ask for maximum police powers in a community, as opposed to those which insist that police power is undue interference with individual freedom.

Certainly it cannot be inferred that complete transition to imprisonment *as* punishment, rather than *for* punishment, has been made. Physical punishments in forms such as whipping, punitive labor, securing hands in a position high above the head, and battering with a high-pressure stream of water are still used in some prisons. Moreover, restriction of liberty is almost universally interpreted to mean deprivation of some *physical comforts*, with the result that the suffering imposed is physical as well as psychological. For example, within prisons, solitary confinement as punitive restriction of liberty is always supplemented by physical discomforts in the form of a restricted diet and denial of a bed as comfortable as the beds in the rest of the institution. In some cases, the offender in solitary is handcuffed to the bars so that he cannot sit during working hours. Mere restriction of recalcitrant inmates' liberty is viewed as insufficiently punitive. More generally, the practice of sentencing a man to incarceration *under conditions of physical discomfort*, not just to incarceration, is widely accepted in our society. Even in model minimum-security institutions, cells are not equipped with "luxuries" such as comfortable beds, davenports, bathrooms, and overstuffed chairs. Prisoners "do not deserve" such things. Restriction of liberty continues to mean restriction of some degree of comfort, and hence physical as well as psychological punishment.

Nevertheless, significant interest groups with power to control prison practices are, like the society itself, sharply divided on this issue. Prison administrators are under almost constant harassment from interest groups holding that physical deprivation must supplement deprivation of liberty and maintaining that "sentimentalists" are turning our penal institutions into country clubs. They also are under similar harassment from interest groups holding that there can be no punishment at all beyond that stemming from deprivation of liberty and maintaining that "barbarians" and undemocratic "dictators" deprive prisoners of a level of living comparable to that of the middle class, do not permit them to have sexual relationships with their wives, and so on.

Despite the fact that prisoners continue to be physically deprived, there has been a distinct trend in the United States, and in most of the world, toward decreasing use of corporal punishments and punitive labor to supplement the pain coming from loss of liberty. Many contemporary wardens have in their tenure witnessed tremendous humanitarian changes in their own prisons. There also has been a trend toward reducing the degree of control maintained over prisoners. This means that some of the deprivations stemming from loss of liberty, as well as many physical deprivations, have been eliminated. When pain is inflicted by forcing the criminal to live under authoritarian conditions rather than in conditions of freedom, then reduction in the degree of control is a reduction in punishment.[8]

It is possible, of course, to be restrictive and custodial without being punitive. It was specified above that punishment is pain and suffering that are intentionally imposed. It follows that pain and suffering which are unavoidably imposed are not punishment. Thus, a prisoner who has a painful surgical operation performed on him is not being punished, for the pain is an unavoidable part of the treatment. Similarly, neither a man who is drafted into the army, a child who is compelled to attend school, nor a patient who is compelled to live in a hospital is being punished, despite the fact that each loses some degree of freedom. The principal difference between committing a criminal to prison and a psychotic to a mental hospital is that society officially *wants* the criminal, but not the psychotic, to suffer from the loss of liberty. The psychotic might suffer from confinement behind bars, just as prisoners do, but imposition of the suffering is an unavoidable correlate of treating him and protecting society from him. No educated person believes that committing a psychotic to a hospital should be based on the assumption that the suffering resulting from his incarceration will, by itself, have value in rehabilitation or in deterring others from becoming patients. This, as indicated, is precisely the assumption behind committing men to prison.

In addition to becoming places where the level of suffering for inmates has been reduced, prisons have increasingly become places where positive, nonpunitive, and nonrestrictive services are offered to offenders. These nonpunitive services are called "treatment." Prisons have almost always relied upon some positive action, as well as on restrictive punishment, to reform criminals, but the degree of interest in changing prisoners by nonpunitive means has increased over the years, principally because new services have been added to those already existing. Thus, religious instruction was introduced shortly after imprisonment was invented, academic education was added about a century ago, vocational education was added in the early twentieth century, and psychological, psychiatric, and social work services of various kinds have been in evidence for a generation. Although the conception of the prison as a place of nonpunitive treatment, rather than as a place of punishment and restriction, has not permeated all institutions to the same degree, the social welfare movement and the growth in popularity of psychiatric interpretations of criminal behavior have meant that prisons have been increasingly concerned with establishing positive programs for rehabilitating prisoners by altering their values, habits, atti-

---

[8] Cressey, "Rehabilitation Theory and Reality, II: Organization and Freedom," *California Youth Authority Quarterly*, 10 (1957): 40–47.

tudes, psychic structures, and points of view. Despite the fact that in 1958 less than 5 percent of the 27,000 persons employed in American prisons were directly concerned with the administration of treatment or training,[9] it is correct to say that the *idea* that we should attempt to understand the forces and mechanisms of criminality and develop efficient methods of reformation based on that understanding has gained increasing popularity in the last fifty years, and especially in the years since World War II.

In summary, at present there are three popular sanctioned reactions to crime in contemporary American society. One is hostility, with insistence that the criminal be made to suffer in prison, whether the suffering is physical or psychological. Another reaction is one of humanitarian concern that the punishments in prisons not be too harsh, severe, cruel, or inhuman. A third is inquiry designed to secure comprehension of the social and psychological processes in criminal behavior, so that control can be based on knowledge.

---

[9] A. C. Schnur, "The New Penology: Fact or Fiction?," *Journal of Criminal Law and Criminology,* 49 (1958): 331–34.

31. THE MALE INMATE SOCIAL SYSTEM

Gresham M. Sykes and Sheldon L. Messinger

In recent years increased attention has been paid to the custodial institution in terms of general sociological theory rather than in terms of social problems, notably with reference to aspects of prison life commonly identified in the relevant literature as the "inmate culture," the "prisoner community," or the "inmate social system." This system of social relationships—its underlying norms, attitudes, and beliefs—as found in the American prison is examined in this paper. After summarizing the salient features of the society of prisoners as presented in the sociological literature of the last two decades, we comment briefly on the major theoretical approach that has been used in discussing prison life in the past. Then we develop a theory of the structure and functioning of the inmate social system, primarily in terms of inmate values and their related roles, and finally we outline some possibilities for future research.

THE PRISON SOCIETY

Despite the number and diversity of prison populations, observers of such groups have reported one strikingly pervasive value system. This value system of prisoners commonly takes the form of an explicit code, in which brief normative imperatives are held forth as guides for the behavior of the inmate in his relations with fellow prisoners and custodians. The maxims are usually asserted with great vehemence by the inmate population, and violations call forth a diversity of sanctions ranging from ostracism to physical violence.

Examination of many descriptions of prison life[1] suggests that the chief

---

[1] The following contain relevant material:

David Abrahamson, "Evaluation of the Treatment of Criminals," in *Failures in Psychiatric Treatment*, ed. Paul H. Hoch (New York: Grune & Stratton, 1948), pp. 58–77.

Holley Cantine and Dachine Rainer, eds., *Prison Etiquette* (Bearsville, N.Y.: Retort Press, 1950).

Donald Clemmer, "Leadership Phenomena in a Prison Community," *Journal of Criminal Law and Criminology*, 28 (March–April 1938): 861–72; *The Prison Community* (Boston: Christopher Publishing House, 1940); "Observations on Imprisonment as a Source of Criminality," *Journal of Criminal Law and Criminology*, 41 (September–October 1950): 311–19.

R. J. Corsini, "A Study of Certain Attitudes of Prison Inmates," *Journal of Criminal Law and Criminology*, 37 (July–August 1946): 132–40; R. J. Corsini and Kenwood Bartleme, "Attitudes of San Quentin Prisoners," *Journal of Correctional Education*, 4 (October 1952): 43–46.

George Devereux and Malcolm C. Moos, "The Social Structure of Prisons, and the Organic Tensions," *Journal of Criminal Psychopathology*, 4 (October 1942): 306–24.

Patrick J. Driscoll, "Factors Related to the Institutional Adjustment of Prison Inmates," *Journal of Abnormal and Social Psychology*, 47 (July 1952): 593–96.

Maurice L. Farber, "Suffering and Time Perspective of the Prisoner," *University of Iowa Studies in Child Welfare*, 20 (1944): 153–227.

Joseph F. Fishman, *Sex Life in American Prisons* (New York: National Library Press, 1934).

Vernon Fox, "The Effect of Counseling on Adjustment in Prison," *Social Forces*, 32 (March 1954): 285–89.

L. M. Hanks, Jr., "Preliminary for a Study of Problems of Discipline in Prisons," *Journal of Criminal Law and Criminology*, 30 (March–April 1940): 879–87.

James Hargan, "The Psychology of Prison Language," *Journal of Abnormal and Social Psychology*, 30 (October–December 1935): 359–65.

Ida Harper, "The Role of the 'Fringer' in a State Prison for Women," *Social Forces*, 31 (October 1952): 53–60.

Frank E. Hartung and Maurice Floch, "A Social-Psychological Analysis of Prison Riots: An Hypothesis," *Journal of Criminal Law, Criminology and Police Science*, 47 (May–June 1956): 51–57.

Norman S. Hayner, "Washington State Correctional Institutions as Communities," *Social Forces*, 21 (March 1943): 316–22; Norman S. Hayner and Ellis Ash, "The Prisoner Community as a Social Group," *American Sociological Review*, 4 (June 1939): 362–69; and "The Prison as a Community," *ibid.*, 5 (August 1940): 577–83.

F. E. Haynes, "The Sociological Study of the Prison Community," *Journal of Criminal Law and Criminology*, 39 (November–December 1948): 432–40.

Hans von Hentig, "The Limits of Penal Treatment," *Journal of Criminal Law and Criminology*, 32 (November–December 1941): 401–410.

Alfred C. Horsch and Robert A. Davis, "Personality Traits and Conduct of Institutionalized Delinquents," *Journal of Criminal Law and Criminology*, 29 (July–August 1938): 241–44.

John James, "The Application of the Small Group Concept to the Study of the Prison Community," *British Journal of Delinquency*, 5 (April 1955): 269–80.

Benjamin Karpman, "Sex Life in Prison," *Journal of Criminal Law and Criminology*, 38 (January–February 1948): 475–86.

tenets of the inmate code can be classified roughly into five major groups:

1. There are those maxims that caution: *Don't interfere with inmate interests*, which center of course in serving the least possible time and enjoying the greatest possible number of pleasures and privileges while in prison. The most inflexible directive in this category is concerned with betrayal of a fellow captive to the institutional officials: *Never rat on a con*. In general, no qualification or mitigating circumstance is recognized; and no grievance against another inmate—even though it is justified in the eyes of the inmate population—is to be taken to officials for settlement. Other specifics include: *Don't be nosey; don't have a loose lip; keep off a man's back; don't put a guy on the spot*. In brief and positively put: *Be loyal to your class—the cons*. Prisoners must present a unified front against their guards, no matter how much this may cost in terms of personal sacrifice.

2. There are explicit injunctions to refrain from quarrels or arguments

---

Robert M. Lindner, *Stone Walls and Men* (New York: Odyssey Press, 1946); "Sex in Prison," *Complex*, 6 (Fall 1951): 5–20.

Walter A. Lunden, "Antagonism and Altruism among Prisoners," in P. A. Sorokin, *Forms and Techniques of Altruistic and Spiritual Growth* (Boston: Beacon Press, 1954), pp. 447–60.

Richard McCleery, *The Strange Journey: A Demonstration Project in Adult Education in Prison*, University of North Carolina extension bulletin 32 (1953); "Power, Communications and the Social Order: A Study of Prison Government" (unpublished doctoral dissertation, University of North Carolina, 1956).

Lloyd W. McCorkle and Richard Korn, "Resocialization Within Walls," *Annals of the American Academy of Political and Social Science*, 293 (May 1954): 88–98.

Hermann Mannheim, *Group Problems in Crime and Punishment* (London: Routledge & Kegan Paul, 1955).

William R. Morrow, "Criminality and Antidemocratic Trends: A Study of Prison Inmates," in T. W. Adorno *et al.*, *The Authoritarian Personality* (New York: Harper, 1950), pp. 817–90.

Victor F. Nelson, *Prison Days and Nights* (Boston: Little, Brown, 1933).

Paul Nitsche and Karl Wilmanns *The History of Prison Psychosis*, Nervous and Mental Disease Monograph Series no. 13 (1912).

Norman A. Polansky, "The Prison as an Autocracy," *Journal of Criminal Law and Criminology*, 33 (May–June 1942): 16–22.

Harvey Powelson and Reinhard Bendix, "Psychiatry in Prison," *Psychiatry*, 14 (February 1951): 73–86.

Donald Rasmussen, "Prisoner Opinions about Parole," *American Sociological Review*, 5 (August 1940): 584–95.

Hans Riemer, "Socialization in the Prison Community," *Proceedings of the American Prison Association, 1937*, pp. 151–55.

Clarence Schrag, "Social Types in a Prison Community" (unpublished master's thesis, University of Washington, 1944); "Crimeville: A Sociometric Study of a Prison Community" (unpublished doctoral dissertation, University of Washington, 1950); "Leadership among Prison Inmates," *American Sociological Review*, 19 (February 1954): 37–42.

Lowell S. Selling, "The Pseudo Family," *American Journal of Sociology*, 37 (September 1931): 247–53.

Gresham M. Sykes, "The Corruption of Authority and Rehabilitation," *Social Forces*, 34 (March 1956): 257–62; "Men, Merchants, and Toughs: A Study of Reactions to Imprisonment," *Social Problems*, 4 (October 1956): 130–38.

Donald R. Taft, "The Group and Community Organization Approach to Prison Administration," *Proceedings of the American Prison Association, 1942*, pp. 275–84.

Ruth Sherman Tolman, "Some Differences in Attitudes Between Groups of Repeating Criminals and of First Offenders," *Journal of Criminal Law and Criminology*, 30 (July–August 1939): 196–203.

with fellow prisoners: *Don't lose your head.* Emphasis is placed on the curtailment of affect; emotional frictions are to be minimized and the irritants of daily life ignored. Maxims often heard include: *Play it cool* and *Do your own time.* As we shall see, there are important distinctions in this category, depending on whether the prisoner has been subjected to legitimate provocation; but in general a definite value is placed on curbing feuds and grudges.

3. Prisoners assert that inmates should not take advantage of one another by means of force, fraud, or chicanery: *Don't exploit inmates.* This sums up several directives: *Don't break your word; don't steal from the cons; don't sell favors; don't be a racketeer; don't welsh on debts.* More positively, it is argued that inmates should share scarce goods in a balanced reciprocity of "gifts" or "favors," rather than sell to the highest bidder or selfishly monopolize any amenities: *Be right.*

4. There are rules that have as their central theme the maintenance of self: *Don't weaken.* Dignity and the ability to withstand frustration or threatening situations without complaining or resorting to subservience are widely acclaimed. The prisoner should be able to "take it" and maintain his integrity in the face of privation. When confronted with wrongfully aggressive behavior, whether of inmates or officials, the prisoner should show courage. Although starting a fight runs counter to the inmate code, retreating from a fight started by someone else is equally reprehensible. Some of these maxims are: *Don't whine; don't cop out* (cry guilty); *don't suck around.* Prescriptively put: *Be tough; be a man.*

5. Prisoners express a variety of maxims that forbid according prestige or respect to the custodians or the world for which they stand: *Don't be a sucker.* Guards are *hacks* or *screws* and are to be treated with constant suspicion and distrust. In any situation of conflict between officials and prisoners, the former are automatically to be considered in the wrong. Furthermore, inmates should not allow themselves to become committed to the values of hard work and submission to duly constituted authority—values prescribed (if not followed) by *screws*—for thus an inmate would become a *sucker* in a world where the law-abiding are usually hypocrites and the true path to success lies in forming a "connection." The positive maxim is: *Be sharp.*

In the literature on the mores of imprisoned criminals there is no claim that these values are asserted with equal intensity by every member of a prison population; all social systems exhibit disagreements and differing emphases with respect to the values publicly professed by their members. But observers of the prison are largely agreed that the inmate code is outstanding both for the passion with which it is propounded and the almost universal allegiance verbally accorded it.

In the light of this inmate code or system of inmate norms, we can begin to understand the patterns of inmate behavior so frequently reported; for conformity to, or deviation from, the inmate code is the major basis for classifying and describing the social relations of prisoners. As Strong has pointed out, social groups are apt to characterize individuals in terms of crucial "axes of life" (lines of interests, problems, and concerns faced by the groups) and then to attach distinctive names to the resulting roles or types.[2] This process may be discerned in the society of prisoners and its argot for the patterns of behavior or social roles exhibited by inmates; and in these roles the outlines of the prison community as a system of action[3] may be seen.

An inmate who violates the norm proscribing the betrayal of a fellow prisoner is labeled a *rat* or a *squealer* in the vocabulary of the inmate world, and his deviance elicits universal scorn and hatred.[4] Prisoners who exhibit highly aggressive behavior, who quarrel easily and fight without cause, are often referred to as *toughs*. The individual who uses violence deliberately as a means to gain his ends is called a *gorilla;* a prisoner so designated is one who has established a satrapy based on coercion in clear contravention of the rule against exploitation by force. The term *merchant*, or *peddler*, is applied to the inmate who exploits his fellow captives not by force but by manipulation and trickery, and who typically sells or trades goods that are in short supply. If a prisoner shows himself unable to withstand the general rigors of existence in the custodial institution, he may be referred to as a *weakling* or a *weak sister*. If, more specifically, an inmate is unable to endure prolonged deprivation of heterosexual relationships and consequently enters into a homosexual liaison, he will be labeled a *wolf* or a *fag*, depending on whether his role is an active or a passive one.[5] If he continues to plead his case, he may soon be sarcastically known as a *rapo* (from "bum rap") or *innocent*. And if an inmate makes the mistake on allying himself with officialdom by taking on and expressing the values of conformity, he may be called a *square John* and ridiculed accordingly.

However, the individual who has received perhaps the greatest attention in the literature is one who most nearly fulfills the norms of the society of prisoners, who celebrates the inmate code rather than violates it: the *right guy*, the *real con*, the *real man*—the argot varies, but the role is clear-cut. The *right guy* is the hero of the inmate social system, and his existence gives meaning to the villains, the deviants such as the *rat*, the *tough*, the *gorilla*, and the *merchant*. The *right guy* is the base line, how-

---

[2] Samuel M. Strong, "Social Types in a Minority Group," *American Journal of Sociology*, 48 (March 1943): 563–73; Schrag, in "Social Types in a Prison Community," notes the relevance of Strong's discussion for examination of the inmate social system.

[3] See Schrag, "Social Types in a Prison Community," and Sykes, "Men, Merchants, and Toughs," for discussion of this approach to the prison as a system of action.

[4] The argot applied to a particular role varies somewhat from one prison to another, but it is not difficult to find the synonyms in the prisoners' lexicon.

[5] The inmate population, with a keen sense of distinctions, draws a line between the *fag*, who plays a passive role in a homosexual relationship because he "likes" it or "wants" to, and a *punk*, who is coerced or bribed into a passive role.

ever idealized or infrequent in reality, from which the inmate population takes its bearings. It seems worth while, therefore, to sketch his portrait briefly in the language of the inmates.

A *right guy* is always loyal to his fellow prisoners. He never lets you down no matter how rough things get. He keeps his promises; he's dependable and trustworthy. He isn't nosey about your business and doesn't shoot off his mouth about his own. He doesn't act stuck-up, but he doesn't fall all over himself to make friends either—he has a certain dignity. The *right guy* never interferes with other inmates who are conniving against the officials. He doesn't go around looking for a fight, but he never runs away from one when he is in the right. Anybody who starts a fight with a *right guy* has to be ready to go all the way. What he's got or can get of the extras in the prison—like cigarettes, food stolen from the mess hall, and so on—he shares with his friends. He doesn't take advantage of those who don't have much. He doesn't strong-arm other inmates into punking or fagging for him; instead, he acts like a man.

In his dealings with the prison officials, the *right guy* is unmistakably against them, but he doesn't act foolishly. When he talks about the officials with other inmates, he's sure to say that even the hacks with the best intentions are stupid, incompetent, and not to be trusted; that the worst thing a con can do is give the hacks information—they'll only use it against you when the chips are down. A *right guy* sticks up for his rights, but he doesn't ask for pity: he can take all the lousy screws can hand out and more. He doesn't suck around the officials, and the privileges that he's got are his because he deserves them. Even if the *right guy* doesn't look for trouble with the officials, he'll go to the limit if they push him too far. He realizes that there are just two kinds of people in the world, those in the know and the suckers or squares. Those who are in the know skim it off the top; suckers work.[6]

In summary, then, from the studies describing the life of men in prison, two major facts emerge: (1) Inmates give strong verbal support to a system of values that has group cohesion or inmate solidarity as its basic theme. Directly or indirectly, prisoners uphold the ideal of a system of social interaction in which individuals are bound together by ties of mutual aid, loyalty, affection, and respect, and are united firmly in their opposition to the enemy out-group. The man who exemplifies this ideal is accorded high prestige. The opposite of a cohesive inmate social system— a state in which each individual seeks his own advantage without reference to the claims of solidarity—is vociferously condemned. (2) The actual be-

---

[6] We have not attempted to discuss all the prison roles that have been identified in the literature, although we have mentioned most of the major types. Two exceptions, not discussed because they are not distinctive of the prison, are the *fish*, a novitiate, and the *ding*, an erratic behaver. The homosexual world of the prison, especially, deserves fuller treatment; various role types within it have not yet been described.

havior of prisoners ranges from full adherence to the norms of the inmate world to deviance of various types. These behavioral patterns, recognized and labeled by prisoners in the pungent argot of the dispossessed, form a collection of social roles which, with their interrelationships, constitute the inmate social system. We turn now to explanation of the inmate social system and its underlying structure of sentiments.

THEORETICAL APPROACH TO THE INMATE SOCIAL SYSTEM

The literature shows that few explicit attempts to develop a theory accounting for the norms and behavior of imprisoned criminals have been made. As in literature on other areas of intense public concern, polemics compete with scientific hypotheses, and descriptive anecdotes outnumber empirical generalizations. It may be of greater importance that when the inmate social system has been approached from a theoretical viewpoint, attention has usually been focused on the induction of the individual into inmate society, i.e., the problem of "prisonization."[7] There has been little concerted effort to account for the structure and functioning of the system into which the individual becomes socialized.[8]

It is not difficult to understand why the transformation of the novitiate into a fully accredited convict has received so much emphasis. Penology in the past has been the province primarily of the moralizer and the social reformer, and the major questions have related to how current patterns of adjustment may affect the offender's *future* readjustment to the free community. Thus, the nature of the inmate social system has tended to remain a "given," something to be accepted without systematic explanation, and its functions for current behavior have tended to remain unproblematic. As suggested in the introduction, however, the prison is important as an object of study in its own right; and even from the viewpoint of interest in criminal reform, study only of the socialization process in prison is insufficient, on both theoretical and practical grounds.

On the theoretical side, study of the socialization process in prison leaves a serious hiatus: it does not illuminate the conditions determining the presence (or absence) of inmate society. Acting on the implicit assumption that an inmate behaves like an inmate because of the presence of other inmates who exhibit a distinctive culture, sociologists concerned with the prison have largely failed to provide a theory explaining the remarkable similarity of the inmate social systems found in one custodial institution after another. This fact presses for theoretical consideration at the present

---

[7] Cf. Clemmer, *The Prison Community*, pp. 298ff., on the use of this term.

[8] Albert K. Cohen, in *Delinquent Boys* (Glencoe, Ill.: Free Press, 1955), especially pp. 18–19, makes a similar point relative to discussions of "delinquency."

time; and if we are to understand the fact, more attention must be given to the social setting in which the inmate population must live and to the problems generated by this setting. We want to know why inmate society "is there," as well as how inmates sustain it.

On the practical side, the major administrative directive that may be traced to studies of socialization in the prison is to separate the "prisonized" from the "nonprisonized." Aside from the financial and administrative imponderables involved in any attempt to carry out this directive, however, we believe that in the long run it would not resolve the basic problem: the development of inmate society under the conditions of imprisonment, only one of which is the presence of formerly incarcerated inmates. Any satisfactory solution to this problem will depend on the development of an adequate theory of the social structure of the inmate world; and only as such a theory is developed will knowledge of the socialization process gain perspective.

A NEW THEORY

The loss of liberty is but one of the many deprivations or frustrations inflicted on imprisoned criminals, although it is fundamental to all the rest. As Hayner and Ash have pointed out, inmates are deprived of goods and services that are more or less taken for granted even at the lowest socioeconomic levels in the free community.[9] Inmates must live in austerity as a matter of public policy. Barnes and Teeters have discussed the constraints imposed by the mass of institutional regulations under which prisoners are required to live.[10] Clemmer, Fishman, and others have stressed the severe frustrations imposed on prisoners by the denial of heterosexual relationships.[11] Numerous other writers have described the various pains of confinement in conditions of prolonged physical and psychological compression.

Although the inmate population may no longer suffer the brutality and neglect that in the past aroused the anger of John Howard and similar critics of penal institutions, prisoners still must undergo a variety of deprivations and frustrations which flow either by accident or intent from the fact of imprisonment. Furthermore, it is of greatest significance that the rigors imposed on the inmate by the prison officials do not represent relatively minor irritants which he can somehow endure; instead, the conditions of custody involve profound attacks on the prisoner's self-image or

---

[9] "The Prisoner Community as a Social Group."

[10] Harry E. Barnes and Negley K. Teeters, *New Horizons in Criminology*, 2nd ed. (New York: Prentice-Hall, 1951), pp. 438–39.

[11] Clemmer, *The Prison Community*, pp. 249–73; Fishman, *Sex Life in American Prisons*.

sense of personal worth, and these psychological pains may be far more threatening than physical maltreatment.[12] Brief analysis of the nature of these attacks on the inmate's personality is necessary, for it is as a response to them that we can begin to grasp the rationale of the inmate social system.

The isolation of the prisoner from the free community means that he has been rejected by society. His rejection is underscored in some prisons by his shaven head; in almost all, by his uniform and the degradation of no longer having a name but a number. The prisoner is confronted daily with the fact that he has been stripped of his membership in society at large, and now stands condemned as an outcast, an outlaw, a deviant so dangerous that he must be kept behind closely guarded walls and watched both day and night. He has lost the privilege of being *trusted* and his every act is viewed with suspicion by the guards, the surrogates of the conforming social order. Constantly aware of lawful society's disapproval, his picture of himself challenged by frequent reminders of his moral unworthiness, the inmate must find some way to ward off these attacks and avoid their introjection.[13]

In addition, it should be remembered that the offender has been drawn from a society in which personal possessions and material achievement are closely linked with concepts of personal worth by numerous cultural definitions. In the prison, however, the inmate finds himself reduced to a level of living near bare subsistence, and whatever physical discomforts this deprivation may entail, it apparently has deeper psychological significance as a basic attack on the prisoner's conception of his own personal adequacy.

No less important, perhaps, is the ego threat that is created by the deprivation of heterosexual relationships. In the tense atmosphere of the prison, with its perversions and constant references to the problems of sexual frustration, even those inmates who do not engage in overt homosexuality suffer acute attacks of anxiety about their own masculinity. These anxieties may arise from a prisoner's unconscious fear of latent homosexual tendencies in himself, which might be activated by his prolonged heterosexual deprivation and the importunity of others; or at a more conscious level he may feel that his masculinity is threatened because he can see himself as a man—in the full sense—only in a world that also contains women. In either case the inmate is confronted with the fact that the celibacy imposed on him by society means more than simple physiological frustration: an essential component of his self-conception, his status as male, is called into question.

Rejected, impoverished, and figuratively castrated, the prisoner must face still further indignity in the extensive social control exercised by the custodians. The many details of the inmate's life, ranging from the hours

---

[12] A. H. Maslow, "Deprivation, Threat, and Frustration," *Psychological Review*, 48 (July 1941): 364–66.
[13] McCorkle and Korn, "Resocialization Within Walls," p. 88.

of sleeping to the route to work and the job itself, are subject to a vast number of regulations made by prison officials. The inmate is stripped of his autonomy; hence, to the other pains of imprisonment we must add the pressure to define himself as weak, helpless, and dependent. Individuals under guard are exposed to the bitter ego threat of losing their identification with the normal adult role.[14]

The remaining significant feature of the inmate's social environment is the presence of other imprisoned criminals. Murderers, rapists, thieves, confidence men, and sexual deviants are the inmate's constant companions, and this enforced intimacy may prove to be disquieting even for the hardened recidivist. As an inmate has said, "The worst thing about prison is you have to live with other prisoners."[15] Crowded into a small area with men who have long records of physical assaults, thievery, and so on (and who may be expected to continue in the path of deviant social behavior in the future), the inmate is deprived of the sense of security that we more or less take for granted in the free community. Although the anxieties created by such a situation do not necessarily involve an attack on the individual's sense of personal worth—as we are using the concept—the problems of self-protection in a society composed exclusively of criminals constitute one of the inadvertent rigors of confinement.

In short, imprisonment "punishes" the offender in a variety of ways extending far beyond the simple fact of incarceration. However just or necessary such punishments may be, their importance for our present analysis lies in the fact that they form a set of harsh social conditions to which the population of prisoners must respond or *adapt itself*. The inmate feels that the deprivations and frustrations of prison life, with their implications for the destruction of his self-esteem, somehow must be alleviated. It is, we suggest, as an answer to this need that the functional significance of the inmate code or system of values exhibited so frequently by men in prison can best be understood.

As we have pointed out, the dominant theme of the inmate code is group cohesion, with a "war of all against all"—in which each man seeks his own gain without considering the rights or claims of others—as the theoretical antipode. But if a war of all against all is likely to make life "solitary, poor, nasty, brutish, and short" for men with freedom, as Hobbes suggested, it is doubly so for men in custody. Even those who are most successful in exploiting their fellow prisoners will find it a dangerous and nerve-wracking game, for they cannot escape the company of their victims. No man can assure the safety of either his person or his possessions, and eventually the winner is certain to lose to a more powerful or more skillful exploiter. Furthermore, the victims hold the trump card, since a word to the officials

---

[14] Bruno Bettelheim, "Individual and Mass Behavior in Extreme Situations," *Journal of Abnormal and Social Psychology*, 38 (October 1943): 417–52.

[15] Gresham M. Sykes, *Crime and Society* (New York: Random House, 1956), p. 109.

is frequently all that is required to ruin the most dominating figure in the inmate population. A large share of the "extra" goods that enter the inmate social system must do so as the result of illicit conniving against the officials, which often requires lengthy and extensive cooperation and trust; in a state of complete conflict the resources of the system will be diminished. Mutual abhorrence or indifference will feed the emotional frictions arising from interaction under compression. And as rejection by others is a fundamental problem, a state of mutual alienation is worse than useless as a solution to the threats created by the inmate's status as an outcast.

As a population of prisoners moves toward a state of mutual antagonism, then, the many problems of prison life become more acute. On the other hand, *as a population of prisoners moves in the direction of solidarity, as demanded by the inmate code, the pains of imprisonment become less severe.* They cannot be eliminated, it is true, but their consequences at least can be partially neutralized. A cohesive inmate society provides the prisoner with a meaningful social group with which he can identify himself and which will support him in his struggles against his condemners. Thus it permits him to escape at least in part the fearful isolation of the convicted offender. Inmate solidarity, in the form of toleration of the many irritants of life in confinement, helps to solve the problems of personal security posed by the involuntary intimacy of men noteworthy for their seriously antisocial behavior in the past.

Similarly, group cohesion in the form of a reciprocity of favors undermines one of the most potent sources of aggression among prisoners, the drive for personal aggrandizement through exploitation by force and fraud. Furthermore, although goods in scarce supply will remain scarce even if they are shared rather than monopolized, such goods will be distributed more equitably in a social system marked by solidarity, and this may be of profound significance in enabling the prisoner to endure better the psychological burden of impoverishment. A cohesive population of prisoners has another advantage in that it supports a system of shared beliefs that explicitly deny the traditional link between merit and achievement. Material success, according to this system, is a matter of "connections" rather than skill or hard work, and thus the imprisoned criminal is partially freed from the necessity of defining his material want as a sign of personal inadequacy.

Finally, a cohesive inmate social system institutionalizes the value of "dignity" and the ability to "take it" in a number of norms and reinforces these norms with informal social controls. In effect, the prisoner is called on to endure manfully what he cannot avoid. At first glance this might seem to be simply the counsel of despair; but if the elevation of fortitude into a primary virtue is the last refuge of the powerless, it also serves to shift the criteria of the individual's worth from conditions that cannot be altered to his ability to maintain some degree of personal integration; and the latter, at least, can be partially controlled. By creating an ideal of endurance in the face of harsh social conditions, then, the society of prisoners opens a path to the restoration of self-respect and a sense of independence that can exist despite prior criminality, present subjugation, and the free community's denial of the offender's moral worthiness. Significantly, this path to virtue is recognized by the prison officials as well as the prisoners.

One further point should be noted with regard to the emphasis placed on the maintenance of self as defined by the value system of prisoners. Dignity, composure, courage, the ability to "take it" and "hand it out" when necessary—these are the traits affirmed by the inmate code. They are also traits that are commonly defined as masculine by the inmate population. As a consequence, the prisoner finds himself in a situation where he can recapture his male role, not in terms of its sexual aspects, but in terms of behavior that is accepted as a good indicator of virility.

The effectiveness of the inmate code in mitigating the pains of imprisonment depends of course on the extent to which precepts are translated into action. As we have indicated, the demands of the inmate code for loyalty, generosity, disparagement of officials, and so on are most fully exemplified in the behavior of the *right guy*. On the other hand, much noncohesive behavior occurs on the part of the *rat*, the *tough*, the *gorilla*, the *merchant*, and the *weak sister*. The population of prisoners, then, does not exhibit perfect solidarity in practice, in spite of inmates' vehement assertions of group cohesion as a value; but neither is the population of prisoners a warring aggregate. Rather, the inmate social system typically appears to be balanced in an uneasy compromise somewhere between these two extremes. The problems confronting prisoners in the form of social rejection, material deprivation, sexual frustration, and the loss of autonomy and personal security are not completely eliminated. Indeed, even if the norms of the inmate social system were fully carried out by all, the pains of imprisonment would only be lessened; they would not disappear. But the pains of imprisonment are at least relieved by whatever degree of group cohesion is achieved in fact, and this is crucial in understanding the functional significance of the inmate code for inmates.

One further problem remains. Many of the prisoners who deviate from the maxims of the inmate code are precisely those who are most vociferous in their verbal allegiance to it. How can this discrepancy between words and behavior be explained? Much of the answer seems to lie in the fact that almost all inmates have an interest in maintaining cohesive behavior on the part of others, *regardless of the role they play themselves,* and vehement vocal support of the inmate code is a potent means to this end.

There are, of course, prisoners who "believe" in inmate cohesion both for themselves and others. These hold the unity of the group as a high personal value and are ready to demand cohesive behavior from their fellow prisoners. This collectivistic orientation may be due to a thorough identification with the criminal world in opposition to the forces of lawful society, or to a system of values that transcends such divisions. In any case, for these men the inmate code has much of the quality of a religious faith and they approach its tenets as true believers. In a second category are those prisoners who are relatively indifferent to the cohesion of the inmate population as a personal value, but who are quick to assert it as a guide to behavior because in its absence they would be likely to become chronic victims. They are committed to the ideal of inmate solidarity to the extent that they have little or no desire to take advantage of their fellow captives, but they do not go so far as to subscribe to the ideal of self-sacrifice. Their behavior is best described as passive or neutral; they are believers without passion, demanding adherence from others, but not prepared to let excessive piety interfere with more mundane considerations. Third, there are those who loudly acclaim the inmate code and actively violate its injunctions. These men suffer if their number increases, since they begin to face the difficulties of competition; and they are in particular danger if their depredations are reported to the officials. The prisoners who are thus actively alienated from other inmates and yet give lip service to inmate solidarity resemble a manipulative priesthood, savage in their expression of belief but corrupt in practice. In brief, a variety of motivational patterns underlies allegiance to the inmate code, but few inmates can avoid the need to insist publicly on its observance, whatever the discrepancies in their actions.

* * *

We have drawn a picture of the inmate social system as a set of interlocking roles that are based on conformity to, or deviance from, a collection of dominant values; and we have suggested that these values are firmly rooted in the major problems posed by the conditions of imprisonment. The maxims of the inmate code do not simply reflect the individual values of imprisoned criminals; rather, they represent a system of group norms that are directly related to mitigating the pains of imprisonment under a custodial regime having nearly total power. It is hoped that this view of the prison opens fruitful lines of inquiry, which may lead to better understanding of the structure and functioning not only of prison populations but of social groups in general.

32. THE FEMALE INMATE
SOCIAL SYSTEM

Rose Giallombardo

A neglected area in deviance studies of the adult prison setting concerns female forms of deviation. The study of deviance in the prison setting has typically been concerned with male forms of deviation. Indeed, with the exception of Harper's analysis of the "fringer" role[1] and the recently reported study of a women's prison by Ward and Kassebaum,[2] which describes the homosexual adaptation of female inmates, scientific description and analysis of the informal organization of the adult female prison have been overlooked.[3] In the present paper, inmate social roles and social

Reprinted by permission of the author and the Society for the Study of Social Problems from *Social Problems*, 13 (Winter 1966): 268–88. Original title: "Social Roles in a Prison for Women."

The complete study is reported in *Society of Women: A Study of a Women's Prison* (New York: Wiley, 1966).

[1] Ida Harper, "The Role of the 'Fringer' in a State Prison for Women," *Social Forces*, 31 (October 1952): 53–60.

[2] David A. Ward and Gene G. Kassebaum, "Lesbian Liaisons," *Trans-action*, 1 (January 1964): 28–32. Also David A. Ward and Gene G. Kassebaum, "Homosexuality: A Mode of Adaptation in a Prison for Women," *Social Problems*, 12 (Fall 1964): 159–77. In this institution, the authors found little evidence of the differentiated social types or of inmate solidarity that is typical of the male prison.

[3] In this connection, it should be pointed out that in addition to the aforementioned studies of the adult women's prison, there are several reports of institutions for juvenile

organization in a women's prison will be described in some detail; comparisons of this informal social structure will be made with relevant literature on the social roles assumed by male prisoners; and the social structure inside the prison setting will be viewed in relation to the external environment.

Previous accounts of the male prison have taken the view that the most important features of the inmate culture emerge as a response to the conditions of imprisonment. The features of this system are well known and need not be repeated here.[4] The point to be stressed, however, is that the functional interpretation which is made for the emergence of the inmate system typically views the culture that forms within the prison as a response to the problems found in the internal world of the prison and the crucial ways in which it differs from the external world. It is argued that while the prisoner cannot completely eliminate the pains of imprisonment, a cohesive inmate system which has group allegiance as its dominant value provides the inmate with a meaningful reference group that may reinstate the inmate's self-image, or in some sense neutralize the deleterious effects of its loss. This formulation derives from case studies of single institutions, and therefore it is extremely difficult to ascertain the validity of the conclusions drawn as previous writers have not explored systematically the interaction of the external culture with the conditions for survival faced by the prison aggregate. Nor has anyone assessed several adult prisons

---

girls which reveal homosexual practices and/or the presence of "family" groups among the delinquent girls. These reports are unsystematic investigations and impressionistic reports. See, for example, Charles A. Ford, "Homosexual Practices of Institutionalized Females," *Journal of Abnormal and Social Psychology*, 23 (January–March 1929): 442–44; Margaret Otis, "A Perversion Not Commonly Noted," *Journal of Abnormal Psychology*, 8 (June–July 1913): 112–14; Lowell S. Selling, "The Pseudo Family," *American Journal of Sociology*, 37 (September 1931): 247–53; Seymour L. Halleck and Marvin Hersko, "Homosexual Behavior in a Correctional Institution for Adolescent Girls," *American Journal of Orthopsychiatry*, 32 (October 1962): 911–17; Sidney Kosofsky and Albert Ellis, "Illegal Communication among Institutionalized Female Delinquents," *Journal of Social Psychology*, 48 (August 1958): 155–60; Romolo Toigo, "Illegitimate and Legitimate Cultures in a Training School for Girls," *Proceedings of the Rip Van Winkle Clinic*, 13 (Summer 1962): 3–29. Ward and Kassebaum, however, reported that there were no indications of family groups in the prison they studied ("Homosexuality").

[4] See esp. Gresham M. Sykes and Sheldon L. Messinger, "The Inmate Social System," in Richard A. Cloward et al., *Theoretical Studies in Social Organization of the Prison* (New York: Social Science Research Council, 1960), pp. 5–19 [and pp. 413–25 of this volume]; Gresham M. Sykes, *The Society of Captives* (Princeton, N.J.: Princeton University Press, 1958); Erving Goffman, "On the Characteristics of Total Institutions: Staff-Inmate Relations," in *The Prison: Studies in Institutional Organization and Change*, ed. Donald R. Cressey (New York: Holt, Rinehart & Winston, 1961), chaps. 1 and 2; Richard A. Cloward, "Social Control in the Prison," in *Theoretical Studies in Social Organization of the Prison*, pp. 20–48. See also Donald Clemmer, *The Prison Community* (New York: Holt, Rinehart & Winston, 1958 [reissue of the 1940 edition]); Morris G. Caldwell, "Group Dynamics in the Prison Community," *Journal of Criminal Law, Criminology, and Police Science*, 46 (January–February 1956): 648–57; Norman S. Hayner, "Washington State Correctional Institutions as Communities," *Social Forces*, 21 (1943): 316–22; Norman S. Hayner and Ellis Ash, "The Prison as a Community," *American Sociological Review*, 5 (August 1940): 577–83; Hans Riemer, "Socialization in the Prison Community," *Proceedings of the American Prison Association, 1937*, pp. 151–55.

simultaneously so that a comparative analysis could be made.[5] I think we are just beginning to understand the variability of one prison from another as they are affected by organizational goals, the composition of staff and inmates. Indeed, recent systematic studies of socialization in the male prison by Wheeler and Garabedian call into question the solidary opposition model of inmate culture even within single institutions, as these scholars found that prisoners varied in their support of the inmate culture over time and according to type of prisoner.[6]

Moreover, Irwin and Cressey have advanced the thesis that there are three subcultures in the prison which they maintain reflect the presence of different types of prisoners. These differences presumably are a reflection of the values and attitudes particular inmates bring into the prison and are related to latent identities.[7] Similarly, Schrag attempts to account for inmate deviants with respect to internalization of inmate culture and support of the inmate code in terms of their preprison characteristics and identities.[8] Thus, the developing theoretical considerations tend to emphasize values and attitudes learned by inmates prior to entering the prison.

The present findings from a case study of a women's prison bear on this matter. In the adult female prison which the writer studied, it was found that in order to cope with the major problems of institutional living, the female inmates have also labeled the reactions of prisoners according to the mode of response exhibited by the inmate to the prison situation and the quality of the inmate's interaction with other inmates and staff. However, although the deprivations of imprisonment were present and felt keenly by the female prisoners, the female argot roles differ in structural form and in the sentiment attached to them from the roles assumed by male prisoners. In addition, it should be pointed out that homosexual dyads cast into marriage alliances, family groups, and other kinship ties formed by the inmates integrate the inmates into a meaningful social system and represent an attempt to create a substitute universe within the prison.[9]

---

[5] It is interesting that an analysis of variations in organizational goals and an examination of data on the inmates of several juvenile correctional institutions for boys call into question the "solidarity opposition" model of the inmate group. See David Street, "The Inmate Group in Custodial and Treatment Settings," *American Sociological Review*, 30 (February 1965): 40–55.

[6] Stanton Wheeler, "Socialization in Correctional Communities," *American Sociological Review*, 26 (October 1961): 696–712; Peter C. Garabedian, "Social Roles and Processes of Socialization in the Prison Community," *Social Problems*, 11 (Fall 1963): 139–52.

[7] John Irwin and Donald R. Cressey, "Thieves, Convicts, and the Inmate Culture," *Social Problems*, 10 (Fall 1962): 142–55.

[8] Clarence Schrag, "Some Foundations for a Theory of Correction," in *The Prison: Studies in Institutional Organization and Change*, ed. Donald R. Cressey (New York: Holt, Rinehart & Winston, 1961), pp. 309–57.

[9] Marriage, family, and kinship in the female prison will be discussed in a forthcoming paper. However, in this context it might be worthwhile pointing out that the differentiation of sex roles is crucial as it structures at the outset many other roles which the inmate may legitimately play. Once an inmate has adopted a sex role, it automatically closes off some family roles, while at the same time it opens up legitimate avenues for other roles.

The empirical evidence to be presented supports the thesis that differences in the informal social structure in male and female prison communities can be understood in terms of the differential cultural definitions ascribed to male and female roles in American society. More specifically, it is suggested that the prison structure incorporates and reflects the *total* external social structure in that the differential cultural definitions ascribed to male and female roles in the external world influence the definitions made within the prison, and function to determine the direction and focus of the inmate cultural system.

CULTURAL EXPECTATIONS OF MALE AND FEMALE ROLES

Are sex roles so sharply differentiated in American society that we would expect wide variations in behavior patterns to be found in the two prison communities? There are a number of areas in which American society differentiates male and female roles. In the main, it may be said that in contrast to the male, who is expected to prepare for an occupational role, and whose prestige rank is established by the nature of his lifework, the female's life goal is achieved through marriage and child-rearing. Although the "career woman" is an important social type,[10] the percentage of women who pursue uninterrupted careers is very small in our society. So long as women bear children, there must be some social arrangement to ensure that the functions of nurturing and training during the period of dependency are fulfilled.

And we may point to other areas in which American culture tends further to differentiate male and female roles. It does not discourage and accepts a public display of affection between two women such as the use of terms of endearment, embracing, holding hands, and kissing. Such behavior on the part of the male, however, would immediately be defined as homosexual. Moreover, women are said to be more dependent, emotional, less aggressive, and less prone to violence than men. It is said that women generally show less initiative in openly defying authority, whereas men have been defined as independent, violent, and aggressive.[11] This *generalized popular culture* persists for women on another level—the woman-to-woman popular culture. In this vein, the mass media perpetuate the stereotype that a "woman's worst enemy is another woman." Because of the

---

[10] Robin M. Williams, Jr., *American Society*, rev. ed. (New York: Knopf, 1960), pp. 64–65. Although many married women at one time or another do some kind of work outside the home for which they earn a salary, marriage and family are the primary goals for most American women. Indeed, despite the marked increase in the number of married women in the labor market, the worker role of women continues to be regarded by society as secondary to the traditional role of women as mothers and homemakers.

[11] Indeed, the architecture of the male prison has been historically oriented upon the general belief that the male criminal is aggressive and dangerous.

female's orientation to the marriage market, it is argued that she tends
see other women as rivals.[12] This view finds its significance and signature
underscored in the highly stylized type of the best friend "betrayed." A
similar theme is operative when we find that working women state preferences for male supervisors rather than female supervisors.

To the extent that this generalized popular culture persists in the prison
setting, a situation of calculated solidarity may be said to obtain between
the female inmates. Calculated solidarity is defined as a social unity based
not upon automatic conformity to a set of common norms perceived to be
morally binding, but rather a unity which is subject to constant interpretation by the inmate as she perceives each situation from the point of view of
her own interests. Common responsibility in any particular situation,.
then, exists only to the extent that the individual perceives her own interests to be served.[13] Unless the formal organization can supply the inmates with all of their wants, then perforce inmates must turn to one
another for the satisfaction of those needs which are attractive and agree-
able to them, and which cannot be fulfilled by the formal organization.
Clemmer's finding is relevant here. In response to questionnaire items, 70
percent of his subjects concluded that "friendships in prison result from
the mutual help man can give man rather than because of some admired
trait."[14] However, if the popular culture on the woman-to-woman level is
imported into the prison environment, then we would expect that violations of much tabooed behavior may not be severely punished, or may be
overlooked, as the very nature of the case implies that expectations of behavior cannot be consistent. Possible latent dysfunctions of the popular
culture, then, would be expected to neutralize deviant acts.

METHOD OF STUDY

I was fortunate to have the opportunity to undertake field work for a
period of one year in a large women's prison in a correctional system generally regarded as one of the most progressive. Data were gathered by personal observation of the inmates as they participated in formally scheduled

[12] Simone de Beauvoir, *The Second Sex*, trans. and ed. H. M. Parshley (New York:
Bantam Books, 1961), p. 514. She argues that the marriage market from one age period to
another is very unstable for the female. Consequently, the process of acquiring a husband becomes an urgent matter, and this concern is often destructive of feminine friendships, for the young girl sees rivals rather than allies in her companions. In this connection, Jules Henry has stated that the self-orientation of the female begins at an early age;
see *Culture Against Man* (New York: Random House, 1963), pp. 150–55.

[13] As Malinowski has cogently pointed out, however, automatic conformity does not
exist empirically. But we may conceive of automatic conformity and lawlessness as ideal
types with the prison approximating calculated solidarity. See Bronislaw Malinowski,
Crime and Custom in Savage Society (New York: Harcourt, Brace, 1932), esp. chaps. 3, 4,
and 5.

[14] Clemmer, *The Prison Community*, p. 123.

inmate activities: work assignments, vocational and avocational classes, group counseling sessions, academic educational classes, recreational and religious activities. At all inmate functions, the observer sat with the inmates. Other sources of data were obtained by personal observation of informal interaction patterns in the cottage units and on the grounds. During the year it was possible to get to know all the inmates who were at the prison when the study began, approximately 650, and many of the inmates who were committed during the course of the year as well. Interviews of one hour to three hours in length were held with these inmates. These interviews provided basic information on the nature and meaning of the cultural experiences and activities of the group, as well as the social values attached to them. The sociological characteristics of the inmate population were obtained by an examination of the record files of 653 inmates who were confined at the same time.

Other data were obtained by attendance at classification and subclassification meetings; the disciplinary court; meetings of the lieutenants and correctional officers; and other scheduled staff meetings. Informal interviews with correctional officers, prison administrators, and other staff members provided additional data. During the last week of the study, an anonymous questionnaire was administered to all the correctional officers to obtain data on the sociological characteristics of the correctional officers and perceptions of their role function.

THE DEPRIVATIONS OF IMPRISONMENT

Sykes has noted in his study of the Trenton prison that the pains of imprisonment for the modern prisoner are not rooted in physical brutality, but rather may be seen as attacks on the psychological level.[15] The "residue of apparently less acute hurts," he argues, such as the deprivation of liberty, goods and services, heterosexual relations, autonomy and security, "may indeed be the acceptable or unavoidable implications of imprisonment, but we must recognize the fact that they can be just as painful as the physical maltreatment which they have replaced."[16]

What would constitute deprivations for women? Interview data revealed that although the perceptions of the female inmates vary from one another in this regard, depending upon the stage of the inmate's prison career, one's former commitment history,[17] and/or the relative ease with which

---

[15] Sykes, *The Society of Captives,* p. 64.

[16] *Ibid.*

[17] On a selected day the records revealed that 52.1 percent had been previously jailed or imprisoned. The commitment age of the inmates ranged from fifteen to sixty-seven years, with a mean of 32.2 and a median of 30.5. Fifty-six percent of the inmate population were white and 44 percent were Negro. The marital status of the inmates indicated that 27.1 percent were single; 31.5 percent were married; 20.7 percent were separated; 16.4 percent were divorced; and slightly over 4 percent were widows.

the individual may adjust to the inmate social system, there is nevertheless a "hard core of consensus" among the female prisoners that prison life *is* depriving and frustrating.

In the female institution studied, it is quite true that in some areas the deprivations of imprisonment are less harsh. The physical surroundings are more pleasant; the cottages, although starkly simple, are clean and provide the inmate with adequate physical living conditions; with some ingenuity and mutual aid, the inmates enjoy limited opportunity for variety in the matter of dress.[18] The list could doubtless be expanded.

In spite of the mitigation of the pains of imprisonment, however, the differences cited are merely peripheral to the major concerns of prison life. The problems to be solved by the female inmate in this institution are the same conditions for survival as those for which the male prisoner has found it necessary to provide solutions in order to survive psychically in the prison environment. These problems have their basis in the disorientation resulting from the abrupt termination of the individual's freedom: the lack of opportunity for heterosexual relations—the fracturing of every influence favorable to the cultivation of emotional reciprocity as a result of being cut off from family and friends; withholding of material goods; attacks on the self through the humiliating experiences incidental to a prison commitment; the loss of autonomy and responsibility to which life in a prison inevitably leads; and the lack of security and privacy.

The loss of liberty and autonomy are among the most uniformly felt deprivations of imprisonment among the female inmates. Restraints on the inmate's freedom are keenly felt, and the transition from liberty to rigidly restricted movement is a matter with which the female must come to terms in order to survive psychically in the prison world.

Whatever the material circumstances may have been for the individual inmate in civil society, the punishing aspect of denying the inmate ownership of personal goods in prison is that it removes the last resource the inmate possesses to express individuality, and therefore the abrupt removal of personal effects tends to destroy the inmate's self-image. The stripping and mortifying process[19] occurs immediately after the inmate's entrance into the prison; the personal clothing and other possessions of the inmate are replaced by the prison issue, which is fairly uniform, certain to have been worn by generations of prisoners, and to be either sizes too large or sizes too small. When one recalls that it is always open season on women's

---

[18] Yarn may be purchased at the commissary store. Knitted items such as socks and sweaters provide another means by which the loss of goods may be mitigated.

[19] Stripping and mortifying practices are discussed in Erving Goffman, *Asylums* (New York: Doubleday, 1961); see esp. pp. 14–25. In the prison, no clothing may be kept by the inmates except girdles (if they are not the panty type), brassieres, and shoes of simple (relatively low-heeled) closed styles. Medals, simple style earrings and wedding rings which are not studded with precious or semi-precious stones may be kept by the inmate, as well as wrist watches which are valued under fifteen dollars.

fashions, it is not surprising to learn that the attack on the individual's self-image with reference to clothing is particularly acute for the female inmate. The strategies employed by some of the inmates in the admission and orientation unit to individualize the prison issue by monograms, embroidery, or the strategic placement of pleats on a surplus WAC jacket in an attempt to make them "more like free-world clothes" are all evidence of the subtlety of deprivation.

For the male prisoner, it has been pointed out that lack of heterosexual intercourse is frustrating and depriving, and the evidence indicates that the same holds true for the great majority of the female inmates. Most inmates have enjoyed the company of men outside, and sex constitutes a major problem of adjustment for almost every inmate. Women do not choose to live their lives entirely apart from men, and the necessity of doing so in prison is frustrating for the individual.[20] Indeed, the situation for the imprisoned female may perhaps be seen to be more serious than for the male. "[American] culture," writes Jules Henry, "gives women no firm role except an erotic one."[21] In this regard, Parsons has discussed three broad categories of adjustment for the American female: (1) the "good companion" role; (2) the "glamour girl" role; and (3) the "domestic" role.[22] Thus with the closing of the prison gate the female prisoner finds herself cut off from the structure of American society conducive to the cultivation of a female role, which is the avenue through which she achieves self-respect and status.

The evidence, however, suggests that the other major deprivation suffered by the male prisoner, namely, the loss of security,[23] occurs on another level of experience for the female inmate, which is consistent with the popular culture. In the words of the inmates: "The hardest part of living in a prison is to live with other *women*." Commonly expressed attitudes of the nature of women are: "You can't trust another woman"; "Every woman is a sneaking, lying bitch." Hence, it is not so much the constant fear of violence or sexual exploitation, such as is the case for the male prisoner, which creates a hardship for the female inmates, but rather the strain involved in being in the forced company of women who are believed to

---

[20] The obvious exceptions to this, of course, are the homosexuals who have practiced homosexuality in the free community. Approximately 5 percent of the inmate population falls into this category. For this group, it cannot be said that this aspect of imprisonment is depriving. In a sense, the imprisonment of the homosexual—whether male or female—is ironical, for the loss of liberty, except in a few countries, is always accompanied by the denial of contact with the opposite sex so as to increase the burden of punishment. The homosexual in prison, however, is actually in a favored position, because the competition of the opposite sex has been excluded.

[21] Jules Henry, *Culture Against Man*, p. 61; also cf. Margaret Park Redfield, "The American Family: Consensus and Freedom," *American Journal of Sociology*, 52 (November 1946): 182. "Beyond the roles of glamor girl and nursemaid, the part to be played by women is but vaguely defined in our society."

[22] Talcott Parsons, "Age and Sex in the Social Structure of the United States," *American Sociological Review*, 7 (October 1942): 610–13.

[23] Sykes, *The Society of Captives*, p. 78.

be untrustworthy, capable of predatory tactics. Thus, the female inmate is apt to fear the consequences of aroused jealousy transformed into vitriolic verbal attacks;[24] and she suffers acute insecurity in confronting and handling the frequent attacks of *penitentiary darby*—gossip which takes place at all times and on all sides within the prison. Moreover, there is enough differentiation among the inmates so that some women experience insecurity in adjusting to living in the forced company of others whom they consider to be socially inferior; some of the white women, for example, find living in close proximity with Negroes to be distasteful; others feel repulsion at having to associate with prostitutes, women who are untidy in their personal habits, or who use vulgar language.[25]

As does the male prisoner, the female prisoner soon discovers that escape routes in prison are few. Psychological and physical withdrawal are not significant modes of adaptation to mitigate the pains of imprisonment for the inmates in this institution. What follows now is a description of the informal social structure which provides a complex of clearly defined social roles for the female prisoners and sets the limits of mutual accommodation.

THE SOCIAL ROLES

Snitchers and Inmate Cops or Lieutenants

Communication across caste lines is strictly forbidden in the female prison studied except for matters of urgent business, and all such interaction is expected to be handled with swift dispatch. Indeed, to violate the ban placed on legitimate communication flowing from inmates and staff is considered to be a very serious matter. The female inmates argue that no inmate should jeopardize the successful execution of activities based upon the common interests of the inmates in connection with the performance of illegal functions to relieve the pains of imprisonment; and secondly, supplying information to officials may result in the withdrawal of privileges or other forms of punishment, thereby adding to the pains of imprisonment for the inmate.

In the female prison, the role of the *snitcher* is the female counterpart to the "rat" in the male prison. To accuse an inmate of snitching is the most serious accusation which one inmate may hurl at another because it

---

[24] This is not to say, however, that there are no fights which take place among the inmates, but the real violence that occurs in the prison, however, tends to be in connection with a homosexual triangle. And in this connection the great fear is not so much for one's life, as the fear of *disfigurement*—the fear that an inmate "out to get" another will use razor or scissors to disfigure one's face. It is worthwhile noting that the prison officials issue scissors to each inmate; the blades are fairly blunt, but, nevertheless, this indicates the widely held belief of women as nonaggressive types.

[25] Types of contaminative exposures have been discussed by Erving Goffman in *Asylums,* pp. 25–35.

clearly signifies the division of loyalty between the staff and the inmates. The importance placed upon the "no snitching" norm is apparent as it covers every range of behavior and is put in the imperative to the new inmate or the deviant: "See and see nothing! Hear and hear nothing!"

Although the female prisoners agree that inmates should never give any information concerning an inmate to the staff, any prisoner according to the female inmates may occasionally engage in snitching when it is believed to serve the individual's interest. Moreover, the female's self-orientation and the tendency to see one another as rivals both function to decrease general expectations of rigid alliance with one another. Consequently, the female inmate rarely expresses any surprise when she suspects another inmate of deviating from the norm prohibiting communication of inmate affairs across caste lines—only a kind of bitterness that the status of inmate is not sufficient to bind and solidify the inmates completely into a cohesive group. The popular culture, then, in connection with the extent to which any female may be trusted, functions to neutralize many deviant acts in the prison. As a result, many deviant acts are overlooked, or are not severely punished; in contrast to the situation in the male prison, we find that violation of the "no snitching" norm does not often result in violence. In the words of one prisoner: "A lot is said about what will be done if you catch a snitch, but you know women! They talk loud, draw a crowd, and that's as far as it goes. When it comes to a showdown, they chicken out." This does not mean, however, that negative sanctions are not imposed. Panning and signifying are common modes of punishment to control behavior in the female inmate community.

Panning is general derogatory gossip about an inmate when the inmate is not physically present. *Signifying,* on the other hand, is a more compelling negative sanction because the offending inmate is physically present. A group of inmates will discuss a deviant act in considerable detail with biting sarcasm, scorn, and mimicry; the inmate's name is not at any time mentioned, but little doubt is left as to the inmate's identity. Both panning and signifying are extremely effective modes of social control. But sanctions need not always be so obvious to be effective. The fact that the prison is isolated,[26] of course, makes the prisoners extremely dependent upon one another for emotional reciprocity, and this in itself serves to check much continued deviant behavior. In the words of an inmate: "It's rough when the group ignores you." Inflection in one's voice, then, pretense that one has not seen another, and turning the head to avoid a greeting can be exquisite punishment in the prison community, and can often be quite as devastating as the more pointed panning and signifying.

---

[26] Most women, as a matter of fact, serve their entire sentence without a visit from the outside world. In the year 1962, for example, an examination of the records revealed that 79 inmates, or about 12 percent of the inmate population, received visits during the entire year.

Inmates who violate the ban on communication are watched closely and pertinent information concerning their activities is circulated quickly to other inmates. The snitcher, in short, is *persona non grata* in the prison community, and any common cause with an inmate assuming this role would in all certainty hurt one's reputation and close off interaction with the great majority of inmates. The snitcher is condemned by the female inmates because she denies the cohesion of the inmate community and jeopardizes the successful execution of the many illegal activities that take place in the prison to mitigate the pains of imprisonment. And the fact that the snitcher is disloyal to the inmate group adds to the burden of imprisonment.

The behavior subsumed under "center man" in the male prison finds expression in the role of *inmate cop* or *lieutenant*. The inmate cop is a prisoner who is in a position of authority over other inmates, and in the process of executing her work function will issue orders to other inmates or report infractions of rules in connection with work. The prison experience is considered to be the "great equalizer"[27] and inmates resent taking orders from other inmates. As one prisoner said contemptuously: "She tries to act just like an officer. She forgets that she came through the gate and she's got five numbers across her chest just like the rest of us. She's an officer without a uniform, and she tries to tell another inmate what to do. They're always in the officer's face. . . ." The inmate cop or lieutenant in effect takes the role of the officer and thereby violates an important tenet of the inmate code: she denies the egalitarian ethos of the inmates.

The inmate cop's disloyalty is despised not only because it is open to view, but also because it is often flaunted in the face of other inmates. Here is an open and shut case of identification with staff values, and the inmate cop's actions deny the solidarity of the inmate body and weaken the bonds of interdependence which bind them together. Moreover, the inmate cop is apt to rationalize her actions in terms of noncriminal values which according to the inmate code have no place in the prison. Unless this inmate can be persuaded to "see the light" through socialization into the inmate culture, she cannot be reasoned with or bought. In this sense she poses a real threat to the inmate community, because the inmate cop is an added bulwark to the staff's forces, and the fact that an inmate is adding to the pains of imprisonment by joining forces with the staff makes her doubly despised.

Squares and Jive Bitches

Along with the snitchers and the inmate cops, the *squares* are truly the pariahs of the inmate community. "Square" is a derisive label pinned on

---

[27] Cf. Judge M. Murtagh and Sara Harris, *Cast the First Stone* (New York: Cardinal, 1958), p. 244.

inmates who are considered to be accidental criminals. The behavior of the square in the prison community clearly betrays her alien status, as she is oriented to the prison administration and tends to possess "anti-criminal" loyalties. Degrees of "squareness" are recognized by the female inmates, ranging from the inmate who is said to be "so square that she's a cube" to the inmate designated as a "hip square." The "cube square" is very definitely oriented to societal values and the prison administration, whereas the "hip square" tends to sympathize with the inmate code and adheres to some of its principles, sometimes going so far as to *pin*—act as a lookout —for other inmates. Her sympathy tends to take the form of stated tolerance for inmate activities. The distinguishing characteristic of the "hip square," however, is that she does not engage in homosexual activity, as well as the fact that she is oriented to the administration and societal values. In the female prison studied, it should be pointed out that anyone who does not engage in homosexual activities in the prison in one form or another is automatically labeled a square.

Not only are squares outside the mainstream of inmate activities—excluded and ostracized by the inmate population—but more important for the inmate social system, squares are pitied. It is said that squares "don't know any better," and, further, it is widely believed that the square is not "woman enough" to commit a crime. "They're suckers and fools—gullible without even knowing it." And herein lies the key to understanding the threat that the square poses for the inmate community. Like the inmate cop or lieutenant, the square tends to identify with the institutional officials. In the case of squares, however, association is considered to be doubly hazardous, for in their presumed gullibility squares may unwittingly divulge information to the officials. It is for this reason that squares are apt to be "fed with a long-handled spoon," that is, information concerning inmate activities is carefully sifted and censored.

While the deviance of the square is often the consequence of an artless simplicity, and presumably leaves open the possibility that induction into the inmate culture may remedy the situation (indeed, the pressures applied are so great that this frequently does occur), the deviance of the *jive bitch*, on the other hand, is a deliberate, calculated strategy to cause conflict. In short, the *jive bitch* is a troublemaker whose strategy often involves a distortion of the facts, as in the case, for example, when she is interested in breaking up an established homosexual relationship: she will often volunteer information about *kites* (prison letters) and illicit rendezvous to the injured party, who in many cases would prefer not to be the recipient of such information—as it will mean that ignorance is no longer bliss—and who may be goaded into terminating an affair, which, although perceived not to be perfect, may be felt to be better than none.

Moreover, the jive bitch can't be trusted to keep her word when she gives it, indicating her disloyalty to the inmate group. Although female inmates claim that women are not trustworthy, it is normatively demanded that once you give your word to a prisoner, you should keep it—particularly in connection with matters concerning mutual aid. An example of a jive bitch supplied by an inmate follows:

> You're out of cigarettes, and you go to a girl and say, "Look, I'm out of cigarettes, and I won't have any money until next week. When you go to Commissary, would you buy me a carton, and I'll pay you back next week?" She says, "Sure, baby, sure. I'll get them for you on Friday." When Friday comes, you go to her house to get the cigarettes and when you say, "Did you get the cigarettes?" she opens her mouth like she's surprised and maybe slaps her cheek and she looks at you and says, "Oh, baby, I forgot all about it. I'm sorry, baby, honest!" That's a jive bitch 'cause she had no intention of getting you those cigarettes in the first place.

The jive bitch, in short, is an example *par excellence* of the woman-to-woman popular culture translated into role behavior. And the fact that she cannot be depended upon weakens even the bonds of calculated solidarity which exist among the female inmates.

Rap Buddies and Homeys

While no inmate trusts another woman completely—"You pick your people and even then you only go so far"—within the limitations imposed by this definition of the situation, an inmate may single out another prisoner as a special friend. She is one with whom an inmate can converse easily, and, further, assume reasonably that the conversation will be mutually binding as secret. Any two people who find one another compatible in this way may become *rap buddies* to one another. This relationship is dissolved if the expectations concerning the relationship are not honored by either of the incumbents of the rap buddy role; or if the relationship develops into a homosexual relationship, the inmates become a "couple" and assume the obligations relevant to a homosexual relationship.

The *homey* role is probably as close to "blood" relationship as one comes in the female prison, and the relationship holds a special place in the lexicon of the inmates. Technically speaking, even if conflict ensues between homeys, the relationship still holds. The homey is the inmate who is from another inmate's hometown or nearby community. Homeys may or may not have known one another before incarceration; but whatever the case, within the prison these inmates become homeys to one another. Contact is made as soon as the presence of a homey becomes known; information is usually obtained from inmate orientation helpers or inmate office workers. Inquiries as to whether a homey's needs in the orientation unit have been met are immediately made: cigarettes, soap, toothpaste, facial tissues, and any other commissary items which she needs will somehow be routed to her. The special bond of reciprocity which is established between homeys is of a vastly different degree of intensity than that between rap buddies, and is expected to cover a wide range of behavior; homeys have the right to turn to one another when material need arises, and the further expectation exists that if economically possible, the mechandise is to be returned at a later date.

Although superficially the rap buddy and homey roles may appear to be quite similar, the basis for the allocation of these roles and functions is quite different. What is the basis for allocation of functions with respect to the homey role? While there is a special relationship that exists between homeys, significantly the homey relationship excludes homosexuality. Indeed, an inmate will express great indignation if the suggestion—however lightly veiled—is made that a homosexual relationship exists between her and a homey. "That's my homey. I wouldn't do that to her" certainly suggests the exploitative evaluation many inmates have of the homosexual relationship. But when we examine other aspects of the role this explanation adds little to our understanding of the function the role plays in the lives of the female inmates.

A significant aspect of the homey relationship lies in the fact that inmates sharing this status address and refer to one another by the term "homey," emphasizing to the incumbents of the role and the inmate community alike the nature of the special relationship involved. Indeed, a novitiate who calls a homey by her given name is promptly corrected by other inmates. One is quite reasonably led to ask why it is that mutual aid and mode of address are patterned between homey and not, for example, between rap buddies. Does the answer lie in the fact that they are from the same geographical area? Given the self-orientation of the female, it is not very likely that this would seem to be a plausible explanation. Actually the occupants of the homey role are, as it were, buying insurance for the future. The extension of mutual cooperation between homeys insures both role occupants that the possibility will not arise that a homey will "read" her —that is, speak derogatively of her behavior in prison to anyone in civil society. Presumably, the inmate who resides in the same geographical area would most likely be in a favored position to do so.

The homey relationship is a splendid example of the refinement in social roles which takes place in the female community to solve the special problems of the inmates stemming from the cultural definition females have of one another.

Connects and Boosters

The fifteen dollars which inmates are permitted to spend per month at the commissary store is not a large sum when one takes into account that it covers almost all purchases, including cigarettes.[28] Furthermore, even this

---

[28] It is possible to make special withdrawals for yarn purchases.

modest sum is beyond the reach of most inmates. Few legitimate channels are open to the female inmates to improve their economic lot in the prison. Like the male prisoners, the female inmates also find it necessary to exploit the environment in order to improve their material circumstances. Here it takes the form of stealing from institutional supplies. Significantly, a role based upon aggressive physical tactics, such as the "gorilla" reported by Sykes who takes what he wants from other inmates by force, does not emerge in the female inmate community. By contrast, in the female prison the *connect* is any inmate with a "good job" who will cooperate in the procurement of scarce goods and/or information. Connects are also those inmates who are in a position to negotiate with other inmates to obtain information or goods, that is, acting both as middleman and distributor. Thus, this role includes the procurement of both goods and services.

In this connection, the inmates draw a sharp line between the connect, who often takes a dual role, and the *booster*, whose exploitation of the environment consists solely of stealing from official stores and carries on a successful business enterprise. Of course, it should be made clear that stealing from the officials is universal at the prison. Even inmates designated by sister inmates as squares and inmate cops declare they will sometimes take a pot of coffee out of the dining room "on principle." Inmates, however, make a clear distinction between the petty boosting which is engaged in by all the inmates—say a few teaspoonfuls of sugar placed in a napkin, a sandwich, and the like, while in the dining room—and the stealing engaged in by the booster. The difference lies mainly in the source of supply, the regularity with which the goods may be procured, and the purpose for which the items are stolen. Items stolen sporadically for individual consumption tend to be classified under the category of petty boosting. The booster is the inmate who is in a position to steal desired objects regularly and in fairly large quantities.

Now in the male prison, regardless of the source of supply, giving and sharing are normatively demanded by the inmate code—especially if the materials have been stolen from the officials. The "pedlar" or "merchant" has been described as "a man so alienated from other prisoners, so selfish in his pursuit of material advantage, that he is willing to thrive on the misery of his companions. He places his own well-being above the well-being of the inmates as a whole. He does not share the goods in short supply but exploits, instead, the needs of others."[29] Interestingly, the same behavior for which the "merchant" is despised in the male prison is that which receives words of praise from female inmates. To "get a good thing going," that is, to engage in a successful enterprise, is to draw forth admiration from the inmates. It is held: "If you get a little racket going, more

---

[29] Sykes, *The Society of Captives*, p. 94.

power to you." And yet at the same time inmates rationalize many of their actions by saying, "If I don't get there first, someone else will," which clearly indicates the self-orientation of the inmates. In a real sense, boosters are inmates who have "gotten there first," and for this feat there is admiration—albeit tinged with not a little envy. In addition, inmates tend to feel gratitude to the booster, for it is recognized that the booster's role involves a certain amount of risk. Whatever recompense is necessary to enjoy the pleasure of making a cup of coffee at odd hours of the day is thought to be well worth the price. The inmates will gladly exchange a carton of cigarettes for a pound of coffee,[30] and if this transaction can be made a weekly matter, prison life is made more tolerable.

In contrast to the male prisoner, no sharp line is made by the female inmates between selling and giving, except between homeys, inmates participating in a homosexual marriage, and other "family" members. Who are the inmates that become the clients for the supply of illicit goods? All prisoners do not have an opportunity to enjoy these luxury items, regardless of their financial situation. Low-caste inmates, such as snitchers, squares, and inmate cops or lieutenants, of course, lie outside the boundary of legitimate giving, as these inmates have deviated from the inmate code, and therefore have roped themselves off from the privilege of sharing in the scarce goods that circulate about the prison. They are in the same boat as "rats," "center men," "weaklings," and "fish" in the male prison. Apart from the pariahs in the female prison, mutual aid is greater near the locus of high intensity of emotional reciprocity. As intensity of emotional reciprocity decreases, mutual aid decreases proportionately.

Pinners

Since complete elimination of detection is never possible in the performance of many illicit activities, the female inmates find it necessary to minimize the risk of being detected by the prison officials. For this reason, the role of *pinner* is very crucial in the prison.

The pinner in the female prison is a lookout, stationed as a sentry to prevent a surprise attack upon inmates engaging in illicit activities from all unauthorized persons—whether they be staff or inmates. With discovery always imminent and punishment a certainty, the pinner's role is not one to allocate to amateurs or to inmates whose loyalty is in doubt. The pinner must be an inmate who can be trusted, stand up under pressure, and she must be "in the know." Depending upon the task at hand, sometimes the female inmates find it necessary to mobilize a team of pinners—each of whom must share the responsibility that the task at hand be carried out successfully. The interdependence of the inmates requires the cooperation

---

[30] Cigarettes are the most important nexus of exchange among the inmates.

of other inmates in order to carry out their activities successfully. In the words of an inmate:

> Even if you wanted to go it alone, it's almost impossible to do. The situation is such that you need the help of other inmates. For example, if you're makin' it with someone, you need a pinner. This means initiating the aid of a third party—maybe more. And you might be called up to help two other people in the same situation. . . . The way pinning works is this—maybe I've got two friends who are involved with each other. O.K., well, I'll go into the office and keep the officer busy for an hour talking about a problem I have or I make one up. She can't be in two places at one time, so usually this is a safe procedure. Or a girl will stand at the foot of the stairs with a tin can in her hands. If the officer or a person known to be a snitcher goes up the stairs, she drops the can, or she whistles loudly. These signals are understood.

Now while it is important to the female inmates that the pains of imprisonment be mitigated, it is also imperative that in the process of doing so their deviant actions do not result in disciplinary action which will increase the burden of punishment. The pinner, therefore, is a valued individual, as she imparts a measure of reasonable security to the inmates that their deviant performances will not result in loss of days or other forms of punishment.

The Homosexual Cluster: Penitentiary Turnouts, Lesbians, Femmes, Stud Broads, Tricks, Commissary Hustlers, Chippies, Kick Partners, Cherries, Punks, and Turnabouts

The problems and concerns of the female inmates in adjusting to deprivation of heterosexual relationships are revealed by the number of roles channeled into homosexual behavior. Moreover, the female inmate's *role refinement* with respect to the categories of homosexual activity illustrates its function both as a motivating force in the lives of the inmates and as an organizing principle of social organization.

The inmates apply a number of labels to homosexual behavior in the prison, depending upon the specific role assumed, the adeptness with which the assumed role is played, and the motivation for the behavior. Broadly speaking, the inmates differentiate between penitentiary turnouts and lesbians. The *penitentiary turnout* is the prisoner who resorts to homosexuality in the prison because heterosexual relationships are not available; in contrast, the *lesbian prefers* homosexual relations in the free community. In this respect she resembles the "fag" in the male prison. The lesbian is labeled as a sick person by the inmates because it is argued that the preference and selection of homosexual relations in a situation where choice is possible clearly constitute a true perversion. It is only in the penitentiary world, where men are unavailable, that the values and norms regarding homosexual behavior are redefined by the inmates and—within the limits imposed by this definition—accepted as a temporary substitute for heterosexual relations.

Stylized symbolic devices make it possible for the female inmates to attach new meanings to a culturally defined sex *role* representation seen as a variation of a sex *type* based upon biological attributes. The institutionalized character of the differential sex roles orders the behavior of the inmates and defines the limits of permissible behavior and regulates the interaction between the inmates.

The *femme*[31] or *mommy* is the inmate who plays the female role in a homosexual relationship. The femme role is a highly sought-after role in the prison because most of the inmates want to continue to play the feminine role in a meaningful way in the prison. Cast in the context of a "marital" relationship, the femme continues to act out many of the functions assigned to the role of wife in civil society. The complementary role to the femme is the *stud broad*[32] or *daddy*, who assumes the male role. The stud broad is accorded much prestige by other inmates for these reasons: First, the stud is said to provide the prison with the male image; second, the role is considered to be a more difficult one for an inmate to assume and sustain over a period of time, because it is thought to be "unnatural" for a female to assume the guises of the male. Moreover, the role is considered to be difficult because studs not only assume certain external symbols of sex differentiation, but in addition are expected to incorporate into role behavior the many social expectations of the male role.

As far as homosexual relations are concerned, the evidence is consistent with that reported by Ward and Kassebaum; that is, homosexual relations are established voluntarily between the principals involved. No physical coercion is applied in obtaining a homosexual partner.[33] In seeking a solution to the problem engendered by the lack of heterosexual relations, interpersonal relations in connection with homosexuality play a major part in the lives of the female inmates. Cast in the context of a "marital" relationship, the homosexual dyad is viewed by the inmates as a meaningful personal and social relationship. From the mass of interview data it is clear, however, that this mode of adjustment (with the exception of homosexuals who practice homosexuality in the free community) would be repugnant for most prisoners, but the uniqueness of the prison situation compels the inmate to redefine and attach new meanings to this behavior within the prison structure.[34]

---

[31] This role is also reported in Ward and Kassebaum, "Homosexuality," p. 169.

[32] Cf. the role of the butch in *ibid.*, pp. 168–69.

[33] *Ibid.*, p.171.

[34] Estimates of the number of inmates who are involved in homosexuality vary. Inmates who are very much involved in this phase of inmate culture place the figure at 90 or 95 percent. The associate warden (treatment) estimated that 80 percent of the inmates were involved in homosexual relations. Correctional officers tended to set the figure at 50 or 75 percent, which agrees with the usual estimates I obtained from squares. Some officers and other staff members set the figure at 100 percent. At one point in the study,

The inmates are not able to resolve their sense of isolation within the formal organization, and therefore develop relationships and behavior patterns within an informal structure. For the vast majority of the inmates, adjustment to the prison world is made by establishing a homosexual alliance with a compatible partner as a marriage unit. Although we cannot discuss the dynamics of mate selection, courtship, and marriage in this paper, it should be pointed out that when a stud and femme have established a homosexual alliance, they are said to be "makin' it" or to be "tight"; that is to say, they are socially recognized as constituting a legitimate married pair. Since one of the important goals in establishing a homosexual marriage alliance is to strive for what is referred to as a "sincere" relationship, which is translated to mean a stable relationship and one based upon romantic love, the *trick* is held in low esteem by the inmates because she allows herself to be exploited, rather than to develop a relationship that is sincere. And the trick permits exploitation in a variety of ways—usually economically and as a source of labor. Any individual who allows herself to be exploited in this manner is considered "weak." Moreover, tricks are regarded as "suckers" and "fools" because they may be kept dangling with promises.

Who are the inmates who utilize exploitative tactics? The *commissary hustler* is so labeled as an individual who establishes a single homosexual alliance with an inmate who lives in the same cottage, but in addition establishes relationships with one or more inmates in other cottages for economic purposes. This is called "mating for commissary reasons," and any femme other than the inmate who lives in the stud's cottage is labeled as a trick in the relationship. The commissary hustler presents a commissary list to the tricks scattered throughout the prison, and they, in turn, supply the commissary hustler with needed material items. The function of all the tricks in this "polygynous" system is an economic one. The "wife" in the cottage takes precedence over all others. She shares in the bounty and usually knows of the existence of other femmes, i.e., tricks. Indeed, if the "couple" is in serious economic difficulty, she may suggest to her stud that this role be assumed. Or the stud may consult the femme in arriving at a decision to "work a few tricks."

So long as the "wife" shares the same household as the stud, the existence of other femmes (tricks) in the relationship is tolerable. As the inmates put it: "The nearest is the dearest, and the closest gets the mostest." In addition, it should be pointed out that the "wife" who lives in the same household as the stud also derives security from the public recognition of

---

I made a cottage count of inmates assuming the male role, and the studs totaled 215 inmates. The number of "males" in the prison tends to vary slightly from day to day, depending upon inmate releases and individual role choice. And the same is equally true of the inmates playing the femme role. At this time, there were 336 femmes out of a total of 639 inmates. At any rate, it is apparent that femmes are competing for a scarce commodity.

the relationship as legitimate. They are recognized as a "couple." The additional wife (or wives) merely serves an economic function. One would be well advised to ask why an inmate enters into a trick role. The stud population is outnumbered by the femme population, and competition for studs is very keen. Actually, each trick in this situation anticipates and plans for the day when the relationship will become a permanent one; each trick anticipates displacing the cottage "wife" in the affections of the stud. And since the trick is, after all, an inmate with a commissary account, the possibility that this might occur is a good one. While it is more or less understood that she will wait for an invitation to move to the stud's cottage, sometimes a trick may lose patience and forgo prison etiquette. Such cottage moves present complicating triangular situations, often leading to violence.

The role of commissary hustler is one which requires a certain amount of adroitness to carry out successfully. The inmates argue that in the free community, the commissary hustler would tend to exploit men, but since there are no men in prison, they expoit women. Although there may be individual personality factors involved, there are structural features in the prison which precipitate this role. Every inmate is not compensated for work performed in the prison, and the role of commissary hustler provides an avenue whereby an inmate may solve her economic needs.

The dyad configuration cast into the framework of a marital relationship covers a wide range of behavioral expectations. The commissary hustler, although in some respects exploitative, nevertheless does maintain a stable and sincere relationship with the femme who shares the same cottage. However, when the individual exploits *each* situation with a partner for its unique possibilities, whether it be sexual gratification or material, the inmate is said to occupy a *chippie* role. This role differs from the commissary hustler in a very important way. Although the commissary hustler actually establishes one sincere relationship and exploits other inmates in order to provide for the femme in the relationship, the chippie establishes no single relationship of this type. Chippies are said to be "makin' it," but not to be "in love" with any individual. The chippie, in the inmates' eyes, is the prison prostitute. The inmate who "chippies from one bed to another"—i.e., terminates affairs too quickly—is held in scorn by the inmates, as her behavior is held to be promiscuous. This behavior draws forth words of scorn from the inmates because the ideal cultural pattern in the prison is to establish a permanent relationship. The chippie clearly deviates from the ideal pattern, as the affairs of this inmate are characterized by their striking temporary quality.

The female inmates distinguish clearly between homosexual activity that is considered to be promiscuous and that which is engaged in solely for sexual gratification. Although *kick partners* are also not involved as "lovers," there is, nevertheless, a predictable permanence in the relationships maintained between kick partners, but the motivation for entering into the partnership is clearly understood to be solely for physical gratification. There is usually no economic exchange in this relationship, and the inmates exhibit no jealousy. An inmate is apt to enter such a relationship when she does not wish to assume the responsibilities that a more permanent tie would entail. The object of this relationship is to release sexual tension. Kick partners sometimes consist of a group of several women among whom partners are exchanged and friendly relations exist between all members concerned. To the extent that kick partners are "discreet," the behavior is not looked down upon by the inmates.

Every society has a reserve of members from which potential mates may be obtained. When resources are limited, or because of cultural prescriptions, mates may be drawn from other groups. In the female prison, the kick partner is an individual who may be drawn into a permanent tie. And there is also the possibility that the square will in time come to "see the light" and enter into the inmate social organization. But there is one category of inmates in prison, namely, those labeled *cherries*, who constitute an uncommitted sizable reserve for potential mates, as they are the inmates who have never been "turned out"—initiated into homosexual practices. Cherries, however, are not squares. Often they are young and first offenders, and they are usually initiated by older women. Cherries in this context are "hep" individuals, i.e., know what the score is from the point of view of the prisoners, but for one reason or another have not engaged in homosexuality. Sometimes a short sentence may be the deciding factor; a preference not to become emotionally involved; or it may be that the individual decides that this mode of adjustment may not be desirable.

One who assumes a false part or assumes a character other than the real is despised for his hypocrisy both within and without the prison gates. Within the female prison, the *punk* is despised for pretense and deceit. In the male prison, it will be recalled that the "punk" is an inmate who plays the submissive part in a homosexual relationship because he is coerced into doing so. In this respect it is said that "punks" differ and may be distinguished from "fags," who it is said are "born," not "made." In a sense, "fags" resemble the lesbians, for it is said by the inmates that they are "born that way," or "something happened to them in their childhood."

The punk in the female prison, on the other hand, is the inmate so designated because she acts like a female, that is, takes on the coquettish mannerisms of a woman when the expected behavior is that of the male. The behavior of the punk elicits a combination of anger and ridicule from the inmates. The tendency is to heap blame upon the punk, because the punk's "impotence" is not a constitutional failure, but rather is due to incomplete role learning. Responsibility, therefore, is placed upon the individual. Punks are, as it were, self-proclaimed studs without substance—unconvincing sexual deviates. The punk is despised and ridiculed by the inmates.

While the punk is guilty of incomplete role learning, the *turnabout,* on the other hand, claims expertise at playing both male and female roles. As a matter of fact, she not only describes herself glowingly in terms of her versatility, that is, "good either way," but stands ready to put her boasted skill to the test. Such protean versatility, however, is viewed with amused contempt by the inmates. As a prisoner put it, "There's a lot of talk, but not the right kind of talk. She should know what she is and stay that way. And we tell them, 'Get yourself together and find out what you are!' "

The female inmates prefer a structured situation in their prison world, and inmates playing male roles one day and female roles the next confuse the issue greatly, especially for the inmate who may be planning a strategy of conquest. In addition, anything which tends to decrease the "male" population in the prison is apt to be alarming to the inmates. It is not surprising, therefore, that the turnabout is held in low esteem.

CONCLUSION

The social roles as distinguished and labeled by the female inmates constitute the basic structure of social relationships formed by the inmates in response to the problems of a prison commitment. While it is apparent from the previous discussion that some argot roles are mutually exclusive, other roles clearly are not. Furthermore, an inmate may assume one role soon after commitment, for example, such as square, but may assume many other roles at a later point in time if drawn into the inmate social organization.

In addition to the comparisons with the male prison community that have already been made, there are other important differences that may be pointed out at this time. Consistent with the cultural definition of the female as nonaggressive, the roles of violence that emerge in the male prison, namely, those of "wolf," "tough," "gorilla," "hipster," and "ball buster," are notably absent among the female inmates. Also significant is the fact that a role resembling the structure of the "right guy" who is such a dominant figure in the male prison does not emerge in the female prison. Concepts such as "fair play," "courage," and the like—which are consistent with the concepts of endurance, loyalty, and dignity associated with the "right guy"—are not meaningful to the female. Although it is true that the norm of inmate loyalty exists in the prison world, the popular culture of women as untrustworthy is imported into the prison world and serves both to neutralize many deviant acts and to furnish the rationale for their commitment.

The need to assert or defend one's femininity, in the same way that the male inmate must prove his masculinity in the group if his manhood is called into question, clearly does not arise for the female inmate. This is a reflection of the self-orientation of the female, and the fact that the female validates her femininity by proving she can attract men. In other words, it appears that general features of American society in connection with the cultural definitions ascribed to male and female roles are imported into the prison and are reflected in the structure of social relationships formed by the inmates. Nowhere is this more dramatically revealed than in the extraordinary function of the homey role, with its extended implications for the reentry of the inmate into civil society. From the same vantage point, we saw that the function of the pinner's role serves to control the physical distance between inmates engaging in illicit activities, on the one hand, and the snitcher on the other, in order to make it possible for the female inmates to avoid discovery and punishment.

The number of roles clustered about homosexual behavior clearly reveals the problems and concerns of the female inmates in connection with adjustment to deprivation of heterosexual relationships. Moreover, the distinctions made by the inmates as to motivation, role assumed, adeptness with which the assumed role is played, and so on, indicate the values and expectations of the inmates with respect to this behavior. But the rights and obligations attached to a legitimate "marital" relationship automatically close off much interaction among the inmates, as inmates assuming this type of relationship must account for all of their contacts with members of the "opposite sex." As the inmates move closer to legitimate relationships in the prison, then, the refinement of roles becomes necessary in order to control and to account for the behavior of every inmate in the system.

The cultural orientation of males, however, precludes legitimate marriage and family groupings as a feasible alternative solution for the male prisoners, as the serious adoption of a female role is contrary to the definition of the male role as masculine. Hence, family groups do not emerge in the male prison. It is noteworthy that in the male prison the "fags" and "punks" are both held in derision by the vast majority of male inmates, as it is felt that they have sacrificed their manhood, but the homosexuality of "wolves" is looked upon as a temporary adjustment to sexual tensions generated by the prison setting. The absence of sentiment and the aggressive behavior of the "wolf" is consistent with the cultural definition of the *masculine* role, and thus homosexuality loses the taint of femininity in the prison that male homosexuality tends to carry in civil society. In addition, the cultural orientation of the male role with respect to demonstrations of affection toward another member of the same sex clearly precludes the adoption of legitimate feminine roles by male inmates in informal kinship groupings such as those found among the female inmates. The ease with which women may demonstrate acts of affection, both verbally and physically, toward members of the same sex perhaps may provide a *predisposition* to widespread homosexuality and its ready acceptance under the extreme conditions of isolation in the prison setting. This fact alone, however, is not enough to account for the emergence of the female inmate social system.

Why do these remarkable differences in inmate culture emerge in the two prison communities? Two theoretical positions have already been posed. The first of these is the typical structural-functional analysis of total institutions which asserts that behavior systems of various types of inmates are a result of the conditions of imprisonment. However, when we consider that the deprivations of imprisonment were found to be present in the female prison studied and keenly felt by the female prisoners—yet the typical cultural system which emerges in the adult male prison is not present—we must conclude that the differences in structural form found in the two prison communities are inadequately explained by current functional analysis *solely* as a response to the deprivation of imprisonment. The deprivations may provide necessary conditions for the emergence of an inmate system, but they are not in themselves sufficient to account for the structural *form* that the inmate social system assumes in the male and female prison communities.

The second interpretation views inmate culture as somehow imported into the prison world from the external world by the inmates who compose that culture, through the particular attitudes and values which inmates learned prior to entering the prison. This position has been most forcibly suggested by Schrag, Irwin, and Cressey, and calls our attention to the thesis that the behavior patterning of inmates is influenced by preprison experiences, social identities, and cultural background. Simply stated, the behavior patterns in the prison are the result of the inmates' relations in the external world; however, the external world is important only in providing the particular cultural elements that the inmates learn. Inasmuch as the individuals who enter the prison world are not a random sample of the population, the values and attitudes brought into the prison do not comprise a random sample of the elements of outside culture; hence, prison culture differs—especially by the presence of increased hostility, violence, and traffic in illicit goods. The three subculture groups (thief, convict, and legitimate) in Irwin and Cressey's typology presumably demonstrate this thesis,[35] as these authors maintain that their three subculture groups share learned behaviors which are common and peculiar to them in or out of prison. Elsewhere, it has been cogently pointed out that Irwin and Cressey do not demonstrate that this is so.[36] Nevertheless, they have called atten-

---

[35] Irwin and Cressey, "Thieves, Convicts, and the Inmate Culture," esp. pp. 148–53.

[36] Julian Roebuck, "A Critique of 'Thieves, Convicts, and the Inmate Culture,'" *Social Problems*, 11 (Fall 1963): 193–200. It should be pointed out that Schrag's analysis also remains unclear, for at one point he comments: "Juxtaposed with the official organization of the prison is an unofficial social system originating within the institution and regulating inmate conduct with respect to focal issues, such as length of sentence, relations among prisoners, contacts with staff members and other civilians, food, sex, and health,

tion to the important thesis that the behavior patterning of inmates may be influenced by social identities and cultural backgrounds.

We suggest, rather, that the culture that forms within the prison by males and females can be understood in these terms: The prison inmate social system is not an intrinsic response to the deprivations of imprisonment, although the deprivations of imprisonment may be important in precipitating inmate culture; nor can inmate culture be viewed as a mere reflection of the values and attitudes inmates bring into the prison world. The evidence presented here suggests that the male and female cultures *are* a response to the deprivations of prison life, but the nature of the response in both prison communities is influenced by the differential participation of males and females in the external culture. The culture that emerges within the prison structure may be seen to incorporate and reflect the total external social structure; that is, the way in which roles are defined in the external world influence the definitions made within the prison. General features of American society with respect to the cultural definitions and content of male and female roles are brought into the prison setting and they function to determine the direction and focus of the inmate cultural system. These general features I have suggested are those concerned with the orientation of life goals for males and females; second, cultural definitions with respect to dimensions of passivity and aggression; third, acceptability of public expression of affection displayed toward a member of the same sex; and, finally, perception of the same sex with respect to what I have called the popular culture.

It is the *system* of roles and statuses that is imported into the prison setting, and not merely the values and attitudes of the individuals who enter the prison world. It is in these terms that the importance attached to the female role, marriage ties, and family groups can be understood as salient elements of prison culture in the female prison community, but not in the male prison community. It would seem, then, that there is greater unity between the inner and outer worlds than has heretofore been thought. Accordingly, greater understanding of the prison communities may be accomplished by focusing our attention on the relationship of the external and internal cultures rather than trying to understand the prison as an institution isolated from the larger society.

---

among other things." This suggests that all inmates face a number of common problems of adjustment as a result of incarceration and that social organization develops to provide solutions. See Clarence Schrag, "Some Foundations for a Theory of Correction," in *The Prison,* ed. Cressey, p. 342.

33. INFORMAL ORGANIZATION AND INMATE ATTITUDES IN THREE TYPES OF PRISONS

Bernard B. Berk

While sociological interest in informal organization dates back to the time of Cooley, there has been little exploration of the relationships between formal and informal organization. Earlier research efforts have been more concerned with documenting the existence of informal organization and demonstrating that it had an impact upon organizational functioning than in trying to establish relationships between it and the organizational context. Different conclusions have been reached in regard to its contribution to the formal organization's ability to achieve its goals, with Roethlisberger and Dickson highlighting its subversive aspect in limiting productivity in economic organizations, while Shils and Janowitz suggest it can facilitate the goals of military organizations by developing social cohesion.[1] Recon-

Reprinted by permission of the author and the publisher from *American Journal of Sociology*, 71 (March 1966): 522–34. Copyright © 1966 by the University of Chicago. Original title: "Organizational Goals and Inmate Organization." Footnotes have been renumbered.

[1] F. J. Roethlisberger and W. J. Dickson, *Management and the Worker* (Cambridge: Harvard University Press, 1939); Edward A. Shils and Morris Janowitz, "Cohesion and Disintegration of the Wehrmacht in World War II," *Public Opinion Quarterly*, 12 (1948): 280–315. Informal organization has also been found to contribute positively to economic organizations by reducing absenteeism, and negatively to military ones by generating norms which foster "goldbricking." Lewin's study contrasting the consequences of different patterns of control upon informal relations specifies in more detail relationships be-

ciling these findings rests upon the notion that organizations with different goals, structures, and contexts should produce different patterns of informal organization, and informal organization would also have different effects upon the functioning of such diverse types of organizations. What is needed is specification of relationships between the parameters of formal and informal organization and identification of those aspects of organizations which generate oppositional informal organization. By limiting this investigation to one particular type of organization and by examining variation in one of its parameters—its goals—it is hoped some clarification of the problems may emerge.

Specifically, this paper examines relationships between organizational goals and informal organization in a variety of correctional institutional settings. The study had major objectives. First, we sought to replicate Grusky's study of the consequences of treatment goals for the informal organization of prison inmates.[2] Second, we were concerned with extending existing formulations concerning the relationship between the formal and informal structure of total institutions and, in particular, the conditions which generate informal organizations that are fundamentally opposed to the existing administration.

DESCRIPTION OF RESEARCH SITES

The three institutions selected for study were minimum-security prisons which differed in their emphasis of treatment goals. The criteria used to determine the extent to which treatment goals were dominant were: (1) the presence of a full-time counselor or of treatment personnel; (2) the existence of a rehabilitative program; and (3) the active implementation of

---

tween organizational parameters and informal relations (K. Lewin, R. Lippitt, and R. K. White, "An Experimental Study of Leadership and Group Life," in *Readings in Social Psychology*, ed. G. E. Swanson, T. M. Newcomb, and E. L. Hartley, rev. ed. [New York: Holt, Rinehart & Winston, 1952]). For an excellent study dealing with similar concerns in juvenile institutions which was published too late for comment in this paper, see David Street, "Inmates in Custodial and Treatment Settings," *American Sociological Review*, 30 (February 1965): 40–56.

[2] The replicated study was: Oscar Grusky, "Organizational Goals and the Behavior of Informal Leaders," *American Journal of Sociology*, 65, no. 1 (July 1959): 59–67. Sociology is characterized by a lack of replication studies, particularly in the area of social organization. In his analysis of replication studies, Hanson noted fewer than twenty-five such studies in the field of sociology, with fully one-third of these refuting the original hypothesis. This would appear to leave sociology in the position of having relatively few sets of propositions which have been independently tested in different research sites. This condition neither contributes to the development of a cumulative fund of reliable knowledge, nor does it permit of the development of a set of standardized instruments which can be used to compare different types of organizations. See Robert Hanson, "Evidence and Procedure Characteristics of 'Reliable' Propositions in Social Science," *American Journal of Sociology*, 63 (January 1958): 357–71. This replication was enhanced by the use of the same instruments in two new prison camps in addition to a repeat investigation of the prison originally studied by Grusky. Moreover, we utilized Grusky's questionnaire items and Guttman scales.

educational, vocational, or other auxiliary-type programs. The three prisons (to be called Benign, Partial, and Lock) were ranked on a continuum ranging from a strong treatment orientation to a strong custodial orientation.[3]

Camp Benign ranked as the most treatment-oriented institution, as all three criteria were present. In addition, it was the smallest, containing only ninety-seven inmates. This prison was characterized by considerable staff-inmate interaction, maximal opportunities for counseling and guidance,[4] and a sincere effort directed at changing the inmate. Camp Partial was slightly larger (127 inmates) and had both a full-time counselor and a limited educational program. However, it did not have an official treatment program. Treatment techniques employed in this institution tended to be subverted to custodial ends, such as securing inmate conformity. Camp Lock, which had 157 inmates, was the most custodially oriented institution, the sole rehabilitative program being an Alcoholics Anonymous group. Its primary goal was containment, and there was little official pretense or concern about treatment or rehabilitation. The officials sought to run an institution which attracted as little attention as possible from the community.

THE FINDINGS

Inmate Attitudes

The first area investigated was the differences in attitudes of inmates of the treatment and custodial prisons. Numerous observers have asserted that the relationship between guards and inmates in custodial institutions is characterized by hostility, mistrust, suspicion, and fear, promulgated by both the official dictates of the prison and the informal norms among the inmates.[5] Grusky, Vinter and Janowitz, and others have argued that a

---

[3] It is important to keep in mind that all three prison camps would be located on the treatment end of the continuum if compared with maximum-security institutions.

[4] One cannot overlook the possible importance of the size of the prisons, which could provide an additional explanation to the one offered in this paper. However, the fact that Benign almost doubled in size between the original study and the replication, while inmate attitudes remained relatively unchanged, casts some doubt on its usefulness in accounting for our findings. Also, similar data collected on three other juvenile institutions did not show attitudes to be related to size as such; rather, it confirmed the importance of organizational goals. This it not to discard the importance of size, since it may have important ramifications for organizational structure which, in turn, influences informal organization. There was also a selectivity in the inmates sent to Benign, which will be dealt with in this paper.

[5] Donald Clemmer, *The Prison Community* (New York: Holt, Rinehart & Winston, 1958), chap. 2; Donald Clemmer, "Observations on Imprisonment as a Source of Criminality," *Journal of Criminal Law and Criminology*, 41 (September–October 1950): 311–19; R. J. Corsini, "A Study of Certain Attitudes of Prison Inmates," *Journal of Criminal Law and Criminology*, 37 (July–August 1946): 132–42; Donald Cressey, ed., *The Prison: Studies in Institutional Organization and Change* (New York: Holt, Rinehart & Winston, 1961); Lloyd W. McCorkle and Richard Korn, "Resocialization Within Walls," *Annals of the*

positive and cooperative type of staff-inmate relationship is a prerequisite for and a consequence of treatment goals. This is due primarily to accepting attitudes on the part of the staff, the overall replacement of formal controls by more informal ones, and the general reduction of inmate deprivations.

Grusky found support for the hypothesis that more positive attitudes among inmates are found in treatment, rather than in custodial, institutions. By comparing attitudinal responses of inmates in three institutions, each situated in a different position along the treatment-custodial continuum, we were able to test this hypothesis more carefully than could be done in the original case study.

As in the original study, inmate attitudes in three areas were examined: attitudes toward the prison, staff, and treatment program. Table 1 demon-

TABLE 1

INMATE ATTITUDES TOWARD THE PRISON, STAFF, AND PROGRAM

	Benign (Percent) (N = 95)	Partial (Percent) (N = 124)	Lock (Percent) (N = 138)
Attitudes toward the prison:[a]			
Favorable (Scale Types I–II)	63.1	48.2	39.1
Attitudes toward the staff:[b]			
Favorable (Scale Types I–II)	44.3	29.2	23.4
Attitudes toward the program:[c]			
Favorable (item response "yes")	88.8	81.9	74.8

[a] For a description of scale see O. Grusky, "Treatment Goals and Organizational Behavior" (unpublished Ph.D. dissertation, University of Michigan, 1958), p. 141. The coefficients of reproducibility for this scale were Benign .91, Partial .90, and Lock .93. The coefficients of scalability were .54, .77, and .81, respectively. A difference of over 12.5 percent between the camps is significant at the .05 level by a difference-of-proportions test.

[b] The coefficients of reproducibility for this scale were Benign .88, Partial .91, and Lock .92; for scalability, they were .53, .75, and .77, respectively.

[c] Only a single item, "Do you feel [the program] has helped you in any way?" was available. No answer: Benign 2, Partial 3, Lock 19.

strates a positive relationship between favorable inmate response toward the prison and the degree of development of its treatment goals. Where about six out of ten of Benign's inmates were positively oriented toward

American Academy of Political and Social Science, 293 (May 1954): 88–98; Hans Reimer, "Socialization Within the Prison Community," Proceedings of the American Prison Association (1937), pp. 151–55; Gresham M. Sykes, The Society of Captives (Princeton, N.J.: Princeton University Press, 1958); Gresham M. Sykes and Sheldon L. Messinger, "The Inmate Social System," in Richard A. Cloward et al., Theoretical Studies in Social Organization of the Prison (Social Science Research Council Pamphlet no. 15 [March 1960]), pp. 5–19 [and 413–25 of this volume]; Robert Vinter and Morris Janowitz, "Effective Institutions for Juvenile Delinquents: A Research Statement," Social Service Review, 33 (June 1959): 118–30.

the prison (63 percent), not quite five of ten of Partial's inmates (48 percent) and less than four of ten of the inmates at Lock (39 percent), the most custodially oriented prison of the three, had positive feelings toward their institutions. A similar pattern is revealed concerning attitudes toward the staff. At Benign, 44 percent of the men had favorable attitudes toward the staff, whereas only 29 percent at Partial and 23 percent at Lock were as positively oriented toward the staff. The third area of inmate attitudes investigated were those toward existing programs. These attitudes were also found, as expected, to be related to the goals of the prison. At Benign, 89 percent of the men felt that the program had helped them, as compared with 82 percent of the men at Partial and 75 percent of the men at Lock who expressed similar views. Attitudes toward the programs were the most positive, and reflected, in part, the salience of the program, which in turn was due to the official support for treatment goals. In short, Grusky's original hypothesis was strongly confirmed.[6] Significant differences were found between the prison which was most custodially oriented and the one most treatment-oriented.

The Effects of Socialization

In order to give a sharper test to the proposition, the length of residence in the institution was held constant. In this manner, the consequences of official socialization could be examined. It would be expected that the longer the inmate was exposed to the values and programs of the prison, the more likely he would be influenced by them; that is, inmates who have spent a long time in the prison should most clearly reflect the impact of the prison on their attitudes, and those who have been there only a short time should be least affected.

The data presented in Figure 1 show a strong relationship between attitude toward the staff and length of time spent in the prison. Inmates who had spent longer time in the custodially oriented prison were more likely to hold negative attitudes than those who had been there only a few months, whereas the reverse was true at the treatment-oriented prison, where inmates who had spent a long time in the prison were more likely to hold positive attitudes than negative ones.[7] When those inmates at Benign who had spent fewer than three months in the prison were compared with those who had spent more than eight months there, we found

---

[6] In comparing Grusky's results with our own, there was remarkable agreement in the percentages of positive responses.

[7] In an excellent study of socialization within the prison, Wheeler demonstrates similar findings in regard to "prisonization," a phenomenon related to attitudes toward both society and the prison. His findings show that the longer the time the inmate spent in the prison, the less conforming his attitudes were with those of the staff, reflecting his internalization of the prison culture. See Stanton Wheeler, "Socialization in Correctional Communities," *American Sociological Review*, 26 (October 1961): 697–712.

that only about one of three (35 percent) of the former, as contrasted with about half (56 percent) of the latter, fell into the most favorable scale type. At Camp Lock the reverse was found true. The proportion of positive responses dropped sharply from 27 percent of the inmates who had been

FIGURE 1

RELATIONSHIP OF ATTITUDES TOWARD STAFF
TO LENGTH OF TIME SPENT IN PRISON

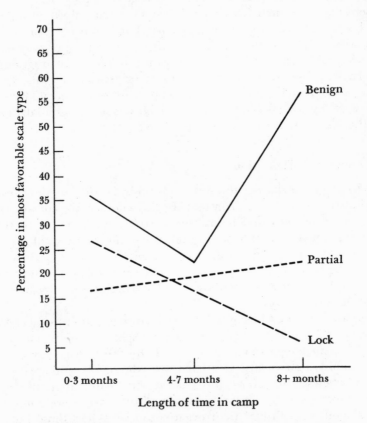

The N's from which percentages were based for the 0–3-month period were: Benign 26, Partial 33, and Lock 55. For the 4–7-month period, they were 36, 35, and 44, respectively. And for the 8+-month period, they were 30, 59, and 35.

there less than three months to less than 9 percent of those who had been there eight or more months. Camp Partial exhibited a mild positive influence, reflecting its intermediate position.[8]

---

[8] It should be pointed out that a smaller proportion of fairly recent (0–3 months) inmates of Partial than those from the more custodial Lock demonstrated favorable atti-

In Figure 2, the same general relationship is revealed with respect to attitudes toward the prison, but not as clearly. The proportion of inmates at Lock who were favorably oriented decreased slightly from 36 percent of

FIGURE 2

RELATIONSHIP OF ATTITUDES TOWARD PRISON
TO LENGTH OF TIME SPENT IN PRISON

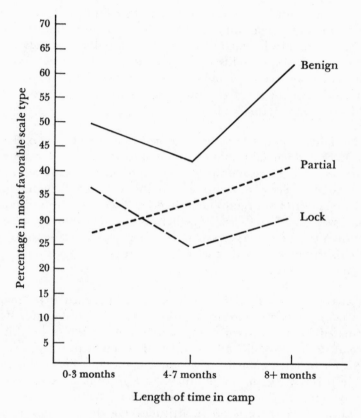

The N's from which percentages were based are the same as for Figure 1.

tudes toward the staff. However, the percentage of favorable responses increased steadily with experience in the former institution, and decreased steadily in the latter. A greater proportion of favorable responses was evidenced at all time periods among inmates of the highly treatment-oriented Benign than among those of both the other prisons. We inferred that inmates of Benign were apparently more receptive to the staff initially, their receptivity then declined, but ultimately responses were most favorable among those inmates with eight or more months of experience. Of course, the sample survey design which we used has the weakness of providing data only for a particular slice of time. Resurveys or panel studies are required to assess clearly the effect of prison experience on attitudes.

those whose stay was short-term to 31 percent of those having a longer-term stay in the prison. In contrast, the percentage of favorable responses increased at Benign from 50 percent of those having less than three months' experience to 64 percent of those who had eight or more months in prison. However, in both prisons, inmates with four to seven months' experience were most negative.[9]

Influence of Other Variables

Before any conclusions could be drawn from these findings, it was necessary to control for other relevant variables, since an important obstacle to studies of this nature is that inmates are not usually randomly assigned to treatment institutions. This was true of this study as well, in that inmates at Benign were younger and likely to have been less serious offenders. However, this type of selectivity does not appear to have accounted for the results obtained in this study.

Age. Initially, it might have been argued that the older age of the inmates at Lock and Partial would be sufficient to account for the more negative attitudes found there. Our findings, on the contrary, show age to be inversely related to negative attitude at both Lock and Benign, with the younger inmates in both camps more likely to hold negative attitudes. No difference was found at Partial. Furthermore, young inmates were more positive than their counterparts at Lock. The same was true for older inmates. This would suggest that selectivity in regard to age would operate against the hypothesis.

Type of Offender. It similarly could have been argued that inmates at Partial and Lock were more experienced and hardened criminals, well indoctrinated in the ways of crime, and would therefore exhibit more negative attitudes. We may ask, first, whether this is true and, second, if so, is this factor large enough to account for the differences obtained between the prisons? Again, the findings show, in contradiction to what is commonly believed, that the more serious offenders, by a variety of measures, did not have more negative attitudes. On the contrary, these two variables were generally unrelated. In the few cases where differences were found, they were small and variable. Furthermore, the direction of this relationship was reversed in the treatment institution, where the more serious offenders were more likely to hold more positive attitudes than the less serious offenders. And, finally, when comparable groups of types of offend-

---

[9] Wheeler ("Socialization in Correctional Communities") found a similar U-shaped pattern in regard to conforming attitudes held by inmates and attributed this to the stage of the inmate's institutional career. Inmates in the last phase of their institutionalization were believed to shed prison culture as they anticipate leaving the prison and returning to society.

ers were compared in the various camps, they were more positive in their attitudes at Benign than at Lock.[10]

It would appear (see Table 2) that the selectivity in regard to age and type of offender would not be sufficient to account for the differences ob-

TABLE 2

INMATE ATTITUDES TOWARD THE PRISON BY AGE AND TYPE OF OFFENDER
(Percent in Most Favorable Scale Type)

	Benign		Partial		Lock	
	Per-cent	Num-ber	Per-cent	Num-ber	Per-cent	Num-ber
Age:						
25 years and under	47.6%	86	36.3%	11	11.1%	18
26+	77.7	9	35.4	111	35.9	114
Number of prison sentences:						
1	48.6	70	37.1	62	34.2	76
2 or more	56.0	25	35.1	61	29.3	58
Number of charged crimes:						
1–3	45.9	61	31.9	47	35.5	45
4+	65.3	26	39.6	63	33.3	70
Seriousness of crimes:[a]						
Less serious crimes	50.0	18	47.5	59	30.8	39
More serious crimes	50.0	74	34.7	59	31.6	76

[a] When more than one crime was charged, the most serious was coded. Serious crimes were regarded as murder, rape, and assault. The less serious crimes consisted in robbery, burglary, larceny, etc.

tained in this study, and certainly could not account for the differences between Partial and Lock, since there was little difference in the types of inmates sent to those two camps. It should be pointed out, however, that inmates at Benign were more positive during the early period than inmates at the other camps, which may have been partly due to a selectivity, or may have resulted from the camp having had an initial positive impact on inmate attitudes. In any case, whatever differences existed in the nature of the inmates in the organization initially as a result of differential recruitment procedures, inmates became more positive over time in the treatment

---

[10] The total time spent by the inmate in confinement in any institution was also found to be related to negative attitudes; the longer the time spent in custodial institutions, the more negative the attitude. This, of course, supports the argument that it is the prison experience as such which is largely responsible for the development of negative attitudes. Selectivity did exist, however, in that all inmates sent to prison camps to begin with were not believed to be security risks by the prison officials. It should be pointed out in this connection that inmates in all camps were, as a whole, positively oriented toward their institutions, staff, and programs. Whether this finding can be attributed to an initial selectivity in inmates sent to camps, or whether this is a reflection of the differences between maximum- and minimum-security prisons generally, cannot be settled by this research design. The amount of variance accounted for by characteristics of members in an organization has not been clearly established by research findings.

institution and more negative in the custodial one, reflecting the differential impact of the organization upon its members.

By these tests, then, it appears that, regardless of any selectivity in input, the differences between prisons were responsible for attitudinal differences.

Informal Organization. These attitudinal differences between prisons reflected major differences in the nature of the informal organization among prison inmates. Support for this assertion is reflected in the finding that attitudes of inmates were related to the degree of their involvement in the inmate subculture. Attitudes appeared to be acquired as a result of informal socialization and participation in prison subculture, and reflected those informal standards held by its members.

Involvement and participation in the subculture was measured by the number of friendship choices the inmate received from other inmates. Three types of inmates were distinguished: the uninvolved or isolate, who received no choices; the moderately involved, who received from one to three choices; and the highly involved, who received four or more friendship choices. Table 3 shows that at Benign isolates were the most negative

TABLE 3

DEGREE OF INVOLVEMENT IN INFORMAL SYSTEM
AND ATTITUDES TOWARD THE PRISON[a]
(Percent in Most Favorable Scale Type)

	Benign		Partial		Lock	
	Per-cent	Num-ber	Per-cent	Num-ber	Per-cent	Num-ber
Isolates (received no choices)	33.3%	15	32.4%	37	33.3%	75
Moderately involved (received 1–3 choices)	50.6	63	38.5	78	30.2	59
Highly involved (received 4+ choices)	64.6	17	25.0	12	20.0	5

[a] Involvement measured by the number of friendship choices received by the inmate.

and the highly involved inmates the most positive in their attitudes toward the prison. At Lock the reverse was true, with the highly involved inmates the most negative and the uninvolved inmates the most positive in their attitudes. At Partial, negative attitudes were related to both high and low involvement in the subculture. It is not immediately clear why moderately involved inmates at Partial were more positive than isolates. In all three prisons, however, favorableness of attitude was related to degree of involvement with the informal organization.[11]

---

[11] Wheeler's study "Socialization in Correctional Communities" also demonstrated a relationship between the speed and degree of "prisonization" and involvement in informal inmate organization.

Informal Leadership. Further evidence of the impact of custodial and treatment goals on informal organization among prison inmates was found in the kinds of attitudes held by informal leaders in the various prisons.

Both Schrag's and Grusky's studies[12] dealt with the relationship between leaders and organizational goals. Schrag asserted that leaders were uniformly selected from among the most negative inmates. In contrast, Grusky hypothesized that orientation of the leader would vary with the type of total institution; specifically, informal leaders in treatment institutions were seen as more likely to be cooperative than their counterparts in custodially oriented prisons.

Consistent with Grusky's hypothesis, leaders at Benign were more positive in their attitudes than were leaders at Partial, who in turn were more positive than those at Lock.[13] However, this might have been true for any sample of inmates, because inmates were, as a whole, more positive at Benign than at Lock. By comparing the leaders with the nonleaders within each prison, a more precise test of this relationship was obtained. Tables 4 and 5 show leaders were more positive than the nonleaders at Benign, while the reverse was true at Lock, where the leaders were more negative than the nonleaders. This relationship was found to hold for attitudes toward both the prison and the institution's programs.

TABLE 4

LEADERSHIP AND ATTITUDES TOWARD PRISON
(Percent in Most Favorable Scale Type)

	Benign		Partial		Lock	
	Per-cent	Num-ber	Per-cent	Num-ber	Per-cent	Num-ber
Leaders	61.3%	31	47.5%	50	23.3%	37
Nonleaders	45.3	66	35.5	77	34.3	97

TABLE 5

LEADERSHIP AND ATTITUDES TOWARD PROGRAM[a]
(Percent Favorable)

	Benign		Partial		Lock	
	Per-cent	Num-ber	Per-cent	Num-ber	Per-cent	Num-ber
Leaders	74.2%	31	47.6%	50	39.3%	37
Nonleaders	62.5	66	48.0	77	63.5	97

[a] The particular item asked if they thought the programs in the camp were a good idea.

[12] Clarence Schrag, "Leadership among Prison Inmates," *American Sociological Review*, 19 (February 1954): 37–42; Grusky, "Organizational Goals and the Behavior of Informal Leaders."

[13] Leaders were designated in accordance with Grusky's and Schrag's studies (*ibid.*).

OBSERVATIONS ABOUT INFORMAL ORGANIZATION

Having replicated Grusky's study and substantiated the hypothesis, we sought to develop a fuller explanation of the findings. Inmate attitudes reflect the nature of inmate subculture and informal organization, which in turn are conditioned by formal organizational characteristics, such as the formal structure and the official objectives.

Informal organization develops in prison because: (1) inmates are isolated from society; (2) institutionalization generates common problems of adjustment[14] which require cooperation for their solution while simultaneously providing a situation with opportunity for effective interaction with others similarly situated;[15] and (3) inmates are members of a formal organization which, by its very nature as a system of action, can never fully anticipate or coordinate all behavior through the formal system alone; hence, informal organization serves to close the gaps of the formal organization.

Two kinds of informal organization have been identified in the prisons studied—one supportive of the official structure and the other in opposition to it. We submit that the goal of treatment encourages the development of the former, and the goal of custody the latter.

Inmate subcultures develop as solutions to the problems and deprivations experienced by inmates in the prison situation. They would therefore differ in their form and content as the nature of the problems experienced by inmates differ, particularly those created by the institutional experience itself. The two different types of informal organization developed because the inmate subsystem performed contrasting functions in the treatment and custodial institutions.

Two reasons may be suggested to explain the character of the inmate subculture in the custodial institution; first, the problems faced by inmates tend to be more severe there; in addition, inmates perceive the custodial institution itself to be responsible for their problems. As a result, they band together in opposition to the prison and its administration, which they see as the source of their frustrations.[16] Consequently, inmate subcultures

---

[14] In the typical custodial prison, social rejection, pervasive and rigid social control, and loss of liberty, autonomy, respect, affection, heterosexual relationships, security, and self-esteem have been identified as problems which inmates experience. Because these problems often require the cooperation of others for their solution, strong pressures for a collective response are built up. As cohesion develops among the inmates, a reduction of deprivations is experienced; and, conversely, as it decreases, an increase in the irritants of prison life is experienced. In this manner systematic pressures for a collective solution are created (cf. Sykes and Messinger, "The Inmate Social System").

[15] Cf. Albert K. Cohen, *Delinquent Boys* (Glencoe, Ill.: Free Press, 1956), chap. 3, for a penetrating analysis of the formation of subcultures.

[16] McCorkle, for example, has argued that the major problem the inmate social system attempts to cope with is social rejection, and that inmates defend threats to their self-esteem by "rejecting the rejectors," a process which allows inmates to maintain favorable self-images in a situation where the formal organization imposes self-definitions which are

tend to become more and more dominated by the values of professional criminals, which already emphasize a strict demarcation between the guards and inmates, since these groups are seen as fundamentally in opposition to one another.

The emergence of this subculture compounds an already difficult problem—a central concern, in fact, of the custodial institution—that of maintaining social control within the prison. Since techniques for insuring conformity are inadequate, guards resort to various methods of accommodation and bargain for conformity with the means available to them.[17] One method, as Sykes points out, is to "buy compliance at the cost of tolerating deviance." In return for the guards' overlooking selected infractions of the rules, inmates are expected to comply with the rest. In this fashion, inmates begin to regulate their own behavior and, in so doing, begin to fulfill, in part, the formal organization's task of maintaining internal order. The more effectively they are able to exert control over their behavior, the more advantageous is their bargaining position vis-à-vis the guards—a process which itself has a further consolidating effect upon inmate subculture. In this manner, inmates are able to gain some degree of freedom from the demands and pressures of the formal organization, thereby increasing the relative amount of control they can exercise over the conditions of their existence.[18] This newly gained mastery over their environmental conditions is, however, illusory. It would appear that they have merely traded their previous situation and its attendant deprivations for subjugation to an even more despotic ruling group—other inmates who have less compunction and fewer limitations about the use of force and violence to gain compliance with their ends. Thus, in reality, freedom is usually only temporary, as inmate leaders quickly replace the official demands for conformity with new demands for conformity to new rules which sustain their dominance.

In contrast to this picture of informal organization in custodial institutions, we can view the development of informal organization in treatment institutions. While inmate organization can also be found in treatment institutions, it does not generally take on an oppositional character, simply because many of the psychological deprivations of imprisonment have

---

unacceptable or threatening. This is accomplished by devaluing either the importance or legitimacy of persons imposing such definitions. See McCorkle and Korn, "Resocialization Within Walls," pp. 86–95.

[17] Sykes, *The Society of Captives;* Cloward, "Social Control in the Prison," in *Theoretical Studies in Social Organization of the Prison,* and others have pointed out problems endemic to the custodial institution in maintaining social control, the most important of these being the lack of an internalized sense of duty on the part of inmates, the limitations upon the use of force, the difficulties involved in segregating rule violators, the lack of effective inducements, and the strains inherent in the role of the guard.

[18] See Richard McCleery, "Communication Patterns as Bases of Systems of Authority and Power," in Cloward *et al., Theoretical Studies in Social Organization of the Prison,* for a discussion of relations between formal and informal power structures.

been reduced and a shift in patterns of control has occurred. Inmates are treated with more respect by the organization, and as a result the institution is not perceived by inmates to be totally against them or antithetical to their interests. In addition, the treatment institution is more flexible in regard to its rules, and treatment needs of inmates are considered in its demands for conformity. Furthermore, in its attempt to regulate behavior, formal methods of control are replaced by more informal ones, thus reducing resentment and hostility. This leads to a greater tolerance in the range of inmate conformity and, concomitantly, "control" becomes less important in the hierarchy of organization objectives. Accordingly, there is little payoff from the administration for inmates' regulation of their own behavior.

Selected aspects of the formal organization's structure also have an impact on informal organization. Particularly in total institutions, the formal authority structure serves as a model for the informal. The custodially oriented prison, which is usually highly centralized, tends to produce a similar type of informal inmate leadership; for such an adaptation serves, on the one hand, to strengthen official control and administration of the prison and, on the other, to stabilize inmate relations by focusing attention on the deprivations inflicted by the authorities. Because inmate subculture there is dominated by criminal values emphasizing a strict demarcation between guards and inmates, informal leadership must thereby justify itself by securing special concessions from the oppressors, the "screws," in return for which the leaders prevent their men from stepping too far out of line. The typical inmate in such a situation is confronted with few alternatives and usually accepts the values and the leadership as they are presented to him, thereby perpetuating the subculture.

The inmate subsystems are seen as performing different functions within their respective institutions, which, as we have seen, are directly linked to the goals of the prison. In the custodial prison, even though the inmate subsystem was oppositional and subversive to the organization, it also functioned to assist it in the maintenance of internal order by regulating inmate behavior, though this was usually at the cost of the "corruption of the formal authority system." In contrast, control of inmate behavior was not a primary function of informal organization in the treatment institution. Informal organization there was more compatible with the formal organization and was more oriented toward meeting the particular needs of inmates and integrating and coordinating their behavior.

The functioning of informal leaders was, in turn, directly linked to the functions performed by the inmate subsystem, and, as a consequence, the informal leaders' main task in the custodial prison was one of exercising control over the behavior of other inmates. In order effectively to implement this end, the informal leadership employed the same techniques as the formal organization and developed a highly consolidated and centralized power structure. And, like the formal organization, it also relied upon coercion and force, rather than on consensus or cooperation, to ensure conformity.

In contrast, the informal leaders in the treatment institution, because the treatment goal allowed for a broader range of inmate adaptation, performed a variety of functions depending on the particular needs of the inmates, and functioned more as coordinators and integrators of behavior than as controllers, as they did in the custodial prison. Not only did the informal leaders play very different roles in the two types of prisons, but techniques of leadership differed as well, since the inmate subsystem in the treatment institution tended to be based more upon consensus and cooperation than was true of the custodial prison.

These speculations led to a new hypothesis about the structure and functioning of informal leadership in the different types of prisons. As we have pointed out, one of the techniques for maintaining order in the custodial prison was the *centralization of control* by informal leadership. Because this function was less important for the inmate subsystem in the treatment institution, it was hypothesized that the more treatment-oriented the prison, the less centralized the informal leadership structure would be and the proportionately greater number of inmates who would emerge as top leaders.

The data supported this hypothesis. At Benign, 9.3 percent of the inmates were chosen as top leaders (that is, received nine or more choices), while at Partial 6.3 percent were chosen, compared with only 1.3 percent of the inmates at Lock. When inmates were asked: "Who are leaders?" similar results were obtained. Forty-three percent of the inmates at Benign were named, compared with 38 percent at Partial and 23 percent at Lock.[19] Both measures indicated greater concentration of power and centralization of control in the custodial prison.

A second technique adopted by inmate leaders in the custodial prison to control inmate behavior was the use of coercion to secure conformity and to maintain power. This led to a hypothesis dealing with types of persons likely to rise to positions of leadership or influence in the two types of prisons. Because *control* was an important function of the inmate leaders in the custodial prison, individuals disposed toward such behavior would be more likely to rise to positions of leadership there than would be true of treatment prisons, where a more charismatic, socioemotional, or consensus-oriented type of leader would be expected to develop. Therefore, it was hypothesized that leaders in the custodial institution would be more

---

[19] In part, some of the differences between camps in the proportions of top leaders was a function of the numbers of nominations made by respondents in the different camps. Whether the number of nominations reflects the number of actual leaders is directly linked to the difficult problem of validity in the use of sociometric techniques, which cannot be dealt with here.

authoritarian, reflecting their "tough-minded" orientation toward the use of power, and would be "less well liked," due to their reliance upon coercion and emphasis upon control, than leaders in treatment institutions. Support for this hypothesis comes from the finding that leaders were selected from the most authoritarian inmates at Lock, whereas the reverse was true at Benign, where leaders were selected from the least authoritarian inmates.[20] Not only was the leadership structure more decentralized at Benign, but the leadership positions were occupied there, as well, by less authoritarian persons. Furthermore, leaders at Benign were less authoritarian than those at Partial, who in turn were less authoritarian than the leaders found at Lock. No difference in authoritarianism was found among the general populations of inmates at the three prisons. In addition to their being less authoritarian, the leaders at Benign were liked better, friendlier, and more approachable by other inmates than was true of the leaders at Lock.[21] This style of leadership is reflected in the findings that leaders at Benign were more likely to be chosen by other inmates as "well liked," a "best buddy," and as someone with whom they could discuss their personal problems than was true of the leaders at Lock. Partial once again was found to exhibit an intermediate position with regard to its leaders.

SUMMARY AND CONCLUSIONS

The purpose of this study was twofold: (1) to replicate a study conducted by Grusky; and (2) to examine the consequences of treatment and custodial goals upon the inmate subsystem within correctional institutions, with particular emphasis on the conditions generating oppositional informal organization. Three areas of concern were inmate attitudes, the effect of socialization, and the development of informal leadership.

1. The findings on the whole supported Grusky's major hypothesis: Inmates were more positive in their attitudes toward the institution, staff,

---

[20] Leaders were more authoritarian than nonleaders at Lock and less authoritarian than nonleaders at Benign. At Lock, 48.3 percent of the leaders as compared with 39 percent of the nonleaders gave authoritarian responses to a question asking if they would harshly discipline an angry employee, while at Benign only 33.3 percent of the leaders as compared with 47.6 percent of the nonleaders responded in such an authoritarian fashion. At Partial, 40.5 percent of the leaders and 52.0 percent of the nonleaders responded in an authoritarian fashion.

[21] Leaders were also less well liked and more socially distant from nonleaders in the custodial institution. At Benign, 77.4 percent of the leaders were also chosen as a "best buddy" by other inmates as compared with 66 percent of the leaders at Partial and 40.6 percent of those at Lock. The same pattern was found in regard to being chosen as "best liked" by other inmates; 77.8 per cent of the leaders at Benign, 52 percent of the leaders at Partial, and only 48 percent of the leaders at Lock were so chosen. These relationships were also found to hold in regard to a question asking who they would discuss personal problems with in the prison; inmates at Lock were much less likely to discuss personal problems with their leaders than were inmates at Benign.

and programs in the treatment institution than those in the custodial one. Furthermore, they became more positive or negative with the length of time they spent in the prison, depending upon the type of organizational goal, thereby suggesting that it was the prison experience which was primarily responsible for the development of negative attitudes.

2. Differences between prisons were found to be related to differences in inmate organization. Two facts suggested this: First, attitudes were found to be related to degree of involvement with inmate organization, and second, leaders' attitudes were found to vary systematically with the prison's goals, being more positive in the treatment institution and more negative in the custodial one.

3. The informal leadership structure was also found to be more centralized in the custodial institution in an attempt to maintain more effective control over inmate behavior. The informal leaders among the inmates played different roles, depending upon organizational goals and contexts; and these roles were directly linked to the function of the inmate subculture within the prison. Leaders in the custodial prison were also found to be more authoritarian and less well liked than leaders in the treatment prison, reflecting the differences in their roles.

The goal of "custody," with its concomitant centralized and formal authority structure and increased deprivations for inmates, contributed significantly to the development of the hostile informal organization in the custodial prison. The disenfranchisement of inmates from possible rewards of the institution encouraged the development of negative attitudes and a hostile informal leadership.

Criminology and
the Sociology of Law

PART EIGHT

Early sociological jurisprudence was almost entirely the province of legal scholars such as Pound, Brandeis, and Holmes. While these and other eminent members of the legal profession were raising some significant issues about the law as one form of social regulation, sociologists failed to reciprocate in bringing their professional skills and knowledge about research technique to an understanding of behavior and the legal order. This was in part because sociologists narrowly viewed the law as a body of regulations concerning the control and treatment of criminal behavior; in fact, this conception of the law became a central part of formal criminology. Reflecting the absence of a social science perspective, issues debated in legal circles were settled by opinions based upon rich and varied experience in legal affairs, not by systematic empirical investigation.

A second period may be distinguished in which the major emphasis has been upon applying sociological analysis to problems of legal institutions and the evolution of legal doctrine. Recent work by sociologists of law developed at least two major thrusts. The first of these has as its goal the understanding of values as determinative of legal process, an interest long debated in jurisprudence but only recently documented with empirical data. Typical studies have revealed normative conflicts as they impede the exercise of legal control in such areas as public morality and deviant subcultures. Other research has focused upon the social consequences of legal regulation, as seen in studies of taxation, business practices, and race relations. Most recently, considerable interest has been shown in the legal regulation of individual rights, both in the spheres of protection (e.g., preservation of reputation and the right to privacy) and privilege.

The other major activity of legal sociologists has been the examination of the structure of legal organization. This is the most recent and rapidly developing field, and it owes its emergence substantially to the growth of law and social science centers at Berkeley, Wisconsin, Northwestern, and the University of Denver. Funded by the Russell Sage Foundation, these four have an interdisciplinary emphasis similar to programs in the law schools of Chicago, Michigan, and Columbia, and to social science departments at Indiana and New York University. The range of research interests and publications of these programs is prodigious.

Broadly speaking, "legal organization" refers to several distinct but hopefully cumulative interests. As a reflection of sociological interest in professions such as medicine, dentistry, and business, investigators have turned to the profession of law. Representative here are studies of the recruitment of lawyers, the process of socialization in law schools, factors associated with various career trajectories, and increasing specialization. As a consequence of these studies, a great deal is now known about the occupational features of a legal career and the development of professional self-conceptions.

Second, there has been considerable investment of resources in the study of justice administration and court structure. Probably the innovative work by University of Chicago sociologists on jury behavior has the longest tradition, but this has been supplemented by studies of judicial selection and judicial decision-making. It should be noted, however, that political scientists, social psychologists, and law faculty members have collaborated in many of these investigations, since the subject matter transcends the boundaries of a single discipline.

Third, legal organization refers to the body of knowledge accumulating on the solicitation and use of information (for example, scientific evidence) in legal decision-making. Recent work in this tradition has attempted to assemble findings on the problems citizens define as appropriate for legal assistance, and the attempts persons make at problem-solving through contact with attorneys.

The paper by Philip Selznick that opens this section, "Legal Institutions and Social Controls," formulates a number of propositions about the decline of nonlegal sources and agencies of social control. Prominent among these are the projected consequences of increasing "mass society" and the growth and influence of large-scale organization.

The concept of mass society, in which persons are seen as gaining in freedom and equality of opportunity and enjoying a broadened range of interpersonal relationships, is sometimes viewed in association with personal disengagement and loss of identity. Jerome Skolnick, in "Justice Administration in Mass Society," reviews a number of issues posed by justice administration in the context of mass organization.

Richard D. Schwartz' and Sonya Orleans' paper "On Legal Sanctions" is derived from a two-part study of legal compliance. The first section, reprinted here, assesses the literature on preventive effects of sanctions, their severity, the social costs incurred, and alternative modes of securing compliance. (The second part, not reprinted in this volume, reports findings from a field experiment on motivational factors affecting compliance with federal income-tax laws.)

"Research on the Legal System in America," by Edwin M. Schur, is taken from a more extensive review of selected empirical studies in the sociology of law. Included is a consideration of four areas important to the development of a comprehensive sociology of law: courts, judges, and juries; administration of criminal justice; styles of legal work; and the public and the law.

Further reading in the theoretical and empirical study of law and the social order is to be found in the following selections:

1. *Some General Essays on the Nature and Scope of Legal Sociology*

Auerbach, Carl A. "Legal Tasks for the Sociologist," *Law and Society Review* 1 (November 1966): 91–104.

Aubert, Vilhelm. "Researches in the Sociology of Law," *American Behavioral Scientist* 7 (December 1963): 16–20.

Donnelly, Richard; Goldstein, Joseph; and Schwartz, Richard D. *Criminal Law* (New York: Free Press, Macmillan, 1962).

Evan, William M., ed. *Law and Sociology* (New York: Free Press, Macmillan, 1962).

Gibbs, Jack P. "Crime and the Sociology of Law," *Sociology and Social Research* 51 (October 1966): 23–38.

Pound, Roscoe. "Sociology of Law," in *Twentieth Century Sociology*, ed. Georges Gurvitch and Wilbert E. Moore (New York: Philosophical Library, 1945), pp. 297–341.

Rose, Arnold M. "Law and the Causation of Social Problems," *Social Problems* 16 (Summer 1968): 33–43.

———. "Some Suggestions for Research in the Sociology of Law," *Social Problems* 9 (Winter 1962): 281–84.

Schur, Edwin M. *Law and Society: A Sociological View* (New York: Random House, 1968).

Selznick, Philip. "Sociology of Law," in *International Encyclopedia of the Social Sciences* (New York: Free Press, Macmillan, 1968), vol. 9, pp. 50–57.

———. "The Sociology of Law," in *Sociology Today: Problems and Prospects*, ed. Robert K. Merton, Leonard Broom, and Leonard S. Cottrell, Jr. (New York: Basic Books, 1959), pp. 115–27.

Simon, Rita James, ed. *The Sociology of Law: Interdisciplinary Readings* (San Francisco: Chandler, 1968).

2. Sociology and Properties of the Criminal Law

Dreher, Robert H. "Origin, Development, and Present Status of Insanity as a Defense to Criminal Responsibility in the Common Law," *Journal of the History of the Behavioral Sciences* 3 (January 1967): 47–57.

Geis, Gilbert. "Sociology, Criminology, and the Criminal Law," *Social Problems* 7 (Summer 1959): 40–47.

Goldstein, Abraham S. *The Insanity Defense* (New Haven: Yale University Press, 1967).

Mannheim, Hermann. "Crime: Its Meaning in Relation to Law, Religion, Custom, and Morals," *Comparative Criminology* (Boston: Houghton Mifflin, 1965), pp. 22–34.

Quinney, Richard. "Introduction: Toward a Sociology of Criminal Law," in *Crime and Justice in Society*, ed. Quinney (Boston: Little, Brown, 1969), pp. 1–30.

Wellford, Charles F. "The Status of Theory in the Sociology of Law" (paper read at the American Sociological Association meetings, Boston, August 1968).

3. Some Representative Empirical Studies in the Sociology of Law

Hazard, Geoffrey C., Jr. "Reflections on Four Studies of the Legal Profession," in *Law and Society*, a special supplement to *Social Problems* 13 (Summer 1965): 46–54.

Ladinsky, Jack. "Careers of Lawyers, Law Practice, and Legal Institutions," *American Sociological Review* 28 (February 1963): 47–54.

Lortie, Dan C. "Laymen to Lawmen: Law School, Careers, and Professional Socialization," *Harvard Educational Review* 29 (Fall 1959): 363–67.

Mayhew, Leon, and Reiss, Albert J., Jr. "The Social Organization of Legal Contacts," *American Sociological Review* 34 (June 1969): 309–318.

Reichstein, Kenneth. "Ambulance Chasing: A Case Study of Deviation and Control Within the Legal Profession," *Social Problems* 13 (Summer 1965): 3–18.

Schwartz, Richard D., and Orleans, Sonya. "On Legal Sanctions," *University of Chicago Law Review* 34 (Winter 1967): 274–300.

—————— and Skolnick, Jerome H. "Two Studies of Legal Stigma," *Social Problems* 10 (Fall 1962): 133–42.

Zeisel, Hans. "The Law," in *The Uses of Sociology*, ed. Paul F. Lazarsfeld, William H. Sewell, and Harold L. Wilensky (New York: Basic Books, 1967), pp. 81–99.

4. The Courts and Justice Administration

Blumberg, Abraham S. *Criminal Justice* (Chicago: Quadrangle Books, 1967).

Cicourel, Aaron V. *The Social Organization of Juvenile Justice* (New York: Wiley, 1968).

Newman, Donald J. *Conviction: The Determination of Guilt or Innocence Without Trial* (Boston: Little, Brown, 1966).

——————. "Sociologists and the Administration of Criminal Justice," in *Sociology in Action: Case Studies in Social Problems and Directed Social Change*, ed. Arthur B. Shostak (Homewood, Ill.: Dorsey Press, 1966), pp. 177–87.

The President's Commission on Law Enforcement and Administration of Justice. *Task Force Report: The Courts* (Washington, D.C.: U.S. Government Printing Office, 1967).

Rose, Arnold M. "The Social Scientist as an Expert Witness in Court Cases," in *The Uses of Sociology*, ed. Paul F. Lazarsfeld, William H. Sewell, and Harold L Wilensky (New York: Basic Books, 1967), pp. 100–118.

Schroeter, Gerd. "Protection of Confidentiality in the Courts: The Professions," *Social Problems* 16 (Winter 1969): 376–85.

Simon, Rita James. *The American Jury—The Defense of Insanity* (Boston: Little, Brown, 1967).

Skolnick, Jerome H. "Social Control in the Adversary System," *Journal of Conflict Resolution* 11 (March 1967): 52–70.

5. *Issues in Legal Sanctions and Deterrence*

Ball, John C. "The Deterrence Concept in Criminology and Law," *Journal of Criminal Law, Criminology, and Police Science* 46 (September–October 1955): 347–54.

Gibbs, Jack P. "Crime, Punishment, and Deterrence," *Southwestern Social Science Quarterly* 48 (March 1968): 515–30.

———. "Sanctions," *Social Problems* 14 (Fall 1966): 147–59.

Tittle, Charles R. "Crime Rates and Legal Sanctions," *Social Problems* 16 (Spring 1969): 409–423.

34. LEGAL INSTITUTIONS
AND SOCIAL CONTROLS

Philip Selznick

When the architects of this program asked me to discuss nonlegal social controls, I assume they had in mind the need for greater humility within the legal profession. So proud an occasion as this calls for sober reflection on the limits of the distinctively legal—on the contingent, derivative, and partial place of formal adjudication and control within the larger ordering of human society.

I have no objection to communicating such a perspective, thereby adding an appropriate note of piety to these proceedings. Nevertheless, I think it may be more important for us to consider some of the great social changes that are occurring in modern society, how they affect the balance between legal and nonlegal controls, and what problems this changing balance poses for the legal order. The humility we ask of lawyers may be all too welcome to them. The real message may be a summons to responsi-

Reprinted by permission of the author and the publisher from *Vanderbilt Law Review*, 17 (December 1963): 79–90.

This paper reflects in part the work being carried on at the Center for the Study of Law and Society, University of California, Berkeley, particularly studies of the administration of criminal justice by Jerome H. Skolnick, and of corrections by Sheldon L. Messinger.

bility and joint effort, not a suggestion that lawyers retreat to what they know best.

My assigned topic covers a very large part of what sociology (or more broadly, behavioral science) is about. For we are interested in all the ways social order is created and sustained. We study control in small groups and large ones; we study gross mechanisms of control and subtle ones; we see in every human setting the forces that encourage and enforce responsible conduct. Of course, we also give much attention to the breakdown of social control and to the emergence of what is, from the standpoint of the group or situation, irresponsible or "deviant" behavior.

Paralleling every major legal concern is a much larger and more finely textured system of codes and relationships. Interests of personality are recognized and protected in many areas of the law, yet how little we really depend on law for the day-by-day comfort we gain from orderly arrangements that save us from embarrassment, unwanted intrusions, or worse. The law of contracts facilitates and protects concerted activity, but the bonds of organization rest far more on practical and informal reciprocity and interdependence than they do on the availability of formal sanctions. Society is still held together by self-help and not by the intervention of legal agencies. Claims of right are asserted, adjudicated, and enforced for the most part outside the formal legal system.

Having said this much, I must hasten to add that there is considerable variation, at different times and places, and in different sectors of society and law, in the effectiveness of self-help and in reliance on legal controls. It is here, at the point of variation, that real inquiry begins.

I.

The evolution of modern society is marked by two master trends that have brought with them decisive changes in social control and in the role of law. The first of these trends is often referred to as the drift toward mass society. The second and closely related master trend is the increasing bureaucratization and centralization of industrial society.

There is a cruel contrast in these twin lines of evolution. In a mass society there is more freedom, more participation, more mobility, more equality. On the other hand, the bureaucratic trend creates a world of complex organizations, of more formalized controls, of centralized power, of individual helplessness and dependency. Yet both trends have the same source—the creation of an industrial society that imposes a remorseless logic on every human community that comes within its sway.

In contemporary social science there is much interest in studying the effects of industrialization on the non-Western world. These societies, rapidly emerging out of a preindustrial past, are breaking the bonds of tradition, family, and locality. Reaching out for modern technology and its fruits, they are indeed experiencing great strains. To a certain extent, the history of industrialization in Europe and the United States is being recapitulated. All this is of great importance and eminently worth pursuing. On the other hand, I venture to suggest that we have not yet fully absorbed the significance for *our own* institutions of the industrial and urban revolution.

For a long time, our society has had much to cushion it against the full impact of modernization. Until quite recently we continued to have a fairly strong rural and small-town counterweight. Our large immigrant population had its own resources of social organization. Political, economic, and cultural diversity set limits to change and helped give men roots. The inertia of tradition could sustain for generations a sense of identity and of moral continuity.

The loosening of social bonds, and the concomitant weakening of nonlegal controls, is manifest in many ways. The most important, of course, is the decline of kinship as the major unit of social organization and therefore of social control. That the functions of the family have changed in recent history is a familiar sociological tale. What was once an enterprise and a nuclear community, a unit of production and an indispensable alliance against a forbidding external world, has now become a more specialized and limited institution. What it can do for its members, and what it may ask of them, have both been radically curtailed.

This is not to say that the family is unimportant. Of course it is still the chief source of personal gratification, the main agency for socializing the young, the true staff of life for most men and women. But the family has become a significantly weaker reed, both for the individual and for society. After all, we are not speaking here of complete social breakdown, but of shifts that markedly aggravate our problems of social control. We still ask much of the family, but we have not fully recognized that its resources as an institution, its tools for doing the job, have become more and more limited.

As I see it, we are not dealing primarily with moral atrophy, the corrosion of personal values. If that exists, it is a symptom and not a cause. The main reasons for the waning role of the family in social control are practical and stem from larger changes in our economic life. The truth is that discipline in the family is less effective today because its practical significance in the routines of life has sharply declined. In an important but limited sense, it is no longer needed. When the family is really a going concern, and the activities of its members must be coordinated, if not for production, then at least as a condition of survival, the need for discipline is apparent. Authority makes sense to the individual because it is justified by urgent necessity. Moreover, the family member is heavily dependent on this small social world and its resources. Given such a setting, it is easy for appropriate moral sentiments to be created and sustained.

Let us remember that for the most part society must rely on the willing acceptance of discipline. Without consent, discipline may be enforced, but that is always less effective and has heavy costs. Now what is the foundation of this consent? It may be that some societies have won consent to authority by creating an irresistible cake of custom, a communicated sense of what is right and wrong, respectable and disreputable. I suspect that this sort of thing is greatly exaggerated. The natural habitat of the human being is a world of opportunity and constraint, of alternatives set by the practical exigencies of making a living and winning self-esteem. Customs are enforced, not abstractly and mechanically, but in the course of giving guidance to activities that make sense in their own terms. When the activites no longer make sense, we can expect social codes and symbols to attenuate and lose their force.

That the adolescent needs discipline in his own psychic interests I do not doubt. That society would be better off if the family could exercise more effective control may also be true. But such a function cannot be simply "assigned" to the family. It will not be performed at the desired levels if it does not flow naturally out of the requirements of everyday life.

The weakening of the family as an agency of social control is only a phase, although a major one, of the broader trend toward a looser, less disciplined social order. Thus another feature of our society is the steady decline of *fixed status* as a vehicle of social control. For today's Americans, of all groups and classes, status-seeking is a sign of a society on the move. It is a good guess that many fewer people today than two generations ago "know their place" and limit their actions and their aspirations accordingly. We sometimes forget, I think, how much even our own society has depended on the proprieties of status, on the giving and receiving of deference. Perhaps most important, we have counted on a large amount of voluntary segregation, so that the more privileged and the better integrated member of the community might live out his respectable life without being much affected by his more vulgar fellow citizens.

This comfortable scheme of things already seems unreal. It will soon be gone forever. The dispossessed are knocking at the door. They are making their presence known, refusing to accept the rightness of middle-class values, appealing to a broader sense of justice. The revolution of rising expectations is far from restricted to the underdeveloped countries. On the contrary, it is no less important right here.

One way of observing the breakdown of group barriers is to take note of the spread of working-class patterns of dress and leisure-time activity among middle-class children. In our open, fluid society, styles do not flow only from the top down. They also move up from below. The result is a cultural diffusion that adds little to the stability of community life. We have created a society that makes these things possible and even inevitable. This we have done for good and sufficient reasons, but we must be ready to pay the price.

It seems obvious to me that we are in no position to deplore this waning of nonlegal controls. Dedicated as we are to personal autonomy and well-being, we cannot very well yearn for the submergence of the individual in family or community. We expect and value his self-assertion; we shall honor in due course his new claims of right. Committed as we are to political freedom and legal equality, we cannot fail to accept the social transformations born in part of those ideals. Perhaps it is not logically necessary that political freedom be translated into social opportunity, or that legal equality produce a social leveling. But our political and legal concepts have, for better or worse, been hooked on to large-scale industry, the mass market, and mass communications. Together they create a revolutionary thrust that loosens and tears the social fabric.

The changes to which I have referred must inevitably increase the burdens of our legal institutions. If society cannot depend on an informal, autonomous, self-regarding, person-centered order for the maintenance of social control, it will turn to more explicitly organized agencies and to more powerful instruments of surveillance and regulation. Not only the police, but the schools, social work agencies, and perhaps other institutions, will be called upon to serve the needs of social control.

Traditionally, the formal agencies of control have been relatively weak. Their resources were limited, their techniques crude. Their effect on the life of the community was softened by a recognition of their own dependence on the people around them and by the continuity of the official and the ordinary citizen. The cop on the beat belonged to the community and he manifested his membership in dress and demeanor. Are we not already describing things remembered, a fading era?

The combination of social demand and technical competence will, in the not too distant future, create far more effective agencies of legal control. They will be more efficient and more honest, more isolated from the community and less dependent on it. They will be expert monitors of the round of life and will naturally tend to move from partial to total surveillance. Perhaps most important, the new agencies will have absorbed a prophylactic orientation, a doctrine of prevention to supplement repression.

When coercive authority enlarges its competence and adopts new, more positive goals, we have an obligation to sit up and take notice. The chief barrier to unbearable despotism has always been the limited competence of the ruler. It is one thing to have the ideology of autocracy, and its trappings; it is another to have the means to put it into practice. Thirty years ago Charles Merriam could write of the "poverty of power"—the "wide gap between the apparent omnipotence of authority and the actual operation of power, between the iron fist of force and its incidence upon human flesh and feeling."[1] This is still very largely true. But is it not the deeper lesson of our century that effective, total power *can* be mustered and sustained, if not forever, then at least long enough to exact a memorable toll in suffering and degradation?

When an institution has low capabilities, it tends to conserve its strength, to be passive rather than active. It waits for things to happen, to make themselves visible. Increase its capabilities and a subtle transformation may occur. Now the agency can exercise more initiative and reach out to deal with potential trouble. Such a prospect raises very real questions regarding the security of citizens who occasionally run afoul of the law.

As agencies of control become more rational and efficient, we may well hope for more searching study of how our institutions actually operate and what values lie half-hidden in accustomed practice, in administrative use and wont, in the traditional way of doing things. For example, how much do we depend on the policeman's role as a kind of magistrate, a dispenser of rough and ready justice as he exercises discretion in the streets? What will happen to this role in the motorized and mechanized elite corps of the future?

The ideal of equal justice seems to require that all offenders be treated alike. Yet there is evidence that the police routinely attempt to distinguish, especially among juveniles, the apparently casual offender from the committed delinquent. Lawyers and other social scientists may see in this a violation of even-handed justice. And indeed this is so, especially where racial and class bias are operative. But when confronted with these facts I am moved to ask: If the law is administered with prudence, does this not require some differential treatment at the first point of contact and not only after judgment, when ultimate disposition is made? Do we need or want agencies of control so efficient and so impartial that every actual offender has an equal chance of being known and processed? In considering this point we should bear in mind that offenses of all kinds are probably very much more numerous in fact than in record.

As you can see, I am concerned that we do not respond too eagerly and too well to the apparent need for more effective mechanisms of social control. In the administration of justice, if anywhere, we need to guard human values and forestall the creation of mindless machines for handling cases according to set routines. Here vigilance consists in careful study of actual operations so that we may know what will be lost or gained when administrative changes are proposed.

I have emphasized the dangers of competence, particularly in the technology of surveillance. Other problems arise, however, because of institu-

---

[1] Charles Merriam, *Political Power* (New York: Whittlesey House, McGraw-Hill, 1934), p. 156.

tional *in*competence. I refer to the quest for rehabilitation, for trans-forming punishment into treatment, for a mode of organization and de-cision that will permit the courts and other agencies to act in the offender's own interests.

The most remarkable feature of our criminal law is indeed this effort to seek new ways of doing justice. The civilized impulse manifest here does honor to us all. And yet, some doubts are raised. If a man is to be rehabili-tated, he must be accessible. What are the limits of this access, both physical and psychological? If injustice occurs, what are the principles to which appeal can be made? Are the institutions within which this work goes on really capable of doing more than providing, at best, humane custody? If these institutions cannot provide treatment, yet purport to do so, what are the actual rules according to which time is served? Are these rules subject to criticism and control?

I do not mean to throw cold water on the attempts being made, notably in my own state, to transform the administration of corrections. In the long run there is hope for it. In the shorter run, there are limitations. Among these limits are the administrative resources, including appropriate knowledge, available for carrying out the intent of the law. The more we ask of the law, from the standpoint of creative change, the more important is this administrative base. And the problem is exacerbated when the legislature offers, in response to public sentiment, a murky mixture of incompatible demands.

Perhaps the most important issue raised by these developments is the violation of personal privacy. It is one of the ironies of our age that men of good will are concerned about privacy but, at the same time, support the most ruthless invasions of it. When official control is combined with sensitivity to personality, the outcome may be greater protection of basic human rights, including the right to be secure in one's private fears and fantasies. Another possibility, however, is the kind of intrusive probing and exposure that is incompatible with personal dignity.

The answer to this cannot be a withdrawal from or rejection of the "treatment" perspective. With the weakening of more intimate settings, and the persistence, nevertheless, of humane ideals, society will inevitably assume responsibility, through more formal agencies, for personal help and guidance. The question is, have we worked out the legal consequences of this uneasy and conceivably virulent combination of coercive power and moral persuasion?

Much of what I have said thus far adds up to a plea for more intensive study, by lawyers and other social scientists, of the organizational aspects of legal procedure. The legal order is more than a set of rules and princi-ples. It is a congeries of administrative agencies whose ways of working must decisively affect how the law actually impinges on the citizen and what its contribution is to the broader life of the community. Presumption of innocence is no empty slogan in our system, yet we have reason to believe that in actual operation there is an administrative presumption of guilt. I do not say that this, if true, is shocking or deplorable. It may be, in the end, perfectly compatible with the legal assumption properly understood. Yet this is the kind of thing that needs to be opened up for examination, if only because there is always a serious possibility that administrative exigencies will subvert a legal ideal.

For it is still true that legal policy, like any other, needs effective social supports. The more sensitive the policy, the more readily subject it is to distortion, and the more urgent are these supports. Some laws, as we know, are self-administering, because they stimulate and channel private initiative. Historically our system has depended on that, but the more we ask of the law, the more often shall we find that this private initiative is lacking or ineffective. A recent study of National Labor Relations Board cases involving union members who lost their jobs because of union discrimination touches on this problem.[2] The workers were interviewed and a full story of the context of the case, including what happened after the NLRB decision, was obtained. The results are illuminating. When the worker is a lone individual who has run afoul of union rules or otherwise given offense, the NLRB proceeding may be better than nothing, but on the whole it is quite ineffective. The worker has a hard time pursuing his case and faces an even rougher time if he is rehired. The law, as administered, offers little to the isolated individual confronted with great organizational power. On the other hand, in those cases where the member belonged to a faction, and thus had group support both during the litigation and after it, he fared rather well. In that setting, as in many others, a nonlegal, autonomous order lends its strength to the law.

For many purposes, we are not going to be able to depend on this prior social organization, this force in being, this socially given capability of implementing legal norms. The legal order of the future will strive to develop the conditions of its own effectiveness. This suggests, again, more emphasis on the organizational side of things. In addition to new, more or less distinctively legal institutions, such as the juvenile court and the public defender, we should expect that other parts of government, and some private associations as well, will play a part in adding to the resources of the legal order. The coordination of these activities and agencies, within the framework of a unitary legal system, will stretch the minds and perhaps try the souls of legal analysts.

For example, how deep is our commitment to the adversary principle in the administration of justice? Is that principle fully compatible with new modes of adjudication and control? How much variation in the adver-

[2] Manuscript in preparation by Bernard Samoff. The study was sponsored by the Trade Union Project, Fund for the Republic.

sary idea is acceptable? How far should it be built into administrative structure and process? It seems clear that this hallowed if sometimes embattled procedural canon needs a great deal more study to assess its relevance for the legal system of the future.

Another problem is the emergence of new bodies of law, founded in dimly understood principles, confused by the *ad hoc* character of our legislation and case law. Have we been witnesses to the development of a law of welfare whose concepts and doctrines, including implications for procedure, need explication? What is the relation between this emergent branch of the law, if it is one, to the rest of the system, especially the law of crimes? Is contemporary legal scholarship prepared to do the job of cutting across old categories and creating new ones? These things are suggested, not by an abstract concern for doctrinal clarity or symmetry, but by the compelling pressures of the living law, the law in action.

II.

Earlier I suggested that we must accept a secular trend toward the waning of nonlegal social control. To the sociologist, this is a phase of the drift toward mass society. I have also suggested that, at the same time, legal agencies of control will have increased responsibilities thrust upon them.

There is another and rather different part of this picture to which I should like to call attention. I refer to the growth of the large-scale organization as the representative institution of modern life. In industry, government, education, medicine, philanthropy—you name it!—the principle of rational coordination, the bureaucratic principle, holds sway. Self-perpetuating leadership and centralized authority are fixed stars in our firmament. In these areas there is no waning of social control. Quite the contrary. But is it *nonlegal* control? That question might provoke a prolonged debate.[3]

In an important sense, we are of course speaking of the private sector of economy and society. On the other hand, many observers have noted a blurring of the public and the private. A striking feature of this development is the *convergence* of governmental and nongovernmental forms of organization and modes of action. A great deal of government activity is similar to that carried on by private groups. Government today includes many activities and agencies that have little to do with the distinctive functions of the sovereign and to which, therefore, the traditional logic of public law may not properly apply. At the same time, discussions of the modern corporation and trade union have increasingly stressed their

---

[3] The following comments draw upon my paper "Private Government and the Corporate Conscience," prepared for a Symposium on Business Policy at the Graduate School of Business Administration, Harvard University, April 1963.

"quasi-public" status. It is asked quite seriously whether such institutions are really so different from large public enterprises or service agencies.

Furthermore, and perhaps more important, a kind of legality seems to develop within these large enterprises. In both public and private bureaucracies, authority and rule-making tend to take on the impersonality, the objectivity, and the rationality of a legal system. The elaboration of formal rules creates expectations regarding the consistency and fairness of official action. In modern management there is an inner dynamic tending toward a progressive reduction in the arbitrariness of decision-making. In ever wider areas of administration there is a demand that decisions be made in the light of general principles.

We are coming to see the private association as a group organized for defined and public ends—public, that is, from the standpoint of the group itself rather than the general community. Known and acknowledged purposes provide the basis of adherence and discipline. Given such ends, rational criteria may be developed to assess the means used to attain them. Thus membership in an association is a way of participating in a system of rationally coordinated activities. Objective and impersonal standards, determined by the requirements of that system, may be invoked for the assessment and control of organizational members. The members in turn may claim the protection of those same rational criteria.

It is this commitment of professional management to an atmosphere of legality—a commitment derived more from the necessities of modern enterprise than from goodwill or ideology—that underlies the widespread acceptance of private bigness as compatible with freedom. In our society the fear of corporate power has eased considerably. Criticism is muted in temper, reformist in intent. I believe that this is mainly due to the growing conviction that the large corporation is not necessarily a "rough beast." It is obscurely understood that the enterprise is enmeshed in circumstances that brake its power and create, indeed, a corporate conscience.

What and where is the corporate conscience? The corporate conscience is the internally accepted system of fair dealing, of respect for personal rights, of authority constituted and justified by rational necessity in the light of public ends. In a familiar phrase, it is corporate "due process."

This emerging ethic has its chief source in the practical necessities of industrial management. We see a convergence of three major tendencies in the institutional history of the firm:

1. The growing importance of impersonal procedures in the conduct of the enterprise—something I have already noted.
2. The recognition of "human relations" as a critical factor in management, especially the significance of respect and status-protection for employee morale.
3. The widespread adaptation of management to the power of trade

unionism and the creation thereby of systematic procedures for the formulation and redress of grievances.

To say that a corporate conscience exists is not to say that we can rely on it. In questions of power and justice, we do not rely upon the individual conscience either. Our legal and political system necessarily postulates the existence of evil, especially the danger that some merely human form, believing itself free of error, will attempt to match its claimed perfection with unlimited power. Because of that risk, we cannot rely upon goodwill, personal or institutional.

We should distinguish, however, what we can rely upon from what we can aspire to. The ethic of rational coordination provides the foundation for new expectations, new claims of right, new legal controls. The existence of internal order within the enterprise validates external control and, at the same time, makes it feasible. It is just because fairness is already institutionalized to a large extent in the private sphere that an appeal to the larger political community, to the legal order, is warranted. The firmer the sense of legitimate expectation, the more likely it is that there will be an appeal beyond the immediate setting. Moreover, if a quasi-legal system of fair dealing already exists, there is some assurance that the routine case will be handled satisfactorily. Therefore, enforcement of exceptional claims for redress of grievances becomes feasible.

I take the view, that, in the evolving law of private associations, we are responding to opportunities rather than resisting oppression. I do not say that private power is not abused, but the really important fact is that we now have the possibility, a product of modern history, of extending the ideals of due process to private associations. This might always have been a worthy objective, but the development of an inner order within the modern enterprise brings that objective into close accord with what historical reality makes possible.

These reflections suggest that we take a long, leisurely look at the so-called "limits of effective legal action." Can we assume fixed legal resources? What if changing institutions, both inside and outside the legal sphere, offer new opportunities for enriching the sense of justice? The answer may require a radical revision of that hard-nosed legal philosophy which celebrates the settlement of disputes and the curbing of irresponsible conduct. Today the law is summoned to fulfill aspirations, not merely to meet the minimal needs of social order. The business of taking that truth seriously may occupy us for some years to come.

35. JUSTICE ADMINISTRATION IN MASS SOCIETY

Jerome H. Skolnick

There is no doubt that America is a "mass society" if measured by such criteria as urbanization, population mobility, communication facilities, and, most simply, size and growth—of population, government, industry, prisons, educational institutions, and automobile accidents. I do not intend in this paper to be caught in the debate between pessimistic theorists of mass society and optimistic critics[1]—whether such growth is associated with, on the one hand, a weakening of fundamental values and human relations and perhaps an increased proneness to accept demagogues and extremist solutions to social problems; or, on the other, increased educational and cultural opportunities for the masses along with rewarding interpersonal relations, as compared with realities rather than myths of small towns and earlier ages. Whatever may be the *general* truth of the assertions of the mass-society theorist, there is no doubt that the qualities of a mass society—for instance, its tendencies toward size, depersonalization,

Reprinted by permission of the author and the Society for the Study of Social Problems from *Law and Society,* supplement to *Social Problems,* 13 (Summer 1965): 15–28. Original title: "The Sociology of Law in America: Overview and Trends." Footnotes have been renumbered.

[1] Harold L. Wilensky and Charles N. Lebeaux, *Industrial Society and Social Welfare* (New York: Russell Sage Foundation, 1958), pt. 1.

and shifting population—have significant implications for the legal order.

One of these is the shift in the law from an adjudicative to an administrative character. A classic sociological research in this area is Paul Tappan's case study of the Wayward Minor Court of New York, unpretentiously, and from a theoretical point of view uninvitingly, entitled *Delinquent Girls in Court*.[2] The study itself, however, is a major one in highlighting conflicts inherent in the trend toward administrative processing of juveniles. Tappan traces the history of values, attitudes, and philosophies associated with a strongly punitive heritage in approaching offenders against the criminal law. At more or less the same time, humanitarian interests were seeking to "help" the juvenile offender with individualized "treatment" of "delinquents"—"the very term," as Karl Llewellyn cogently remarks, "being a device to lessen stigma and to enlist and focus the 'education'-attitude we associate with youth as contrasted with the 'retribution'-attitude we associate with 'public enemies.' "[3]

Tappan neatly traces the incorporation of both sets of values into the juvenile court. The process emerges in three stages: legislation, adjudication, and correction. At the legislative stage there are sumptuary prohibitions associated with juvenile statutes—such juvenile offenses as "waywardness" and "incorrigibility" typically encompass a wider spectrum of behavior than those specified in adult criminal codes. At the adjudication stage, the juvenile may not be afforded the same rights as the adult, e.g., the right to counsel. Finally, because he is being "treated" rather than punished, the juvenile may be confined for a longer period of time for the same conduct. The upshot of this process is to give society far more arbitrary authority over the juvenile than over the adult offender—frequently to give punitive tendencies freedom to operate within a procedural context suggesting clinical aid.

Critical analysis of juvenile court law and proceedings by Tappan and others[4] has brought about a change from an easy acceptance of the notion

---

[2] Paul W. Tappan, *Delinquent Girls in Court* (New York: Columbia University Press, 1947).

[3] Karl N. Llewellyn, writing in the Foreword to Tappan, *Delinquent Girls in Court*, p. viii.

[4] See David Matza, *Delinquency and Drift* (New York: Wiley, 1964); *Comparative Survey of Juvenile Delinquency*, Part 1 (prepared by Paul Tappan) (New York: United Nations Department of Economic and Social Affairs, 1958); Francis A. Allen, "The Borderland of the Criminal Law," *Social Service Review*, 32 (June 1958): 107–119; and "Criminal Justice, Legal Values, and the Rehabilitative Idea," *Journal of Criminal Law, Criminology, and Police Science*, 50 (September–October 1959): 226–32; Margaret K. Rosenheim, ed., *Justice for the Child* (New York: Free Press, Macmillan, 1962); Lewis Diana, "The Rights of Juvenile Delinquents: An Appraisal of Juvenile Court Procedures," *Journal of Criminal Law, Criminology, and Police Science*, 47 (January–February 1957): 561–69; Robert G. Caldwell, "The Juvenile Court: Its Development and Some Major Features," *Journal of Criminal Law, Criminology, and Police Science*, 51 (January–February 1961): 493–511; Sol Rubin, *Crime and Juvenile Delinquency* (New York: Oceania, 1961), chaps. 4–5. For an article critical of Tappan on grounds that the court he studied was a special type of youth court, see F. James Davis, "The Iowa Juvenile Court Judge: A Study in

of "treatment" to an interpretation of any sort of forced institutionalization as a form of punishment. This analysis has also produced a clearer appreciation of the nature of the adjudicative proceeding as contrasted with
the more "efficient" and "scientific" administrative mode. As Tappan says:

> There is one telling argument against wholesale abandonment of
> legal rule and procedural form to accomplish social objectives: wholly
> to free the law from the "dead hand of the past" one must entrust
> unlimited discretion to judge, reformer, or clinician and his per-
> sonal views of expedience. Unless he be circumscribed in some degree
> by established instrumental or traditional rule and form, the fate of
> the defendant, the interest of society, the social objectives themselves
> must hang by the tenuous thread of the wisdom and personality of the
> particular administrator.[5]

These problems are not confined to juveniles alone. There is an extensive literature discussing the implications of "treating" an individual
within a custodial context.[6] To the extent that this context allows great
hegemony over a human being because he is being "corrected," there is
always the risk that the correctional mechanism will be abused by those in
charge of it. It is very likely that the pressures and anxieties engendered by
the mass processing of offenders inevitably encourages a favorable and
frequently uncritical view of correctional claims. Thus, one major administrative problem associated with mass society is the size of the prisoner
population. The magnitude of this group is largely caused by recidivism,
i.e., the repeated commission of criminal acts by the same persons, who
thus continually repopulate the institutions designed to correct them. Consequently, a major issue, which continues to be examined, is the extent to
which correctional efforts influence future criminality.[7]

The field of criminology is replete with studies bearing some relation to
the sociology of law. The question is, on what basis do we distinguish
those which are more relevant from those which are less? I would suggest
that the standard to be used is the relevance these studies have to identifying and understanding a presently operating or incipient adjudicative system—broadly speaking, a system of rules under which decisions are made
to sanction human beings in some important way. For instance, there is in
criminology a considerable literature dealing with the issue of prediction
methods, and ability to make predictions is relevant to a number of adjudi-

---

Role-Definition," *Journal of Criminal Law, Criminology, and Police Science,* 42 (September–October 1951): 338–50.

[5] Tappan, *Delinquent Girls in Court,* p. 22.

[6] See Sheldon L. Messinger and Vilhelm Aubert, "The Criminal and the Sick," *Inquiry,*
1 (1958): 137–60; Erving Goffman, *Asylums* (Garden City, N.Y.: Doubleday, 1961); and
Thomas S. Szasz, *Law, Liberty, and Psychiatry: An Inquiry into the Social Uses of Mental
Health Practices* (New York: Macmillan, 1963).

[7] This idea is usually expressed as the idea of "secondary deviance." See Edwin Lemert,
Social Pathology: A Systematic Approach to the Theory of Sociopathic Behavior (New
York: McGraw-Hill, 1951), esp. pp. 75–76.

cative settings. One of these, bail, was referred to earlier. Parole prediction studies have long been an interest of criminology,[8] and there are also the well-known—and often criticized—attempts by the Gluecks to predict criminality, especially among juveniles.[9]

For the field of sociology of law, the questions to be raised concerning prediction studies are not technical ones.[10] Although the legal sociologist must be competent to assess various prediction methods, this is basically the concern of the criminologist. The main job of the sociologist of law would not be to develop better prediction methods, but to understand their effect on modes of adjudication. Similarly, in studies of prisons, the sociologist of law would not be primarily interested in the ethnography of prisons, but instead would look at the prison as a setting which requires a highly developed system of social control. When prisoners break rules, what are the grounds upon which violations are perceived as having taken place, what norms are used to deal with perceived violations, and what are the general issues faced by having this adjudicative task within the setting of prisons having different modes of government?[11]

The trends associated with the growth and expansion of society pose for criminal law administration a sociological dilemma—although the ideals of the law emphasize individual rights and protections, the everyday mass processing of offenders takes place under conditions which increasingly invite systematic violations, denials, and evasions of these rights and protections. An absolute increase in the number of criminal offenders (a function of overall population rise) coupled with limited criminal administrative resources encourages the growing majority of criminal cases to be settled by the accused's pleas of guilty, giving the criminal process a quality which Donald Newman has ably described as "bargain justice." Newman points out the effect of informal conviction methods on selection for probation by showing that in 34.5 percent of the cases reporting bargaining, probation was bargained for. "With such informal tactics," Newman comments, "selection for placement on probation is determined by the skill of the offender or his lawyer in bargaining, rather than on factors

---

[8] Among others, see the following studies: Karl F. Schuessler, "Parole Prediction: Its History and Status," *Journal of Criminal Law, Criminology, and Police Science*, 45 (November–December 1954): 425–31; Lloyd Ohlin, *Selection for Parole: A Manual of Parole Prediction* (New York: Russell Sage Foundation, 1951); Daniel Glaser, "A Reconsideration of Some Parole Prediction Factors," *American Sociological Review*, 19 (June 1954): 335–41; Jerome H. Skolnick, "Toward a Developmental Theory of Parole," *American Sociological Review*, 25 (August 1960): 542–49.

[9] Sheldon Glueck and Eleanor T. Glueck, *Unraveling Juvenile Delinquency* (New York: Commonwealth Fund, 1950); Sheldon Glueck, *The Problem of Delinquency* (Boston: Houghton Mifflin, 1959).

[10] Leslie T. Wilkins, "Problems in Prediction Methods," in *The Sociology of Crime and Delinquency*, ed. Marvin E. Wolfgang, Leonard Savitz, and N. Johnston (New York: Wiley, 1962), pp. 96–100.

[11] See Richard A. Cloward *et al.*, *Theoretical Studies in Social Organization of the Prison* (New York: Social Science Research Council, 1960).

of the case which would have more relevance to successful rehabilitation by field rather than institutional placement."[12] Newman will shortly be publishing a more comprehensive study of factors leading to the plea of guilty, derived from observations made by the American Bar Foundation's studies of the administration of criminal law.[13] An interesting discussion of "bargain justice" is also contained in a recently published work by Arnold Trebach.[14]

I have also been working in this area, but with a somewhat different emphasis than Newman or Trebach. Where Newman's interest tends to be criminological and Trebach's is in constitutional law, I am interested primarily in the institutional aspects of the system of "justice without trial." In examining police, prosecutor, defense attorney, the question is how institutional values and requirements combine to affect such traditional jurisprudential concerns as the adversary system, the presumption of innocence, and the relationship between substantive law and criminal procedure. When one looks at "bargain justice" in this light, classic issues in the administration of large-scale organizations emerge—e.g., the development of informal rules and structures, conflict between line and staff, conflict between the requirement to *produce* and interest in *quality* of product.[15]

Abraham S. Blumberg has just completed a doctoral dissertation in this area, of which I have read only the abstract. Attempting to understand what happens to traditional norms of due process of law when placed in the institutional apparatus of a functioning court, Blumberg states that a "new due process" model is generated, based upon organizational efficiency.[16]

David Sudnow has completed a study of the use of categories of crime to facilitate pleas of guilty. On the basis of field observations of a California Public Defender's office, Sudnow proposes that the facilitation of pleas of guilty is predicated upon a stereotyping of the sorts of people associated with the charged offense; a "normal" criminal is one who conforms to the stereotype. His case is therefore easier to cope with routinely. Categories of crime are an important part of the social structure of criminal law administration in a manner not contemplated by the state criminal code.[17]

---

[12] Donald J. Newman, "Pleading Guilty for Considerations: A Study of Bargain Justice," in Norman Johnston et al., The Sociology of Punishment and Correction (New York: Wiley, 1962), p. 30.

[13] Donald J. Newman, The Decision as to Guilt or Innocence (New York: American Bar Foundation, 1962).

[14] Arnold S. Trebach, The Rationing of Justice: Constitutional Rights and the Criminal Process (New Brunswick: Rutgers University Press, 1964).

[15] Center for the Study of Law and Society, Annual Report (Berkeley· University of California Press, 1963), pp. 4–6.

[16] Abraham Blumberg, Criminal Justice (Chicago: Quadrangle Books, 1967).

[17] David Sudnow, "Normal Crimes: Sociological Features of the Penal Code in a Public Defender Office," Social Problems, 12 (Winter 1964): 255–76.

LAW AND MORALITY

Another issue concerning the mass administration of justice is the relation between law and conventional morality. Typically, the enactment of moral convictions into criminal law results in "victimless crime"—crimes in which complainants are primarily law-enforcement officials rather than citizens. Such enactments may have negative effects on the administration of criminal law and related behavior. Thurman Arnold pointed out in 1935, for example, that:

> Before . . . prohibition . . . the problem of search and seizure was a minor one. Thereafter, searches and seizures became the weapon of attack which could be used against prohibition enforcement. For every "dry" speech on the dangers of disobedience, there was a "wet" oration on the dangers of invading the privacy of the home. Reflected in the courts the figures are startling. In six states selected for the purpose of study we find 19 search-and-seizure cases appealed in the 12 years preceding Prohibition and 347 in the 12 years following.[18]

This problem has been aggravated especially by laws related to the control of drug and marijuana use, and by laws designed to prevent the practice of homosexual activities. Alfred Lindesmith has cited some of the problems in his recently published *The Addict and the Law*,[19] and an able summary is contained in Edwin Schur's *Crimes Without Victims*.[20] My own work on law enforcement[21] examines the issue in some empirical detail, and it has been given legal and philosophical treatment by Herbert Packer[22] and H. L. A. Hart.[23]

The side effects of such laws extend beyond institutions dealing with criminality. Packer and Gampell have published a study revealing the consequences of abortion laws for hospital abortion practice.[24] Noting the increase of therapeutic abortions for psychiatric reasons (within an overall decline in the total incidence of therapeutic abortion), the authors sent questionnaires to twenty-nine hospitals regarding the *procedure* for arriving at a decision to therapeutically abort. Of the twenty-four questionnaires returned, eighteen indicated they believed there was a failure to

---

[18] Thurman W. Arnold, *The Symbols of Government* (New Haven: Yale University Press, 1935).

[19] Alfred R. Lindesmith, *The Addict and the Law* (Bloomington: Indiana University Press, 1965).

[20] Edwin M. Schur, *Crimes Without Victims* (Englewood Cliffs, N.J.: Prentice-Hall, 1965).

[21] Jerome H. Skolnick, *Justice Without Trial: A Sociological Study of Law Enforcement* (New York: Wiley, 1966).

[22] Herbert L. Packer, "Two Models of the Criminal Process," *University of Pennsylvania Law Review*, 113 (November 1964): 1–68.

[23] H. L. A. Hart, *Law, Liberty, and Morality* (Stanford: Stanford University Press, 1963).

[24] Herbert L. Packer and Ralph J. Gampell, "Therapeutic Abortion: A Problem in Law and Medicine," *Stanford Law Review*, 11 (May 1959): 417–55.

conform strictly to the legal standards for abortion as understood by the hospitals and the physicians themselves. In effect, to avoid legal culpability, individual physicians rarely perform therapeutic abortions in their private offices. Instead, therapeutic abortion cases are taken to the hospital, where a therapeutic abortion committee or its equivalent dilutes *individual* responsibility with institutional responsibility. Here we find another instance of a "victimless crime" having an unanticipated procedural effect.

Packer, who has been a consistent critic of legal incursions into areas of morality, has analyzed the economic advantages to the seller of designating "demanded" goods or services as illegal. He characterizes the commercial process as, in effect, governmental support of undesirable conduct through the inadvertent creation of a protective tariff. He describes the situation as follows:

> As we know from current experience . . . people go on buying narcotics even if they have to steal money to pay the price. Economic theory explains this phenomenon by introducing the concept of elasticity of demand. It is only when the demand is quite elastic that increases in price will reduce the amount demanded. People who are willing to pay two thousand dollars for a car will not ordinarily want the same car if its price is suddenly doubled. But when the demand is inelastic, when the commodity is something that people want so badly that they will pay almost any price to get it, if its sale is illegal, the crime tariff goes into operation. Regardless of what we think we are trying to do, if we make it illegal to traffic in commodities for which there is an inelastic demand, the actual effect is to secure a kind of monopoly profit to the entrepreneur who is willing to break the law.[25]

If procedural modifications and protective criminal tariffs are two of the most consequential side effects of "crimes without victims," the most important and controversial of all is the extent to which such laws "create" criminality among persons who would otherwise be relatively law-abiding. Probably the leading sociologist opponent of the legal enforcement of morality is Howard S. Becker, who sees the "labeling" of criminals—especially marijuana users and addicts—as a form of "moral enterprise."[26] If, as sociologists of law, we are interested in understanding how societies achieve higher or lower level legal orders, we might propose that the wider the range of prohibited conduct, the less likely that law can be administered fairly. Thus, the most general issue to be raised in this area is the capacity of a legal system to be a successful "enterprise" under increasing demands that it be society's instrument for the resolution of pressing social problems.

This issue is certainly not confined to criminal law and in some respects is not as serious there since citizens charged with crimes at least can depend upon a constitutional right to a speedy trial. It is the civil courts in crowded

[25] Herbert L. Packer, "The Crime Tariff," *American Scholar*, 33 (1964): 551–57.
[26] Howard Becker, *Outsiders* (New York: Free Press, Macmillan, 1963).

urban areas—as evidenced by research on court congestion and delay[27]—which are literally packed with cases. And ordinarily, criminal cases do not account for the civil backlog. As one article on the subject states, "For its increasing mobility, spreading cities, and booming technology, modern society pays a fearful price in accidental injuries. Each year accidents claim 10,000,000 victims of whom 100,000 are fatalities. In a nation of 180,000,000 people this means that over 5 percent of the population annually become accident statistics."[28]

SOCIAL-SCIENTIFIC KNOWLEDGE AND LEGAL NEEDS

The sociologist can play several roles in responding to the pressures put upon judicial administration by a rapidly expanding society. One role will almost inevitably be pushed upon him—that of the technical specialist whose scientific training includes methodological, analytical, and statistical skills relevant to the clarification or amelioration of problems which lawyers and related administrators are quick to see as important.[29] This is the applied research role, and is the sort Hans Zeisel played in studying court congestion. Here, in effect, the social scientist acts as a management consultant to courts or other bodies concerned with the administrative side of justice.

The social scientist may also attempt to introduce facts directly into the judicial process itself. Here again, Zeisel has written a comprehensive piece on the problems of introducing survey research evidence into a legal setting.[30] The three most important obstacles to the acceptance of surveys by the courts are that: (1) they are typically based upon samples, rather than entire populations; (2) the inferences are often drawn from hearsay evidence; (3) there is reluctance on the part of the survey researcher to do away with the anonymity of his informants. None of these would seem to be an insuperable barrier to the introduction of survey evidence—the U.S. Census has all these characteristics but the courts take judicial notice of its data, trusting in its disinterested character and its expertness.

In considering the introduction of facts into the judicial process, one

---

[27] Hans Zeisel, Harry Kalven, Jr., and Bernard Buchholz, *Delay in the Court* (Boston: Little, Brown, 1951). The Columbia University Project for Effective Justice is also doing work in this area. See, for example, Marc A. Franklin, Robert H. Chanin, and Irving Mark, "Accidents, Money, and the Law: A Study of the Economics of Personal Injury Litigation," *Columbia Law Review*, 61 (January 1961): 1–39.

[28] Franklin, Chanin, and Mark, "Accidents, Money, and the Law," p. 1.

[29] I would include my work on lie detection in this category. It is of little interest to sociologists but probably could not have been written by someone trained solely in law. See "Scientific Theory and Scientific Evidence: An Analysis of Lie Detection," *Yale Law Journal*, 70 (April 1961): 694–728.

[30] Hans Zeisel, "The Uniqueness of Survey Evidence," *Cornell Law Quarterly*, 45 (1960): 322, 325.

distinction which must be taken into account is that between data allowed and disallowed by the preferential and exclusionary rules of evidence. An even more central distinction is that between adjudicative and legislative facts. Kenneth Culp Davis calls this "the cardinal distinction which more than any other governs the use of extra-record facts by courts and agencies. . . ." He goes on to explain that:

> When a court or an agency finds facts concerning the immediate parties —who did what, where, when, how, and with what motive or intent— the court or agency is performing an adjudicative function, and the facts are conveniently called adjudicative facts. When a court or an agency develops law or policy, it is acting legislatively; the courts have created the common law through judicial legislation, and the facts which inform the tribunal's legislative judgment are called legislative facts.[31]

Sociological and psychological research usually will provide the courts with legislative facts, while psychiatric findings are more likely to be used to establish adjudicative facts. Thus in the restrictive-covenant cases[32] sociologists and psychologists testified regarding family life within racially demarcated areas and the detrimental consequences of overcrowding and *de facto* segregation on a variety of urban social problems. This was a precursor to the Social Science Statement appended to the appellants' brief in the school-segregation cases.[33]

In playing the role of expert witness, the sociologist or psychologist will often be faced with value-laden issues, and the temptation to act as an advocate rather than scholar is likely to be correspondingly strong. Moreover, legal questions may be framed so narrowly that the social scientist is hard put to answer the precise question called for by the law. Thus, in the school-segregation cases, the question was whether separation of the races in schools was harmful to Negroes, provided the facilities were equal. Professor Kenneth Clark testified in a South Carolina case that it was, offering as evidence certain negative responses to a psychological test. He neglected to mention, however, that negative responses occurred with greater frequency in northern *desegregated* schools. It is noteworthy that the first report of Clark's omission appear in a *Yale Law Journal* "comment"[34] and not in a social science periodical until some years later (after the *Brown v. Board* decision).

Obviously Clark was in a dilemma. He was onto a finding of scientific import which should have been pursued further—that people in a deprived

---

[31] Kenneth Culp Davis, *Administrative Law Treatise* (St. Paul, Minn.: West, 1958).

[32] *Shelley* v. *Kraemer*, 334 U.S. 1 (1948); *McGlee* v. *Sipes*, 316 Mich. 614, 25 N.W. 2d 638 (1947); *Hurd* v. *Hodge*, 162 F. 2d 233 (D.C. Cir. 1947).

[33] Appendix to Appellants' Briefs, "The Effects of Segregation and the Consequences of Desegregation: A Social Science Statement," *Brown* v. *Board of Education*, 347 U.S. 483, reprinted in *Minnesota Law Review*, 37 (1953): 427ff.

[34] "Grade School Segregation: The Latest Attack on Racial Discrimination," *Yale Law Journal*, 61 (1952): 730–39.

status fare better in certain respects under conditions where the deprivation is consistent rather than uneven. This finding does not betoken the
superiority of a segregated system. It does suggest, however, that the subtler
prejudices of the North may be more damaging psychologically than the
overt discriminatory practices of the South. Had such a finding occurred in
a strictly professional setting, rather than in the context of an adversary
proceeding, it probably would not have been reported without further research. But since Clark made his findings as the witness for one side in a
law case, he was hamstrung. He was obliged to report under these circumstances, and the legal question was framed so narrowly he could neither
investigate nor testify with the precision requisite for scientific accuracy.
This case illustrates some of the problems of directly introducing social
science evidence into judicial proceedings.

Having indicated problems of social science testimony, it is also appropriate to report some less controversial instances. For example, Harold
Lasswell and some of his assistants appeared in court during World War II
to testify that the propaganda put out for American consumption by
"native fascist" organizations was in many cases identical with that prepared by the German propaganda ministry—this testimony was meant to
show that such organizations were in communication with the German
government.[35] Arnold Rose has been involved in several cases, mainly involving racial and religious issues. In one, where a young Negro woman
was being returned to Florida from Minnesota, it was alleged she was destined to become a public charge. This allegation was supported on grounds
that an illegitimate pregnancy was an indication of the young woman's
mental incompetence, and that an intelligence test showed her to be feeble-
minded. Rose testified as to general facts: (1) that there is no necessary relation between pregnancy outside of marriage and feeble-mindedness,
especially since 20 percent of all Negro births in Florida were illegitimate;
and (2) that low IQ scores, especially under certain conditions of test administration, are not necessarily evidence of mental incompetence. Citing
Klineberg's and other studies, he explored the difficulties of IQ test interpretation.[36]

There are other, less adversary, ways for social scientists to make practical
contributions to legal issues. The separate orientations of legal scholars
and social scientists are most likely to converge at the so-called "policy"
level.[37] This is a broad notion with various and divergent connotations in

---

[35] Harold D. Lasswell, "Application: Detection; Propaganda Detection and the Courts,"
in H. D. Lasswell, N. Leites, and Associates, *Language of Politics* (New York: G. W. Stewart, 1949).

[36] Arnold M. Rose, "The Social Scientist as Expert Witness in Court Cases," *Minnesota
Law Review*, 40 (1956): 205–18. This article is to appear in a forthcoming volume edited
by Paul F. Lazarsfeld on *The Uses of Sociology*.

[37] General areas of research opportunity are outlined by Arnold Rose in a paper entitled "Some Suggestions for Research in Sociology of Law," *Social Problems*, 9 (Winter
1962): 281–83.

the legal context. It may refer to the production of facts of which the judge may take notice in creating law; or it may refer, as Norval Morris[38] puts it, to the judge's difficult duty of choosing between varying types of treatment to effect a reform. Policy may also hark back to such substantive issues as whether there ought to be reform in narcotics legislation[39] or income taxation.[40] And a related issue would be the effect of substantive reform in one area on procedure in another, for instance, the consequences of Prohibition on search and seizure practices. In sum, although policy issues may have varying contents, all have to do with the effects of change—either substantive or procedural—on the legal order.

To rank policy studies on a scale of centrality in the sociology of law, a good rule of thumb is that those are most central which reflect back upon the working of the legal order. Such a study is Gerver's description of the social psychology of witness behavior. He analyzes how the ceremonial aspects of legal procedure and the legal rules of evidence account for much of the stressful character of witness behavior.[41] Studies in delinquency rehabilitation are of interest to sociology of law to the extent that they lead to an understanding of adjudicative behavior. If the main contribution relates to the efficiency of correctional officials, the interest of such studies —no matter their quality—would be mainly criminological.

On the other hand, certain studies, like Stewart Macaulay's, obtain results which are central to sociology of law and at the same time rich in policy implication. Macaulay's findings indicate that "businessmen often fail to plan exchange relationships completely, and seldom use legal sanctions to adjust these relationships or to settle disputes."[42] Even in a mass society we find that certain kinds of business relations are treated as status relations, without formal resort to contract law. Macaulay's study, as William Evan comments,[43] invites further investigation of the conditions under which business organizations resort to contract enforcement and the conditions under which different degrees of "contractualness" are found in business transactions. Such findings would not only be important for sociological theory, by adding to our understanding of social behavior as an exchange relationship; they should also be of interest to lawyers

---

[38] See Norval Norris, review of Max Grunhut, *Juvenile Offenders Before the Courts*, in *Yale Law Journal*, 66 (May 1957): 962–72.

[39] For example, see Edwin M. Schur, *Narcotic Addiction in Britain and America: The Impact of Public Policy* (London: Tavistock, 1962); and Lindesmith, *The Addict and the Law*.

[40] Two recent books treating this are Louis Eisenstein, *The Ideologies of Taxation* (New York: Ronald Press, 1961); Jerome R. Hellerstein, *Taxes, Loopholes, and Morals* (New York: McGraw-Hill, 1963). See also Philip Stern, *The Great Treasury Raid* (New York: Random House, 1964).

[41] Israel Gerver, "The Social Psychology of Witness Behavior with Special Reference to the Criminal Courts," *Journal of Social Issues*, 13 (1957): 23–29.

[42] Stewart Macaulay, "Non-contractual Relations in Business: A Preliminary Study," *American Sociological Review*, 28 (February 1963): 55.

[43] William M. Evan, "Comment on Macaulay's Article," *American Sociological Review*, 28 (February 1963): 67–69.

whose task it is to draft commercial codes. Indeed, Llewellyn's interest in law in action was whetted by just this sort of obligation.

One question frequently posed as a practical issue is whether a particular policy for preventing a certain behavior actually works; usually the question is posed as whether a particular criminal sanction deters. Stated this way, it would seem that a researcher could come up with a yes-or-no answer. In fact, common sense tells us that anticipated punishment deters—the real issue is how much of it deters whom from doing what under which set of conditions; or, stated negatively and perhaps more interestingly, which persons are not deterred by the threat of punishment and why not?

One of the more suggestive studies along these lines is Harry Ball's investigation of rent-control violations. He found that different procedures in developing rent-control ceilings elicited varying feelings of unfairness and opposition to the controls. Degree of violation, in turn, was empirically demonstrated to be correlated with procedure for arriving at control, rather than severity of sanction alone.[44]

There are, unfortunately, few research situations where the applied social scientist can manipulate the environment sufficiently to come up with this sort of specific finding.[45] One of the more interesting technical possibilities for policy research is the field experiment. One of these attempted to understand the practical consequences of various types of criminal law labels (accused, acquitted, certified innocent) on a job applicant's ability to get menial work. The results suggested that an accusation is virtually as stigmatic as a conviction on a criminal charge of assault.[46] Another study is testing which sanctions are most effective in achieving compliance with income-tax laws.[47] In the United States, the currently best known instance of sociologists working within the legal process is the "Provo experiment," where the authority of the court was used to assign youths on a random basis to alternative rehabilitational projects.[48] One problem of all such attempts is that results are rarely clear-cut, and may not be generalizable to other settings. La Mar T. Empey, who was senior researcher in this experiment, has an illuminating discussion of such problems in a later article.[49] For the development of sociology of law, however, participation in

[44] Harry Ball, "Social Structure and Rent-Control Violations," *American Journal of Sociology*, 65 (May 1960): 598–604.

[45] The distinguished Polish sociologist Adam Podgorecki offers several examples of "legal engineering" in Poland and also attempts to develop a set of principles for a "science of legal policy." See his "Law and Social Engineering," *Human Organization*, 21 (Fall 1962): 177–81.

[46] Richard D. Schwartz and Jerome H. Skolnick, "Two Studies of Legal Stigma," *Social Problems*, 10 (Fall 1962): 133–42.

[47] R. D. Schwartz and J. H. Skolnick, "Televised Communication and Income Tax Compliance," in *Television and Human Behavior*, ed. L. Arons and M. A. Way (New York: Appleton-Century-Crofts, 1963), pp. 155–65. Schwartz is now carrying out a study based upon a modified and elaborated version of this design.

[48] La Mar T. Empey and Jerome Rabow, "The Provo Experiment in Delinquency and Rehabilitation," *American Sociological Review*, 26 (October 1961): 679–96.

[49] La Mar T. Empey, "The Application of Sociological Theory to Social Action," *Social Problems*, 12 (Summer 1964): 56–67.

action projects is less relevant than a scholarly attempt to understand the possibilities of the role of law and legal institutions in social reform.

In my opinion, although the line between the applied and the theoretical is not easily drawn, the most important work for the sociologist of law is the development of theory growing out of empirical, especially institutional, studies. In this respect, Tappan's study of the juvenile court is exemplary. He has, on the one hand, suggested reforms in juvenile legislation and administration; and on the other, he has done so in terms of detailed empirical research based upon a fairly explicit contrast between juvenile court proceedings and a traditional model of the adjudicatory enterprise. Finally, he has stated conditions under which the "administrative" or "judicial" model is more or less likely to prevail.[50]

Now it may be that because of the constitutional requirements associated with criminal law, it is easier to develop such a model or models for the criminal process than for the civil, but it is no less necessary to abstract a procedural model for the civil process. Judges seem to spend most of their time on tasks which would not conventionally be considered judging— arranging dates for hearings, meeting with psychiatrists, and so forth. Furthermore, the general tenor of discourse about trial courts is so preoccupied with the issue of efficiency in the management of the court's work load that one wonders whether there is something distinctive about courts, or whether these should be regarded as simply another administrative agency. Or with a different stress, it might be asked whether procedures and claims of right associated with conventional court proceedings should be limited to such tribunals, or expanded to include a variety of proceedings in which claims of an individual are to be decided by an agent of government.

Whatever the policy resolution may ultimately be, it needs to be informed by contemplation and research which will attempt to infer—from observation of a variety of such proceedings—whether there are distinctive behavioral modes associated with particular types of decisions (for instance, deciding the guilt of accused traffic violators, the inheritance of estates, the custody of children, the value of loss of limb, or the amount of welfare or unemployment insurance to be dispensed to a particular claimant). The issue is whether factors which appear to distinguish one type of proceeding from another (e.g., the number of claimants who must be processed in relation to a limited number of authorities, the social status of the claimants, the social distance between claimant and agent of government, the value of the claim) can be drawn together coherently and consistently enough to permit the specification of distinctive modes of adjudication. Moreover, with this sort of theoretical basis drawn from observations, it should be easier to inform such specific issues as the advisability of employing the adversary principle in novel contexts of decision-making

---

[50] Tappan, *Delinquent Girls in Court.*

that have characteristics commonly associated with the act of judging. Finally, it may be possible, and certainly desirable, to consider varied proceedings separately, in order to determine whether their different contents and structures are linked systematically to the emergence of one or another adjudicatory model.[51]

Let me illustrate from the 1964–65 crisis at the University of California in Berkeley. This situation has been described in a number of recent publications.[52] I want to deal here, and only briefly, not so much with the particular situation, but with the issue of the appropriateness of certain kinds of sanctioning processes in varying institutional settings. The prevailing conception of the status of university administration with respect to sanctioning of students is that of *in loco parentis*.[53] The college is seen as the student's home away from home, and the administrators of the university as surrogate fathers. Under this doctrine, the sanctioning model for the university is the family.

A family, as an institution, does not encompass the idea of due process of law. Unlike a policeman or a judge, a father may act arbitrarily. He may in anger confine a child to a room for conduct that was not clearly defined and prospectively announced. The principle of *nulla poena sine lege* does not prevail, standards of behavior are not required to meet stringent tests of specificity and clarity, and such standards need not be strictly construed in favor of the "accused." A family is presumably an institution in which there are no accusers and accused—the norm is precisely that of benevolent paternalism. The relationship is based upon love and kinship, and therefore, short of physical cruelty, a father is permitted wide latitude in discipline, even the use of corporal punishment, for which we use the euphemism "spanking."

Transfer this conception through a doctrine of *in loco parentis* to an institution having several deans and 27,000 students, many of whom are married and have children, and the absurdity of the analogy is apparent. At one time, perhaps, a university might have been an institution akin to a family, a true *alma mater*. Today, however, it can no longer depend upon the give and take, the familiarity, and the uniformity of interests of the familial setting as guarantees of an ultimately just administration of sanctions. More important, a father is typically *independent* in a way that the president of a large, research-oriented university may not be. In such an institution, major economic, political, and social interests are at stake, and it is inevitable that sanctioning decisions may be influenced by these. It is

[51] These ideas were suggested by working papers prepared by Jerome Carlin and Geoffrey Hazard as part of the Civil Justice Project of the Center for the Study of Law and Society, Berkeley.

[52] S. M. Lipset and S. Wolin, eds., *The Berkeley Student Revolt* (Garden City, N.Y.: Doubleday–Anchor, 1965).

[53] See "Private Government on the Campus—Judicial Review of University Expulsions," *Yale Law Journal*, 72 (June 1963): 1362ff.

now public knowledge, for example, that the Regents of the University of California have insisted upon charges being brought against students.

The conception of institutional rule by familial principles has strong totalitarian overtones. It is the conception that underlies Soviet legality. As one of the leading scholars on the subject has written:

> Soviet law cannot be understood unless it is recognized that the whole Soviet society is itself conceived to be a single great family. . . . As the state, it acts officially through the legal system, but its purpose in so acting is to make its citizens into obedient children, good students, ardent believers, hard workers, successful managers.
>
> This, indeed, is the essential characteristic of the law of a total state. We have seen that legal consequences follow from this conception of the role of law. Court procedure is informal and speedy; the judge protects the litigants against the consequences of their ignorance, and clarifies to them the nature of their rights and duties; there is elaborate pre-trial procedure directed toward uncovering the whole history of the situation. The rule "Let the punishment fit the crime" is supplemented (though not supplanted) by the rule "Let the punishment fit the man."[54]

On the other hand, should the university be required to maintain strict standards of due process of law in its sanctioning? Shall a student who is accused of violating a university regulation be permitted to have counsel? If so, should failure to advise him of right to counsel constitute grounds for dismissal of charges? Should standards of conduct be required to meet the stringent tests of specificity and clarity demanded of criminal laws? In short, if the sanctioning apparatus of a university is no longer analogous to that of a family, should it be held to the standards required of a criminal court? This is a major issue facing the University of California. I think that almost all would agree that neither sanctioning model, the family or the criminal court, is *entirely* appropriate to the university as an institution. The emergence of a new sanctioning structure will grow out of much thought and will be the cause and consequence of further conflict. At the heart of the dispute will be the institutional character of the university. If campus officials are not independent, if the total situation induces arbitrariness, then controls on official conduct will need to approximate those in criminal courts; anything less will lead to discontent; possibly future turmoil, and, worst of all, injustice. If, however, the social interests of campus administrators and students could truly be brought together, so that students were able to depend upon the fairness of administration, the need to control authority would be lessened. The "multiversity" is not exactly a polity—but it is far from being a family.

This situation, however, is not confined to the University of California alone, or to the university as an institution. As Charles Reich has pointed

---

[54] Harold J. Berman, *Justice in the U.S.S.R.* (New York: Random House [Vintage ed.], 1963), p. 366.

out, Americans are increasingly living on government largesse, a "new property" in the form of benefits, services, contracts, franchises, licenses, employment, and, I would add, education. Associated with this trend are new claims of right, and new demands for a rule of law in the adjudication of such claims. As Reich puts it:

> We cannot safely entrust our livelihoods and our rights to the discretion of authorities, examiners, boards of control, character committees, regents, or license commissioners. We cannot permit any official or agency to pretend to sole knowledge of the public good. We cannot put the independence of any man . . . wholly in the power of other men.[55]

The problem of reconsidering and revising adjudicative tribunals must become increasingly more salient in an era of an automated industrial revolution and a revolution of rising demands for egalitarian social status.

JURIMETRICS

The question of the judge's role in society has been raised most provocatively by those political scientists and lawyers interested in jurimetrics,[56] a discipline which seeks generalizations for programming judicial decision-making into an electronic computer. The very idea that the work of exalted judges, such as those of the United States Supreme Court, may be broken down into a number of variables predicting outcomes, raises the hackles of those who find such a notion simple-minded and overdeterministic, as it undoubtedly is.[57] At the same time it must be acknowledged that the issue—the basis of judicial decision-making—has long been a central concern to American law professors interested in jurisprudence.[58]

Perhaps the most interesting aspect of this development for the sociology of law is not whether machines can predict better than men, or whether one computer program predicts better than another; rather, it is the use to

---

[55] Charles A. Reich, "The New Property," *Yale Law Journal,* 73 (April 1964): 787.

[56] Hans W. Baade, ed., "Jurimetrics," *Law and Contemporary Problems,* 28 (Winter 1963) : 1–270. See also Glendon A. Schubert, *Quantitative Analysis of Judicial Behavior* (New York: Free Press, Macmillan, 1960); and *Mull,* the quarterly newsletter of the Electronic Data Retrieval Committee of the American Bar Association, founded at Yale Law School under the editorship of Layman E. Allen.

[57] See, for example, Joseph J. Spengler, "Machine-Made Justice: Some Implications," in *Law and Contemporary Problems,* 28 (Winter 1963): 36–52.

[58] See especially Karl N. Llewellyn, *The Common-Law Tradition: Deciding Appeals* (Boston: Little, Brown, 1960); *Jurisprudence: Realism in Theory and Practice* (Chicago: University of Chicago Press, 1962). See also Wechsler, "Toward Neutral Principles of Constitutional Law," *Harvard Law Review,* 73 (1959) : 1ff.; Pollack, "Racial Discrimination and Judicial Integrity: A Reply to Professor Wechsler," *University of Pennsylvania Law Review,* 108 (1959) : 1ff.; Bickel and Wellington, "Legislative Purpose and the Judicial Process: The Lincoln Mills Case," *Harvard Law Review,* 71 (1957) : 1ff.; Arnold, "Professor Hart's Theology," *Harvard Law Review,* 73 (1960): 1298ff.; and Addison Mueller and Murray L. Schwartz, "The Principle of Neutral Principles," *U.C.L.A. Law Review,* 7 (July 1960): 571–88.

which this knowledge will be put in the legal order. If we have a society placing great pressure upon the judicial system, one issue which arises is whether machine judgment cannot be substituted for human judgment. It is already perfectly clear, for instance, that machines can and will do many of the routine bibliographic tasks of lawyers. Julius Stone, in a recent *Stanford Law Review* article,[59] suggests that their services

> might even extend to prediction of future appellate holdings as to the law, so far as these may safely serve the practitioner in advising clients and thus relieve office and court congestion. Once a high degree of reliability is reached, conscientious lawyers may well and properly undertake more responsibility in securing settlement of cases out of court. . . . [S]uch predictions might [even] be of service . . . to lower court judges where their decisions depend on a point of law still to be clarified at the appellate level.[60]

Stone rues such a development in the hands of appellate court judges as a possible subversion of the legal order. The problem as Stone sees it is not that the machine will not predict well enough from a judge's own past behavior or the average past behavior of a group of judges; on the contrary, what Stone fears is that the machine may corrupt justice by predicting too perfectly and so ruling out change within the system. What Stone has not taken into account is that, at least theoretically, the factors which have led to transformations as well as the factors accounting for stability in law could possibly be programmed.

Actually, of course, it is not likely that the work of judges will be largely automated within the near future. If such automation should occur, however, or even if its introduction should be seriously contemplated, the processes by which it is introduced and the consequences for the adjudicative setting should be of central interest to the sociologist of law.

---

[59] Julius Stone, "Man and Machine in the Search for Justice," *Stanford Law Review,* 16 (May 1964): 515–60.
[60] *Ibid.,* pp. 558–59.

36. ON LEGAL SANCTIONS

Richard D. Schwartz and Sonya Orleans

Sanctions are officially imposed punishments aimed at enforcement of legal obligations. They are said to constitute the core, if not the defining characteristic, of the legal order. Inadequate sanctions are blamed for the failures of legal control in such divergent areas as international law, domestic crime, and civil rights. Despite the presumed importance of sanctions in the legal process, however, serious attention has rarely been paid to the topic.[1]

This paper examines sanctions from the perspective of the social sciences. It consists of . . . an oversimplified account of conventional wisdom in the area of sanctions, uses some research findings to show the inaccuracy of many of these conventional beliefs, and suggests the complexity of the problem. . . . [It is] presented here in a frank effort to elicit suggestions which will make the final report more useful as a social scientific contribution to jurisprudence.[2]

Reprinted by permission of the authors and the publisher from *The University of Chicago Law Review*, 34 (Winter 1967): 274–82.
[1] Arens and Lasswell, *In Defense of Public Order* (1961).

[2] Writers in jurisprudence have long stressed the importance of sanctions, but often without systematizing the questions in this area. Notable efforts to deal systematically with the topic range from Bentham, *An Introduction to the Principles of Morals and Legislation* (1823), to Carlston, *Law and Organization in World Society* (1962).

Notwithstanding the frequency with which the concept of sanction is used, there exists at present little empirical knowledge as to how, when, and whether sanctions work. For the most part, we rely on conventional wisdom in this area. Many legislators and administrators speak and act as if they believed some very primitive assumptions about sanction:

1. That it tends to reduce the frequency with which punished acts will be performed in the future by the offender and others.
2. That its effectiveness is an increasing function of its severity.
3. That it can be employed without incurring substantial costs to the society.
4. That other modes of increasing compliance need not be considered as alternatives, or at least not as incompatible alternatives, to punishment.[3]

A brief survey of information bearing on these assumptions casts doubt on each of them. It also accentuates the scattered and inadequate nature of the evidence available and points to the need for relevant research.

PREVENTIVE EFFECT OF SANCTIONS ON THE OFFENDER AND OTHERS

The preventive effects of punishment on the offender are open to question. High rates of recidivism, in regard to crimes of property in particular, suggest that prison terms do little more than delay the recurrence of crime for one-third of the prisoners.[4] The period in prison serves in many instances to alienate the offender further from society and to train him systematically in techniques for escaping future punishment.[5] Prison imposes on him,

---

For a cogent appeal to social scientists to attend to the issues of jurisprudence, see Harry Jones, "A View from the Bridge," *Social Problems*, 13 (1965): 41–42.

[3] These assumptions do not exhaust all the ideas concerning sanction effectiveness currently held by practitioners. In addition, policy makers seem to be guided by the belief that sanction impact increases with such elements as advance knowledge and clarity of the norm, compatibility with other norms, and the certainty of enforcement. These and other conditions—all presumably heightening the legitimacy of the norms—have been formally included in the literature of jurisprudence, most recently in Fuller, *The Morality of Law* (1964), pp. 33–94. Although Fuller seems primarily concerned with moral imperatives, his eight conditions may be read as hypotheses bearing on the probable effectiveness of legal sanctions.

[4] Glaser, *The Effectiveness of a Prison and Parole System* (1964), pp. 13–35, presents the most complete statistics to date. Glaser's figures are lower, but probably sounder, than previous estimates. A much higher figure is given by Arens and Lasswell, *In Defense of Public Order*, p. 276.

[5] Sykes, *The Society of Captives* (1958), is the best single description of the process. Cf. *The Prison: Studies in Institutional Organization and Change,* ed. Cressey (1961), and especially therein: Goffman, "On the Characteristics of Total Institutions: The Inmate World" and "On the Characteristics of Total Institutions: Staff-Inmate Relations"; and McCleery, "The Governmental Process and Informal Social Control."

moreover, a stigma which tends to impede his economic and social adjustment upon release.[6]

In civil cases, other mechanisms may lighten the effect of sanction. In medical malpractice cases, for instance, doctors routinely insure themselves against the threat of court action[7] and deduct the cost as a business expense.[8] Even those convicted of malpractice benefit from the sympathy of their colleagues, so that in one recent study doctors found liable for malpractice reported that their practices had increased after losing their cases, because of referrals from sympathetic colleagues.[9] Businessmen, potential targets of litigation, are usually able to avoid court action despite technical breaches of contract because of the culture and control system of the business community.[10] When they are found liable, they apparently react to such sanction—following Mr. Justice Holmes' advice[11]—less as moral condemnation than as a business cost to be paid in return for the privilege of breach.

Similarly, the deterrent effect is open to question. In interviews conducted informally some years ago, a few instances were found in which tax violations *began after* the prosecution of a widely publicized case. The primary reasons given were that the convicted offender had been incredibly stupid and that his evasions had been of major proportions. "If that is the kind of thing the government waits for," said one informant, "they'll never come after me."[12] Deterrence is supposed to work through fear of punishment. But if enforcement reduces fear of punishment, there is reason to suppose that the deterrent influence may vanish or even be replaced by an incentive. Nor is it certain that fear of punishment deters. Andenaes twice searched the literature for evidence that it did and came

---

[6] Schwartz and Skolnick, "Two Studies of Legal Stigma," *Social Problems,* 10 (1962): 133; Rubin, *Crime and Juvenile Delinquency* (1958); McSally, "Finding Jobs for Released Offenders," *Federal Probation* 24 (1960): 12. One author suggests the possibility of reversing the process of status degradation, but successful techniques for doing so are yet to be invented (Goldstein, "Police Discretion Not to Invoke the Criminal Process—Low Visibility Decisions in the Administration of Justice," *Yale Law Journal,* 69 [1960]: 543, 590). For a theoretical treatment of the status degradation process, see Garfinkel, "Conditions of Successful Degradation Ceremonies," *American Journal of Sociology,* 61 (1956): 420.

[7] A nationwide survey of 20,000 physicians, conducted in 1963 by the Law Department of the American Medical Association, indicated that 94.3 percent of the 14,000 respondents had liability insurance (AMA Law Department, "1963 Professional Liability Survey," *A.M.A. Journal,* 189 [1964]: 859, 862).

[8] Deduction for malpractice insurance, apparently assumed as a legitimate business expense for private practitioners, was extended to company physicians under Rev. Rul. 60–365, 1961–62 *Cum. Bull.* 49.

[9] Schwartz and Skolnick, "Two Studies of Legal Stigma," pp. 138–39.

[10] Macaulay, "Non-contractual Relations in Business: A Preliminary Study," *American Sociological Review,* 28 (1963): 55.

[11] Holmes, *The Common Law* (1923), pp. 299–307.

[12] "The Effectiveness of Legal Controls—Factors in the Reporting of Minor Items of Income on Federal Tax Returns" (paper presented at the annual meeting of the American Sociological Association, Chicago, 1959).

up with very little the first time, substantially more the second.[13] One of his best finds was a report on crime rates in Copenhagen before, during, and after a seven-month period in which the police were rendered ineffectual because disarmed and reorganized by the German army of occupation. During these seven months "without police," robbery and larceny in Copenhagen apparently increased tenfold, whereas embezzlement, fraud, and homicide rates remained virtually constant.[14] This suggests that the perceived danger of punishment serves as an immediate deterrent to the first type of crime but not to the second. It is difficult to interpret these findings with reference to a theory of sanction. The stability of crime in the second category might mean that such crime is not primarily deterred by fear of sanction, or it might mean that fear of detection and sanction remains high even in the absence of police because such crime can be readily detected without police help. If the first explanation carries any weight, it raises questions as to the circumstances in which fear of sanction explains compliance. Instead of accepting the blanket generalization that deterrence works universally (or the converse, that it never works), it seems more realistic to assume that sanction deters some violations under some circumstances. If this is so, it falls to the social scientist to try to specify the conditions under which deterrence works and, if possible, the intervening variables which explain why it does or does not.

SEVERITY OF SANCTIONS

Historical materials, case studies, and experimental evidence raise serious doubts about the proposition that sanction effectiveness is a linearly increasing function of severity of prescribed punishment. For one thing, when the threat of severe punishment is extended to a variety of offenses which are not considered serious hazards to community welfare, the penalties are unlikely to be enforced. In the classic instance of this, British law in the eighteenth century specified nearly two hundred capital offenses, including the stealing of goods valued at five shillings from a shop, at forty shillings from a dwelling place, and so forth. Juries reacted to these severe penalties by regularly specifying, in the face of sworn testimony to the contrary, that the stolen goods were worth one shilling less than the amount which would make the act a capital offense. Parliament abolished the death penalty on all but four offenses by 1861, in important part be-

---

[13] Andenaes, "General Prevention—Illusion or Reality," *Journal of Criminal Law, Criminology, and Police Science,* 43 (1952): 176; Andenaes, "The General Preventive Effects of Punishment," *University of Pennsylvania Law Review,* 114 (1966): 949.

[14] Trolle, *Syv Maaneder uden Politi* (Seven Months Without Police, 1945). This account is taken from Andenaes, "General Prevention—Illusion or Reality."

cause of pressure from commercial interests, whose avowed purpose was to secure reliable enforcement of property laws by making their penalties more acceptable to juries.[15] Even where severe punishment can be effectively administered, it may not deter. Orsted describes a period in eighteenth century Norway when homicide rates increased because of the belief of suicidal persons that execution for murder was the only technique of suicide which might excuse them from eternal damnation. This led to the abolition of the death penalty in such cases on the ground that it acted as an incentive to, rather than a deterrent from, murder.[16]

The literature of contemporary psychology also casts doubt on the severity assumption. In general, psychologists studying animal learning agree that punishment reduces the likelihood of the punished behavior occurring only when it contributes to the learning of alternative responses.[17] If the punished individual for some reason repeats the punished response after punishment ($R \rightarrow Pun \rightarrow R$), that response may subsequently become *more* likely as a result.[18] Under other conditions, punishment may temporarily inhibit the response it follows, but the response increases in frequency following the cessation of punishment.[19] The more severe the punishment under such circumstances, the greater the motivation for the punished response. Even where a socially approved alternative is available, severe threat may not be the most effective way of promoting its adoption. This has been suggested by Janis and Feshbach in an experiment which shows that behavioral change can be greater under mild than under extreme threat.[20] Subsequent experiments[21] qualify this finding but do not eliminate the possibility hypothesized in the original research.

---

[15] Cantor, *Crime and Society* (1939), pp. 222–24.

[16] Orsted, *Eunomia* (1815–22), vol. 3, p. 147.

[17] Skinner, *Science and Human Behavior* (1953), pp. 182–93. The leading experiment is Estes, "An Experimental Study of Punishment," *Psychological Monographs,* 57 (1944): 263.

[18] Experimental findings on the subject are slim but suggestive. The leading animal experiment is reported by Muenzinger and Pawloski, "Motivation in Learning—Comparison of Electric Shock for Correct Turns in a Corrective and a Noncorrective Situation," *Journal of Experimental Psychology,* 42 (1951): 118.

[19] Azrin, "Effects of Punishment Intensity During Variable-Internal Reinforcement," *Journal of Experimental Analysis of Human Behavior,* 3 (1960): 123. More recently, the same experimenter reported data which suggested that punishment accomplishes this effect by raising the level of aggression. Thus, the observation might hold particularly for responses which are hostile toward others or destructive toward self. Azrin, "Motivational Aspects of Escape from Punishment," *Journal of Experimental Analysis of Behavior,* 8 (1965): 31. We are indebted to Frank Zimring, a third-year student at the University of Chicago Law School, for bringing this work to our attention, as well as for other valuable suggestions.

[20] Janis and Feshbach, "Effects of Fear-Arousing Communications," *Journal of Abnormal and Social Psychology,* 48 (1953): 78.

[21] Berkowitz and Cottingham, "The Interest, Value, and Relevance of Fear-Arousing Communications," *Journal of Abnormal and Social Psychology,* 60 (1960): 37; Leventhal and Niles, "A Field Experiment on Fear Arousal with Data on the Validity of Questionnaire Measures," *Journal of Personality,* 32 (1964): 459; Leventhal, Singer and Jones, "Effects of Fear and Specificity of Recommendation upon Attitudes and Behavior," *Journal of Personal and Social Psychology,* 2 (1965): 20.

SOCIAL COSTS OF PUNISHMENT

Also open to question is the assumption that punishment can be employed without consideration of its costs to society. The sanctioned person, as well as those who identify with him, may become alienated from those who invoke or impose the deprivation. In civil matters, this can lead to an intensification of hostility between parties whose continued cooperation is necessary for their own interests and/or for the welfare of society. It was this danger that led Harry Shulman strongly to advocate nonadversary proceedings as a substitute for winner-take-all judgments in labor-management relations.[22] The same effect figures importantly in the philosophy of the family courts, as advanced by such proponents as Judge Alexander.[23] When the opponent is the entire society, as represented by the prosecution in criminal cases, antagonism generated by punishment can produce alienation from the society. This may lead to withdrawal from social participation and/or an increased tendency to strike back at the society in varying ways.[24] Such acts may be directed specifically against the kind of compliance enforced by the punishment. In the case of taxation, for instance, it may take the form of individual evasion, a culture of noncompliance such as is represented by moonshining, or a sociopolitical movement such as Poujadism, focused on thwarting tax collection. In addition, alienation from the state can result in more general resistance ranging from political apathy to revolution.

This is not to say, of course, that the imposition of sanction inevitably produces such effects. But there is enough evidence that they can occur to merit attention by policy makers and theorists alike. We need to know the conditions under which sanction produces side effects which nullify its contribution to social order. To what segments and proportions of the population may sanction be applied without impairing the equilibrium of the social system? What is the effect of perceived legitimacy in reducing the socially disturbing side effects of sanction? How does legitimacy interact with varying degrees and types of sanctions? What are the conditions —such as power distribution, sanction invocation, value consensus—which affect the sense of legitimacy in various sociocultural settings? This is only a sample of the questions which must be articulated and explored if we are to understand the range of consequences which flow from the administration of sanctions.

---

[22] Shulman, "Reason, Contract, and Law in Labor Relations," *Harvard Law Review*, 68 (1955): 999. See Mentschikoff, "Commercial Arbitration," *Columbia Law Review*, 61 (1961): 846. See also Coons, "Approaches to Court-Imposed Compromise in the Uses of Doubt and Reason," *Northwestern University Law Review*, 58 (1964): 750.

[23] Alexander, "Constitutional Rights in the Juvenile Court," in *Justice for the Child*, ed. Rosenheim (1962), p. 82.

[24] For a thoughtful discussion of the phenomenon among youth, see Matza, *Delinquency and Drift* (1964).

ALTERNATIVE MODES OF SECURING COMPLIANCE

It is interesting to note that sanctions are rarely weighed against alternative means of securing compliance. Our legal system contains very few instances in which people are explicitly rewarded for compliance, rather than punished for deviance. The exceptions are most likely to be found in the regulation of economic behavior through devices such as tax incentives for investment and subsidies for crop limitation. Other countries have used incentives such as bonuses for larger families. But for the most part, incentives have been left to nonlegal and especially nongovernmental agencies, such as insurance companies which provide lower rates for accident-free drivers. It was this lack of emphasis on incentives in legal policy which led Swift's Gulliver to the following comment:

> Although we usually call Reward and Punishment the two hinges upon which all government turns; yet I could never observe this maxim to be put in practice by any nation, except that of *Lilliput*. Who ever can there bring sufficient proof that he hath strictly observed the laws of his country for seventy-three moons, hath a claim to certain privileges, according to his quality and condition of life, with a proportionable sum of money out of a fund appropriated for that use: He likewise acquires the title of *Snilpall*, or Legal, which is added to his name, but does not descend to his posterity. And these people thought it a prodigious defect of policy among us, when I told them that our laws were enforced only by penalties without any mention of reward.[25]

The disinclination to use explicit rewards for legal compliance can be variously explained. The subject is too complex to explore in detail here. We suggest, however, that for reasons of economy explicit rewards tend to be employed where only small segments of the population are supposed to be their recipients. Legal norms, as Simmel pointed out, characteristically provide minimal standards which a majority are expected to observe.[26] For the violator, the appropriate consequence is a deprivation. It would be possible in principle to give rewards to violators when they cease their violations, but this would seem likely to provide a motive for violation. Extension of rewards to all who observe the law would be expensive, difficult to administer, and ineffectual if the recipients were too numerous. If incentives were limited to the exemplars of legality—as semiseriously proposed by Swift—it might carry the implication that obedience to law is optional rather than obligatory. Moreover, emphasis on strict and manifest compliance with law might jeopardize a major benefit of a minimal, negatively defined code of conduct: the freedom of the individual to innovate, an especially necessary element in a dynamic social order.

Some of the same considerations apply to the use of conscience as a mo-

---

[25] Swift, *Gulliver's Travels* (Modern Library, 1931), p. 64.
[26] See particularly "On the Significance of Numbers for Social Life," in *The Sociology of Georg Simmel*, trans. Wolff (1950), pp. 99–104.

tivational support of law. Although religious systems have included appeals to conscience, as in the Ten Commandments and canon law, this element is largely absent in secular legal systems such as our own. While some of our statutes contain preambles giving the purposes of the legislation, such statements are characteristically used more for interpreting the meaning of the law than for moral exhortation. The body of the statute itself is almost invariably confined to a description of the standard of conduct and to a matter-of-fact statement of consequences which will befall the violator. Avoidance of appeals to conscience was noted by Holmes as an evolving characteristic of our legal system.[27] It has been explained by Cahn[28] and Fuller[29] on the ground that conscience alone cannot adequately enforce conduct for the majority. This consideration does not explain, however, why conscience is not combined with the threat of sanction. Among the possible explanations are the difficulty of the making of a direct appeal to conscience by the state, and the implicit assumption (as yet inadequately tested) that a combination of conscience and threat reduces the effectiveness that either would have separately.

Heavy, if not exclusive, reliance on sanction rests only in part on the absence of alternatives. Some evidence has been noted above which points to the effectiveness of sanction as a means of enforcing compliance in certain circumstances. In addition to rational justifications for enforcing law through sanction, certain nonrational elements may also enter. The frustration-aggression hypothesis of the learning theorists may be interpreted as giving one such reason.[30] Violation of socially approved norms may be assumed to act as a frustration to many in the society. The imposition of legal sanction may serve as the most convenient socially approved expression of aggression against the source of the frustration. Sanction, in these terms, appears to be a more gratifying response than the provision of reward to nonoffenders or to the offender when he complies with the standard. Another explanation, proposed by Freud in *Totem and Taboo*, interpreted the punitive response to illegality as reflecting in part an attempt by sanctioners to repress their own impulses for comparable deviant activity. Exploring the subject in another context, Freud suggested that sanction tendency has a second powerful, unconscious source:

> In our unconscious we daily and hourly deport all who stand in our way, all who have offended or injured us. . . . Indeed our unconscious will murder even for trifles . . . it knows no other punishment for crime

---

[27] Holmes, *The Common Law, passim.*
[28] Cahn, *The Moral Decision* (1956), pp. 9–49.
[29] Fuller, *The Morality of Law* (1964), pp. 3–32.
[30] Dollard, *Frustration and Aggression* (1939). The original hypothesis asserted that frustration was a necessary and sufficient condition for aggression. It was later modified to make frustration only a necessary condition (Miller, "The Frustration-Aggression Hypothesis," *Psychological Review*, 49 [1941]: 337). Evidence for the hypothesis is summarized in Berelson and Steiner, *Human Behavior—An Inventory of Scientific Findings* (1964), pp. 266–71. For an alternative explanation of aggression, see Lorenz, *On Aggression* (1963).

than death: and this has a certain consistency, for every injury to our almighty and autocratic ego is at bottom a crime of *lèse-majesté*.[31]

Ranulf argued that sanction is often irrational in the sense that it exceeds the social needs for effective control and that this reflects an inclination toward "disinterested cruelty."[32] This impulse he found particularly characteristic of the middle class; he suggested, by way of explanation, the distinctively insecure social position of that stratum.

Whatever the merits of such explanations, and of many more like them, they have in common the view that punishment does not inevitably serve its manifest purpose. Yet the argument can be sustained in the final analysis only if alternative means of securing compliance can be demonstrated to be at least as functional as punishment. Only when such information is available can the persistence of punishment be legitimately scored as gratuitous and hence irrational.

---

[31] Freud, *On War, Sex, and Neurosis* (1947), p. 272.
[32] Ranulf, *Moral Indignation and Middle-Class Psychology* (1938).

37. RESEARCH ON THE LEGAL SYSTEM IN AMERICA

Edwin M. Schur

A study of the law in action obviously encompasses an enormous array of potential topics for investigation, which vary in terms of legal substance, legal procedure and setting, and general questions of interest to the sociologist. There is almost no end to the empirical studies that might be undertaken with a view to further understanding the real workings of any modern legal system. A number of areas for such research and specific projects have already been mentioned. Studies of the legal needs of the poor and the extent to which these needs are met represent a good example of concentration on the actualities, rather than on the doctrines and formal organization, of the legal order. Similarly, the issue of the effects of law—as a deterrent, as an instrument of social change, and so forth—is another subject falling into this category and is one on which undoubtedly a great deal more research will be done. Furthermore, some research that we might not immediately associate with the phrase "law in action" nonetheless has relevance to a general empirical orientation to legal systems. Thus, historical and comparative perspectives, which cannot be considered further here, may be very useful in throwing additional light on present content and procedures in a particular legal order.[1] Likewise, patterns of legal education, admittedly somewhat removed from the actual processes involved in lawsuits and other legal "events," may indirectly shape a legal system, through their influence (the nature and extent of which require empirical investigation) on the perspectives of lawyers and judges and on their approaches to their work.

Clearly, then, it is beyond the scope of this necessarily brief chapter to explore all the possibilities for research on the "law in action." Instead, we shall consider four areas which . . . seem particularly important to the development of a comprehensive sociology of law. It should be noted too that . . . the focus will be almost entirely on the present-day American legal system, although many of the specific issues and findings very likely have wider relevance.

COURTS, JUDGES, AND JURIES

The legal realists and sociological jurists, in writings both theoretical and concerned with policy, drew attention to the very real social action that constitutes the life of the courts. Jerome Frank, in particular, emphasized the key roles of judge and jury at the trial-court level. In recent years, social scientists have begun to explore systematically the court as an arena of legal behavior.

Without doubt, the most impressive effort at an empirical analysis of the courts in action has been the extensive and continuous research of the Chicago Jury Project. This study, by a team of social scientists working closely with legal experts (and maintained as an ongoing research unit of the University of Chicago Law School), has focused mainly on the behavior of jurors; but it has also produced numerous findings illuminating other aspects of court process and organization. The early history of this project is interesting because it suggests some of the problems of interrelationship between sociologists on the one hand and lawyers and the public on the other, which may be activated by the sociological study of legal phenomena.

In 1954, five jury deliberations in a federal court in Kansas were recorded by microphones concealed in the jury room. This research technique was adopted with the permission of the judges and attorneys involved in the cases, but without informing individual jurors. The recordings were edited in such a way that neither the specific case nor the identities of the jurors could be recognized. Over a year after the recordings were made, they were played (at the request of one of the judges) at an official conference of

---

[1] See, for example, William J. Chambliss, "A Sociological Analysis of the Law of Vagrancy," *Social Problems*, 12 (Summer 1964): 67–77.

judges in Colorado, so that those present could have a more accurate picture of how juries really deliberate and of whether the judges' instructions to juries are properly understood. The event was picked up by the national press; there followed expressions of editorial outrage at such invasion of the sanctity of the jury room. Eventually there were hearings by a U.S. Senate subcommittee, at which leaders in the Association of American Law Schools supported carefully controlled research using concealed microphones, while the American Civil Liberties Union completely disapproved of the practice. The controversy culminated in the passage of a federal law making any attempt to record, observe, or listen to jury deliberations in any court of the United States a criminal offense.[2] While certainly the matter of jury secrecy raises important policy issues, there is some evidence that in this instance legislators may have partially miscalculated the nature of informed opinion concerning the research practices in question. Although there are no data on reactions of the general public, one sociologist did survey samples of lawyers, sociologists, and political scientists. As might have been predicted, the social scientists overwhelmingly approved of recording jury deliberations for research purposes. What is more surprising is that the lawyers, while much more critical, showed surprisingly strong support for the practice.[3] It is quite likely, therefore, that the clamor in the news about "jury bugging" blew the incident completely out of proportion, with the result that an important research effort received a serious setback.

Subsequent work by the project reveals an ingenious adaptation to this curb on their investigations. A decision was reached to record mock-jury deliberations, but the problem presented itself of ensuring that this artificial research situation be as similar as possible to the real thing. The following procedure was adopted.[4] Transcripts of actual cases that had been decided by the courts were edited, condensed, and recorded—with law-school faculty usually playing the principal parts of attorneys, witnesses, judge, and so on. Through the cooperation of presiding judges and bar associations (in Chicago, St. Louis, and Minneapolis), jurors for the study were drawn by lot from regular jury lists and assigned, as part of regular jury duty, to hear these recorded cases. After the jury received an explanation of the study, from a judge, and before listening to the trial, each juror completed a questionnaire (similar to a lawyer's examining of prospective jurors) on which various social-background data were recorded. Jurors

[2] For excerpts from the Senate hearings and text of the federal law, see R. C. Donnelly, J. Goldstein, and R. D. Schwartz, *Criminal Law* (New York: Free Press, 1962), pp. 82–84.

[3] Waldo Burchard, "A Study of Attitudes Toward the Use of Concealed Devices in Social Science Research," *Social Forces,* 36 (December 1957): 111–16; and Waldo Burchard, "Lawyers, Political Scientists, Sociologists—and Concealed Microphones," *American Sociological Review,* 23 (December 1958): 686–91.

[4] As summarized by Rita James Simon, "Trial by Jury: A Critical Assessment," in *Applied Sociology,* ed. Alvin Gouldner and S. M. Miller (New York: Free Press, 1965), p. 306.

then listened to the recorded trial, after which, but prior to group deliberation, they completed another short questionnaire stating how they would
then have decided the case. The jury then retired to its deliberations (including selection of a foreman, as well as reaching a verdict), all of which
were recorded for subsequent analysis. After having reached the verdict,
the jurors were again questioned, as to their reactions to the experiment,
among other things. The jury was then taken back to the judge to report its
verdict and to receive the thanks of the court for its service.

Through this technique, the Chicago researchers have produced a wealth
of data concerning the behavior of juries. Social-status factors, for example,
have been found to exert a considerable influence on jury deliberations:
"Men, in contrast with women, and persons of higher in contrast with
lower status occupations have higher participation, influence, satisfaction,
and perceived competence for the jury task." Likewise, "it appears that the
foreman is expected to be a male, preferably, a male of higher educational
status."[5] The project has also examined jury behavior on a wide variety of
specific substantive and procedural legal issues, ranging from whether or
not the jury takes into account probable attorneys' fees in determining the
amount of damages to award in personal injury suits to how the jury
evaluates expert psychiatric testimony in criminal trials.[6] Much attention
has been devoted to determining which factors weigh most heavily with
jurors in reaching decisions and how well they understand the proceedings
and in particular the instructions they receive from the court. According
to one recent report, the general nature of these findings is such as to allay
many of the fears concerning the prejudice and incompetence of the typical
jury. Simon writes that "when a group of laymen of diverse backgrounds
are brought together as a jury, they function and arrive at verdicts in a
manner unexpected by many persons. . . . The law imposes a universalistic
and impersonal set of expectations which the jurors internalize, even
within as short a period of time as their first trial." While juries do not
always proceed with their deliberations in the most "efficient" manner,
and while emotional factors certainly influence such deliberations, "Our
data suggest that these feelings become socialized. They are redefined so
as to be functionally responsive to the expectations of the judicial system
and of popular sentiments."[7] If these data do not necessarily provide a
complete and definite picture of all aspects of jury behavior, they certainly
constitute the closest approximation available at this time. Any subse-

---

[5] Fred L. Strodtbeck, Rita M. James, and Charles Hawkins, "Social Status in Jury Deliberations," *American Sociological Review,* 22 (December 1957): 718. See also Fred L.
Strodtbeck and R. D. Mann, "Sex Role Differentiation in Jury Deliberations," *Sociometry,*
19 (March 1956): 3–11; and Rita M. James, "Status and Competence of Jurors," *American
Journal of Sociology,* 64 (May 1959): 563–70.

[6] See Hans Zeisel, "Social Research on the Law," and Fred L. Strodtbeck, "Social
Process, the Law, and Jury Functioning," both in *Law and Sociology: Exploratory Essays,*
ed. William M. Evan (New York: Free Press, 1962); and Simon, *op. cit.*

[7] Simon, *op. cit.,* p. 304.

quent evaluation of the jury system (and debate as to whether it advances or impedes "legality") must surely take these findings into account.

Recognition that jury deliberations must be placed in a larger institutional context has led the Chicago researchers also to inquire more broadly into the workings of the trial courts. Thus the project's first book-length publication, *Delay in the Court*,[8] reports on an extensive survey of the work of the Supreme Court of New York County—analyzing the distribution of types of cases making up the court's work load, the extent of delay and the apparent reasons for it, and the likely consequences of various proposed remedies. The authors also provide cross-jurisdictional data corroborating the existence of variations in "claims consciousness," "in the sense that a comparable series of accidents will give rise to a greater number of claims in some areas or communities than in others."[9] In view of the heavy component of personal-injury suits in the work of the trial courts, such matters are of the utmost policy importance, as indeed are all the aspects of work load and delay considered in this study.[10] Sociologists elsewhere have studied the work patterns of the trial courts, as in the California Civil Justice Project. Preliminary findings there revealed not only that the work load is likely to be excessive, but furthermore that only a small proportion of the judges' time is indeed spent deciding contested cases, and that judges (because of differences in prestige, time and energy required, legal issues posed, and procedures employed) would rather handle certain types of cases in preference to others.[11] Such findings may be extremely important for the light they throw on the role conceptions of judges and on the types of tribunals and staffs most likely to handle specific kinds of judicial work expeditiously and conscientiously.

A rather different body of knowledge about courts and judges is being developed through so-called behavioral studies of judicial decision-making.[12] This mode of research, which has appealed particularly to political scientists, draws heavily on the legal realists' conception of the nature of the judging process. Although some formulations of the realists undoubtedly exaggerated the arbitrary element in decision-making (as seen in

---

[8] Hans Zeisel, Harry Kalven, Jr., and Bernard Buchholz, *Delay in the Court* (Boston: Little, Brown, 1959). A second volume based on the project's studies has just been issued. See Kalven and Zeisel, *The American Jury* (Boston: Little, Brown, 1966).

[9] Zeisel, Kalven, and Buchholz, *Delay in the Court*, p. 237.

[10] See Maurice Rosenberg, "Court Congestion: Status, Causes, and Proposed Remedies," in *The Courts, the Public, and the Law Explosion*, ed. Harry W. Jones (Englewood Cliffs, N.J.: Prentice-Hall, 1965). See also Maxine Boord Virtue, *Survey of Metropolitan Courts: Final Report* (Ann Arbor: University of Michigan Press, 1962).

[11] Jerome Carlin, "Preliminary Notes on Adjudication and the Administration of Justice" (Center for the Study of Law and Society, University of California, Berkeley, May 1964, duplicated).

[12] See Glendon Schubert, ed., *Judicial Behavior* (Chicago: Rand McNally, 1964); and Glendon Schubert, ed., *Judicial Decision-Making* (New York: Free Press, 1963). See also symposium on "Jurimetrics," *Law and Contemporary Problems*, 28 (Winter 1963); and symposium on "Social Science Approaches to the Judicial Process," *Harvard Law Review*, 79 (June 1966).

apocryphal references to "gastronomical jurisprudence," according to which the quality of the judge's breakfast might be the key determinant of his decisions), the belief that environmental and predispositional factors have importance has strongly persisted. Efforts to discern "voting patterns" among appellate judges, especially those of the United States Supreme Court, have focused on the influence of some of these factors.

This research has taken a variety of forms. Some investigations have centered on the social-background characteristics of judges.[13] Studies have documented these characteristics (one historical analysis found a disproportionate representation of white Anglo-Saxon Protestants among U.S. Supreme Court justices; another survey reached similar findings concerning state-court judges), and some have gone on to test interrelationships between personal background and affiliations and patterns of decision-making. Thus, it has been found (perhaps not surprisingly, though such data at least systematically confirm what one might suspect) that Democratic and Republican judges differ in the tendencies of their decisions across a wide range of legal situations. Democratic judges are more likely (and Republicans less likely) to decide in favor of defendants in criminal cases, unions in labor-management disputes, claimants in unemployment compensation cases, the libertarian position in free-speech cases, the government in tax matters, the claimant in personal-injury suits, and so on. While such findings may be interesting, refined statistical analyses make clear the difficulty of definitely attributing decision patterns to particular factors of background or affiliation. Many variables seem to be involved, and the weighting of each relative to the others is uncertain.

Another approach has been to concentrate on the composition of particular courts as small groups containing coalitions in the form of "voting blocs," a conception developed originally by C. Herman Pritchett in pioneering analyses of the work of the U.S. Supreme Court.[14] This focus, which has interested sociologists as well as political scientists, has produced useful further documentation of the "bloc" tendency, as well as suggestive data concerning possible factors in changing alignments. It also may increase our understanding of judicial leadership,[15] although this quality is particularly difficult to assess through available sources of data. Direct

---

[13] For example, John R. Schmidhauser, "The Background Characteristics of United States Supreme Court Justices," and Stuart Nagel, "The Relationship Between the Political and Ethnic Affiliation of Judges, and their Decision-Making," both in *Judicial Behavior*, ed. Schubert. See also Joel Grossman, "Social Backgrounds and Judicial Decision-Making," *Harvard Law Review*, 79 (June 1966): 1551–64.

[14] C. Herman Pritchett, *The Roosevelt Court* (New York: Macmillan, 1948). See also Eloise C. Snyder, "Uncertainty and the Supreme Court," *American Journal of Sociology*, 65 (November 1959): 241–45; Eloise C. Snyder, "The Supreme Court as a Small Group," *Social Forces*, 37 (March 1958): 232–38; and Walter F. Murphy, "Courts as Small Groups," *Harvard Law Review*, 79 (June 1966): 1565–72.

[15] S. Sidney Ulmer, "Leadership in the Michigan Supreme Court," in *Judicial Decision-Making*, ed. Schubert; and Walter F. Murphy, "Leadership, Bargaining, and the Judicial Process," in *Judicial Behavior*, ed. Schubert.

observation of the decision-reaching processes is rarely possible. At the same time, secondary evidence, such as the personal papers of justices, may sometimes usefully supplement analysis of recorded judicial voting behavior.

Out of this recognition of voting blocs and patterns has come the development of efforts to predict the voting behavior of particular judges (and hence the decisions of particular courts) on the basis of past decisions and through varied methods including cumulative scaling, "games theory," and refined mathematical and computer techniques.[16] If it is true that the responses of Judge A to situations of types X, Y, and Z recurrently fall into a neat cumulative ordering ("scale"), then we may be in a good position to predict future responses to similar situations (or to situations related to these in a clearly defined way). Likewise, if a specific judge clearly favors one side on a particular legal issue, then a games-theory analysis based on the steps he is likely to take to maximize desired outcomes may also help us to predict his future judicial behavior.

Such analyses have, however, been subjected to some rather intense criticism. According to the critics, while research of this sort may apply methodological techniques of great sophistication, it may incorporate oversimplified or incorrect assumptions about the nature of the judicial process.[17] Thus, it has been argued that often the behaviorists' categorizations of decisions and justices are artificial or misguided. Judicial votes and the justices themselves are arbitrarily forced into one or the other of the categories established by the researcher. A judge's vote in a particular case is determined to be pro or con civil liberties, for example, even though he might in fact have reached his decision on completely different grounds. As Fuller notes:

> A judge votes to declare invalid or unlawful some exercise of power by a labor union. Does this prove he is "against" labor unions? It is quite possible that he has a deep faith in the labor movement, but is convinced that the greatest threat to it lies in irresponsible actions by unions. It may even be that his friendliness toward labor has enabled him to obtain an understanding of such problems denied to those who stand at a greater distance from the battle.[18]

Because the researchers have been interested in judicial voting differences, unanimous decisions have been left out of their analyses, and this omission may distort the overall patterns that emerge. Likewise, they have

---

[16] See Joseph Tanenhaus, "The Cumulative Scaling of Judicial Decisions," *Harvard Law Review*, 79 (June 1966): 1583–94; Glendon Schubert, "The Certiorari Game," in *Judicial Behavior*, ed. Schubert; and readings in *ibid.*, chap. 5, "Mathematical Prediction of Judicial Behavior."

[17] Wallace Mendelson, "The Neo-Behavioral Approach to the Judicial Process: A Critique," *American Political Science Review*, 57 (September 1963): 593–603; and Lon Fuller, "An Afterword: Science and the Judicial Process," *Harvard Law Review*, 79 (June 1966): 1604–28.

[18] Fuller, *op. cit.*, p. 1612.

scored or ranked judges according to votes, not opinions. Sometimes a judge may "vote" a particular way because of a procedural technicality, whereas a written opinion reveals (or would reveal, if he were to write one) a strong and opposing tendency in making decisions, with reference to the substantive issues in the case. Nor is there any definite way of classifying the possible outcomes in a dispute. Thus, it may not always be clear which outcome is pro and which con civil liberties, or even that a civil-liberties issue is necessarily involved in the first place. This sort of problem is best seen in cases in which two liberal causes are competing with each other—as, for example, in disputes concerning pretrial newspaper publicity alleged to prejudice a criminal defendant's case, where the libertarian beliefs in a free press and fair trial are set off one against the other.

Behavioral research, in other words, may oversimplify what is at stake in a legal case. It is not simply a matter of voting pro or con on a single dimension. And as Fuller notes with reference to games theory, such approaches are "concerned with the 'pay-off' and not with the rewards of the game itself. . . . Judges may derive rewards from collaborative efforts that transcend individual 'pay-offs.'" Indeed, "what a judge may want (some of us are naïve enough to hope that this is what he will always want) is a decision that is just, proper, and workable."[19] The behaviorists may thus slight the judge's conception of his professional role, and his interest in preserving the consistency and integrity of the overall legal order as he sees it. Decisions are attributed solely to political predilection; "contradictory" votes reflect shifting attitudes. Behaviorists have been charged with following the legal realists at their most extreme, with taking the position that the law as a developing body of rules is more or less a myth: "Indeed, it appears that a major burden of their studies of the judicial process is to demonstrate that law is not an important element in court decisions."[20]

At any rate, it should be emphasized that these studies have focused largely on the content of decisions and on the work of appellate courts. This focus is not surprising, given the interest of political scientists in constitutional development and in general issues of public policy. Nor is there any question that research of this sort may produce interesting data, which are relevant to a full understanding of the judicial system. Nonetheless, it is likely that the work of sociologists will center mainly on the trial courts and on general processes rather than on specific doctrinal outcomes and trends.

A somewhat different area altogether, and one that should be of mutual interest to political scientists and sociologists, is that of the organization

---

[19] *Ibid.*, p. 1607.
[20] Mendelson, *op. cit.*, p. 593.

and staffing of the courts. As we have already seen, sociologists have examined the work load of courts and problems of delay, matters that have obvious relevance for the organization of the court system. Thus far the matter of judicial recruitment has not been of central interest to sociologists. An example of research in this area, which is of sociological as well as political relevance, is the study by Joel Grossman, a political scientist, of the workings of the American Bar Association's Standing Committee on Federal Judiciary.[21] Grossman provides a comprehensive, empirically grounded analysis of this influential committee (which advises on appointments to the federal bench)—including its history, its composition, the general nature of its activities, its relationships with the Attorney General's office and the Senate Committee on the Judiciary, and the extent to which its work has affected judicial recruitment patterns. Noting that "for the first time a private group of national scope has become an integral part of the federal recruitment process," Grossman's study concludes that the committee has achieved some effectiveness in maintaining minimum standards of qualification, but has not gained the power completely to control specific nominations. Although it "operates on the sufferance of both the Attorney General and the Senate Judiciary Committee . . . it has nonetheless altered the previously existing distribution of recruitment power."[22]

Patterns of judicial selection at the state-court level are also of sociological significance, in particular as a revealing indicator of the intersection between our society's legal order and the political system (in the specific party-politics sense). The qualifications of state judges have long concerned analysts of the American judicial system, including such astute observers as James Bryce, who found that in at least some states,

> a place on the bench of the superior courts carries little honour, and commands but slight social consideration. It is lower than that of an English county court judge or [stipendiary] magistrate, or of a Scotch sheriff-substitute. It raises no presumption that its holder is able or cultivated or trusted by his fellow-citizens. . . . Often he stands below the leading members of the State or city bar in all these points and does not move in the best society. . . . A judge is not expected to set an example of conformity to the conventional standards of decorum.[23]

To Bryce, as to subsequent students of the courts, the method of appointment, invariably operating through "the agency of party wirepullers," was seen as a crucial factor in lowering the quality of state judges. As a

---

[21] Joel B. Grossman, *Lawyers and Judges: The ABA and the Politics of Judicial Selection* (New York: Wiley, 1965). See also Jack Peltason, *Federal Courts in the Political Process* (New York: Random House, 1955), chap. 4, "Recruiting Judges."

[22] Grossman, *Lawyers and Judges*, pp. 208, 209. For a survey of lawyers' opinions of the committee's work, see Jack Ladinsky and Joel Grossman, "Occupational Consequences of Professional Consensus: Lawyers and the Selection of Judges," *Administrative Science Quarterly*, 11 (June 1966): 79–106.

[23] James Bryce, *The American Commonwealth*, 2nd ed. rev. (New York and London: Macmillan, 1891), p. 513.

recent analysis of New York politics has indicated, there is indeed a close functional interdependence between the judicial system and the political party system. Control over court staffing provides the parties with a means of rewarding party workers (and therefore indirectly promoting the incentives to working for the party), of securing party revenues (through the "purchase" of judgeships), of satisfying the demands of religious and ethnic elements in the party, and of protecting its general interests through the recruitment of favorably disposed judges. At the same time, the parties provide the court system with a workable, if somewhat corrupt, means of recruitment, machinery for supporting candidates for electoral judicial posts, and an organized base from which may emanate pressure for higher judicial salaries.[24] The belief that such systems of "mutual accommodation" are detrimental to the soundness of the judiciary has created, at least among lawyers, much discussion of schemes for the "merit selection" of judges.[25] These schemes should be of interest to the sociologist, for clearly the mode of selection employed may have far-reaching implications for the norms and patterns emerging in the work of the courts, as well as for the place of the courts in relation to outside forces in society.

These political aspects of the judicial system also suggest the importance of placing the work of the courts within a general context of competing pressures from opposed interest groups within the society. This point was made above, in connection with power elements in the legal order, and can be seen to be particularly relevant to the question of law as an instrument of conscious social change. The concept of "pressure group" is not one that has been much in vogue with sociologists, but it is difficult to see how the influence of such groups on court action can be ignored. Similarly, while the point is well made that judges seek to develop their rulings without open reference to outside pressures, the opposing positions between which they must choose have to come from somewhere. Interest groups shape these positions in a number of ways, including direct backing or representation of individual litigants and sometimes the filing of *amicus curiae* ("friend of the court") briefs. And these are not the only possibilities. Peltason nicely summarizes the role of groups as follows:

> . . . following certain established procedures, groups enter the judicial forum. Represented by formal litigants, interests seek the support of judges. Part of the action centers in the courtroom, where arguments are addressed to the judges and facts are brought to their attention in order to persuade the judges to decide that the "law" is on a particular side. But groups do not limit their action to the courtroom. They seek to influence opinion generally, to secure the support of law writers, and the other agencies of government.[26]

[24] Wallace Sayre and Herbert Kaufman, *Governing New York* (New York: Russell Sage Foundation, 1960).

[25] Glen R. Winters and Robert E. Allard, "Judicial Selection and Tenure in the United States," in *The Courts, the Public, and the Law Explosion*, ed. Jones.

[26] Peltason, *op. cit.*, p. 54.

ADMINISTRATION OF CRIMINAL JUSTICE

There is, of course, a long tradition of sociological research in the areas of criminology and penology. Sophisticated criminologists have recognized that in a sense, since crimes are "established" through laws, the legal aspect of crime is central. Thus Sutherland and Cressey hold criminology to include within its scope "the processes of making laws, of breaking laws, and of reacting toward the breaking of laws. These processes are three aspects of a somewhat unified sequence of interactions."[27] Yet American research on crime has until very recently been almost totally preoccupied with studying only the breaking of laws (and more specifically the individuals who break laws). Studies of prisons represented the primary effort to assess the processes of "reacting toward the breaking of laws." The notion that the law itself was a significant indicator of society's reaction to particular forms of behavior was generally slighted. As Hermann Mannheim stated:

> We have made considerable efforts to discover what sort of person the offender is and why he has broken the law, and we rack our brains to find out what to do with him. . . . Hardly ever do we pause for a moment to examine critically the contents of that very law the existence of which alone makes it possible for the individual to offend against it.[28]

Nor was there much direct interest in enforcement processes, as such.

Deviance and Societal Reactions

There is a developing reaction, in deviance studies, against the earlier and almost exclusive concentration on the personal and social characteristics of individual offenders. For a long time, the major research method in criminology involved comparing a "sample" of institutionalized or otherwise readily identifiable "offenders" with a matched sample of supposed "nonoffenders." Not only are sociologists becoming more alert to the methodological deficiencies of this procedure (it is now pretty well accepted that such samples are not in fact representative of *actual* offenders and nonoffenders), but increasingly they are also questioning the theoretical assumptions underlying the earlier work. In particular, there is now a greater willingness than before to abandon what has been termed the "assumption of differentiation"[29]—the belief that deviating individuals (apart from their deviance) significantly differ in their personal characteristics from nondeviating individuals, and that such differentness somehow accounts for their deviance. On the contrary, it is now being maintained that the dis-

---

[27] Edwin Sutherland and Donald Cressey, *Principles of Criminology*, 7th ed. (Philadelphia: Lippincott, 1966), p. 3. See also Gresham Sykes, *Crime and Society* (New York: Random House, 1956), chap. 1.

[28] Hermann Mannheim, *Criminal Justice and Social Reconstruction* (New York: Oxford University Press, 1946), p. 1.

[29] David Matza, *Delinquency and Drift* (New York: Wiley, 1964), chap. 1.

tinguishing characteristic of deviating individuals is the very fact of their having been socially defined as deviant. In this view, deviance is essentially characterized not by "causal factors" but by processes of social definition. As Howard S. Becker puts it:

> Deviance is *not* a quality of the act the person commits, but rather a consequence of the application by others of rules and sanctions to an "offender." The deviant is one to whom that label has successfully been applied; deviant behavior is behavior that people so label.[30]

If one adopts this approach, then the "audience" of reactors, rather than the deviating individual, becomes the crucial object of research.[31] While this perspective is being given renewed emphasis today, it has in fact a substantial heritage in sociological theory—both in such general formulations as the "self-fulfilling prophecy" and in more specific analyses of the social functions of deviance and conflict.[32] In any event, focus on the labeling process is bound to direct increased attention to the ongoing behavior that indeed constitutes the administration of criminal justice. Just as societal reactions "cause" deviance, so also sociolegal reactions (or the "criminalization of deviance," as this writer put it in *Crimes Without Victims*) in a sense cause "criminal" behavior or at least shape problems of crime. Whereas the key research question used to be, "Why does A commit crimes, while B does not?" today sociologists are more and more asking, "Why does society label X behavior a crime?" "What specific processes and reacting agencies are involved in this labeling?" and "What are the social consequences, particularly in terms of the development of criminal self-images and role commitment, of attaching this label to X behavior?"

The consequences of imposing criminal sanctions may be considerable, quite apart from the specific and intended punishments that may be inflicted at any stage in the sanctioning process. Prosecution for a criminal offense constitutes a "status-degradation ceremony," which has the capacity to produce significant modifications of personal identity. As Harold Garfinkel notes:

> The work of the denunciation effects the recasting of the objective character of the perceived other: The other person becomes in the eyes of his condemners literally a different and new person. . . . The former identity stands as accidental; the new identity is the "basic reality." What he is now is what, "after all," he was all along.[33]

---

[30] Howard S. Becker, *Outsiders* (New York: Free Press, 1963), p. 9.

[31] Kai T. Erikson, "Notes on the Sociology of Deviance," *Social Problems,* 9 (Spring 1962): 307–314.

[32] A classic criminological statement on "labeling" is Frank Tannenbaum's discussion of the "dramatization of evil" (early stigmatization of youngsters as delinquent), in *Crime and the Community* (New York: Columbia University Press, 1957). A major statement of deviance theory in processual terms is Edwin Lemert, *Social Pathology* (New York: McGraw-Hill, 1951).

[33] Harold Garfinkel, "Conditions of Successful Degradation Ceremonies," *American Journal of Sociology,* 61 (March 1956): 421–22.

Likewise, research on prisons, and on other "total institutions" such as mental hospitals, indicates that a severe process of "mortification" and stripping persons of their identity is one of the most significant features of life in such an environment.[34] Sometimes the adverse consequences of labeling deeds as crimes may even be felt by individuals who have no direct contact with official agencies of law enforcement. Thus, in *Crimes Without Victims*, the present writer suggests that the mere knowledge that one's behavior has been socially defined as criminal may have important effects on an individual's self-conceptions and behavior.

That the ramifications of this labeling extend well beyond the law-enforcement processes themselves was documented in a field experiment testing the responses of potential employers to an individual's past prosecution for crime.[35] A researcher, purporting to be an employment agent, presented to one hundred prospective employers at resort hotels information concerning an applicant for an unskilled job. Similar information was given in all instances except with respect to the applicant's involvement with the law: twenty-five employers were shown a record indicating no such involvement; twenty-five others saw a record indicating trial and acquittal on an assault charge and including a letter from the judge certifying acquittal and reminding readers of the presumption of innocence; in another twenty-five instances, trial and acquittal for assault were similarly revealed but without a judge's letter; and finally twenty-five employers were confronted wtih a record of trial and conviction on the assault charge. Nine of the employers receiving the "no record" folder responded positively to the applicant; among employers shown the folder containing the acquittal plus the judge's letter, there were six positive reactions. Only three of the employers learning of acquittal without the judge's letter indicated they would consider the applicant, and but a single employer among those receiving the "conviction" folder expressed any interest in him. On the other hand, in a related inquiry reported by the same authors, doctors who had been sued for malpractice did not (at least as inferred from interviews with them) experience serious occupational curtailment or harm. While recognizing that the two studies were not strictly comparable, Schwartz and Skolnick concluded that the difference in status (including professional group support) might account for the contrasting sets of consequences in the two situations. On the other hand, as a critic noted, the different kinds of proceedings involved in the two inquiries (criminal prosecution for an act of violence in the one case, and civil suit for professional misconduct in the other) may well have influenced the results.[36] At any rate, the research seems to indicate that the formal legal

---

[34] Erving Goffman, *Asylums* (New York: Anchor Books, 1961).
[35] Richard D. Schwartz and Jerome H. Skolnick, "Two Studies of Legal Stigma," *Social Problems*, 10 (Fall 1962): 133–42.
[36] See comments of H. Laurence Ross, and rejoinder by Richard D. Schwartz and Jerome H. Skolnick, *Social Problems*, 10 (Spring 1963): 390–92.

distinctions between accusation and conviction, and the presumption of innocence that supposedly applies in the absence of the latter, are considerably less potent as shapers of real social action than as abstract legal principles.

Enforcement Discretion

A matter that has been of special interest to legal analysts of the criminal process is the discretion accorded officials at various stages of enforcement as to which procedures shall be followed from that point on, and even as to whether further proceedings of any sort shall occur.[37] In the past, sociologists were concerned with this discretion primarily because of the effect it had on official criminal statistics, leading to "case mortality" at each stage and hence rendering statistics about conviction and especially about prisoners quite misleading. There was also some interest in the fact that informal deals were made in the administration of criminal justice, with the result that a "bargain" model of criminal justice might be applicable.[38] Recently there has been a significant increase in intensive research on these informal social processes underlying the formal structure of criminal-law administration.

A good illustration of this work is provided by a recent report of observational research into the nature of police officers' contacts with juveniles.[39] Because of the philosophy and practice of our juvenile court system, the extent of discretionary power resting with officials at almost every stage is even greater in juvenile cases than in those dealing with adult offenders. In an intensive study of police work with juveniles, Piliavin and Briar noted the officer's discretion to invoke a variety of alternative dispositions, ranging from outright release to arrest and confinement in a juvenile detention center. Their study revealed that both the decision as to whether to bring a boy into the police station in the first place and the subsequent decision as to which particular disposition to invoke were based largely on

> . . . cues which emerged from the interaction between the officer and
> the youth, cues from which the officer inferred the youth's character.
> These cues included the youth's group affiliations, age, race, grooming,
> dress, and demeanor. Older juveniles, members of known delinquent
> gangs, Negroes, youths with well-oiled hair, black jackets, and soiled
> denims or jeans (the presumed uniform of "tough" boys), and boys who

---

[37] Joseph Goldstein, "Police Discretion Not to Invoke the Criminal Process: Low Visibility Decisions in the Administration of Justice," *Yale Law Journal*, 69 (1960): 543–94; and Sanford Kadish, "Legal Norms and Discretion in the Police and Sentencing Processes," *Harvard Law Review*, 75 (March 1962): 904–931.

[38] Donald J. Newman, "Pleading Guilty for Consideration: A Study of Bargain Justice," *Journal of Criminal Law, Criminology, and Police Science*, 46 (March–April 1956): 780–90.

[39] Irving Piliavin and Scott Briar, "Police Encounters with Juveniles," *American Journal of Sociology*, 70 (September 1964): 206–214.

in their interactions with officers did not manifest what were considered to be appropriate signs of respect tended to receive the more severe dispositions.

Other than prior record, the most important of the above clues was a youth's *demeanor*.[40]

As the authors point out, such reliance on stereotypes may have self-fulfilling consequences, leading not only to closer surveillance of Negro and other supposedly "tough" youths (with consequent higher rates of apprehension and disposition of them), but also to increased hostility of entire social categories of juveniles toward law and law enforcers with the likelihood of real increases in offending behavior.

There are signs that the growing interest in the sociology of law, together with the societal-reactions emphasis in deviance studies, are combining to generate a comprehensive body of sociological knowledge about police and other enforcement practices. To such important but somewhat isolated early studies as William Westley's analysis of the police use of violence[41] are being added new theoretical contributions, such as Stinchcombe's recent treatment of the relation between police practice and institutions of privacy in a society,[42] as well as increasingly systematic and long-term observational and survey research. Jerome Skolnick's book *Justice Without Trial*,[43] based on intensive observational studies, provides a wealth of valuable data about the police, with special attention to practices in the area of the enforcement of laws against "vice." Attempting to sketch the policeman's "working personality," the author considers the general position of the police within the social structure, the pressures and exigencies of the police role, and the values and situational factors that determine patterns of everyday police activity. Emphasizing elements of discretion in the enforcement process, Skolnick goes on to discuss thoroughly police behavior relating to such matters as processing of traffic violations, narcotics control, burglary, and prostitution. He considers in some detail the use of informers and police decoys and the issues surrounding search-and-seizure—matters that should be of sociological as well as legal interest, since behavior of this sort is central to enforcement activity in certain areas of the criminal law. In his general discussion, Skolnick illuminates the ways in which the values of public order and the rule of law may come into conflict and the mechanisms through which the police attempt to reconcile such conflict and at the same time act in a way that is

---

[40] *Ibid.*, p. 210.

[41] William A. Westley, "Violence and the Police," *American Journal of Sociology*, 49 (August 1953): 34–41.

[42] Arthur L. Stinchcombe, "Institutions of Privacy in the Determination of Police Administrative Practice," *American Journal of Sociology*, 69 (September 1963): 150–60.

[43] Jerome H. Skolnick, *Justice Without Trial: Law Enforcement in Democratic Society* (New York: Wiley, 1966). See also David J. Bordua, *The Police: Six Sociological Essays* (New York: Wiley, 1967).

consistent with their own professional values and social perspectives. Also noteworthy in Skolnick's work is the concept of a "criminal law community"—a fairly close-knit, interacting network of judges, lawyers, police, and other officials involved in the enforcement and adjudication process —which must be examined in its entirety by the researcher if the constituent elements are to be fully understood.

The workings of such a community are further revealed in a recent report on extended observation of the work of a public defender's office.[44] Notwithstanding the ostensible role of the public defender as the protector of the indigent in their dealings with the apparatus of prosecution, it may well be that the relationship between the defender and the prosecutor is much closer than that between the defender and his client. Noting, in line with the concept of "bargain justice" mentioned above, that most cases are settled by a plea of guilty, Sudnow discloses that the public defender rarely prepares to try cases in the conventionally understood sense of seeking to win. Rather, his efforts are concentrated on securing an appropriate "deal," the possibilities for which are more or less routinely established through past dealings with the cooperating prosecutors. In this connection, his contact with the client need be only extremely limited and is largely aimed at placing the particular offense within one of a variety of categories through which he has come to conceptualize "typical" offense patterns. Such "normal crimes" represent "knowledge of the typical manner in which offenses of given classes are committed, the social characteristics of the persons who regularly commit them, the features of the settings in which they occur, the types of victims often involved, and the like."[45]

Significantly, in this study the public defender was found to share with the prosecutor the presumption that individuals coming before the courts are in fact guilty of the offenses charged. Rather than "defending the interests" of such persons, as the ideal legal norms would have it, the defender's office essentially represents one cog in the machinery by which charged individuals are "processed." The defender is part of the team that accomplishes this processing and is not particularly interested in challenging the system:

> . . . the district attorney, and the county which employs them both, can rely on the P.D. not to attempt to morally degrade police officers in cross examination; not to impeach the state's witnesses by trickery; not to attempt an exposition of the entrapment methods of narcotics agents; not to condemn the community for the "racial prejudice that produces our criminals" (the phrase of a private attorney during closing argument); not to challenge the prosecution of "these women who are trying to raise a family without a husband" (the statement of another private attorney during closing argument on a welfare fraud

---

[44] David Sudnow, "Normal Crimes: Sociological Features of the Penal Code in a Public Defender Office," *Social Problems*, 12 (Winter 1965): 255–76.
[45] *Ibid.,* p. 259.

case); in sum, not to make an issue of the moral character of the administrative machinery of the local courts, the community or the police. He will not cause any serious trouble for the routine motion of the court conviction process.[46]

Clearly these recent intensive researches into underlying processes in criminal justice are highly relevant for our understanding of the legal system in action. No examination of substance and procedure in the field of criminal law can be completely satisfactory, unless it takes into account the emergence (largely through informal interaction between individuals occupying the related roles that constitute the system of criminal justice) of working patterns of accommodation to situational imperatives and of routinized modes of everyday operation. Such developing patterns reflect or even generate a significant amount of strain between ideal and actual legal norms. They reveal, in particular, that it is difficult for the legal system to do all things for all people (no matter how contradictory the desired functions of the system may be) at the same time. This difficulty is most clearly brought out in Skolnick's discussion of the tremendous strain imposed on the system by the effort to institutionalize both "law" (in the sense of adherence to high standards of procedural legality) and "order" (in the sense of protection of the public from direct harm and outrage) through police activities.

Also glaringly evident in these patterns is the intersection between the legal order and the general system of social stratification, partly discussed earlier. Wherever informal "justice" dominates the proceedings, the widening of official discretion provides room for social stereotypes and even prejudices to come into play. We have seen this tendency quite clearly in police encounters with juveniles, and it is an element of serious risk attaching to all discretionary police activity. The stratification factor itself has, in certain ways, been institutionalized as an impediment to evenly dispensed criminal justice. Apart from the systematic "legal" discrimination against Negroes in some American jurisdictions, the most blatant example of this process may be the continuing inequities built into the administration of bail. As Ronald Goldfarb has noted:

> Millions of men and women are, through the American bail system, held each year in "ransom" in American jails, committed to prison cells often for prolonged periods before trial. Because they are poor or friendless, they may spend days, weeks, or months in confinement, often to be acquitted of wrongdoing in the end. A man is accused of stealing a few dollars from a subway change-booth, spends six months in jail before trial, and is finally acquitted. . . . His only crime is poverty—he could not afford the $105 fee for a bondsman to put up the $2,500 bond set by the judge. . . . Yet a man with means, accused of far more serious crimes and eventually to be found guilty, may have

---

[46] *Ibid.*, p. 273.

to spend no time in jail before trial; his only virtue the fact that he could pay his way out of jail and wait comfortably at home for his trial to begin.[47]

As Goldfarb also points out, in the discretion to set bail lies the power to punish (before trial) individuals or groups that are particularly troublesome or unpalatable to the social establishment (civil-rights demonstrators and pacifists may be two examples). In actual practice, the manifest function of bail, to secure the subsequent appearance of the defendant, often has been lost sight of, with a resulting increase in social pain to individuals, which is often completely unjustified, and an unnecessary expense to society. Alternatives to the bail system—such as the Manhattan Bail Project, in which intensive interviews with detainees are used to establish those individuals who constitute good risks, and under which many who would previously have been held are now released on their own recognizance[48] —are bound to influence the patterns of criminal justice in action, and should therefore be of interest to the sociologist.

STYLES OF LEGAL WORK

Another avenue to an understanding of the law in action involves studying the organization and routine work patterns of the legal profession. As was mentioned earlier, some of the current sociological interest in the legal system developed out of research focused on the general analysis of occupations and professions. From this standpoint a broad array of sociological concepts may be applicable to analyzing the positions and work of the individuals who man the legal order—ranging from "professional self-image" to occupational "role set," from "recruitment" and "socialization" to colleague relationships and possible "role conflicts." Similarly, at least for other than lone practitioners, organization theory may be relevant, with such concepts as "bureaucracy," organizational "commitment," and organizational "goals" coming into play.

It has been suggested by at least one legal critic that research along these lines may produce an overly narrow concentration on certain small-scale and mundane aspects of the realm of law. Thus, it is argued that law is much more than simply what lawyers do and further that the lawyer's role is, in some essential aspects, not at all like other occupational and professional roles. Hazard states that "the term 'lawyer' refers less to a social function than to a type of training, a type which in fact is shared by people doing a bewildering variety of tasks." The same writer also insists that for

---

[47] Ronald Goldfarb, *Ransom: A Critique of the American Bail System* (New York: Harper & Row, 1965), p. 1.
[48] *Ibid.*, chap. 5.

full understanding of legal work one must recognize that with respect to any important legal problem "there is a long, a rich and a demanding intellectual culture."[49] Certainly it is true, and most sociologists accept the fact, that lawyers operate in a great many different settings, that any conception of *the* lawyer (believed to apply to the entire profession) would be misleading. Likewise, sophisticated social analysts are aware of both the relevant heritage of legal philosophy and the significant technical formulations embodied in the legal system. Yet these factors do not vitiate an investigation of law as a profession. Such research represents one of a number of complementary, rather than mutually exclusive, approaches to the study of legal institutions. Nor is it an absolute prerequisite for such research that the sociologist have extensive training in the law. Clearly, some familiarity with legal substance and procedure will be of great help to the investigator. At the same time, it should be kept in mind that to require of the researcher lengthy formal and technical training in the discipline or occupational field to be investigated would greatly hamper sociological research in any number of fields, such as the sociology of science, of medicine, of religion, and indeed the social analysis of any occupation or profession. There is no greater need for specialized knowledge in studying the legal profession than in these other instances. Of course, a very good argument can be made for better communication and more cooperative interaction between sociologists and lawyers; cross-disciplinary team research will often provide a useful means of averting some of the problems just mentioned.

We have already seen that there is a very real social stratification within the legal profession, and that the lawyer's general standing and specific work patterns may be partly determined by his social background and type of legal education. The interplay between the numerous variables involved here is complex, but the overall relationship between recruitment and professional role is well summarized in the following statement: "Social background prescribes two major career contingencies: level of technical skill and access to clients."[50] Whereas all lawyers theoretically share a common body of technical knowledge and special skills, as well as a dual commitment to serve the client (in a personal and confidential relationship) and the public (as "servant of the court"), in practice there is an enormous amount of variation not only in what particular types of lawyers do but also in how they relate to their clients and other individuals and agencies and in how they view their professional roles. If we examine actual work situations, a few dominant patterns emerge.

---

[49] Geoffrey C. Hazard, Jr., "Reflections on Four Studies of the Legal Profession," in *Law and Society*, supplement to *Social Problems*, 13 (Summer 1965): 50, 51.

[50] Jack Ladinsky, "Careers of Lawyers, Law Practice, and Legal Institutions," *American Sociological Review*, 28 (February 1963): 53.

The Large Law Firm

The major law firms maintain a position of considerable power in modern American society. They wield a substantial influence in the business community and on public policy in general. Members of such firms tend to be held in high social esteem. Under these circumstances, it is probably not surprising that the large, well-established firms tend to recruit as new members individuals of relatively high socioeconomic status. Members of large firms are much more likely than are members of small firms or individual practitioners to be Protestant; to have fathers who were in business, managerial, or professional positions; to have attended an Ivy League or other high-quality college; and to have attended (and done well at) one of the major, nationally known law schools or at least some other full-time, university-connected law school (as compared with nonuniversity-connected and night law schools).[51] In particular, a man who obtains top grades (and is on the "law review," the prestigeful and influential student-edited journal) at the top, nationally known schools (primarily Harvard, Yale, and Columbia) may be "ticketed for life as a first-class passenger on the escalator for talent." As David Riesman goes on to comment, there is a "self-confirming myth" in legal education, in which the law-review men get the top jobs, make the contacts, and gain the experience necessary for advancement, and hence attain a success that "proves" that the law-school marking system (which, in the first year, determines law-review membership) is an accurate indicator of talent. At an early point in their training, such men gain a high level of confidence and the conviction that they are destined for important jobs.[52]

This conviction is usually upheld through their work experience in the large firms. As one observer puts it, "What the Wall Street lawyers do in their professional capacity is nothing less than to provide prudential and technical assistance in the management of the private sector of the world economy."[53] Surveys reveal significant differences in work patterns and clientele between large-firm lawyers on the one hand and small-firm members and individual practictioners on the other. The former are more likely than the latter to serve business clients (mainly large corporations in the field of heavy industry and finance) and wealthy, Protestant individual clients, to have an overwhelming concentration of work in the areas of business and probate law, to spend much less time in court, and to deal with federal and appellate courts (rather than local ones) when such contact does occur. There is also a pronounced pattern of higher income for lawyers in the larger firms.[54]

[51] Jerome Carlin, *Lawyers' Ethics* (New York: Russell Sage Foundation, 1966), chap. 2, "The Social Structure of the Metropolitan Bar"; and Ladinsky, *op. cit.*

[52] David Riesman, "Law and Sociology: Recruitment, Training, and Colleagueship," in *Law and Sociology*, ed. Evan.

[53] Hazard, *op. cit.*, p. 53.

[54] Carlin, *Lawyers' Ethics;* and Ladinsky, *op. cit.*

At the very top of the bar's status hierarchy, in the major New York firms described in Smigel's *The Wall Street Lawyer*, the lawyer deals almost exclusively with the corporate and financial problems of big business. Here too the incoming lawyer gains membership in a substantial organization, which is impressive in its own right. He finds himself part of an establishment that may occupy three or four floors of a downtown office building and that may comprise as many as 50 to 150 lawyers and up to 250 nonprofessional staff. The firm is likely to have a long and renowned history, an atmosphere all its own, and an almost tangible aura of importance. Lawyers in the firm hold positions within a well-elaborated hierarchy—as reflected in the distribution of income and general prestige in the allocation of status symbols, such as office space, secretaries, and so forth, and of professional tasks and responsibilities. Although the young lawyer's initial work may be of a segmental or highly specialized variety, not involving direct contact with clients and perhaps dealing with only one small facet of a broader matter, he is likely at once to be impressed by the wealth and power of the clients and the sizable nature of their business transactions. Nor is he dealt with as a mere underling. He has been hired for his demonstrated competence and his potential for leadership in the profession, and in many respects he is treated as a colleague, albeit a junior one.[55]

Work in such a setting is not, of course, without its difficulties. Some lawyers feel that the firms engender too early and too great specialization; most of the large firms have separate departments, officially or unofficially, to deal with such areas of work as corporate law, tax law, litigation, and so on. Others find troublesome the very keen competition for advancement to full partnership. Then too, some lawyers may be concerned that the work in the impersonal bureaucratic setting seems to have little relation to the ideal of the lawyer as a "free professional," as a free-wheeling and confidential adviser to trusting clients. A few of the lawyers may even be defensive about the close ties between the Wall Street firms and big business and conscious of the fact that the bulk of their work contributes little to protecting the underdog, an important theme in popular conceptions of the lawyer's role. And notwithstanding the firms' attempts to maintain a spirit of colleagueship, the fact that they are salaried employees who must in the last analysis take orders is disturbing to some. Finally, the pervasive pressures to conform—personally, socially, and even politically—may cause irritation.[56]

For most of its members most of the time, however, the large law firm provides good earnings, excellent experience, and satisfying work. The prospect of a partnership holds out the possibility of a really sizable in-

---

[55] Erwin O. Smigel, *The Wall Street Lawyer* (New York: Free Press, 1964).

[56] *Ibid.*, chap. 10, "Strains and Dilemmas." For excellent fictional accounts of life and work in the large law firm, see Louis Auchincloss, *Powers of Attorney* (Boston: Houghton Mifflin, 1963).

come combined with enormous prestige and entrée to the inner circles of the corporate and financial worlds. And for those not destined to achieve partnership, or for those who may be dissatisfied with the firm for one reason or another, there is the possibility of using their positions in the large firm as stepping stones to other favorable situations—in industry, government, teaching, or in somewhat smaller but still very successful law firms.

Individual Practice

Sharply contrasting with the situation of the elite, large-firm lawyer is that of the typical individual practitioner in a large city. As we have already seen, there are significant differences between lawyers in the two types of practice, both in social background and in the kinds of work they do and the success they achieve. The lone practitioner is likely to be the son of an immigrant, who has worked his way up; he is likely to have attended either a "proprietary" or a Catholic night law school and not to have completed college, which at one time was not always a requirement for admission to such law schools. At least at the lower levels of individual practice, he is earning a precarious living, and his clientele tends to be a transient one of lower-income individuals. His legal work involves mainly small-scale and routine business matters and litigation between individuals. His contact with agencies and courts (the latter being particularly frequent) tends to be at the local level. As Jerome Carlin points out in *Lawyers on Their Own*, an important study of individual practice in Chicago, these men constitute something like a "lower class" of the metropolitan bar. Their practice consists largely of "those residual matters (and clients) that the large firms have not pre-empted"—such as matters too inconsequential (financially or otherwise) for such firms to handle, and "the undesirable cases, the dirty work, those areas of practice that have associated with them an aura of influencing and fixing and that involve arrangements with clients and others that are felt by the large firms to be professionally damaging. The latter category includes local tax, municipal, personal injury, divorce, and criminal matters."[57]

Carlin distinguishes between upper-level and lower-level individual practitioners; the former may have a more stable and secure small-business clientele for whom they perform a wider range of less routine services. It is primarily the lower-level solo practitioners who are bogged down in the dirty work of the law, whose financial circumstances are perilous, and for whom getting business represents a continuous battle.

At the outset, many lawyers trying to establish practices of their own

---

[57] Jerome E. Carlin, *Lawyers on Their Own* (New Brunswick, N.J.: Rutgers University Press, 1962), pp. 17–18; generally, on the background and work of these lawyers, see chaps. 1–3.

are closely tied to the local neighborhood, a situation that few find satis-factory. As a fairly successful neighborhood practitioner told Carlin:

> "People don't look at the neighborhood lawyer as on the same profes-sional level as the lawyer in the Loop—but on the same level as service people, real estate and insurance brokers, and similar types of nonpro-fessional categories. He's looked at more as a neighborhood business-man rather than as a professional. Doctors don't have that problem; you don't consider Loop doctors to be on a completely different level."[58]

Going beyond the neighborhood, the solo lawyer seeks contact with po-tential clients through membership in a range of communal organizations, which usually have an ethnic or religious basis. Politics is also seen as a use-ful means of extending one's clientele, as well as developing helpful court and other official contacts. But often these methods are insufficient, and it becomes necessary to rely on individuals who, for one reason or another, may be in a position to channel legal business in his direction. As Carlin notes, such a "broker" (between lawyer and client) may be "another lawyer, an accountant, a real estate or insurance broker or agent, a building contrac-tor, a doctor, a policeman, bondsman, precinct captain, garage mechanic, minister, undertaker, plant personnel director, foreman, etc."[59] Personal injury cases often are referred by a variety of individuals who may serve as "runners"; waitresses and bar girls may refer divorce matters, policemen criminal matters. At the same time, and especially in connection with wills, business, and real estate matters, these lawyers face continuous and increas-ingly strong competition from nonlegal sources, such as banks, real estate brokers, and accountants. These competitors often have the edge in both specialized skill and visibility; and as Carlin points out, the lawyer cannot today claim exclusive access to the agencies that process the matters in question.

Apart from the sheer difficulty of earning a decent living under these circumstances, the less sucessful of the individual practitioners experience a generalized and severe status dilemma. Whereas "law appeared to provide the easiest and cheapest avenue to professional status . . . they find that ac-cess to the higher status positions is all but closed to them and that the positions they do manage to achieve are often marginal, their practice residual, and their foothold in the profession precarious."[60] Not only is much of their work relatively insignificant by the dominant standards of the profession, but they have very little contact (and virtually no sense of real colleagueship) with the more successful, large-firm lawyers. Individual prac-titioners rarely attain positions of leadership in the bar, and in fact they

---

[58] *Ibid.*, p. 125.
[59] *Ibid.*, pp. 135–36.
[60] *Ibid.*, p. 173.

are not even as likely as large-firm lawyers to maintain membership in the leading professional associations, often finding it more valuable to be active in the smaller, ethnic bar associations. While solo lawyers can at least pride themselves on being their own bosses, most seem to recognize that this independence is a very mixed blessing.[61]

Of course, it must be kept in mind that the "Wall Street lawyer" and the lower-level individual practitioner represent the extreme points of a continuum along which legal practices vary. In between are numerous gradations involving membership in a variety of middle-sized and small firms, many of which are very successful and handle a considerable range of interesting legal work. Also, it should be noted that there certainly are some individuals who practice on their own and attain a high degree of success, both financially and in terms of professional standing. This attainment may occur particularly when a lawyer develops a reputation for great skill in a highly specialized field, such as patent law, literary property, civil liberties, or even matrimonial or criminal law. Indeed, all of the comments made thus far concerning stratification within the metropolitan bar must be recognized as reflecting statistical regularities only. They refer to large classes of individual instances, and to each generalization there are undoubtedly specific exceptions.

Furthermore, the major studies of legal practice have concentrated almost exclusively on lawyers in the largest metropolitan centers. As Carlin mentions, "In comparison with the highly stratified metropolitan bar, the smaller city bar has over the years remained a fairly homogeneous professional community." Attributing this homogeneity partly to the absence of huge "law factories," he noted that (in 1958) there were no firms with as many as fifteen lawyers in American cities of less than 200,000 population, and very few with more than five or six lawyers.[62] Similarly, there has been virtually no sociological analysis of the position and functions of the small-town lawyer. Legal practice in such a setting undoubtedly varies a good deal from that of the lone practioner in the metropolis. It is quite possible that some lawyers in small towns may be able satisfactorily to combine the independence of individual practice with a considerable measure of financial success and professional and social standing within the local community.[63] Other varieties of legal work—including positions in government agencies, in prosecutor's and legal-aid offices, and as "house counsel" on corporation staffs—also deserve further attention from researchers. Undoubtedly each type of legal practice has its peculiar recruitment and work patterns, compensations, drawbacks, strains, and dilemmas.

---

[61] *Ibid.*, chap. 5, "The Anatomy of Dissatisfaction."

[62] *Ibid.*, pp. 23, 39.

[63] For an interesting fictional portrayal of the lawyer in a small community, see James Gould Cozzens, *The Just and the Unjust* (New York: Harcourt, Brace & World, 1942).

Legal Ethics and Role Strain

Within any profession, just as within society in general, there is always a problem of social control. While dominant norms regulating behavior may provide a workable amount of stability, there is never complete consensus about them nor full adherence to them. Considering the various and sometimes conflicting personal and societal expectations of the lawyer, it is not surprising that there are, as Parsons has noted, certain strains in his professional role that may lead to deviant behavior.[64] Conflicts of interest, and hence a built-in likelihood of committing some impropriety, seem to stalk the lawyer wherever he goes. He is supposed to act in a cool, dignified manner befitting a professional man, yet he is called upon to deal with human problems often baffling in their complexity and sometimes heavily freighted with conflict, irrationality, exploitation, cruelty, or greed. His reasonable interest in earning a good living is perpetually challenged by his fiduciary role as a trusted agent. Often he is privy to information about his clients or their business that he could easily turn to his own financial advantage, yet the interest of the client must always override his own.

Sometimes conflicting too will be the lawyer's obligation to the client and his role as a public servant. In the criminal law, the possibilities for such conflict are ever present. A criminal court seeks the facts and aims at judgments designed to maximize societal interests; yet under our adversary system the proceeding cannot go beyond those facts brought forth by the parties, and each party is committed to presenting the best possible case for its side. To what extent, under these circumstances, is the defense lawyer obligated to provide full disclosure of all facts in his possession? What are the ethics governing the lawyer's intentionally conveying a misleading or false impression in a criminal trial? These are questions that have yet to be answered definitely and to the satisfaction of all legal experts.[65] Conflict between obligation to the client and to the public may also arise in connection with business matters and other noncriminal legal work. The lawyer advising a corporation in the preparation of a securities prospectus is supposed not only to be safeguarding the interests of his client, but also to be indirectly helping to ensure that the securities-buying public is protected against misrepresentation. Without doubt, the strain on the lawyer imposed by this sort of situation is most glaringly evident in the field of tax law. There is in our present legal system but a tenuous line between the more or less institutionalized game of "tax avoidance" and the

---

[64] Talcott Parsons, "The Law and Social Control," in *Law and Sociology*, ed. Evan.

[65] See articles by law professor Monroe H. Freedman and others to appear in a forthcoming issue of the *University of Michigan Law Review*, concerning the question of whether defense lawyers in criminal cases always must be truthful and candid in court (reported in *Boston Globe*, June 5, 1966, p. A–5). See also Walter F. Murphy and C. Herman Pritchett, *Courts, Judges and Politics* (New York: Random House, 1961), chap. 9, "The Bar."

socially and legally proscribed behavior known as "tax evasion." In one sense, tax evasion may sometimes be little more than an effort at avoidance that doesn't work. Of course, this is a bit of an oversimplification; the sensible (and secure) lawyer advises prudence and follows the many specific legal guidelines that are available to him. But as Parsons points out, the lawyer is expected to be "both permissive and supportive in his relation with his clients," and yet at the same time he must often "resist their pressures and get them to realize some of the hard facts of their situations."[66] It should be clear that such a complex undertaking, even for a lawyer who is unusually skillful and subtle in interpersonal relations and in legal craftsmanship, can generate serious ethical dilemmas and produce a great deal of tension and strain.

Having in mind the dual concept of the lawyer as a "free professional" and a public servant, and in line with that independence of the legal profession that is often considered a key feature of a system grounded in the rule of law, the profession has long sought to regulate conduct within its own ranks through a formal system of social control embodying stated ethical norms (canons of legal ethics) and machinery for their enforcement. The operation of this system is now coming under empirical investigation by sociologists. As mentioned earlier, an important study by Jerome Carlin, based on a survey of the New York City bar, has revealed a "moral division of labor" in which patterns of adherence to and deviation from these stated norms relate closely to stratification within the profession.[67] Asked how they had behaved or would behave in a variety of situations of ethical conflict, most lawyers in large firms (fifteen or more lawyers) turned out to be high conformers to the ethical canons. There was decreasing conformity among members of medium-sized firms (five to fourteen lawyers), small firms (fewer than five lawyers) and individual practitioners. (Carlin also found that the formal grievance machinery of the bar association was not the effective control mechanism; rather, a combination of inner disposition, client pressure, court and agency atmosphere, and colleague controls operated to permit or deter violations.)

Although the large-firm lawyer may encounter substantial temptation to deviate, his financial security and the relative stability of his clientele enable him to sustain a cultural pattern in which serious ethical violations may be considered out of the question. The individual practitioner, on the other hand, has both opportunity to transgress and little motivation to conform. Not only is he subjected to severe economic problems but he has no stable clientele on which to rely. Since he must constantly be concerned with attracting business, he is heavily dependent on the activities of nonprofessional intermediaries. And the clientele he does attract often requires

---

[66] Parsons, *op. cit.*, p. 69.
[67] Carlin, *Lawyers' Ethics.*

that he act in manipulative and ethically questionable ways in order to secure compliance or even mere action on the part of minor officials. It is hardly surprising, under these circumstances, that individual practitioners often tend to view law as a business rather than as a profession. Carlin found, in his Chicago study, that "close to half the respondents were unable to say without hesitation that the practice of law is a profession and a little over a fourth, including practically all the lawyers in the personal injury field, were clearly convinced that it is not."[68]

As this last point suggests, the substance and administration of particular fields of law may crucially affect the propensity to violate ethical norms. Personal injury suits—in which the client is typically a one-shot proposition and in which a "contingent fee" arrangement (the lawyer gets a percentage of the verdict) usually prevails—breed not only improper solicitation of legal business and the stirring up of litigation (both proscribed by the canons of ethics) but also active efforts to misrepresent evidence, and other types of ethical violation.[69] Recognition of these tendencies, along with the desire to reduce court congestion and delay for the litigant, has led to proposals for new methods of processing automobile accident claims, including schemes modeled on workmen's compensation procedures.

Matrimonial work also introduces ethical dilemmas and imposes considerable strain on the lawyer's image of himself as a dignified professional. In a study of New York lawyers who specialized in matrimonial practice,[70] O'Gorman found widespread criticism of that state's divorce laws, which at that time provided only one ground for divorce, adultery. These laws were held to be unrealistic, to be discriminatory (since the wealthy could go out of state and the poor could not), and systematically to generate deviant behavior. As O'Gorman points out, the need to engage in collusion and perjury in order to establish the necessary evidence of "fault" in such cases (and thus satisfy the client's wish to dissolve the marriage) is a potent source of role conflict and strain for the lawyer. Some of his respondents indicated this strain:

> Ninety percent of the undefended matrimonials are based on perjury. They are all arranged. The raids are made with the consent of the defendant. We all know this. The judges know it. *It's embarrassing to go [to court]*.

> [The laws] are a farce. . . . I have in mind especially the undefended matters before official referees. You have these black nightgown routines with the man in the blue shorts. *I tell you it's insulting to a lawyer*.[71]

---

[68] Carlin, *Lawyers on Their Own*, p. 192.

[69] Kenneth J. Reichstein, "Ambulance Chasing: A Study of Deviation and Control Within the Legal Profession," *Social Problems*, 13 (Summer 1965): 3–17; and Carlin, *Lawyers on Their Own*, pp. 71–91.

[70] Hubert J. O'Gorman, *Lawyers and Matrimonial Cases* (New York: Free Press, 1963).

[71] *Ibid.*, pp. 33, 34. (Italics in original.)

The lawyer's situation in matrimonial cases is further complicated by the need to deal with clients many of whom are in an extremely emotional state and tend to demand extravagant settlements. As in the personal injury field, these conditions have led to proposals for reform of both the substance and procedures of the law. Likewise (and again, a similar situation holds true for personal injury work) many lawyers avoid divorce matters completely or wherever possible. Since O'Gorman's study was conducted, the New York statutes have been revised to allow a number of grounds for divorce rather than the single one that previously existed. A follow-up investigation, after enough time had elapsed for any impact of the change to be felt, might produce some interesting results.

These comments may point up the inadequacy of a sociology of law that either considers legislation outside its realm or determines that the substance of law should never be considered worthy of social investigation. Clearly, there is a reciprocal relationship between the substantive law (including statutes) and the way lawyers go about and react to their work. Just as unworkable criminal legislation puts special pressures on the police, which may significantly influence enforcement behavior and the policeman's professional self-image, substantive law of any sort with which he must deal affects the lawyer's activities and self-conceptions. Thus, in assessing the factors that shape the lawyer's situation, we must add to training, stratification of the bar, and the organization of legal practice, the institutionalized legal arrangements within which he must operate.

THE PUBLIC AND THE LAW

Although the desirability of specific legislation or judicial rulings is not a direct professional concern of sociology, the somewhat elusive interplay between public opinion and the law must be taken into account in any analysis of the legal order.[72] The importance of this relationship is evident in those discussions that stress the "living law" as a necessary grounding for effective legislation, and such importance would more generally seem central to any conception of legal institutions in which the law is seen (at least partly) as a means for achieving identifiable social ends. If research on the effectiveness of specific laws is to have an adequate focus, it is necessary first to know the goals toward which such laws are directed. Thus to the analysis of actual social effects of laws and legal procedures, the sociologist should add research into the relevant public attitudes and understandings. Such research may also have an indirect benefit for policy-makers, some of whom, for example, might agree that "the question, What sorts of behavior

---

[72] See the classic study by A. V. Dicey, *Lectures on the Relation Between Law and Public Opinion in England During the Nineteenth Century* (London: Macmillan, 1905); and more recently Morris Ginsberg, ed., *Law and Opinion in England in the Twentieth Century* (Berkeley: University of California Press, 1959).

should be declared criminal? is one to which the behavioral sciences might contribute vital insights. This they have largely failed to do, and we are the poorer for it."[73] Notwithstanding his recognition that he cannot, as scientist, *answer* basic questions of policy, the sociologist may provide useful data and analysis that will facilitate the process of reaching intelligent answers.

Two recent instances of official and quasi-official decision-making on controversial legal issues illustrate the potential relevance of sociological research of this sort. In connection with a naturalization proceeding, the question was raised whether the individual seeking citizenship (who had deliberately put to death his thirteen-year-old son—blind, mute, and horribly deformed since birth through brain injury—and who for this offense was found guilty of second-degree manslaughter and given a five- to ten-year suspended sentence) could be said to be of "good moral character" as required by the Nationality Act.[74] Asserting that the conduct in question had to be tested against "the generally accepted moral conventions current at the time," Judge Learned Hand, speaking for the court, concluded: "Quite independently of what may be the current moral feeling as to legally administered euthanasia, we feel reasonably secure in holding that only a minority of virtuous persons would deem the practice morally justifiable, while it remains in private hands, even when the provocation is as overwhelming as it was in this instance." He therefore ruled that the petition for naturalization be dismissed, without prejudice to the filing of a new petition, which would, because of the later filing date, avoid consideration of this offense, since the statute only insisted on good moral character for five years prior to the date of petition. Judge Jerome Frank, dissenting, stated his belief that "the attitude of our ethical leaders" would be the most appropriate test in such matters. If, as the governing precedents indicated, general public opinion should be the guide, then, Frank argued, the case should have been remanded to the lower court so the litigants could "bring to the judge's attention reliable information on the subject, which he may supplement in any appropriate way. All the data so obtained should be put on record. On the basis thereof, the judge should reconsider his decision and arrive at a conclusion."[75] Clearly, a systematic survey of opinion might have been of assistance in this situation.

The same kind of problem arose in connection with the deliberations of the American Law Institute concerning a draft provision in its Model Penal Code under which homosexual offenses between consenting adults would not be held criminal. As it turned out, this issue, which was hotly

---

[73] Francis A. Allen, *The Borderland of Criminal Justice* (Chicago: University of Chicago Press, 1964), p. 31.

[74] *Repouille* v. *U.S.*, 165 F. 2d. 152 (2d Cir., 1947); reprinted in Donnelly, Goldstein, and Schwartz, *op. cit.*, pp. 124–26.

[75] *Ibid.*

debated within the Institute, was finally resolved by a vote of its members, who upheld the view that such behavior should be removed from the list of criminal offenses. In subsequent publications, various observers examined this procedure—some insisting that a survey by social scientists would have provided a valuable guide to action, others arguing either that the behavior in question was clearly a violation of moral standards about which no research was necessary, or that in any case public opinion would not necessarily provide a sound basis for formulating principles of criminal law.[76]

A major attempt at "ascertaining the moral sense of the community" by scientific means was made by an interdisciplinary research team at the University of Nebraska. Through interviews with a large sampling of the adult population of that state, the researchers sought public reactions to a variety of issues bearing on the law as it related to the allocation of authority and responsibility between parent and child. While there was not a clear-cut consensus among the respondents on all of the issues, the findings did suggest the existence of a considerable discrepancy between the general tendency of opinion and some of the prevailing legal norms. Above all, this study provides an example (imperfect as it may be in some methodological details) that could suggest to lawmakers some of the ways in which social scientists may assist them.[77]

Several other investigations have focused on public attitudes toward specific provisions of the criminal law. In a 1955 study, a sample of university students was asked to rank in seriousness various hypothetical behaviors that constituted violations of the penal code (of California).[78] In a Michigan study, reported in 1958, a sample composed of three subgroups—a group from the general population, a group of convicts in a Michigan prison, and male students in two criminology classes—ranked in seriousness some nineteen felonies, and imposed hypothetical sentences for the various offenses.[79] Such research may be quite useful in pointing up possible discrepancies between stated norms and public sentiments, particularly with respect to borderline criminal offenses. A recent inquiry, in which the present author's study *Crimes Without Victims* was taken as a point of departure, explored social reactions to such borderline behavior. A sample of adults in the San Francisco Bay Area was questioned regarding information and attitudes relating to abortion, homosexuality, and drug

---

[76] See the materials reprinted in Donnelly, Goldstein, and Schwartz, *op. cit.*, pp. 126–32.

[77] Julius Cohen, Reginald A. H. Robson, and Alan Bates, *Parental Authority: The Community and the Law* (New Brunswick, N.J.: Rutgers University Press, 1958). For critical comment, see Jerome Skolnick, "The Sociology of Law in America: Overview and Trends," in *Law and Society*, supplement to *Social Problems*, 13 (Summer 1965): 31.

[78] Arnold M. Rose and Arthur Prell, "Does the Punishment Fit the Crime? A Study in Social Valuation," *American Journal of Sociology*, 61 (November 1955): 247–59.

[79] G. M. Gilbert, "Crime and Punishment: An Exploratory Comparison of Public, Criminal, and Penological Attitudes," *Mental Hygiene*, 42 (1958): 550–57.

addiction. By concentrating on a few specific types of behavior, this survey was able to elicit considerable information on attitudes toward each. The data also suggested a likely relationship between misconceptions and stereotypes and low tolerance of the deviating behaviors, and they showed an interesting comparison of tolerance levels for the three "offenses." Thus: "Citizens appear to be most tolerant or permissive regarding abortion, less tolerant of proposed changes in laws and practices regarding homosexuals, and least accepting of changes in the handling of drug addicts. This rank order of tolerance for victimless crimes holds for all of the subgroups compared."[80] The study of public information about, and conceptions of, behavior subject to the criminal law takes us one step beyond mere expressions of agreement or disagreement with specific legal provisions. Growing interest in research on attitudes toward, and stereotypes concerning, deviant behavior should indirectly enhance our understanding of some important aspects of our legal system.[81]

So far, most of these investigations have been limited in scope. While they may contribute to policy-making, it should certainly be emphasized that in no sense can they be expected to eliminate the final value assessments that must go into determining whether or not certain behavior should be legally proscribed. At the same time, systematic study of this sort provides a useful antidote to glib statements concerning the state of public opinion on such matters. It is often claimed, without any empirical substantiation, that public opinion simply will not accept a proposed reform, or that "all right-thinking people" condemn a particular form of behavior. Often the law lags behind changes in public opinion, and this lag can be revealed through the social survey. (Of course, the very concept of "lag" here really suggests a value judgment, for we could decide, alternatively, that the law in such situations is preserving worthwhile values that the public is misguidedly abandoning.) On the other hand, social reformists may insist that at certain times the law must move ahead even if it is in advance of public opinion. In any event, it must be recognized that the social scientist has not yet fully convinced the legislator that systematic surveys are a major adjunct to the policy-making process. Sophisticated legal analysts are alert to the technical limitations of such research,[82] while less sophisticated lawyers may still view the social analyst as a perhaps well-meaning but probably misguided interloper in the policy realm.

---

[80] Elizabeth A. Rooney and Don C. Gibbons, "Social Reactions to 'Crimes Without Victims,' " *Social Problems,* 13 (Spring 1966): 407.

[81] See John Kitsuse, "Societal Reaction to Deviance: Problems of Theory and Method," *Social Problems,* 9 (Winter 1962): 249–56; and J. L. Simmons, "Public Stereotypes of Deviants," *Social Problems,* 13 (Fall 1965): 223–32.

[82] W. J. Blum and Harry Kalven, Jr., "The Art of Public Opinion Research: A Lawyer's Appraisal of an Emerging Science," *University of Chicago Law Review,* 24 (1956): 1–12; reprinted in Donnelly, Goldstein, and Schwartz, *op. cit.,* pp. 132–36.

In addition to surveying public opinion relating to specific laws or legal proposals, sociology could usefully explore public understandings and attitudes regarding the legal system in general. Such research would probably reveal considerable ignorance or misunderstanding of legal procedures and substance. Attitudes toward, and feelings about, the overall legal order, and the role of the legal profession, would very likely show variation between different groups and strata in society. We have already seen the value of exploring the distribution within the social system of objective legal needs and of legal services available for meeting those needs. An important and related dimension consists of attitudes and values. Do people believe that lawyers are helping them or exploiting them? Do they think that the legal order is there for their benefit and that it really dispenses justice? What goals do they believe the legal system, and the legal profession, should advance?

We have touched on such issues from time to time throughout this study. It seems evident that conceptions of the legal system will vary according to a person's position in the social structure. For the Negro American, justice all too often appears to be "white man's justice," with the entire legal order being seen as a systematic mechanism for racial oppression. For the lower-class consumer, legal procedure may frequently represent a source of bureaucratic entanglement making an already precarious financial situation even more trying, or a clever device through which unscrupulous dealers take advantage of him. Most likely it is only within the upper socioeconomic strata that there develops the notion of a continuing relationship with a lawyer who serves as a trusted adviser. In the realm of attitudes toward the law and lawyers, we can expect to find a reflection of the "moral division of labor" within the bar itself, which, as we saw, shapes lawyers' attitudes toward their work and their clients. It is interesting that when a middle-class white man literally puts himself in the position of a lower-class Negro, as lawyer-writer William Stringfellow tried to do when he went to live and work in Harlem, he finds it exceedingly difficult to maintain the positive conceptions of the legal system that he previously accepted without reservation.[83] Undoubtedly the nature of actual encounters with legal practitioners, or with their nonprofessional surrogates, and procedures has important bearing on the development of attitudes toward law. Further research concerning such encounters, and the "definitions of the situation" of parties to them, will contribute greatly to our total understanding of the law in action. In this connection, it should be noted that sometimes the individual's impressions of the law may actually develop through contacts with nonlawyer intermediaries, as

---

[83] William Stringfellow, *My People Is the Enemy* (New York: Holt, Rinehart & Winston, 1964).

when an insurance claims adjuster seeks to settle an automobile accident case prior to actual "legal" intervention.[84]

It has often been said that American attitudes toward law and the lawyer are ambivalent. The lawyer is respected as an important and powerful figure, yet at the same time regarded with great suspicion and even fear. Systematic research on the "images of law" will make clear whether, and if so, to what extent and under what conditions, these stereotyped notions are grounded in empirical reality.

---

[84] An ongoing study of the role of one such intermediary, the claims adjuster, is described by H. Laurence Ross, "Settled Out of Court: An Interim Report" (New York University, 1966, duplicated).